1976

HISTORY AND SYSTEMS
OF
PSYCHOLOGY

HISTORY AND SYSTEMS
of
PSYCHOLOGY

- - - - - - - - - - - - - -

WILLIAM S. SAHAKIAN

Schenkman Publishing Company

HALSTED PRESS DIVISION
JOHN WILEY & SONS
New York – London – Sydney – Toronto

Distributed solely by Halsted Press, a Division of John Wiley & Sons, Inc., New York

Library of Congress Cataloging in Publication Data

Sahakian, William S.
    History and systems of psychology.

        Bibliography: p.
        Includes index.
        1. Psychology — History. I. Title.
        [DNLM: 1. Psychology — History. BF81 S131ha]
BF81.S23   150'.19'09   74-26354
ISBN 0-470-74975-X
IBSN 0-470-74977-6 pbk.

Dedicated to
the memory of
my father
JACOB SAHAKIAN

CONTENTS

Behavior. The Group Mind. Experiments on Lamarckian Theory. Concluding Comments. **FRANCIS GALTON (1822-1911): Founder of Psychometrics.** Hereditary Genius. Galton's Principal Contributions to Statistics. Method of Ranks. Method of Correlation. **KARL PEARSON (1857-1936): The Biometric School at London University. CHARLES SPEARMAN (1863-1945): Founding of Factor Analysis.** Two Factor Theory and Factor Analysis. Noegenetic Laws. Spearman's Influence. **CYRIL BURT (1883-   ): Perpetuation of the Factor Analytic Tradition at London.** Four Factor Theory. **RAYMOND B. CATTELL (1905-   ): Multivariate Experimental Psychology. H. J. EYSENCK (1916-   ): Dimensional Approach to Personality.**

(B) EXPERIMENTAL PSYCHOLOGY AT CAMBRIDGE

JAMES WARD (1843-1925): England's First Psychological Laboratory. GEORGE FREDERICK STOUT (1860-1944): Ward's Distinguished Pupil. WILLIAM HALSE RIVERS RIVERS (1864-1922): The First Experimental Psychologist at Cambridge. CHARLES SAMUEL MYERS (1873-1946): The Cambridge Laboratory. FREDERIC CHARLES BARTLETT (1886-   ): Memory as a Social Psychological Phenomenon. Socio-Psychological Factors of Remembering. Social Psychology of Thinking.

Berlin: Physiological Psychology Makes Its Appearance

The *Privatdozent* and His Habilitation. American Students at German Universities During the Nineteenth Century. Berlin and Its University. **JOHANNES PETER MÜLLER (1801-1858): Father of Experimental Physiology.** The Birth of Experimental Psychology. **Bell-Magendie** Law on Spinal Nerve Roots. Specific Energy of Nerves. **HERMANN LUDWIG FERDINAND HELMHOLTZ (1821-1894): Greatest Experimental Psychologist of the Nineteenth Century.** First Law of Thermodynamics. Reaction-Time Experiment. Helmholtzian Empiricism. Unconscious Inference or Unconscious Conclusion. Theory of Perception. Pre-Helmholtzian Psychology of Sound. The Helmholtz Resonance Theory of Hearing. Perception of the Quality of Tone. Post-Helmholtzian Auditory Theory. **Rutherford's** Frequency Theory or Telephone Theory. **Wever's** Volley Theory. **Békésy's** Traveling Wave Theory. **Young's** Theory of Color. **Isaac Newton's** Color Theory. Helmholtz's Theory of Color. Conclusion. **Johannes Kries (1853-1928): Duplicity Theory.** Evolutionary Theories of Color: **Ladd-Franklin** Theory of Color Evolution. **Ewald Hering (1834-1918): Four Color Theory. Purkinje** Phenomenon. Hering's Theory of Opponent Colors. Hering's Nativistic Visual Space Perception Theory. **HERMANN EBBINGHAUS (1850-1909): Experiments on Memory.** Ebbinghaus: Heir of Fechner. Experiments on Memory. Rapidity of Learning a Series of Syllables as a Function of Their Length. Meaningful Material versus Meaningless Material. Overlearning and the Savings Method. Grouping Material. The Curve of Forgetting. Experimental Psychology of Memory. **LEWIS WILLIAM STERN (1871-1938): Psychometrics by Ebbinghaus' Protégé.** Stern's Personalistic Psychology. The I.Q. and the Era of Testing. Binet-Simon Intelligence Scale. Stanford-Binet Intelligence Scale. Army Alpha and Beta Tests. An Era of Psychometrics. Stern's Aussage Test. Rorschach, Bender Gestalt, TAT, and Other Tests.

der of the Phenomenological Movement.Psychologism and Intentionality. Phenomenology. DAVID KATZ (1884-1953): Phenomenology of Color. Color Theory. EDGAR RUBIN (1886-1951): Visual Perception of Figure-Ground Phenomena. Figure-Background Phenomena. Figural After-Effect.The End of an Era.

faction and Tension Release. **Vera Mahler** (1899-   ): Degrees of Substitute Activity. **Kate Lissner:** Substitute Value. Environmental Forces and Topological Psychology. Conflict. Field Theory in Social Science. Social Space. Group Dynamics. **LEON FESTINGER (1919-   ): Cognitive Dissonance.** Gestalt Migrates to America.

Ego, and Supergo. Instincts: Their Pressure, Aim, Object, Source, Classes, and Sublimation. The Ego as the Conscious Executor of the Personality. The Superego and Conscience. Psychodynamics of Neurosis and Psychosis. Psychoanalytic Therapy. Topography of the Mind: Conscious, Preconscious, and Unconscious. Libidinal Development: Psychosexual Stages of Mental Development. Psychoanalytic Social Psychology. Group Psychology. Freudian Psychology of Religion. Concluding Comments on Psychoanalysis. **CARL GUSTAV JUNG (1875-1961): Analytical Psychology.** The Founding of Analytical Psychology. The Word Association Test. The Collective and Personal Unconscious. The Collective Unconscious and Its Archetypes. Mandala (Including the Concepts: Self, Ego, Persona, and Individuation Process). Other Archetypes: Syzygy (Anima and Animus). The Shadow. Psychological Types: Introversion and Extroversion. The Four Functions: Sensing, Thinking, Feeling, and Intuiting. **Ernst Kretschmer (1888-1964): Constitutional Types. William H. Sheldon (1899-   ): Constitutional Psychology.**

(B) NEO-FREUDIAN CULTURAL ANALYSTS

ALFRED ADLER (1870-1937) and The Cultural Analysts. Adler's Individual Psychology. Inferiority and Superiority Feelings. Striving for Superiority. The Life Style. Finalism and Fictional Finalism. Social Feeling or Social Interest. Adlerian Psychotherapy. Early Memories. The Trend toward Cultural Explanations of Personality Development: **Ruth Benedict (1887-1948) and Margaret Mead (1901-   ).** Cultural Determinants of Personality. **Karen (Danielsen) Horney (1885-1952):** Neo-Freudianism and the Sociological School. **Erich Fromm (1900-   ):** Humanistic Psychoanalysis. Harry Stack Sullivan (1892-1949): Interpersonal Theory of Psychiatry.

(C) PHENOMENOLOGISTS AND EXISTENTIALISTS

VICTOR E. FRANKL (1905-   ) Logotherapy: The Will to Meaning. Tenets of Logotherapy. Will to Meaning. **EXISTENTIAL ANALYSIS: Ludwig Binswanger (1881-1966) and Medard Boss (1903-   ). Carl R. Rogers (1902-   ):** Client-Centered Therapy. Nondirective Psychotherapy. Phenomenological Theory of Personality. **J. L. MORENO (1892-1974): Psychodrama and Group Psychotherapy.** Moreno's Psychotherapy.

(D) NEUROPHYSIOLOGICAL PSYCHOTHERAPISTS

JULIUS WAGNER-JUREGG (1857-1940) and MANFRED J. SAKEL (1900-1957): The Birth of Shock Therapy in Vienna. Sakel's Insulin Shock Therapy for Schizophrenia. **Lazlo Joseph Meduna (1896-1964):** Metrazol Convulsive Shock Therapy. **Ugo Cerletti (1877-1963):** Electroshock Therapy. **Egas Moniz (1874-1955):** Prefrontal Leucotomy. **Walter Freeman (1895-   ) and James W. Watts (1904-   ):** Prefrontal Lobotomy.

(A) Development of Early American Psychology. Four Stages of American Psychology Since 1640. American Psychology: Stage One (1640-1776); Period of Moral Philosophy and Mental Philosophy. American Psychology: Stage Two (1776-1886); Period of Intellectual Philosophy. American Psychology: Stage Three (1886-1896); The American Renaissance. American Psychology: Stage Four (1896 to the Present); American Functionalism. (B) The First Generation of American Psychologists: James, Ladd, Hall.

(A) HARVARD DURING THE TENURE OF JAMES

WILLIAM JAMES (1842-1910): Harvard's Luminary. The Principles of Psychology. Functionalism. The Stream of Consciousness. Theory of the Self. Psychology of Temperament: Tender-minded and Tough-minded. **James-Lange** Theory of Emotions. **CANNON'S Thalamic Theory of Emotions.** Cannon's Homeostasis Theory. Evaluation of Cannon's Theory. **Selye's** General Adaptation Syndrome (G.A.S.). **HUGO MÜNSTERBERG (1863-1916): Psychology Applied and Harvard's Laboratory.**

(B) HARVARD DURING BORING'S TENURE

MURRAY and the Harvard Psychological Clinic. Harvard's Psychological Laboratory. Boring's Star Pupil: **SKINNER (and His Operant Behavior Theory). STEVENS and Harvard's Psycho-Acoustic Laboratory. ALLPORT and the Department of Social Relations.** Fritz J. Roethlisberger (1898-1974): and Field Studies.

Mass Action and Equipotentiality. **Cerebral Localization: Descartes; Gall; Flourens; Broca; Fritsch and Hitzig; Ferrier; Munk; and Goltz.**
DECLINING INFLUENCE OF UNIVERSITIES AND SCHOOLS OF PSYCHOLOGY

Soho Takuan (1573-1645); Baigan Ishida (1685-1744); Toan Tejima (1718-1786); Ho Kamada (1753-1821); Mabuchi Kamo (1697-1769); Seisho Fujitani (1737-1778); Mitsue Fijitani (1767-1832); Norinaga Motoori (1725-1801): PRE-TWENTIETH CENTURY JAPANESE PSYCHOLOGY. Early Japanese Philosophical Psychology.

(B) FOUNDERS OF JAPANESE EXPERIMENTAL PSYCHOLOGY

YUJIRO MOTORA (1858-1912): Japan's First Experimental Psychologist. MATATARO MATSUMOTO (1865-1943). Psychocinematics.

(C) BEHAVIORISM MAKES ITS DEBUT IN JAPAN

Matsumoto's Disciples: **Asataro Narasaki (1882-   )** and **Kwanichi Tanaka (1882-1962)**. **Narasaki:** Importer of Watsonian Behaviorism into Japan. Behaviorism Meets with Opposition: **Chiba** and **Kido.** Proposed Behavioristic Reconciliations: **Masuda. Kuroda:** Japan's Prominent Animal Psychologist.

(D) INTRODUCTION OF GESTALT PSYCHOLOGY INTO JAPAN

KANAE SAKUMA (1888-1970): Psycholinguistics

(E) THE RETURN OF ZEN PSYCHOLOGY

SHOMA MORITA (1874-1938) AND KOJI SATO (1905-1971): Zen Psychology. Morita Therapy: The Application of Zen Buddhism to Psychotherapy. Shinkeishitsu and Arugamama. Four Stages of Morita Therapy. Koji Sato's Zen Psychology. Psychology of Zen. Relation of Zen Psychology to Western Psychology.

PREFACE

What makes this book new and different is its schools approach to the history and systems of psychology. Not schools of thought merely—although they are present—but centers, university centers from which the major ideas in psychological thought germinated throughout the centuries. These centers are as trunklines feeding the branch lines that spread in a variety of directions as offshoots.

While teaching and researching in the field of systematic and history of psychology, the author became increasingly aware that psychology develops in integrated clusters, rather than haphazardly or accidentally. Yet, only minimal attention is accorded this fact in texts on the history of psychology and in systems of psychology. Most texts call attention to a school of functional psychology at Chicago University, a Würzburg school of imageless thought, or even an Austrian school of act psychology. But the striking fact is that schools abound everywhere throughout the history of psychology. It is only when the reader is made aware of this ''cartel-like'' existence of schools or universities radiating psychologies peculiar to their interests, that he gains an insight enabling him both to appreciate and grasp the fundamental course of development assumed by a school of psychology, and realizes why, with understanding.

A serious attempt has been made to treat the adherents important to each school in detail, with their satellites (or precursors) examined along with the major figure. The book is further characterized by offering many more quotations than are generally supplied the reader in histories of psychology. Quotations from primary sources often lend appreciation, insight, and the flavor of the influential founders of psychology. Where necessary, a chapter is introduced with an overview offering a running summary or synopsis, which enables the reader to gain a bird's eye view of the whole before engaging in the particulars of the tenets of each psychologist sufficiently noteworthy to command attention in the history of psychology.

In sum, this book's distinctiveness lies in its (1) university or school approach, (2) quotations where deemed necessary from original sources, (3) summary overview followed by an analysis in depth, and (4) extended scope which includes, in addition to traditional Western psychologists, psychologists from Russia, Japan, India, and Latin America, as well as the development of clinical and social psychology.

WILLIAM S. SAHAKIAN

Beacon Hill,
Boston, Massachusetts

If men cannot always make history have a meaning,
they can always act so that their own lives have one.
Camus

PART ONE

PRECURSORS
OF
MODERN PSYCHOLOGY

Although it was not until the period of the Renaissance that the term *psychology* was coined by *Philipp Melanthon* (1497-1560), psychology nevertheless was studied systematically at least as early as the time of *Aristotle,* "the Stagarite" (384-322 BC), when he treated the psyche in his *De Anima* (On the Soul) or *Psychology.* The term psychology, of Greek derivation *(psyché* and *logos),* etymologically signifies a discourse on the soul. As the term was employed throughout the history of psychology, it acquired a number of meanings, or at least its content as an academic study at universities did. Among these meanings or definitions are "the science of mind," "the science of immediate experience" (Wundt), and in more recent times, "the science of behavior."

The first textbook containing the term psychology in its title, written by *Johann Friedrich Herbart* (1776-1841), is significant also for its treatment of the subconscious mind and its introduction of mathematical psychology. Titled *Lehrbuch der Psychologie* (1816), it was translated as *A Text-Book in Psychology: An Attempt to Found the Science of Psychology on Experience, Metaphysics, and Mathematics.* Despite its long history of over two and a half millennia as ancillary to other disciplines (such as philosophy, religion, physiology, and medicine), psychology has risen to the stature of a respected and independent discipline and profession, comparable to the natural sciences and the medical profession. The first historian of psychology, *Aristotle,* provided more than a text in psychology, he offered by way of his *De Anima,* the first history of psychology.

CHAPTER 1

Overview of the
History of Early Psychology

(A) ANCIENT GREEK PSYCHOLOGY AT ATHENS

The Greek psychologists were predominantly Athenian, the exceptions being a few of the very earliest researchers: Alcmaeon, Empedocles, and Democritus, who were influenced by the Greek philosopher *Pythagoras* (c. 580-c. 500 BC) of Samos, Greece. Driven out of Samos, Pythagoras left for southern Italy, where he established his academy at Crotona, and from where his influence emanated, spreading from southern Italy throughout the greater part of Magna Graecia.

The propagation of his ideas was principally owing to the spread of a scientific mode of religion that he founded, one in which the material goods of life were little esteemed compared to art and science. An individual's important activity was that of fostering science and art. Even Aristotle and especially Plato were influenced by Pythagoras, but these two Athenians seem to be conversant with the "so-called Pythagoreans" rather than with Pythagoras, the two being merged to a point of indistinguishableness.

Alcmaeon: The First Physiological Psychologist

The first important product for psychology that sprang from Pythagoras' Academy at Crotona was the Greek physiologist and physician, *Alcmaeon of Crotona,* who flourished in the sixth century BC. Thought to be the first person to undertake anatomical dissections for research purposes, Alcmaeon possibly was also the first vivesectionist. By applying the Pythagorean notion of a cosmic harmony between a pair of contraries, he theorized that normalcy or good health consists of a balance, equilibrium, or isonomy of the laws of nature, hence anticipating Hippocrates.

The Pythagorean physiologist Alcmaeon accounted for vision "by reflection in the diaphanous element" of the eye, the eye seeing through its environing water. Hearing is accomplished through a resonant vacuum in the ear by transmitting sound inwardly by air waves, the vacuum (or vacua) being resonant. Thus he provided the antecedent of Helmholtz's resonance theory of hearing. Taste he explained by the tongue's moisture, warmth, and softness.

Empedocles: Theory of Perception

Empedocles (c. 495-435 BC) of Agrigentum, another disciple of Pythagoras, was the first to introduce a sense perception hypothesis by theorizing that like perceives like. By virtue of the senses, a person perceives through effluences found in the pores of the various senses. The effluences (that which flows or issues from a body) pass through the senses untouched or else are inhibited altogether.

3

The Greek philosopher who succeeded Aristotle as the head of the Peripatetic school, *Theophrastus* (c. 377-287) of Lesbos, summarized the Empedoclean theory of vision:

> Hearing . . . is caused by sounds outside. For when [the air] is set in motion by the voice there is a sound in the ear, for hearing is like a bell sounding in the ear which he calls a "fleshy nodule." And the air when set in motion strikes on the solid parts and makes a sound (Dox. 478).

Animism played an important role in the psychology of ancient Greek thinkers. Empedocles, along with Anaxagoras and Democritus (and many others) theorized that plants possess a mind and intelligence. Thinking he identified with sensation or something close to it. By his theories of "emanation" and "like perceives like," Empedocles surmised that "with earth we see earth, with water we see water; with air we see the bright air; with fire we see destroying fire; just as with love we [perceive] love, and with hate, baleful hate" (Aristotle, *De Anima*, bk. 1, ch. 2, 404).

Democritus: The Specific Energy of the Sense Organs

The Greek philosopher *Democritus* (460-370), "the Abderite," refined the perception theory of Empedocles and the atomic theory of *Leucippus* of Abdera (5th century BC). The first behaviorist in psychology, Democritus held that the mind *(psyché)* consists not of conscious states, but of atoms, the atomistic structure accounting for perception. The atomic structure comprising the mind or soul is the same as that of the make-up of fire. Perception is accounted for by the activity arising from objects encountering the psyche's fire atoms, thus creating a phenomenon (appearance) of reality. Effluxes (emanating from objects) set the sense organs in motion, and through the vehicle of fire atoms, images (copies of the real external object) are produced. Perception then is the impression of these on fire atoms, for the motion of fire atoms constitutes psychological activity.

Each organ of sense, because it is capable of accepting only those images corresponding to its peculiar motion and formation, results in a Democritan *specific energy of sense organ theory*. Each sense organ is capable of receiving its own peculiar effluxes, so that effluxes foreign to the sense of sight would be visually imperceptible, though perceptible by another sense capable of receiving them. Perceptions, as miniature copies, are like the genuine object in the real external world. The physiological psychology espoused by Democritus prevailed throughout the ages until contemporary times. It was even supported by John Locke, the English empiricist who coined the expression "association of ideas." Furthermore, Democritus anticipated Locke's theory of primary and secondary qualities. Democritus' psychology accounted for dreams as images which found their way into the body by weak or imperceptible (subconscious or subliminal consciousness) motion during a waking state or during the state of sleep. The motion exerted by the finest images evokes thought, that is, a genuine insight into the object's atomic structure.

Democritus also introduced the doctrine of mechanical necessity in nature, the theory that each effect must have its mechanical cause. Consequently he traced psychological functions to their respective components: thought to the brain, perception to the sense organs, emotions to the heart, and appetite to the liver.

Anaxagoras: Adaptation Level Theory of Perception

The Athenian philosopher *Anaxagoras* (499-428 BC) of Clazomene was, like Leucippus and Democritus, an atomist. The objects in the universe are comprised of minute atomic particles, natural objects being a mixture of all qualities. By the psyche acting upon these masses of particles, perception results. However, perception is effected not by like perceiving like but by opposites or contrasting stimuli. Perceptual discrimination requires contrasting or opposing elements, otherwise a neutral perception results. Theophrastus, explaining Anaxagoras' theory of perception, wrote:

> Perception is by opposites; for like is not affected by like. . . . Seeing, for example, is occasioned by the image on the pupil of the eye; but no image is cast on what is the same color, but only on what is of a different color. . . .
>
> In the same way touch and taste discriminate their objects. For what is just as hot or just as cold as we are neither warms us nor cools us by its presence. . . . By the warm we know the cold, by the brackish water the fresh, by the sour the sweet—according to our deficiency in each case. . . .
>
> Further, all sensation is accompanied by pain. . . . The contact of unlike with unlike is in every case painful. This pain is conspicuous in the case of sensations long continued or very intense; for brilliant colors and loud noises cause pain, and one cannot stand the same sensations very long (*De. Sens.* 27; dox. 507-8).

Thus we find in Anaxagoras' perception theory the antithesis of that espoused by his predecessors and contemporaries.

Another fifth century BC Greek philosopher, *Diogenes of Appollonia,* taught in Athens that intra-organic air accounts for sensation and mental activity. Like his contemporaries and predecessors, he theorized the pupillar image as the chief factor in visual perception. He imputed intelligence to air which was the fundamental principle of the psyche. The brain, as the central organ of sense, receives sensory impressions in its proximity by the air conducted in specific sense organs.

Protagoras: The Perception Theory of Personality

Protagoras (481-411 BC) of Abdera in Thrace, the first of the Sophists, lectured in Athens. This friend of Pericles debated his position against Socrates. His psychogenetic approach to the psyche led to his identifying perceiving and thinking. Accordingly, personality is the product of sensations. His psychology is predicated on his hypothesis that "man is the measure of all things, of things that are, that they are; and of things that are not, that they are not" (Plato, *Cratylus,* 385 E). His theory, which resulted in the subjectivity of sense perception, held that perception is the result of the forces of two motions directed toward each other, the first motion that of the object being perceived and the second that of the percipient organ sensing. Perception is a product, a *gestalt,* a concomitant of perceiving subject and perceived object. While the two are necessary conditions of perception, neither one by itself is a perception. An individual's knowledge is contingent on the moment of his personal or private perception rather than as things objectively are in reality, hence *Protagorean relativism.* Perception provides the individual only with things as they appear, that is, the represented content rather than the real thing itself. The relativism of Protagoras has come to be known as phenomenalism, the precursor of phenomenology that plays such an important role in contemporary psychology. Thus the important factor in the psychology of Protagoras is not actual reality, but the phenomenon of perception arising from motion.

Socrates: Founder of the Inductive Method

The Athenian philosopher *Socrates* (470-399 BC) left no writings, his views being recorded by Plato and Xenophon. Aristotle correctly attributed to Socrates the founding of inductive method that became so important a scientific technique. From multifarious particular instances Socrates sought that which these data shared in common, that being their definition, truth, or concept.

The Socratic or *maieutic method* in which Socrates played the role of midwife in extracting truths hidden in the unconsciousness of individuals simply by asking questions resulted in discovery of the unconscious mind that proved so fundamental in the psychoanalytic psychology of Freud. The Socratic method of responding to questions by raising questions became basic to the client-centered therapy or the nondirective psychotherapy of Carl R. Rogers. Thus in Socrates is found the base to the two leading psychotherapies current in the United States.

It was more than the personal unconscious that Socrates introduced, it was the collective unconscious, the premise on which C. G. Jung constructed his analytical psychology. With this concept of the universal unconscious, the repositor of truth and knowledge, Socrates opened the scientific world to the doctrine of nativism that was to play an important role in the history of psychology. Socrates also introduced the *intellective will,* a quasi-determinism in which the will responds to the dictates of reason.

Plato: Founder of Biological Psychology

Socrates' most distinguished student, *Plato* (427-347 BC) of Athens, contributed to psychology with a biological theory of personality, an interpretation of dreams, unconscious motivation, the association of ideas, and a psychology of perception. After a period of wandering from Megara to Egypt, Cyrene, Sicily, and Magna Graecia, Plato returned to his native city, Athens, in 387 BC when he established the Academy, the world's first university. It lasted until 529 AD when Justinian closed it.

Like Freud who was to follow two and a half thousand years later, Plato also had a triune structure of the personality which he (like Freud) constructed on a biological base. The structure of personality is characterized by the *intellect, will* (volition), and *appetite,* each with its biological base: head, heart, stomach (liver) respectively. A person is psychologically dichotomized into his reasoning self (intellect) and his dual affective (emotional) aspect (activity of will and appetitive activity). The psyche (soul) is seen as a unity with its three activities. Mental abnormality or maladjustment results from their imbalance or lack of harmony, integrative wholeness being normalcy. It is only the mind *(nous),* however, with its intellective (logical) function that survives to immortality, but it also possessed a pre-existence. Owing to this pre-existence, the mind is the repository of dormant or unconscious truths, knowledge, primordial achetypes, as Jung was to term them, or innate ideas, as Descartes called them. Mental development was therefore the surfacing of these unconscious truths or knowledge to conscious awareness. Wholesome or normal personality development calls for the maximal development *(excellence)* of the intellectual activity *(logistikon)* to maintain a harmonious balance (justice) over other components (volitional activity and appetitive activity) of the personality. The resultant of this balance or harmony (justice) is a psychological adjustment with its attendant happiness, owing to the development of each personality component to a state of excellence so that the intellect attains a state of wisdom, conation the state of will-power, and appetitive activity the state of self control. Virtue for Plato was equated with excellence, the specific virtues being wisdom, courage (will-power), and temperance (self-control); their harmonious or balanced interplay producing the concomitant virtue of justice or righteousness. Thus like Freud who was to follow later, the intellective aspect exerts a regulative control over other aspects of the personality.

Plato was also the first to introduce a *psychology of individual differences, constitutional psychology,* and *genetic psychology,* for he believed that a person adjusts psychologically only when he cultivates his most dominant trait and finds his suitable place in society where he can best function with respect to that trait. To do otherwise would result in a societal misfit, maladjustment, and frustration with its attendant misery. A society in which each person functions at that which he is best suited by his psychological nature produces more than individual adjustment, it results in individual happiness and social justice. In order to effect this desired result, persons must be tested so that their individual differences and personality characteristics can be ascertained. To enhance the native acquisition of the finest possible innate capacities, Plato advocated that psychological aristocrats (persons endowed by nature with the finest personality qualities) be mated so that they produce superior psychological progeny. Education can do no more than develop to its finest peek those natural endowments or psychological constitution with which a person is born.

Association of Ideas. Credit as precursor of associational psychology should go to Plato, for it was he who first noted that one idea leads to another. In the *Phaedo* he queried:

> What is the feeling of lovers when they recognize a lyre, or a garment, or anything else which the beloved has been in the habit of using: Do not they, from knowing the lyre, form in the mind's eye an image of the youth to whom the lyre belongs? . . .

May you not also from seeing the picture of a house or a lyre remember a man? and from the picture of Simmias, you may be led to remember Cebes (steph. 73).

Also the precursor of unconscious motivation and the interpretation of dreams, Plato noted that pleasures and appetites that were socially objectionable were satisfied in dreams. He spoke of "those which are awake when the reasoning and human and ruling power is asleep" (*Republic*, bk. 9, steph. 571). In the *Phaedo*, Plato discussed "the meaning of certain dreams."

Aristotle: Founder of Functional Psychology

Plato taught in his Academy for almost four decades, attracting superlative scholars, but his greatest was Aristotle (384-322 BC), "the Stagarite." However, Aristotle, not content to remain in the Academy, founded his own university in Athens, the Lyceum, the members of which were dubbed the *peripatetic school* owing to their promenading about in a grove of shade trees during lectures. Aristotle too had a celebrated student in Alexander the Great (356-323 BC), tutoring him in 343 BC when Alexander was a thirteen year old youth. Aristotle rose to the height of preëminence as a scientist, holding the title of "the philosopher" for over two millennia. Even today when the layman thinks of a person as having five senses, he still shows the influence of Aristotle.

Like Plato before him, Aristotle grounded his psychology on biology, empirically investigating animal psychology, hence was the first animal or comparative psychologist. While his animal psychology is a novel contribution, Aristotle's human or speculative psychology rests heavily on the Platonic. Although he adopted Plato's association of ideas theory, he too did little with it except to use it as the explanation of how a person can recall at will.

Aristotle's researches uncovered a dual psyche, one almost equated with life that is found as characteristic of animal souls, and in addition to it a *nous* or mind characterizing the human soul. Thus the human being has two souls; the higher, capable of reasoning, survives bodily destruction to immortality. Whereas his approach to the animal soul is empirical, that to the human is speculative. The animal soul (life) differs from the vegetable soul (life) in that the former is typified by unity and concentration, with sensation its fundamental activity. Each sense is capable of receiving its own peculiar type of perception. Senses come to a combined unity by virtue of the "common sense," the central sense organ which is seated in the heart. Responsible for the individual's knowledge, the common sense retains ideas as images after the cessation of stimuli and as such they become memories or copies of prior perceptions. The series in which these ideas in memory are bound to one another, that is, the association of ideas, makes it possible for an individual to recall matter committed to memory at will. Notions or ideas arise from sense impressions registering on the *tabula rasa* (blank tablet) mind so that reasoning by induction results. In his *De Anima* Aristotle asserted that

The mind is potentially the object of thought, though perhaps not actually so until thought takes place. It must be that the case here is similar to that of the tablet on which nothing has been actually written. This is what takes place in the case of mind, and it is the object of thought as other things are (bk. 3, ch. 4, 429^b-430^a).

For Aristotle nothing is in the mind which was not first in the senses.

Hence (1) no one can learn or understand anything in the absence of sense, and (2) when the mind is actively aware of anything it is necessarily aware of it along with an image; for images are like sensuous contents except in that they contain no matter (*De Anima,* bk. 3, ch. 8, 432^a).

Aristotle's Self-Actualization Psychology. Aristotle's functionalism assumes the form of self-actualizationism or self-realizationism. He viewed the soul as the *entelechy* (self-contained purpose) of the body, that is the human personality (as is true of all things) is made with a purpose which must be fulfilled otherwise frustration or misery results. The person who actualizes himself fully, i.e., realizes his every major potential capacity or ability, is adjusted in the sense that he finds himself in a state of *eudaimonia* (beautiful state of mind) or which signifies the same thing for Aristotle, happiness. Within the personality there exists a propensity for what is good for himself, thus the goal of every action of a human being is to achieve good which is realized by activity, that is, the actualization of his potentialities.

Aristotelian Social Psychology. Inasmuch as the human being is a social or political animal by nature according to Aristotle, an individual has an inner psychological need for society. Without society it is impossible to fulfill one's potentialities. Thus suitable psychological adjustment and happiness are found in living with others.

With the only possible exception of Plato, Aristotle is the first social psychologist, his social psychology extending even to the area of attitudinal psychology. In his *Rhetorica* Aristotle treated both attitudes and the psychology of persuasion. In fact he defined rhetoric as "the faculty of observing in any given case the available means of persuasion" (bk. 1, ch. 2). Three means of effecting persuasion are: (1) the credibility or personal character of the speaker; (2) the ability to place the audience in the right frame of mine; and (3) the ability to prove the words uttered by the speaker. The social psychology of persuasion has come to occupy an important place in current social psychology, especially the investigations undertaken since World War II by C. I. Hovland and his team at the Yale Communication Research Program.

Aristotelian Conception of the Psyche or Soul. For Aristotle three kinds of souls exist: (1) the vegetative soul, found in plants, is limited in function to propagation and assimilation; (2) the sensitive soul, possessed by animals, has in addition: appetite, sense, and locomotion; and (3) the rational soul, found only in human beings (who also possess the lower two types of souls). The activity of the soul in question defines the purposiveness or goal of the organism, each organ with its own teleological objectives. Teleologically, however, the lower functions exist for the higher, their functions being an activity of life in the following ascending order: (1) nutrition (vegetative life); (2a) perception (life of sensation); (2b) kinetic soul (life of creative power, desire, and locomotion); and (3) dianoetic or rational soul (life of intellect or reason).

The soul, as unitary life, is indivisible, hence found in each organism as a unit. Defined by Aristotle the soul is the "entelechy or complete realization of a natural body endowed with the capacity of life" (*De Anima*, bk. 2, ch. 1, 420^a), entelechy being full realization or the form giving energy activating realization or actualization. As a unity the soul pervades the body, is found in every part of it. Since the heart is the vital organ it must be the psychological and physiological center of an organism. Thus the psyche or soul is a unitary life or indivisible mind functioning with its faculties or potentialities of nutrition, sense-perception, imagination, memory, and reasoning.

Aristotle's Psychology of Sensation and Perception. Sensation is the distinguishing characteristic between the vegetative soul and the animal soul. While sensation per se is psychical, the organ of sense is physical. Of the five senses recognized by Aristotle (seeing, hearing, smelling, tasting, and touching), sight is the most valuable for living, while hearing is more significant for the intellectual life. While sight is transmitted by a fluid, air is the medium for hearing. Smell entails both air and water, whereas touch and taste are correlated with the physical—earth. Whereas light is the medium of vision, air and water are media of sound. Unlike light, sound travels. Air serves as the medium for smelling, but for aquatic creatures, it is water. As a variety of touch, these two senses have a medium that is not external to the body, the tongue being the medium of taste with moistness its vehicle. While flesh is the medium of touch, the sense of touch is comprised of a combination of senses.

Unlike contemporary psychologists, the ancient Greek psychologists did not distinguish between sensation and perception. They did, however, attempt to analyze the essential feature of sensation which would be comparable to perception. The faculties of the soul Aristotle listed in ascending order as (1) nutrient (vegetative), (2) sentient together with appetite and locomotion (animal), and (3) intellectual (human).

Aristotelian Clinical Psychology: Catharsis. Approximately two dozen centuries before the advent of Freud, Aristotle was aware of the psychological phenomenon of catharsis as the purging away of emotion. Freud initially employed the term abreaction to express the cleansing or expurgation of emotion, but later turned to the Aristotelian catharsis (purgation, purification, or cleansing). The orgiastic effect of music, poetry, and tragedy was observed by Aristotle, who described cathartic experience in his *Politics:*

> Some persons fall into a religious frenzy, whom we see as a result of the sacred melodies—when they have used the melodies that excite their soul to mystic frenzy —restored as though they had found healing and purgation *(catharsis)*. Those who are influenced by pity or fear, and every emotional nature, must have a like experience, and others in so far as each is susceptible to such emotions, and all are in a manner purged and their souls lightened and delighted (bk. 8, ch. 7, 1342^a).

Aristotle's contributions to psychology do not end here, for his psychological investigations encompassed dreams and even after-images. The works of this one man that dominated the intellectual world for over two millennia are so pervasive and enormous that some scholars believe them to be the product of the combined faculty of his university.

Stoical Psychology

Sensation and Perception. In accord with Aristotelian psychology, the stoics viewed the mind as a *tabula rasa* (blank tablet), acquiring its content as the senses furnish it with data or rational content from the outer world. Perceptions are essentially physical processes, impressions of objects in the outer world on the soul. One stoic, Chrysippus, regarded perception as the alteration of the soul's qualities. He held that all original ideas are impressions on the psyche and effect changes in it. The stoics also introduced the term *spirit (pneuma)*, connoting more than mere soul *(psyché)*.

While ideas refer to particular objects, concepts (originating in perception but nevertheless the product of the reasoning faculty) are pictures awakened in memory by recall. Concepts, being common to everyone alike, serve as the *consensus gentium* (universal agreement) criterion of truth.

Epictetus: Stoical Psychotherapy. The Greek stoic from Hierapolis in Phrygia, Epictetus (50-120 AD), who was once a slave, taught in Rome until 90 AD, when he with other philosophers was exiled from there by Emperor Domitian, spending the remainder of his life in Nicopolis. Like Socrates before him, he left no writings, his philosophy being preserved by his pupil Flavius Arrian in the *Discourses* and the *Enchiridion*. Stoicism was spawned in Athens by *Zeno* of Citium (c. 340-265 BC).

Stoic psychology is basically one of attitude characterized by stoical indifference and endurance. Tranquility or complete freedom from life's vicissitudes is the ideal objective. Essentially it is keynoted by an independent will and freedom from the passions achieved through apathy or emotionlessness by refusing to submit to excess of desire. Their criterion of normalcy and their greatest virtue was to live in accord with nature, passionate desire being an aberration. As an important personality component, the will must remain inviolate. Let no one break your will; yield it to no one.

Stoical psychotherapy is essentially one of attitude change: to "accept all things in a spirit of content" *(Discourses,* bk. 1, ch. 12). "The essence of good and evil," asserted Epictetus, "lies in an attitude of will" *(Discourses,* bk. 1, ch. 29). Epictetus thought exemplary the attitude of Socrates when the politicians Anytus and Meletus successfully effected his conviction, hoping to break his spirit. Socrates attitude was: "Anytus and Meletus have power to kill me, but not to harm me" *(Discourses,* bk. 2, ch. 2). In this way peace of mind, psychological adjustment, or mental tranquility is achieved. Mental composure is the greatest good, for there is nothing in the world worth becoming disturbed about. The root cause of anxiety lies in a state of desire or want. Epictetus remarked: "When I see a man in a state of anxiety, I say, 'What can this man want?', If he did not want something which is not in his power, how could he still be anxious?'' (*Discourses,* bk. 2, ch. 13).

Freedom is found in self-mastery. One must never regard a loss as a setback but as returning what was never truly owned. Freedom from fear and a troubled mind is preferred even if it means dying from hunger. If one does not gain self-mastery, he will find many masters—those things upon which he depends or the objects of his desires. Psychological adjustment or happiness is then ''freedom from passion and disturbance, the sense that your affairs depend on no one'' (*Discourses,* bk. 4, ch. 4). A person must repudiate what is not within reach—what is beyond his power. Welcome the problems of life as spiritual or mental exercise, so that your spirit is strengthened to cope with life's severest difficulties. Alfred Adler was later to adopt the stoic philosophy and psychology, especially this admonition. Adler held that a child protected from problems will find difficulty in dealing as an adult with life's problems and be vulnerable to mental ailment. The stoical goal of psychological adjustment is peace of mind, freedom, and tranquility, but it does not come cheap.

Although stoicism lasted in a variety of forms, finding its way into the philosophy of Spinoza and Shakespeare as well as Christian thought, in the third century (AD) it encountered its antithesis in Neo-Platonism. Notwithstanding their combating stoical ideas, the Neo-Platonists did nevertheless accept the ethical theory and pantheism of the stoics.

(B)   ALEXANDRIAN AND PATRISTIC PSYCHOLOGY

With the passing of the great Greek and Roman stoics (the later Roman stoics merely reiterating the views of the Greek stoics), psychology moved from one of sensationalism and rationalism to one of mysticism. The sensible and supersensible worlds, in sharp contrast to each other, led to Neo-Platonism with its principal center Alexandria in Egypt and the school's chief exponent *Plotinus* (c. 205-270). The founder of Neo-Platonism, *Ammonius Saccas,* an Alexandrian philosopher of the first half of the third century (AD), taught not only Plotinus but *Origen Adamantius* (c. 185-254), a Greek father of the Christian Church who succeeded Clement of Alexandria as head of the Christian Catechetical School in Alexandria. Ammonius sought a harmonization of the philosophies of Plato and Aristotle.

Plotinus: The First Empirical Psychologist

The importance of *Plotinus* (c. 205-270) to psychology is due chiefly to his being the first to approach psychology empirically, notwithstanding his introspective orientation. Born in Egypt of Roman parentage, Plotinus, who lectured in Rome from 244 AD, developed his psychological views in his *Enneades.*

Plotinus observed that the ''higher soul's'' cognitions, as a conscious activity, are contingent on data furnished by the senses. Owing to their being mere receptive physical states or excitatory states of the ''lower soul,'' the body together with its sensations, passions, and feelings is passive. Conscious perception, a function of the "higher soul," is reflection. In this manner Plotinus was led to the experience of self-consciousness in which the mind is aware of its own state, function, being, and content. Self-consciousness is the intellect actively aware of itself as existing and as knowing. Mingling his mysticism with his psychology, Plotinus cited the characteristics of the soul as

> sprung from the breath of God, immortal, possessing body, having form, simple in its substance, intelligent in its own nature, developing its powers in various ways, free in its determinations, subject to the changes of accident, in its faculties mutable, rational, supreme, endued with an instinct of presentment, evolved out of one [archetypal soul] (*Enneades* IV, 22).

The intellectual heir, successor, and climax of neo-Platonic psychology is St. Augustine. However, before examining his contributions it seems advisable to pause and consider some views antedating his.

Alexandrian Psychology: Philo and Origen. Philo Judaeus or *Philo of Alexandria* (c. 20 BC-c. 40 AD), dubbed the "Jewish Plato," was influenced by Platonism, Pythagoreanism, and stoicism. His dualistic psychology of the individual, derived principally from Plato, views the human as twofold, possessing a higher and lower self, the higher being a spiritual self *(pneuma)* and the lower soul a vital force of the body or the realm of sense. Evil (id forces) arises from the latter. Thus the person of sense experience must be distinguished from the self made in God's image. The individual's higher self is preexistent as Plato taught and is probably capable of transmigration as the Pythagoreans believed. Inasmuch as body and soul are not substantially united, the soul sheds the body at death.

The anthropological dualism of Philo continued in the psychology of another Alexandrian, *Origen Adamantius* (c. 185-254). With the exception of St. Augustine, he was, as the founder of Christian theology, probably the greatest theologian of the early Christian Church. Like Philo, Origen too distinguished between the higher or spirit *(pneuma)* self of an individual and his bodily *(soma)* nature, resulting in a rational soul and an animal soul. The animal soul with its instincts and passions (Freudian id) must be suppressed in order that a personality resembling God's might prevail. The soul's dichotomous nature is evident in his *On First Principles* where he mentions that

> there exists within us, besides the heavenly and rational soul, another one which is by its nature contrary to the first and which is called either the flesh, or the wisdom of the flesh, or the soul of the flesh (bk. 3, ch. 4).

Origen's psychology, which carried him into an empirical investigation of the will, found its antecedent in the empirical observation of the will by St. Paul. Origin, in his *On First Principles,* reasoned:

> We must inquire, therefore, what exactly this will is, which is intermediate between the flesh and the spirit, above and beyond the will which is said to belong to the flesh or to the spirit. For a certainty we should hold that everything which is said to belong to the spirit is due to the will of the spirit and whatever deeds are called 'works of the flesh' are due to the will of the flesh. What then above and beyond these is the will of the soul, which is

given a separate name and which the apostle [Paul] wishes us not to do when he says, 'So that ye may not do the things that ye will to do'? [Galatians 5:17] It seems to be here indicated that this will must be attached to neither of these two, that is, neither to the flesh nor to the spirit. But some one may say that just as it is better for the soul to do its own will than to do the will of the flesh, so again it is better for it to do the will of the spirit than its own will. Why then does the apostle say, 'So that ye may not do the things that ye will to do'?—since in that contest which is waged between the flesh and the spirit, the spirit is by no means certain of victory; for it is clear that in many cases the flesh obtains the mastery (bk. 3, ch. 4).

Anthropological or psychological dualism was endorsed by many of the patristic writers, including *Irenaeus* (c. 120/140-200/203), who distinguished between the psychical breath of life and the animating spirit, the former inextricably woven to and perishing with the body and the latter possessed of an eternal nature. *Tertullian* (155/160-after 220) of Carthage (north coast of Africa), regarded as the first Christian psychologist (by Roback and Kiernan, 1969), did likewise. Tertullian, however, drew a distinction between the mind and soul, the soul permeating the body rather than being spiritual or incorporeal in character. Despite its being the breath of God, the soul is not spiritual, i.e., an incorporeal substance, a point with which St. Augustine took issue.

Before proceeding further it seems advisable to review the psychology found in the Bible that the patristic psychologists (and for that matter those that are to come, e.g., St. Augustine and St. Thomas) commented upon and incorporated into their own psychologies.

Psychology of the Old and New Testaments

Numerous terms have been employed connoting the structure of the human personality. While most terms used to convey the vital principle, ego, self, or soul of a person stem from the same root meaning (breath or wind), many of them vary in their functional significance. Old Testament words for soul, such as those used by *Moses* (13th century BC), refer to the vital principle, including animal life. While the functional use of *nefesh* (breath) is used interchangeably for the life of a person as well as the animal soul, *ruah* (breath, wind) denotes the spiritual or immortal aspect of humans. "Then the Lord God formed a man from the dust of the ground and breathed into his nostrils the breath of life. Thus the man became a living creature" (Genesis 2:7). The apparent difference between the soul of a person and that of an animal is that the former's soul is made in the image of God.

Generally speaking, the Bible holds to an anthropological dualism, dichotomizing the personality into spirit (soul) and flesh (body), but occasionally, as is the case with St. Paul, the personality is viewed as triune: soul, spirit, and body. Paul's benediction to the Thessalonians reads: "The God of peace . . . make you holy in every part, and keep you sound in spirit, soul, and body" (I Thessalonians 5:23). The writer of the book of Hebrews also views the human personality as triune, comprised of psyche, spirit, and body. He asserted:

For the word of God is alive and active. It cuts more keenly than any two-edged sword, piercing as far as the place where life *(psuché)* and spirit *(pneumatos)* . . . divide (Hebrews 4:12).

Psychology of Personality in the New Testament. New Testament terms for soul, *psuché* (soul, breath) and *pneuma* (wind, breath, spirit) also stem from the same root. While most terms used in the New Testament to depict the ego or self of the human personality overlap, functional distinctions are perceptible. While *psyché* (or *psuché*) pertains to the life of humans and the animal souls, *pneuma,* a more humanistic concept, connotes the spiritual character of a person, a higher element than soul.

Other personality constructs found in the New Testament include *nous* (mind) signifying the rational operations of the personality, such as reflective consciousness, perception, understanding, judging, evaluating. Luke reported that Jesus "opened their minds *(nous)* to understand the scriptures" (24:45). *Phronema* (mind) is the contemplative self, the thought-contents. St. Paul asserted: "For the mind *(phronema)* of the flesh is death" (Romans 8:6). *Kardia* (heart) is the affective, attitudinal, and emotional construct of the personality, and is used to designate the hidden resources or unconscious aspect of the personality. Peter wrote: "Your beauty should reside, not in outward adornment . . . but in the inmost centre of your being *(kardia)*" (I Peter 3:4). *Thelesis* (will) denotes the personality as willing. *Sarx* (flesh) is used in the New Testament with overtones of the Freudian id as well as in contrast to the spirit, e.g., "Everything the world affords, all that panders to the appetites *(sarx)* or entices the eyes, all the glamour of its life, springs not from the Father but from the godless world" (I John 2:16). *Jesus* (4 BC-30 AD), dichotomizing the individual into spirit *(pneuma)* and flesh *(sarx)*, said: "The spirit *(pneuma)* is indeed willing, but the flesh *(sarx)* is weak" (Matthew 26:41). St. Paul linked *sarx* with sensuality and instinctual urges. Writing to the Ephesians, he admonished: "We all lived our lives in sensuality, and obeyed the promptings of our own instincts and thoughts" (Ephesians 2:3). St. Paul, well aware of the conflicts existing among the Freudian personality components of ego, id, and superego, wrote to the Romans:

> We know that the law is spiritual; but I am not. . . . I do not even acknowledge my own actions as mine, for what I do is not what I want to do, but what I detest. But if what I do is against my will, it means that I agree with the law and hold it to be admirable. But as things are, it is no longer I who perform the action, but sin that lodges in me. For I know that nothing good lodges in me—in my unspiritual nature. . . . The good which I want to do, I fail to do; but what I do is the wrong which is against my will; and if what I do is against my will, clearly it is no longer I who am the agent (Romans 7:14-20).

Although the psychology of the early Christians was unsystematic, they had little difficulty identifying mental constructs, especially the various components of the personality.

St. Augustine (354-430): Father of Introspectionist Psychology

Arelius Augustine (354-430), Bishop of Hippo in North Africa, was influenced by Plotinus, Plato, and St. Paul, thus synthesizing Platonism with Christianity. With the possible exception of Plotinus, Augustine should be credited with introducing introspectionism as a method into psychology. From Plotinus, Augustine derived an interest and insight into self-consciousness as a phenomenological entity. His concern for self-consciousness led him to the Cartesian *cogito* which in turn led him to conclude that in the act of doubting the self, one finds himself in the predicament of proving it. Accordingly in addition to the external five senses, there is an internal one of inner perception enabling a person to become aware of his own private mental processes. Humans are capable of more than objective observation, they are capable of self-observation of inner private mental states or operations. In *On the Trinity,* Augustine explained:

> For whence does a mind know another mind, if it does not know itself? For the mind does not know other minds and not know itself, as the eye of the body sees other eyes and does not see itself; for we see bodies through the eyes of the body, because, unless we are looking into a mirror, we cannot refract and reflect the rays into themselves, which shine forth through those eyes, and touch whatever we discern. . . . But whatever is the nature of the power by which we discern through the eyes, certainly, whether it be rays or anything else, we cannot discern with the eyes that power itself; but we inquire into it with the mind, and if possible, understand even this with the mind. As the mind, then, itself gathers the knowledge or corporeal things through the senses of the body, so of incorporeal things through itself. Therefore it knows itself also through itself (bk. 9, ch. 3).

Thus is Augustine's account of how the human mind, without sensory data or the utilization or the senses, can apprehend itself.

Anthropological Dualism. Also subscribing to an anthropological dualism of mind and body, Augustine emphasized the dichotomy sharply. While his dualism of mind and body was adopted by Descartes and other psychologists, it was bypassed by St. Thomas Aquinas as well as St. Paul for a triune man. Augustine takes his lead from Plotinus in regarding the body as a sinful, material, and inferior aspect of the individual. Despite soul and body being united, the soul does not require the body for its existence. Even in sensation, the body does not act on the soul, for it is the soul's action by which sensation, as an aspect of attending, is a continuous act. The soul senses and animates the body. Without the soul, physical sensations are disordered. Accordingly a person is defined as ''a rational soul using a mortal and earthly body'' *(De moribus eccl.,* 1, 27, 52).

The Empirical Mind. Unlike many of his intellectual predecessors in Christianity, Augustine did not espouse a mind devoid of content. True, there is as an innate quality on the one hand, but there is also the empirical mind replete with experiences derived from sense data that have been added to the innate mind. Mind and soul being interchangeable terms for Augustine, he spoke of mind or soul as lying

> more deeply within, not only than those sensible things, which are clearly without, but also than the images of them; which are indeed in some part of the soul, *viz.,* that which beasts also have, although these want understanding, which is proper to the mind. As

therefore the mind is within, it goes forth in some sort from itself, when it exerts the affection of love towards these, as it were, footprints of many acts of attention. And these footprints are, as it were, imprinted on the memory, at the time when the corporeal things which are without are perceived in such way, that even when those corporeal things are absent, yet the images of them are at hand to those who think of them. Therefore let the mind become acquainted with itself, and not seek itself as if it were absent; but fix upon itself the act of [voluntary] attention (*On The Trinity,* bk. 10, ch. 8).

The perceptive reader will recognize in this quotation the anticipation of certain Lockean empirical views, including the "blank tablet" mind upon which impressions ("footprints") are made.

The Mind's Cardinal Activities: Memory, Understanding, and Will. The continuity of sensation in the mind is possible owing to the ability to remember. Beginning with the premise of immediate certainty of inner experience, Augustine holds that the act of doubt establishes the existence of the doubter, hence the reality of the person as a conscious being. A person might be mistaken about everything in the universe except his own existence, for to err at all, it is necessary to exist. This basic certainty encompasses the three fundamental states of consciousness: memory, understanding, and will because the individual who doubts is aware of more than his existence merely, he at the same time remembers, knows, and wills inasmuch as his doubt is grounded on previous ideas. Thought, knowledge, and judgment are present in the assessment of the moving force of doubt.

Who ever doubts that he himself lives, and remembers, and understands, and wills, and thinks, and knows, and judges? Seeing that even if he doubts, he lives; if he doubts, he remembers why he doubts; if he doubts, he wishes to be certain; if he doubts, he thinks; if he doubts, he knows that he does not know; if he doubts, he judges that he ought not to assent rashly. Whosoever therefore doubts about anything else, ought not to doubt of all these things; which if they were not, he would not be able to doubt of anything (*On the Trinity,* bk. 10, ch. 10).

The soul or mind in the Augustinian view is the living whole of the personality, the life of which is a unity with a self-consciousness that is certain of its existence. Memory, understanding, and will are essentially one, aspects of a single unity or mind. "These three, memory, understanding, will, are not three lives, but one life; nor three minds, but one mind. . . . And hence these three are one, in that they are one life, one mind, one essence . . . , they are called also together, not plurally, but in the singular number" (*On the Trinity,* bk. 10, ch. 11). In order to establish their unity empirically, Augustine observed:

For I remember that I have memory and understanding, and will; and I understand that I understand, and will, and remember; and I will that I will, and remember, and understand; and I remember together my whole memory, and understanding, and will (*On the Trinity,* bk. 10, ch. 11).

Thus the personality for Augustine is a unity, a self-conscious unity, one that is indubitable.

The Close of the Platonic Era. Due to his empirical approach, Augustine the neo-Platonist was able to avoid some of Plato's difficulties. However, Platonism did not end with Augustine but dominated the entire first period of the Middle Ages from 529 AD when Justinian closed the Academy to the rise of the universities in the twelfth century. Progress in psychology during this period was negligible, arising once again during the second or Aristotelian period of the Middle Ages, and extending approximately from 1200 to the fall of Constantinople in 1453, the dominant figure during this period being St. Thomas Aquinas.

St. Thomas Aquinas (1225-1274): The Person as a Psychophysical Unity

The Italian scholastic, Aquinas, was born at Roccasecca, near Aquino. He studied at the universities of Naples and Paris, being a pupil of Albertus Magnus at the latter institution. He taught at the University of Paris in 1256, and spent almost a decade (1259-1268) as adviser and lecturer to the papal Curia. The era of the founding of universities was getting underway during the life of Aquinas, the University of Paris opening in 1205; Padua in 1222; Lyons in 1223; Naples in 1224; Oxford in 1249; and Cambridge in 1284.

Although Aquinas belongs to the Christian tradition, and in this work he is so ordered, he intellectually belongs with and following the Arabian Aristotelians, for it was from them that Aristotelianism was acquired during the Medieval Period. Like the Arabian psychologists, he posits an *agent intellect,* i.e., a power in the intellect rendering things intelligible in act or actuality. The individual is a *psychophysical unity,* that is, a soul actuating a body. The human soul, unlike the animal and vegetable soul, as intellect or mind is an incorporeal, subsisting substance. An individual, however, is more than a soul, he is a composition of soul and body, hence human nature is a unity. Nevertheless, while the body is perishable, the soul is not. Inasmuch as without a body, sense experience is impossible, it must be part of the human person. By uniting with a body, the intellectual soul is provided with a suitable sense organ, the union being one of form to matter. As an all-pervasive entity, the soul permeates every portion of the body. Aquinas is also in accord with Aristotle regarding five exterior senses. The *intellect* is not the essence, but the power or potential of the soul.

> Potentiality has a double relation to act. There is a potentiality which is always perfected by its act. . . . There is another potentiality which is not always in act, but proceeds from potentiality to act. . . . The human intellect, which is the lowest in the order of intellects and most remote from the perfection of the divine intellect, is in potentiality with regard to things intelligible, and is at first *like a clean tablet on which nothing is written,* as the Philosopher [Aristotle] says. This is made clear from the fact that at first we are only in potentiality towards understanding, and afterwards we are made to understand actually. And so it is evident that with us to understand is *in a way to be passive.* . . . Consequently the intellect is a passive power (*Summa Theologica,* Q. 9, art. 2).

However, the human possesses more than a passive intellect (*tabula rasa* mind); there also exists an agent intellect, rational powers.

> Nothing is reduced from potentiality to act except by something in act; as the senses are made actual by what is actually sensible. We must therefore assign on the part of the

intellect some power to make things actually intelligible, by the abstraction of the species from material conditions. And such is the necessity for positing an agent intellect (*Summa Theologica*, Q 79,-art. 3).

The *agent intellect*, being in the soul as one of its powers, renders the soul an intellective soul. Unlike the neo-Platonic Arabian thinkers, Aquinas held that the agent intellect is not one, but there are as many as there are persons (souls).

The soul also possesses *appetitive powers*, inclination and natural appetite, among them being sensuality or sense appetite with its irascible and concupiscible powers. While the irascible and concupiscible appetites at times may resist reason, they nevertheless obey it.

The *will*, as subordinate to reason, does not will nilly willy, but responds to the intellect. Since the human is a free agent, the will as agent motivates each of the soul's powers to that action which is suitable, the exception being the vegetative aspect of the soul which is not subject to a person's will. Free choice, however, is more than a judgment, it is a power.

Scholastic psychology climaxed with Aquinas, in whom rational psychology reached its apex. Notwithstanding the attempt of St. Thomas to unify the human personality, the spiritual soul or mind and the physical or material body remained, at least in the opinion of the author, a dichotomy. Rather than attempting a unification of body and mind, Descartes maintained a dualism. It remained for two Cartesian successors, Spinoza and Leibniz, to effect the most suitable unity in a psychophysical parallelism. However, the mind-body problem remains a perennial one for psychology.

(C)   ARABIAN PSYCHOLOGY AT BAGDAD AND CORDOVA

Psychology during the second period of the Middle Ages shifted from a Platonic influence to one that fell under that of Aristotelianism. The pervasive influence of Aristotle is apparent in the psychology and philosophy of the three major religious bodies in the Western world, viz., Christian, Arabian, and Jewish. Christian thinkers, the last to be introduced to Aristotle's psychology, derived their manuscripts on Aristotelianism from the Arabs who provided them with both Aristotelian treatises together with their own commentaries on Aristotle and original monographs. Jewish writers also made their contributions to Christian scholars. Thus Christian contact during the twelth and thirteenth centuries with Arabian and Jewish thinkers benefited Christian scholars considerably, especially with respect to Aristotelian psychology. By the eighth century the Moslem empire spanned from Spain tô Persia.

The Aristotelianism that first entered the Arabian world was of a neo-Platonic character with an emphasis on Aristotle's second entelechy, i.e., the human intellect that survives to immortality. The neo-Platonic element is evident in the introduction of a number of "Intelligences" arranged hierarchically in ascending order from the material world to that of the Supreme Being, the human intellect being the last of these pure intelligences as well as the least perfect. This view found its obscure grounding in an Aristotelian text which cites the active intellect as divine and immortal whereas the passive understanding (*tabula rasa* mind) originates and terminates with the body.

Each of the two important centers of Arabian psychology, Bagdad and Cordova, had a distinguished scholar, Avicenna at Bagdad and Averroës at Cordova in Spain. Neither scholar was of Arabian descent, the former being a Persian and the latter a Spanish Moor. However, both, Moslems by religion, wrote in the Arabian language. Laboratory psychology can find its antecedent in physiology and physics that is ultimately rooted in Arabian medicine, optics, and mathematics.

Avicenna (980-1037): Bagdad Psychology

Bagdad, the leading city of ancient Mesopotamia (Iraque), had a scientific school founded by *Abbassid Caliph al-Ma'mūm* (813-833). At this school, where distinguished thinkers such as Avicenna studied, Greek literature, both philosophical and scientific, was translated. One of the early savants of the Bagdad school was *Alfarabi* (d. 949/950), an Aristotelian who wrote commentaries on the works of "the philosopher." The most important member of the Bagdad school, *Abū 'Alī al-Hasayn ibn 'Abd Allāh ibn Sīnā* (known to the West as Avicenna), succeeded Alfarabi whose predecessor was *Alkindi* (d. 873). The physician-philosopher Avicenna was an Aristotelian with a neo-Platonic bent.

From God, the perfect intelligence and one necessary being, an intellectual order proceeds. The series of intelligences continues in descending order to the tenth and final which is the "active intellect" or the "agent intellect," from which springs individual souls. Since according to the neo-Platonic principle "thinking is creating," from the consciousness of the second intelligence arises the soul, owing to its knowing its relationship to God as necessary. From it also the body is engendered, due to its knowing itself as conscious of being possible. Thus from a single source emerges both soul and body as well as intellectual acts. The soul's essence, a spiritual substance, possesses powers of intelligence, sense, and vegetation. The highest, the "possible intellect," is so designated owing to its capacity for knowing, but the actual knowing process is a synthesis of the agent intellect and the power of sense. The forms (e.g., natural or scientific laws or universals) are impressed on minds with the capacity to receive them (human minds) by the agent intellect (cosmic intellect). Knowing (grasping essenses) proceeds from a perception of sense objects by the external sense organs, their images retained by internal faculties (imagination, common sense, and the power of cogitation). Internal senses abstract the essential qualities from accidental characteristics of objects. However, it is the agent intellect rather than the human intellect per se that effects the process of abstraction, producing pure forms. Even if a person were devoid of all sense perception, he would, nevertheless, be aware of his existence.

Algazel or *Algazzali* (1058-1111), an Arabian philosopher who taught at Bagdad from 1091-1095, summarized the views of Avicenna (and Alfarabi) in a work translated as *Philosophia*. It was this work that provided the Medieval period with the Avicennian system of thought.

Although Scholastic thinkers of the Medieval period contested and repudiated some of Avicenna's psychology and philosophy, they also modified a considerable portion of it for their own purposes. Its neo-Platonism, with overtones of Augustinianism, proved so palatable to certain of the thirteenth century Augustinians that some of the views of these scholastics were termed Avicennian-Augustinianism. With the passing of Avicenna, Arabian psychology declined in Bagdad and the East, but in Cordova, Spain, it was rejuvenated, especially by Spain's leading thinker of the time, Averroës.

Averroës (1126-1198): Cordovan Psychology

From the tenth to the thirteenth centuries, Spain was an important scientific center, with Christians, Arabians, and Jews in common intercourse and living with a liberty of thought. Spanish-Arabian philosophy is traced to *Abenmasarra* of the ninth century who enunciated the theory of pseudo-Empedocles. In Cordova there was, in the eleventh century, *Aben-Hazam*. However, the foremost thinker of them all was the physician Averroës of Cordova. For a time he lived in Morocco and Seville before returning to Cordova. He was dubbed "the commentator," owing to the esteem in which his commentaries on the writings of Aristotle were held. Even more than Arabian thought, he influenced subsequent Jewish and Christian views. Averroism and Christian scholasticism of the second period of the Middle Ages were in striking resemblance. It was Averroës who first realized that the sensitive organ of vision was not the lens of the eye but the retina.

Unlike Avicenna, Averroës repudiated the intelligences arising one from the other in descending order. Everything stems from a direct creation by God. However, the ultimate substance consists of intelligences, characterized by immaterial forms and pure acts. The body's substantial form is the soul. Although the soul has a "possible intellect" (capacity to understand), it is not a spiritual substance, but a corporeal form united with the body, accordingly perishing with it at death. Union with the agent intellect is by virtue of the highest corporeal power, the imagination or passive intellect (*tabula rasa* mind). Common scientific knowledge (natural laws and universals) is made possible by the agent intellect (cosmic or universal intellect).

Accused of heresy, Averroës was exiled from Cordova, but returned to favor and to Cordova. While a kind of astrology had crept into the psychology of Avecinna inasmuch as he held that the moon had a tie-in with human psychology, the notion that stars and planets affect the human mind was roundly rejected by another Spaniard, the humanist Vives.

Moses Maimonides (1135-1204) Judaistic Psychology at Cordova. The greatest of the medieval Jewish philosophers was the Cordovan, Moses Maimonides, known as Rambam. The physician Maimonides, who studied under Arabic scholars, left for Cairo in 1148 when the Moslem's captured Cordova. There he practiced medicine, and in 1177 he became the celebrated Rabbi of Cairo.

Mental conflicts arising from the clash of Greco-Arabian thought with Judaism prompted him to reconcile Greek science with the Jewish faith, the result being his

The Guide to the Perplexed, written in Arabic from 1176 to 1191. The cosmogony of Avicenna, complete with motor intelligences of the celestial spheres, was borrowed by Maimonides. Also adopted from Avicenna was the identification of the agent intellect with the last (ninth) of the intelligences, allocating the functioning of illuminating human minds to it. Unlike his predecessors, Maimonides regarded the soul as one, the physical, vital, and psychical being aspects or activities of a single soul. Like Averroës, Maimonides sought truth in science, which to the two men constituted a universal religion.

Juan Luis Vives (1492-1540): The Birth of Inductive Method in Psychology

Born in Valencia, Spain, Vives, a student of the humanist Erasmus, sought a more humane treatment of mental patients. For a period of time he taught at the universities of Louvain and Oxford. His distinction in psychology is that he introduced current empirical and inductive methods for psychological research together with a phenomenological approach. He broke away from the scholastic approach which seemed to be interested merely in the nature and reality of the soul for a phenomenological psychology as enunciated in his *De Anima et Vita* (1538). Not what the soul is, but its phenomenon was of psychological interest, or as he articulated it: "What the soul is, is of no concern for us to know; what it is like, what its manifestations are, is of very great importance." Introspection, or the exploration of an individual's own inner life of the mind is the object and method of investigation.

One of the early writers to discuss associational psychology, Vives was the first to introduce the emotional origin of association, i.e., the ability of emotionally toned thoughts to revive other emotions or thoughts. He mentioned that during his boyhood years while ill with a fever he ate cherries that tasted peculiar owing to the illness. Since that time, whenever he ate cherries he more than recalled the fever, he seemed to re-experience it. In some unconscious manner (though the word "unconscious" is not in his vocabulary), emotions enhance memory. He even treated human egoistic drives, appetites, and the ambivalence of feelings, such as love mitigated with hate.

Nevertheless, the orientation of Vives, like so many of his contemporaries and predecessors, was Aristotelian. Nor was he the first of the Renaissance thinkers to note the significance of emotions, for the Italian statesman, *Niccolò Machiavelli* (1469-1527), considered by some to be the first social psychologist, noted the role of emotions in human motivation. He held that a person is dominated by his passions. The empirical psychology of Vives contributed to the development of psychology and influenced some thinkers, among them being the French skeptic *Michel (Eyquem) de Montaigne* (1533-1592). In a very real sense the psychology of Vives serves as the transition from Renaissance to modern psychology.

(D)   CONTINENTAL RENAISSANCE PSYCHOLOGY: FRANCE/HOLLAND/GERMANY

During the seventeenth and eighteenth centuries three prominent figures emerged as leaders of a school that came to be known as *Continental rationalism*. The three: Descartes from France, Spinoza from Holland, and Leibniz from Germany were chiefly guided by Galileo's method of mathematical deduction. One consequence of this method was a direct confrontation with the scholasticism that dominated the academic world for centuries throughout the Middle Ages. Another outcome was a new conception of psychology. The problem that the scholastics disguised as nonexistent (the mind-body problem), the Continental rationalistic psychologists boldly confronted. These thinkers treated psychological issues in the light of their new science, viewing phenomena mathematically and mechanically, regarding nothing in the physical universe as mysterious.

Unlike other psychologists treated in this work, the Continental rationalists had no university affiliation, one principal reason being their desire for intellectual freedom, which would not be theirs as a college professor. Descartes spent a lifetime avoiding any offense to the Inquisition, and Spinoza avoided danger by taking refuge in obscurity as well as withholding publication of his manuscripts (except one) which were posthumously published. Leibniz avowed that his intention was the reconciliation of science with religion.

Since the Medieval period, Descartes is the principal personality in the development of scientific thought. In his attempt to resolve the psycho-physical dualism of the human being, he was led by anatomical dissections to discoveries in physiological psychology, hence becoming the father of physiological psychology.

René Descartes (1596-1650): Father of Physiological Psychology

The first of these Continental rationalists, Descartes, was born in La Haye, France and resided in Holland from 1629 to 1649. Even more than his interest in psychology, he was a mathematician, philosopher, and scientist. Out of the French culture of his times he built his system on (1) the skepticism that pervaded the life of France; (2) the Augustinianism that dominated Protestant as well as Roman Catholic thinking; and (3) the mathematics for which Paris was celebrated.

The Cartesian Cogito. The *Cartesian method,* one of provisional doubt, did not admit of any fact or truth which was not known with certainty, hence indubitably. The result was that matter was ultimately an assumption, and the soul or mind (interchangeable terms for Descartes) was (as Augustine before him had established) beyond doubt, accordingly known with certainty. He concluded: *Cogito, ergo sum* (I doubt, therefore I exist). Inasmuch as the process of doubt is one of thinking, it follows that in doubting the existence of consciousness is experienced and asserted. Not only is the existence of the soul more certain than the body, but existence continues contemporaneously with thought processes. Inasmuch as external sense data are not required to establish the mind's (soul's) existence, it follows that knowledge concerning it as a reality is innate, that is to say, the soul is an innate idea. On the other hand, the reality of matter is vouched for by God, since it cannot be indubitably proved. The British empiricists, Berkeley and Hume, later denied the existence of matter, terminating their views with phenomenalism, the theory that the objects of sense exist but without any underlying material substance designated reality.

Interaction of Mind and Body. When Descartes accounted for the organism's integrative activity as an automatic, self-acting mechanism, he became the father of physiological psychology and of reflex action (or reflexology). Unlike the mind, Descartes theorized that the body is a machine subject to causation according to mechanical laws. The machine, called the body, is acted upon indirectly by the mind, the soul's location being in the pineal gland in the brain. Sensory action is accounted for by the activity of "delicate threads" extending from the sense organs to the brain. Motor action or reflex activity is effected by inflating muscles with animal spirits via nerve conduits. In his *Treatise of Man* (1662) Descartes explained:

> To understand . . . how external objects that strike the sense organs can incite [the machine] to move its members in a thousand different ways: think that (a) the filaments (I have already often told you that these come from the innermost part of the brain and compose the marrow of the nerves) are so arranged in every organ of sense that they can very easily be moved by the objects of that sense and that (b) when they are moved, with however little force, they simultaneously pull the parts of the brain from which they come, and by this means open the entrances to certain pores in the internal surface of the brain; [and that] (c) the animal spirits in its cavities begin immediately to make their way through these pores into the nerves, and so into muscles that give rise to movements in this machine quite similar to [the movements] to which we [men] are naturally incited when our senses are similarly impinged upon.
>
> Thus . . . , if fire A is near foot B, the particles of this fire . . . have force enough to displace the area of skin that they touch; and thus pulling the little thread . . . , they simultaneously open the entrance to the pore [or conduit] . . . where this thread terminates [in the brain]: just as, pulling on one end of a cord, one simultaneously rings a bell which hangs at the opposite end ([1662] 1972, p. 33-4).

No sharp distinction is drawn between sensory and motor nerves. Animal spirits were potent fluids subject to the laws of mechanics.

The seat of the soul through which interaction is effected is the pineal gland. Although the soul is united to every portion of the body conjointly, the locus of interaction is in the pineal gland. In his *Passions of the Soul* (1650), Descartes explained:

> There is a small gland in the brain in which the soul exercises its functions more particularly than in the other parts. . . . It seems to me quite evident that the part of the body in which the soul immediately exercises its functions is neither the heart, nor even the brain as a whole, but solely the most interior part of it, which is a certain very small gland, situated in the middle of its substance, and so suspended above the passage by which the spirits of its anterior cavities communicate with those of the posterior, that the slightest motions in it may greatly affect the course of these spirits, and, reciprocally, that the slightest changes which take place in the course of the spirits may greatly affect the motions of this gland ([1650] 1911, art. 31).

Explaining reflex action, Descartes asserted:

> But the greater part of our motions do not depend on the mind at all. . . . When a man in falling thrusts out his hand to save his head he does that without his reason counselling him so to act, but merely because the sight of the impending fall penetrating to his brain, drives the animal spirits into the nerves in the manner necessary for this motion, and for producing it without the mind's desiring it, and as though it were the working of a machine (*Fourth Set of Objections,* 1911, pp. 103-4).

While the reflex type of action is beyond the will's control, it is modifiable indirectly by the soul's action. In addition to his physiological psychology, Descartes contributed to the psychology of emotions, visual perception, will, and memory.

The intellectual successors of Descartes, Spinoza and Leibniz, were dissatisfied with his explanation of psychophysical interaction. Consequently they provided their own account of the mind-body problem.

Benedict Spinoza (1632-1677): Psychophysical Parallelism

Born in Amsterdam of Jewish-Portuguese parents, Spinoza earned his living grinding optical lenses. He declined the chair of philosophy at Heidelberg when it was offered to him because he feared its acceptance would be at the cost of intellectual freedom. At twenty-four he was excommunicated from the Synagogue, and accordingly changed his name from the Hebrew *Baruch* to the Latin *Benedict,* feeling that he could be blessed (Baruch in Hebrew) in Latin as well as Hebrew.

His geometric approach to psychology reads like a treatise on Euclidian geometry, with its axioms, propositions, scholia, and corollaries. So impressed was Spinoza with the Cartesian mathematical method that he declared: "I will therefore write about human beings as though I were concerned with lines and planes and solids." The person as well as the universe is a mechanical system, mechanics itself being spiritual and all things divine. Hence he is a pantheist and metaphysical monist. It was Spinoza's pantheistic monism which equated God with substance that led him to his psychophysical parallelism.

The Doctrine of Psychophysical Parallelism. Descartes espoused a dualism of mind and body, holding that reality is composed of substance thinking (mind) and substance extended (body). However, for Spinoza there is but one substance with an infinite number of attributes, two of which are mind and body. "Consequently, substance thinking and substance extended are one and the same substance" (*Ethics,* pt. 2, prop. 7). Mind and body are accordingly phases of the same organism. Therefore whatever occurs to body affects mind as well and vice versa because "the order and connection of ideas is the same as the order and connection of things" (*Ethics,* pt. 2, prop. 7). Thus Spinoza anticipated the gestalt doctrine of isomorphism. Interaction of mind and body does not occur owing to their being the same organism; whatever affects the organism automatically affects its attributes of mind and body. Spinoza's intellectual successor, Leibniz, pursues this line of thought further, arguing that interaction is not a genuine reality but that mind and body merely appear as if the two were interacting. Leibniz and Spinoza effected their parallelism by removing the Cartesian dualism of mind and matter and by ascribing a genuine unity to the human person.

Other contributions of Spinoza to psychology include his premise of rationalism which contends that everything in the universe permits of a rational explanation, even the strangest behavior of the psychotic. In this respect he anticipated Freud. He also made a case for emotional control through self-understanding, that is, by understanding the nature of emotional behavior. ''An emotion, which is a passion, ceases to be a passion,'' he declared, ''as soon as we form a clear and distinct idea thereof'' (*Ethics*, pt. 5, prop. 3), that is, when we clearly understand ourselves. His attempt at a geometrical approach to the study of personality is anticipatory of contemporary mathematical psychology. His intellectual successor, Leibniz, though a mathematical genius like Descartes owing to his discovering the differential calculus (independently of Isaac Newton), did not utilize mathematics in his psychological research.

Gottfried Wilhelm Leibniz (1646-1716): The Human Mind as an Activity

With the Cartesian tradition in Paris and Holland, with Malebranche in Paris and Spinoza in Holland, and with Leibniz the first of a long line of German scientists, modern scientific culture was inaugurated. With Leibniz the curtain closes on the Renaissance, and the Enlightenment is ushered in with the publication of *An Essay concerning Human Understanding* in 1690, written by his British contemporary, John Locke (1632-1704). Thus in Leibniz is found the transition from the Renaissance to the Enlightenment. While Spinoza uttered the definitive statement on scholastic realism of the Renaissance and the Medieval period, Leibniz, breaking with tradition, forecast the coming individualism. Substance, forms, universals, particulars, and the rest of the scholastic notions in Spinoza were to look backward to the Renaissance and the Middle Ages, while Leibniz is anticipating the future with his concept of mind not as a substance but as an activity, his substance not as inert matter but as dynamic activity, and his dynamic view of the human mind as unconscious to barely conscious to fully conscious.

Born in Leipzig, Leibniz was educated at the universities of Leipzig, Jena, and Mainz, obtaining his doctorate from the latter in 1666. In addition to his bachelor's thesis, *The Principle of Individuation* (1663), only his *Theodicy* (1710) was published during his lifetime. It was in this book that he argued that this was the best of all possible worlds, an idea derided by Voltaire in his *Candide*. Leibniz stayed in Paris from 1672 to 1676, visiting London in 1673, with the last three decades (1687-1716) of his life devoted to scientific and philosophical studies. During this period (1676-1716) he served as librarian and privy councilor to the duke of Brunswick.

Mind-Body Problem: Doctrine of Pre-established Harmony. Whereas Descartes premised his system on mind and matter as ultimate and Spinoza predicated his on substance, Leibniz structured his on *monad* (the Greek for one, individual, or unity), and articulated it in his *Monadology* (1714), the study of monads. The notion that he wanted to convey is that the ultimate nature of a human being is that of individuality, oneness, activity, consciousness (and unconsciousness as well as preconsciousness), and a unity. Negatively stated it means that inert matter (inactive, dead matter) does not exist nor do soul*less* bodies or bodies without souls. Hence nothing is dead, for reality including human personality or mind is activity. "Substance cannot exist without action, and there is indeed never a body without movement" ([1704] 1896, p. 47). Intelligence is activity as is all other mental activity. In this view, termed *panpsychism* (all of nature possesses a psychic characteristic or psychical quality), act psychology of the late nineteenth and early twentieth century was anticipated.

Accordingly the monad, and consequently each personality, is characterized by *individuality*, for "every monad must be different from every other" (*Monadology*, no. 9); substance, and therefore personality, "is a being capable of action" (1714, no. 1) and "has no parts." While the body is an organic activity, the soul is a monadic activity. Their co-ordinated activities function in perfect harmony owing to a pre-established harmonious arrangement of their respective natures. Hence interaction is unnecessary. What appears as interaction is but a pre-established character of each (body and mind) operating in unison. Interaction is therefore not genuine but merely appears to be taking place. Interpreting Leibniz, one could say that body and mind because of their complementary natures work together to produce a unified whole comparable to hydrogen and oxygen which produce water. Thus in the Leibnizian doctrine of pre-established harmony, which is his theory of psychophysical parallelism, is found the antecedent of gestalt psychology, holism and isomorphism.

Petites Perceptions: Degrees of Consciousness. Basic in the system of Leibniz is his *law of continuity* according to which "nature makes no leaps," that is everything occurring in nature is by gradual (almost indistinguishable) increments. Nothing is abrupt. The same holds true in psychological phenomena in which a gradual change occurs along a continuum from a virtual state of unconsciousness to one of full conscious awareness. In psychology, which Leibniz termed *pneumatology* ("psychology" was coined by *Philipp Melanchthon* [1497-1560]), there is a gradual intensification of consciousness from near consciousness *(petites perceptions)* to full conscious attention *(apperception)*. In his *New Essays concerning the Human Understanding* (1704), Leibniz orders unconscious states along a continuum to consciousness.

> There are at every moment an infinite number of *perceptions* in us, but without apperception and reflection, *i.e.* changes in the soul itself of which we are not conscious, because the impressions are either too slight and too great in number, or too even, so that they have nothing sufficiently distinguishing them from each other; but joined to others, they do not fail to produce their effect and to make themselves felt at least confusedly in the mass. . . . Thus there were perceptions of which we were not conscious at once, consciousness arising in this case only from the warning after some interval, however small it may be ([1704] 1896, p. 48).

Hence Leibniz is not only the legitimate founder of the subconscious mind, but he anticipated discrimination in psychology as well as figure and ground of gestalt or Helson's adaptation theory.

Critique of the Human Mind as a Tabula Rasa. When John Locke wrote his *An Essay concerning the Human Understanding* (1690), he did so with considerable attention to attacking the Cartesian innate ideas theory by holding that the mind is a "white paper" or *tabula rasa* at birth awaiting data to be furnished it from the senses. Thus Locke was in accord with Aristotle in maintaining that there is nothing in the mind which was not first in the senses. In writing his *New Essays concerning the Human Understanding* (1704), Leibniz came to the defense of his Continental rationalist colleague. Noting that animals share sense experience with humans, yet lack scientific knowledge, Leibniz concluded that the human mind is more than an animal or *tabula rasa* mind. "There is nothing in the intellect which was not previously in the senses," asserted Leibniz, "provided we make the reservation, except the intellect itself" (bk. 2, ch. 1).

Stimulated by the Leibnizian assertion that there is more to the mind than a *tabula rasa*, another German, Immanuel Kant, decided to investigate the nature of the mind, i.e., its innate character, resulting in *nativism*, a theory which remained permanently in psychology.

(E)   MODERN GERMAN PHILOSOPHICAL PSYCHOLOGY

German philosophical psychologists have made unquestionable inroads into both clinical and experimental psychology. Kant's nativism has found a lasting place in psychology, and the psychology of Schopenhauer and Nietzsche have found their way into Viennese clinical psychology, especially that of Freud, Adler, and Frankl.

Immanuel Kant (1724-1804): Kantian Nativism

Born in Königsberg, Kant was educated at the University of Königsberg where he remained the rest of his life as its most distinguished professor. The major influences upon him included the pietism of ethical Puritanism in which he was reared, the Leibnizian-Wolffian philosophy acquired while a student at the University of Königsberg, the physics of Newton from his college days, the humanitarianism of Rousseau acquired in his late thirties, and the skepticism of Hume.

The A Priori Intuition of Space and Time. Kant's nativism is emphasized in his theory of sense perception. Space and time are innate in the subject rather than introduced from external sense experience. As such, they constitute part of the understanding. A person cannot sense except by the categories of spatial and temporal relations. Sense perception is comprised of two elements: the necessary (constant) and the changing (accidental), the former being time and space. These two universals (because time and space are the same everywhere) are also necessary because data cannot be perceived except in temporal and spatial categories. As the necessary forms of experience, time and space are requisite if experience is to occur at all. Thus the mind synthesizes whatever data sense provides it with space and time. Consequently there is no pure sense, for everything entering the human mind bears the stamp of a fact that exists somewhere and at some time. The mind is not a tabula rasa, but a very active entity, as Leibniz contended, which requires percepts in order to manufacture knowledge. Sense data, on the other hand, are meaningless or lack the scientific brand without the activity of mind synthesizing them into experiential knowledge. "Without sensibility," asserted Kant, "no object would be given to us, without understanding none would be thought. Thoughts without content are empty, perceptions without conceptions are blind" (1781, I, pt. 2, 1).

Time is then according to Kant "nothing but the form of inner sense," and as such it is "the form a priori condition of all phenomena without exception. Space, as the pure form of all external phenomena, is the a priori condition only of the external phenomena" (1781, I, pt. 1, sect. 2). Space and time are not in the objects themselves but are transcendentally found within the perceiving individual. Far from being a tabula rasa, the human mind is capable of three stages of syntheses or transcendental activity (subjective a priori activity transpiring within the mind). The first, transcendental aesthetic, is one of perception being a synthesis of sense data with time and space. The second, transcendental analytic, is one of logical understanding. The third, transcendental dialectic, is one of reasoning in order to integrate systematically the facts of experience into a coherent whole. The transcendental process of synthesis belongs to the understanding, and is defined as the "nonsensuous faculty of knowledge." Only the realm of the phenomenal world results in legitimate knowledge, the world of reality (noumena or thing-in-itself) remaining unknowable inasmuch as it transcends sense perception, and scientific knowledge is the synthesis of sense data with the machinery of understanding. Reality at most is a mental reconstruction in the mind of what is understood to be the ultimate thing-in-itself producing phenomenal objects. Thus "the world is my representation."

Arthur Schopenhauer (1788-1860): Psychology of Will

Schopenhauer, quickly seizing upon Kant's declaration of the world as representation or idea, developed his own system in his multivolume The World as Will and Idea (1818), contending the world in which we live is a mere representation (phenomenal) and reality or the thing-in-itself that Kant termed noumena will (force). Thus the phenomenal world is idea (representation) and the real world is will (irrational force).

Schopenhauer is labelled a pessimist because he contends that the forces of reality underlying and controlling natural phenomena are irrational ones, unresponsive to reason. In the human being, suffering results from such forces owing to their being conscious as well as irrational, assuming the form of instinctual forces. The irrational driving forces of instinct, rather than being concerned for the individual, contribute merely to the enhancement of the race. Accordingly, a person who is no longer desirous of living (someone with a terminal disease or in a concentration camp, to cite a modern example) cannot bring himself to suicide owing to the drive of self-preservation which is concerned only for the human race and not the individual and his plight. The same holds true for the irrational forces of the sex drive.

Conflicts arise from the sex drive's being in collision with the intellect, the intellect yielding by resorting to the mechanism of rationalization. Accordingly, a person is by definition "at once impetuous and blind striving or will (whose pole or focus lies in the genital organs), an eternal, free, serene subject of pure knowing (whose pole is the brain)" (*World as Will and Idea,* sect. 39). While sex is essentially selfishness, seeking its own satisfaction, love is concerned for the welfare of others. "*Eros* is selfishness, *agape* is sympathy" (sect. 67). Owing to the instinctual drives, a person is either in a state of want (suffering) or ennui.There is no instinctual fulfillment, only a repetition compulsion (as Freud later termed it). "The nature of man consists in this, that his will strives, is satisfied and strives anew, and so on for ever. . . . For the absence of satisfaction is suffering, the empty longing for a new wish, languor, *ennui*" (sect. 52). The only sane course to take in order to escape the human predicament is sublimation.

Sublimation. Schopenhauer anticipated the Freudian doctrine of sublimation by recommending escape or relief from the irrational instinctual forces through a form of sublimation entailing becoming lost in Platonic philosophy, or in music and poetry, or even sympathic love, for these activities have a calming effect on the will. "All these reflections," wrote Schopenhauer,

> are intended to bring out the subjective part of aesthetic pleasure; that is to say, that pleasure so far as it consists simply of delight in perceptive knowledge as such, in opposition to will. And as directly connected with this, there naturally follows the explanation of that disposition or frame of mind which has been called the sense of the *sublime* (*World as Will and Idea,* sect. 39).

Other than sublimation, the extinction of instinctual desires or a life of asceticism is encouraged by Schopenhauer.

The influence exerted by Schopenhauerian psychology on Freud is evident, but his influence extends to a number of other psychologists, including Viktor E. Frankl with respect to existential neurosis. Although Frankl speaks of an existential or noögenic neurosis as a Sunday neurosis, the experience was anticipated by Schopenhauer who commented that "as want is the constant scourge of the people, so ennui is that of the fashionable world. In middle-class life ennui is represented by the Sunday, and want by the six week-days" (*World as Will and Idea,* sect. 57). Another psychologist influenced by Schopenhauer, Nietzsche, accepted him as his mentor before later repudiating him. While the pessimistic Schopenhauer viewed the irrational drive (principally sex) as primary, for Nietzsche it was the will to power. Whereas Freud took the lead of Schopenhauer, Alfred Adler followed Nietzsche's will to power.

Friedrich Nietzsche (1844-1900): The Will to Power

Some psychologists indulge in tracing an individual's philosophy to his psychological orientation. William James, for example, held that a person's philosophical *Weltanschauung,* idealistic or materialistic, is discernible from his psychological orientation. Consequently some psychologists feel justified in tracing Schopenhauer's and Nietzsche's philosophy to their lives. Although this may prove an interesting endeavor, it does not serve as valid disproof of their conclusions as some psychologists mistakenly assume. Both Schopenhauer and Nietzsche quit their university posts, Schopenhauer because of lack of students. While a *Privatdozent* (lecturer) at the University of Berlin, Schopenhauer arrogantly scheduled his courses during the hours that the celebrated Hegel lectured, hopefully to win Hegel's students away from him. As it turned out, he was left without a sufficient number of students to continue, consequently he left teaching permanently, living on his father's inheritance. He studied at the universities of Göttingen and Jena, obtaining his Ph.D. in 1813 from the latter institution.

Nietzsche attended the universities of Bonn and Leipzig, where he studied Schopenhauer's writings. In 1868, at the age of twenty-four, he was offered the chair of philology at the University of Basel, notwithstanding his not having received his doctorate. In the light of these events, the University of Leipzig decided to grant him a degree supposedly on the strength of his record while at that institution. He taught for a decade (1869-1879) at Basel, retiring on a pension (owing to failing health). He became psychotic (apparently general paresis) in 1889 and died the following year in Weimar.

Neitzsche's Power Drive. Contrary to Schopenhauer, Nietzsche believed that the instincts should not be repressed but given full vent, for they are life-giving. Guilt, a symptom of illness, should be repudiated. Instincts should be expressed, never repressed. A healthful joy is experienced in the feeling and venting of the will to power. "Life itself appears to me," stated Nietzsche in *The Antichrist,* "as an instinct for growth, for survival, for the accumulation of forces, for *power:* whenever the will to power fails there is disaster" (no. 6). Instinctual loss is tantamount to corruption. Power is lost through pity, and through it suffering is rendered contagious.

***Ressentiment* and Repressed Hostility.** Nietzsche termed *ressentiment* that form of behavior arising out of repressed hostility. Emotions that are not vented owing to a sense of frustration or impotency in striking back at one's superior foe fester, resulting in perverted forms of behavior in which natural values are supplanted by "denaturized" ones. He fancied that the norms of Judaism and of modern Christianity were of the "denaturized" order. In his *A Genealogy of Morals (*[1887]1897), Nietzsche explained:

> Whereas, on the one hand, the life of the noble man is self-confident and sincere . . . , the man of resentment, on the other hand, is neither sincere, nor naïve, neither honest nor straightforward against himself. His soul *squints;* his mind loves hiding-places, alleys and back-doors; everything hidden appeals to him as *his* world, *his* shelter, *his* comfort; he is master in the art of keeping silence, of forgetting nothing, of waiting, of provisional self-diminution, of self-humiliation (Essay 1, sect. 10).

Behavior stemming from *ressentiment* is secretive. To illustrate it in a non-Nietzschean example, it would be to vent one's hatred of his employer by insidious behavior in which he does not know who it is that is causing him harm. The person who vents his emotions behaves differently, for he experiences not *ressentiment* (repressed agression) but conscious resentment. Consequently "the resentment of the superior man, when it appears in him, acts and exhausts itself in the reaction which follows at once, hence it does not *poison*" (1956, p. 38).

Long before Freud, Nietzsche, well aware of the consequences of repression, asserted in *Beyond Good and Evil* ([1886] 1955):

> "I did this," says my memory. "I cannot have done this," says my pride, remaining inexorable. Eventually, my memory yields (no. 68).

Other contributions of Nietzsche include his analysis of sublimation, thus anticipating Freud, and a discussion of sadism. In the *Genealogy of Morals,* he observed:

> To see another suffer is pleasant; to make another suffer is still more pleasant. . . . For we are told that, in the devising of bizarre cruelties, the apes abundantly announce and, as it were, "prelude" man. No festival without cruelty: thus the oldest and longest history of man teaches us—and in punishment, also, there is so much that is *festival!* (Essay 2, Sect. 6).

Nietzsche also contributed to Frankl's logotherapy by providing him with the dictum: "If we possess our *why* of life we can put up with almost any *how*" (*Twilight of the Idols* ([1889]1968), "Maxims and Arrows," no. 12). Frankl rendered this to mean that if a person has a meaningful reason for which to live, then he can surmount any of life's vicissitudes. Freud too believed that a person who has a cause for which to live, adjusts more readily than one without a cause.

The perceptive reader will note that the British philosophical psychologists were bypassed. The reason is that they have their own psychological orientation, and consequently are treated in the succeeding chapter on British Empiricism, Associationism, and Evolutionism.

PART TWO

DEVELOPMENT OF BRITISH PSYCHOLOGY

British associationism has its roots in British empiricism, and in turn British empiricism is rooted in Aristotelianism for its epistemology. Epistemology, the study of the nature and extent of human knowledge, was the principal interest of the great train of British empiricism which received its definitive inauguration with the appearance of John Locke's *An Essay concerning Human Understanding,* marking the opening of the period of the Enlightenment with its publication in 1690. The mission of Locke was the critical examination of the limits and foundation of knowledge.

CHAPTER 2

British Empiricism, Associationism, and Evolutionism

(A) BRITISH EMPIRICISM

British empiricism is the offspring of the ideas of Aristotle, for it was he who first expressed the idea that there is nothing in the mind which was not first in the senses and its concomitant of a *tabula rasa* mind, a mind which was a blank tablet at birth. These Aristotelian ideas became the Lockean foundation for his epistemological views as enunciated in his *An Essay concerning Human Understanding*.

Locke's tabula rasa thesis is actually an antithesis, an antithetical position to the Cartesian thesis of *innate ideas* and rationalism. But later, the Germans such as Leibniz countermanded by amending the Lockean thesis "there is nothing in the mind which was not first in the senses" with "except the mind itself." It was left to Kant to synthesize Continental rationalism with British empiricism.

THOMAS HOBBES (1588-1679):
Father of British Empiricism and Associationism

Born in Malmesbury, Wiltshire in England, Hobbes, a close friend of Francis Bacon (1561-1620), was Oxford trained but claimed that he had learned little from the university that graduated him in 1608. Exiled to France, owing to his political convictions, he returned to England in 1652, and from 1660 became a member of the household of the Earl of Devonshire. Hobbes, pensioned by Charles II, encountered such notables in his travels as Galileo and Gassendi on the Continent, and Ben Johnson, Harvey, and Cowley in England. His books important to psychology include two of his most famous classics: *Human Nature* (1650) and *Leviathan* (1651).

The value of Hobbes' contributions must be appreciated for their influence on subsequent British empiricism and associationism. It was he who charted the lines that later British thinkers were to follow, though he did no more than merely outline the laws of associative connection, basing them on one class of phenomena, viz., memory. It was as true of Hobbes as it was with Bacon that mental phenomena were to be viewed in physical terms and thus he entertained a mechanical conception of the mental. Basing his position on the premise that "all is body or body in motion," Hobbes viewed the empirical psychical life and consciousness as corporeal. Consequently idea, volition, and other mental phenomena of experience are bodily activity. To speak of anything else (such as something spiritual rather than mental) is to lapse into theological matters. Thus

35

Hobbes' anthropological materialism reduces the mind to body and its functions. For him, "whatever exists is matter, and whatever changes is motion."

The problem, first introduced by Bacon, was left for resolution to Hobbes, who did so by resorting to associational psychology, and thereby becoming the father of this school. By regarding the elements of consciousness as mere sense impressions, Hobbes proceeded to explain memory and thought as the combination and transformation of these impressions of sense. All other psychical elements such as feelings and mental activity are reduced to the impulse (instinct) of self-preservation and the feelings of pleasure and pain which are attendant upon these sense impressions. Accordingly he also fathered psychological hedonism, the view that human behavior is not by choice but the natural avoidance of pain and the pursuit of pleasure. "Will therefore is the last Appetite in Deliberating" (1651, I, ch. 6). The determinist, Hobbes, rejected freedom of the will and developed a natural history explanation of the emotions.

For Hobbes, psychological association is tied to the coherence of former ideas.

> The *cause* of the *coherence* or consequence of one conception to another, is their first *coherence* or consequence at that time when they are produced by sense: as for example, from St. Andrew the mind runneth to St. Peter, because their names are read together; from St. Peter to a *stone*, for the same cause; from *stone* to *foundation*, because we see them together; and for the same cause, from foundation to *church*, and from church to *people*, and from people to *tumult*: and according to this example, the mind may run almost from anything to anything (1650, ch. 4, 2).

Using *coherence* to signify *contiguity*, Hobbes did in effect initiate British associationism though in inchoate form. Furthermore his "terminism," (the nominalistic theory that concepts are merely terms) influenced and had an effect on the Enlightenment in England.

JOHN LOCKE (1632-1704): Tabula Rasa Mind

Born in Wrington in Somersetshire six years after Bacon's death and a third of a year before Spinoza, the Englishman, Locke, was the son of a Puritan, a small landowner attorney. Entering Christ Church (Oxford University) in 1652, he remained there for thirty years, receiving a bachelor's degree in 1656 and a master's in 1658. Though he studied and practiced medicine and was called Dr. Locke among his friends, he never graduated in that field, and abandoned it in 1666. The following year began his friendship with Lord Ashley (later Earl of Shaftesbury) and a subsequent move to Ashley's London home for fifteen years as his confidential advisor. Beginning in 1675 he studied medicine in France for four years. Because Shaftesbury was suspected of plots and he of complicity with him, Locke fled to Holland in 1684, returning with William and Mary during the revolution to become commissioner of appeal, a post he held from 1689 to his death in 1704. His classic, *An Essay concerning Human Understanding* (1690), was the product of seventeen years of labor and appeared when he was nearing sixty years of age. Owing to it he has been considered by some as siring modern psychology.

Association of Ideas. Not until the *An Essay concerning Human Understanding* had gone into its fourth edition in 1700 did Locke include a chapter on the "Association of Ideas," which was to become the watchword for association psychology for two centuries. But having coined the term *association of ideas,* he scarcely employed it and then only to mean connections among experiences. He wrote:

> Some of our *ideas* have a natural correspondence and connexion one with another; it is the office and excellency of our reason to trace these, and hold them together in that union and correspondence which is founded in their peculiar beings. Besides this, there is another connexion of *ideas* wholly owing to chance or custom: *ideas,* that in themselves are not at all of kin, come to be so united in some men's minds that it is very hard to separate them, they always keep in company, and the one no sooner at any time comes into the understanding but its associate appears with it; and if they are more than two which are thus united, the whole gang, always inseparable, show themselves together (1706, II, ch. 32, sect. 6).

Locke assumed the leadership of the Enlightenment while developing an empirico-psychological exposition of the world based on the Cartesian conception. Because ideas stem from two sources, there are two classes: ideas of *sensation* and ideas of *reflection,* idea signifying any kind of experience. By attention or repetition they are fixed in memory. Ideas are associated by contiguity. Locke's association theory is essentially one of a combination of ideas.

Mind as a Blank Tablet. Much of Locke's impetus and ideas originated as a polemic against Descartes' "innate ideas." Whereas Descartes saw the mind laden with knowledge at birth, Locke developed the antithesis that the mind at birth is a *tabula rasa,* a blank tablet or white paper.

> Let us then suppose *the mind to be, as we say, white paper* void of all characters, without any ideas. How comes it to be furnished? Whence comes it by that vast store which the busy and boundless fancy of man has painted on it with an almost endless variety? Whence has it all the materials of reason and knowledge? To this I answer, in one word, from *experience;* in that all our knowledge is founded, and from that it ultimately derives itself. Our observation, employed either about *external sensible objects,* or about the *internal operations of our minds perceived and reflected on by ourselves,* is that which supplies our understandings with all the materials of thinking. These two are the fountains of knowledge, from whence all the ideas we have, or can naturally have, do spring (1706, II, ch. 1, sect. 2).

Ideas, the object of thinking, arise from sensation or reflection (mind) as their source. Those from reflection come later since "the soul begins to have ideas when it begins to perceive." Ideas may be either *simple* or *complex,* the latter abstractions of the former. The mind constructs complex ideas out of the simple ones. Compounding simple ideas into complex ones marks the beginning of the notion of "mental chemistry" that J. S. Mill was later to underscore. Simple ideas, those the mind can neither make nor destroy, are also in the mind like the complex, but qualities (both primary and secondary) are in external objects.

Whatsoever the mind perceives in itself, or is the immediate object of perception, thought, or understanding, that I call idea; and the *power to produce any idea in our mind, I call quality* of the subject wherein that *power is.* Thus a *snowball* having the power to produce in us the ideas of white, cold, and round, the power to produce those ideas in us as they are in the snowball *I call qualities;* and as they are sensations or perceptions in our understandings, I call them ideas; which ideas, if I speak of sometimes as in the things·themselves, I would be understood to mean those qualities in the objects which produce them in us (1706, II, ch. 8, sect. 8).

Qualities may be either *primary* or *secondary,* the former inhering in the bodies themselves but the latter are of a psychological nature producing ideas that are not perceived in the object. Those inseparable from the bodies are primary qualities.

These I call original or primary qualities of body; which I think we may observe *to produce simple ideas* in us, viz. *solidity, extension, figure, motion* or *rest,* and *number.*
Secondly, such qualities which in truth are nothing in the objects themselves but powers to produce various *sensations* in us by their primary qualities, i.e. by the bulk, figure, texture, and motion of their insensible parts, as colours, sounds, tastes, etc. These *I call secondary qualities.* To these might be added a *third sort,* which are allowed to be barely *powers,* though they are as much *real qualities in the subject* as those which I, to comply with the common way of speaking, call qualities, but for distinction, *secondary qualities.* For the power in fire to produce a new colour, or consistency in wax or clay, by its primary qualities, is as much a quality in fire as the power it has to produce in me a new idea or sensation of warmth or burning, which I felt not before, by the same primary qualities, viz. the bulk, texture, and motion of its insensible parts (1706, II, ch. 8, sect. 9-10).

By "powers" insensible primary qualities produce sense qualities. Power is also used in the sense of bringing about a change such as the sun possessing power to make lead fluid or wax white.

Perception, the simplest idea obtained from reflection, is the actual production of an idea in mind, e.g., fire may burn people with the same effect it does a billet except for brain activity (a sense of heat, experience of pain that is produced in the mind in which the actual perception exists). Substance, the underlying reality of sensed objects, remains a mystery for Locke which he termed an *I-know-not-what.* Hence he is a metaphysical agnostic. One does not perceive reality. What is termed substance is merely a "collection of a certain number of simple ideas," joined in a unity. "For our *idea* of substance is . . . obscure . . . : it is but a supposed I-know-not-what, to support those ideas we call accidents" (1706, II, ch. 23, sect. 15). Locke repudiated the notion of substance as knowable. Substance is supposed to be the entity (object in external reality) producing the qualities that people sense (accidents). Substance is the unknown supporter of known qualities.

If anyone should be asked, what is the subject wherein color or weight inheres, he would have nothing to say but the solid extended parts. And if he were demanded, what is it that solidity and extension inhere in, he would not be in much better case than the Indian . . . who, saying that the world was supported by a great elephant, was asked, what the elephant rested on; to which his answer was, a great tortoise; but being again pressed to know what gave support to the broad-backed tortoise, replied—something, he knew not what . . . The idea, then, we have, to which we give the *general* name substance, being nothing but the supposed, but unknown, support of those qualities we find existing, which we imagine cannot subsist *sine re substante,* "without something to support them," we call that support substantia: which, according to the true import of the word, is, in plain English, standing under, or upholding (1706, II, ch. 23, sect. 2).

Isaac Newton (1642-1727), Locke's younger contemporary, was pleased with Locke's banishment of "substantial forms," and warned: "Beware of metaphysics!" Newton preferred the mathematico-mechanical explanation of phenomena, with analysis preceding synthesis. Removing the substratum that philosophers have termed *substance* created a lasting problem since the time of Locke. His intellectual successor, Berkeley, while retaining sense qualities, repudiated material substance, thus creating the doctrine of universal immaterialism or what is commonly known as *phenomenalism.*

GEORGE BERKELEY (1685-1735): The New Principle

Born in Kilkenny County, Ireland of an English customs officer who had come to Ireland, Berkeley, Ireland's greatest philosopher, attended Kilkenny College (the "Eton of Ireland") before graduating from the University of Dublin with his bachelor's in 1704 and again in 1707 with a M.A. degree. He lectured in divinity and Greek at Dublin until 1724 when he became dean of Derry. Having obtained a charter for a college in the Bermudas the following year, he left in 1728, spending three years in Rhode Island, where his daughter is buried. When it became apparent that the government grant was not forthcoming, he returned and was made Bishop of Cloyne in 1734. He retired in 1752 to Oxford where his son was studying, died suddenly the following year, and was buried in Christ Church, Oxford University.

The University of Dublin, where Locke's *An Essay concerning Human Understanding* stirred keen discussions, was the intellectual climate into which Berkeley entered. He assisted in forming a group for the discussion of Locke, Newton, and Boyle in 1705. In Dublin at the young age of 25 he published a classic, the *New Theory of Vision* (1709) and one year later his *magnum opus,* the *Principles of Human Knowledge* (1710). His *new principle* has been numerously termed: "subjective idealism," "phenomenalism," "universal immaterialism." By employing Hobbes' nominalism and Locke's empiricism, Berkeley annihilated corporeal substance. "There is no *senseless unperceived* substance" (1710, I, sect. 71). Inasmuch as all qualities are within a person's mind, then substance or matter as the substrate of sensible qualities does not exist since it is unknowable as Locke had established. Substance is a fictitious notion perpetuated throughout the ages. Bodies are precisely what they are perceived to be, rather than something behind what is actually perceived. External objects are exactly what is sensed (seen, touched, tasted, heard, and smelled), i.e., they are the stuff of experience. For a thing to exist it must be perceived. *"Esse is percipi."* To be is to be experienced.

> Some truths are so near and obvious to the mind that a man need only to open his eyes to see them. Such I take this important one to be, viz. that all the choir of heaven and furniture of the earth, in a word all those bodies which compose the mighty frame of the world, have not any subsistence without a mind—that their being is to be perceived or known; that consequently so long as they are not actually perceived by me, or do not exist in my mind or that of any other created spirit, they must either have no existence at all, or else subsist in the mind of some Eternal Spirit—it being perfectly unintelligible, and involving all the absurdity of abstraction, to attribute to any single part of them an existence independent of a spirit. To be convinced of which, the reader need only reflect, and try to separate in his own thoughts the being of a sensible thing from its being perceived (1710, I, sect. 6).

Only spirits (minds) and their functions (ideas, volitions, and understanding) exist. Objects are reduced to a complex of ideas, their only reality is in being perceived, accordingly they are a bundle of ideas, the sum of their qualities. Whereas Locke reduced ideas to sense, Berkeley accorded them a primacy.

A spirit or mind, on the other hand, is a simple, undivided, active being that perceives ideas and possesses an understanding and will, as two principle powers. "By the word *spirit* we mean only that which thinks, wills, and perceives." Whereas a spirit is active, an idea is passive.

Doctrine of Divine Arbitrariness. The laws of nature or science are merely the continual perception of a continuous succession of ideas. The laws of causation producing cause and effect relationships are the habitual ways in which God operates, the arbitrarily established habits of God. The sense data and the laws by which they are governed do not respond to my will, hence are the creatures of another will, viz., the deity.

> The ideas imprinted on the Senses by the Author of nature are called real things: and those excited in the Imagination being less regular, vivid, and constant, are more properly termed ideas, or images of things, which they copy and represent. But then our sensations, be they never so vivid and distinct, are nevertheless ideas, that is, they exist in the mind, or are perceived by it, as truly as the ideas of its own framing. The ideas of Sense are allowed to have more reality in them, that is, to be more strong, orderly, and coherent than the creatures of the mind; but this is no argument that they exist without the mind. They are also less dependent on the spirit, or thinking substance which perceives them, in that they are excited by the will of another and more powerful Spirit; yet still they are ideas, and certainly no idea, whether faint or strong, can exist otherwise than in a mind perceiving it (1710, I, sect. 33).

As John Stuart Mill later contended, Berkeley is a realist believing in objective reality, for he argued that "the things I see with my eyes and touch with my hands do exist, really exist, I make not the least question. The only thing whose existence we deny is that which *philosophers* call Matter or corporeal substance" (1710, I, sect. 35). A distinction is drawn between imagination and perception, the latter being orderly, distinct, and more affecting. Association among phenomena is divinely established, instituted as the divine habitual behavior or arbitrary will of God.

Berkeley's New Theory of Vision. While distance itself is invisible, remote distance is perceived by experience rather than by sense. Ideas suggesting distance are: (1) the sensation resulting from the eyes turning and (2) confused appearance. When distance is judged with both eyes, it is the result of experience. "For *distance* being a line directed end-wise to the eye, it projects only one point in the fund of the eye. Which point remains invariably the same, whether the distance be longer or shorter" (1709, sect. 1). By an idea that is perceived in the act of seeing, distance is "suggested" to the mind. The secondary criteria of vision (interposition, aerial perspective, and relative size), Berkeley had likewise discussed. He also cited three primary criteria: (1) distance between the pupils (convergence), (2) the occurrence of blurring when objects are placed too close to the eyes, and (3) straining of the eye when objects are too close to the eyes (accommodation). A man born blind would have no idea of distance immediately on receiving his sight.

> Distance or outness is neither immediately of itself perceived by sight, nor yet apprehended or judged of by lines and angles, or anything that hath a necessary connexion with it; but that it is only suggested to our thoughts by certain visible ideas and sensations attending vision, which in their own nature have no manner of similitude or relation either with distance or things placed at a distance; but, by a connexion taught us by experience, they come to signify and suggest them to us, after the same manner that words of any language suggest the ideas they are made to stand for; insomuch that a man born blind and afterwards made to see, would not, at first sight, think the things he saw to be without his mind, or at any distance from him (1710, I, sect. 43).

Perception of distance is from "an habitual or customary connexion" among ideas. The association principle as found in Berkeley is one of contiguity of ideas, ideas as being observed to go together constantly. By the principle of association Berkeley developed his theory of visual space perception. The retina's surface accounts for the horizontal and vertical, but not for depth perception which entails tactual experiences. Experiences gained through reach and touch become gradually associated with retinal phenomena. Tactual memories in combination with visual impressions explain the three-dimensional quality received by the retina. His theory of the mind's compounding of sensory qualities makes Berkeley one of the early entrants into associational psychology.

Not only is distance not perceived, magnitude is not either. Magnitude is contingent upon distance; without accounting for it by distance, it cannot be perceived.

> It hath been shown, there are two sorts of objects apprehended by sight; each whereof hath its distinct magnitude, or extension. The one properly tangible, i.e. to be perceived and measured by touch, and not immediately falling under the sense of seeing: the other, properly and immediately visible, by mediation of which the former is brought in view. Each of these magnitudes are greater or lesser according as they contain in them more or fewer points; they being made up of points or minimums. For, whatever may be said of extension in abstract, it is certain, sensible extension is not infinitely divisible. There is a minimum tangibile, and a minimum visibile, beyond which sense cannot perceive. This every one's experience will inform him.

> The magnitude of the object which exists without the mind, and is at a distance, continues always invariably the same: but the visible object still changing as you approach to, or recede from the tangible object, it hath no fixed and determinate greatness (1709, sect. 54-5).

Thus even the idea of size lacks objectivity.

Whereas Hobbes introduced matter as the sole substance, Locke eliminated the notion of substance. Berkeley, with his *psychologism,* discarded material substance for sense phenomena but retained the notion of spirit or mind, the entity necessary for the perception of ideas. Berkeley's intellectual successor in the British empirical movement, Hume, repudiated even the spirit, mind, or notion of self, leaving nothing but a "bundle of perceptions" as the human personality.

DAVID HUME (1711-1776): Personality as a Bundle of Perceptions

The Edinburgh-born philosopher, historian, and political economist, Hume, was educated at the University of Edinburgh. After studying law he became judge advocate to General James Sinclair in 1747, and in 1752 keeper of Advocates' Library in Edinburgh. In 1765 he was in Paris as a staff member of the British embassy, and two years later appointed under-secretary of state for a couple of years in London. He retired to Edinburgh in 1769. During this period he had an unhappy quarrel with Jean Jacques Rousseau, whom he had befriended. By 1775 his health failed steadily and he succumbed to death the following year.

Most of his contributions to psychology are found in his *Treatise of Human Nature, being an Attempt to Introduce the Experimental Method of Reasoning into Moral Subjects,* written during his stay in France and published in London in 1739 in three volumes, the third volume appearing the following year. Reviewing his own work, he asserted: "Never literary attempt was more unfortunate; it fell *dead-born from the press,* without reaching such distinction as even to excite a murmur among the zealots" (1777, p. 233). He published his *Philosophical Essays* (later entitled *An Inquiry concerning Human Understanding*) in 1748 as an abbreviated and simplified version of his *Treatise.* "The principles are the same in both," he commented.

Association of Ideas. Adopting Berkeley's phenomenalism and extreme nominalism that only particular ideas of sense exist, Hume replaced Locke's distinction of outer and inner perception with original (impression) or copy of an original (idea) as the content of consciousness. Ideas, copies of impressions, are simple or complex. Impressions may be of inner as well as of outer experience, for impressions are of two types: those of sensation and those of reflection.

Noting that ideas, by some principle of connection, associate with a certain degree of regularity, Hume asserted:

> Though it be too obvious to escape observation, that different ideas are connected together; I do not find that any philosopher has attempted to enumerate or class all the principles of association; a subject, however, that seems worthy of curiosity. To me, there appear to be only three principles of connexion among ideas, namely, *Resemblance, Contiguity* in time or place, and *Cause* or *Effect* (1777, sect. 3).

Not that the uniting principle is an inseparable connection, but it is guided by a principle of uniformity. Ideas that are simple become complex by virtue of a bond or union, an associating quality. He cited examples of each: (1) resemblance: "a picture naturally leads our thoughts to the original," (2) contiguity: "the mention of one apartment in a building naturally introduces an enquiry or discourse concerning the others;" and (3) cause and effect: "if we think of a wound, we can scarcely forbear reflecting on the pain which follows it." Some "gentle force" prevails in associating ideas.

Yet, Hume finds no necessary connection in cause and effect relationships, no observable cause, but only a *sequence* of events rather than a consequential relationship.

> When we look about us towards external objects, and consider the operation of causes, we are never able, in a single instance, to discover any power or necessary connexion; any quality, which binds the effect to the cause, and renders the one an infallible consequence of the other. We only find, that the one does actually, in fact, follow the other. The impulse of one billiard-ball is attended with motion in the second. This is the whole that appears to the *outward* senses. The mind feels no sentiment or *inward* impression from this succession of objects: Consequently, there is not, in any single, particular instance of cause and effect, any thing which can suggest the idea of power or necessary connexion (1777, sect. 7).

If causes were indeed perceptible then it would be possible to ascertain the cause of any effect on first experiencing the event. Cause, rather than being a real entity, is an association of sequential events.

The Mind as a Bundle of Perceptions. The phenomenalism of Hume eliminated all metaphysical entities including matter, substance, soul, God, and the laws of science or of nature, hence his philosophy of skepticism or nihilism. Inasmuch as the laws of science (nature) are imperceptible then they do not exist, a fact that awoke Kant from his dogmatic slumber. Although agreeing with Berkeley's psychologism that only perceptions exist, he rejected the Berkeleian position that the soul was necessary in order to have perceptions. The mind is no more than the perceptions active within it.

> We may observe, that what we call a *mind*, is nothing but a heap or collection of different perceptions, united together by certain relations, and suppos'd, tho' falsely, to be endow'd with a perfect simplicity and identity. Now as every perception is distinguishable from another, and may be consider'd as separately existent; it evidently follows, that there is no absurdity in separating any particular perception from the mind; that is, in breaking off all its relations, with that connected mass of perceptions, which constitute a thinking being (1739, bk. 1, pt. 4, sect. 2).

Descartes thought of the soul as indubitable, an inner ego, for a thought without a thinker cannot exist. Similarly Berkeley held that there can be no perceptions without a perceiver. But Hume, to the contrary, disagreed because one does not have a perception or idea of himself. In order to have an impression of the self it must remain invariably the same thoroughout the entire course of one's life. Yet no such impression exists.

If any impression gives rise to the idea of self, that impression must continue invariably the same, thro' the whole course of our lives; since self is suppos'd to exist after that manner. But there is no impression constant and invariable. . . .

When I enter most intimately into what I call *myself,* I always stumble on some particular perception or other, of heat or cold, light or shade, love or hatred, pain or pleasure. I never can catch myself at any time without a perception, and never can observe any thing but the perception. . . .

I may venture to affirm the rest of mankind, that they are nothing but a bundle or collection of different perceptions which succeed each other with an inconceivable rapidity, and are in a perpetual flux and movement (1739, bk. 1, pt. 4, sect. 6).

The soul, without a power that remains the same, is like a theatre where perceptions, having made their successive appearances, pass on.

Some credit Hume as the impetus behind associational psychology. Certainly he had considerable effect with the Scottish associationists. Others reacted to him by seeking refuge in realism, but in the naive realism that objects are genuinely and objectively real, their reality being exactly as the senses depict them. Hume also had considerable influence over current schools of thought, especially logical positivism.

(B)   BRITISH ASSOCIATIONISM

Associational Psychology. Associationism, while as old as the psychology of Aristotle, gained currency with David Hartley, despite its coinage being that of John Locke who introduced it in the fourth edition of his classic *Essay concerning Human Understanding* in 1700 (as the 33rd chapter of book II, "Of the Association of Ideas." Locke used it to convey connections among experiences, as illustrated in paragraphs six and seven of that work:

This strong combination of *ideas,* not allied by nature, the mind makes in itself either voluntarily or by chance; and hence it comes in different men to be very different, according to their different inclinations, educations, interest, etc. . . . A musician used to any tune will find that, let it but once begin in his head, the *ideas* of the several notes of it will follow one another orderly in his understanding, without any care or attention, as regularly as his fingers move orderly over the keys of the organ to play out the tune he has begun. . . . That there are such associations of them made by custom in the minds of most men, I think nobody will question. . . . (1706)

But Locke's treatment of association is as a principal cause of error rather than a human process of knowledge. While *association* is the term accorded widest acceptance, other terms were also used such as *suggestion* by Thomas Brown, *mental discourse* by Thomas Hobbes, and *translation* by Tucker.

Association as the principal mental function was scarcely used since the time of Plato and Aristotle until the period of Hobbes and British empiricism, especially the thinkers Locke, Berkeley, and Hume. These British empiricists were interested in association psychology as ancillary to their epistemological theories. But the theory of knowledge of the British empiricists served to catapult the association psychology so that with Hartley's *Observations on Man* (1749), the era of association psychology was launched.

The precursors of association psychology, writers from the time of Plato, Aristotle, and *John of Salisbury* (c. 1115-1180) to the Spaniard *Juan Luis Vives* (1492-1540), touch upon association psychology only in passing, and consequently must be regarded as only forerunners of associationism. But they explicitly touch upon association psychology as the following excerpt from Plato's Phaedo attests:

> What is the feeling of lovers when they recognize a lyre or a garment or anything else which the beloved has been in the habit of using? Do not they from knowing the lyre form in the mind's eye an image of the youth to whom the lyre belongs? And this is recollection: and in the same way anyone who sees Simmias may remember Cebes. . . . And from the picture of Simmias you may be led to remember Cebes. . . . And in all these cases the recollection may be derived from things either like or unlike. . . . When we perceive something either by the help of sight or hearing or some other sense, there was no difficulty in receiving from this a conception of some other thing, like or unlike, which had been forgotten and which was associated with this (1890, 73-76).

Aristotle, likewise, in his *De Memoria et Reminiscentia (On Memory and Reminiscence)* wrote:

> Acts of recollection, as they occur in experience, are due to the fact that one movement has by nature another that succeeds it in regular order. . . . Whenever, therefore, we are recollecting, we are experiencing certain of the antecedent movements until finally we experience the one after which customarily comes that which we seek. This explains why we hunt up the series of movements, having started in thought either from a present intuition or some other, and from something either similar, or contrary, to what we seek, or else from that which is contiguous with it (1941, p. 612).

Yet it was not until the time of Hume that the principles of association were sought. Reducing the principles of association to three, Hume had cited them as: resemblance, contiguity (in time and place), and cause and effect. Taking his lead from Hume, another Scot, Dugald Stewart (1753-1828), offered resemblance, contrariety, and vicinity (in time and place) in addition to accidental coincidence with respect to the sounds of words. He also added cause and effect, means and end, and premises and conclusion as cases of relation in one's train of thought.

Although the association school of psychology is principally British, in Germany mental association was treated by Wolff; and in France by Condillac and the French sensationalists. In Baldwin's *Dictionary of Philosophy and Psychology*, G. F. Stout defined associationism as "the theory which, starting with certain simple and ultimate constituents of consciousness, makes mental development consist solely or mainly in the combination of these elements according to certain laws of association. . . . According to this theory . . . all genesis of new products is due to the combination of pre-existing elements" (1901, p. 80)

Considering the British empiricists as the first stage of development of association psychology, the second stage extended from the publication of Hartley's

Observations on Man in 1749 to the publication of *Analysis of the Phenomena of the Human Mind* by James Mill in 1829, and would include Thomas Brown's *Lectures on the Philosophy of the Human Mind* (1820). The third period, opening with Mill's *Analysis* in 1829, ran to the publication of Spencer's *Principles of Psychology* in 1855 which opened the fourth period. With this publication, British psychology enters its evolutionary period.

Hartley's formulation was grounded in a physiological process entailing vibrations of a brain substance stimulated externally through the senses from which ideas arise and are associated. Repudiating Hartley's fusion of psychology with physiology, Brown based his associationism on intuitional psychology in which the ideas associated are new entities rather than the mere revival of earlier sensations and introduced the concept of "mental chemistry" that John Stuart Mill was to adopt as an integral part of his system. According to James Mill the mind was merely machinery for the associative process, stressing the indissolubility of associations, whereas his son, John Stuart Mill, abandoned his father's mechanism for the chemical view, i.e., mental chemistry. With Bain, introspectionism is rejected for the physiological as Hartley had done originally, thus making the circle complete. But Bain's physiology is far more sophisticated so that the pendulum of the Hegelian dialectic swung more in the form of an upward spiraling cycle. Nevertheless the associative process remained for Bain of fundamental importance.

DAVID HARTLEY (1705-1757): Association of Ideas

The classic work of Hume's contemporary, David Hartley's *Observations on Man* (1749) antedates the work of Hume. An English physician from London and recognized founder of the associationist school of psychology, Hartley was a University of Cambridge graduate. His *Observations on Man* (1749), expounding his associationism, appeared three years after Condillac's *Essay on the Origin of Human Knowledge,* coincidentally containing common views.

But he did derive the idea for his theory from another Cantabridgian work, John Gay's (1699-1745) *Dissertation concerning the Fundamental Principles of Virtue or Morality* (1731), consequently making Gay the immediate precursor of the association school of psychology. In that work, Gay wrote:

> We first perceive or imagine some real good. . . . Hence . . . we annex pleasure to those things. Hence those things and pleasure are so tied together and associated in our minds, that one cannot present itself, but the other will also occur. And the association remains even after that which at first gave them the connection is quite forgot (1781, 884).

Known principally for his two major theories: (1) doctrine of *vibrations* and (2) doctrine of *associations,* Hartley sought to establish a correspondence between neural and mental activity by the medium of vibrations, utilizing the *association principle* as his explanation. The first doctrine is hinted in the last paragraph of Newton's *Optics* in the *Principia,* and the second from Locke and the empiricists. Accepting Locke's *tabula rasa* mind as his premise, Hartley traced sensations to vibrations of minute particles in the medullary substance of the nerves and brain.

Borrowing Newton's world-ether doctrine, he developed a "physics of the soul," grounded on nerve mechanics.

> External objects impressed upon the senses occasion, first in the nerves on which they are impressed, and then in the brain, vibrations of the small, and, as one may say, infinitesimal, medullary particles (1749, I, prop. 4).

Moderate vibrations produce pleasure, while pain results from the more violent ones. He accounted for memory by vibration depositing in the brain *vibratiuncles* (fainter vibrations) resembling the original and corresponding to ideas of sensation. One's past experiences determine the nature, intensity, and extent of vibrations in the brain that account for reminiscences and thoughts.

His proposition regarding associations states:

> Any sensation *A, B, C,* etc. by being associated with one another a sufficient number of times, gets such a power over the corresponding ideas *a, b, c,* etc. that one of the sensations *A,* when impressed alone, shall be able to excite in the mind *b, c,* etc. the ideas of the rest (1749, I, prop. 10).

The oft associated sensations become associated with corresponding ideas, as well as the ideas associating themselves with each other. "Sensations may be said to be associated together, when their impressions are either made precisely at the same instant of time, or in the contiguous successive instants" (1749, prop. 10). Accordingly there are two types of association: (1) synchronous and (2) successive. The two, aspects of contiguity, establish association on the basis of contiguity.

Relying constantly on Locke's coinage, the "association of ideas," which Hartley used throughout his work, he sought to account for sense phenomena, emotions, memory, and the like in terms of his two major laws of vibration and association.

Reducing passions, emotions, or affections to "aggregates of simple ideas united by association," Hartley stated that they were "excited by objects" and were "traces of the sensible pleasures and pains, which make up by their number, and mutual influence upon one another, for the faintness and transitory nature of each singly taken" (1749, p 368). The implication of this explanation is a mechanistic theory of will.

The determinist Hartley explained voluntary action as resulting from the firm connection existing between motion and sensation (idea); or, in physical terms, between an ideal and motory vibration. He enunciated his position accordingly:

> By the mechanism of human actions I mean, that each action results from the previous circumstances of body and mind, in the same manner, and with the same certainty, as other effects do from their mechanical causes; so that a person cannot do indifferently either of the actions *A,* and its contrary *a,* while the previous circumstances are the same; but is under an absolute necessity of doing one of them, and that only. Agreeably to this I suppose, that by free-will is meant a power of doing either the action *A,* or its contrary *a;* while the previous circumstances remain the same.
>
> If by free-will is meant a power of beginning motion, this will come to the same thing;

since, according to the opinion of mechanism, as here explained, man has no such power; but every action, or bodily motion, arises from previous circumstances, or bodily motions, already existing in the brain, i.e. from vibrations, which are either the immediate effect or impressions then made, or the remote compound effect of former impressions, or both (1749, I, pp. 500-1).

Thus Hartley's system, is association theory synthesized with a theory of vibratory motion. He was the first to distinguish between association by contiguity and by similarity.

   Joseph Priestly (1733-1804): Hartley's Disciple. A quarter of a century after the publication of Hartley's *Observations on Man,* Joseph Priestley, an English chemist and clergyman, developed Hartley's theory further in his *Hartley's Theory of the Human Mind on the Principle of the Association of Ideas* (1775). It was Priestley's *Essay on the First Principles of Government* (1768) that suggested "the greatest happiness of the greatest number" principle to Jeremy Bentham as his criterion of moral good and right.

   Pleased with Hartley's repudiation of instinct, soul, and faculties, Priestley carried Hartley's materialism and associationism further. He saw education with unlimited possibilities. Children exposed to the right experience would by associative laws develop habits of good behavior. Explaining his extreme form of empiricism and associationism, Priestley wrote:

> Till the mind has been affected with a sense of pleasure or pain, all objects are alike indifferent to it; but some, in consequence of being always accompanied with a perception of pleasure, become pleasing to us while others, in consequence of being accompanied with a sense of pain, become displeasing; and to effect this nothing can be requisite but the association of agreeable sensations and ideas with the one, and of disagreeable ones with the other. Admitting, therefore, the doctrine of association or that two ideas often occurring together will afterwards introduce one another, we have all that is requisite to the formation of all our passions or affections, or of some things being the objects of love and others of hatred to us (1777, sect. 4).

   Julien Offray de la Mettrie (1709-1751): Man as a Machine. Whereas Priestley replaced Hartley's psychology with a complete nerve physiology, the French physician Julien Offray de la Mettrie carried this anthropological materialism to its ultimate, reducing a human being to a machine. In his *Histoire Naturelle de l' Âme (Natural History of the Soul,* 1745; translated as *Man a Machine,* 1912), La Mettrie taught that organic changes occurring in the brain and nervous system account for all mental phenomena. He argued that

> the human body is a machine which winds its own springs. It is the living image of perpetual movement. It is the function of nourishment to continue those bodily functions originally produced by heat. Without nourishment for the body, the soul also languishes, goes mad, or dies through exhaustion. The soul is not unlike a taper, which flares up briefly a moment before it goes out. But nourish the body, pour into its veins vigorous juices and strong liquors and the soul becomes strong again, and the soldier who would have been put to flight by water becomes fierce, and gallantly rushes forward to his death to the sound of drums. It is in this fashion that a hot drink excites the blood, where a cold drink calms it (1912, p. 21).

Believing that physical death terminated the mental life, La Mettrie advocated a life devoted to the enjoyment of pleasure. La Mettrie was pursuing the psychology of Locke in restricting the contents of the mental life to elements derived from the excitation of the senses.

Étienne Bonnot de Condillac (1715-1780): French Sensationalism. It was another Frenchman, Condillac, who, more so than La Mettrie expounded Locke's empiricism in its extreme form, sensationalism. During the period of the French Enlightenment, Condillac developed his association psychology in his *Traité des Sensations* (1754), (translated as *Treatise on the Sensations,* 1930). Earlier in his *Essai sur l'Origine des Connaissances Humaines* (Essay on the Origin of Human Knowledge, 1746), he, premising his position on Locke's empiricism, theorized that a person's mental development is due to his use of language, for without words, ideas are impossible; without learning to speak, mental reflection is impossible.

By the time Condillac wrote his *Treatise on Sensations,* he no longer accepted Locke's theory that sensation and reflection are the sole sources of ideas. Rather he limited the mental life to sensations alone. Utilizing a fantasy to explain his view, Condillac imagined a marble statue in human form. In turn the statue acquired senses: first smell, then taste, hearing, sight, and touch as the final sense. He concluded that without touch the other senses, singly or in combination, would be incapable of giving one an idea of an object that was external to consciousness. He equated attention with a vivid sensation, memory with a recalled sensation (transformed sensation), instinct with a habit (but its reflection is obliterated), and feeling with thinking, for thought is a consequence of sense. Love, hate, fear, volition, hope, and other activities of the mind are simply transformed sensations, sensation as experienced being either pleasurable or painful. Thus Condillac felt justified in concluding:

> The history of our statue's faculties make the progress of all these things clear. When it was limited to fundamental feeling, one uniform sensation comprised its whole existence, its whole knowledge, its whole pleasure. In giving it successively new modes of being, and new senses, we saw it form desires, learn from experience to regulate and satisfy them, and pass from needs to needs, from cognitions to cognitions, from pleasures to pleasures. The statue is therefore nothing but the sum of all it has acquired. May not this be the same with man? (1930, pp. 239-8).

During the French Enlightenment the psychology of Locke had dominated the French, completely eclipsing that of their own countryman and founder of physiological psychology, René Descartes. The psychology of sensationalism met with intense opposition among the Scottish psychologists, especially Thomas Reid and his successors.

THOMAS REID (1710-1796): Sensation and Perception

The Scottish philosopher and psychologist, Reid, was graduated from the University of Aberdeen in 1726, remaining there as librarian, and in 1752 to be elected to the chair of philosophy for a dozen years. The year that he published his *Inquiry into the Human Mind on the Principles of Common Sense* (1764), he succeeded to the chair of Adam Smith as Professor of Moral Philosophy at the University of Glasgow, where he remained for sixteen years. A founder of the Aberdeen Philosophical Society, Reid was abruptly stimulated by the theories of his compatriot, Hume, which affected him as they did Kant by awakening him from his dogmatic slumbers. Resigning from his professorship in 1780 in order to enable himself to write, Reid published the *Essays on the Intellectual Powers* (1785) when he was 75 years of age and his *Essays on the Active Powers* (1788) three years later.

Reid rebelled against the skepticism of Descartes and Hume, and the subjective idealism of Berkeley. Reacting to them, he developed his "common sense" philosophy, which became popular in Scotland and filtered down to the present time as *naive realism*. One of the axioms of common sense is that, Hume to the contrary, sensations without a sentient being do not exist. Since Hume's reasoning appeared to Reid as "just," it was necessary therefore either "to call in question the principles upon which it was founded, or to admit the conclusion" (1765, p. v). He thought it unreasonable "to admit a hypothesis, which . . . overturns . . . common sense," hence the start of the common sense school in Scotland, theories of which were to play an important role in England, Russia, and the United States as well.

Theory of Sensation and Perception. Known in the history of psychology for his theory of sensation and perception, Reid dealt with them in his *Inquiry into the Human Mind* (1764) and in his *Essays on the Intellectual Powers* (1785). Distinguishing sensation from perception (the rose itself external to a person), he differentiated the two accordingly:

> When I smell a rose, there is in this operation both sensation and perception. The agreeable odour I feel, considered by itself, without relation to any external object, is merely a sensation. It affects the mind in a certain way; and this affection of the mind may be conceived, without a thought of the rose, or any other object. This sensation can be nothing else than it is felt to be. Its very essence consists in being felt; and, when it is not felt, it is not. There is no difference between the sensation and the feeling of it — they are one and the same thing. It is for this reason that we before observed that, in sensation, there is not object distinct from that act of the mind by which it is felt — and this holds true with regard to all sensations.
>
> Let us next attend to the perception which we have in smelling a rose. Perception has always an external object; and the object of my perception, in this case, is that quality in the rose which I discern by the sense of smell. Observing that the agreeable sensation is raised when the rose is near, and ceases when it is removed, I am led, by my nature, to conclude some quality to be in the rose, which is the cause of this sensation. This quality in the rose is the object perceived; and that act of my mind by which I have the conviction and belief of this quality, is what in this case I call perception (1785, Essay 2, ch. 16).

Though not technically an associationist, Reid initiated among the associationists the theory that sensations possess objective reference. To the naive realists he contributed the dictum that sensation is a natural or original principle of belief.

Reid's work was continued by his disciple, *Dugald Stewart* (1753-1828) from Edinburgh, but his contributions to that of Reid were virtually nil. The most that he accomplished was to popularize Reid's position. But Stewart did produce an original thinker of the association school in the form of his disciple, Thomas Brown, who attended his lectures at the University of Edinburgh, later to become his colleague.

THOMAS BROWN (1778-1820):
Primary Laws of Suggestion (Association)

Abandoning the practice of medicine for philosophy and literature, Brown, a graduate from the University of Edinburgh with an M.D., distinguished himself in the history of psychology with his association theory which was more in the tradition of the English associationists than the Scottish thinkers. He died at the height of his career, leaving to his successors the publication of his classic three volume work in psychology *Lectures on the Philosophy of the Human Mind* (1820). When objection was raised to the appointment of John Leslie as a professor of mathematics in 1805 because he was charged with being an infidel and a skeptic as a follower of Hume, Brown wrote an able defense in support of Hume's doctrine of causality, *Inquiry into the Relation of Cause and Effect.* Hume's skepticism also engendered a disenchantment for associationism. In need of a principle comparable to association psychology in order to account for the unity of the soul, Brown turned to what he termed the *law of suggestion.*

Primary and Secondary Laws of Suggestion. The phrase *association of ideas* was unacceptable to Brown because it lacked a "suggesting principle" to ideas. Thus his preference for the term "suggestion" rather than "association" shows the influence of Hobbes from whom it derives. He noted that the suggesting principle is influenced by similarity; resemblance is a connecting principle in one's train of thought. Suggestion, he asserted, depends "on prior coexistence, or at least, on such immediate proximity as in itself, very probably, a modification of coexistence" (1820, II, p. 11).

Citing three primary laws of suggestion: (1) *resemblance,* (2) *contrast,* (3) *nearness of place or time,* Brown proceeded to discuss secondary laws of suggestion. He illustrated resemblance by stating that "no one can be ignorant of the effect of strong similarity, in recalling objects, as when a pictured landscape recalls a familiar scene, or a portrait a familiar countenance" (1820, II, pp. 11-12). Contrast, as a suggesting principle, is readily seen by the following contrasting illustrations. "The *palace* and the *cottage,*—the *cradle* and the *grave,*—the extremes of *indigence* and of luxurious *splendour,* are not connected in artificial *antithesis* only, but arise, in ready succession, to the observer of *either*" (1820, II, 34). Hume's principle of contiguity is the third law (nearness in place or time). "To think of one part of a familiar landscape, is to recall the whole" (1820, II, p. 41).

The *secondary laws of suggestion,* those modifying the influence of the primary by inducing one association rather than another, consist of the following nine:

In addition then, to the primary laws of suggestion, which are founded on the mere relations of the objects or feelings to each other, it appears that there is another set of laws, the operation of which is indispensable to account for the variety in the effects of the former. To these I have given the name of *secondary laws of suggestion;*—and we have seen, accordingly, that the suggestions are various as the original feelings have been, 1st, Of longer or shorter continuance; 2dly, More or less lively; 3dly, More or less frequently present; 4thly, More or less recent; 5thly, More or less pure, if I may so express it, from the mixture of other feelings; 6thly, That they vary according to differences of original constitution; 7thly, According to the differences of temporary emotion; 8thly, According to the changes produced in the state of the body; and, 9thly, According to general tendencies produced by prior habits. (1820, II, p. 53)

Whereas the primary laws are founded on the mere relations of objects or feelings to each other, the secondary laws of suggestion account for the modifications that situations or conditions bear on the primary. The principle of habit likewise modifies the primary laws of suggestion with its potent influence.

Also introducing a theory of *relative suggestion,* Brown defined it as that tendency of mind "by which, on perceiving or conceiving objects together, we are instantly impressed with certain feelings of their mutual relation" (1820, II, p. 273). The relative suggestion is to be distinguished from *simple suggestion,* the mind's tendency to think of an idea owing to an experience by which the two are connected by proximity.

The theory of *mental chemistry* which was to become an issue with John Stuart Mill originated with Brown's hypothesis that complex mental states arise from fusions as well as compositions of simple and relative suggestions.

From the very instant of its first existence, the mind is constantly exhibiting phenomena more and more complex,—sensations, thoughts, emotions, all mingling together, and almost every feeling modifying, in some greater or less degree, the feelings that succeed it;—and as, in chemistry, it often happens, that the qualities of the separate ingredients of a compound body are not recognizable by us, in the apparently different qualities of the compound itself,—so, in this spontaneous *chemistry* of *the mind,* the compound sentiment, that results from the association of former feelings, has, in many cases, on first consideration, so little resemblance to these constituents of it, as formerly existing in their elementary state, that it requires the most attentive reflection to separate, and evolve distinctly to others, the assemblages which even a few years may have produced. (1820, I, p. 156).

Mental chemistry was not the only influence exerted on subsequent psychologists by Brown, nor was it limited to the laws of association which he adamantly termed suggestion. He assisted in lending prominence to the muscle sense and its associated experiences as well as bringing to the fore the experience of relation.

WILLIAM HAMILTON (1788-1856): Law of Redintegration

Reid's *Works* were prepared, annotated, and introduced by the Glasgow-born *William Hamilton,* who was an unsuccessful candidate for Thomas Brown's chair of philosophy at the University of Edinburgh but successful in obtaining one of his own in logic and metaphysics in 1836.

More of a critic than a member of the association school, Hamilton is known in psychology for his theory of *redintegration,* found in his posthumous *Lectures on Metaphysics* published in 1858. Redintegration, a theory in the tradition of associationism, is the view that a stimulus which is an integral part of a whole complex will activate the entire complex when it is itself activated, such as a few notes from a song will cause one to recall the entire melody. By redintegration entire trains of thoughts are stimulated since they are connected like links of a chain.

> The faculty of Reproduction is governed by the laws which regulate the Association of the mental train. . . . Brown divides the circumstances affecting association into primary and secondary. Under the primary laws of Suggestion, he includes Resemblance, Contrast, Contiguity in time and place,—a classification identical with Aristotle's . . . Now all the laws which I have hitherto enumerated may be easily reduced to two,—the law of Simultaneity, and the law of Resemblance or Affinity, of Thought. Under Simultaneity I include Immediate Consecution in time; to the other category of Affinity every other circumstance may be reduced (1858, p. 431).

After reducing all laws to his two—resemblance and affinity—, Hamilton then reduces these two to the one supreme law of redintegration.

The law of redintegration or totality, which Hamilton discovered in *The Confessions* of St. Augustine, he explained as follows:

> Those thoughts suggest each other which had previously constituted parts of the same entire or total act of cognition. Now to the same entire or total act belong, as integral or constituent parts, in the first place, those thoughts which arose at the same time, or in immediate consecution; and in the second, those thoughts which are bound up into one by their mutual affinity. Thus, therefore, the two laws of Simultaneity and Affinity are carried up into unity, in the higher law of Redintegration or Totality; and by this one law the whole phenomena of Association may be easily explained (1858, p. 435).

Augustine's account of association psychology from which Hamilton obtained his redintegration theory follows:

> But what when the memory itself loses any thing, as falls out when we forget and seek that we may recollect? Where in the end do we search, but in the memory itself? and there, if one thing be perchance offered instead of another, we reject it, until what we seek meets us; and when it doth, we say, "This is it;" which we should not unless we recognized it, nor recognize it unless we remembered it. Certainly then we had forgotten it. Or, had not the whole escaped us, but by the part whereof we had hold, was the lost part sought for; in that the memory felt that it did not carry on together all which it was wont, and maimed, as it were, by the curtailment of its ancient habit, demanded the restoration of what it missed? For instance, if we see or think of some one known to us, and having forgotten his name, try to recover it; whatever else occurs, connects itself not therewith; because it was not wont to be thought upon together with him, and therefore is rejected, until that present itself, whereon the knowledge reposes equally as its wonted object. And whence does that present itself, but out of the memory itself? for even when

we recognize it, on being reminded by another, it is thence it comes. For we do not believe it as something new, but, upon recollection, allow what was named to be right. But were it utterly blotted out of the mind, we should not remember it, even when reminded. For we have not as yet utterly forgotten that which we remember ourselves to have forgotten. What then we have utterly forgotten, though lost, we cannot even seek after (1907, 10, XIX, 28).

Hamilton is also known for his theory of logic which clashed with the formulation of *Augustus de Morgan* (1806-1871), notable in psychology, logic, and mathematics for *De Morgan's theorem,* a new logic of relations. In his *Formal Logic* (1847) containing his laws, De Morgan offered an algebra of logic comparable to the English mathematician *George Boole* (1815-1864), published the same year in his *Mathematical Analysis of Logic,* and in a more developed form in *Laws of Logic* (1854). De Morgan's laws were known in verbal form by *William of Ockham* (1280-1347), especially known for *Ockham's razor.* Hamilton's memory has been perpetuated by John Stuart Mill's *Examination of Hamilton's Philosophy* (1865), containing important doctrines for philosophy and psychology. A member of the Scottish school and an able critic, Hamilton stimulated subsequent associationists to reexamine the fundamental principles of association psychology.

JAMES MILL (1773-1836): Association of Ideas

With the writings of James Mill and his son, John Stuart Mill, association psychology embarks on a more systematic basis by an orderly analysis of associationism. The father, a Scot historian and philosopher who moved to London, virtually failed as a clergyman of the Scottish church before becoming editor of the *Literary Journal* in 1803. His acquaintance with Jeremy Bentham (1747-1832) led to his complete adoption of Bentham's utilitarian theories. With Bentham and others, he contributed to the founding of London University in 1825. His principle contribution to psychology, *Analysis of the Human Mind* (1829), was published four years later. With the publication of his greatest literary achievement, *History of India* in 1818, he entered a successful career as an official in the India House. With Mill, association psychology reached its apex. Some believe that Mill is the only pure or genuine associationist to follow Hartley.

Association Psychology. Like Hartley, Mill concerned himself with only *contiguity,* that is, impressions repeated synchronously or in immediate succession. But Mill sought to establish a *law of frequency* in order to resolve the principle of similarity and of contrast. Instead of Brown's formulation of mental phenomena, Mill preferred Hartley's. Whereas Hartley's *Observations on Man* (1749) was the classic of association psychology of the eighteenth century, Mill's *Analysis of the Human Mind* (1829) was the classic of the nineteenth. Mill purported to adduce proofs for association psychology that Hartley lacked.

Mill, who has been regarded as the second founder of association psychology, relegated mental phenomena into sensations ("primary states of consciousness") and ideas, the latter arising from the former. E.g., to see a horse is a sensation, then to think of his master is an idea, and one idea may set off a chain reaction of a number of other ideas. Sensations (eight in number) occur in a (1) synchronous order or (2) successive order. "The synchronous order, or order of simultaneous existence, is the order in space; the successive order, or order of antecedent and consequent existence, is the order in time" (1869, I, p. 71).

Unlike sensations, ideas are not derived from objects but from sensations, and respond to the general law of the association of ideas, viz., "our ideas spring up, or exist, in the order in which the sensations existed, of which they are the copies" (1869, I, p. 78). Association is not a force, power, or cause, but simple contiguity. Implicit in this law are the following:

1. Of those sensations which occurred synchronically, the ideas also spring up synchronically. . . .

2. As the ideas of the sensations which occurred synchronically, rise synchronically, so the ideas of the sensations which occurred successively, rise successively. . . .

3. A far greater number of our sensations are received in the successive, than in the synchronical order. Of our ideas, also, the number is infinitely greater that rise in the successive than the synchronical order.

4. In the successive order of ideas, that which precedes, is sometimes called the suggesting, that which succeeds, the suggested idea; not that any power is supposed to reside in the antecedent over the consequent; suggesting, and suggested, mean only antecedent and consequent, with the additional idea, that such order is not causal, but, to a certain degree, permanent.

5. Of the antecedent and consequent feelings, or the suggesting, and suggested; the antecedent may be either sensations or ideas; the consequent are always ideas. An idea may be excited either by a sensation or an idea. . . .

6. As there are degrees in sensations, and degrees in ideas; for one sensation more vivid than another sensation, one idea more vivid than another idea; so there are degrees in association. . . .

7. The causes of strength in association seem all to be resolvable into two; the vividness of the associated feelings; and the frequency of the association. . . .

8. Where two or more ideas have been often repeated together, and the association has become very strong, they sometimes spring up in such close combination as not to be distinguishable. . . .

9. Some ideas are by frequency and strength of association so closely combined, that they cannot be separated. If one exists, the other exists along with it, in spite of whatever effort we make to disjoin them. . . .

10. It not unfrequently happens in our associated feelings, that the antecedent is of no importance farther than as it introduces the consequent. . . .

11. Mr. Hume, and after him other philosophers, have said that our ideas are associated according to three principles; Contiguity in time and place, Causation, and Resemblance. The Contiguity in time and place, must mean, that of the sensations; and so far it is affirmed, that the order of the ideas follows that of the sensations. Contiguity in time, means the successive order. Contiguity of two sensations in place, means the synchronous order (1869, I, pp. 78-110).

Mill's principles of vividness and frequency are his replacements of Brown's secondary laws, and Hume's three laws of association are interpolated for assimilation into his own system. Resemblance arises from our being accustomed to seeing like things together a number of times, hence is reducible to frequency. Mill's son John took issue with this aspect of his father's theory.

Summarizing the phenomena of the human mind, Mill enumerated them as: (1) sensations, (2) ideas (copies of sensations), (3) simple ideas (copies of one sensation) and complex ideas (copies of several sensations in such combination that they give the appearance of being only one idea), and (4) trains of ideas (one idea succeeding another indefinitely). Ratiocination or syllogistic reasoning he explained as association of terms of a proposition grouped into a train. Reflection is reduced to consciousness, and consciousness in turn to possessing sensations and ideas. An idea of reflection is more than a "generalization of particular states of consciousness" (1869, II, p. 179). The will he defined as a peculiar conscious state preceded by action.

One objection to Mill's explanation of the growth of mental complexity is his mechanical account of the associative process, viewing the mind and its experiences merely as complex and successive mental states comparable to the workings of a machine. Later, his son, seeking to correct his father's short-comings, accounted for these processes by "mental chemistry." Nevertheless association in its pure form culminated in James Mill's *Analysis* which followed in the Hartley tradition.

JOHN STUART MILL (1806-1873): Permanent Possibilities of Sensation

The precocious son of James Mill, John Stuart Mill, was taught Greek by his father at three, to read Plato and study Latin and algebra by eight, and logic at twelve. He remembered the chilling sternness of his reserved, undemonstrative father. The London-born Mill joined the East India House at seventeen, rising to the chief of the office. When he was about fourteen to fifteen years of age he spent over a year in France with Jeremy Bentham's brother Samuel. After the dissolution of the East India Company in 1858 he, being pensioned, turned to a literary and political life, being elected to parliament after refusing to canvass for political office in 1865.

Mill added his own notes to his father's *Analysis of the Human Mind* in 1869, thus developing his own position on association psychology while at the same time criticizing his father's viewpoint. His psychology is also found in his *Logic* (1843) as well as in his *Examination of Sir William Hamilton's Philosophy* (1865). Hamilton's incisive criticisms spurred him and other associationists to re-examine the premises of association psychology.

Mental association that Hartley saw as inseparable, James Mill explained as ideas combined inseparably by frequency and association. John Stuart Mill, moderating his father's stand, said that the "inseparable associations" are dissoluble by subsequent experiences. John Stuart Mill postulated two important hypotheses: (1) expectation of sensation, and (2) laws of association of ideas. According to the first hypothesis, the mind, capable of expectation, forms concepts of possible sensations, i.e., sensations, though presently not experienced, can be, if given the necessary conditions, conditions that have been learned by experience. Matter, he defined as "the permanent possibility of sensation." He added, "the reliance of mankind on the real existence of visible and tangible objects, means reliance on the reality and permanence of possibilities of visual and tactual sensations, when no such sensations are actually experienced. We are warranted in believing that this is the meaning of matter" (1884, I, pp. 243-4). In this respect Mill is a realist in the sense of Berkeley, for both believe in external reality, but not in inert matter devoid of sense content. Later, William James followed suit with his doctrine of *radical empiricism*. Mill sought to formulate a "psychological theory of the belief in an external world" by theorizing the mind's ability to proceed from actual sensation to possible sensations, concluding that matter is merely the "permanent possibilities of sensations." It is by association that certain permanent possibilities of sensations are grouped in given configurations, and hold according to the associative law of inseparability (resembling the context theory of his father and Berkeley).

Laws of Association. Mill enunciated the following four laws of association:

> 1st. Similar phaenomena tend to be thought of together. 2nd. Phaenomena which have either been experienced or conceived in close contiguity to one another, tend to be thought of together. The contiguity is of two kinds; simultaneity, and immediate succession. Facts which have been experienced or thought of simultaneously, recall the thought of one another. Of facts which have been experienced or thought of in immediate succession, the antecedent, or the thought of it, recalls the thought of the consequent, but not conversely. 3rd. Associations produced by contiguity become more certain and rapid by repetition. When two phaenomena have been very often experienced in conjunction, and have not, in any single instance, occurred separately either in experience or in thought, there is produced between them what has been called Inseparable, or less correctly, Indissoluble Association: by which is not meant that the association must inevitably last to the end of life—that no subsequent experience or process of thought can possibly avail to dissolve it; but only that as long as no such experience or process of thought has taken place, the association is irresistible; it is impossible for us to think the one thing disjoined from the other. 4th. When an association has acquired this character of inseparability—when the bond between the two ideas has been thus firmly riveted, not only does the idea called up by association become, in our consciousness, inseparable from the idea which suggested it, but the facts or phaenomena answering to those ideas, come at last to seem inseparable in existence: things which we are unable to conceive apart, appear incapable of existing apart; and the belief we have in their co-existence, though really a product of experience, seems intuitive. (1884, I, pp. 234-5).

The four laws are respectively: (1) *similarity*, (2) *contiguity*, (3) *frequency*, and (4) *inseparability*. Mill had earlier listed the three laws of (1) *similarity*, (2) *contiguity*, and (3) *intensity* in his *Logic:*

> Of these laws the first is, that similar ideas tend to excite one another. The second is, that when two impressions have been frequently experienced (or even thought of) either simultaneously or in immediate succession, then whenever either of these impressions or the idea of it recurs, it tends to excite the idea of the other. The third law is, that greater

intensity, in either or both of the impressions, is equivalent, in rendering them excitable by one another, to a greater frequency of conjunction (1846, p. 532).

"Contiguity" is combined with "frequency" or "habit." The earlier rendition of the laws has the third and fourth missing, but "intensity" is missing in the later formulation. In disagreement with his father, "similarity," rather than being reduced simply to "frequency," is made the first principle of association, "frequency" being merely ancillary to contiguity.

Unlike his father, Mill believed that complex ideas, rather than consisting of simple ones, are generated by them by a "mental chemistry." "Seven colors when they rapidly follow one another *generate* white, but not that they actually *are* white: so it appears to me that the Complex Idea, formed by the blending together of several simpler ones, should, when it really appears simple, . . . be said to *result from,* or be *generated by,* the simple ideas, not to *consist* of them" (1846, p. 532). Although the idea of an orange consists of simple ideas, complex ideas derived from a combination of senses must be accounted for by mental chemistry. "These therefore are cases of mental chemistry: in which it is proper to say that the simple ideas generate, rather than that they compose, the complex ones" (1846, p. 532). Thus mental coalition is superseded by mental chemistry as Mill's major contribution to association theory (and criticism of his father's system). Not that associative coalescence was repudiated, for ideas can coalesce by a rapid association formation resulting in some of them that are left unattended being eliminated, disappearing, or being forgotten. Fusion is more than a mere coalescence, it is a mental chemistry producing a new entity which is more than the mere sum of the individual parts in agglomeration.

Canons of Causation. To support his theory, Mill abandoned his father's philosophical rationalism for the inductive techniques of experimentalism. In order to ascertain whether a complex idea has been generated from simple ones or not, Mill recommended the employment of his canons of causation, especially the "method of difference" supporting the "method of agreement." Mill's five canons for determining the cause of any effect are:

First Canon   *Method of Agreement*

If two or more instances of phenomenon under investigation have only one circumstance in common, the circumstance in which alone all the instances agree, is the cause (or effect) of the given phenomenon. . . .

Second Canon   *Method of Difference*

If an instance in which the phenomenon under investigation occurs, and an instance in which it does not occur, have every circumstance save one in common, that one occurring only in the former; the circumstance in which alone the two instances differ, is the effect, or cause, or a necessary part of the cause, of the phenomenon. . . .

Third Canon   *Joint Method of Agreement and Difference*

If two or more instances in which the phenomenon occurs have only one circumstance in common, while two or more instances in which it does not occur have nothing in common save the absence of that circumstance; the circumstance in which alone the two sets of instances differ, is the effect, or cause, or a necessary part of the cause, of the phenomenon. . . .

Fourth Canon   *Method of Residues*

Subduct from any phenomenon such part as is known by previous inductions to be the effect of certain antecedents; and the residue of the phenomenon is the effect of the remaining antecedents. . . .

Fifth Canon   *Method of Concomitant Variation*

Whatever phenomenon varies in any manner whenever another phenomenon varies in some particular manner, is either a cause or an effect of that phenomenon, or is connected with it through some fact of causation (1846, pp. 224-33).

When Mill read Whewell's *History of the Inductive Sciences* immediately on its publication 1837, his formulations for an inductive logic chrystallized, resulting in the publication of his classic *Logic* in 1843.

One year later his *Essays on Some Unsettled Questions in Political Economy* appeared, distinguishing him as a political economist. His interest in political economy continued resulting in the publication in 1848 of *Essentials of Political Economy*. But further significant ideas in psychology, especially association theory, finally appeared 22 years after the publication of *Logic;* he published in 1865 in two volumes under the title of *An Examination of Sir William Hamilton's Philosophy* because Hamilton had revived British empiricism following its severe attacks by Reid and the Scottish realists.

ALEXANDER BAIN (1818-1903):
Retentiveness, Agreement, and Compound Association

Another Aberdeen Scot, Bain, was educated at Marischal College (became the University of Aberdeen in 1858) where in 1860 he was appointed to the new chair of logic and English. When in 1840 he became a contributor to the *Westminster Review,* it led to a friendship with John Stuart Mill that endured throughout life. The year before Mill published his *Logic* (1843), he assisted him with the manuscript revision. It was Bain also who wrote the biography of *James Mill* (1882), a preliminary portion of which he compiled for the first issue of *Mind,* the world's first journal of psychology, published in 1876 under the editorship of Bain's pupil Croom Robertson. He distinguished himself with the publication of his classic in psychology, *The Senses and the Intellect* in 1855, and what was to be its sequel or second volume, *Emotions and the Will* (1859), was delayed for four years owing to the publisher's concern for the first volume's poor sales. Later he added *The Study of Character* (1861), but these volumes proved too large to be suitable as textbooks for class use so that in 1868 he produced them in condensed form in his *Manual of Mental and Moral Science.* Another text designed for students, *Logic* (1870), was based on Mill's treatise. Still another text in psychology was to follow, *Mind and Body,* published in 1872. His articles were collected for a volume in 1884 titled *Practical Essays.* Nevertheless Bain's two classics, *The Senses and the Intellect* and *Emotions and the Will,* underwent three revisions each and were standard texts in Britain for most of the latter half of the nineteenth century when they were replaced by Stout's *Manual of Psychology* (1898).

In addition to association theory, Bain's contributions to psychology include theories in physiological psychology, the doctrine of will, and psychophysical parallelism. Though he has been credited with originating the theory of psychophysical parallelism, the theory antedates him, going back to Leibniz and Spinoza. Bain is known for his applications of the findings of physiology to psychology, and his work marks the transition from empirical associationism to physiological experimentalism.

In his *Logic,* he devoted a section to "Logical Methods of Psychology," the important aspect of which is the analysis of psychological phenomena entailing experimental methods. From inductive techniques laws are established, such as the law of *relativity* (borrowed from Spencer) and the "intellectual" laws of *retentiveness* and *similarity* (laws of associational psychology).

Psychophysical Parallelism. By psychophysical parallelism is meant the concomitance of mind and body, the two invariably accompanying each other. "Mind and extended matter—are found in union" (1870, p. 505). Every feeling has both its mental side as well as its physical. "The concomitance of the two radically distinct phenomena gives the peculiar characteristic of the science. Every fact of mind has two sides" (1870, p. 506). Consequently psychology is on the one hand "animal biology" and subject to its laws, while on the other it treats the unique phenomenon of individual self-consciousness. Mill's methods of agreement and difference are the inductive or experimental methods by which the law of psychophysical parallelism is established.

> The great Law of Concomitance of Mind and Body must be proved by the Method of Agreement. We must show that the whole of the facts of mind—Feelings, Volitions, Thought, are at all times accompanied by bodily processes. . . .
> We can do more than establish a law of concomitance of mind and body generally. We can, by the methods of Elimination, ascertain the exact bodily processes connected with mental processes (1870, p. 513).

Mill's method of residues and concomitant variation would also be involved.

Doctrine of Association. Mind is defined as an unextended subject possessing three attributes: (1) *feeling,* (2) *volition,* and (3) *intellect.* "Feeling is exemplified by pleasures and pains; Volition is action prompted by Feelings; Thought, or Intellect, contains the processes known as Memory, Reason, Imagination, etc." (1870, p. 505). While all of the emotions are feelings, sensations are only partly feelings and partly intellectual states. But each feeling has both a mental and physical side. Phenomena in psychology include: *(a) consciousness, (b) sensation, (c) emotion, (d) volition,* and *(e) intellectual states.*

Three fundamental processes characterize intellectual states: (1) *discrimination* (relativity or contrast), (2) *similarity* (or agreement in difference), (3) *retentiveness, revivability,* and *contiguous association* (idea, memory, and recollection). "In order to make us feel, there must be a change of impression; whence all feeling is two-sided" (1870, p. 2) is Bain's definition of the law of discrimination or relativity. "When an impression is repeated, after an interval, we are affected with a new and peculiar consciousness, the shock or consciousness of Agreement in difference" is Bain's explanation of Agreement or similarity.

Of the four "laws of mental association," two are simple and fundamental and two are complex: (1) *law of contiguity*, (2) *law of similarity*, (3) *law of compound association*, and (4) *law of constructive association*. Contiguity is an old familiar one equivalent to Hamilton's "redintegration," and can be substituted by the terms: adhesion, mental adhesiveness, or acquisition. "Actions, Sensations, and States of Feeling, occurring together or in close succession, tend to grow together, or cohere in such a way that when any one of them is afterwards presented to the mind, the others are apt to be brought up in idea" (1855, p. 318). Included in the law of contiguity is the law of repetition. Whereas objects are juxtaposed or simultaneous when joined by contiguity, the law of similarity joins things that are alike though separated in time. It is Hamilton's law of repetition which was first enunciated by Aristotle.

> Contiguity joins together things that occur together, or that are, by any circumstance, presented to the mind at *the same time;* as when we associate heat with light, a falling body with a concussion. But, in addition to this link of reproductive connexion, we find that one thing will, by virtue of similarity, recall another *separated from it in time*, as when a portrait recalls the original (1868a, p. 457).

An association that is not sufficiently strong to revive past ideas may be able to do so in concert with other associations which Bain's law of compound association stated as: "Associations, separately too weak, may, conjointly, be strong enough to revive past experience" (1868b, p. 151). This law treats the plurality of links of contiguous association. Bain stated the law of constructive association accordingly: "By means of association, the mind has the power to form new combinations or aggregates, *different* from any that have been presented to it in the course of experience" (1868, bk. 2, ch. 4). This law accounts for those operations termed imagination, creation, constructiveness, and origination by which the artist, poet, musical composer, and inventor are able to construct new and ingenious forms. The intellectual processes are reduced by Bain to these laws of association.

Doctrine of the Will. Though not a fact of consciousness, will is a mental phenomenon with its intellectual and emotional aspects. Its two fundamental components are: "first, the existence of a spontaneous tendency to execute movements independent of the stimulus of sensations or feelings; and, secondly, the link between a present action and a present feeling, whereby the one comes under the control of the other" (1888, p. 303). Preceding sensation, movement is independent of external stimuli. Volition begins when the "clear consciousness of movements sensibly remedial comes into play, that consciousness has the power of stimulating a concurring activity" (1855, p. 296). Sucking may be the reflex action of an infant when a nipple is placed in his lips, but it is a genuine voluntary act when he continues to do so out of a sensation of hunger and ceases on the cessation of hunger. Bain provided a summary of his theory of volition:

(1.) There is a power of spontaneous movement in the various active organs anterior to, and independent of, the feelings that such movement may give birth to; and without this no action for an end can ever be commenced.

(2.) There exists consciousness, feeling, sensation or emotion, produced from movements, from stimulants of the senses and sensitive parts, or from other causes. The physical accompaniment of this is a diffused excitement of the bodily organs constituting the outburst or expression of it, as the start from a blow.

(3.) There is a property of consciousness—superadded to and by no means involved in, this diffused energy of expression,—whereby a feeling can influence any present active exertion of the body so as either to continue or abate that exertion. This is the property that links feeling to movement, thereby giving birth to volition. The feelings that possess this power—including nearly all pain and many states of pleasure,—I have hitherto described as volitional feelings; those that are deficient in this stimulus, being principally of the pleasurable class, are the pure, un-volitional, or serene emotions (1855, pp. 297-8).

Volition entails motive, deliberation, resolution, desire, and belief. In a later discussion of the will, Bain modified his position in *Mind and Body: The Theories of Their Relation* (1883). Here he asserted:

The Will, volition, or voluntary action is, on the outside, a physical fact; animal muscle under nervous stimulation is one of the mechanical prime movers; the motive power of muscle is as purely physical as the motive power of steam; food is to the one what fuel is to the other. The distinguishing peculiarity of our voluntary movements is that they take their rise in Feeling, and are guided by Intellect; hence, so far as Will is concerned, the problem of physical and mental concomitance is still a problem either of Feeling or of Intellect (p. 76).

The will's two primitive, instinctive, or primordial elements are spontaneous energy or surplus activity (disposition of moving organs coming into self-operation prior to feeling or sense stimulation), and pleasure and pain. Resorting to pleasure and pain as instinctive motivation reduces Bain's theory of will to psychological hedonism, apparently influenced by the British utilitarians, Bentham and his successors. The will also has a third element usually acquired through the educative process that extends or improves volitional powers under the guidance of the intellect.

Conclusion and Transition. As is evident, association psychology is chiefly a Scottish movement notwithstanding its English origin with Hartley. With the exception of John Stuart Mill, all of the associationists treated were Scots. One may even argue that the movement began with Hume, another Scot, with his theory of causation as contiguity. Although Berkeley preceded him on this matter with his doctrine of divine arbitrariness, it was Hume who developed it and who exerted considerable influence on the Scottish philosophers both positively and by causing them to react in opposition. British Associationism did not terminate with Bain; in England it was fostered by the evolutionist Herbert Spencer in the form of evolutionary associationism. Another evolutionary associationist, *George Henry Lewes* (1817-1878), took his lead from Spencer and Darwin, but his influence failed to command much attention. Known for his *Problems of Life and Mind,* that was written in five volumes from 1873 to 1879, Lewes' two distinctive contributions to association theory are: (1) stressing the social factor in the evolution of mind; and (2) dividing mental phenomena into a threefold classification of: *(a)* sensations (of feelings), *(b)* images, and *(c)* ideas (conceptions) instead of the traditional twofold sensations and ideas. The social factor is attributed to the influence of the French philosopher or social psychologist, Comte.

(C) BRITISH EVOLUTIONISM

The association principle was perpetuated by some of the British evolutionary psychologists, but it soon waned, yielding completely to evolutionism. British evolutionary psychology subsequently assumed the form of statistical psychology or the psychology of individual differences. These latter two tendencies (evolutionism and Galton's psychology of measurement) provided the foundation of the functional psychology that was to pervade virtually all of American psychology in the last quarter of the nineteenth century into the first half of the twentieth.

HERBERT SPENCER (1820-1903): Evolutionary Associationism

Although exerting a negligible influence currently, Herbert Spencer, one of the most prominent proponents of the evolutionary movement, coined the phrase "survival of the fittest" that Darwin was to adopt for a title chapter of later editions of his *Origin of Species By Means of Natural Selection or the Preservation of Favoured Races in the Struggle for Life* (1859). Chapter six carries the title "Natural Selection; or the Survival of the Fittest." Moreover, it was Spencer who brought the term "evolution," which initially appeared in 1854, into currency. His definition of evolution as "a change from an indefinite, incoherent homogeneity, to a definite, coherent heterogeneity; through continuous differentiations and integrations" (p. 216) of his earlier edition of *First Principles* (1862) was in later editions more technically rendered:

> Evolution is an integration of matter and concomitant dissipation of motion; during which the matter passes from an indefinite, incoherent homogeneity to a definite, coherent heterogeneity; and during which the retained motion undergoes a parallel transformation (1900, p. 367).

For his definition of evolution, Spencer was inspired by the English physiologist at the University of London, *William Benjamin Carpenter* (1813-1855), author of *The Principles of General and Comparative Physiology* (1839) and *Principles of Human Physiology* (1846). Reviewing Carpenter's publication as subeditor of the *Economist,* Spencer was impressed with a formula that he found in it, "von Baer's formula expressing the course of development through which every plant and animal passes—the change from homogeneity to heterogeneity" (1926, vol. 1, p. 384). This Spencer recognized as the law of individual development. The Estonian naturalist and embryologist *Karl Ernst von Baer* (1792-1876), discoverer of the human ovum, observed that diverse vertebrate organs derive through differentiation from germ layers. He is known for his *Über Entwicklungsgeschichte der Thiere* (1828-1837) and *Untersuchungen über die Entwicklung der Fische* (1835). Predicated on his new found notion, Spencer, who supplanted the doctrine of special creation with his theory of development by successive modifications, reported it in his "The Development Hypothesis" as early as 1852, seven years before the appearance of Darwin's *Origin of Species*.

Lamarck's Theory of the Inheritance of Acquired Characteristics. Depending on others to gather his data for him, Spencer (in addition to von Baer's ideas) relied on John Stuart Mill's *Logic* and on insights sired by the reputed father of modern geology, the British geologist *Charles Lyell* (1797-1875), author of *Principles of Geology* (1830-1835). However, whereas Lyell rejected Lamarck's theory of inherited acquired characteristics, Spencer adopted it. The French naturalist, *Jean Baptiste Pierre Antoine de Monet Lamarck* (1744-1829), who antedated Darwin in proposing his evolutionary theory, hypothesized in his *Philosophie Zoologique* (1809) that environmental changes are responsible for structural alterations in animals and plants, particularly by the greater use of those aspects of the organism contributing most to adaptation or development. While through disuse organs atrophy, those of greatest utility (acquired characteristics) are transmitted to offspring in subsequent generations (inheritance). Thus the organism modifies itself through effort in survival or adaptation, passing these acquired desirable characteristics via inheritance to its progeny.

Spencer's Evolutionary Psychology. Predicating his psychology on the evolutionary hypothesis, Spencer reasoned that the way to understand the mind is by observing how it evolved from an undifferentiated mass to a highly integrated, heterogeneous organism. Defining life as "the continuous adjustment of internal relations to external relations" (1879, p. 21), Spencer hypothesized

> that life consists in the maintenance of inner actions corresponding with outer actions, was confirmed on further observing how the degree of Life varies as the degree of correspondence. It was pointed out that, beginning with the low life of plants and of rudimentary animals, the progress to life of higher and higher kinds essentially consists in a continual improvement of the adaptation between organic processes and processes which environ the organism. We observe how along with complexity or organization there goes an increase in the number, in the range, in the speciality, in the complexity, of the adjustments of inner relations to outer relations. And in tracing up the increase we found ourselves passing without break from the phenomena of bodily life to the phenomena of mental life (1910, vol. 1, sect. 131).

Spencer's evolutionary psychology found its way into social psychology. His *The Study of Sociology* (1872), which culminated in his *Descriptive Sociology* (1873-1934), sought to establish sociology as a science. If it did not accomplish its objective, it did nevertheless establish Spencer as the founder of sociology as a systematic, comparative, and inductive science.

Spencer's Associationism. Basing his association psychology on the premise that the elemental components of the mind are "feelings and the relations between feelings," Spencer proceeded to define feelings as "any portion of consciousness which occupies a place sufficiently large to give it a perceivable individuality; which has its individuality marked off from adjacent portions of consciousness by qualitative contrasts; and which, when introspectively contemplated, appears to be homogeneous" (1910, vol. 1, sect. 65). In addition to feelings, cognitions also are regarded as states of consciousness. Not only are feelings associated with one another, relations are too. Feelings, as composites, derive from "mental shocks" (nervous shocks).

> When considering the composition of Mind, we saw that relations as well as feelings cohere with one another in consciousness; and what was there described as cohesion of relations is otherwise describable as association of relations (1910, vol. 1, sect. 117).

Coherence (and nervous revivability) are aspects of association. Association of relations and association of feelings obey the same law:

> Every relation then, like every feeling, once being presented to consciousness, associates itself with like predecessors. Knowing a relation, as well as knowing a feeling, is the assimilation of it to its past kindred; and knowing it completely is the assimilation of it to past kindred completely (1910, vol. 1, sect. 120).

Spencer's association law should be recognized as the law of association by contiguity.

Essentially a self-made man, Spencer, who was born in Derby, studied for a short period of time with his uncle, but ran away owing to the severity of the discipline. His father's laissez faire approach to learning in which Spencer was allowed to study whatever he chose remained with him throughout life. His later social Darwinism, which he promoted, advocated individualism and laissez faire to such an extent that he did not believe that the poor should be accorded relief since the sooner unfit individuals were eliminated from society through natural selection, the better the race would benefit biologically. He predicated his social psychology on individualism and the laissez-faire doctrine to such an extent that social psychology merely served for the better understanding of individual psychology. Spencer refused to accept college appointments, rather he worked for the Birmingham and Gloucester Railway when he was seventeen, studying fossils which came from railroad cuts.

Practically all of Spencer's psychology is merely of historical value today, though he was quite influential when he was alive. His psychology, however, is immensely valuable in understanding the thinking that prevailed in the latter half of the nineteenth century. His contemporary, Charles Darwin, not only wielded a decisive influence during his own lifetime, but continues to be a vital factor in current psychology. Nevertheless, Spencer, who never had a college education, exerted enormous influence in his era, evidenced by men of stature, such as William James adopting his books as texts, among them being Spencer's *Principles of Psychology* and his *First Principles*.

Spencer's Intellectual Heir: Leonard Trelawny Hobhouse (1864-1929): Evolving Mind Theory. Strongly influenced by Spencer's evolutionary psychology, and to a lesser extent by John Stuart Mill and Auguste Comte, Hobhouse was interested in the evolutionary development of mind in animals and in humans. The Oxford trained Hobhouse held the chair of sociology at the University of London. The Cornwall-born Hobhouse, unhappy with Spencer's survival of the fittest theory, developed his own in which absolute mind attains self-consciousness in an historical process.

His thesis, advanced in his *Mind in Evolution* (1901) purports to trace the phases of mental development or the trend of mental evolution of animals and humans. A work essentially on comparative psychology, its view resembles that of *Outlines of Sociology* (1897) by Lester Ward (1841-1913). Synopsizing his theory, Hobhouse wrote:

> The normal tendency of evolution is not towards a higher, but a divergent type. In the resulting diversity old types survive, and there is deterioration as well as improvement. Within these divergencies there is one line of true development. This is the evolution of Mind. The generic function of Mind is to organise Life by correlating its parts. Its growth consists in the widening scope and increasing articulateness of correlation, with which it replaces that organisation of life which rests on heredity. . . .
>
> Orthogenic evolution consists in the rise of higher organisation—the higher organisation being that in which unity is more complete and scope greater. The basis of the process is an improved physical organisation on which the higher, intelligent organisation rests. Organisation is the most efficient means of maintaining life, and this is true of the special forms of organisation by Intelligence and social co-operation. Fundamental antithesis [exists] between the organisation of life and the struggle for existence. With the growth of organisation comes a modification of plan, substituting pleasure, and later happiness for bare existence as the end of action. Effort towards a higher development is made possible by a mitigation of the struggle for existence, and finally becomes the explicit end upon which the whole plan of organisation is seen to rest. . . .
>
> In the absence of mind, life is relatively anarchic, and evolution planless. The evolution of mind consists in the introduction of order and purpose. It is organic growth, and yet, at least in its higher stages, the working out of a purpose. As the purpose becomes realised, the movement itself becomes more sure and swift (1901, pp. ix-xiv).

Development in its highest stage is purposive. Methodologically behaviorism appealed to him. "In the last analysis," he asserted, "the phenomena of our own consciousness are also the behaviour of those complex wholes which are ourselves and this radical Behaviourism is the one and only method of all psychology" (1944, p. 168).

CHARLES DARWIN (1809-1882):
Emotions as Serviceable Associated Habits

Although Darwin is principally known as a biologist, his theory of biological evolution has had an overwhelming and lasting effect upon the subsequent course of psychology. Furthermore he is a psychologist in his own right, at least his book on *The Expression of the Emotions in Man and Animals* (1872) is an unquestionable psychological work. Like Spencer, Darwin too was captivated with Lyell's *Principles of Geology*, both the book and the man having a decided influence upon him, for Lyell was one of three of Darwin's closest friends. Of the other two, Joseph Hooker and *Thomas Henry Huxley* (1825-1895), the latter, an English biologist, was the coiner of the terms *epiphenomenalism* and *agnosticism*. Although never an atheist, Darwin, influenced by Huxley, did die an agnostic. Epiphenomenalism views the mental life as a byproduct of the physical. Huxley, who was dubbed "Darwin's bulldog," championed Darwinism. "In my most extreme fluctuations," wrote Darwin, "I have never been an Atheist in the sense of denying the existence of a God. I think that generally (and more and more as I grow older), but not always, that an Agnostic would be the more correct description of my state of mind" (1889, p. 274). Lamarck also influenced Darwin.

Unlike Spencer, Darwin had an excellent formal education, initially at the University of Edinburgh for the study of medicine (which did not agree with him) and then at the University of Cambridge with the intention of becoming a clergyman. But his love and devotion to natural history won out, when Darwin, a person of independent means, accepted an unpaid post to board the *H. M. S. Beagle* as a naturalist for a five-year expedition around the world (1831-1836). The trip produced his *Journal of Researches* (1830) and in 1859 fructified into the celebrated *Origin of Species*, containing his doctrine of natural selection or the famous theory of evolution.

Darwin's Theory of Evolution. Credit for evolutionary theory (natural selection) is shared by Darwin with *Alfred Russel Wallace* (1823-1913), an English naturalist who published it a year before Darwin in his *On the Tendency of Varieties to Depart Indefinitely from the Original Type* (1858), which he sent to Darwin. However, accounts by both men were published in a joint paper by the Linnaean Society in 1858. Wallace gathered his data from the Amazon (1848-1852) and from Malay Archipelago (1854-1862).

It was the classic *An Essay on the Principle of Population* (1798) by the English economist *Thomas Robert Malthus* (1766-1834) that provided the catalytic effect Darwin needed to gain the insight for his theory. Darwin reminisced:

Being well prepared to appreciate the struggle for existence which everywhere goes on from long-continued observation of the habits of animals and plants, it at once struck me that under these circumstances favourable variations would tend to be preserved, and unfavourable ones to be destroyed. The result of this would be the formation of new species (1958, p. 120).

Implications of the theory were profound. Darwin had reasoned that man and brute were qualitatively alike, hence modern psychologists, especially animal comparative psychologists were to regard as valid data extrapolated from psychological research on the infrahuman and apply it to the human. Among the first psychologists to be enamoured with the theory for its viability in psychology were the American functionalists. In more recent times the behavioral psychologists (rather than their antitheses—the humanistic psychologists) such as Watson and Hull and their heirs have exploited Darwinism. Thus Darwin is to be credited for the introduction of the psychological investigation of animal behavior into psychology.

Psychology of Emotions. It was not Darwin's second major work, *The Descent of Man and Selection in Relation to Sex* (1871), that was rich in psychological value, but his book on animal psychology and emotion titled *The Expression of the Emotions in Man and Animals* (1872) published the year following. In this work he described expressions of emotions, such as fear from its initial state of surprise to its extreme of terror or horror. Habit, inheritance, and the association psychology accounted for some of the emotional signs. Note that the British were profoundly influenced by association psychology for an extended period of time. Darwin explained:

> Some of the signs may be accounted for through the principles of habit, association, and inheritance,—such as the wide opening of the mouth and eyes, with upraised eyebrows, so as to see as quickly as possible all around us, and to hear distinctly whatever sound may reach our ears. For we have thus habitually prepared ourselves to discover and encounter any danger. Some of the signs of fear may likewise be accounted for, at least in part, through these same principles. Men, during numberless generations, have endeavoured to escape from their enemies or danger by headlong flight, or by violently struggling with them; and such great exertions will have caused the heart to beat rapidly, the breathing to be hurried, the chest to heave, and the nostrils to be dilated. As these exertions have often been prolonged to the last extremity, the final result will have been utter prostration, pallor, perspiration, trembling of all the muscles, or their complete relaxation. And now, whenever the emotion of fear is strongly felt, though it may not lead to any exertion, the same results tend to reappear, through the force of inheritance and association (1965, pp. 306-307).

Darwin believed that many of the symptoms of emotion were probably attributable to a large part to a disrupted transmission of nerve energy from the cerebrospinal system to different portions of the body because of the mind's being so potently affected.

Darwin's Heir in Psychology: George John Romanes (1848-1894): Founder of Comparative Psychology. Romanes, the Canadian-born biologist and physiologist, early established a friendship with Charles Darwin. Born of an old Scottish family that moved to London the year of his birth, Romanes was educated at the University of Cambridge. Owing to his father's inheritance, he turned to his own private research, the only position he held during his life being a part-time lectureship with the University of Edinburgh.

Encouraged by Darwin, Romanes sought to apply his mentor's theory of natural selection to the evolution of the animal and human mind. The outcome was a series of books, resulting in the founding of *comparative psychology*. The first, *Animal Intelligence* (1882), delineated his objectives:

> First, I have thought it desirable that there should be something resembling a text-book of the facts of Comparative Psychology, to which men of science, and also metaphysicians, may turn whenever they may have occasion to acquaint themselves with the particular level of intelligence to which this or that species of animal attains. . . .

My second, and much more important object, is that of considering the facts of animal intelligence in their relation to the theory of Descent (1882, pp. v-vi).

Although the work amassed data on animal behavior, it failed to cope directly with the continuity of mind between animals and humans. While Romanes regarded the first book as merely laying the foundation of fact upon which to construct his vindication of mental evolution, his second work, *Mental Evolution in Animals* (1883), fared no better. He strove vainly to establish ''mental evolution in man as well as in animals'' (1884, p. 1). The book, thoroughly oriented from the evolutionary standpoint, defined reason as ''the faculty which is concerned in the intentional adaptation of means to ends'' (1884, p. 318). Earlier Romanes offered his criterion of mind in terms of adaptation. He queried:

> Does the organism learn to make new adjustments, or to modify old ones, in accordance with the results of its own individual experience? If it does so, the fact cannot be due merely to reflex action . . . , for it is impossible that heredity can have provided in advance for innovations upon, or alterations of, its machinery during the lifetime of a particular individual (1882, pp. 4-5).

The third book of the trilogy, *Mental Evolution in Man* (1887), proved best in defending the evolutionary argument.

British association psychology, which penetrated the psychology of the British evolutionary movement, is also found in the psychology of Romanes. In a sense, Romanes reverted to the earliest stage of associationism, regressing to the psychology or empiricism of Locke. He imputed Locke's simple ideas to animals, complex ideas (the ability to associate) to both humans and animals, and notional ideas (abstract conceptions) to the ''unique prerogative of man.''

In his vindication of Darwinism, Romanes launched out in opposition to the neo-Darwinians (Alfred Russel Wallace and August Weismann) who restricted the sole factor of organic evolution to natural selection, while Darwin regarded it as merely the principal factor, that is, the Lamarckian factor of transmission by inheritance of acquired characteristics was not to be excluded. Darwin held that the Lamarckian factor probably played an important role.

Neither a creative scientist nor profound thinker, Romanes, whose research predominantly dealt with the nervous system of jelly-fish, star-fish, and sea-urchins, is known for his pioneering efforts in comparative psychology.

Huxley's Psychological Heir: Conwy Lloyd Morgan (1852-1936): Morgan's Canon. Charles Darwin and Thomas H. Huxley, in initiating the drive for the advancement of evolutionary theory, succeeded in enlisting champions for their common cause. While Darwin won over Romanes, Huxley enlisted C. Lloyd Morgan, principally known in psychology for his canon. The London-born Morgan had planned on a mining engineer's career at the School of Mines, London, when as fortune would have it he encountered T. H. Huxley at a dinner, the two seated together. At Huxley's encouragement, he undertook biological work with his mentor at the Royal College of Science, there to become the disciple of the celebrated evolutionist. Morgan's entire career, an academic one, was spent at

University College, Bristol, where he began as a lecturer in 1883 and retired as Professor of Psychology and Ethics in 1919.

Known in psychology as a comparative psychologist, Morgan published his *An Introduction to Comparative Psychology* in 1894, the year Romanes died. Romanes, it will be recalled, coined the term *comparative psychology,* ironically during the year in which Darwin died. Morgan, who sought to correct the errors of Romanes whom he greatly admired, objected to Romanes' abuses, such as crediting his monkey with the mechanical principle of the screw which Morgan rejected as an unsatisfactory misuse of terms, and crediting the animal with abstract emotions and sentiments of beauty and a sense of justice and morality. Morgan remonstrated: "A sense of beauty, a sense of ludicrous, a sense of justice, and sense of right and wrong—these abstract emotions or sentiments, as such, are certainly impossible to the brute" (1890, p. 403). In consequence of such objections, Morgan formulated the canon of interpretation identified by his name:

> In no case may we interpret an action as the outcome of the exercise of a higher psychical faculty, if it can be interpreted as the outcome of the exercise of one which stands lower in the psychological scale (1894, p. 53).

Morgan's *Emergent Evolution* (1923), viewing evolution as discrete steps rather than gradual, expressed ideas congenial with *Samuel Alexander* (1859-1938) as found in his *Space, Time, and Deity* (1920), and shows the influence of *Henri Bergson's* (1859-1941) *élan vital,* found in his *Creative Evolution* (1907). Ironic, is it not, that the leading evolutionists, Alexander and Bergson, were born the year Darwin published his *Origin of Species* (1859)? Another evolutionist important to psychology, Graham Wallas, was also born during that same year.

Evolutionism in British Social Psychology

Shortly after Darwin and Spencer enunciated their evolutionary theories, they were quickly adopted and assimilated in psychology, social psychology as well as comparative psychology, and later into the psychology of learning.

Walter Bagehot (1826-1877): Darwinistic Social Psychology. Within a decade after Darwin published his *Origin of Species* (1859), an English economist and journalist, Walter Bagehot, a University College, London graduate who was editor of the *Economist,* developed an evolutionary theory of social psychology in his *Physics and Politics* (1869). Bagehot's social Darwinism, an imitation theory of social psychology, holds that the irresistible attraction of "chance predominance" actually "rules all but the strongest men to imitate" (1875, p. 36) with the result that "an unconscious imitation determines their words, and made them say what of themselves they would never have thought of saying" (1948, p. 36). The conquering nations predominate over the weaker and are emulated by the vanquished either consciously or unconsciously, because of the advantages gained through imitation. Influenced by Spencer, Bagehot held that "progress is an increase of adaptation of man to his environment, that is, of his internal powers and wishes to his external lot and life" (1875, p. 208). With advancing civilization, imitation and its force subsides. Appropriately enough Bagehot subtitled his *Physics and Politics* with *Thoughts on the Application of the Principles of "Natural Selection" and "Inheritance" to Political Society* (1869). Spencerian evolution lent itself to application to social psychology, for Spencer emphasized that survival is facilitated in numbers, in society, better than by attempting to fend for oneself on an individual basis.

Graham Wallas (1859-1932): Britain's First Social Psychologist. The English political scientist Graham Wallas developed an instinct theory of social psychology. Wallas, who was a faculty member of the London School of Economics before becoming a professor at the University of London, articulated his views in *The Great Society* (1914). The Oxford trained Wallas repudiated intellectualistic or rationalistic interpretations of social or socio-psychological behavior in his *Human Nature in Politics* (1908), but a half dozen years later in his *The Great Society* he recognized intelligence as a reliable guide, owing to its relatively late appearance in evolutionary development. Complex modern society, the great society, is the heritage of twentieth century humanity. Influenced by Spencerism, Wallas asserted that "we have become biologically more fitted to live with the help of social heritage, and biologically less fitted to live without it. We have become biologically parasitic upon our social heritage" (1921, p. 17). Human social behavior must be explained in terms of social heritage rather than accounted for by instinct, argued Wallas in his *Our Social Heritage* (1921).

Evolutionism in sociology and social psychology found its way to the United States where it was strongest during the first quarter of the twentieth century. In America it was pursued by *James Mark Baldwin* (1861-1934), who found a psychophysical parallelism in evolution, which he explicated in his *Development and Evolution: Including Psychophysical Evolution, Evolution by Orthoplasy, and the Theory of Genetic Modes* (1902). Baldwin, who edited the first dictionary of psychology, the three volume *Dictionary of Philosophy and Psychology* (1901-1902), taught at Toronto, Princeton, and Johns Hopkins universities. He developed an imitation and recapitulation theory of social psychology along the lines of Hegelian and Comtean evolutionary thought. Baldwin viewed the individual's genetic growth as corresponding to the developmental stages of human history (recapitulation theory). G. Stanley Hall, another evolutionist, shared a similar recapitulation theory, asserting that "the best and only key to truly explain mind in man is mind in the animals he has sprung from and in his own infancy, which so faintly recapitulates them" (1904, vol 2, p. 65).

CHAPTER 3

Psychology
At the Universities
of Cambridge and London

In England the major role of psychology as a science has unfolded principally at the University of Cambridge and at London. The only universities in all of England to have established a chair in psychology prior to World War II were the University of Cambridge, where Frederic C. Bartlett (1866-   ) first occupied the chair in 1931; King's College (London), where Charles S. Myers (1873-1946) assumed the first chair in 1906; and at University College, London, where Charles E. Spearman (1863-1945) was the chair's initial occupant in 1928. Although Oxford, the nation's first university, was founded as early as the twelfth century, it never had a chair in psychology until 1947, when G. Humphrey (1889-1966) was appointed to it.

Academic ranks at University College, London are ascendantly structured accordingly: Lecturer; Senior Lecturer; Reader; and ultimately to the rank of Professor. At Cambridge University the ordering begins with Demonstrator (or Assistant Lecturer) and proceeds to Lecturer (or Senior Assistant in Research), then to Reader, and finally to Professor. A Lecturer in a university in the United States is usually in part-time employ, the ascent in these universities being from Instructor; Assistant Professor; Associate Professor; to the rank of full Professor.

(A) PSYCHOLOGY OF INDIVIDUAL DIFFERENCES
AND STATISTICAL METHOD
AT UNIVERSITY COLLEGE, LONDON

University College, London, modeled to an extent after the University of Berlin (which was founded in 1809), received its royal charter in 1836, though it was taking shape in 1825. Intended as a center of liberal education in the natural sciences, it was to have no Faculty of Theology. Although two chairs (one of Logic and the Philosophy of the Human Mind) were established in 1828, neither had occupants when the lecture course began that year because no one of sufficient distinction applied for either. In 1830 the Chair of Logic and the Philosophy of the Human Mind was finally occupied by John Hoppus (with the concurrence of James Mill. Both Jeremy Bentham and James Mill were among the university's founders. Bentham's remains, handsomely clad, sit in a glass case in the university's library, the school's benefactor, Bentham, having willed it so).

George Croom Robertson (1842-1892): Founder of *Mind*, England's First Psychological Journal. Although philosophy of mind was psychology, lectures under the designation of psychology were first offered by George Croom Robertson, successor to Hoppus in 1867. Thus it was that psychology was introduced into a major British university. A Scottish psychologist trained in the psychology of Bain and British associationism, Robertson founded (in 1876) and edited England's first journal treating psychology, *Mind*. Robertson was without peer because his rival at the University of Cambridge, *James Ward* (1843-1925), was only at the point of presenting his dissertation, *The Relation of Physiology and Psychology*, in 1875 for a Fellowship at Trinity College, Cambridge University. Robertson, responsible for an original view of psychological perception, held that every act of perception entails both discrimination and comparison. Unless a person can discriminate and differentiate one sense quality from another, he cannot be said to be perceiving. Bare and simple sensations as facts of conscious experience do not exist, for the conscious mind at any precise moment constitutes more than sensations. Conscious experience is more than pure sense.

James Sully (1842-1923): The Era of Textbooks. Robertson, becoming ill, resigned in 1892, dying later that year. James Sully, who had been undertaking some of Robertson's work during his illness, succeeded to the chair at fifty years of age. Trained at the University of Göttingen (1867-1868) under Lotze, and at the University of Berlin (1871-1872) with Helmholtz, Sully is distinguished in history of British psychology as a textbook writer, publishing his *Sensation and Intuition* in 1874, and his *Outlines of Psychology* (1884) a decade later. Lotze profoundly influenced him. In the latter work this orientation was quite apparent:

> I hold that psychology, while a science of *mind,* is a *science* of mind. By this I mean, first of all, that it deals with events or processes which agree with the phenomena of the external world in exhibiting orderliness or uniformity of succession, and so are suscepti- ble of being brought under definite laws; and, secondly, that it has in its own instruments and methods of research, when properly understood, an adequate means of ascertaining these laws (1884, p. v).

Mind as a substance belongs to the province of philosophy, but "as a science psychology is concerned only with the phenomena of mind, with mental states, psychical facts, or whatever else we choose to call them" (1884, p. 1). Thus psychology is the study of consciousness, with introspection its methodology.

Happy with the reception his texts had received, Sully published a two-volume tome in 1892, *The Human Mind: A Textbook of Psychology.* The new work, an elaboration of the ideas presented in his *Outlines of Psychology,* accorded fuller treatment to physiological and experimental psychology. His definition of psychology remained pretty much the same, defining it in the new text "as the science that investigates and explains the phenomena of mind, or the inner world of our conscious experience" (1892, vol. 1, p. 1).

While good textbook writers have rightfully earned their place in the history of psychology, Sully's prominence in the history of psychology is overestimated, owing to his success as an author of texts. Nevertheless it was through the initiative of Sully that University College, London was to have its Laboratory of Experimen- tal Psychology in October of 1897, with *William Halse Rivers Rivers* (1864-1922) as its director. Rivers, however, left later that year for the University of Cambridge, but not without going down in the history of psychology as London's first experimental psychologist. Futhermore, it is to Sully's credit that the British Psychological Society was launched, for Sully summoned its first meeting on October 24, 1901 at University College, London, with ten psychologists present. Edgell reported the others as:

> Dr Sophie Bryant, Headmistress of the famous North London Collegiate School, Mr Boyce Gibson, Lecturer on Philosophy and Psychology at Westfield College and also at Hackney College and New College, Mr F. N. Hales, a Scholar of Cambridge, Dr Robert Armstrong Jones, Senior Resident Physician at the London County Council Asylum at Claybury, Dr W. McDougall, Fellow of St John's College, Cambridge, and a student under Dr Rivers, and co-operating with Prof Sully at University College by holding a weekly class in experimental psychology, Dr F. W. Mott, Pathologist at Claybury and Professor of Physiology at Charing Cross Hospital Medical School, Dr W. H. R. Rivers, Lecturer in Experimental Psychology and the Physiology of the Special Senses at Cambridge, Dr W. G. Smith, Lecturer in Psychology at King's College, London, and Mr A. F. Shand, a moral science graduate at Cambridge, interested in psychology for its own sake (1937, p. 113).

It was the psychiatrist Mott, *Henry Maudsley's* (1835-1918) pupil, who, on returning from Kraepelin's clinic in Munich, pled the cause of a university psychiatric hospital devoted to research as well as treatment. With a £ 30,000 grant from Maudsley, the idea fructified into the Maudsley Hospital in London.

It was Sully who read the new-born society's first paper on February 2, 1902 on "The Evolution of Laughter," publishing later his *An Essay on Laughter* (1902), thus making him an early psychologist of esthetics, as well as a pioneer in child psychology with his *Studies of Childhood* (1895).

Although it was *Carveth Read* (1848-1931) who succeeded Sully in 1903, joined by *George Dawes Hicks* (1862-   ), occupant of the chair of moral philosophy, descent in the psychological line is from Sully to McDougall, who was in charge of the psychological laboratory, and then to Charles Spearman, McDougall's successor in 1906. When Carveth Read resigned in 1911, reorganization of the department resulted in Spearman's becoming Professor of Psychology. Both Read and Hicks published in psychology and were members of the British Psychological Society, the latter, a Leipzig Ph.D. (1896), having published with W. H. R. Rivers. Two years after Spearman's appointment, the psychoanalytically oriented psychologist, *John Carl Flugel* (1884-1955), who did his studies in psychology under McDougall at Oxford, joined the University College staff in 1909 as Demonstrator. In addition to his psychoanalytical contributions, Flugel is Britain's first major historian of psychology, having published his *A Hundred Years of Psychology* in 1933. A second student of McDougall's at Oxford who went on to distinguish himself in psychology, *Cyril Lodowic Burt* (1883-   ), also joined the University of London psychologists, but not until 1924, when that institution was being characterized as the London school of psychology.

WILLIAM McDOUGALL (1871-1938):
The First Social Psychology: Hormic Psychology

When Rivers left for Cambridge University, for a few years (1898-1899) E. T. Dixon served as the interim director, until William McDougall came in 1900 to head the post. The laboratory equipment was supplied by Hugo Münsterberg, Francis Galton, and other contributors, but mostly from the apparatus accumulated from Münsterberg's laboratory of psychology at the University of Freiburg when he was about to embark for the directorship of the psychological laboratory at Harvard University, where James had summoned him in order to make Harvard the nation's leading research center in psychology.

The University College, London atmosphere in which the British Psychological Society was to have its birth is related by McDougall:

> During my teaching at University College, a little group of persons interested in psychology began to gather for informal discussions in my laboratory. After a time we made ourselves into a formally constituted group, the British Psychological Society, with, I think, twelve original members; and presently we held larger and more formal meetings in various centers, and undertook to publish a journal, the *British Journal of Psychology* (1930, p. 206).

Like his colleague, Sully, McDougall also did graduate work at the University of Göttingen (with Müller in 1900), and like Sully brought the Göttingen psychological atmosphere with him to London. However, McDougall, who fancied himself a disciple of William James and G. F. Stout, proved influential as Münsterberg's successor at Harvard in 1920. The Lancashire-born McDougall, a product of the universities of Manchester and Cambridge, qualified for a career in medicine at St. Thomas' Hospital in London in 1897. Thus he was the most credentialed British psychologist of his time, with fourteen years of training for his profession.

McDougall at Oxford. The restless McDougall, always out of step with his colleagues and forever looking for more productive opportunities, left his part-time readership at University College, London in 1906 after accepting the Wilde Readership in Mental Philosophy at Oxford in 1904, where he remained an uncomfortable decade. Far from ideal, Oxford was not the preferred place for a serious psychologist, since it lacked a psychological laboratory until 1936 and its chair of psychology was deferred until a decade later. It was T. H. Huxley who quipped that a punishment for a wicked scientist is condemnation as a science professor at Oxford. McDougall's puny laboratory in the physiology department at Oxford did not conduce to producing great work, but some of his finest publications stem from this period, owing to his two lectures per week schedule that afforded him time for research.

The First Social Psychology Text. From his first paper in 1899, McDougall was interested in psychophysics of vision, brain functioning, synaptic functions, and the phenomena of attention, but most of his early papers were "still-born" and went without recognition. In 1905 his *Physiological Psychology* appeared, and though outdated today, it served its purpose for that generation. Three years later he published his *An Introduction to Social Psychology* (1908), a book that saw twenty-three editions in a score of years, with reprintings as late as the 1960s. A remarkable feat indeed, since this was the first text that a psychologist anywhere in the world published with social psychology as its title. How ironic that McDougall, who had an abiding aversion for behaviorism, should be the one who provided American behaviorists with their definition of psychology as the science of behavior, offering it as early as 1905 in his *Primer of Physiological Psychology*, and again in 1908 in his *An Introduction to Social Psychology*. He dauntlessly proclaimed that

> psychologists must cease to be content with the sterile and narrow conception of their science as the science of consciousness, and must boldly assert its claim to be the positive science of the mind in all its aspects and modes of functioning, or, as I would prefer to say, the positive science of conduct or behaviour (1960, p. 13).

Four years later he let the world know the character of psychology by publishing his *Psychology, the Study of Behavior* (1912). The small volume was expanded in 1923 as *Outline of Psychology*, and dedicated to William James. Because he objected to his psychology being confused with Watsonism, he redefined psychology in the latter text as "the science of the human mind" (1923, p. 38). Explaining the difference between the two, he wrote:

> The two principal alternative routes are (1) that of mechanistic science, which interprets all its processes as mechanical sequences of cause and effect, and (2) that of the sciences of mind, for which purposive striving is a fundamental category, which regard the process of purposive striving as radically different from mechanical sequence (1923, p. vii).

The prime objective of McDougall was to advance a hormic theory of behavior in his *An Introduction to Social Psychology*, a theory that remained with him throughout life, and by which his psychology was identified.

McDougall's Hormic Theory of Behavior. Hormic theory (purposive striving) and the instinctual source of hormic energy are the two principal theses advanced in McDougall's *Social Psychology*. The concept hormic implies autonomy (will), for hormic means an "active striving towards a goal" (1960, p. 446). McDougall was not out of line in England with his purposive psychology because his systematic orientation harmonized with that of James Ward, his evolutionary outlook with Darwin, his functionalism with Americans and Britains, and his dynamic approach with Robert S. Woodworth at Columbia University. Yet most of his energies were exhausted in polemics, defending his position against critics. As late as 1925 in the Powell Lecture at Clark University, McDougall found himself apologetically saying:

> I am responding to an invitation to defend Purposive Psychology, or, in other words, to defend the proposition that man's acting and thinking are purposive. . . . I am expected to support by argument a fact familiar to all men through first-hand experience. . . . This is a strange and embarrassing position for any man of science (1926, p. 273).

While behavior of the brute is determined by the driving force of instinct, in human behavior instinct supplies the driving power. "Instincts are the prime movers of all human activity" hypothesized McDougall, and

> by the conative or impulsive force of some instinct (or of some habit derived from an instinct), every train of thought . . . is borne along towards its end, and every bodily activity is initiated and sustained. The instinctive impulses determine the ends of all activities and supply the driving power by which all mental activities are sustained: and the most highly developed mind is but a means towards these ends, is the instrument by which these impulses seek their satisfactions, while pleasure and pain do but serve to guide them in their choice of the means.
>
> Take away these instinctive dispositions with their powerful impulses, and the organism would become incapable of activity of any kind (1960, p. 38).

Instinct he defined as "an inherited or innate psycho-physical disposition which determines its possessor to perceive and to pay attention to, objects of a certain class, to experience an emotional excitement of a particular quality upon perceiving such an object, and to act in regard to it in a particular manner, or, at least, to experience an impulse to such action" (1960, p. 25). Although McDougall provided an elaborate. list of instincts and corresponding emotions (e.g., the instinct of flight and the accompanying emotion of fear), he encountered considerable difficulty with respect to classification. Unable even to agree with his own list, he tended to supersede instinct with *propensity,* and also to reduce instincts to different aspects of the will to live.

Regarding the formation of character as his greatest psychological contribution, McDougall adopted the concept *sentiment* from his London colleague, *Alexander F. Shand* (1858-1936). His revised view now held that a pure instinct occurs only once (on its maiden appearance), after which it is modified by personal and interpersonal experiences, thus becoming a *sentiment,* defined as "an organised system of emotional dispositions centred about the idea of some object" (1960, p. 137). Following Shand (1896, 1914), McDougall treated emotion as a passing phase of mind, whereas sentiment was regarded as an enduring structure of the mind, a result of growth rather than inherited constitution. Self-regard, the overriding sentiment, has pride and self-respect as its two forms, two other principal sentiments being love and hate. Not only are the sentiments a social product, but the social chararacter of instincts is explained in terms of the influence exerted by a person's social environment.

The Group Mind. His *Social Psychology* was seen as a preparation or propaedeutic to McDougall's *The Group Mind* (1920), which was to be his *magnum opus*. However, "its reception was so unfavorable," lamented McDougall, "that the *magnum opus* went a-glimmering. For, as I have said, I have found it increasingly difficult to believe in the value of my work" (1930, p. 212). This is now the Harvard era, for McDougall in 1920 had assumed the Chair of Psychology left vacant by Münsterberg's death in 1916. Out of step with the psychologists at Harvard, as he had been most of his life with colleagues elsewhere and plagued because of his support of unpopular or extreme causes in psychology, McDougall left Harvard for Duke University in 1927 in search of a congenial atmosphere.

The *Group Mind* postulated that a "social aggregate has a collective mental life, which is not merely the sum of the mental lives of its units, it may be contended that a society not only enjoys a collective mental life but also has a collective mind" (1920, p. 10). This was not the first time that McDougall imposed upon the psychological community (which was striving to move from the occult to scientific investigation) highly speculative notions. In 1911 he issued his *Body and Mind* with the annoyingly provocative subtitle *A History and a Defense of Animism,* and the startling conclusion: "the empirical evidence . '. . seems to weigh very strongly against parallelism and in favour of animism" (1911, p. 356). He sought to prove the existence of a human soul as a serious scientific hypothesis.

The evolutionist McDougall, emulating Darwin or at least under his influence, went to the Torres Strait with the Cambridge Anthropological Expedition in 1898. This evolutionary orientation is maintained in the *Group Mind.* The objective in this book was the investigation of the more highly evolved mind, a group spirit, a national mind of a higher order than the individual mind. A person's thought and behavior is not the same in an interpersonal setting as when he is alone. Among other things, the group spirit, curbing individual self-interests, contributes toward the continuity and development of group organization.

Experiments on Lamarckian Theory. While at Harvard and later at Duke University, McDougall's evolutionary psychology was carried into the laboratory where his experiments on rats sought to establish the Lamarckian theory of the transmission of acquired characters, publishing his findings as "An Experiment for the Testing of the Hypothesis of Lamarck" in 1927. Seventeen years were consumed in this abortive research.

Concluding Comments. Reflecting on the life of McDougall, Donald Keith Adams, his colleague at Duke University, commented that "anyone who has read his illuminating autobiography can not have failed to note its profoundly pessimistic tone" (1939, p. 5). On reading his autobiography, Robert Mearns Yerkes, who preceded him at Harvard, remarked that his life is a major tragedy. It is becoming increasingly obvious that it was more than his psychology of supporting unpopular causes that proved unacceptable, it was also the phraseology in which he couched his theories. For example, instead of instinct, need or drive would have proved acceptable to psychologists; and for "group mind," a "social force field" would have fared as a preferable construct.

Nevertheless, it is as L. S. Hearnshaw observed: "British psychology was largely shaped by McDougall's *Social Psychology"* (1964, p. 212). J. Drever's assessment is probably accurate when he commented that McDougall's *Social Psychology* "is perhaps as much undervalued today as it was overvalued then" (1968, p. 504).

Although Charles Spearman succeeded McDougall at the University of London, it seems advisable first to treat Francis Galton and Karl Pearson, also associated with that institution, for it was these two who began not only to set the trend at London in psychometrics and the psychology of individual differences, but whose efforts produced England's greatest contribution to the history of psychology, and whose works, along with Darwin's, gave American psychology its distinctive character, *American functionalism.*

FRANCIS GALTON (1822-1911): Founder of Psychometrics

It fell to the cousin of Charles Darwin, Francis Galton, to wield an enormous influence on American experimental psychology, statistical analysis, and its resultant functional psychology. His efforts produced the journal devoted to the theory and practice of statistics, *Biometrika,* in 1901 and the establishment of the Eugenics Laboratory at University College, London, with Karl Pearson its first director. The Galton chair then fell to R. A. Fisher, who was succeeded by L. S. Penrose.

A Cambridge University graduate (1844) and a man of independent means, Galton did not produce his classic *Hereditary Genius: An Inquiry into Its Laws and Consequences* (1869) until his late forties, a decade after his cousin Charles Darwin gave the world his work that revolutionized subsequent psychology, the *Origin of Species* (1859). The Birmingham-born Galton, who served in British civil service, has many firsts to his name, but he is known best for his anthropological study of heredity and its attendant statistical analysis, and as the founder of the science of eugenics. Identification of individuals by fingerprint in 1892 is also to his credit as is the Galton whistle, which is well known to any student of psychology. Thus Galton is the first psychologist of individual differences, having developed the technique of statistical correlation. His motto was: "Whenever you can, count" (Pearson, 1924, vol. 2, p. 340). The anthropometric laboratory that he established as early as 1884 was subsequently transferred to University College, London.

Galton's statistics and its application to psychology entered American psychology through James McKeen Cattell, who assisted Galton in setting up his Anthropometric Laboratory in South Kensington. Cattell, the primary force in introducing statistics into American psychology, initially taught it in his first psychology course at the University of Pennsylvania in 1888. The previous year it was taught at the same institution by Roland P. Faulkner, the first Professor of Statistics in the United States. Helen Mary Walker, in assessing Cattell's role in statistical psychology, reported

> There appears to be general agreement that Cattell's teaching, both at the University of Pennsylvania and, more especially later at Columbia, combined with his use of statistics in his own writings, was the greatest single factor making for the adoption of statistical methods by American psychologists (1929, p. 152).

Hereditary Genius

In an ethnological investigation, Galton noted mental peculiarities of different races, hence derived the idea of studying the subject of hereditary genius. He set out to prove that "high reputation is a pretty accurate test of high ability," and that there is a "hereditary transmission of physical gifts" (1869, p. 2). His studies, undertaken in the 1860s, culminated in the publication of *Hereditary Genius: An Inquiry into Its Laws and Consequences* (1869). Applying statistical analysis to his findings, he reasoned that

> there must be a fairly constant average mental capacity in the inhabitants of the British Isles, and that the deviations from that average—upwards toward genius, and downwards towards stupidity—must follow the law that governs deviations from all true averages (1869, p. 32).

Noting that "characteristics cling to families," Galton sought to establish a hereditary explanation for genius running in certain families. In addition to genius as such, specific forms of greatness are also inherited. Relying on statistical average and deviations from it on either side of average, Galton concluded that "eminently gifted men are raised as much above mediocrity as idiots are depressed below it" (1869, p. 36). He referred to his method as the law of deviation from an average, and credited the Belgian statistician and astronomer, *Lambert Adolphe Jacques Quételet* (1796-1874), for it. Quételet is credited with formulating the average man *(l' homme moyen)* as a basic type, and also with the application of the theory of errors.

Seeing the need for homogeneity, Galton, by random selection, counted groups wherever there was variation governed by a dominant such as age, size, etc., noting the variation of precisions according to the square root of the number of observations. Owing to the *law of deviations,* he recommended *ranking* characteristic traits of individuals, with the mid (500th) point of measurement being what was later termed the median, and the 250th and 750th ranks the quartiles. He observed that the ranking produced an ogive (cup-shaped) curve, his entire objective being to obtain individual differences of people for purposes of practical application.

Galton's Principal Contributions to Statistics

Method of Ranks. Aware of the need to develop a method for assessing differences in intellectual ability and achievement, Galton devised a method of percentiles. His objective in *Hereditary Genius* (1869) was to establish that "a man's natural abilities are derived by inheritance, under exactly the same limitations as are the form and physical features of the whole organic world" (1869, p. 1). Inspired by Darwin's evolutionary theory, he noted the power each generation has over the succeeding one.

By an eminent man, Galton meant someone who achieved a position that only 250 out of a million persons attain, or one person in 4,000. Galton, who claimed to be the first to apply statistics to heredity and psychology of individual differences, introduced the law of deviation from an average. He asserted that

> the range of power between . . . the greatest and least of English intellects is enormous. There is a continuity of natural ability reaching from one knows not what height, and descending to one can hardly say what depth. I propose in this chapter to range men

according to their natural abilities, putting them into classes separated by equal degrees of merit, and to show the relative number of individuals included in the several classes. . . .

The method I shall employ for discovering all this, is an application of the very curious theoretical law of "deviation from an average" (1869, p. 26).

He then went on to conclude that the number of eminent men above average is equal to the number of idiots below the mean.

The statistical concept of *grades,* also appeared historically for the first time in Galton's *Hereditary Genius,* which classified the most eminent men out of a million persons in the highest rank and the stupidest in the lowest, the remaining 999,998 falling into fourteen classes equally graded.

Probable error and the *ogive curve,* also introduced into statistics by Galton, were offered in 1875 in his "Statistics by Intercomparison, with Remarks on the Law of Frequency of Errors." He sought a method by which to obtain simple statistical results, yet "applicable to a multitude of objects lying outside the present limits of statistical inquiry." Apparently implying what was to be termed in statistics, the median, he asserted, "The object then found to occupy the middle position of the series must possess the quality in such a degree that the number of objects in the series that have more of it is equal to that of those that have less of it" (1875, p. 34). He continued:

the most convenient measure of divergency is to take the object that has the mean value, on the one hand, and those objects, on the other, whose divergence in either direction is such that one half of the objects in the series on the same side of the mean diverge more than it does, and the other half less. The difference between the mean and either of these objects is the measure in question, technically and rather absurdly called the 'probable error' (1875, p. 34).

In an article on the "Statistics of Mental Imagery" (1880), Galton explicated his finding, introducing the terms first suboctile, first octile, first quartile, middlemost (median), last quartile, last octile, last suboctile (1880).

Scales of merit or *percentiles scales* developed by Galton called for grouping members according to an order of merit. He arranged Cambridge University students according to their grades earned, classifying them by intervals of 500 up to 8,000. The object was to determine the grade of an individual with respect to a given faculty when he is compared with other individuals, so as to have that grade meaningful. Knowledge of an average value, such as the average income of an Englishman is $10,000 a year is meaningless, unless one has knowledge of the distribution of income among all Englishmen, i.e., what is the barest minimum required to ward off starvation and what signifies living in luxury. Consequently,

in respect to the distribution of any human quality or faculty, a knowledge of mere averages tells but little; we want to learn how the quality is distributed among the various members . . . and to express what we know in so compact a form that it can be easily grasped and dealt with. . . .

A knowledge of the distribution of any quality enables us to ascertain the Rank that each man holds among his fellows, in respect to that quality. This is a valuable piece of knowledge in this struggling and competitive world, where success is to the foremost, and failure to the hindmost, irrespective of absolute efficiency. A blurred vision would be above all price to an individual man in a nation of blind men, though it would hardly enable him to earn his bread elsewhere. When the distribution of any faculty has been ascertained, we can tell from the measurement, say of our child, how he ranks among other children in respect to that faculty, whether it be a physical gift, or one of health, or of intellect, or of morals (1889, pp. 36-7).

By knowing an individual's rank, one can determine whether he is making progress through the years or whether he is losing ground. Galton referred to these as *centisimal grades* (precentiles), the mid point of the scale being the *median,* and *quartiles* for the 75% and 25% grades. Graphically diagrammed, the real measure that corresponds to each percentile rank produces an *ogive* (S-shaped) curve. Ogive is from an old French word for cup, *augive.* Galton held that "the object of statistical science is to discover methods of condensing information concerning large groups of allied facts into brief and compendious expressions suitable for discussion" (1883, p. 33).

Method of Correlation. Correlation in statistics is also credited to Galton, with Karl Pearson. F. Y. Edgeworth, and W. F. R. Weldon subsequently refining it. Thus the method of ogives and percentiles has in some measure been superseded, while that of correlation survived. In an important paper titled "Co-relations and Their Measurement, Chiefly from Anthopometric Data" (1888), Galton explained the meaning of "co-relation or correlation of structure."

> Two variable organs are said to be co-related when the variation of one is accompanied on the average by more or less variation of the other, and in the same direction. Thus the length of the arm is said to be co-related with that of the leg, because a person with a long arm has usually a long leg, and conversely. . . . It is easy to see that co-relation must be the consequence of the variations of the two organs being partly due to common causes (1888, p. 135).

Correlation, an idea borrowed from biology, was anticipated by the German mathematician and astronomer from Göttingen, *Karl Friedrich Gauss* (1775-1855) and the celebrated French astronomer and mathematician *Auguste Bravais* (1811-1863). Galton, in devising the *coefficient of correlation,* a concept he derived from his research on inheritance, found that children are partially determined by parental traits and partially by the race as a whole. This tendency toward the general mean, he termed *regression.* Experimenting with sweet peas, he found the diameter of the daughter seeds positively related to that of the parent, yet with a tendency toward the general mean. He observed:

> When the deviations of the subject and those of the mean of the relatives are severally measured in units of their own Q, there is always a regression in the value of the latter. . . . The statures of kinsmen are co-related variables; thus, the stature of the father is correlated to that of the adult son, and the stature of the adult son to that of the father; that stature of the uncle to that of the adult nephew, and the stature of the adult nephew to that of the uncle, and so on; but the index of co-relation, which is what I there called

"regression," is different in different cases. In dealing with kinships there is usually no need to reduce the measures to units of Q, because the Q values are alike in all the kinsmen, being of the same value as that of the population at large. It however happened that the very first case that I analysed was different in this respect. It was the reciprocal relation between the statures of what I called the "mid-parent" and the son. The mid-parent is an ideal progenitor, whose stature is the average of that of the father on the one hand and of that of the mother on the other, after her stature had been transmuted into its male equivalent by the multiplication of the factor of 1 · 08. The Q of the mid-parental statures was found to be 1 · 2, while that of the population dealt with was 1 · 7. Again, the mean deviation measured in inches of the statures of the sons was found to be two-thirds of the deviation of the mid-parents, while the mean deviation in inches of the mid-parent was one-third of the deviations of the sons (1888, pp. 143-4).

Expressing each measure by its deviation from the average, with the standard unit being the semi-interquartile range of each distribution, then the coefficient of correlation will be found to be the slope of the regression line. Galton concluded:

> The prominent characteristics of any co-related variables, so far as I have as yet tested them, are four in number. It is supposed that their respective measures have been first transmuted into others of which the unit is in each case equal to the probable error of a single measure in its own series. Let y = the deviation of the subject, whichever of the two variables may be taken in that capacity; and let x_1, x_2, x_3, &c., be the corresponding deviations of the relative, and let the mean of these be X. Then we find: (1) that $y = r$X for all values of y; (2) that r is the same, whichever of the two variables is taken for the subject; (3) that r is always less than 1; (4) that r measures the closeness of co-relation (1888, p. 145).

The *index of correlation* (which came to be called r) states that "where there is no relationship at all, r becomes equal to 0; when it is so close that Subject and Relative are identical in value, the $r = 1$." Galton continued, "therefore the value of r lies in every case somewhere between the extreme limits of 0 and 1" (1908, p. 303).

By 1889 Galton had utilized his findings in his *Natural Inheritance*, a work that influenced Pearson and others to pursue the investigation of correlation, and led consequently to the founding of the London school of mathematical statistics, as well as the founding of the psychology of individual differences and psychometrics.

Karl Pearson (1857-1936): The Biometric School at London University. While it was Galton who initially hit upon the technique of statistical correlation in 1877, it remained for his intellectual successor and loyal friend, Karl Pearson, Galton Professor of National Eugenics at University College, to develop the theory into its present mathematical form. Owing to Pearson's technical and mathematical abilities, the true brilliance and promise of Galton actualized. Also materialized was the Biometric Laboratory at the University of London under Pearson, together with their journal *(Biometrika)*, in 1901. The London-born Pearson, a University of Cambridge graduate, joined the London faculty at twenty-five years of age, two years later to assume the Chair of Applied Mathematics and Mechanics at University College, London, where he remained a lifetime. In 1911 he occupied the newly-endowed Chair of Eugenics, one endowed by Galton. While many of his papers are found in the journal *Biometrika* of which he was editor from 1902 to 1935, he is best known for his *The Grammar of Science* (1892), a work exhibiting his inimitable canny for solving problems. His early papers were collected in a volume titled *Early Statistical Papers* in 1948, and summaries of his lectures in his daughter's biography *Karl Pearson: An Appreciation of Some Aspects of His Life and Work* (1938).

Pearson's niche in the history of psychology was the mathematical basis he provided Galton's statistical methods, thus extending their scope and range for application in psychology, as well as in the area of eugenics and heredity.

It was one of the founders of *Biometrika*, the zoologist *Walter Frank Raphael Weldon* (1860-1906), a professor at University College, London from 1891 to 1899, who coined the term *Galton's functions* for Galton's use of the term *index*. While Galton introduced the theory and word *correlation*, the term *coefficient of correlation* was coined by the British economist *Francis Ysidro Edgeworth* (1845-1926), the *Economic Journal's* initial editor in 1891. The term's maiden appearance was in his paper "On Correlated Averages" (1892). While Galton referred to the *normal curve* as the Gaussian Law of Error (1908, p. 304), it was Pearson who first coined the term, as well as *standard deviation* (σ), resulting in the elimination of measuring deviation by quartiles or probable error. Pearson introduced the standard deviation in 1893, and the symbol (σ) for it in his "Contributions to the Mathematical Theory of Evolution" (1894). In it, referring to his normal curve, he wrote:

> In most cases, as in the case of errors of observations, they have a fairly definite symmetrical shape and one that approaches with a close degree of approximation to the well-known error or probability-curve. A frequency-curve, which for practical purposes, can be represented by the error curve, will for the remainder of this paper be termed a *normal curve*. When a series of measurements gives rise to a normal curve, we may probably assume something approaching a stable condition; there is production and destruction impartially round the mean. In the case of certain biological, sociological, and economic measurements there is, however, a well-marked deviation from this normal shape, and it becomes important to determine the direction and amount of such deviation (1948, p. 2).

Preferring Bravais' formula for correlation, coined by Pearson *product moment* in 1896, which has come to be known as the Pearson *r*, the formula reads: $r = \Sigma xy/N\sigma x\sigma y$. In 1896 Pearson developed his method of multiple correlation, and two years later one for the probable error of a correlation coefficient. In addition to his contributions to the technique of correlation to psychological statistics, Pearson is credited with the chi-square (χ^2) test for goodness of fit in his "On the Criterion that a Given System of Deviations from the Probable in the Case of a Correlated System of Variables is such that It Can Be Reasonably Supposed to Have Arisen from Random Sampling" (1900). In 1904 and 1905 he elaborated the chi-square test of goodness of fit into the mean square coefficient of contingency

(C), i.e., the association of two different sets of data are measured in order to determine to what degree the variables are not dependent upon one another as well as the extent of chance involved. Pearson phrased it:

> With a view of lessening the number of coefficients in use, I adopt the following convention: Any expression of function of either the mean square contingency ($\bar{\phi}^2$) or the mean contingency (Ψ) (or indeed of any other measure of the contingency), which, when the grouping is sufficiently small, is theoretically equal to the coefficient of correlation—on the hypothesis of normal frequency—shall be termed a coefficient of contingency (1904, p. 9).

The indebtedness of psychologists to Pearson for the wide variety of statistical tools that he furnished them is attested by their constant use and dependence upon statistical data for the verification of their psychological findings.

CHARLES SPEARMAN (1863-1945):
Founding of Factor Analysis

One of the psychologists who reaped the benefits of Galton's accomplishments (and of Pearson's) was McDougall's successor at University College, London, Charles Spearman. The London-born Spearman obtained his Ph.D. from Leipzig (1904) under Wundt, where he acquired his expertise in experimental methods of psychology. His apprenticeship in Germany terminated in 1906 after a brief period of time with Külpe at the University of Würzburg and Müller at the University of Göttingen. He was the first at University College, London to occupy the Chair of Psychology, for none was established until 1928. His long tenure at London University began in 1906 and lasted until his retirement in 1931.

Spearman's two most notable contributions to psychology are *general intelligence* and *factor analysis,* having founded the factor school of psychology and the general factor of ability which came to be called *g*, with its complement of specific abilities, collectively termed *s*. Consequently his psychological stance is dubbed *two-factor theory.*

Two Factor Theory and Factor Analysis. Although the beginnings of factor analysis are possibly traced to Pearson's accomplishments, Spearman's development exceeds Pearson's to such an extent that the roots are hardly noticeable. Spearman, the formulator of factor analysis, employed a common factor together with a number of specific factors, permitting individual differences to be accounted for by tests scoring a single general ability together with a specific factor of each test. According to Spearman's two-factor theory of intelligence, a cognitive performance must be a function of two factors (1) *general ability* ordinarily found in any cognitive performance (general factor called *g*), and (2) *specific ability* found in a particular test (specific factors; specific to each different ability). Spearman, introducing his theory in 1904 in his classic paper, "'General Intelligence,' Objectively Determined and Measured," defended it emphatically in 1930, as well as throughout the years. He explained:

> One part depends on an element or factor which remains always the same in all the

abilities of the same individual. The other part depends on a second factor which, even for the same individual, differs freely from one ability to another. The former factor has been named "general intelligence" or "general ability." . . . Prudence recommended that the names of "general intelligence" or "general ability" should be replaced by the non-committal letter of the alphabet *g*. A further reason for preferring the bare letter is that the terms "general intelligence" or "general ability" are apt to suggest some separate mental power capable of existing on its own account, whereas in truth no such "general ability" has ever been found apart from some "special ability," which constitutes the other factor and has been denoted by *s*. The two factors are, for the general theory at any rate, nothing more than two values derived from one and the same real thing; this itself is the whole score obtained by any individual for the whole of some concrete mental operation (1930, pp. 342-3).

In addition *g* and *s* are given "weight" according to their relative influences. Spearman measured *g* by a "hotch-potch" procedure, initiated into practice by Binet. A collection of numerous tests produced a scale, their mean being an individual's intellectual level. The six foundation pillars upon which two factor theory rests are: (1) correlation coefficients, (2) calculated deviations of tetrad differences from zero, (3) observation of these deviations, (4) proof of the two factors, (5) their relative weights in abilities, and (6) their actual measurements in individuals. When various abilities correlate perfectly unity is approached, the opposite being a zero correlation. The procedure used is correlation coefficients. Results showed that rather than perfect correlation, only intermediate values were obtained. The tetrad difference, currently superseded by factor analysis, was Spearman's technique of ascertaining whether there is more than a single factor present in a group of intercorrelations.

When Spearman's major book, *The Nature of 'Intelligence' and the Principles of Cognition* was published in 1923, he was anxious to confirm the existence of a general factor *(g)* with a distinct concept of intelligence, but when his second book, *The Abilities of Man* (1927) appeared four years later, Spearman was content to accept a number of group factors. "With this failure to explain the law of span goes also . . . a similar inability to explain any of the three characters found by us to be mentally universal, *g,* perseveration, or oscillation" (1927, p. 404). Perseveration, oscillation, fluency, and persistence are included in group factors. Without realizing it, this concession on Spearman's part led to what is today called multiple factor analysis, and his general factor is currently viewed as secondary, consisting perhaps of fluid and crystallized general intelligence.

Noegenetic Laws. Spearman, developing three qualitative laws, termed them *noegenetic* (creative mind) because the mind creates a new *fundament* (a new mental content). They are: (1) the law of apprehension of experience, (2) the law of eduction of relations, and (3) the law of eduction of correlates. Influenced by the British associationists (Locke, Bain, etc.), he viewed the laws as evoking a relation between two fundaments, resulting in a new one. Whereas the association psychology laws merely reproduced mental content, his explained the genesis of new mental content.

In addition to these qualitative laws, he offered five quantitative laws on which the noegenetic processes occur: (1) *the law of mental span:* "Every mind tends to keep its total simultaneous output constant in quantity, however varying in quality" (1923, p. 131); (2) *law of retentivity of dispositions:* "The occurrence of any cognitive event produces a tendency for it to occur afterwards" (1923, p. 132); two manifestations or corollaries of the law of retentivity are *(a) law of inertia:* "Cognitive events always both begin and cease more gradually than their (apparent) causes" (1923, p. 133), and *(b) law of association:* "Cognitive events by occurring in company tend to do so with greater ease" (1923, p. 134); (3) *law of fatigue:* "The occurrence of any cognitive event produces a tendency opposed to its occurring afterwards" (1923, p. 134); (4) *law of conative control:* "The intensity of cognition can be controlled by conation" (1923, p. 135); and (5) *law of primordial potencies:* "Every manifestation of the preceding four quantitative principles is superposed upon, as its ultimate basis, certain primordial but variable individual potencies" (1923, pp. 136-7). The laws, which appeared in his *Nature of Intelligence* and were elaborated in his *Abilities of Man,* failed to make any appreciable impact on psychologists.

Spearman's Influence. The severe and relentless opposition encountered by Spearman from his contemporaries was met with equally strong defenses. His computation methods were supplanted by others, and his two factor theory radically modified, but nevertheless pangs he experienced gave birth to a new and developing field of multiple factor analysis, even if his own theories were aborted. His approach to psychology was not only perpetuated by his successor at University College, London, but by two students at University College, London who distinguished themselves: Hans J. Eysenck and Raymond B. Cattell.

Thus while Spearman gave birth to two factor theory in 1904, devoting the remainder of his professional life (forty years) to it, and accordingly is the father of factor theory, his original theory of general and specific factors yielded to theories of many group factors. "Then it naturally followed that some workers explored the possibility of extracting several factors directly from a matrix of correlations among tests, and thus arose the concept of multiple-factor analysis" (Harman, 1955, p. 2). In the United States *multiple factor analysis* was popularized by L. L. Thurstone, coiner of the term. The major contribution of Thurstone, observed Harman, is "the generalization of Spearman's tetrad-difference criterion to the *rank* of correlation matrix as the basis for determination of the number of common factors" (1955, p. 2). Currently there are numerous factor analytic schools. Thus combined with the efforts of Spearman over a score of years, Karl Pearson (1901), Cyril Burt, Godfrey H. Thomson (1951), J. C. Maxwell Garnett, L. L. Thurstone (1931, 1947, 1948), and Karl Holzinger aided in the development of factor analysis.

CYRIL BURT (1883-   ): Perpetuation of the Factor Analytic Tradition at London

By the time Cyril Burt succeeded to Spearman's chair in 1931 at University College, London, factor analysis at that institution had become a tradition. The

London-born Cyril Lodowic Burt was one of McDougall's bright students at Oxford, where, after receiving his degree in 1907, he spent the following year at the University of Würzburg studying under Külpe. Burt came to know Francis Galton, owing to his father's being physician to the Galton family. When the first volume of *Biometrika* (founded by Galton, Pearson, and W. F. R. Weldon in 1901) appeared, he purchased a copy containing the article "Anthropometry and the Identification of Criminals," which provided him with a table of intercorrelations (based on physical measurements of criminals) in terms of *index-characters* (factors). Perceiving that Pearson's analysis might be extrapolated for application in psychology by way of mental measurement, he developed his *centroid formula* by simplifying Peason's complex equations. The consequence of his findings was the confirmation of Galton's twofold theory: (1) general factor of intelligence which was principally innate, and (2) group factors (special aptitudes). The results, published as "Experimental Tests of General Intelligence," appeared in 1909 as his first work in psychology. The paper set the keynote of his professional or theoretical life in psychology, with other publications to come, such as "General and Specific Factors Underlying the Primary Emotions" (1915). This interest followed him throughout the years, as his "The Factorial Analysis of Ability" written as late as 1939 attests.

It is not to be assumed that Burt independently of Spearman arrived at his two factor theory, for he was well aware of Spearman's classic paper on "General Intelligence Objectively Measured and Determined" (1904), and the very first paragraph of Burt's important 1909 paper acknowledges Spearman's efforts. Even the term *general intelligence,* in Burt's title, was introduced by Spearman.

Four Factor Theory. Burt's leading sentence in his important 1909 article reads: "The experimental determination of the mental characters of individuals is admittedly a problem of wide theoretical interest and of vast practical importance." He added: "The particular mental character which in importance is perhaps above all supreme, is that traditionally termed 'General Intelligence' " (p. 94). Interested in validating Spearman's mathematical methods, he saw his investigations of general intelligence presenting three queries: "(i) can its presence be detected and its amount measured? (ii) can its nature be isolated and its meaning analysed? (iii) is its development predominantly determined by environmental influence and individual acquisition, or is it rather dependent upon the inheritance of a racial character or family trait? (1909, p. 96). Furthermore experimentation is required in order to ascertain "Whether Intelligence consists of a single elementary faculty; whether it is the complex resultant of a number of faculties, all working in co-operation; or whether there is really no such thing as 'General Intelligence' " (1909, p. 96).

He was convinced that a considerable portion of disagreement in the factor theory debate (especially between Thomson and Spearman) would vanish if psychologists would restrict themselves to the primary meaning and definition of the term factor.

The matrices that define factors in psychology have the essential properties of 'selective operators.' Hence a factor is primarily a principle of classification and nothing more: it is expressed in quantitative form simply because the items, whose characteristic pattern constitutes the distinguishing mark of the class described by it, vary continuously and in degree rather than discontinuously and in kind (1939, p. 84).

Taking his cue from Aristotelian logic of classes in which he noted four kinds of predicables (genus, species or differentiae, individual propria, and accidents), he found corresponding to them four kinds of factors: (1) general, (2) group or difference, (3) specific, and (4) accidental. All multiple factor theories (including two and three factor theories) are special derivatives of four-factor theory.

According to Burt, all factor methods are reducible to the same basic set of values, differences among factors being merely superficial, with matrix algebra the preferred procedural methodology for dealing with issues of factor analysis. In a 1911 paper on "The Experimental Study of General Intelligence" he was formulating his definition of intelligence that he finally offered in *Mental and Scholastic Tests* (1921), reiterating it in *The Subnormal Mind* (1935) as an "inborn, general cognitive efficiency" (1935, p. 23). Thus intelligence is essentially hereditary, innate and universally common with respect to an intellective factor. Not that social or environmental factors play no role, but that the innate is decidedly the more decisive. Nor did he overlook the *orectic* (emotional) aspect of life, having turned considerable attention to it in the 1930s, with his articles on "The Analysis of Temperament" (1938) and "The Factorial Analysis of Emotional Traits" (1938) in which he espouses his theory of a factor of *general emotionality*. In these publications, and in his *The Factors of the Mind* (1940), Burt introduced bipolar emotive factors of temperament types of extroversion and introversion. This aspect of his work was pursued by his student *Hans J. Eysenck,* who exploited factor analysis in clinical psychology and personality theory. Another of Burt's students, Raymond B. Cattell, contributed to the development of factor psychology to the extent that in 1966 he was able to publish a *Handbook of Multivariate Experimental Psychology* that ran close to 1,000 pages, with Burt contributing a chapter on "The Appropriate Uses of Factor Analysis and Analysis of Variance." This late publication reiterated Burt's earlier position, stating:

> Both factor analysis and analysis of variance seek to investigate, by suitable statistical techniques, what are variously termed the "components," "factors," "dimensions," or "sources" of a complex set of variations. That means that both are essentially concerned with problems of classification of variables. In factor analysis we *end* by determining what the "factors" are, i.e., what the appropriate classification appears to be, and when we seek to measure the relative importance: in analysis of variance we *begin* with a knowledge of what the factors presumably are, and we test their statistical significance (1966, p. 286).

Not only did Burt remain faithful to factor theory throughout his professional life, he maintained it at University College, London, making of it a tradition there. Reminiscing about the situation, he reported in his "Autobiography:"

During the twenty years that I have occupied the Chair of Psychology at University College, my main aim has been to preserve its original traditions, and to make it a focus for that branch of psychology which was founded and developed there by Galton—"individual" or, as Stern used to call it, "differential psychology"—the study of the mental differences between individuals, sexes, social classes and other groups (1952, p. 72).

When Burt assumed the Chair of Psychology at University College, London in 1931, he had but a half dozen students pursuing an undergraduate degree in psychology together with a dozen research students. After a score of years his students totalled over 200, 80 of them involved in research, his more distinguished ones being (in addition to Cattell and Eysenck) *Frederick C. Bartlett* (1866-   ) of Cambridge University and *Peter Lovell Broadhurst* (1924-   ) of the University of Birmingham. When Burt retired in 1951, he was succeeded by R. W. Russell (1914-   ).

Raymond B. Cattell (1905-   ): Multivariate Experimental Psychology. Born in Devonshire, England, Raymond Bernard Cattell took his Ph.D. in psychology under Charles Spearman and a decade later a D.Sc. under Burt at the University of London. During the late 1930s he migrated to the United States, and has been Research Professor of Psychology at the University of Illinois since 1945, and subsequently that institution's Director of the Laboratory of Personality and Group Analysis. Founder of the Society of Multivariate Experimental Psychology for the development of factor psychology, Cattell has developed a *factor theory of personality*. His objective is the establishment of a quantitative, experimental, and mathematical basis for the investigation of personality and human motivation.

Since Wundt experimented with but one variable in psychology, his approach may be called univariate experimental psychology; the factor theorists, owing to their dealing with a number of variables at a given time, are involved in *multivariate experimental psychology*. Cattell, basing his system on Thurstone's (1931) refinement of Spearman's factor theory, included not only Spearman's general and specific factors but group factors as well, the result being a multivariate factor theory.

Preferring the *inductive-hypothetico-deductive method,* Cattell's investigations assumed the order of an upward spiral proceeding from observation of an experiment to the final deduction along the following ascending steps: (1) experiment observation, (2) inductive reasoning to some regularity, (3) hypothesis, (4) deduction of consequences for experiment or observation. The process is continuously repeated, but upward progress is regularly being made, hence the spiralling upward rather than a circular process of getting nowhere.

Defining personality of an individual tentatively as "that which enables us to predict what he will do in a given situation" (1950, p. 21), Cattell proceeded to a conclusive definition:

Personality can be defined, first, factorially, as the dimensions of behavioural space for human beings, secondly, biologically, as the patterns of reaction to the environment required to maintain internal chemical states (homeostasis), thirdly, clinically, as a more or less integrated set of originally discrete dynamic trends, fourthly, sociologically, as a transmitting and creating element in the culture pattern, and so on (1950, p. 220).

Viewing personality as "that which determines behaviour in a defined situation," Cattell, owing to his factor orientation, produced a *trait theory of personality,* couched in mathematical terms. While all persons share "common traits," each has his singularly own "unique traits," the latter being subdivided into "relatively unique" and "intrinsically unique." It is necessary to draw a distinction between "surface traits" (manifest variables) and "source traits" (covert or underlying variables), the latter being the more important, for they are the real structural influences, and the former an interaction of source traits. From another standpoint traits may be classed as "dynamic traits" (action or goal motivating), "ability traits" (effectiveness in goal achievement), and "temperament traits" (constitutional factors, e.g., speed, energy, or emotional reactivity).

Data concerning personality derive from *L-data* (life record), *Q-data* (self-questionnaire rating), and *T-data* (objective test). Personality traits are ascertained from factor analytic studies involving the three tests which are the principal sources of personality data. Factor analytic techniques: *P-technique, R-technique,* and *Q-technique,* Cattell defined accordingly:

> *P-technique:* A factor analytic design which measures a single person on the same set of variables repeatedly over a number of different occasions. Correlations between the variables are computed over these occasions as entries, then factor analysed. P-technique and incremental factor analysis are the two main methods for determining dimensions of personality change-over-time (or states). . . .

> *R-technique:* Ordinary factor analysis in which tests are given to people and correlated over people (1965, pp. 372-3).

> *Q-technique:* A factor analysis from correlating persons instead of tests. The transpose of R technique (1957, p. 899).

In recent years Cattell became Director of the Institute for Research on Morality, Colorado, in consequence of which his attention has turned to ethics, an *ethics of beyondism,* articulated in his *A New Morality from Science: Beyondism* (1972), a subject which has held his interest since 1938. Cattell's (1950c) is a psychological approach to ethical problems.

H. J. Eysenck (1916-   ): Dimensional Approach to Personality. With a factor theory psychology derived from the same sources as Cattell's, Hans Jurgen Eysenck developed a dimensional approach to personality. The German-born Eysenck left his native land in 1934 with the rise of Nazism for England, obtaining his Ph.D. at the University of London in 1940. This former student of Burt was a Reader in Psychology at the University of London, becoming Professor of Psychology at the institution's Institute of Psychiatry, as well as senior psychologist at its two affiliated hospitals, Bethlem Royal and Maudsley.

While Cattell's is a statistical approach to personality investigation, Eysenck's (1947) is dimensional; furthermore while the former employed a larger number of factors, Eysenck's (1952) treatment is limited to only two or three, such as introversion-extroversion (Jung's influence). Eysenck's (1950) method, hypothetico-deductive, calls for an hypothesis of personality followed by deductive tests.

(B)   EXPERIMENTAL PSYCHOLOGY AT CAMBRIDGE

One of the world's oldest universities (founded in the thirteenth century), the University of Cambridge has been a leader in British psychology, boasting of that Commonwealth's first laboratory of psychology (founded by James Ward in 1891). As early as 1877 (if James Ward and the distinguished diagrammatic logician John Venn (1834-1923) had had their way), Cambridge would have had the world's first psychological laboratory. But it was not until 1891 that the university made a grant of £50 for the purchase of psychological apparatus to be utilized in connection with Ward's lectures. In 1888 the American James McKeen Cattell was resident as a fellow-commoner at the university, offering instruction in experimental psychology, having acquired it from Hall at Johns Hopkins and from Wundt at Leipzig. At the invitation of Michael Foster, W. H. R. Rivers was invited to Cambridge in 1893 to lecture on the physiology of the special senses. Consequently because of Rivers' appointment as University Lecturer of Physiological and Experimental Psychology, he became the first officially recognized instructor of experimental psychology at the University of Cambridge. Yet a Chair of Psychology was not established at Cambridge until 1931; F. C. Bartlett was appointed to the Chair of Experimental Psychology, occupying it until his retirement in 1952, when O. L. Zangwill succeeded him.

JAMES WARD (1843-1925):
England's First Psychological Laboratory

Having appreciated the fact that it was through the efforts of Ward that Cambridge acquired its first laboratory of psychology, the student of psychology will also learn that it was also with Ward that Cambridge psychology in any modern sense of the term had its start, for it was Ward who broke away from British empiricism and associationism. Known especially in the history of psychology for his famous article "Psychology" in the ninth edition of the *Encyclopaedia Britannica* in 1886, Ward, owing to the views expressed in the article, altered the course of British psychology. From the time of the publication of his *Britannica* article to the mid-twentieth century, he was a potent force in charting the course of British psychologists.

Born in Hull, Ward attended the universities of Berlin, Göttingen, and Cambridge as well as working in the University of Leipzig physiological laboratory. Originally he prepared for the Congregational ministry, serving a church in Cambridge before setting his course for psychology at the age of thirty. At Berlin he worked with Ludwig, and at Röttingen with Lotze. His professional connection with the University of Cambridge began in 1881 as lecturer, rising to the Chair of Mental Philosophy and Logic in 1897 until his retirement in 1925.

Unsympathetic toward behaviorism and with a negligible interest in physiological psychology, Ward and his psychology constitute a decisive break with the empiricism, associationism, and sensationalism then prevailing in British psychology. Ward's systematic psychology viewed experience as a continuum. By the action of selective attention (consciousness) distinctions among experiences are introduced gradually into this continuum of experience, the subject of these experiences becoming an important consideration. Operation in development of subjective selection (in addition to natural) is emphasized.

Ward elaborated his 1886 *Britannica* article in the 1911 edition, and expanded it with new material for his *Psychological Principles* ,(1918). His definition of psychology as "the science of individual experience—understanding by experience not merely, not primarily, cognition, but also, and above all, conative activity or behaviour" (1920, p. 28), keynotes his systematic psychology. Opposed to the atomism of the Lockean tradition, he preferred the Leibnizian tradition, viewing personality not as a bundle of sensations (Hobbes) but as the source of acts. Repulsed from British empiricism, he was attracted toward the German outlook of Leibniz, Kant, Lotze, and Brentano. The Britannica article defined psychology also as "the science of individual experience," adding that its objective is "first, to ascertain its ultimate constituents, and secondly, to determine and explain the laws of their interaction" (11th ed., p. 548). Ward analyzed the individual or subject as possessing: (1) cognition, (2) feeling, and (3) conation, the vehicles by which objects are ascertained, the first providing presentation of the sensory, and the third presentation of the motor. He provided the following diagram (11th ed., p. 554):

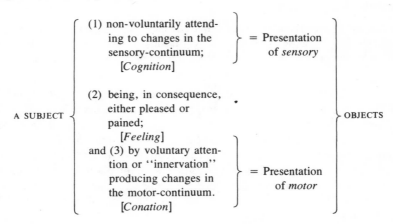

The self, instead of being "congeries of faculties," he termed attention, a term he preferred to consciousness. The self, as subject of experience, always is. Subconsciousness he dismissed as "nothing more than the application to the facts of presentation of the law of continuity," a concept that Leibniz introduced into psychology. As for sensation, he held that within the fields of consciousness, every sensation "has sensibly some continuous duration and seems sensibly to admit of some continuous variation in intensity and extensity" (1911, p. 562).

Association psychology he repudiated, holding that association by similarity is neither fundamental nor free from confusion, and association by contiguity is inexplicable. While mental contents are comprised of sensory and motor *presentations,* they are part of a continuum rather than isolated units.

George Frederick Stout (1860-1944): Ward's Distinguished Pupil. The University of Cambridge graduate, G. F. Stout, began his long tenure at St. Andrews University in 1903, remaining there until his retirement in 1936. An "armchair psychologist," Stout distinguished himself by authoring the most notable and widely adopted British textbook of the first half of the twentieth century, *A Manual of Psychology* (1899), that saw its fifth edition in 1938. Like Ward, he was both influenced by Brentano and vehemently opposed the British associationists. While an undergraduate student at the University of Cambridge, he was recruited for psychology by Ward. Stout too wielded an influence, not merely through his widely read text, but through the journal *Mind* which he edited from 1891 to 1920. While sharing views with Ward, he also acknowledged indebtedness to Spinoza, Hume, Herbart, Brentano, and Kant. More than the *Manual,* his first work, the two volume *Analytic Psychology* (1896) was original.

Defining psychology as "the study of mental facts or as the study of mental life," (1932, p. 1), Stout held that the psychologist's method was introspective analysis, and his task the systematic establishment of the conditions and laws accounting for the course of the mental life of people. Characteristic of the psychic life is a persistent unity (unlike anything in the material world of things). Hence mind is viewed as a unity of consciousness, rather than simply processes or states. He asserted that

> psychology is concerned with modes of consciousness as connected within the unity of consciousness. But we are unable to speak of modes of consciousness and their unity without reference to a conscious individual, a mind or self which owns them (1932, p. 15).

British empiricism with its psychology without a soul is repudiated along with its psychical atomism. In concert with Ward, Stout rejected the mental chemistry that John Stuart Mill introduced, for the realm of mind is a sui generis with its own peculiar laws. His genetic and evolutionary psychology emphasized human development, the psychic life being essentially purposive and effortful. Attention and conation too are important concepts, as they were for Ward. His approach, the descriptive analysis of all data that is present in consciousness, is reminiscent of the method of Husserl and Meinong. He became increasingly aware of his phenomenological orientation.

Along with Ward, Stout became an important pioneer in British psychology, his influence being felt in Anglo-Saxon psychology. His publications continued even to his becoming a septuagenarian. Like Ward before him, he founded no school of psychology, yet the voluntaristic psychology that Ward introduced and Stout continued was perpetuated by William McDougall. Stout's papers, including a chapter on "Ward as a Psychologist," have been published in a volume titled *Studies in Philosophy and Psychology* (1930).

William Halse Rivers Rivers (1864-1922): **The First Experimental Psychologist at Cambridge.** Rivers, who was trained at Tonbridge School and St. Bartholomew's Hospital in London and held a degree in medicine, began lecturing in experimental psychology at Guy's Hospital in London. Owing to the influence of the Cambridge physiologists, Hughlings Jackson and Henry Head, Rivers charted the future course of his life in psychology, with a decided interest in anthropology stemming from his Cambridge Anthropological Expedition to the Torres Straits. His Freudian influence is apparent from his later writings: *Instinct and the Unconscious* (1920), *Conflict and Dreams* (1923), and *Medicine, Magic, and Religion* (1924). Reviewing his life, Bartlett reported:

> In 1893 Rivers was invited to Cambridge by Sir Michael Foster, to lecture on the physiology of the special senses, and in 1897 a movement, initiated many years before by Professor James Ward and Dr. Venn for the official recognition by the University of Experimental Psychology, produced its definite result, and Rivers was made University Lecturer of Physiological and Experimental Psychology. He was thus the first officially recognized teacher of experimental psychology at Cambridge and the first person in England to plan and carry out a systematic course of practical teaching in the subject (1928, p. 275).

Although it was through Sully's initiative that the Laboratory for Experimental Psychology was founded at University College, London in 1897, it was Rivers who became its first director, notwithstanding his being there for only a matter of months.

From 1908 when Rivers made his initial journey to Melanesia to the outbreak of World War I, he became increasingly involved in sociological and ethnological issues. Rivers, having relinquished his position as Lecturer in Experimental Psychology, the post was transferred to C. S. Myers, making him the first University of Cambridge lecturer with the sole responsibility of teaching experimental psychology. Rivers was also coparticipant with Ward and others in the founding of the *British Journal of Psychology* in 1904, becoming its first co-editor.

Charles Samuel Myers (1873-1946): **The Cambridge Laboratory.** The University of Cambridge graduate (Sc.D., 1909), Myers, joined Rivers in the Cambridge psychological laboratory as Demonstrator in 1904, becoming Lecturer in Experimental Psychology from 1909 to 1922, leaving to become Director of the National Institute of Industrial Psychology which he (with H. J. Welch) founded. During a leave of absence from the University of Cambridge he completed his first book on industrial psychology, which appeared in 1921 as *Mind and Work*. From 1911 to 1924 he edited the *British Journal of Psychology*.

Perhaps more than anyone else in the early years of the laboratory of psychology, Myers saw to its development. Like his predecessor, Rivers, he too was qualified in medicine, and with him and William McDougall they left on the Cambridge Anthropological Expedition to Torres Straits (New Guinea) and Sarawak (Borneo). In 1903 he saw the psychological laboratory moved to a cottage on the River Cam belonging to the University Press, where the then director, Rivers, was granted £ 50 for new apparatus and an annual £ 50 for expenses to maintain the laboratory. When Myers undertook directing the psychological laboratory in 1909 he published *A Text-book of Experimental Psychology*, the purpose being to inform one of the nature and scope of psychological experiments. Thus the leadership in psychology at Cambridge had fallen to C. S. Myers, who received a stipend of £ 50 (less than $125) per year. The small laboratory on Mill Lane, too small and unsuitable, prompted Myers to launch a drive in 1908, and by 1913 the new laboratory was opened, with Myers its unpaid director. By the close of World War I, Myers (with Rivers) successfully established a Diploma in Psychological Medicine at the University of Cambridge.

When Myers resigned as Director of the Psychological Laboratory, F. C. Bartlett, who came to Cambridge in 1909, succeeded him as Director of the Psychological Laboratory. In 1931 Bartlett was to occupy the first chair of psychology, the Chair of Experimental Psychology, at Cambridge.

FREDERIC CHARLES BARTLETT (1886-   ): Memory as a Social Psychological Phenomenon

It was in 1922 that Bartlett succeeded Myers as Director of the University of Cambridge Laboratory of Psychology, an appointment he relinquished to Oliver Louis Zangwill (1913-   ) on his retirement in 1952, together with the newly created Chair of Psychology established in 1931. The Cambridge educated Bartlett does not regard himself as belonging to any school of psychology. When asked, his reply is simply, "I am a Cambridge psychologist" (1930, p. 40). Stout's *Manual* was the first psychology book that he ever read, followed by his *Analytic Psychology*. Then he travelled 18 miles to the nearest library to take notes on Ward's *Britannica* article weekly. Small wonder that he considers himself a Cambridge psychologist. Bartlett's role in British psychology has been a dominant one, for the majority of Chairs of Psychology in Britain in 1960 were occupied by his students who graduated from Cambridge, among them being the present occupant of the Cambridge chair, O. L. Zangwill.

Bartlett's approach to psychology has been one of dealing with real life situations, one free from statistics, which he dismisses as a scientific make-shift. This attitude has spread to his students, with but few exceptions. In Bartlett, the psychological laboratory had the first nonmedic as its director.

Socio-Psychological Factors of Remembering. In the book for which he is best known, *Remembering: A Study in Experimental and Social Psychology*, which appeared in 1932 and has been in print even in the late 1960s, Bartlett advanced the thesis that remembering, rather than being a reproductive process, is actually a *reconstructive* one. Changes, occurring during the process of remembering, indicated that remembering entailed attitudes and "schemata," rather than solely sense data. Thus initial experiences, affected by a number of factors, such as a person's cultural background as well as his social and emotional interests, undergo extensive changes. An individual ordinarily does the same with respect to perception in the sense that what passes for perception is actually recall. Bartlett observed:

All people who have at any time been concerned with the nature and validity of everyday observation must have noticed that a great amount of what goes under the name of perception is, in the wide sense of the term, recall. Some scene is presented for observation, and a little of it is actually perceived. But the observer reports much more than this. He fills up the gaps of his perception by the aid of what he has experienced before in similar situations, or, though this comes to much the same thing in the end, by describing what he takes to be 'fit,' or suitable, to such a situation. Yet, in almost all cases, he is certainly doing the first, and in many instances he is demonstrably doing the second (1932, p. 14).

Bartlett, whose experiments on remembering began as early as 1914, a year after the new laboratory of psychology opened, hit upon the idea when participating with Myers in demonstrations arranged for visitors. He noted that the observers' visual perception was determined by more factors than the sense data presented before them. Remembering, concluded Bartlett is not mere re-excitation, but

an imaginative reconstruction, or construction, built out of the relation of our attitude towards a whole active mass of organised past reactions or experience, and to a little outstanding detail which commonly appears in image or in language form. . . . The attitude is literally an effect of the organism's capacity to turn round upon its own 'schemata,' and is directly a function of consciousness. The outstanding detail is the result of that valuation of items in an organised mass which begins with the functioning of appetite and instinct, and goes much further with the growth of interests and ideals (1932, p. 213).

The functionalist Bartlett, who first reported on his experiments in 1920 in "Some Experiments on the Reproduction of Folk Stories," derived his "method of repeated reproduction" from J. Phillipe (1897).

Social Psychology of Thinking. Over a quarter of century later Bartlett issued his sequel to remembering titled *Thinking: An Experimental and Social Study.* Interested in thinking in connection with social activities, Bartlett regarded thinking as high-level skill, comparable to motor skills, and sharing many characteristic properties. Unlike *Remembering,* this work provided no new theory. Nevertheless he observed that experimental thinking acquired a social character. Thinking "is fundamentally co-operative, social and cannot proceed far without the stimulus of outside contacts" (1958, p. 123).

Although *Thinking* was published after Bartlett had been in retirement for a half dozen years, his intent to develop an experimental study of thinking dates from 1932, the year *Remembering* was published.

Neither of these two books was Bartlett's first. The first work, one of lesser importance and centering on his anthropological interests, is titled *Psychology and Primitive Culture* (1923). He sought to derive from this study some fundamental psychological laws applicable to modern society, since he felt that the psychological mechanisms operative in any society hold true for other societies. The level of social development is not a crucial factor. In this work, also oriented from the standpoint of social psychology, Bartlett held that since between primitive and civilized people there is no fundamental difference, it follows that the best insight into contemporary social psychological situations is through primitive culture, owing to its relative simplicity. He concluded that both primitive and civilized societies

> display the same tendencies, though these vary considerably in their relations one to another, at different times. And since in modern times the root tendencies may be checked, controlled, and constantly directed in their sphere of operation by derived impulses having a specific character, it is well to begin with the problems afforded by primitive culture. The latter are not essentially different, but they are less complicated (1923, p. 287).

When Bartlett retired from Cambridge, a great era had come to a close, for experimentation at the laboratory under his successor had increasingly taken the form of American physiological and neurological psychology, and the study of animal behavior, as evidenced by two publications of his successor *Oliver Louis Zangwill* (1913-   ): *Cerebral Dominance and Its Relation to Psychological Function* (1960) and (with W. H. Thorpe) *Current Problems in Animal Behaviour* (1961).

PART THREE

DEVELOPMENT OF GERMANIC PSYCHOLOGY

Although psychology in some form (philosophical, physiological, etc.) was transpiring in many of the German universities (such as Königsberg, Bonn, and Heidelberg), two principal epochal centers stand out as citadels, viz., Berlin and Leipzig. While Johannes Müller, Helmholtz, Ebbinghaus, and Stumpf were constructing a citadel for psychology at the University of Berlin, Weber, Fechner, Wundt, and others were seeing that the University of Leipzig was the celebrated hub of the psychological universe. During the nineteenth century these two strongholds of psychology were setting the pace but not without serious competition, for several other universities were conducting important research and producing valuable findings. Among them were: the University of Göttingen where Herbart founded mathematical psychology and published the first textbook of psychology, with Lotze and G. E. Müller contributing to the stature of psychology there, and where Husserl brought phenomenology to fruition; the University of Würzburg that Külpe made famous for imageless thought; and the Austrian universities of Vienna, Graz, and Prague which contributed significantly to act psychology and phenomenology through the efforts of such men as Brentano, Meinong, and Ehrenfels.

During the early period of experimental psychology, at the two bastions of learning that advanced the cause of psychology, Berlin and Leipzig, it was physiologists who initiated experimental research in psychology, J. Müller at the former institution and Weber at the latter. But at each center these two physiologists were followed by magnificent experimentalists who accelerated the pace with a sharp upward mobility and thrust. Helmholtz accomplished this at Berlin, while Fechner followed suit at Leipzig. After Fechner, Wundt saw that psychology as a new and experimental science was permanently entrenched in the annals of science; by his singular efforts at Leipzig he established the first psychological laboratory there in 1879, and in 1881 instituted a journal for reporting research in psychology. Hence was born   the new   psychology, a scientific psychology experimentally based.

Many of the giants of the new physiological psychology in Germany used the vehicle of medicine to attain their objectives, entering medicine on an undergraduate level and utilizing it for the study of physiology and anatomy rather than for the sake of practicing medicine. The closest analogue today is perhaps the number of aspirants to a political life who prepare for it by studying law, never intending to practice law. Much of the psychology was medical psychology *(medizinisch Psychologie)*, though not the clinical psychology or psychiatry that is familiar to many today, but a medical psychology closer to psychoneurology except that normal processes rather than pathological ones were emphasized in the history of psychology.

These psychological physiologists saw the ramifications physiology had for psychology as in the case of Johannes Müller. Later, with the work of Fechner the isomorphic arrangement of body and mind in parallel functioning became the base or impetus of psychological investigation from a physiological experimental orientation. Furthermore, the bulk of these "new psychologists" were still deeply enmeshed in philosophy both from the standpoint of interest and the fact that many held positions in departments of philosophy from which psychology eventually sprang and severed the umbilical cord.

The Privatdozent and His Habilitation

The intermittent appearance of the term *Privatdozent* and *Habilitation* will be found in this part devoted to German psychology. Inasmuch as there is no equivalent in the United States to them, it seems advisable to comment on the matter. In the German universitites and systems based on it, a *Privatdozent* is a lecturer, the first and lowest stage in a university career. An unsalaried lecturer, the *Privatdozent* is remunerated from student fees so that his income increases according to his popularity. But despite his popularity, his income is never large. Nor does he have tenure or faculty standing in the university's governing body. His lectures, however, rank with those of a professor.

Other German academic ranks in ascending order include: *Ordentlicher Professor* (ordinary professor, comparable to assistant professor), *Ausserordentlicher Professor* (extraordinary professor, i.e., comparable to associate professor), and ultimately the highest rank of "chair" or full *Professor*.

Qualification as a full faculty member requires "habilitation," the earning of a doctorate and the successful defense of one's thesis (the product of one's research). To candidate as a full faculty member, a person is required to submit his *Habilitationsschrift*, a thesis beyond the doctoral dissertation dealing with a research project. It is presented as a lecture before the faculty and passed upon by the vote of those holding full professorships. The usual means of achieving a university professorship is via that of *Privatdozent* as was true of distinguished scholars such as Kant, but owing to prejudice it was rare for a Jewish *Privatdozent* to attain the position of full professor in Prussia.

American Students at German Universities During the Nineteenth Century

Almost nine thousand Americans attended German universities in the hundred-year span from 1820-1920, the reason being that residence at a foreign university (especially German) would give a person the competitive edge in seeking a position in the United States. The German doctorate accorded one a decided prestige. Prior to 1870, the United States was almost entirely devoid of scientific psychology, but still worse it was without professional schools of any type of science, including medicine. Education in medicine made its initial appearance in 1859 in Chicago and continued in 1871 at Harvard. It was not until 1893 that a degree was required for the study of medicine: first at Johns Hopkins, and in 1901 at Harvard. The Harvard graduate program was not only too expensive, it provided little opportunity for independent work, for it was merely a glorified continuation of undergraduate study.

The migration of American students of psychology to Germany began in the 1870s. Before the decade ended, the number of students in social science outnumbered even those in theology and law. It was not until the turn of the century that the universities in the United States undertook to any extent the task of professional education. Once this occurred, the reaction antagonistic to German psychology was firmly established, with German influence waning and finally perishing.

Matriculation at German universities by Americans was *pro forma*, requiring merely previous acceptance at any college of repute. The Ph.D. was granted often in three years, but occasionally for only two years of study accompanied by a dissertation and the passing of a comprehensive oral examination. By the turn of the century a German doctorate (such as one from the University of Berlin) was notoriously easy in comparison to one earned in the United States! At least that was the claim of the Association of American Universities.

The universities at Halle and Göttingen were the first to command the interest of students in the United States, dating to the eighteenth century when Benjamin Franklin was the first to visit Göttingen in 1766. Göttingen was a favorite of American students of science, attracting almost a hundred Americans in the 1850s to over three hundred in the 1890s, the attraction being professors of distinction, such as Carl Friedrich Gauss, Johann Friedrich Herbart, Wilhelm Weber, Rudolf Hermann Lotze, Friedrich Wöhler, Georg Elias Müller, and others. However, the University of Berlin gradually outdistanced the rest, with over half of all students coming to Germany from the United States spending at least a semester there during the 1820-1920 hundred-year span. The University of Leipzig in the 1870s attracted more students than Halle and Göttingen, thus being second only to the University of Berlin. With respect to psychology, the most popular German universities were Berlin and Leipzig.

CHAPTER 4

Berlin: Physiological Psychology Makes Its Appearance

Berlin and Its University

To speak of Berlin as the house that Müller, Helmholtz, Ebbinghaus, Stumpf, and Köhler built is not to say that they are to be credited for the proud history of the University of Berlin. Rather, they built the renowned department of psychology. The university itself, though relatively young among German universities, prides itself on its venerable tradition and choice of professors for distinguished excellence. It has been considered the most prestigious one in all Germany, and although these men contributed to its distinction, others did so as well. To be called to the University of Berlin not only distinguished a person, but it was also a recognition of his distinction.

The University of Berlin was founded in 1810, in consequence of the Napoleonic victories when Prussia had lost its celebrated University of Halle, by the then minister of education, Wilhelm Humbolt. He was followed by two distinguished philosophers: Johann Gottlieb Fichte (1762-1814) and Friedrich Schleiermacher (1768-1834) who became its first two deans. The list of scholars who dignified the university with their singular contributions over the years include Hegel, who was there within eight years of its founding. Numbered among succeeding generations of scientists were: Müller, Du Bois Reymond, Helmholtz, Ebbinghaus, Beneke, and Stumpf; while the philosophers included Friedrich W. J. Schelling, Wilhelm Dilthey, and Ernst Troeltsch. Adolf Harnarck (theologian), Albert Einstein (physicist and mathematician), Ernst Cassirer (philosopher), and Wolfgang Köhler (psychologist) are the more recent luminaries. At the turn of the century its library (together with the state library in front of it) housed millions of volumes (including manuscripts and musical works).

JOHANNES PETER MÜLLER (1801-1858):
Father of Experimental Physiology

The Birth of Experimental Psychology

The "new" or experimental psychology was spawned in the laboratories of physiologists and anatomists. Although J Müller (not to be confused with G. E. Müller of Göttingen) is cited as the father of experimental physiology, nevertheless experimental research in physiology antedates him by many years as evidenced by the experimental work of the following: *Charles Bell* (1772-1842),

Scottish anatomist and professor of surgery at the University of Edinburgh; *François Magendie* (1783-1855), the French physiologist and physician who held the chair of anatomy at the Collège de France; *Marie Jean Pierre Flourens* (1794-1867), physiologist and physician, as well as professor in the Collège de France, who developed a physiological theory of sensation in 1821, assigning special functions to the cerebrum based on experimental evidence as recorded in his paper *Recherches expérimentales sur les propriétés et les fonctions du système nerveux dans les animaux vertébrés* (1824) and in *Expériences sur le système nerveux* (1825); and *Marshall Hall* (1790-1857) the English physician and physiologist who discovered reflex action in 1832, publishing it the following year as *Reflex Function of the Medulla Oblongata and Medulla Spinalis* (1833). Hall was not alone in the discovery of reflex action, for Descartes long before him and *Robert Whytt* (1714-1766) of Edinburgh in 1751 initiated it as well as Bell. Müller in his major work, *Handbuch der Physiologie des Menschen* (1833-1840), translated as *Elements of Physiology* (1842), devoted considerable space to the work of Hall.

Bell-Magendie Law on Spinal Nerve Roots

Among the number of discoveries of *Sir Charles Bell* (1772-1842) was the distinct functions of the sensory and motor nerves enunciated in his *Idea of a New Anatomy of the Brain* in 1811 and confirmed in his *The Nervous System of the Human Body* (1830). He found special sensory filaments that served to transmit impressions to the brain, and special motor filaments carrying signals from the brain to the muscles. While some nerves possess a sole sensory function, others provide a motor function only, ideas anticipatory of Müller's theory of the specific energy of nerves. Bell wrote:

> It has been acknowledged that the anterior roots of the spinal nerves bestow the power of muscular motion; and the posterior roots sensibility. When the anterior roots of the nerves of the leg are cut in experiment, the animal loses all power over the leg, although the limb still continues sensible. But if, on the other hand, the posterior roots are cut, the power of motion continues, although the sensibility is destroyed. When the posterior column of the spinal marrow is irritated the animal evinces sensibility to pain; but no apparent effect is produced when the anterior column is touched (1852, p. 21).

Bell's contemporary, *François Magendie* (1783-1855), furnished independent data in France in 1822 attesting to the distinct functions of the posterior (sense function) and anterior (muscular function) roots. Magendie related his experiment:

> Using a very sharp scalpel I was able . . . to lay bare the posterior half of the spinal cord. . . . I saw it [dog] move, although its sensibility was completely removed. . . . I began to consider it probable that the posterior roots of the spinal nerves had different functions from those of the anterior roots, and that they were particularly concerned with sensibility.
>
> It occurred to me, of course, that the next step was to cut the anterior roots while leaving the posterior ones intact. . . . The limb was completely immobilized and flaccid, although there could be no doubt that its sensibility remained unimpaired (1822, p. 276).

A concomitant of the Bell-Magendie law of spinal nerve roots is the *law of forward conduction*, the theory that the flow of conduction in nerve fibers travels in only one direction. It was this law that opened the way for Marshall Hall's successful work on reflex function and reflex arc.

Specific Energy of Nerves

The specific energy of nerves theory was introduced by *Johannes Müller* (1801-1858), who also offered the view that color sensations are produced on the retina by pressure, as well as some contributions to reflex action. A little over a score of years after Bell published his spinal nerve root theory, Müller developed his specific energy of nerves theory, which not only grew out of Bell's findings but lent permanent verification to the Bell-Magendie law, yet at the same time eclipsed Bell and his discovery.

The German physiologist Müller was born in Coblenz, Prussia approximately a quarter of a century after Bell and Magendie. After studying at Berlin and Bonn, he received his doctorate from the latter institution in 1822, the year that Magendie published his work on the Bell-Magendie law of spinal nerve roots. He remained at Bonn as a *Privatdozent* (private instructor) and later as assistant professor until 1833 when he left for the University of Berlin's chair of anatomy and physiology where he became the world's foremost authority in physiology as well as the world's first to hold the title of Professor of Physiology. His immense influence is readily apparent in his students: Helmholtz, Ernst Wilhelm Brücke (1819-1892) (Freud's professor), Emil du Bois-Reymond (1818-1896), and Carl Friedrich Wilhelm Ludwig (1816-1895), a founder of nonvitalistic physiology. All were pioneers in German physiology.

Though some of his ideas were found in his earlier work, *Zur vergleichenden Physiologie des Gesichtsinns* (1826), Müller developed thoroughly his specific energy of nerves theory in his epoch-making *Elements of Physiology* (1833-1840). Müller, who developed a science of physiology thereby emancipating it from medicine, stated his law of specific energy of nerves in terms of the following propositions:

External agencies can give rise to no kind of sensation which cannot also be produced by internal causes, exciting changes in the condition of our nerves.

The same internal cause excites in the different senses different sensations;–in each sense the sensations peculiar to it.

The same external cause also gives rise to different sensations in each sense, according to the special endowments of its nerve.

The nerve of each sense seems to be capable of one determinate kind of sensation only, and not of those proper to the other organs of sense; hence one nerve of sense cannot take the place and perform the function of the nerve of another sense (1842, II, p. 1069).

Whereas Bell and Magendie had merely mentioned that there were only two types of nerves, one for sense and the other for muscular activity, Müller, grasping the significance of the finding, reasoned that the entire nervous activity of man could be comprised of nerves specializing in the activity peculiar to them so that a blow on the head could cause nerves in the skin to feel pain, nerves in the ears to give a ringing sound, nerves in the eyes to see "stars," i.e., each nerve has its own function regardless of what stimulates it so that nerves conveying visual sensation will do so not only from light but from eyeball pressure or surgical activity performed upon them. *"The peculiar sensations of each nerve of sense can be excited by several distinct causes internal and external"* (1842, III, p. 1064). Different stimuli affect the same nerve in the same way. One nerve is incapable of usurping the function of another. Müller queried as to whether it was the brain that produced the sensation or the nerve itself, or was the nerve merely the transmitter? He favored the specific energies in the nerves view.

With regard to reflex activity (or reflective motion as it is often translated), Müller formulated a law:

> *When impressions made by the action of external stimuli on sensitive nerves give rise to motions in other parts, these, are never the result of the direct reaction of the sensitive and motor fibres of the nerves on each other; the irritation is conveyed by the sensitive fibres to the brain and spinal cord, and is by these communicated to the motor fibres* (1842, I, p. 709).

Müller drew from Descartes, Bell, and Hall for his formulation of reflex action.

HERMANN LUDWIG FERDINAND HELMHOLTZ (1821-1894): Greatest Experimental Psychologist of the Nineteenth Century

One of the greatest scientists of the nineteenth century, Hermann von Helmholtz, was born in Potsdam (near Berlin) of a philosopher father and a mother who descended from the Quaker William Penn (1644-1718), founder of Pennsylvania. Because his parents were without means, Helmholtz studied medicine on a scholarship at Friedrich-Wilhelm Institute in Berlin, earning his doctorate in 1842 with the publication of his dissertation *De Fabrica Systematis Nervosi Evertebratorum,* proving that nerve fibers originate in ganglion cells and are connected individually with nerve fibers leading from them, thus foreshadowing the neuron theory. By viewing nerve fibers as prolongations of the cell body, Helmholtz had demonstrated Müller's hypothesis. He credited Müller as his guiding influence and inspiring teacher in his intellectual development.

Helmholtz held a succession of academic posts including professor at Könisberg (1848-1855), Bonn (1855-1858), and Heidelberg (1858-1871) before going to the University of Berlin in 1871 where he remained for the last 23 years of his life. While attempting to explain the nature of the glow of reflected light such as that seen in an animal's eye in one of his classroom lectures at Königsberg in 1850, he hit upon the invention of the opthalmoscope which became of enormous value to medicine. The full title of the work in English declaring the invention explains the nature of the instrument: *Description of an Ophthalmoscope for the Investigation of the Retina in the Living Eye* (1850). The ophthalmoscope illuminates the retina and produces a distinct image of the retina "by means of the light which, returning from the retina of the observed eye, falls into the eye of the observer [so that] we may be able to receive distinct images of the retina itself, and of the picture of the light-source cast upon it" (1916, p. 19). He also invented the ophthalmometer, an instrument for measuring the eye, the radii of curvature of the crystalline lens in order to ascertain near and far sightedness. Moreover he offered an explanation of accommodation to explain how the eye focuses for depth vision. The great work containing these accomplishments as well as his theory of color vision (Young-Helmholtz three color theory of vision) is his *Physiological Optics,* appearing in three parts in 1856, 1860, and 1866.

Furthermore he distinguished himself in physiological and psychological acoustics with another classic published in 1862, *On the Sensations of Tone as a Physiological Basis for the Theory of Music,* and published the first treatise on the anatomical, physiological, and mathematical aspects of the ear, *The Mechanism of the Ossicles of the Ear and Membrana Tympani* (1869). He is credited with founding the fixed-pitch theory of vowel tones, the view that vowel pitch is contingent on resonance provided by the formation of the oral cavity of the mouth rather than the pitch of the note itself.

Psychological science is indebted to Helmholtz for his contributions to experimental psychology which produced: (1) the Young-Helmholtz three-color theory of vision, (2) the application of the theory of specific energies to experiences of the distinctive qualities of sense such as loudness and color, (3) the resonance theory of hearing, (4) the empirical theory of perception, (5) the theory of unconscious inference, (6) the reaction time experiment, and (7) the energeticist doctrine as implied in the theory of the conservation of energy.

First Law of Thermodynamics

Before the Physical Society of Berlin, Helmholtz delivered the address that came to be published in 1847 as *On the Conservation of Force,* an epoch-making paper that established him as one of the founders of the law of the conservation of energy, the first law of thermodynamics. Actually, the first law of thermodynamics (conservation of energy) was formulated five years earlier by the German physician and physicist *Julius Robert Mayer* (1814-1878) in 1842 in his paper *Bemerkungen über die Kräfte der unbelebten Natur* (which appeared in Liebig's *Annalen*). Three years later Mayer more explicitly enunciated the doctrine in *Die organische Bewegung in ihren Zusammenhange mit dem Stoffwechesel* (1845). Mayer's claims were contested.

A year after Mayer's initial discovery, the English physicist, *James Prescott Joule* (1818-1889), a student of John Dalton, read what is today known as *Joule's law* in a paper delivered before the British Association at Cork in 1843, titled "The Calorific Effects of Magneto-electricity and the Mechanical Value of Heat." He held that when mechanical force is expended, then an exact equivalent of heat is invariably obtained. The unit of work energy, the joule, was named after him.

With these and other precursors, Helmholtz was able to state the principle of the conservation of force explicitly and in the modern sense in which heat, chemical reactions, electricity and the like are transformable into mechanical energy. On introducing the theory of potential energy, Helmholtz stated his law regarding the conservation of force accordingly: "The *quantity of force which can be brought into action in the whole of Nature is unchangeable,* and can neither be increased nor diminished" (1910, p. 184). Quantity of force is equivalent to the amount of work. His psychological theory was grounded on his energeticist hypothesis. In 1848 he viewed the muscles of animals as the seat of heat production. More than a physicist, Helmholtz made contributions engulfing the fields of physiology, mathematics, medicine, mechanics, and acoustics. Later, Freud and Jung translated these findings into terms of *psychic energy.*

Reaction Time Experiment. An early classic demonstration of Helmholtz (in 1850) involved his experiment on nerve time, the speed at which nerve impulse travels, thus he was the first to introduce reaction time experiments in psychology. While Müller believed that the measurement of the velocity of the nerve impulse would never be ascertained, Helmholtz reasoned that if molecular changes were entailed in nerve conduction then it must proceed at a measurable rate. At Königsberg he invented the myograph in order to measure muscle twitch delays for varying lengths of nerve. Because the Bell-Magendie law established a distinction between motor and sensory nerves, it would not do to assume that the properties of the sensory compare equally with motor nerves.

Consequently he developed reaction experiments along the lines of those in use by astronomers for calculating the human factor or personal equation. Using a frog, Helmholtz successfully measured speed conduction in the frog's motor nerve simply by stimulating the nerve in close proximity to the muscle and then at some distance from the muscle, the muscular response being delayed depending on the distance travelled by the stimulation. He ascertained that nerve impulse travels along the motor nerve at a velocity of approximately 90 feet per second. Extending his experiment to measure the speed of the sensory nerves of man, he administered a mild electrical shock to the skin both near and distant from the brain, requiring the individual to produce a given hand reaction on sensing the shock. As with frogs, he also alternately stimulated toe and thigh of humans, instructing the subject to depress a key (or else having the response registered on his invention, the myograph, as soon as the sensation was experienced). The finding was that sensory impulses travel from 160 to 200 feet per second; the same held for motor impulses.

The experiments for procuring the rate of speed of nerve conduction were not fully satisfactory because while the speed of nerve conduction was quite brief, the reaction time was by comparison lengthy and variable. Nevertheless these experiments led the way to extensive research on reaction time and association time both in Europe and America.

It was a Dutchman, *Frans Cornelis Donders* (1818-1889), a physiologist and ophthalmologist who introduced prismatic and cylindrical lenses for eyeglasses, who saw the psychological significance of Helmholtz's finding, and in 1868 had measured physiological time entailing choice and discrimination. The mental processes of discrimination and choice intervened between stimulus and response. In effect the disjunctive reaction time experiment was born.

In 1873 *Siegmund Exner* (1846-1926), a University of Vienna physiologist and an editor of *Zeitschrift,* contributed still further by showing the importance of *preparatory set;* he coined the term *reaction time.*

By the time Wundt established his psychological laboratory or institute in 1879 at Leipzig, pioneering work having prepared the course for him, he proceeded to conduct experiments on timing mental operations with the consequence that two of his influential students Cattell (who earned his Ph.D. under Wundt in 1886 at the University of Leipzig) and Külpe (who did likewise a year later) carried the technique to their own laboratories later, Cattell to Bryn Mawr College and Columbia University, and Külpe to the University of Würzburg.

Helmholtzian Empiricism

Rather than following the Continental rationalists, Helmholtz took his lead from the British empiricists by denying nativism or innate ideas while holding to the empiricist premise that all knowledge derives from experience, either acquired or hereditarily transmitted. Forsaking the nativism of Kant and Fichte, Helmholtz repudiated the intuitionism that allowed for a priori judgments, intuition of perception such as the intuition of space and time enunciated by Kant, and the theory of innate ideas. When this dispute later in psychological circles came to be one of geneticism versus nativism in perception, Helmholtz along with Lotze and Wundt embraced geneticism as it was promoted in evolutionary theories in opposition to the nativism of Müller, Hering, and Stumpf.

Kant at the University of Königsberg (and Fichte following suit) espoused a theory of the a priori intuition of time and space. But Helmholtz, while he was still in Kant's stronghold at Königsberg, was in the process of forming his empiricistic doctrine as early as 1855.

> It may often be rather hard to say how much of our apperceptions (Anschauungen) as derived by the sense of sight is due directly to sensation, and how much of them, on the other hand, is due to experience and training. The main point of controversy between various investigators in this territory is connected also with this difficulty. Some are disposed to concede to the influence of experience as much scope as possible, and to derive from it especially all notion of space. This view may be called the empirical theory (empiristische Theorie). Others, of course, are obliged to admit the influence of experience in the case of certain classes of perceptions; still with respect to certain elementary apperceptions that occur uniformly in the case of all observers, they believe it is necessary to assume a system of innate apperceptions that are not based on experience, especially with respect to space-relations. In contradistinction to the former view, this may perhaps be called the intuition theory (nativistische Theorie) of the sense-perceptions (1925, III, p. 10).

Helmholtz rejected the nativistic or intuition theory on the grounds that (1) it is an unnecessary hypothesis, (2) its consequences, applicable to perceptual images of space, accord with reality in but a few instances, (3) it is unclear, and (4) the

doubtful value of innate space sensations aiding the explanation of visual percep:
tion is vague at best. Nevertheless he was quite aware of his inability to refute
intuition theory outright.

Unconscious Inference or Unconscious Conclusion

Closely related to his empiricism, unconscious inference (sometimes translated
unconscious conclusion) is a conclusion or inference at which one arrives without
consciously reflecting upon it, such as: "All men are mortal." "Conclusions of
this sort are reached without conscious reflection, because in our memory the same
sort of thing in cases previously observed unites and reinforces them" (1925, III,
p. 25). Helmholtz carried this doctrine into the realm of sense perception, arguing:

> Now we have exactly the same case in our sense-perceptions. When those nervous
> mechanisms whose terminals lie on the right-hand portions of the retinas of the two eyes
> have been stimulated, our usual experience, repeated a million times all through life, has
> been that a luminous object was over there in front of us on our left. We had to lift the
> hand toward the left to hide the light or to grasp the luminous object; or we had to move
> toward the left to get closer to it. Thus while in these cases no particular conscious
> conclusion may be present, yet the essential and original office of such a conclusion has
> been performed, and the result of it has been attained; simply, of course, by the
> unconscious processes of association of ideas going on in the dark background of our
> memory. Thus too its results are urged on our consciousness, so to speak, as if an external
> power had constrained us, over which our will has no control.
>
> These inductive conclusions leading to the formation of our sense perceptions cer-
> tainly do lack the purifying and scrutinizing work of conscious thinking. Nevertheless, in
> my opinion, by their peculiar nature they may be classed as conclusions, inductive
> conclusions unconsciously formed (1925, III, pp. 26-7).

Helmholtz regarded unconscious inferences as irresistible because they are unconscious, formed by experience, and arrived at inductively. The ill-chosen term met
with severe opposition, partly owing to the fact that Schopenhauer also used it but
in another context. Others charged that the term was self-contradictory because a
conclusion implies a conscious one. Sechenov, who spent some time working in
Helmholtz's laboratory, employed the term as did his intellectual successor Pavlov
who exclaimed: "What the genius Helmholtz referred to as 'unconscious conclusion' corresponds to the mechanism of the conditioned reflex" (1928, p. 126).

Theory of Perception

Perception is that sensory pattern which has a direct dependence on the object
stimulating it. Helmholtz's position, based on Locke's view and J. Müller's law of
the specific energies of the sense nerves, distinguished sensations with respect to
modality (e.g., blue, warm, sweet, high-pitched, etc.) and *quality*.

> Every sensory nerve . . . when excited by even the most varied stimuli, produces a
> sensation only within its own specific circle of quality. The same external stimulus,
> therefore, if it strikes different nerves, produces diverse sensations, which are always
> within the circles of quality of the nerves excited. The same vibrations of the ether which

the eye experiences as light, the skin feels as heat. The same vibrations of the air which the skin feels as flutter, the ear hears as sound (1971, p. 370).

According to Helmholtz's empirical theory of perception, "knowledge of the field of vision is acquired," and the fact that it appears nativistic or innate is due to the "accumulation of memory impressions," that is, unconscious inference. Because of the function of memory and unconscious inference, it is not surprising that there is a paucity of pure perceptions.

Influenced by Locke and J. S. Mill before him, Helmholtz regarded the object as an aggregate of sensations, the formation of such aggregate he explained in terms of experiencing sensations being habitually clustered together. The permanence of objects remains except when one's will makes them disappear and return again to the relations they had earlier with the sense-organ in question. Hence we have Helmholtz's version of Mill's permanent possibilities of sensation.

Pre-Helmholtzian Psychology of Sound

Gross anatomy of the ear was early known, *Empedocles* (c. 495-435) of Agrigentum, Sicily having discovered the inner ear; while *Galen*, the Pergamum-born (Asia Minor) Greek physician who flourished in the second century A.D. named the labyrinth and considered it a nervous organ essential to hearing. The description of the pinna, external meatus, drumskin, and nerve distribution to the labyrinth was Galen's contribution. Particulars of aural anatomy occurred in the sixteenth and seventeenth centuries as evidenced by the contents of the eight-volume *Elementa Physiologiae Corporis Humani* (1757-1766) published by the Swiss physiologist and anatomist, *Albrecht Haller* (1708-1777). Haller, who in 1764 anticipated the resonance theory of hearing of Helmholtz by one hundred years, is known for introducing the theory of the irritability of living tissue, as well as describing the particulars of ear anatomy. Whereas *Alcmaeon,* the Greek physician who flourished in the sixth century B.C. and is regarded as the first to undertake anatomical dissections, had been aware of an aperture from the mouth to the ear, the eustachian tube was named after *Bartolommeo Eustachio* (Eustachius) (1524?-1574), an Italian who is reputed to be one of the founders of anatomy. Eustachio described the tensor tympani and ossicles as well as the eustachian tube in his *De Auditu Organis* (1562). An Italian physician and professor of surgery at the University of Padua, *Giulio Casserio* (1556-1609), offered a more extensive description of the tympanic membrane and ossicles together with their muscular and the cochlea structure.

In his *Anatomy of the Human Body* (1809), *Charles Bell* (1774-1842) reasoned that the cochlea could function with respect to the finer auditory discriminations while the entire labyrinth performs as the organ of hearing. He accurately ascertained the function of the round window. A French physiologist who was a professor in the Collège de France, *Pierre Jean Marie Flourens* (1794-1867), published a work on the operation of the nervous system in 1824 in which he cited the semicircular canals in the ear as the organism's reflex orientation. Johannes Müller theorized the conduction of sound through the tympanum to be dual: by the.

ossicles and by the air to the round window. By mid-eighteenth century microscopic anatomy benefitted research on the ear enabling *Alfronso Corti* (1822-1876), the Viennese-trained Italian anatomist, to uncover the "organ of Corti" in 1851, that complex organ of the ear used to perceive sound directly. It was with such information available to him that Helmholtz was able to proceed with his formulation of the resonance theory of hearing.

For over a century the Helmholtzian resonance theory of hearing has commanded the attention of psychologists. Though his audio interests were stimulated as early as 1852 when he corrected some mathematical errors of Challis, it was not until 1863 that his classic *Sensations of Tone* appeared. The theory relied upon several sources: (1) the function of the round window that Bell observed in 1809, the semicircular canals as a nonauditory function as Flourens noted in 1830, and other facts concerning the acoustical and microscopic physiology of the ear; (2) Müller's theory of specific nerve energies; and (3) Ohm's law, introduced by the German physicist *Georg Simon Ohm* (1787-1854) in 1843. According to Ohm's law, rather than receiving a sensation of a single sound, the human's perception of complex sound is one of sensing those separate components of the complex wave producing the sound. By this acoustic law a person can focus attention on simple harmonic components of an irregular sound wave. The law rested on the theorem of *Jean Baptiste Joseph Fourier* (1768-1830), geometrician, physicist, the French statesman accompanying Napoleon Bonaparte to Egypt. He declared in 1822 that a periodic function can be resolved into sine and cosine terms that entail known constants.

The Helmholtz Resonance Theory of Hearing

The resonance theory of Helmholtz is one form of the *place theory* of hearing because pitch is determined by that portion stimulated in the organ of Corti by a given frequency. Different parts of the basilar membrane of the cochlea are tuned to diverse frequencies, high frequencies at the base where the membrane is narrowest. Utter a sustained note near a harp and resonance will set into sympathetic vibration the particular string that is in tune with the pitch sung. It is also referred to as the *piano theory* because, like the strings of a piano, the transverse fibers are tuned to a given sound and when vibrated they stimulate the nerve endings corresponding to the fibers in question. The vibrating strings send signals to the brain, with the transverse fibers of the basilar membrane serving as the resonant elements. The hair cells and connected nerve fibers serve as signal systems informing the brain as to which particular portion of the basilar membrane is vibrating. In this manner the pitch of a tone is produced, with the number of impulses per second providing tonal intensity. An increment in intensity signifies an increment in pulsation, the longer transverse fibers attuned to the lower frequencies. The piano theory also accounts for tonal gaps, tonal deficiencies.

To draw further conclusions from our hypothesis, when a simple tone is presented to the ear, those Corti's arches which are nearly or exactly in unison with it will be strongly excited, and the rest only slightly or not at all. Hence every simple note of determinate pitch will be felt only by certain nerve fibres, and simple tones of different pitch will excite different fibres. When a compound musical tone or chord is presented to the ear, all those elastic bodies will be excited, which have a proper pitch corresponding to the various individual simple tones contained in the whole mass of tones, and hence by properly directing attention, all the individual sensations of the individual simple tones can be perceived. The chord must be resolved into its individual compound tones, and the compound tone into its individual harmonic partial tones.

This also explains how it is that the ear resolves a motion of the air into pendular vibrations and no other. Any particle of air can of course execute only one motion at one time. That we considered such a motion mathematically as a sum of pendular vibrations, was in the first instance merely an arbitrary assumption to facilitate theory, and had no meaning in nature. The first meaning in nature that we found for this resolution came from considering sympathetic vibration, when we discovered that a motion which was not pendular, could produce sympathetic vibrations in bodies of those different pitches, which corresponded to the harmonic upper partial tones. And now our hypothesis has also reduced the phenomenon of hearing to that of sympathetic vibration, and thus furnished a reason why an originally simple periodic vibration of the air produces a sum of different sensations, and hence also appears as compound to our perceptions.

The sensation of different pitch would consequently be a sensation in different nerve fibres. The sensation of a quality of tone would depend upon the power of a given compound tone to set in vibration not only those of Corti's arches, which correspond to its prime tone, but also a series of other arches, and hence to excite sensation in several different groups of nerve fibres.

Physiologically it should be observed that the present assumption reduces sensations which differ qualitatively according to pitch and quality of tone, to a difference in the nerve fibres which are excited. This is a step similar to that taken in a wider field by Johannes Müller in his theory of the specific energies of sense (1885, ch. 6).

Helmholtz's resonance or piano theory is also referred to as *place theory* because pitch perception is dependent upon the place of greatest stimulation of the basilar membrane.

Perception of the Quality of Tone. Another of Helmholtz's major contributions, his theory of the perception of tonal quality, accounted for the quality of tone by its dependency on the order, number, and intensity of overtones (harmonics) and the roles played by them in the musical tone's structure.

The sound becomes a *musical* tone, when such rapid impulses recur with perfect regularity and in precisely equal times. Irregular agitation of the air generates only noise. The *pitch* of a musical tone depends on the number of impulses which take place in a given time; the more there are in the same time the higher or sharper is the tone. . . .

A tone of the same number of vibrations has always the same pitch, by whichever one of these instruments it is produced. That which distinguishes the note A of a piano, for example, from the equally high A of the violin, flute, clarinet, or trumpet, is called the quality of the tone·

Moreover, he contributed a theory of differential and summational tone in his *Sensations of Tone* (1863), a lasting work on acoustics.

The first class, discovered by Sorge and Tartini, I have termed *differential tones*, because their pitch number is the *difference* of the pitch numbers of the generating tones. The second class of *summational tones,* having their pitch number equal to the *sum* of the pitch numbers of the generating tones, were discovered by myself (1954, p. 153).

Also credited with founding the theory of the fixed-pitch of vowel tones, Helmholtz accounted for vowel pitch by the mouth's resonance, i.e., the cavity formed during the singing of a vowel.

We may certainly assume that in the tones of the human larynx, as in all other reed instruments, the upper partial tones would decrease in force as they increase in pitch, if they could be observed without the resonance of the cavity of the mouth. In reality they satisfy this assumption tolerably well, for those vowels which are spoken with a wide funnel-shaped cavity of the mouth, as A [a in art], or A [a in bat lengthened, which is nearly the same as a in bare]. But this relation is materially altered by the resonance which takes place in the cavity of the mouth. The more this cavity is narrowed, either by the lips or the tongue, the more distinctly marked is its resonance for tones of determinate pitch, and the more therefore does this resonance reinforce those partials in the compound tone produced by the vocal chords which approach the favoured pitch and the more, on the contrary, will the others be damped. Hence on investigating the compound tones of the human voice by means of resonators, we find pretty uniformly that the first six to eight partials are clearly perceptible, but with very different degrees of force according to the different forms of the cavity of the mouth, sometimes screaming loudly into the ear, at others scarcely audible.

Under these circumstances the investigation of the resonance of the cavity of the mouth is of great importance. The easiest and surest method of finding the tones to which the air in the oral cavity is tuned for the different shapes it assumes in the production of vowels, is that which is used for glass bottles and other spaces filled with air. That is, tuning-forks of different pitches have to be struck and held before the opening of the air chamber — in the present case the open mouth — and the louder the proper tone of the fork is heard, the nearer does it correspond with one of the proper tones of the included mass of air (1954, pp. 104-5).

Helmholtz had accurately explained the bone mechanisms of the ear (1869) as well as the action of the cochlea which he based on sympathetic vibration.

Post-Helmholtzian Auditory Theory

Subsequent to the time that Helmholtz advanced his resonance theory of hearing, several others appeared, the most important among them being: (1) the *frequency theory,* (2) the *volley theory,* and (3) the *traveling wave theory.*

Rutherford's Frequency Theory or Telephone Theory. After receiving his M.D. from the University of Edinburgh in 1863, *William Rutherford* (1839-1899) went on to become Professor of Physiology at King's College, London in 1869 before accepting his final appointment at the University of Edinburgh from 1874 to his death in 1899. Rutherford is known in psychology for a paper on "A New Theory of Hearing" that he published in 1886. It was a *frequency theory of hearing* that came to be dubbed descriptively a *telephone theory of hearing* just as Helmholtz's was appropriately termed a "piano theory."

Rutherford, noting that the ear operates along the principle of a telephone, believed that it transmitted both simple and compound frequencies through the auditory nerve to the brain. External sound frequencies after reaching receptors are transmitted unanalyzed to and through auditory nerve fibers to the brain. The organ of Corti, vibrating as a whole, conveys the same number of impulses as the tympanic membrane and stapes have. Auditory centers of the brain analyze these stimuli. The brain converts frequency to sensations of sound. An entering wave stimulates a single impulse of nerve fiber, loudness being dependent upon the number of nerve fibers and receptors stimulated. Louder impulses travel further and stimulate a greater number of hair cells.

> The theory which the lecturer had arrived at, and which he published that night for the first time, might be termed the telephone theory of the sense of hearing — the theory that the cochlea does not act on the principle of sympathetic vibration, but that the hairs of all its auditory cells vibrate to every tone just as the drum of the ear does; that there is no analysis of complex vibrations in the cochlea or elsewhere in the peripheral mechanism of the ear; that the hair cells transform sound vibrations into nerve-vibrations similar in frequency and amplitude to the sound vibrations; that simple and complex vibrations of nerve energy arrive in the sensory cells of the brain, and there produce, not sound again of course, but the sensations of sound, the nature of which depends not upon the stimulation of different sensory cells, but on the frequency, amplitude, and form of the vibrations coming into the cells, probably through all the fibres of the auditory nerve. On such a theory the physical cause of harmony and discord is carried into the brain, and the mathematical principles of acoustics find an entrance into the obscure region of consciousness (1886, p. 167).

Experimenting on a frog, Rutherford was able to obtain only 352 cycles per second tones. Consequently the theory encounters problems with the higher frequencies since man can hear from approximately 20 to 20,000 cycles per second, yet no mammalian nerve fiber is capable of transmitting higher than 1,000 cycles per second.

Wever's Volley Theory. Feeling that the place theory required supplementation, *Ernest Glen Wever* (1902-   ), a Harvard Ph.D. who spent virtually his entire career at Princeton's psychology department, developed a volley theory based on the volley principle that he developed with his Princeton associate, *Charles William Bray* (1904-   ), who earned his Ph.D. from that institution.

The theory, a compromise or synthesis of place and frequency theories, explains pitch by the firing of *volleys* of nerve impulses up to 5000 cycles per second, and in excess of that the *place* of greatest excitation in that portion of the basilar membrane is invoked as the explanation. These two researchers found that the nerve potentials of a cat's auditory nerve impulses could be amplified and sent into a telephone receiver. They heard the same signal tones fed (up to 5200 c.p.s.).

> A pure tone sounded into the ear of the cat is recognized as that same tone in the receiver. Speech is received readily; and the degree of fidelity can be judged from the fact that under good conditions an observer in the sound-proof room is able to recognize who is speaking into the cat's ear if the person's voice is reasonably familiar to him (1930, p. 376).

In order to explain how hearing reaches 20,000 c.p.s., Wever employed the volley frequency theory, illustrated by a captain having the individual members of his company fire their rifles not in unison but in delayed or staggered order so as to produce the effect of a stream of bullets. The auditory nerve fibers operate in a volley manner to a single given wave stimulus, with the volley frequency providing pitch and the number of fibers for each volley producing loudness.

As well as nerve potentials the researchers were picking up cochlear ones.

The representation in terms of nerve impulses gives a faithful indication of the stimulus frequency for all the low and the intermediate tones, but it fails for the high tones. On the other hand, the representation in terms of place is only vague for the low tones and becomes progressively more specific as the frequency is raised (Wever & Lawrence, 1954, p. 409).

Békésy's Traveling Wave Theory. The University of Budapest Ph.D., *Georg Békésy* (1899-   ), a Nobel Prize Laureate in medicine and physiology, who is currently Senior Research Fellow in Psychophysics at Harvard University, formulated a *law of contrast* and developed the *traveling wave theory*. The propagation of sound in the cochlea assumes the form of a wave traveling in the basilar membrane from the base to the apex of the cochlea. A modification of the Helmholtzian resonance theory, this theory explains the maximum amplitude as that point resonating to the frequency of the stimulus at a given point along the basilar membrane.

Each of the vibration patterns of the basilar membrane postulated by the four major theories of hearing can be obtained by varying two elastic properties of the membrane — namely, the coupling between adjacent parts and the absolute value of the elasticity. If these two variables are adjusted to their numerical values in the cochlea of a living animal or a fresh preparation of the human ear, traveling waves are observed along the membrane. These traveling waves have a flat maximum that shifts its location along the membrane with a change of frequency — the place of the maximum determining the pitch. An enlarged dimensional model of the cochlea in which the nerve supply of the sensory organs on the basilar membrane was replaced by the skin of the arm indicates that the inhibitory action in the nervous system can produce quite sharp local sensations, which shift their place with changes in the frequency of the vibrations (1956, p. 783).

Békésy's traveling wave theory is developed fully in his *Experiments in Hearing* (1960) edited by E. G. Wever.

Young's Theory of Color

Thomas Young (1773-1829) formulated his theory of color vision in 1807 in which he hypothesized three primary colors corresponding to three kinds of color sensitive points (nerve fibers) on the retina.

From three simple sensations, with their combinations, we obtain seven primitive distinctions of colours; but the different proportions, in which they may be combined, afford a variety of traits beyond all calculation. The three simple sensations being red, green, and violet, the three binary combinations are yellow, consisting of red and green;

crimson, or red and violet; and blue, of green and violet; and the seventh in order is white light, composed by all three united. But the blue thus produced, by combining the whole of the green and violet rays, is not the blue of the spectrum, for four parts of green and one of violet make a blue differing very little from green; while the blue of the spectrum appears to contain as much violet as green: and it is for this reason that red and blue usually make a purple, deriving its hue from the predominance of the violet (1807, I, p. 40).

Young espoused a psychological theory in which three types of particles on the retina function independently as receptors, producing the various colors on the spectrum.

Isaac Newton's Color Theory

Not that the entire spectrum of colors being reduced to a small number was new, for Isaac Newton (1642-1727) had postulated that idea as early as 1704 in his *Opticks or a Treatise of the Reflections, Refractions, Inflections and Colours of Light*. Even earlier he had presented his "New Theory about Light and Colours" to the Royal Society on February 8, 1672. A University of Cambridge scientist, Newton proposed the theory that "light consists of rays differently refrangible." Newton, a friend of John Locke (1632-1704), wrote a letter to Leibniz (1646-1716) in 1679 contending that he (and not Leibniz) discovered the differential calculus. In the *Opticks*, he theorized that white light separates into a spectrum and proved different refractive indexes for the various colors.

> *Whiteness and all grey Colours between white and black, may be compounded of Colours, and the whiteness of the Sun's Light is compounded of all the primary Colours mix'd in a due Proportion* (1730, Prop. V, Theor. 4).

Helmholtz Theory of Color

Utilizing Young's theory (so that it has come to be referred to as the Young-Helmholtz theory of color), Helmholtz held that all colors are produced from the mixture of three basic colors. His tridimensional theory of color corresponded to his tridimensional theory of tone, for all tones are compounds of pitch, intensity, and timbre. Helmholtz reduced every hue to violet, green and red as the fundamental colors. "When we speak of reducing the colours to three fundamental colours, this must be understood in a subjective sense and as being an attempt to trace the *colour sensations* to three *fundamental sensations*" (1924, pp. 143-4). The eye, provided with three different sets of nerve fibers, senses red when the first is stimulated, green on the second, and violet on the third. "Objective homogeneous light excites these three kinds of fibres in various degrees, depending on its wave-length. The red-sensitive fibres are stimulated most by light of longest wave-length, and the violet-sensitive fibres by the light of shortest wave-length" (1924, p. 143). Although each color of the spectrum stimulates all three kinds of fibers, some are excited intensely and others faintly; e.g., the red light stimulates the red-sensitive fibers intensely; the other two are merely mildly stimulated.

Note that Helmholtz was utilizing Müller's theory of specific nerve energy, but extending it to apply to elements within a specific sense, in this case, sensing color by different nerve fibers, each with its own appointed task, i.e., whenever a given nerve fiber is stimulated it responds always with the same sensation, the red sensitive fibers with the sensation of red. Rather than being Müller's specific nerve energy theory, Helmholtz's was a theory of *specific fiber energy*, or specific energies of the cortical areas (rather than nerves). He assumed that the three elements in the retina had their corresponding cortical activity in the brain whose principal function is the combination of the three to produce color as experienced, accordingly the Helmholtz theory is one of the *specific energies of cortical areas*, a view considered and discarded by Müller.

Conclusion

Although one may take his leave of Helmholtz, he cannot forget his contribution as is evidenced in this treatment of him. His influence is felt by many researchers on the contemporary scene as well as by any freshman student undertaking a course in Introduction to Psychology as his initial entry into the world of psychology.

In 1894 *Punch* (and a week later in *Nature*), the London weekly known for its satirical caricatures of British notables, paused long enough from its usual biting appetite to salute the memory not of a British statesman but of a German scientist:

> What matter titles? HELMHOLTZ is a name
> That challenges, alone, the award of Fame!
> When Emperors, Kings, Pretenders, shadows all,
> Leave not a dust-trace on our whirling ball,
> Thy work, oh grave-eyed searcher, shall endure,
> Unmarred by faction, from low passion pure. . . .
> Distant still that mental goal
> To which great spirits strain; but when calm Fame
> Sums its bold seekers, Helmholtz, thy great name
> Among the foremost shall external stand,
> Science's pride, and glory of thy land (Sept. 22, 1894).

Punch's prophecy thus far has proved true.

Johannes Kries (1853-1928): Duplicity Theory

The one time associate of Helmholtz and contributor to the third (and last) edition of Helmholtz's *Physiological Optics* (1911), Johannes Kries, developed a *duplicity theory (Duplizitätstheorie)* according to which twilight vision was attributed to rod function of the retina, and daylight vision to the function of retinal cones. The duplicity theory is considered as a second stage to the Young-Helmholtz theory of retinal action. Kries explained his theory accordingly:

> By referring to it as the *duplicity theory (Duplizitätstheorie)* . . . the implication is that there is not simply a morphological duality of the elements of the retinal neuro-epithelium, but a corresponding duality of function as well, and that to a certain extent there are two kinds of vision. One kind is that which is active when the eyes are light-adapted and stimulated by strong light — *Tagessehen* (or *daylight vision*,

photopia). . . . Opposed to it is the so-called *Dämmerungssehen* (or *twilight vision, scotopia*), when the eye is dark-adapted and the light stimulus is weak. On the duplicity theory the organ for daylight vision is the "daylight mechanism" or "brightness-mechanism" represented by the totality of cones; the "twilight mechanism" or darkness-mechanism being constituted by the rods along with the visual purple absorbed in their outer segments (Nagel, 1924, p. 345).

The dark-adapted eye (scotopic vision) is monochromatic or tone-free, while the light-adapted eye (photopic vision) is polychromatic or toned. The threshold stimulus intensity is low in scotopic vision, and comparatively high in the photopic (color vision). Daylight vision (color vision) mechanism is in the foveal region of the retina where rods are absent. Among colorblind individuals red-blind were termed *protanopes* by Kries; the green-blind were *deuteranopes*.

Colorblindness was known as early as 1794 when *John Dalton* (1766-1884), an English chemist and physicist, wrote the first detailed description of it, a disorder that he and his brother had from birth (called Daltonism). A few weeks after he was elected to membership in the Manchester Literary and Philosophical Society in 1794 he delivered a paper on "Extraordinary Facts Relating to the Vision of Colours," depicting his predicament in which he sensed only blue, purple, and yellow.

That part of the image which others call red appears to me a little more than a shade or defect of light; after that the orange, yellow and green seem one colour which descends pretty uniformly from an intense to a rare yellow, making what I should call different shades of yellow.

Heinrich M. Müller (1820-1864), a German anatomist, had presented a crucial paper in 1851 on rods, cones, and visual purple. The following year the anatomist *Rudolf Albert Kölliker* (1817-1905), a professor at the University of Würzburg, adopted it in his *Mikroskopische Anatomie* (1852 a, b), these two men distinguishing the two recipient organs of the retina as rods and cones. It was not Helmholtz but a German anatomist, *Max Johann Sigismund Schultze* (1825-1874), who grasped the duplicity aspect of the rods and cones in 1866 and made them more explicit a year later, noting that some retina receptors stimulate sensations of color while others stimulate colorless ones. But Schultze was cued from a paper published the previous year by *Hermann Aubert (1826-1892)*, a professor of physiology at Breslau and later at Rostock. Aubert (1857) noted that as visual acuity and color discrimination approach the periphery of the retina they diminish. This fact gave Schultze the insight that color vision must be the function of the cones. He also noted that cones are absent in some nocturnal animals such as bats. In 1894 *Arthur König* (1856-1901), a physicist at the University of Berlin, cofounder of the *Zeitschrift* (with Ebbinghaus) and loyal backer of Helmholtz, defined the function of visual purple with respect to night vision (rod vision). Reaping the benefits from all of these research findings, Kries was able to construct his duplicity theory in 1894.

Evolutionary Theories of Color:
Ladd-Franklin Theory of Color Evolution.

The contention of Schultze in 1866 was established by Kries in 1894, viz., that rod vision or achromatic twilight vision was of a more primitive nature than cone vision or chromatic daylight vision. Authors writing from the time of Schultze to Kries on the matter intimated an evolutionary character existing between them. Hering (who will be discussed later) assumed that yellow-blue was an earlier development than red-green because yellow-blue color blindness ordinarily accompanies red-green, whereas red-green blindness need not be a concomitant of yellow-blue. The view suggests three stages of color evolution: (1) white-black vision as the earliest and most stable substance, (2) yellow-blue as the second stage, and (3) red-green as the third and least stable substance.

In 1892 Christine Ladd-Franklin (1847-1930) focused in on this evolutionary relationship of the color sense. Christine Ladd, an American psychologist and logician who married Fabian Franklin in 1882, received her graduate training at John Hopkins, Göttingen, and Berlin universities before her long tenure at Columbia University as lecturer. She was also an associate editor of Baldwin's *Dictionary of Philosophy and Psychology* (1901). Whereas in philosophy she is known for having developed a method that reduces all syllogisms to a single formula, in psychology she is noted for a developmental theory of the human color sense.

The Ladd-Franklin theory of color evolution, variously called genetic theory, development theory, and the evolution theory, began in consequence of her semesters spent in the laboratories of G. E. Müller and König as she contemplated the views of Helmholtz and Hering.

While developing the Donders' theory as preferable, her own theory unveiled itself to her in 1892. In 1881 Donders suggested that color vision be accounted for by color molecules decomposing and thereby selectively stimulating the nerves. Ladd-Franklin put the matter in an evolutionary context. It was Donders' idea that the Young-Helmholtz theory maintained at the point of the retina but simple colors are a brain function. While accepting the theory of six colors, he felt that the optic nerve fibers contained only three specific nerve energies. Whereas red, green, and blue constituted the three specific energies, yellow appeared in the brain as a result of red and green in combination exciting it. White is the resultant of all three, and black the absence of all energies. Prompted by the Machian psychophysical parallelism doctrine, Donders reasoned that brain process parallels a simple color.

Ladd-Franklin felt that the Helmholtz and Hering theories had to be reconciled, one trichromatic in the cortex (Helmholtz) and the other tetrachromatic in the retina (Hering school including Donders and G. E. Müller), and that the reconciliation was arranged through a theory of the order of the development of the color sense. The double function and structure of the retina (rod and cone or white and color vision) had already been established by Max Schultze and others, and that yellow-blue cones occurred chronologically prior to the red-green. The Ladd-Franklin theory of color evolution reasons that from white (grey), blue and yellow evolved; from yellow, green and red emerged. The warm side of the blue-yellow is yellow, and is in closest proximity to red-green, differentiating into red and green, whereas white (grey) differentiates into blue and yellow. The theory assumed that

> there occurred, first, a light-sensitive chemical substance in the (low-grade) rods which responded non-specifically to light of any sort within the visible spectrum. The simple cleavage product of this stage of development forms the nerve-excitant which is corre-lated with the sensation of white. This is the only sensation possible when the rods alone function, i.e. in the cases of (a) normal achromatic vision in the extreme periphery, and of achromatic vision in (b) the normal eye in a state of darkness-adaptation and with low objective intensities, and in (c) the totally chroma-blind defectives. Development of the colour-sense takes place in the form of the acquiring of greater specificity in that part of the colour-molecule which undergoes cleavage. Instead of responding alike to all parts of the visible spectrum, part of it, SY, is synchronous in its electronic vibrations with the longer waves, and part of it, SB, with the shorter waves; but whenever both of these nerve-excitant substances are torn off at the same time, they unite chemically to constitute the former whiteness-excitation. This is the stage of development of the normal midperiphery, and of the two types of yellow-blue-vision. In Stage III the complete differentiation of the light-sensitive molecule in the way of greater specificity has taken place, and red and green are added as specific sensations. But the nerve-excitant substances, EG and ER, when they are both dissociated out together, reconsti-tute the yellow nerve-excitant, EY. Again it is plain that yellow and blue nerve-excitants re-unite to constitute the original nerve-excitant, EW, whose sensation effect, when the cortex is reached, is white in quality (1929, p. 131).

Blue apparently did not differentiate into any other hues in the process of evolu-tionary development.

Ewald Hering (1834-1918): Four Color Theory

Opposition to Helmholtz's three color theory came from a University of Leipzig trained physician, Hering. Moreover, the empiricism of Helmholtz was severely challenged by the nativism of Hering, who is regarded by some historians as siring gestalt psychology inasmuch as both form and extension are native. At Leipzig Hering's instructors included E. H. Weber and his brother Wilhelm Eduard Weber, the anatomist, as well as Fechner. Hering went to the chair of physiology at the University of Prague where he succeeded the distinguished Czech physiologist *Johannes Evangelista Purkinje* (1787-1869).

Purkinje Phenomenon. It was as early as 1825 that Purkinje, inspired by Goethe's color studies, described the phenomenon for which he is best known in psychology in his *Neue Beiträge zue Kenntniss des Sehens in subjectiver Hinsicht.* Also called the *Purkinje effect* and *Purkinje shift,* the phenomenon is that which is experienced as twilight approaches. Hues at the short-wave end of the spectrum (violet and blue) appear brighter than those of the long end (red). During the process of dark adaptation sensitivity to red and yellow (the 600 to 700 nanometer end) is lost before the violet and blue end (400 to 500 nanometer end of the spectrum). It was Hering (1895) who explained the Purkinje phenomenon in terms of the eye's dark adaptation, rather than attributing it to a low illumination of stimulus.

Purkinje discovered other visual phenomena including the *Purkinje after-image* (Bidwell's ghost), *Purkinje figures,* and *Purkinje-Sanson images.*

Hering's Theory of Opponent Colors. Known chiefly for his color theory, Hering opposed Helmholtz by arguing that four primary colors exist: red, yellow, green, and blue. Arranging them in antagonistic or opponent pairs of blue-yellow and green-red, he explained that three types of receptors or receiving organs with a dual output for each (one output for the breakdown of photochemicals and one for the resynthesis of photochemicals) could signal the primary colors, one receptor for blue or yellow, a second for red or green, and a third for black or white.

> Therefore since redness and greenness, or yellowness and blueness are never simultaneously evident in any color, but rather appear to be mutually exclusive, I have called them *opponent colors. . . .*
>
> We should conclude from this that in the inner eye a physiological process whose psychological correlate would be simultaneously both red and green or yellow and blue is either not possible at all or is possible only under quite special, unusual circumstances (1964, p. 50).

Four physiological variables exist corresponding to the four primary hues. Visual sensation is the psychical correlate of chemical processes in the visual substance.

Though influenced by the psychophysics of Fechner, Hering constructed his theory on the ideas of such precursors as the poet Johann Wolfgang Goethe (1749-1832), whose treatise on *Farbenlehre* (Science of Colors) appeared in 1810, and *Hermann Aubert* (1826-1892), Professor of Physiology at Breslau and later at Rostock. Aubert, whose hypothesis was referred to by Kries as a "four color theory," asserted: "If we want to be clear about color sensations, then the words black, white, red, yellow, green, and blue suffice as main designations, and I may therefore treat them as principal sensations or principal colors" (1865, p. 186). With respect to isomorphism Hering was influenced by Ernst Mach who contended that "To every psychical there corresponds a physical, and the reverse. To like psychical processes there correspond like physical, to unlike, unlike" (1865, 52 Bd.).

The four major points of Hering's opponent theory of color are: (1) the visual apparatus (including the retina and brain) contains three photochemical substances that light affects. (2) Each substance is the source of chemical processes of decomposition and recomposition (one substance's process provides blue and yellow, and a second red and green, and the third black and white), the retina containing six different chemical processes from which all colors are sensed. (3) Only certain forms of stimuli affect the two hue substances, while every light stimulus affects black and white. (4) Complementary colors falling upon the same portion of the retina produce grey by cancelling each other (as is the case with red and green or blue or yellow) owing to the opposing or antagonistic chemical processes of decomposition and recomposition.

Black and white falling upon the same portion of the retina mix into grey despite their cancelling one another in the retina. His hypothesis reads:

To the two qualities of sensation, which we designate as white or bright and as black or dark, correspond two different qualities of chemical activity in the visual substance; and to the different relations of brightness or intensity, with which these two sensations appear in single transitions between pure white and pure black, or to the relations in which they appear mixed, correspond the same relations of intensities of those two psychophysical processes (1968, p. 147).

Whereas the theory of chromatic colors Hering referred to as the theory of *color sense,* the theory of achromatic colors he called the theory of *light sense.* Although Hering's theory appears sound, his position was not corroborated by later findings. It was modified and raised to a higher level of sophistication by Leo M. Hurvich (1910-   ) and his wife Dorothea A. Jameson (1920-   ) in a paper on "An Opponent-Process Theory of Color Vision" in 1957. The two translated Hering's *Outlines on a Theory of Light Sense* in 1964 (*Grunzüge der Lehre vom Lichtsinn,* 1920). Whereas this work emphasized more the light sense than color sense, the bulk of his theory of color sense is found in *Zur Lehre vom Lichtsinne* (Theory of Light Sensation) which appeared in 1872 to 1874 as papers and reprinted as a volume in 1878.

Hering's Nativistic Visual Space Perception Theory. During the 1860's bitter dialogue transpired between the nativists and empiricists. Nativists regarding space perception include Kant, J. Müller, Stumpf, the gestalt psychologists as well as Hering, while the empiricists number Helmholtz, Wundt, and Lotze among their adherents. According to Lotze both the skin and retina have points serving as qualitative local signs. Whereas the predisposition is innate for locating spatial order, it is through experience that local signs associate with spatial order.

According to Hering space is a priori owing to each retinal point with its own spatial feeling comprised of height, depth, and breadth—qualities of space. But real space and visual direction derives from experience.

> Visual space . . . is the creation of our sensorium and is produced by the combined effects of two factors: (1) the sensations of light and space that are induced directly through the binocular retinal images and are based on an inborn mechanism, and (2) the constantly changing state of the sensorium, which depends upon the infinite number of experiences, opinions, and thoughts by means of which, in the course of our lives, the sensorium is . . . continuously recreated. . . .
>
> There are only three simple spatial feelings and, correspondingly, three systems of spatial relations for the doubled retina. The first simple spatial feeling corresponds to the ability to perceive height, the second to the ability to perceive breadth, and the third to the ability to perceive depth. They are all elicited by every retinal point (1965, pp. 148-9).

Why the debates over nativism and empiricism were so intense is difficult for one immersed in twentieth century psychology to appreciate.

HERMANN EBBINGHAUS (1850-1909): Experiments on Memory

If physiological psychology can be traced to J. Müller's *Elements of Physiology* in 1833, and experimental psychology to Fechner's *Psychophysics* in 1860, then the experimental psychology of learning belongs to Ebbinghaus owing to the publication of his *Ueber das Gedächtnis* (translated as *Memory: A Contribution to Experimental Psychology*) in 1885. The German experimental psychologist, Ebbinghaus, was born in Barmen (near Bonn), studying at the University of Bonn before attending Halle and Berlin, consuming three years at these universities during 1867 to 1870. After seven years he returned once more to Berlin for a few years, and then to France and England for three, both studying and tutoring. In 1880 he became a private instructor at the University of Berlin where he published his classic work on memory in 1885. A year later he was appointed *Ausserordentlicher Professor* at the University of Berlin, his tenure there lasting eight years. For some reason he was not promoted to the chair of philosophy (includes psychology) when it was vacant in 1894. The chair was offered to Stumpf who was then at Munich; Lipps (leaving Breslau) filled Stumpf's position at Munich; and to make the game of musical chairs complete, Ebbinghaus accepted Lipp's chair at Breslau where he remained until 1905 when he went to Halle where he fatally succumbed to pneumonia in 1909 at the age of 59.

In addition to epoch-making *Memory* (1885), Ebbinghaus founded (with Arthur König) the *Zeitschrift für Psychologie und Physiologie der Sinnesorgane* in 1890. Three years later he published his theory of color vision (*Theorie des Farbensehens*, 1893), and within four years (in 1897) his *Ebbinghaus completion test* appeared for assessing the mental capacity of school-children. A small book containing a brief summary of his views on memory was published in 1908, *Abriss der Psychologie* and translated the same year as *Psychology: An Elementary Text-Book*.

Ebbinghaus: Heir of Fechner

During his stay in France in the latter half of the 1880s, Ebbinghaus came across a copy of Fechner's *Elements of Psychophysics* in one of Paris' second-hand bookstalls. Fascinated by Fechner's ability to experiment on sensation, he sought to apply the Fechnerian technique to the higher mental processes. Without a university connection and despite Herbart's contention that investigation of these processes was beyond reach experimentally, he adapted Fechner's psychophysical methodology to measuring memory. While the method came from Fechner, the issue of memory came from British associationism, that is, experimenting with repetition and its frequency as the measure of memory.

Despite Ebbinghaus' utilizing only himself as his subject, he successfully conducted the experiments according to his prescription. Although the book is entitled *Memory*, the term is used in its widest sense engulfing learning, retention, association, and reproduction. His ingenious invention of the *nonsense syllable* (a vowel between two consonants such as *gid, var, mon*) was significant, for it led him to the discovery that meaningful material such as learning Byron's poem *Don Juan* could be learned approximately nine times faster than meaningless material. The experiments, running over two years' duration were undertaken in two periods from 1879 to 1880 and from 1883 and 1884.

Experiments on Memory

Not only did Ebbinghaus spend over two years and employ approximately 2,300 nonsense syllables, he conducted numerous experiments so that a curve of errors was established. Variable errors on either side of the curve could be disregarded. Thus (using Fechner's method) he was dealing with averages, thereby eliminating variable errors. Constant error arising from his idiosyncrasies could not be eliminated. The fact that he utilized nonsense syllables rendered every attempt at memorization of equal difficulty, consequently association techniques were eliminated. Learning is defined as being able to recite the material memorized once without error.

Rapidity of Learning a Series of Syllables as a Function of Their Length. It is quite evident that the longer a list of words is to memorize the longer it takes and the more one has to repeat the list in order to commit it to memory so that to memorize a poem of six stanzas takes longer than two. Although it is three times as much material, it requires more than three times as much time. His mathematical calculations resulted in one reading for a list of 7 nonsense syllables but 16 repetitions if the list were lengthened by only 5 more. His results follow:

Number of syllables in a series	Number of repetitions necessary for first errorless reproduction	Probable error
7	1	
12	16.6	±1.1
16	30.0	±0.4
24	44.0	±1.7
36	55.0	±2.8

Note that a list of 36 nonsense syllables is only 5 times longer than 7, yet it requires 55 repetitions to one.

Meaningful Material versus Meaningless Material. Ebbinghaus found that one could learn meaningful material nine times faster than material that held no meaning for the individual. His test was that of memorizing Byron's *Don Juan* so that he could recite it once flawlessly as compared to the same number of nonsense syllables. Eighty syllables of *Don Juan* required 9 readings, while 70 to 80 repetitions were required for memorizing 80 to 90 nonsense syllables. Thus when material is combined so that it rhymes, has rhythm, and meaning it requires approximately one-tenth of the time in Ebbinghaus' case.

Ebbinghaus concluded:

> When in repeated cases I memorised series of syllables of a certain length to the point of their first possible reproduction, the times (or number of repetitions) necessary differed greatly from each other, but the mean values derived from them had the character of genuine constants of natural science (1913, p. 52).

He had achieved experimental and scientific status for the investigation of higher mental processes.

Overlearning and the Savings Method. Since learning is defined as one faultless repetition of the material to be learned, then to continue memorization beyond this point is *overlearning*. Ebbinghaus found that overlearning provided retention advantages so that retention became a function of the number of repetitions. The problem he formulated was:

> If homogeneous series are impressed to different extents as a result of different numbers of repetitions, and then 24 hours later are learned to the point of the first possible reproduction by heart, how are the resulting savings in work related to each other and to the corresponding number of former repetitions? (1913, p. 52).

His test of overlearning (continuing to recite what has been recited once without error) involved overlearning a list of 16 nonsense syllables so that some were repeated 8 times beyond the required number to memorize, some 32 times, and some 64. For overlearning a list 8 times the savings was 8%, 32 times 32%, and 64 times 64%. His complete table follows:

I After a preceding study of the series by X repetitions,	II They were just memorized 24 hours later in Y seconds		III The result therefore of the preceding study was a saving of T seconds		IV Or, for each of the repetitions, an average saving of D seconds
X =	Y =	P.E.m =	T =	P.E.m =	D =
0	1270	7			
8	1167	14	103	16	12.9
16	1078	28	192	29	12.0
24	975	17	295	19	12.3
32	863	15	407	17	12.7
42	697	14	573	16	13.6
53	585	9	685	11	12.9
64	454	11	816	13	12.8
					m = 12.7

Grouping Material. Associations are not only made between contiguous syllables but the entire group of syllables is knit by association so that it is preferable to memorize the whole rather than divide it into parts for there is a savings in so doing. He found that a new *series* of syllables responded to memorization better than a heterogenous group of new syllables. Apparently the formation of associations takes place not only with contiguous elements of the material memorized but among the more distant. Furthermore, associations are formed in two directions (not just one) backward as well as forward. Syllables retaining their relative position in the series when added to a new series are easier to commit to memory. Series that become units provide bonds of connection.

The Curve of Forgetting. The loss of retention owing to the passage of time was also studied by Ebbinghaus, who found that the major portion of the loss occurs within the first few hours. While half of the forgetting occurs within the first half-hour, only four fifths is lost at the end of a month's time.

One hour after the end of the learning, the forgetting had already progressed so far that one half the amount of the original work had to be expended before the series could be reproduced again; after 8 hours the work to be made up amounted to two thirds of the first effort. Gradually, however, the process became slower so that even for rather long periods the additional loss could be ascertained only with difficulty. After 24 hours about one third was always remembered; after 6 days about one fourth, and after a whole month fully one fifth of the first work persisted in effect (1913, p. 76).

The curve of forgetting is among the most cited contributions of Ebbinghaus. **Experimental Psychology of Memory.** The lasting contributions of Ebbinghaus to the field of experimental psychology as applied to memory include: (1) the introduction of objective methods in preference to introspective ones, (2) the devising of nonsense syllables as material capable of calibration, (3) the successful refutation of the laws of association psychology (especially contiguity and immediate succession), (4) quantitatively investigating remote associations, and (5) the utilization of statistics and mathematics successfully with respect to psychological data of the higher mental processes, viz., memory.

LEWIS WILLIAM STERN (1871-1938): Psychometrics by Ebbinghaus' Protégé

The Berlin-born psychologist and philosopher, William Stern, obtained his Ph.D. at the University of Berlin in 1892 under Ebbinghaus. Of his mentor he wrote:

Much deeper was the impression which the lectures and exercises in experimental psychology, given by the young Hermann Ebbinghaus, made upon my mind. . . . Ebbinghaus' point of view appealed to my love for the empirical. . . . Ebbinghaus' excellent teaching, his spontaneous, plastic, humorously tinged delivery, the picturesqueness of his examples all helped to fire with enthusiasm the little group . . . of his students for psychology as he conceived it (1961, pp. 338-9).

When Stumpf was promoted over Ebbinghaus at the University of Berlin, Ebbinghaus left for Breslau in 1894. While he was at Breslau he was instrumental in having Stern habilitated there, and in 1897 he too went as instructor because an academic post at Berlin seemed "hopeless." In 1915 Stern left Breslau and the following year went to the Colonial Institute in Hamburg as the sole professor covering the fields of philosophy, psychology, and pedagogy. An idea of his materialized in 1919 just after World War I when he and his associates offered returning soldiers university courses on a private basis. The result was the founding of the University of Hamburg, which became a state university. Stern remained there until uprooted by the rise of nazidom in 1933 when he migrated to the United States and to Duke University as a professor of psychology and philosophy. A half-decade later he died in that college town of Durham in North Carolina.

Stern's Personalistic Psychology

Unalterably opposed to elementarism in psychology that was so prevalent in pregestalt Germany, Stern, in anticipation of gestalt psychology, favored phenomenological techniques. He was attracted to the *avant garde* in psychology, to child psychology, intelligence testing, and forensic psychology. Both his psychology and philosophy centered on the individual person as unique rather than as an isolated element as Wundt and others regarded man. The *person* was held in sharp focus as is evidenced by his dictum "No gestalt without a gestalter!" the gestalter being the person.

Enraptured with Fechnerian psychophysics, he saw the person as the physical and psychical interwoven, that is, psychophysically neutral, and defined him in terms of a totality, a *unitas multiplex*. Thus is his doctrine of the psychophysical neutrality of being which volume one of his *Person und Sache* (Person and Thing, 1906-1924) treated.

> The "person" is a living whole, individual, unique, striving toward goals, self-contained and yet open to the world around him; he is capable of having experience (1938, p. 70).

Even psychology is personalistically defined as "the science of the person as having experience or as capable of having experience" (1938, p. 70). Rather than characterizing mind in the established manner in terms of consciousness, he preferred "experience." Life has special meanings to a person, and appears to him in three modalities: (1) *vitality*, corresponding to the biological of the world, (2) *experience*, corresponding to the world of objects, and (3) *introception*, the coalescence of the objective world of values into oneself. In agreement with Kant, Stern held that a person possesses dignity, infinite intrinsic value; the person's defining property is "concrete, purposive activity." Unlike a person, a *thing* is an aggregation neither autonomous nor concretely individual nor a whole but externally determined, relative, and abstract. He espoused *personalistics*, the science of the human person. By delving deeper than consciousness of the physical, one arrives at psychophysical neutrality. In this respect Stern approached William James' neutral entity or neutral monism as the ultimate stuff of mind-body. Stern referred to it as "personalistic monism." His distinction between person and thing anticipates Martin Buber's (1878-1965) *I and Thou* (1923) relationship.

The I.Q. and The Era of Testing

From Ebbinghaus, Stern learned about psychology as it relates to learning. As a pioneer in the field of the psychology of individual differences and especially intelligence testing, Stern introduced the I.Q. (intelligence quotient). Whereas the French psychologist *Alfred Binet* (1857-1911), who founded France's first psychological journal and psychological laboratory, originated intelligence tests and the concept of a mental age, it remained for Stern in 1912 to point out that by dividing a child's mental age by his chronological it would produce the intelligence quotient (I.Q.), an indication of his relative intellectual superiority or inferiority.

> Using age gradation tasks are laid down for every age of childhood corresponding to the normal performance of these ages. If a child is tested with this series the level of

accomplishment that he attains (his so-called "mental age" = MA) may be compared with his chronological age (CA). Binet chose as the measure of intelligence the difference between the mental age and the chronological age; nowadays, following my proposal, the ratio of the two values is generally calculated, giving the intelligence quotient IQ = MA/CA. For the normal child this value is equal to 100.

Example: An eight-year-old child completes the test for six-year-olds, but fails at the tasks normal for those from seven to eight years old. CA = 8, MA = 6, the intelligence difference (following Binet) MA − CA = −2, the intelligence quotient IQ = 6/8 x 100 = 75. Crudely expressed, the child has "three-quarter intelligence" (1938, p. 310).

Binet-Simon Intelligence Scale. Unlike Ebbinghaus, who was measuring memory, and other Germans such as Helmholtz, who were testing speed reaction, Binet's interest was the testing of higher mental functions, e.g., reason, judgment, adaptability and the like. As a result he (with his associate Théodore Simon [1873-1961], a French psychologist) produced the epochal Binet-Simon intelligence test as early as 1905. For example, a child of three years of age enumerates objects in a picture; of four, repeats a sentence of six syllables; of five, compares two weights; of six, defines in terms of use; of seven, names four colors; of eight, counts from 20 to 0; of nine, recognizes monetary denominations; of ten, copies drawings from memory; of twelve, defines abstract terms; of fifteen, gives three rhymes; and adults distinguish between abstract terms. Binet and Simon explained their technique:

> The method here presented is one by which the intelligence of a child may be estimated. The method consists in asking the child some precise questions and having him perform some simple experiments; these questions and experiments are called tests. As much research has revealed which of these tests a normal child passes successfully at a given age, it is easy to ascertain whether the child under examination gives results equal to the normal child of his age, or whether he is advanced or retarded in relation to this norm (1913, p. 7).

The scale, initially appearing in 1905, was published in revised form in 1908, and again in 1911.

Stanford-Binet Intelligence Scale. But it was *Lewis Madison Terman* (1877-1956), an American psychologist at Stanford University from 1916 on, who standardized Binet's test by examining 2,000 children, and publishing his Stanford-Binet Intelligence Scale in a volume on *The Measurement of Intelligence* (1916). His findings revealed the average adult mental age to be 16, and the superior adult mental age to be 18. He explained his findings:

> Native intelligence, in so far as it can be measured by tests now available, appears to improve but little after the age of 15 or 16 years. It follows that in calculating the IQ of an adult subject, it will be necessary to disregard the years he has lived beyond the point where intelligence attains its final development.
>
> Although the location of this point is not exactly known, it will be sufficiently accurate for our purpose to assume its location at 16 years. Accordingly, any person over 16 years of age, however old, is for purposes of calculating IQ considered to be just 16 years old. If a youth of 18 and a man of 60 years both have a mental age of 12 years, the IQ in each case is 12 ÷ 16, or .75.

The significance of various values of the IQ is set forth elsewhere. Here it need only be repeated that 100 IQ means exactly average intelligence; that nearly all who are below 70 or 75 IQ are feebleminded; and that the child of 125 IQ is about as much above the average as the high-grade feeble-minded individual is below the average. For ordinary purposes all who fall between 95 and 105 IQ may be considered as average in intelligence (1916, p. 141).

Army Alpha and Beta Tests. The following year an American comparative psychologist from Yale University, *Robert Mearns Yerkes* (1876-1956), was appointed by the American Psychological Association to head a committee (comprised of: Lewis M. Terman; Arthur S. Otis; Frederic L. Wells, Walter V. Bingham; Guy M. Whipple; T. H. Haines; and Henry H. Goddard) to test American service men in World War I. Goddard (1866-1957), known for coining the term *moron* and for his studies on mental deficiency when he was director of psychological research at Vineland Training School in New Jersey, published his findings *The Kallikak Family: A Study in the Heredity of Feeble-Mindedness* in 1912. Goddard both translated and introduced the Binet test into the United States, in 1908, using it to detect degrees of mental deficiency and modifying it so that it was adaptable for his purposes. Yerkes and his associates devised an Army Alpha test for literates and an Army Beta tests for illiterates in order to determine desirable officer material. He found the average mental age of American service men to be thirteen, as he explained below:

> The psychological examiner is frequently asked this question: "How intelligent is the Army?" There is an inherent difficulty in making an answer, for there are no standards in terms of which the statement can be made. The most familiar measures of intelligence, years of mental age as determined by the Stanford-Binet examination, are the results of investigations of a much smaller group (approximately 1000 cases) than the group studied in the Army. For norms of adult intelligence the results of the Army examinations are undoubtedly the most representative. It is customary to say that the mental age of the average adult is about 16 years. This figure is based, however, upon examinations of only 62 persons; 32 of them high-school pupils from 16 to 20 years of age, and 30 of them "business men of moderate success and of very limited educational advantages." This group is too small to give very reliable results and is further more probably not typical. High-school pupils and business men of moderate success presumably do not represent the average American adult with respect to intelligence. . . . 85 per cent of the men who had been to high school show mental ages above average.
>
> It appears that the intelligence of the principal sample of the white draft, when transmuted from alpha and beta examinations into terms of mental age, is about 13 years (13.08) (1921, p. 785).

At the time the reports were complied, Yerkes was a lieutenant colonel, and the noted historian of psychology *Edwin Garrigues Boring* (1886-1968) who assisted editorially in the enterprise was a captain. The group initiated its program on April 6, 1917 at Emerson Hall, Harvard University.

An Era of Psychometrics

Intelligence testing climaxed in the United States in 1939 with the appearance of

David Wechsler's (1896-   ) Wechsler-Bellevue Intelligence Scale (WAIS).
Wechsler, chief psychologist at Bellevue Psychiatric Hospital in New York City,
published his test in *The Measurement of Adult Intelligence,* covering such areas
as: comprehension, arithmetical reasoning, memory span for digits, similarities,
picture arrangement, picture completion, block design, digit symbols, object
assembly, and vocabulary, eleven in all. The three considerations that served as
criteria of his test selection were:

> (1) that previous studies should have shown that the tests correlated reasonably well with
> composite measures of intelligence, (2) that the tests as a group encompassed sufficient
> diversity of function so as not to favor or penalize subjects with special abilities or
> disabilities and (3) that the nature and character of subjects' failures on the tests have
> some diagnostic implications (1958, p. 63).

Stern's Aussage Test. A number of psychologists attempted to develop objective tests of imagery but most were without success. The objective measure of
imagery that is best known is the *aussage* (testimony) test devised by Stern,
initially employed to assess memory accuracy by displaying a picture briefly and
expecting the observer to recall whatever details he possibly can.

> As an example of how such aussage-tests may be carried out at a very early age, we
> append the result obtained from Eva. . . . A picture she had not seen before, "The
> Breakfast" . . . was laid before her for two minutes, and she was asked to say all she
> could see on it; then the picture was taken away and an account and examination
> followed.
>
> The number of statements given in the "primary aussage" was 35—5 wrong; in the
> secondary, 37—8 wrong; if the extreme youth be taken into account, the sum-total
> remembrance was therefore quite excellent.
>
> In such an "aussage"-test then, in spite of its shortness, we get an insight into the
> different aspects of childish individuality (1930, pp. 267-9).

Rorschach, Bender Gestalt, TAT, and Other Tests. The aussage test was the
forerunner of those tests evaluating personality such as the *inkblot test* devised in
1921 by the Swiss psychiatrist *Hermann Rorschach* (1884-1922) in his
Psychodiagnostics. In this, the most famous of the projective tests, the subject is
shown an accidental form of inkblots on 10 pieces of paper or plates (five in color
and five without) and asked: "What might this be?" The test, one of "perceptive
power of the subject," distinguishes apperceptive types and intelligence types.

> The relationship between movement and color factors represents the relation between
> introversion, the faculty of doing "inner work," and extraversion, the faculty of turning
> to the outer world, in the subject. This relationship expresses a condition in the subject,
> or the form of a psychosis when one is present. This relationship may be formulated in
> terms of the "experience type." The following types may be distinguished:
> 1. *Introversive Experience Type.* Predominance of kinaesthetic responses. (Example:
> Imaginative subjects.)
> 2. *Extraversive Experience Type.* Predominance of color responses. (Example: Practical subjects.)
> 3. *Coartated (Narrowed) Experience Type.* Marked submergence of movement and

color factors. . . . (Examples: Pedants, subjects in depressive mood or actually psychotically depressed, subjects with dementia simplex.)
4. *Ambiequal Experience Type*. Many kinaesthetic and equally many color responses. (Examples: Talented individuals, compulsion neurotics, manics, catatonics.) (1942, pp. 181-2).

Another is the *Thematic Apperception Test* designed by the American psychologists *Henry A. Murray* (1893-) and *Christiana D. Morgan* (1893-1967) in 1935. In the TAT test (as it is commonly called), a subject is shown detailed, vague, abstract, and shadowy pictures to stimulate his fantasy, and then asked to formulate a story regarding each. If a recurrent theme persists throughout the pictures described it is significantly indicative of his personality make-up.

> What we have to show is that subjects project their deepest fantasies into such dramatic pictures and thereby reveal directional tensions of which they are quite unconscious. Though some of their stories are elaborations of conscious fantasies, others are not recognized by the subjects as having any personal reference. It is these — in which the personal reference is suggested by other data — that have been ascribed to unconscious fantasies. Of course, the stories as given are conscious fantasies. Like dreams, they must be interpreted if one is to arrive at the unconscious trends which determine them (1935, p, 293).

The TAT with its applications appeared in Murray's *Explorations in Personality* in 1938.

During the score of years from the 1920s to the forties, the United States saw the rapid development of psychometrics. The year Rorschach's inkblot tests were published, *Gordon W. Allport* (1897-1967) of Harvard University developed his Ascendance-Submission Reaction Study, publishing it in 1928; and *Sir Cyril Burt* (1883-) at the University of London published his *Mental and Scholastic Tests* (1921). In 1926 the Goodenough Draw-a-Man Test was developed by a psychologist at the University of Minnesota's Institute of Child Welfare, *Florence L. Goodenough* (1886-1959), who observed abnormal children tending toward highly individualistic drawings. A Vocational Interest Blank was published the following year by *Edward K. Strong, Jr.* (1884-1963), followed the succeeding year with the publication of A. F. Payne's *Sentence Completions*, and in 1930 the Minnesota Mechanical Ability Tests appeared. In 1928 Edward Spranger assembled a six-fold classification of men in his *Types of Men* (the six ideally basic types of individuality being the theoretic, economic, esthetic, social, political, and religious) that was used for the Allport-Vernon Study of Values in 1931, the year *Louis Leon Thurstone* (1887-1955) published his *The Reliability and Validity of Tests,* assessing test theory as it had thus far progressed. He with *Paul Horst* (1903-) and others founded *Psychometrika* which saw its first issue in 1936, the same year that *Psychometric Methods* was published by *Joy Paul Gilford* (1897-) of the University of Nebraska. Two years later the gestalt influence was felt in this area with the publication of *A Visual Motor Gestalt Test and Its Clinical Use* (1938) by a child psychiatrist at Bellevue Hospital and a professor at New York University, *Lauretta Bender* (1897-), wife of the psychiatrist Paul

Schilder. Bender originally employed it in perception studies, and later for diagnosing organic brain pathology and for differentiating various psychiatric disorders. Explaining her test she wrote:

Visually perceived configurations first used by Wertheimer in his experimentations with visual gestalten have been offered to children and adults and mentally defective and mentally sick patients with the request that they be copied. The final product is a visual motor pattern which reveals modifications in the original pattern by the integrating mechanism of the individual who has experienced it.

The gestalt function may be defined as that function of the integrated organism whereby it responds to a given constellation of stimuli as a whole; the response itself being a constellation, or pattern, or gestalt (1938, p. 3).

One year later Wechsler's WAIS and a more sophisticated version of the Army Alpha called the Army General Classification Test (AGCT) were produced. To complete the decade the Minnesota Multiphase Personality Inventory was authored by *Starke R. Hathaway* (1903-   ) assisted by J. C. McKinley in 1940, and another, the Test of Mechanical Comprehension, was devised by *George K. Bennett* (1904-   ), President of the Psychological Corporation and coauthor of the *Differential Aptitude Tests* in 1947. In 1953 Janet Taylor (Spence) developed the Taylor Manifest Anxiety Scale, and by 1961 Donn Byrne constructed a Repression-Sensitization Scale. Cattell founded the Psychological Corporation with the assistance of Thorndike and Woodworth in 1921 for the purpose of providing psychological services, a major service being the publication of tests and measurements. The year 1940 also saw the initial publication of the journal, *Educational and Psychological Measurement,* and brought to a close a golden era of tests and measurements. This is not to say that testing and the devising of tests did not continue, for it did with the most significant event being in 1947, marking the founding of the Educational Testing Service in Princeton, New Jersey by the College Entrance Examination Board, the American Council on Education, and the Carnegie Foundation for the Advancement of Technology; it emerged as the major center for psychometric research, testing, and the development of tests.

CHAPTER 5

Leipzig: Birthplace of the New (Experimental) Psychology

Though much older than the University of Berlin, Leipzig's university is not as distinguished, especially since World War II (as part of East Germany) when it fell into communist hands, and was renamed Karl Marx University in 1952. In consequence of war devastation, it lost its valuable collections and suffered extensive destruction.

Its founding dates to 1409 when religious differences under the leadership of John Huss erupted, resulting in the establishment of a university at Leipzig, along the order of the University of Prague, by 46 professors and 369 students from Prague. Its inauspicious beginning paralleled that of the universities at Paris and Bologna with lectures conducted at the homes of the faculty. Its early years were humanistically oriented followed by a period influenced by the German Reformation. But the statutes of 1559 suppressed the Reformation movement at the university, resulting in numerous professors and students abandoning the university.

It was in 1830 that it reorganized with a quality faculty, by decree of Frederick August of Saxony, leading to its rapid acquisition of the distinction for which it was known. Such notable psychologists as E. H. Weber, Fechner, Wundt, Ewald Hering, Lotze, Max Frey, Johannes Kries, and Wilibald A. Nagel distinguished the university by their contributions. Several influential American psychologists were products of the University of Leipzig, including James McKeen Cattell, Lightner Witmer, Frank Angell, Edward Wheeler Scripture, Edward Bradford Titchener, and Charles Hubbard Judd, who earned their Ph.D's there, while others such as G. Stanley Hall, James Mark Baldwin, Howard Crosby Warren, and Mary Whiton Calkins studied there. Fourteen Americans obtained their doctorates under Wundt at Leipzig from 1875 to 1919, a period in which Wundt directed 186 doctoral theses, hence earning him the title of "senior psychologist in the history of psychology." Other distinguished students of Wundt's include: the Russian V. Bekhterev; Charles Spearman from the University of London; A. Lehmann from the University of Copenhagen; E. Kräepelin from the University of Munich; H. Münsterberg from Freiburg and later at Harvard; L. Lange from Tübingen; and O. Külpe and K. Marbe both from Würzburg.

The First Laboratories of Psychology. At Leipzig, Wundt had his psychological laboratory operating from 1875 though the date of its founding is cited as 1879. Mistakenly it was thought that 1879 was its formal founding but formal recognition was not accorded it until 1883 accompanied by an appropriation. In turn, his students and others attending the University of Leipzig founded laboratories of psychology the world over, among them being: G. S. Hall at Johns

Hopkins in 1881; A. Lehmann at the University of Copenhagen in 1886; J.McK. Cattell at the University of Pennsylvania in 1887; H. Münsterberg at the University of Freiburg in 1888; J. M. Baldwin at the University of Toronto in 1890; G. Martius at Bonn, F. Angell at Cornell, and M. Calkins at Wellesley College in 1891; E. A. Pace at the Catholic University of America and E. W. Scripture at Yale in 1892; J. M. Baldwin at Princeton and F. Angell at Stanford in 1893; O. Külpe at the University of Würzburg in 1894; W. G. Smith at Smith College in 1895; and G. M. Stratton at the University of California in 1896.

Though laboratories had existed prior to Wundt's in 1879, they were ancillary and were not formally and explicitly used for psychological research exclusively. The room set aside for experimental purposes in psychology by William James in 1875 at Harvard University was more of an anticipatory nature, and Carl Stumpf's (1848-1936) acoustic laboratory of tuning-forks for his research on tonal fusion, were hardly what could be called founded. Wundt's *Psychologisches Institut* (psychological laboratory is the American equivalent) produced an array of names for a Who's Who in Psychology.

Laboratories of psychology and other disciplines find their prototype in the original laboratory of science, the first being a laboratory of chemistry founded at the University of Giessen in 1824 by *Justus von Liebig* (1803-1873). Liebig, reputed founder of organic chemistry, introduced methods of organic analysis with the result that his laboratory became the first practical chemical teaching laboratory.

The laboratory was followed by similar ones: the German chemist *Friedrich Wöhler* (1800-1882) founded one at Göttingen in 1836; the inventor of the Bunsen burner, *Robert Wilhelm Bunsen* (1811-1899) founded a laboratory at the University of Marburg; another German chemist who introduced vaccination and whose laboratory was long regarded as a paradigm, *Otto Linné Erdmann* (1804-1869), founded his laboratory at Leipzig in 1843; the founder of the German Chemical Society, *August Wilhelm von Hofmann* (1818-1892) founded England's first at the University of London (at that time the Royal College of Chemistry) through the influence and offices of Prince Albert in 1845; and the first laboratory in the United States was established at Yale University by the American chemist Benjamin Silliman (1779-1864) and carried on by his son Benjamin Silliman (1816-1885). The Silliman Lectures at Yale University have included some delivered by psychologists, among them being those by Kenneth W. Spence (1907-1967), whose lectures were published in 1956 as *Behavior Theory and Conditioning*. Prior to 1840 America was without an institution worthy of the name university from the scientific standpoint, for scientific schools did not arise until 1847 at Yale and Harvard. Science was for the purpose of training engineers, a task which was performed by the U.S. Military Academy and Rensselaer Polytechnic Institute prior to 1847. Before the period of the scientific laboratories, scientists worked at home, often with their children as subjects and apprentices. Even college courses were conducted in the homes of professors, as was "Philosophy 9," at Harvard offered by William James at his home on 20 Quincy Street in Cambridge where currently stands the Faculty Club. Dissecting rooms can be traced to medieval universities in Italy thereby qualifying anatomy as the mother of the sciences. Chemistry was spawned in alchemy, and the other sciences likewise had humble beginnings, some finding their parentage in astrology.

Wundt's Laboratory at Leipzig: Psychology's First

Tradition in psychology has it that the first laboratory of psychology was founded in 1879 by Wilhelm Wundt, yet William James claimed that his was in operation as early as 1874 at Harvard. Historians of psychology attempt to resolve the discrepancy in terms of a *de jure* establishment and a *de facto* founding. For some reason still unknown Wundt cited the founding of his laboratory in 1879 though his laboratory was in operation as early as 1875, the year Wundt came to the University of Leipzig. In his autobiography (*Erlebtes und Erkanntes, 1920*) Wundt spoke of his *Psychologisches Institut* as a gradual development, producing its first doctoral dissertation by Max Friedrich during the 1879-1880 semester. The Italian psychologist at Rome, Guido Villa, publishing his *Contemporary Psychology* (1899) before the turn of the century, cited 1874 as the founding date of Wundt's laboratory of psychology (p. 67). The laboratory of James in the 1870s and 1880s (of which more will be said later) was ill equipped and could hardly pass qualifications for a psychological laboratory (namely one suitably equipped for student and faculty research and instruction).

Since Wundt's was the world's first psychological laboratory, it seems appropriate to offer a somewhat detailed discussion of it. Wundt not only had his laboratory but laboratory assistants and in 1883 founded the journal *Philosophische Studien* for publishing the results and methods of psychological research emerging from his laboratory, the journal appearing whenever sufficient material amounting to 150 pages was gathered. The journal terminated publication in 1903, continuing as *Psychologische Studien* in 1905. In 1879 Wundt's laboratory had rooms provided by the university with appropriations and in the eighties went from four to six rooms with 19 students conducting original research, the bulk of them Germans, Americans, and Russians. But subjects were not provided except those students mutually serving one another, as such, the successful researches being published and often serving as doctoral dissertations. Wundt's laboratory of psychology provided the model for a great many of the psychological laboratories not only in Germany but in other countries as well, including the United States. The first assistant in a psychological laboratory anywhere in the world was the American James McKeen Cattell, who approached Wundt in 1886 declaring: "Herr Professor, you need an assistant and I shall be your assistant" (1928, p. 545). Wundt's laboratory occupied the top floor of the *Convict* building, one in which students ate their meals. Experimental work conducted at the psychological laboratory included: (1) analysis of sensation, (2) timing mental processes, (3) time-sense, and (4) attention, memory, and the association of ideas. Wundt was not a laboratory worker (nor was G. Stanley Hall, founder of one of America's first psychological laboratories), yet his laboratory won world renown, acquiring international reputation and influence. It was the world's largest and best equipped.

Leipzig: World's Best Equipped Laboratory of Psychology. For its day, the laboratory of psychology at the University of Leipzig was the best equipped in the world, and the apparatus assembled by Wundt became standard for psychological laboratories throughout the world. In the early 1880s when Oswald Külpe (1862-1915) and August Kirschmann (1860-1932) were his laboratory assistants, the laboratory (or institute) comprised six rooms containing:

1. *Hipp Chronoscope* (costing 282 marks)
2. *Kugelfallapparat* (for testing the chronoscope; worth, 64 marks)
3. *Control hammer* (for regulating chronoscope; cost, 275 marks)
4. *Fallapparat* (with slit in plate for displaying a letter or word; 125 marks)
5. *Fall-Chronometer* (145 marks)
6. *Sprecht contact-apparat* (for generating or breaking current by speaking into a membrane-covered drum; 33 marks)
7. *Schall hammer* (electrically connected and striking when current is connected or interrupted)
8. *Metronomes* (one with bell, 12 marks; one without bell, 15 marks)
9. *Electro-magnet* with stative (9 marks)
10. *Color mixers* (clock operated, 54 marks each; governors attached, 64 marks each)
11. *Electric chronographic tuning fork* (250 vibrations, 90 marks).
12. *Helmholtz electric chronographic tuning fork* (1125 vibrations, 75 marks; tuning forks mounted on resonance boxes; varying costs)
13. *Reaction apparat* (10 switch buttons electrically connected, 56 marks)
14. *Pendulum* (with slits in bob; the subject peers through a tube at the swinging pendulum, the object being to discern a word or letter behind the pendulum).
15. *Adjustable magnets* (for reaction-time experiments of light impressions; 275 marks)
16. *Chronograph* (heavy weights rapidly revolving a drum for the purpose of measuring short time intervals; 700 marks)
17. *Zeitsinnapparat* with six contact keys (for judging time intervals between sounds; 124 marks)
18. *Fallapparat* with four electromagnetic ballholders (F. Angell used it for investigating average error while at Leipzig)
19. *Three-fold diaphragm* with adjustable square holes (designed by Kirshmann for experimenting on the relation of color to the apparent size of the surface)
20. *Apparatus for afterimage* experiments (48 marks; another for afterimage duration of light and sound, 60 marks; one for eye movements, 45 marks; one for retinal images, 34 marks)
21. *Rotation-apparat* (lecture room color mixer; 34 marks)
22. *Baltze kymograph* (designed by Baltze, the mechanic of Carl Friedrich Wilhelm Ludwig [1816-1895], head of the physiological laboratory at Leipzig, a founder of nonvitalistic physiology; Wundt's students had the advantage of Ludwig's laboratory [institute] of physiology).

During Wundt's tenure at Leipzig from 1875 to 1917, he directed 186 theses (two theses were not complete until 1919). Of the psychological theses (70 of the 186 were philosophical) growing out of his laboratory, the approximate breakdown on subject matter was:

70% sensation and perception (vision 28%; audition 23%; touch 5%; time-sense 8%)

11% action, association, and memory

10% attention and memory

9% methodology

His students included:

136 Germans (including Austrians)

14 Americans (12 of the 14 obtaining doctorates from 1886 to 1900)

13 Balkans (Roumania, Bulgaria, etc.)

10 English

6 Polish

3 Russian

2 Danish

2 French

Of the 116 students who were investigating psychological issues, only 34 (not quite 30%) became known names in psychology; and of the 34, 13 (including Titchener and Münsterberg) were Americans or became prominent in psychology in the United States. Nineteen of Wundt's doctorates achieved prominence, 13 of them Americans (including Titchener and Münsterberg).

Apparatus equipping modern laboratories of psychology has come a long way since the time of Wundt. The sophisticated equipment currently used takes advantage of modern technology, especially electronics, including computers as well as the advantages of modern chemistry.

The Proliferation of Laboratories of Psychology

Wundt's laboratory of psychology set the pace and became the paradigm for laboratories of psychology throughout the world, many of them instituted by his own students. The burgeoning of laboratories assumed the following pattern:

FOUNDING OF LABORATORIES OF PSYCHOLOGY (to 1900)

Year Founded (De Facto)	Founder or Person in Charge	Institution	Location
1875 (de facto) 1879 (traditional date)	W. Wundt	Leipzig	Germany
1874-6 (de facto)	W. James	Harvard	U.S.A.
1891 (de jure)	H. Münsterberg	Harvard	U.S.A.
1881	G. E. Müller	Göttingen	Germany
1883 (closed in 1887; reopened in 1903 by J. M. Baldwin)	G. S. Hall	Johns Hopkins	U.S.A.
1886	V. Bekhterev	Kazan	U.S.S.R.
1886	H. Ebbinghaus	Berlin	Germany
1886	A. Lehmann	Copenhagen	Denmark

1887	J. McK. Cattell	Pennsylvania	U.S.A.
1888	W. L. Bryan	Indiana	U.S.A.
1888	J. Jastrow	Wisconsin	U.S.A.
1888	Y. Motora	Tokyo	Japan
1888	H. Münsterberg	Freiburg	Germany
1889	H. Beaunis (and A. Binet)	Sorbonne	France
1889	E. C. Sanford	Clark	U.S.A.
1889	G. Sergi	Rome	Italy
1889	C. Stumpf	Munich	Germany
1889	H. K. Wolfe	Nebraska	U.S.A.
1890	J. M. Baldwin	Toronto	Canada
1890	B. Bourdon	Rennes	France
1890	J. McK. Cattell	Columbia	U.S.A.
1890	G. W. T. Patrick	Iowa	U.S.A.
1890	J. H. Tufts	Michigan	U.S.A.
1891	F. Angell	Cornell	U.S.A.
1891	M. Calkins	Wellesley	U.S.A.
1891	G. Martius	Bonn	Germany
1891	Th. Flournoy	Geneva	Switzerland
1891	A. Thiéry, D. Mercier, J. F. Heymans	Louvain	Belgium
1891	J. Ward	Cambridge	England
1892	E. B. Delabarre	Brown	U.S.A.
1892	W. O. Krohn	Illinois	U.S.A.
1892	E. A. Pace	Catholic U.	U.S.A.
1892	E. W. Scripture	Yale	U.S.A.
1892	O. Templin	Kansas	U.S.A.
1892	L. A. Williams	State Normal, Trenton	U.S.A.
1892-3	C. A. Strong	Chicago	U.S.A.
1893	F. Angell	Stanford	U.S.A.
1893	J. R. Angell	Minnesota	U.S.A.
1893	J. M. Baldwin	Princeton	U.S.A.
1893	J. F. Heymans	Groningen	Netherlands
1894	H. A. Aikins	Western Reserve	U.S.A.
1894	C. B. Bliss	University of the City of New York	U.S.A.
1894	H. Ebbinghaus	Breslau	Germany
1894	C. E. Gorman	Amherst	U.S.A.
1894	C. L. Herrick	Denison U.	U.S.A.
1894	O. Külpe	Würzburg	Germany
1894	A. Meinong	Graz	Austria
1894	W. J. Shaw	Wesleyan	U.S.A.
1895	V. Bekhterev	St. Petersburg	U.S.S.R.
1895	F. Kiesow	Turin	Italy
1895	E. W. Runkle	Pennsylvania State	U.S.A.
1895	W. G. Smith	Smith	U.S.A.

1895	A. Tokarsky	Moscow	U.S.S.R.
1896	H. Cohen	Marburg	Germany
1896	G. M. Stratton	California	U.S.A.
1896	A. Tamburini	Reggio Emilia	Italy
1897	G. Dwelshauvers	Brussels	Belgium
1897	B. Erdmann	Halle	Germany
1897	W. Heinrich	Cracow	Poland
1897	W. H. R. Rivers	London	England
1897	C. Wissler	Ohio	U.S.A.
1898	J. H. Leuba	Bryn Mawr	U.S.A.
1898		Texas	U.S.A.
1898	H. C. Piñero	Buenos Aires	Argentina
1900	J. E. Downey	Wyoming	U.S.A.
1900	M. C. Fernald	Maine	U.S.A.
1900	M. F. Meyer	Missouri	U.S.A.
1900		Miami	U.S.A.
1900-1	W. D. Scott	Northwestern	U.S.A.

If those concerned with the founding of laboratories had known the significance that historians of psychology subsequently accorded them, they would have been meticulous in providing posterity with accurate dates concerning them. Cattell cited the founding of Wundt's laboratory in 1879 and then added: "The fiftieth anniversary of the founding of the laboratory was, however, celebrated at Leipzig in 1926" (1928, pp. 543-4), which would date the founding in 1876, the year after Wundt arrived at Leipzig from the University of Zürich. Today considerable debate rages over the dates of the foundings of psychological laboratories. Considerable subjectivity is involved as Boring (1965) noted. The question at issue is one of criterion. Which one (or ones) of the following criteria serves as an acceptable founding date: (1) one in which a psychologist assembles some experimental equipment; (2) one in which he is provided space by his institution; (3) one recognized by his institution by providing a budget; (4) one used for lecture demonstrations only; (5) one in which students as well as faculty carry on research? Other criteria may also be pertinent such as the official founding of a laboratory one year but with a subsequent materialization.

ERNST HEINRICH WEBER (1795-1878): Weber's Law

The German physiologist and anatomist, Weber, was the elder brother of *Wilhelm Eduard Weber* (1804-1891), the celebrated physicist who investigated terrestrial magnetism with the German mathematician and astronomer, *Karl Friedrich Gauss* (1777-1855), known in psychology for the *Gaussian curve* (probability curve). Weber, whose long tenure at the University of Leipzig began in 1818, is prominent in psychology for his research in sensation and the formulation of what came to be known as Weber's law, i.e., *the least discernible increment of a stimulus is a constant that is proportional to the original stimulus.* His formulation was initially presented in *De Tactu: Annotationes Anatomicae et Physiologicae* (Concerning Touch: Anatomical and Physiological Annotations) in

1834 and a dozen years later in a psychological classic *Der Tastsinn und das Gemeingefühl* (The Sense of Touch and the Common Feeling), which first appeared in 1846.

Just Noticeable Difference (j.n.d.). Threshold or *limen* (Latin) is the boundary demarkating responses sensed from two different intensities of stimuli of the same sense. A weight placed in a person's hand may be so light as not to enable the subject to notice it. But to increase the weight gradually will produce a point at which it is sensed. This point (RL from the German *Reiz Limen*) is the lower stimulus threshold, the next point at which any perceptible difference is noticed being the j.n.d. (just noticeable difference) or difference threshold (abbreviated DL for *difference limen*). The point beyond which no greater sensation is experienced by the individual is his *terminal threshold* (TL).

It was just noticeable differences of a specific human sense with which Weber was experimentally concerned that led him to what Fechner termed Weber's law. Thus it was Weber who introduced the experiment of just noticeable differences.

Formulation of Weber's Law. In discriminating between two weights Weber discovered that it is not the actual objective difference (such as a weight scale would do), but merely the ratio of the two weights that is sensed. Not absolute but relative differences are perceived. Although the ratio is constant, it is not the same for all of the senses as some senses possess finer discriminating powers than others, e.g., a person can discriminate differentiations in brightness better than he can for loudness. Weber's law maintains that there is a lawful existence between stimuli and the intensities of stimulation.

The just noticeable difference, however, is always the same for any given sense so that if the addition of a single gram to a fifty gram weight is noticeable then it would require two for a noticeable difference of a 100 gram weight, and four for 200, etc. The ratio remains constant, hence Weber's law: the least discernible increment of a stimulus is a constant that is proportional to the original stimulus. Although the constant is the same, it differs for the various senses. Weber explained his law as follows:

> In comparing objects and observing the distinction between them, we perceive not the difference between the objects, but the ratio of this difference to the magnitude of the objects compared. If we are comparing by touch two weights, the one of 30 and the other of 29 half-ounces, the difference is not more easily perceived than that between weights of 30 and 29 drachms. . . . Since the distinction is not perceived more easily in the former case than in the latter, it is clear that not the weights of the differences but their ratios are perceived. . . .
>
> That which I have set forth with regard to weights compared by touch holds also of lines to be compared by sight. For, whether you compare longer or shorter lines, you will find that the difference is not sensed by most O's [observers] if the second line is less by a hundredth part. . . .
>
> We perceive not the absolute but the relative differences (1968, pp. 108-9).

The law holds that the increment of a stimulus sufficient to produce a noticeable increment of sensation with respect to any sense, rather than being a fixed quantity is contingent upon that portion which the increment bears to the stimulus immediately preceding it. The equation for the law is: Δ I/1 = K. What has been interchangeably referred to as *Weber's constant, Weber's ratio,* or *Weber's fraction* (for a stimulus to be just noticeably different, it is necessary that it be increased by a constant fraction) is expressed Δ I/I. "Delta I" (Δ I) represents the increment yielding a just noticeable difference in sensation; "I" is the symbol for intensity; and "K" for constant.

It has been found that Weber's constant holds rather well in the mid range of intensity for virtually all of the senses. It is a worthwhile index in ascertaining the discriminating abilities of the different senses.

GUSTAV THEODOR FECHNER (1801-1887): Father of the New Experimental Psychology

Intellectual Biography. The German Experimental psychologist and philosopher, Fechner, was born in a parsonage in Gross-Sarchen in southeastern Germany. Largely self-taught, he entered the University of Leipzig at sixteen to study medicine. Fechner, with the exception of the course in physiology offered by E. H. Weber, attended few lectures, acquiring his knowledge on his own from books. At Leipzig where he spent the remainder of his life, he was appointed professor of physics, a post he resigned in 1839 owing to an illness that affected his eyes (probably from experiments entailing gazing at the sun) and mental state as well. Living on his pension while his position was occupied by Wilhelm Weber, brother of Ernst H. Weber, he recovered suddenly and remarkably in October, 1843. As an undergraduate, Fechner studied medicine, receiving his degree in 1822. But his disenchantment with the practice of medicine in which iodine seemed to be prescribed as a panacea prompted him to write some facetious satires on the subject.

Psychophysics Anticipated. Although his revolutionary classic *Elements of Psychophysics* was not published until 1860, the general solution of the problem unfolded itself to him on the morning of October 22, 1850. The basic idea of psychophysics was found in his three volume *Zendavesta, oder über die Dinge des Himmels und des Jenseits (Zend-Avesta, of the Things of Heaven and the Hereafter,* 1851), its influence typifying the new influx of Persian, Chinese, and Indian culture. In it mention is made of his discovery of a mathematical relation existing between the spiritual and physical world. "As our bodies belong to the greater and higher individual body of the earth, so our spirits belong to the greater and higher individual spirit of the earth, which comprises all the spirits of earthly creatures, very much as the earth-body comprises their bodies" (1851, ch. 20, sect. 3). Persian religious philosophy was permeated with dualism, especially ethical dualism.

Fechner was never liberated from his fascination for philosophy of religion, epitomized by his little book *On Life After Death* (1836) in which his panpsychism was apparent to the point of animism, as is evident from his *Nanna, oder über das seelenleben der Pflanzen (Nanna, or the Soul-Life of Plants),* published in 1848. He argued the right to assume the existence of a soul in man, animals, and plants, owing to the suitable interaction of the organs of these beings to react and adapt to external conditions. The plant's (and animal's) soul and body are one, an organic whole.

> True, the plant has no brain like that of the dog, no ganglion ring like that of the insects, but it has something else—it has as a whole the same corporeal constitution as that of the nerve cells. . . .
> When the plant has to procure its nourishment by utilizing the light, and when after its leaves have been stimulated by the light the stem or petiole turns in such a way that the leaf may make the most intensive use of the light, which otherwise would not be possible, the only conclusion we can draw is that the leaf has been sensible of the light (1964a, pp. 186-7).

Beings superior to man (celestial bodies) also possess inward life or soul that is a concomitant of an outward one. Accordingly the universe, rather than being a "dead bulk," is an alive, animated being of the sublimest order.

A distant disciple of Schelling and stimulated by the "philosophy of nature," Fechner, sensing the thrill of life in the entire universe (including plants, earth, and stars), viewed man as standing between the souls of plants and the souls of stars. God's perfection is depicted and unfolded in natural law. His psychophysical orientation is found even in his little book *On Life After Death:*

> Consciousness is present and awake when and where the activity of the body underlying the activity of the mind—the psycho-physical activity—exceeds that degree of strength which we call the threshold. According to this view, consciousness can be localized in time and space. The summits of the waves of our psycho-physical activity move and change about from place to place, though confined, in this life, to our body, even to a limited part of our body, and in sleep they sink below the threshold to rise again in waking (1906, p. 99).

With the rise of Darwinism, Fechner adapted evolutionary theory to his own position, lending Darwinian theory a new foundation while deriving support from it for his own position. It was evident in his *Einige Ideen zur Schöpfungs, und Entwickelungsgeschichte der Organismen (Some Ideas on the Creation and Evolution of Organisms,* 1873).

His final book, *Die Tagesansicht gegenüber der Nachtansicht (The Daylight-View versus the Night-View,* 1879), contrasts the "daylight view" of the world with the dreary, lifeless "night view" characterizing materialism. Referring to his own philosophical stance as "the day view opposed to the night view," he developed an apologetic of his metaphysical theory which was essentially a condensation of subject matter of *Zend-Avesta.* His principles of the daylight view support an optimistic outlook grounded on a faith based on reason:

> That gravitation extends throughout the whole world is a matter of faith; that laws which are traceable in our limited realm extend limitlessly in space and time is a matter of faith; that there are atoms and lightwaves is a matter of faith; the beginning and the goal of history are matters of faith; even in geometry there are things we take upon faith, such as the number of the dimensions of space and the definition of parallel lines. Indeed, strictly speaking everything is a matter of faith which is not directly experienced or logically

established on the basis of this experience. . . . Ultimately the best faith is that which is least contradictory in itself and to all knowledge and to our practical interest (1964b, pp. 248-9).

Experimental Esthetics. Three years before Wundt came to the University of Leipzig, Fechner published his 81 page *Zur experimentalen Aesthetik* (1871) and in 1876 his two-volume *Vorschule der Aesthetik (Introduction to Esthetics),* which marked the founding of experimental esthetics. Having conducted experiments to establish that some abstract forms are by nature pleasing to the senses, he provided novel illustrations of the process of esthetic association. He began with objects that were quite simple (e.g. geometrical figures) analyzing artistic creations, seeking experimentally to discern the laws of esthetic pleasure by uncovering precisely what it is that renders objects pleasant or unpleasant.

Utilizing the Dresden and Darmstadt Madonnas reputed to be the work of Holbein, he experimented by having the two placed together for public observation and public opinion. Though he placed a book beside the paintings for the 11,000 passers-by to comment, only 113 expressed opinions. The experiment was a failure not merely because of the sparse response, but because most of the answers had to be rejected owing to the disregard of the instructions provided.

Development of Psychophysics

With the publication of his *Elements of Psychophysics* in 1860 at the age of 59, Fechner became the father of the new experimental psychology. His contemporary Johannes Müller, who was born in the same year (1801), could not claim that distinction for his experiments were physiological in character, according him the title, father of experimental physiology. Fechner and his contemporary, John Stuart Mill, were breaking from the dualism of mind and body, a view that prevailed over the centuries but was dominant in the psychology of Descartes, who sired modern physiology. Mill and Fechner, taking their lead from Berkeley and Leibniz, abandoned the concept of an inactive, inert matter for a vital one. Hence Fechner is a panpsychist, one who believes that all nature is imbued with some psychic quality.

Defining psychophysics as "an exact theory of the relation of body and mind" (1966, p. xxvii), Fechner regarded it as an exact science comparable to physics. With a sense of indebtedness, he credited a host of scholars from Herbart to his friend and brother-in-law (*Alfred Wilhelm Volkmann* [1800-1877], Professor of Physiology at the University of Halle) for past accomplishments (experiments) contributing to his discovery. Herbart's mathematical approach to psychology and his limen of consciousness proved helpful as did Weber's law (coined by Fechner). The mathematical function relating stimulus intensity and sensation magnitude came from Euler, who applied it a century earlier, and subsequently Herbart and Frobisch in certain cases related it to the dependency of tonal interval perception on their relation to vibration frequences. Even before Euler, this relation was cited by *Daniel Bernoulli* (1700-1782) of the University of Basel, and after him by Laplace and Poisson. Laplace, noting the dependency of *fortune morale* on *for-*

tune physique, theorized that an individual's mental fortune varied with his physical fortune. The same relation noted by Euler held for Steinheil and Pogson with respect to the dependence of various stellar magnitudes (comparable to differences of sensation) on their photometric intensities. Fechner reasoned that a person's material possessions *(fortune physique)* are like inert matter without value or meaning, serving only as instruments for stimulating a sum of psychic values *(fortune morale)* within one. A dollar, for example, is of considerably less value relatively to a wealthy man than to a poor one. Whereas it can excite a beggar's delight, the millionaire would scarcely notice it. The principle, first noted by Daniel Bernoulli, was what Laplace termed *fortune morale* and *fortune physique*, reasoning that any addition to the latter must be proportional to material possessions already owned. While the principle was contributed by Daniel Bernoulli (1738), the terms *fortune physique* and *fortune morale* were coined by *Pierre Antoine de Laplace* (1749-1827) in his *Analytic Theory of Probabilities* (1812-1820). Nevertheless Bernoulli did say: "The gain of 1000 ducats is far more important for poor persons than for rich persons, although the amount is the same for both" and added further: "Any small advantage adds to the ultimate good in reciprocal proportion to the status of the people involved" (1737, p. 177). Fechner noted that a similar phenomenon occurred with respect to the relation existing between sensations and stimuli. The important objective was to ascertain the constant involved, rather than being merely cognizant that as sensations increase arithmetically, stimuli increase geometrically. It was apparent that the sound of one bell added to one hundred would not have the same differential effect on sensation as a second added to a single bell. But the precise formula for the constants for different sense modalities determining the rate of geometrical progression was Fechner's next step—the *Fechner Law*.

Weber-Fechner Law. Fechner's primary task was the measurement or quantification of the psychic or what is experienced. For his formula for psychic measure, he required the "identity hypothesis" or *panpsychism* (everything has a psychic quality); Herbart's limen of consciousness; his own experimental techniques; the psychophysical principle of a functional concomitance between body and mind; and the isolation of the *intensity* of sensation as the variable chosen for measurement rather than sensation as a whole.

According to the *Webner Fechner law* (sensation increases as the logarithm of the stimulus), as the intensity of the sensation increases mathematically, the stimulus increases geometrically. They do not have a one-to-one correspondence or concomitant relationship with each other. Note the following logarithmic relationship between a series of geometric and arithmetic figures in series:

$$\log 1 = 0$$
$$\log 10 = 1$$
$$\log 100 = 2$$
$$\log 1,000 = 3$$
$$\log 10,000 = 4$$

While arithmetic increments are equal, the logarithmic do not increase by equal increments. This phenomenon in everyday life is readily noticeable and appreciated by the person who has had the experience of sitting in a room with but one lighted candle and then lights a second in order to obtain an appreciable increase in illumination. But if he had 100 candles and lit one more, the addition would not be as noticeable. Thus the effects of stimuli are not absolute but relative to the existing sensation experienced. Fechner theorized that there had to be a specific relative increment in the stimulus capable of producing a noticeable intensity of sensation. The ratio between the two (sensation and stimulus) should maintain for the entire series of stimulus increments (from the weakest to the strongest intensity). The formula for Fechner's law (sensation varies or is proportional to the ratio of the logarithm of the stimulus) expressing arithmetical increments in sensations as stimuli increase geometrically is:

$$\gamma = \varkappa \, \log \frac{\beta}{b}$$

From this equation it follows that the sensation magnitude γ is not to be considered as a simple function of the stimulus value β, but of its relation to the threshold value b, where the sensation begins and disappears. This relative stimulus value, $\frac{\beta}{b}$ is for the future to be called the fundamental stimulus value, or the fundamental value of the stimulus.

Translated in words, the measurement formula reads:

The magnitude of the sensation (γ) is not proportional to the absolute value of the stimulus (β), but rather to the logarithm of the magnitude of the stimulus, when this last is expressed in terms of its threshold value (b), i.e. that magnitude considered as unit at which the sensation begins and disappears. In short, it is proportional to the logarithm of the fundamental stimulus value (1968, pp. 112-3).

Simply put the law reads that sensations are proportional to the logarithms of the stimuli by which they are excited, that is:

$$S = C \log R$$

(intensity of sensation is proportional to the logarithm of the stimulus). The relative increase in the strength of the stimulus must be constant as the intensity of a sensation is increased by a given amount. S represents the magnitude of the sensation, C the constant, and R the magnitude of the stimulus (*Reiz,* German for stimulus). C, though a fixed quantity (constant) for a particular series of stimuli, such as brightness or weight, differs from one sense modality (e.g., brightness) to another (e.g., weight).

Methods of Psychophysical Measurement. Fechner's law was based on two presuppositions: *(a)* sensations are measureable and *(b)* each sensation has a zero point at which it is actually sensed. He employed the following three methods: (1) method of just noticeable differences (Weber's method); (2) method of right and wrong cases (originated by K. Vierordt in 1852); and (3) the method of average error. The explanation of each is offered by Fechner:

In the application of the method of just noticeable differences, a person compares the weight of two containers, A and B, by lifting them, after they have first been given slightly different loads. The difference in weight will be felt if it is large enough; otherwise it will not be noticed. The method of just noticeable differences consists in determining how much the weights have to differ so that they can just be discriminated. We may take the reciprocal of this difference as an indication of the degree of sensitivity. . . .

If one takes very small differences of weight one will, upon frequent repetition of the experiment, often be mistaken about the direction of the difference, so that the container that is lighter is taken to be the heavier and vice versa. The more the added weight or the greater the sensitivity, however, the greater will be the number of correct cases compared to the number of wrong or to the total number of cases. The method of right and wrong cases consists essentially in determining the extra weight that is necessary to give the same ratio of right judgments to wrong judgments to the total number of judgments under the various conditions for which the sensitivity is compared. The degree of sensitivity under these different conditions is indicated by the reciprocal of this excess weight.

Doubtful cases should not be omitted but should be counted as belonging half to the right and half to the wrong cases.

One may try, given the true weight of one container on the scale as a standard, to match it by a comparison weight on the basis of judgment of the senses alone. In general, in making this judgment one misses by a certain amount. This error is found when the second container, which had been judged equal to the first, is eventually placed on a scale. On frequent repetition of this experiment many errors are obtained from which one can calculate an average error. We shall consider the reciprocal of the average error obtained in this way as the sensitivity for differences of weight. This is the method of average error (1966, pp. 60-61).

The three methods, representing three techniques of psychological experimentation, are used to derive the threshold value of a sensation, the first giving the upper threshold, the second the lower, and the third the intermediate. The first calls for ascertaining of minimal variations between two sensations by their just barely noticeable or observable differences from a uniform scale of stimuli. Applied to touch, this would mean the application of the two points of a compass to the skin and very gradually increasing or decreasing the interval distance between the two points until the slightest observable difference is noticed by the subject. By the second method, one ascertains how much of a constant discrepancy or difference exists between two points that escape the perception of the subject, i.e., without his noticing any difference between the two compass points. The third, or method of average error, is to take the doubtful cases in which the subject is uncertain (unable to distinguish clearly between the two compass points) and to ascertain from him which seems greater on the whole. On averaging, the right number will predominate over the erroneous ones because the interval will gradually approximate or tend toward a difference that is definitely discernible. Already used in astronomy, the method of average error was adapted by Fechner (in association with Volkmann) to apply to measuring tactual and visual sensations.

Evaluation of Fechner's Psychophysics. Fechner's psychophysics stirred considerable interest, both positive and negative. His creative contributions to psychology as a science have rarely been equalled, despite the disparaging comment of William James that his "law has been attacked on every hand; and as absolutely nothing practical has come of it, it need receive no farther [sic] notice here" (1892, p. 22). James felt that Fechner ignored the fact that "the many pounds which form the just perceptible addition to a hundredweight feel bigger when added than the few ounces which form the just perceptible addition to a pound" (1892, p. 22). Consequently each just perceptible addition to the sensation, which was assumed to be a unit of sensation is not equal to others, i.e., equally perceptible does not mean equally big.

Subsequent objections to Fechner's psychophysics fell into two categories: (1) those impugning the inner structure and questioning its results which include challenging Weber's law as to its validity and the method by which experiments were conducted; also questioned was the mathematical application by which the formula of measurements was derived; and (2) the more critical objection by those who claim that an evaluation produces results differing from Fechner's conclusions.

Even more than his law, Fechner's most significant contribution to psychology has been his methods of measurement. The method remained intact (though what is supposed to be measured was debatable) and has resulted in productive yields for psychological investigation.

WILHELM WUNDT (1832-1920):
Founder of Experimental Psychology

The Baden-born German physiologist, philosopher, and psychologist Wundt is the recognized founder of experimental psychology owing to his establishment of it as an independent science. After studying medicine at Tübingen, Heidelberg, and Berlin, he began lecturing at Heidelberg in 1857; a decade later at this institution he became the first to offer the course "physiological psychology." The lectures that he had started delivering in 1867 materialized into what some historians consider modern psychology's most important book, *Principles of Physiological Psychology,* the first half appearing in 1873 and the latter in 1874 during his career at Heidelberg. This book, the first psychological text and general handbook, underwent six editions from 1873 to 1911, and helped to establish psychology as an independent science.

Wundt, holder of both Ph.D. and M.D. degrees, was a laboratory assistant to Helmholtz prior to his professorial appointments. In 1874 he was elected Professor of Philosophy at the University of Zurich, but the following year resigned it for the same position at Leipzig, founding there the Institute for Experimental Psychology. His long tenure at Leipzig lasted until 1917, three years before his death. A prolific writer, Wundt wrote numerous books in the fields of physiology and philosophy as well as in psychology. His psychological interests were encompassing, engulfing social psychology and hypnotism in addition to physiological and experimental psychology.

Wundt's appointment was in philosophy and so was his journal, but he had made it a scientific philosophy as was his book, *System of Philosophy* (1889). Moreover he contributed to philosophy proper with his two volume *Logic* (1880-1883) and his *Ethics* (1886). Not limited to physiological psychology, his wide interests carried him into *Hypnotism and Suggestion* (1892) and to social psychology, the fruit of which was *Völkerpsychologie* (1900-1909), a natural history of social man. Thus in addition to the experimental method, Wundt also employed the historical.

Definition of Psychology. Defining psychology as the science of immediate experience *(Erfahrungswissenschaft),* Wundt held that physiology was the instrument for constructing a science of psychology.

> The point of view of natural science may, accordingly, be designated as that of *mediate experience,* since it is possible only after abstracting from the subjective factor present in all actual experience; the point of view of psychology, on the other hand, may be designated as that of *immediate experience,* since it purposely does away with this abstraction and all its consequences (1907, p. 3).

As a science, psychology investigates the facts of consciousness together with its relations and combinations in order to uncover the laws by which these relations and combinations are governed. Accordingly psychological investigation ''consists of the sum total of facts of which we are conscious'' (1912, p. 1). The elements of consciousness include sensation, memory, feelings, emotions, motives, and volitional processes.

Physiological psychology, a combination of physiology and psychology deals

> with facts of life at large, and in particular with the facts of human life. Physiology is concerned with all those phenomena of life that present themselves to us in sense perception as bodily processes, and accordingly form part of that total environment which we name the external world. Psychology, on the other hand, seeks to give account of the interconnexion of processes which are evinced by our own consciousness, or which we infer from such manifestations of the bodily life in other creatures as indicate the presence of a consciouness similar to our own (1904, p. 1).

This division, although possessing utilitarian value, is not genuine for the organism as a complex unitary being. But the division is a necessary one for the solution of scientific problems. Yet the dualist Wundt approached psychological data (which he considered phenomena) as a psychophysical parallelist, utilizing the method of introspection. Psychical processes are ascertained through introspection or inner sense. Psychology, as the science of immediate experience, does not distinguish between inner and outer experience since they are merely points of view for considering aspects of experience which are unitary in nature.

Exact observation, the only way to approach psychology, is experimental observation. The contents of psychological science are not permanent objects but *processes* exclusively. Exact investigation of these processes requires their control so that they may be varied at will through experimental techniques. Psychologists must ascertain which ''objective components of immediate experiencè are frequently repeated in connection with the same subject states'' (1907, p. 24).

They must investigate the rise and progress of subjective processes. But this is a difficult assignment since the intention to observe either modifies those facts under observation or suppresses them completely. Accordingly the two exact methods of psychology are the experimental and the observational. The task of the psychologist entails three problems.

> The *first* is the *analysis* of composite processes; the *second* is the *demonstration of the combinations* into which the elements discovered by analysis enter; the *third* is the *investigation of the laws* that are operative in the formation of such combinations (1907, p. 28).

The last calls for the examination of elements into compounds, and from compounds to interconnections, and from interconnections to developments so as to ascertain the actual composition of psychical processes and the discovery of psychical causes expressed in these processes.

Psychical Causality as Mental Law. According to the principle of psychophysical parallelism to which Wundt subscribed, the natural sphere (objective) and psychological sphere (subjective) correspond so that "every elementary process on the psychical side has a corresponding elementary process on the physical side" (1907, p. 364). This view has "empirico-psychological significance" in leading to the recognition of *independent psychical causality*. Psychical causality, arising from the sum total of psychical processes, is obtained by abstracting the *principles of psychical phenomena*, which are: (1) the principle of *psychical resultants*, (2) the principle of *psychical relations*, and (3) the principle of *psychical contrasts*. These laws are as important to psychology as the laws of physical phenomena are to the natural sciences, except that what is studied in psychology are the phenomena (not substances) of immediate experience.

The law of psychic resultants is a principle of creative synthesis in which the psychical phenomena are greater than the sum of the attributes of psychical elements. It is Wundt's version of John Stuart Mill's mental chemistry. The law of psychic relations is Wundt's rendition of the associationist theory of meaning and object. These two laws, psychic resultants and psychic relations, supplement each other, for the former maintains for synthetic processes of consciousness, and the latter for the analytic. The third principle deals with psychical phenomena which stand in contrast to each other.

Laws of Psychical Development. Wundt cited three laws of psychical development: (1) the law of *mental growth*, (2) the law of *heterogony of ends*, and (3) the law of *development toward opposites*. The three laws correspond respectively to the three laws of psychical phenomena. The first applies to the principle of resultants and deals with the continuity of psychical processes; the second, connected with the principle of relations (also with resultants), treats the "larger interconnections of psychical development;" and the third, applicable to the law of the intensification through contrast, is concerned with the "more comprehensive interconnections which form in themselves series of developments."

The Mind as Actuality: Wundt's Theory of Actuality. The human mind is not a passive substance, but an activity, an actuality, a process. In the natural sciences experience is mediate, whereas in psychology experience is "immediate and underived." Appreciating this distinction of the two phases of *one* experience, *"the concept of a mind substance* immediately gives place to *the concept of the actuality of mind* as a basis for the comprehension of psychical processes" (1907, p. 361). The mind is not a thing, a substantial entity, but an ongoing process, a phenomenal activity, a mental process that is active. In the same sense that matter is an indispensable concept to the natural sciences, mind is to psychological investigation. The concept of mind substance is rooted in mythology and metaphysics.

In contrast to the point of view of mind as substance, Wundt advanced an "actuality of mind" concept. "Mental processes are not transient appearance to which the soul stands in contradistinction as . . . permanent" (1912, p. 192); they are real with their own psychical laws, and do not require any substratum.

Our ideas, inasmuch as they are subjective, our feelings and our emotions are immediate experiences, which psychology tries to understand exactly in the way in which they arise, continue, and enter into relations with each other in consciousness. Therefore it is one and the same psycho-physical individual forming a unity, which physiology and psychology have as subject-matter. Each of these, however, views this subject-matter from a different standpoint. Physiology regards it as an object of external nature, belonging to the system of physical-chemical processes, of which organic life consists. Psychology regards it as the system of our experiences in consciousness. Now for every piece of knowledge two factors are necessary — the subject who knows and the object thought about, independent of this subject. The investigation of the subject in his characteristics, as revealed to us in human consciousness, forms therefore not only a necessary supplement to the investigations of natural science, but it also attains to a more universal importance, since all mental values and their development arise from immediately experienced processes of consciousness, and therefore can alone be understood by means of these processes. And this is exactly what we mean by the principle of the actuality of mind (1912, pp. 197-8).

Tridimensional Theory of Feeling. Contemporary factor analysis and its concomitant dimensional theory of personality had its forerunner in Wundt's tridimensional theory of feelings. Feelings vary with respect to three dimensions along a series or a continuum: (1) *pleasantness-unpleasantness,* (2) *strain-relaxation,* and (3) *excitement-calm.* Simple feelings as psychical elements vary in affective quality and intensity. In the center of each dimension is a neutral indifference-zone corresponding to the sensation of luke-warm, being that between hot and cold.

Three such chief dimensions may be distinguished (Fig. 1). We call them the series of *pleasurable* and *unpleasurable feelings* (ab) that of *arousing* and *subduing* feelings (cd) and finally that of feelings of *strain* and *relaxation* (ef). Any concrete feeling may belong to all of these dimensions, or it may belong to only two, or even to only one of them. The last mentioned possibility is all that makes it possible to distinguish the different directions. The fundamental feeling qualities can be represented in the form of a three-dimensional figure the central point (N, Fig. 1) of which is the indifference point. Three lines indicating the three dimensions of feeling pass through this indifference point. A given feeling may lie in one or more of these dimensions (1907, pp. 91-2).

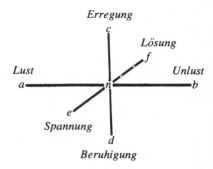

Fig. 1. The Feelings represented by a Three-dimensional System.

1. Erregung = exciting feeling.
2. Beruhigung = quieting feeling.
3. Lösung = feeling of relief.
4. Spannung = feeling of tension.
5. Lust = agreeable feeling.
6. Unlust = disagreeable feeling.

Feeling is related to *apperception* as being the "mark of the reaction of apperception upon sensory content." Apperception in turn is defined as a psychological process in which contents of consciousness come into clear comprehension.

In the simultaneous interconnection of consciousness, for example in a compound clang or in a series of spacial objects, certain *single* components are favored above the others. In both cases we designate the differences in the perception as differences in *clearness* and *distinctness*. Clearness is the relatively favorable comprehension of the object in itself, distinctness the sharp discrimination from other objects, which is generally connected with clearness. The state which accompanies the clear grasp of any psychical content and is characterized by a special feeling, we call *attention*. The process through which any such content is brought to clear comprehension we call *apperception*. In contrast with this, perception which is not accompanied by a state of attention, we designate *apprehension*. Those contents of consciousness upon which the attention is concentrated are spoken of, after the analogy of the external optical fixation-point, as the *fixation-point of consciousness,* or the *inner fixation-point*. On the other hand, the whole content of consciousness at any given moment is called the *field of consciousness*. When a psychical process passes into an unconscious state we speak of its *sinking below the threshold of consciousness* and when such a process arises we say it *appears above the threshold of consciousness* (1907, p. 208).

The concept of apperception acquired increasing importance for Wundt, especially as it became related to the theory of feelings in his later writings. While the theory of apperception did not adapt well to experimentation and observation, the theory of feeling to which it is related did. The concept of apperception derives from Leibniz, who spoke of unconscious perceptions *(petite perceptions)* as well as referring to obscure ideas in consciousness as perceptions, and clear ones as apperceptions. "We may say, then, that the perceived ideas are those which lie in the field of consciousness, while the apperceived are situated at its fixation-point'' (1894, p. 345). An object seen distinctly in the field of vision is apperceived. But apperception can refer to consciousness as a distinct perception.

Folk Psychology. In his *Elements of Folk Psychology* (1916), Wundt provided outlines of a psychological history of the development of mankind as his subtopic reads. The Germans Lazarus and Steinthal introduced the term *folk psychology* in the mid-nineteenth century. Writing at a time when folk psychology was in a relatively established position in psychology, Wundt theorized a social or collective mental life. Phenomena pertinent to folk psychology include "those mental products which are created by a community of human life and are, therefore, inexplicable in terms merely of individual consciousness" (1916, p. 3). Though his "creative synthesis," that new order of psychological synthesis, seems to be a factor, he never successfully extricated himself from his obsession with individual psychology, the upshot of his physiological and experimental psychology. Nevertheless, social phenomena exist in their own right with their own social origin, examples of which are language (which is definitely social in character and creation), myth, and custom, three important socio-psychological phenomena.

While individual psychology is principally experimental in method, the technique for studying folk psychology or social psychology is observational and historical, i.e., a "genetic" approach entailing man's historical development. Despite Wundt's espousal of a "collective consciousness," the product of a mystical type of creative synthesis, his folk psychology was based on individual psychology with a primacy of the individual over the social, i.e., the simple or individual being the foundation of the complex or social. Accordingly social psychology is reduced to individual psychology. Nevertheless, folk psychology, as was true of individual psychology, possessed its own peculiar phenomena for study, viz., language, myth, and custom, and consequently is defined by Wundt as the "study of the developmental principles of language, mythology, and custom."

The New Psychology. This new physiological psychology that was systematized and experimented upon by Wundt set an atmosphere of excitement in psychology, a freshness that stimulated numerous experiments that fructified into a proliferation of findings in psychology. What Wundt termed the "new psychology" quickly spread to the United States.

The great rivalry that existed between the universities of Leipzig and Berlin terminated with the death of Wundt in 1920. At this time gestalt psychology was ushered wholesale into the University of Berlin by Köhler who occupied its chair in 1922 and was acting Director of the Psychological Institute there in 1920.

MAX FREY (1852-1932):
Theory of Four Cutaneous Senses

With the introduction of Müller's doctrine of specific nerve energies, scientists became interested in its potentialities. Helmholtz applied it to specific senses and derived his remarkable findings. The application of specific nerve energies to psychology of sensation introduced by Müller and made fundamental by Helmholtz suggested that one should have as many different kinds of nerves as there are cutaneous sense qualities.

Researching this matter with respect to the cutaneous senses, three physiologists, investigating the sensory spots of the skin, independently arrived at their conclusions at approximately the same time. *Magnus Blix* published his finding on his experiments on cutaneous specific nerve energies in 1882, *Alfred Goldscheider* published his in Germany in 1884, and *Henry Herbert Donaldson* (1857-1938), a Johns Hopkins Ph.D. published his while teaching Psychology and Biology at his alma mater in 1885. But it was not until 1894 that the German physiologist Max von Frey fully demonstrated it. While Blix discovered sensitive spots for cold and warmth, Goldscheider found the same for pressure. Isolation of these spots indicated separate nerve endings. Although the two also had warrant for pain as a fourth sense, (pain spots being so clustered and numerous) it proved infeasible to locate cold, warm, and pressure spots that were insensitive to pain.

The classic theory of four cutaneous senses was advanced by Max Frey, who began at the University of Leipzig as a private instructor *(Dozent)* in 1882 and was elevated in 1891 (three years before his announced discovery) to *ausserordentlicher Professor*. While at Leipzig, he published (from 1894 to 1897) the papers for which he became prominent in psychology. He left for Zurich in 1898 but remained only a year before going on to Würzburg.

Although his predecessors disagreed with him, Frey defended his position of four cutaneous senses, pain as the fourth. He wrote:

> Pain is among that group of sensations that can be produced from the skin. It should be considered, like the cold, warm, and pressure sensations as a fundamental part of consciousness. Even though it often occurs in the presence of other sensations, it is not dependent on them and appears without them under certain circumstances. . . .
>
> The theory stated at the outset was that in every instance where different types of sensations can be produced in a seemingly uniform area different types of nerves and nerve endings are present (1968, pp. 154-5).

In addition to his contribution of pain as the fourth sense modality of the skin, Frey discovered a specific end-organ for each of the four modalities in 1895, and the following year found that in addition to force (stimulus pressure), tension (force per linear unity of the skin area that is depressed) is required.

No system of thought progresses without interruption or challenge. The same held true for Wundtian structuralism which dominated the psychology of the last quarter of the 19th century. The psychology at Leipzig encountered its direct antithesis in Austrian act psychology which set the stage for the beginnings of functionalism.

CHAPTER 6

The Würzburg School
of Imageless Thought

The Würzburg School as the Antithesis of Wundtian Structuralism. The orthodoxy of Wundt, the "founder of experimental psychology," met with reactions on many fronts, the Würzburg school being one of them. Though Külpe's cry for freedom was not intended as a revolt, it tended toward if not fostered the functionalism that proved to be the very antithesis of Wundtian structuralism. While he never left elementarism and embraced content with act, Külpe's systematic experimental introspectionism resulted in functionalism. After all, if Ebbinghaus successfully experimented with memory as a higher mental process, why could not there be other higher thought processes that could be successfully introduced into laboratory experimentation? Whereas the two men shared introspective methodology, Wundt's subjects had advance notice as to what they were expected to observe, while Külpe's did not. The principle issue was the elevation of sophistication of the method of introspection so as to include higher mental processes, rather than restricting it to an analysis of the basic structure of consciousness. The result was a movement of transition from an elemental psychology to a functional one, one of thought processes yielding *imageless thought* (nonsensory mental life) instead of elements of images and the like. Some writers even trace American functionalism to the Würzburg school through James Rowland Angell, an influential member of the functional movement in the United States.

The original University of Würzburg, founded in 1402, which lasted only a few years and was re-established in 1582, is like the University of Frankfurt, situated on the Main River, and only 60 miles southeast of Frankfurt. The medical faculty, at this traditionally Roman Catholic stronghold, is its most famous. It was here that the Nobel prize winning German physicist Wilhelm Konrad Roentgen (1845-1923) discovered X-rays in 1895, called Roentgen rays. In the late 1950s, the university attracted almost 3300 students.

OSWALD KÜLPE (1862-1915):
Founder of the Würzburg School of Imageless Thought

The German psychologist and philosopher, Külpe, born in Candau (Kandava), Latvia, attended the universities of Leipzig, Berlin, Göttingen, and Dorpat before returning to Leipzig where he received his Ph.D. in 1887. At each of these universities he spent from one to three semesters (a common practice of that time), studying psychology, philosophy, and history. Apparently he sought to find himself or the study best suited for him. At Leipzig he came under Wundt's influence and later dedicated his important book in psychology to him in 1893,

Grundriss der Psychologie auf experimenteller Grundlage dargestelt (translated by Titchener as *Outlines of Psychology: Based upon the Results of Experimental Investigation*). Despite having his appetite whetted for psychology and philosophy by Wundt at Leipzig, he left for Berlin, Göttingen, and Dorpat. Nevertheless, he returned to Leipzig in 1886, obtaining his doctorate the following year. With G. E. Müller, he spent three semesters at Göttingen where he initially began his dissertation on feeling, *Zur Theorie der sinnlichen Gefühle* (1887), but the dissertation was presented for acceptance at Leipzig; it was not, however, Wundt but Müller to whom he expressed appreciation.

At Leipzig he remained eight years as a private instructor, as Wundt's second assistant (when his first assistant, Cattell, left for the United States), and in 1894 as extraordinary professor. But that year he left for Würzburg to accept a full professorship. It was here that his fame generated owing to the founding of a psychological laboratory (in 1896) in which his students were to perform such significant and novel experiments as commanded the attention of the psychological world. Research conducted by his students at the Würzburg laboratory led to the expression, "the Würzburg school."

From Würzburg Külpe went to Bonn in 1909, investing fifteen years at Würzburg and four years at Bonn before going on to Munich, building laboratories in all three places thereby propagating the new psychology in Germany more than any other of Wundt's students. Külpe's premature death in Munich during World War I resulted from influenza while calling on wounded German soldiers. Many distinguished students studied under Külpe, among them being the founder of gestalt psychology, Max Wertheimer, who received his Ph.D under Külpe at the University of Würzburg.

Külpe at Leipzig. The Külpe before Würzburg was a psychologist primarily interested in content psychology, with functional psychology and imageless thought a matter for future realization. There was no mention of act psychology, imageless thought, or abstraction when his *Outlines of Psychology* was published in 1893 at Leipzig. In it he defined "psychology as the science of the *facts of experience*," an inductive science whose peculiar "property is the dependency of facts of experience upon experiencing individuals" (1909, p. 2). In his *Introduction to Philosophy*, which first appeared in 1895 and was subtitled "a handbook for students of psychology, logic, ethics, aesthetics and general philosophy," he defined psychology as the "science of those elements in pure, primitive experience which depend upon corporeal experiencing subjects" (1915, p. 62). The *Grundriss* or *Outlines of Psychology* took its departure from the definition of experience offered by Richard Avenarius and Ernst Mach *(Analysis of Sensations,* 1886). However, Külpe believed that he was the first to offer an exposition of psychology from this standpoint in his *Outlines of Psychology*.

> For the developed consciousness, as for the naïve, every experience is an unitary whole; and it is only habit of abstract reflection upon experience that makes the objective and subjective worlds seem to fall apart as originally different forms of existence. Just as a plane curve can be represented in analytical geometry as the function of two variables,

_the abscissae and the ordinates, without prejudice to the unitary course of the curve itself, so the world of human experience may be reduced to a subjective and an objective without prejudice to its real coherence (1915, p. 59).

While Mach and Avenarius contributed the notion of ''experience,'' Külpe tied experience to the experiencing individual so that psychology became the ''science of the facts-of-experience in their dependence upon experiencing individuals.''

Like his teacher Wundt, his book treats the elements of consciousness (sensations and feelings) before moving to the connections of conscious elements (fusion and colligation), his special contribution to the psychology of that period. Though he concluded with a study of attention, will, and self-consciousness as states of consciousness, he dismissed will as if an afterthought.

After discussing fusion of auditory sensation and visual sensation, he treated colligation, another form of spatial and temporal combination.

We should suppose a priori that the mode of interconnection of simple contents would not always be the same. And we can, as a matter of fact, distinguish two principal modes: *fusion* and *colligation*. The former is a more close and intimate connection than the latter. Fusion occurs when the connecting qualities are thrust more or less into the background by the total impression which results from their connection,—when, that is, all or sundry of them lose in distinctness by combination. The total impression itself may be, as it were, the resultant of a balance of qualities, or may be dominated by one or more preponderant elements. A simultaneous connection of tones may stand as a typical example of fusion. Colligation occurs, on the other hand, when the cognisability of the separate qualities is either unaffected by combination, so that they retain their original independence, or is actually increased. The formation of a single qualitative impression is in this case more or less obstructed by the persistent individuality of the elementary constituents. Simultaneous colour contrast (the spatial combination of different colour sensations) may serve as a typical instance of colligation (1909, pp. 20-1).

Imageless thought was completely absent from this book, yet on it depended Külpe's reputation for posterity as far as any major contribution of any consequence to the content of psychology was concerned.

The Functional Psychology of Külpe. Despite his reverent respect for Wundt, Külpe, when he left Wundt in Leipzig for Würzburg, left more than Wundt behind; he also shed his content psychology as well for functional psychology. Not content, but function acquired importance together with the study of higher thought processes, the influential product of which was the school of imageless thought for which the Würzburg school is known in the history of psychology.

The philosophical position of Külpe and his psychological stance went hand in hand, for epistemology was a basic concern. Opposed to both naive realism and idealism alike, the critical realist Külpe felt that the results of his introspective experiments were antagonistic toward the efforts of Ernst Mach and Richard Avenarius who reduced mental processes to sensations. Earlier Külpe was a Machian positivist, but with maturity he abandoned it. He also objected to Berkeley's premise ''to be is to be perceived'' because he distinguished apprehension from both sensation and phenomena. In one type of experiment (apparently influenced in part by Ebbinghaus) in which he offered nonsense syllables of varied arrangements and colors to subjects, Külpe instructed them to report what they observed with respect to one of three variables: pattern, color, or number. Because each subject isolated his own particular interest from the rest and thereby was unaware of the other factors that the cards contained, Külpe reasoned that the *process of abstraction* is contingent upon the subject's apprehension as well as the actual material confronting him.

Discovering abstraction to be a mental function or act that is not subject to direct observation, yet factually evident and retrospectively discoverable, Külpe was led to desert the content psychology of sense for a functional psychology or act psychology. Abstraction, though unobservable directly, is a genuine mental act or function. Consequently *thought processes* exist as well as *thought contents*. Thought processes, nonmaterial acts of thinking, judging, and meaning, are the ego's activities by which actualities of consciousness are transformed into realities, and are not to be dismissed as mere relations among contents. Külpe's distaste for idealism that purports objects are contingent upon consciousness for their existence stems from investigations with respect to egg maturation in which processes occur despite the absence of consciousness. Continuity of development of this nature, an assumption of all sciences, indicates an object's genuine reality whether or not it is consciously present in the mind of a person.

Accordingly Külpe was espousing a dualistic psychology of (1) content, i.e., sensation, and (2) act, i.e., awareness. Machian positivism bewitched Külpe into ushering thought *(unanschauliche Bewusstheit,* the impalpable awareness that in the United States acquired the expression "imageless thought") into the laboratory of psychology for the purpose of subjecting it to direct observation. Caught in the current of the times, Külpe like Freud was investigating unconscious processes.

The Premise of the Würzburg School. It was seen that the mind is capable of abstracting, an act or function that is not subject to direct observation, yet a genuine thought process characterized by impalpable or nonmaterial acts such as thinking and meaning. *Awareness (Bewusstheit)* too was a function, an impalable or imageless content of consciousness, that is, awareness can pertain to meanings of highly abstract terms despite the fact that the words per se are the only perceptible entities.

Meanings are genuine experiences with their own objectivity, independent of the symbols, words, and signs that connote them. Access to this realm of meanings is through retrospective acts. By mental acts meanings are known. Intentionality inheres in the acts of meaning so that they are directed to external objects (atoms, God, etc.). For thought to pertain to that which is independent of it, it is necessary to possess the ability for imageless thought. That the phenomenology of Edmund Husserl and Franz Brentano has penetrated the psychology of Külpe is quite apparent.

Psychology of Esthetics. At Würzburg Külpe's title was Professor of Philosophy and Esthetics, hence his interest in esthetics. In his *Grundlagen der*

Aesthetik (Elements of Esthetics) posthumously published in 1921, he developed a system of esthetics designed to verify the findings of Fechner. Esthetic pleasure was for him as it was for his teacher Wundt, ideally proportioned objects resulting from mental economy. When the whole in relation to its larger part possesses the same ratio as the larger part to the smaller, then it is perceived with the highest degree of diversity but with the smallest expended effort.

Experimenting on esthetic experience as did Fechner before him, Külpe studied the reactions of people as they viewed artistic work on slides. While his research (in contrast to Theodor Lipps' empathy theory of esthetic enjoyment) found sympathetic empathy absent in his subjects, his students, experimenting with what they considered attractive, found a relationship between form, orderliness, harmony, and symmetry. The results of Külpe's experiments are difficult to interpret if not of questionable validity owing to the absence of esthetically inexperienced subjects, persons whose responses could conceivably be quite different.

THE WÜRZBURG SCHOOL (1901 to 1909): (Mayer; Orth; Marbe; Watt; Ach; Messer; and Buhler)

Constituency of the Würzburg School. The Würzburg school is more a product of Külpe's students or junior members of his department and their experiments than anything else. But not until he arrived at the University of Würzburg as full professor did the famous Würzburg school of imageless thought generate. The members include: the Emerschausen-born *Narziss Ach* (1871-1946), who received an M.D. and Ph.D. from the University of Würzburg; of German descent but Paris-born, *Karl Marbe* (1869-1953), who obtained his Ph.D. from the University of Leipzig before joining the faculty at Würzburg as private instructor, being elevated to ordinary professor in 1909, the year Külpe left the University of Würzburg. He succeeded Külpe at Würzburg. When Marbe was at Leipzig, Külpe was a *Privatdozent* there, acting as first assistant in the Leipzig Institute. The two became friends so when Külpe left for Würzburg he took Marbe along with him, hoping to establish a psychological institute.

Born in Meckesheim (Baden), *Karl Buhler* (1879-1963) received an M.D. from the University of Strassburg before attending Berlin and Bonn for his Ph.D., affiliating himself with Würzburg in 1907 as a *Privatdozent,* but leaving with Külpe in 1909. He left for the universities of Bonn, then Munich prior to his professorship at Vienna in 1922.

Others in the Würzburg school were *Henry Jackson Watt* (1879-1925), who became a lecturer in Sherrington's department at Liverpool in 1906, but the following year left for the University of Glasgow for his final tenure as Lecturer in Psychology where he promoted experimental psychology. The musically gifted Watt experimented in the psychology of hearing, publishing his *The Psychology of Sound* in 1917. *Otto Selz* (1881-1944) contributed his psychology of thinking in two volumes, one in 1913 and another in 1922, titled *Die Gesetze des geordneten Denkverlaufs*. The Belgian phenomenological psychologist *Albert Michotte* (1881-1965) was attracted to the Würzburg school by Külpe and went there during the 1907-1908 school year. Michotte, after discovering the works of Brentano, Mach, Meinong, Husserl, Stumpf, von Ehrenfels, and others at Würzburg, established his own school at the University of Louvain, structuring it after the model of the Würzburg school. Close to the phenomenology of Katz and Rubin, he expressed indebtedness to Külpe:

> I was perfectly happy in Würzburg, experiencing a true revelation. Indeed it is to Külpe that I owe my real maturation as a psychologist, not only because of my personal contacts with him and my participation in his seminar and his investigations, but also because it was through him that I discovered the works of Brentano, Mach, Meinong, Husserl, Stumpf, von Ehrenfels and others (1952, pp. 214-5).

Birth of the Würzburg School. Külpe disagreed with Wundt that *thought* was an improper subject for psychological experimentation, and he was anxious to bring it within the scope of the laboratory. The closest experiments to it were the memory experiments that Ebbinghaus successfully conducted in which he subjected *higher mental processes* to the experimental method. Külpe pondered as to whether the processes of thought could also be dealt with experimentally in the laboratory. Consequently he assigned his students subjects related to the psychology of thought for experimental purposes. The positivist Külpe viewed science as empirical with observation its method. The Würzburg program was an undertaking of "the experimental psychology of the thought processes," as Titchener (1909) put it. Actually the school was under the impression that it was investigating a new kind of mental process.

Mayer and Orth on the Qualitative Study of Association (1901). The Würzburg school of imageless thought, higher mental processes, or higher thought processes, is generally traced to 1901, the year A. Mayer and J. Orth published their paper on the qualitative nature of association, *Zur qualitativen Untersuchung der Associationen* (Qualitative Investigation of Associations). The two employed a word method for the qualitative study of association. The course of thought, being a series of associations, should respond to investigation by the method of introspection. The upshot of the study was that a person's response is contingent upon his conscious attitude with its affective overtones. Internal as well as external responses are factors in a person's response.

> Orth, for instance, observed that the word *mustard* touched off a peculiar process which he thought might be characterized as the "suggestion of a familiar form of expression." Then came the associated word *grain*. In all such cases the observer was unable to find in consciousness the least trace of the ideas which he afterwards employed in his report to describe the facts of experience. All these conscious processes we shall conclude, despite their evident and often total differences of quality, under the single name of conscious attitudes. The introspective records show that the conscious attitudes were sometimes affectively toned, sometimes completely indifferent (1901, p. 1).

Bewusstseinslage (conscious attitude or conscious set), introduced by Marbe, became the important topic for experimentation with the Würzburg school.

Marbe's Experimental Study of Judgment (1901). The year that produced

Mayer and Orth's paper saw the publication of Marbe's *Experimentellpsychologische Untersuchungen über das Urteil* (Experimental Investigations of the Psychology of Judgment) in 1901. Two years later Binet's *Experimental Study of Intellect* (1903) appeared. Although logic was widely studied and many psychologists taught and wrote treatises on the matter, amazingly this was the first time it was approached psychologically and empirically.

What attracted Marbe was the fact that widely discrepant opinions were held by logicians on the psychological nature of logic. Accordingly Marbe established conditions under which judgments could be made and accounts of these conscious processes rendered as the judging process transpired. The conclusion was that there is no psychological criterion of judgment. The simple mathematical judgments (e.g., 2 + 7 = 9) were reflexively or automatically given.

Marbe was interested in ascertaining "what experiences must supervene upon a conscious process in order to raise it to the rank of a judgment" (1901, p. 15). As a result, the observer was placed in a situation enabling him to experience different kinds of mental processes in their passage to judgments, and then it was required of him "to report what concomitant experiences supervened upon those processes, and endowed them with the character of judgment" (1901, p. 15).

The experiment called for the observer to lift two different weights (of the same size and shape) with the same hand to the same height and then invert the one that was heavier. It was to the subject's "consciousness, a judgment." The subject reported his conscious processes experienced because it might prove interesting to learn what "conscious processes introduced the act of judgment." "No psychological conditions of the judgment" are disclosed by introspection despite the prevalence of conscious content such as images, sensations, and the course of association. Though conscious content was plentiful, the elements of consciousness played no essential role in the process of judgment. Consequently the judgments of consciousness are correct psychologically, and often objectively, though the observer is unaware of the process. The findings were devastating. For centuries it was assumed that judgments were conscious processes in which the image of the first object was associated with the image of the second in order to draw a conclusion. Marbe's experiment revealed no image, hence *imageless thought*. Judgment with respect to weights is contingent upon muscular contraction in relation to the objective heaviness of the thing lifted, an experience familiar to anyone who has suddenly lifted an empty box expecting it to be loaded with heavy books.

Marbe on "Conscious Set." Marbe's experiment led to the concept of *Bewusstseinslage* (conscious set or conscious attitude). He found that it was inadequate to reduce conscious life to Wundtian elements such as sense perceptions, memory images, and feelings as was generally practiced at the time. He introduced the conscious set of doubt, uncertainty, expectation, surprise, agreement, recognition, and other conscious sets. Wundtian feelings became conscious sets as are the recollections of conversations.

It was Marbe's treatise that prompted Külpe to assign Messer and Watt topics in the experimental psychology of thought. The opening of the century saw a rapid succession of experimental studies on the psychology of thought: in 1904 Watt's *Experimental Contributions to a Theory of Thought;* in 1905 Ach's *Volition and Thought;* and in 1906 Messer's *Experimental Investigation of the Psychology of Thought.* Each of these men employed the Hipp chronoscope and its accessories.

Watt's Experimental Contributions to a Theory of Thought (1904). In the method of associative reaction, the technique employed by Watt, the subject responded to familiar terms (visuálly presented) to be associated with a reaction word. At the conclusion of the experiment the subject reported the contents of his experience. Watt was interested in dealing with thought per se rather than conscious experience as Marbe was. Six series of associations were required of the subject, including associating the stimulus word displayed before him in writing with a superordinate, coordinate, or subordinate idea, or with a whole, part, or another part of a common whole.

. Utilizing a Hipp chronoscope to ascertain an accurate reaction time, Watt then introduced *fractionation* into introspective method to cope with the required lengthy verbal description of everything that occurred in a fleeting conscious moment, resulting in the inability to recall all that rapidly happened.

Consequently he divided consciousness into four stages:

> Series were taken with all the observers, in which they were instructed to make a particular stage of the course of reaction the object of an especially carefully observation. It seemed best to mark off four of these stages: the preparation for the experiment, the appearance of the stimulus-word, the search for a reaction-word (if such search occurred), and lastly the cropping-up of the reaction-word (1904, p. 316).

He found that subjects introspected better when restricted to a single phase or period of the complicated process. The preparatory stage of undertaking the problem or task *(Aufgabe)* provided the key to the thought process. If the subject accepted the task in the preparatory stage, the thought process would proceed facilely on seeing the stimulus word. The results indicated that one's thinking transpiring during the flow of consciousness occurs without his realization. Provided there is proper preparation, thought proceeds automatically; when it does, there is virtually no content. Thought was imageless, devoid of describable mental content.

Ach's Volition and Thought (1905). Ach is credited with three contributions to the Würzburg school: (1) systematic experimental introspection *(systematische experimentelle Selbstbeobachtung),* (2) the determining tendency, and (3) awareness *(Bewusstheit).* Systematic experimental introspection, which was to become the Würzburg school's slogan, expresses the objectives of the Würzburg experimenters well: *systematic* pertaining to "fractionation" of Watt, *experimental* pertaining to the techniques used such as the chronoscope, and *instrospection* the method employed. Ach's fractionation has three periods: a fore, a mid, and an after period. The fore period extends from the signal time to the stimulus, the mid or principal period covers the experience expressly intended by the experiment, and the after period is that indefinite period of time of several minutes duration immediately following the termination of the experiment. The fore and mid periods are introspectively examined during the after period when something of the sort of memory after-images are experienced.

Ach's treatment of the psychology of thought entails an analysis of voluntary action, and he was the first seriously to attempt the development of a psychology of volition based on systematic experimental introspection. The *awareness* of which Ach spoke is a conscious content, an imageless one, comparable to Orth's "conscious attitude." The *determining* tendency is the term used to convey the unconscious manner in which the initial problem of task *(Aufgabe)* proceeds to its intended objective. Thus it is "mental set." For this operatiòn Watt employed Müller's *perseverative tendencies.* The determining tendency reinforces associative ones so that if one's preparatory task has been one of addition, then on observing 3, 3, and 3, his association would be 9, rather that 333 or 27 (3x3x3), etc.

Messer's Experimental Investigation of the Psychology of Thought (1906). During a summer semester at Würzburg in 1905, August Wilhelm Messer (1867-1937) undertook the psychology of thought experimentally by employing the method of free and constrained associations introduced by Watt. As well as possessing mental impressions, the minds of his subjects experienced cognitive and emotional attitudes. Continuing and extending Watt's experimental technique, Messer, unlike his predecessors, had no clearcut program in mind but rambled from experiment to experiment incoherently and lacking direction.

Nevertheless his paper, a huge source of introspective data, is in a sense the most valuable. The *conscious attitudes* of Messer compare with Külpe's "imageless thought," Marbe's "purpose," Watt's "task," Ach's "awareness."

Buhler's Facts and Problems of the Psychology of Thought-Processes (1907). The first portion of Buhler's *Facts and Problems of the Psychology of the Thought-Processes* titled "On Thoughts," appeared in 1907. In order to solve the problem of what people are experiencing when they are thinking, he made his subjects think by reading Nietzsche or some other author to them or by posing a question that had a "yes" or "no" answer, such as: Do you agree that to give every man his own were to will justice and to achieve chaos? The stop watch is used, starting with the stimulus (question) and ending with the reply (yes or no answer). The subject describes his experience, once he has answered.

Buhler's technique, which employs six different types of questions, is termed the *Ausfragemethode,* the method of finding out by asking questions, a method condemned by Wundt as a travesty of the experimental procedure. Buhler's findings yielded thoughts as either imageless or imagery but devoid of sense content, feelings, and attitudes; yet they were clear, vivid, and assuring.

A judgment differs from a conception in that its object is a relation. Moreover "in the act of judgment we take up an attitude towards the subject matter. The specific character of this attitude is conviction, *certainty''* (1930, pp. 126-7). Repetitious sentences lacking conviction are not judgments. Inasmuch as true conviction has reasons, certainty must be based on reasons.

Evaluation of the Würzburg School. With Külpe's tenure at the University of Würzburg terminating in 1909, the school of thought (but not its influence) came to an end. Not only did Wundt criticize the school, but it met opposition both internally and externally. Some of the observers such as E. Dürr (one time assistant of Wundt) were also critical. Wundt held that it was impossible to experiment upon thought. Among the severest strictures were those from the structuralist E. B. Titchener, who devoted two chapters to the school in 1909. The determining tendency was aspersed by G. E. Müller, who dismissed it as mere perseveration.

More than criticism of this nature, others generated a controversy regarding the genuine proprietors and initiators of imageless thought, Binet in France claiming to have introduced it in his *Experimental Study of Intellect* published in 1903. Earlier Stout had argued for the presence in consciousness of imageless thought in his *Analytic Psychology* (1896), which appeared earlier than the publications of the Würzburg school. Woodworth had independently arrived at the same notion in America.

The importance of the Würzburg school is not so much the content or findings of their psychological investigations, as their influence, the new course upon which psychology was set, i.e., the path of function, process, or act psychology. Their discovery of impalpable functions established valid approaches to psychology other that Wundt's criterion of mental content. Brentano's mental acts received support as did all process psychology, accordingly the Würzburg school served as a transition from elemental psychology to act, functional, or process psychology. The introduction of Gestalt psychology also was facilitated, owing to the Würzburg orientation: synthetic rather than analytic; and holistic rather than elementistic (Wundt) or atomistic (associationists).

CHAPTER 7

Göttingen: Transition to Phenomenological Psychology

The City of Göttingen and Its University

The city of Göttingen, a manufacturing one that was first mentioned in the tenth century, is located in West Germany on the Leine River. A South Lower Saxon state, it was in the time of Müller and Husserl a town in the Prussian province of Hanover. The celebrated Georgia Augusta University of Göttingen was founded by George II in 1734, opening its doors three years later in 1737.

In less than a century it had over 1500 students, but the number was cut in half overnight, as it were, with the expulsion in 1837 of seven distinguished professors owing to their protesting the revocation of a liberal constitution. *Die Göttingen Sieben* as they were called included: the physicist brother of E. H. Weber, Wilhelm Eduard Weber (1804-1891); the historian Friedrich Christoph Dahlmann (1785-1860); the semanticist Georg Heinrich August Ewald (1803-1873) whose forced retirement resulted from refusing to swear an oath of allegiance to the Prussian king; a Germanist, Wilhelm Eduard Albrecht (1800-1876); another historian Georg Gottfried Gervinus (1805-1875); and two philologist brothers who are popularly known for the famous *Grimm's Fairy Tales* (1816-1818), Jacob Ludwig Karl Grimm (1785-1863) and Wilhelm Karl Grimm (1786-1859). J. L. K. Grimm, in his *Deutsche Grammatik* (1819-1837), is also known for the philological law named after him, Grimm's law. Karl Friedrich Gauss, known for the Gaussian curve, was also a distinguished member of this university. The town of Göttingen acquired importance owing to its university which indirectly benefited from the events of 1848, such as a large and valuable acquisition of books, manuscripts, zoological and mineralogical collection. When Müller was there in 1903 the university had a teaching staff of 121 and a student body numbering 1529; it had faculties in philosophy (including psychology), law, theology, medicine, and agriculture. Student enrollment in more recent years was between six and seven thousand; in 1968 the university had 6467 students.

The Transition to Phenomenology

The chair of psychology was occupied successively by Herbart, Lotze, and Müller from 1833 to 1921. Though he did not chair psychology, Husserl's influence was felt there from 1901 to 1916. It was during the Husserlian period at Göttingen that psychology strongly turned in the direction of phenomenology, including Müller's orientation, and especially is this true of their students.

Although Müller and his students are given credit for phenomenology at Göttingen, the lasting force for phenomenology stems from the efforts of Husserl both during and subsequent to his tenure at Göttingen. The entire phenomenological movement and the *Yearbook for Phenomenology and Phenomenological Research* belong essentially to Husserl as an undertaking. Müller's students could not have been ignorant of what was transpiring in Husserl's classes, and the spill over of his phenomenology is in evidence. The historian of phenomenology, Herbert Spiegelberg, commented:

> To recapture today the intellectual atmosphere of the Göttingen psychology during the period of Husserl's unfolding phenomenology is no longer possible. What is clear is that, rejected by most of his colleagues, Husserl nevertheless exerted an increasing attraction of the new generation of students, especially the circle which around 1910 became organized in the Göttingen Philosophische Gesellschaft. But it must be realized that this group was by no means "orthodox." Specifically, they did not follow Husserl in the direction of his emerging transcendental phenomenology, with its emphasis on the "reduction" and its incipient idealism. To this group Husserl was primarily the liberator from traditional theories, who invited them to go "to the things" directly and to describe them as they saw them. It must also be realized that at that time the only book of Husserl's available to them in print was his *Logische Untersuchungen* (1972, p. 40).

Though the group was not under Husserl's direction, his inspiration was a factor. A reciprocal influence was felt, with Müller's students coming under the sway of Husserl's phenomenology and Husserl's students sensing Müller's influence. At least each was aware of the other's efforts and objectives. Husserlian phenomenologists participating in experiments conducted at the psychological laboratory at Göttingen include Alexandre Koyré, Jean Hering, and Heinrich Hofmann; presumably they must have carried with them the phenomenology of Husserl. It is not surprising therefore that experimental psychologists such as Erich Jaensch, David Katz, and Edgar Rubin who gravitated to the Göttingen psychological laboratory (because of its prominence in psychological circles at the time) also figured as carriers of the new phenomenological approach to psychological investigation of an experimental nature.

Owing to tension arising between Müller and Husserl, relationships of a personal nature between Müller's experimental psychologists and Husserl were probably strained and minimal. Nevertheless Husserl's influence did penetrate and infiltrate Müller's psychological laboratory. Even if Husserl did not provide the experimental psychologists with their experimental ideas, he probably did serve in the capacity of some sort of catalytic agent.

Although Katz did not participate in any special way in the Philosophische Gesellschaft (Philosophical Society), he did attend the lectures and seminars of Husserl as did Jaensch. In addition to attending Husserl's seminar during the 1905-1906 season, Jaensch corresponded with him from 1906 to 1922.

Katz reported that Rubin

> like other experimental psychologists, was deeply impressed by the phenomenological viewpoint, which at that time had pervaded the scientific atmosphere of Göttingen as a consequence of the spell cast by the ideas of Husserl. This outlook became apparent in his chief work (1951, p. 387).

Another Göttingen psychologist, the Hungarian *Géza Révész* (1878-1955), attended Husserl's lectures, with the phenomenological influence being evident in his *Phänomenologie der Empfindungsreihen* (Phenomenology of the Series of Sensations, 1907) and his two volume work on the sense of touch, *Die Formenwelt des Tastsinnes* (The Forms of the World of the Sense of Touch, 1937). As were his fellow students, *Révész* also was in attendance at the lectures of Husserl. Another of Husserl's students at Göttingen, *Wilhelm Schapp* (1884-1969) contributed to phenomenology by way of a dissertation, *Beiträge zur Phänomenologie der Wahrnehmung* (Contributions to the Phenomenology of Perception), published in 1910 and revised in 1925. Husserl, however, received credit from Schapp.

(A) THE MAKING OF PSYCHOLOGY AT GÖTTINGEN: HERBART, LOTZE, G. E. MÜLLER

The chair of psychology at the University of Göttingen was made famous by the succession of three distinguished psychologists: *Johann Friedrich Herbart* (1776-1841), *Rudolf Hermann Lotze* (1817-1881), and *Georg Elias Müller* (1850-1934). Lotze, who succeeded Herbart, and Müller, who succeeded Lotze, were both trained at the University of Leipzig. The Institute of Göttingen, in constant need of finances, was facetiously referred to by Müller as "the last stronghold of old Prussian parsimony." During Müller's tenure, the insufficient budget reduced the psychological laboratory to the state of a "poorhouse" rather than a laboratory for research. On occasion the water bill was paid by Müller out of his own pocket. Like the chief of staff of a hospital, Müller made daily rounds to obtain dissertation reports from his students, not a single dissertation published without Müller himself being a subject. Müller aspired to establishing psychology at Göttingen with the reputation it enjoyed at Leipzig under Wundt. Even if he did not succeed in matching Wundt's psychological laboratory, he established one second only to that at Leipzig.

Origin of Mathematical Psychology. Réné Descartes (1596-1650) in his search for certitude during the Renaissance found it in mathematics, which he aspired to apply to philosophy in order to gain exactness for that discipline as well, but it remained for another continental rationalist, *Benedict Spinoza* (1632-1677), to apply the Cartesian geometric method with some success to philosophy. In this same spirit and tradition, Herbart applied mathematics to psychology with remarkable success, thus establishing it as a mathematically exact science.

JOHANN FRIEDRICH HERBART (1776-1841): First Mathematical Psychologist

The German philosopher, psychologist, and pedagogue, Herbart, was born in Oldenburg and studied under Fichte at Jena. For four years, beginning in 1805, he lectured at Göttingen before succeeding Kant at Königsberg at the age of 33, spending virtually a quarter of a century at that university, where he instituted a seminary of pedagogy. In 1833 he returned to the University of Göttingen, remaining there for the rest of his life. Rather than Kant, it was Leibniz who influenced him.

His contributions to psychology include: (1) the publication in 1816 of the first textbook in psychology, *Lehrbuch zur Psychologie* (translated as *A Text-Book in Psychology: An Attempt to Found the Science of Psychology on Experience, Metaphysics, and Mathematics);* (2) grounding psychology on a mathematical basis; (3) establishing psychology as a science; (4) repudiating mental faculties; (5) establishing psychology on an empirical basis; (6) developing concepts such as apperceptive mass, threshold of consciousness, and the unconscious; and (7) applying psychology to education. Nevertheless Herbart did not view psychology as experimental, analytical, descriptive or physiological, but rather as empirical, mathematical, mechanical, metaphysical, and dynamic.

Representing the transition of speculative or philosophical psychology (epitomized by Kant, Fichte, and Hegel) to the new psychology (the experimental psychology of Fechner, Helmholtz, and Wundt), Herbart, however, had followers, among them being Friedrich E. Beneke, the empirical psychologist from Berlin; Moritz W. Drobisch (1802-1896) from Leipzig; the first social psychologists Lazarus and Steinthal; and the German philosopher and anthropologist, *Theodor Waitz* (1813-1886), who attempted to base his neo-Herbartian philosophy on psychology.

Apperceptive Mass. The Swiss educational reformer, *Johann Heinrich Pestalozzi* (1746-1827), who sought to implement the pedagogical ideas of Rousseau, emphasized sense perception *(Anschauung)* but failed to note what was responsible for the viability of sense perception, viz., *apperception.* When an object is presented to the senses, explained Herbart, it is *perceived,* but when the new features of its details are identified so that it is recognized, explicated, and interpreted, owing to one's previous accumulation of knowledge enabling him to proceed from the known to the unknown and thereby accumulate still more acquisitions such as classifying it, generalizing concerning it, and relating it, then the object is said to be *apperceived.* It is apperception then that augments one's knowledge. New clues are gained from the apperceptive experience. It is the accumulation of one's past experiences into a unified and coherent whole, an *apperceptive mass.*

> Every new act of perception must work as an excitant by which some will be arrested, others called forward and strengthened. . . . These manifestations must become more complex if, as is usual, the concept received by the new act of perception contains in itself a multiplicity or variety, that at the same time enables it to hold its place in several combinations and series, and gives them a fresh impulse which brings them into new relations of opposition or blending with one another. . . .
>
> Weaker concepts . . . enter into consciousness, act as excitants upon those masses . . . , and are received and appropriated by them (apperceived) just as in the case of a new sense-impression. . . .
>
> The apperceived concepts do not continue rising or sinking according to their own

laws, but they are interrupted in their movements by the more powerful masses which drive back whatever is opposed to them although it is inclined to rise. . . .

The apperceiving mass may be, in its turn apperceived by another mass; but for this to occur, there must be present several concept masses of distinct different degrees of strength (1891, pp. 30-2).

Apperception and apperceptive mass are the Herbartian supplanting of Locke's association of ideas. They constitute his theory of association. From Leibniz he acquired the theory of the monadic soul, apperception, *petites perceptions,* and the unconscious. *Apercevoir* is the French for to perceive, *s'apercevoir* means to notice with attention, the Herbartian *apperception.*

Threshold of Consciousness. The *petites perceptions* of Leibniz are the inhibited ideas (subconscious or subliminal) of Herbart. When these subconscious or inhibited ideas reach consciousness they pass through the threshold, termed by Herbart as the *threshold of consciousness* and defined by him as "that boundary which an idea appears to cross as it passes from the totally inhibited state into some degree of actual ideation" (1961, p. 40).

The passage of a thought from an unconscious state to a conscious one enters the threshold of consciousness as it initially becomes conscious.

A concept is in consciousness in so far as it is not suppressed, but is an actual representation. When it rises out of a condition of complete suppression, it enters into consciousness. Here, then, it is on the threshold of consciousness. It is very important to determine by calculation the degree of strength which a concept must attain in order to be able to stand beside two or more stronger ones exactly on the threshold of consciousness, so that, at the slightest yielding of the hindrance, it would begin to rise into consciousness (1891, p. 13).

Vorstellung (Idea, Presentation, Representation, Mental Image, Concept). Influenced by the Leibnizian theory of activity, Herbart viewed even sense data as active and dynamic. They must be stored up in the mind's apperceptive mass and break through the threshold of consciousness. Ideas in close association form complexes and blendings. The association of ideas or their blending occurs either by contrast or similarity. The soul, a simple entity and a unity, is involved in a process of self-preservation of action and reaction. Self-preservations are ideas or concepts, i.e., the results of the reaction.

Mathematical Psychology. Seeking mathematical applications to psychology, such as the relations of ideas rising to consciousness and falling into unconsciousness, Herbart intoduced the formulas in his *Text-Book in Psychology* (1816) and developed them further in his *Psychologie als Wissenschaft, neu Gegründet auf Erfahrung, Metaphysik und Mathematik* (Psychology as a Science, newly Based upon Experience, Metaphysics, and Mathematics, 2 vols., 1824-25). He furnished three mathematical formulas: (1) "By actual calculation, the remarkable result is obtained that, in the case of the two concepts, the one never entirely obscures the other, but, in the case of three or more, one is very easily obscured, and can be made as ineffective—notwithstanding its continuous struggle—as if it were not present at all" (1891, p.12). The mathematical proof of this formula is found in *Psychologie als Wissenschaft*, (#44).

The calculation of the amount which is to be inhibited by each idea [i.e. the magnitude of ideation which is to be suppressed] must be based upon proportionalities, the first two terms of which derive from the inhibition ratios, and the third term of which is furnished by the sum of the inhibitions.

Let us assume that the ideas *a* and *b* are given as acting against one another in the consciousness, and as being in complete contrast; in this case, in conformity with our previous discussions, the sum of the inhibitions equals the [strength of the] weaker idea, or = *b;* the inhibition ratio, thus, is as *b* : *a*. Consequently, we shall conclude that: the magnitude [of inhibition] to be distributed [throughout the consciousness] (i.e. the sum of the inhibitions [here = *b*]) is to each separate part [of the inhibition] as the sum of the ratio numbers is to each individual ratio number (1961, pp. 32-3).

Between two concepts *a* and *b*, the amount of arrest is expressed in the proportion:

$$a + b : a : : b : \frac{ab}{a + b}$$

So that *a* has a remainder $= a - \frac{b^2}{a + b}$, *while* *b* has a remainder after arrest $= b - \frac{ab}{a + b} = \frac{b^2}{a + b}$; and it is obvious that this can become zero only when *a* is infinite. The case in which there are three concepts, *a, b,* and *c,* give for the remainder of *c* the expression $c - \frac{ab (b + c)}{bc + ac + ab}$, and the conclusion that there may be zero for result—where, for example, *a* and *b* are equal and their sum is equal to three times the value of *c*, (1891, pp. x-xi).

(2) "While the arrested portion of the concept sinks, the sinking part is at every moment proportional to the part unsuppressed" (1891, p. 13). This law is in reference to ideas being suppressed or sinking below the threshold of consciousness. The law, mathematically expressed, is:

$\sigma = S(_{1 - e}{}^{-t})$ in which S = the aggregate amount suppressed, t = the time elapsed during the encounter, σ = the suppressed portion of all the concepts in the time indicated by t, e = the basis of the natural system of logarithms.

(3) The third formula deals with the aid that one idea furnishes another in recalling it to consciousness.

Problem: After an encounter between two concepts, P and Π, the remainders, *r* and *ρ*, are blended (or incompletely united). The problem is to indicate what help one of the two concepts, in case it should be still more suppressed, would receive from the other.

NOTE.—*Solution:* Let P be the helping concept; it helps with a force equal to *r*, but Π can only appropriate this force in the ratio of *ρ* : Π. Hence through P, Π receives the help $\frac{r\rho}{\Pi}$, and in the same way P receives from Π the help $\frac{r\rho}{P}$.

The proof lies immediately in the analysis of the ideas. It is plain that the two remainders, *r* and *ρ*, taken together, determine the degree of union between the two concepts. One of them is the helping force; the other, compared with the concept to which it belongs, is to be considered as a fraction of the whole; and, of the totality of help which could be rendered by the first remainder, it yields that portion which here attains efficient activity.

The following principles may be observed here:

a. Beyond the point of union no help extends its influence.

If the concept $\overline{\Pi}$ has more clearness in consciousness than the remainder ρ indicates, then by the striving of the concept P, which might come to the help of the former, already more than enough has been done; hence for the present it exerts no more influence.

b. The farther the one of the concepts is below the point of union, so much the more effectively does the other help.

NOTE.—This gives the following differential equation:

$$\frac{r\rho}{\Pi}\frac{\rho-\omega}{\rho}\,dt = d\omega,$$

whence by integration $\omega = \rho \left(1 - e^{-\frac{rt}{\Pi}}.\right)$

This equation contains the germ of manifold investigations which penetrate the whole of psychology. It is indeed so simple that it can never really occur in the human soul, but all investigations into applied mathematics begin with such simple presuppositions as only exist in abstraction—e.g., the mathematical lever, or the laws of bodies falling in a vacuum. Here merely the influence of the help is considered, which, if everything depended upon it alone, would bring into consciousness during the time t a quantity ω from Π. Besides, if we take into consideration the single circumstance that Π meets with an unavoidable arrest from other concepts, then the calculation becomes so complicated that it can be only approximately solved by an integration of the following form:

$$d^2\omega = ad^2\omega dt + bd\omega dt^2 + c\omega dt^3.$$

It is self-evident that it much more nearly expresses the facts which are to be observed experimentally. (1891, pp. 18-9).

MORITZ WILHELM DROBISCH (1802-1896): Herbart's Disciple.

A German psychologist and philosopher, who was a professor at the University of Leipzig, Drobisch carried on the Herbartian tradition with the publication of his *Empirische Psychologie nach naturwissenschafticher Methode* (Empirical Psychology according to the Methods of Natural Science) in 1842. Drobisch, Herbart's student, repudiated mental faculties as did his mentor but he also developed an engaging description of the life of consciousness.

Empirical in his approach, he explained ideas as states rather than powers of the mind. Instead of faculties, an "empirical I" exists and a unity of the soul. Speaking of "the refutation of the faculty concept," he claimed that "every return to faculties, or power of forming ideas, in whatever way we may conceive these, appears to lead to no acceptable result" (1898, ¶141). In his continued support of Herbart, he accepted the concept of apperception mass, and dealt with the freedom and inhibition of ideas as well as the inhibition of opposing ideas.

In general the apparent manifestation of the faculties of the mind rests upon combinations, aggregations of ideas in the large, which we can style with Herbart masses of ideas *(Vorstellungsmassen),* which developed with more or less regularity are interwoven out of series, and series of series; and movements and transformations of these masses of ideas appear in place of the activity of the faculties (1898, ¶141).

He saw human development progressing toward a "harmonious form," with its activity tending toward a more peaceful movement.

RUDOLF HERMANN LOTZE (1817-1881): Theory of Local Signs

Biographical Background of Lotze. Known principally in psychology for his theory of local signs, the German philosopher, psychologist, and physician Lotze also gained prominence in psychology for his views on isomorphism, the intuition of space, his opposition to the theory of *vital force,* and for contributing to the founding of physiological psychology. Born in Bautzen, this University of Leipzig graduate earned doctorates in medicine and philosophy before becoming a *Privatdozent* at Leipzig. When he had succeeded to Herbart's chair of philosophy in Göttingen in 1844 at the young age of 27, he had several publications to his name including *Metaphysik* (1841), *Logik* (1843) and the *Allgemein Pathologie* (1842). His classic *Mikrokosmus* appeared in three volumes in 1856, 1858, and 1864 respectively while he was at Göttingen.

Lotze's long tenure at Göttingen lasted 37 years, ending with the date of the publication of his *Outlines of Psychology* in 1881, and with the succession to his chair by G. E. Müller.

At Leipzig, Lotze was influenced by E. H. Weber, A. W. Volkmann, and G. T. Fechner, dedicating his *Medizinische Psychologie oder Physiologie der Seele* (Medical Psychology or Physiology of the Soul), which contained his physiological psychology, to Volkmann in 1852. Though he denied being a Herbartian, Lotze's ideas historically belong to the tradition of Herbart as well as another major German philosopher, Leibniz.

Laws of Psychophysical Mechanism. Lotze's isomorphism or psychophysical mechanism was an attack on Schelling's philosophy, which exerted a dominant influence on medicine. *Friedrich Wilhelm Joseph Schelling* (1775-1854), who taught at Würzburg and Berlin, espoused the theory that only the inorganic realm was subject to mechanical laws, these laws being superseded by powers such as teleological causes. Lotze, who lived at a time when German materialism was at its height and psychophysical parallelism was influential, argued that those laws governing matter in the organic world also control organisms joined to them. He attacked not only Schelling but Hegel and Fichte as well. Although Fechner, Wundt, G. E. Müller, Külpe, and others were psychophysical parallelists, it is not implied that they were metaphysical dualists, for the doctrine could terminate in metaphysical monism if one believed that the parallelism was merely two aspects of one ultimate substance.

Mechanism, the inexorable form connecting and governing all entities in the universe, is all-pervading. While mind is an immaterial entity, its activity on the body (as well as the body's activity on the mind) is exclusively mechanical as dictated by the laws of psychophysical mechanism.

Lotze, who did not feel that his mechanical law theory adversely affected the reality of values, ideals, and dreams, believed in the existence of three distinct realms: regions of facts, laws, and standards of value. Only in a person's thoughts are these separated regions, for in reality they are not. The unity of facts and values is seen in a personal God. Lotze exerted a profound influence on personalism. Despite his viewing the body mechanistically, it was under the direction of a Leibnizian monad-like soul.

Theory of Local Signs and the Theory of Space Perception. The ability to localize became an important issue since the research of Lotze, who employed the term *local sign* to designate the spatial quality of sensations. Lotze, interested in visual and tactual sensations, reasoned that skin contact produces a local sign which has the ability to localize without itself being spatial. The local sign provided the mind by the eye (especially its movements) enables it to construct complex spatial pictures. In visual sensation, the local sign is the movement of the eye (by the object stimulus) that excites the fovea. Points on the retina have their own local signs.

All spatial differences and relations among the impressions on the retina must be compensated for by corresponding non-spatial and merely intensive relations among the impressions which exist together without space-form in the soul; and that from them in reverse order there must arise, not a new actual arrangement of these impressions in extension, but only the mental presentation of such an arrangement in us (1886, p. 33).

The same holds true for the skin with its local signs.

The theory of local signs became influential. E. H. Weber, investigating the ability to localize stimuli that is applied to the skin, ascertained that local signs differed to a considerable extent in various parts of the body. Although Lotze had a proclivity for empiricism, he departed from it with respect to his theory of local signs. Nor was the theory nativism, but a synthesis, a compromise of the Kantian intuition of space, which he agreed with Kant was intrinsic to the mind but also experience generated.

(B) PHENOMENOLOGICAL PSYCHOLOGY AT GÖTTINGEN

Development of Phenomenology at Göttingen

The captivating power of Müller and his productive laboratory magnetically attracted a number of students who became important contributors to psychology as was true in the case of Adolph Jost. Three of these younger men in his laboratory distinguishing themselves in phenomenology were Erich R. Jaensch, David Katz, and Edgar Rubin, the latter two publishing experimental findings compatible and favorable to gestalt psychology. All three men came to Göttingen to obtain their doctorates under Müller.

Phenomenology is not a new term, for it was in coinage with Kant and Hegel, the latter publishing his *Phenomenology of Mind* in 1807. For Hegel it meant the growth of mind from its lowest to its highest stages, and thus represented the growth of knowledge (science). The term was used as early as 1764 by Johann Heinrich Lambert (1728-1777) in his *Neues Organon* (New Organ) as a theory of appearances or illusory features that was fundamental to all empirical knowledge. It was in this sense, though more restricted, that Kant employed it over two decades later in his *Prolegomena* (1783) and *Metaphysical Foundations of Natural Science* (1786). Kant severed phenomena from noumena (things-in-themselves or ultimate reality). By mid-nineteenth century the term came to mean whatever is observed to be an actual fact or to be the case, i.e., a pure descriptive study of data. In his *Lectures on Metaphysics* (1858), William Hamilton, having defined psychology as "the science conversant about the *Phaenomena* of the *mind*," asserted:

> If we consider the mind merely with the view of observing and generalizing the various phaenomena it reveals,—that is, of analyzing them into capacities or faculties,—we have one mental science, or one department of mental science: and this we may call the PHAENOMENOLOGY OF MIND. It is commonly called PSYCHOLOGY— EMPIRICAL PSYCHOLOGY . . . ; we might call it PHAENOMENAL PSYCHOL-OGY (1858, Lect. 7).

It was Hamilton's definition of the term that came into wide use, viz., phenomenology as the descriptive analysis of subjective processes. The German social psychologist, Moritz Lazarus (1824-1903), also used it with the same connotation in his *Leben der Seele* (Life of the Soul, 1856-1857). Edmund Husserl (1900-1901) and Max Scheler (1915) employed it similarly. While Husserl utilized it as a description of the formal structure of phenomena or the ascertaining of their essences, for Scheler phenomenology was the prior or intuitive apprehension of pure facts as they are given in immediate experience. Charles Sanders Peirce (1839-1914) introduced the term in America in 1902 to include a description of illusions, dreams, and imaginations as well as the externally observable. Schumann (who was Müller's assistant at Göttingen and later became Stumpf's assistant at the University of Berlin) was involved in the phenomenological approach with his investigation of perception at the University of Berlin during the opening years of the Nineteenth Century. Stumpf himself was also deeply committed to phenomenology, which meant the study of all experience for him.

It was at Göttingen as well as at Munich from 1913 to 1930 that the phenomenological movement (under the editorship of Husserl) published its organ, *Jahrbuch für Philosophie und phanomenologische Forschung* (Yearbook for Philosophy and Phenomenological Research). During the rise of nazism, the journal was transported to the United States and published at the University of Buffalo (now the State University of New York at Buffalo) by Marvin Farber.

GEORG ELIAS MÜLLER (1850-1934):
Climax of Experimental Psychology at Göttingen

Born at Grimma in Saxony (in the Leipzig vicinity), G. E. Müller did for the University of Göttingen what Wundt did for Leipzig, it ranking second only to

Wundt's as an institution. However, he lacked the originality of Wundt, whatever originality Wundt had. Müller's university training at Leipzig found him under the sway of Drobisch, who instilled Herbartism in him. He never escaped the Göttingen tradition and influence, for even when he left Leipzig for Berlin, he came under the spell of Lotze's writings.

The Franco-Prussian War had interrupted Müller's studies for a year. He returned to Leipzig in 1871, but the following spring in 1872 he found himself studying with Lotze at Göttingen. The two became friends. The German psychologist who distinguished himself in tone psychology, *Carl Stumpf* (1848-1936), was there finishing his studies. Though approximately the same age and at the same institution studying in the same department, the two apparently had slight contact. In 1873 Müller's doctoral dissertation appeared, *Zur Theorie der Sinnlichen Aufmerksamkeit,* theory of sensory attention. His long tenure at Göttingen, opening in 1876 as a private instructor *(Dozent),* closed (with his chairing the department) at the end of four decades with his retirement in 1921. Except for one year in 1880 when he occupied the chair of philosophy at Czernowitz, Müller was professionally associated with only one university, Göttingen, the chair that was offered to him when Lotze left for the University of Berlin where he died within a matter of a few months. The chain at Göttingen extended from an eight-year tenure of Herbart to a 37 one for Lotze before Müller assumed his forty-year command.

At Göttingen, Müller distinguished himself not only for his excellent laboratory, which some consider second only to the one at Leipzig, but also for his work relative to psychophysical method, memory, and color perception. Though he was not original in the sense of the other German luminaries in psychology, he was especially effective in viably developing ideas spawned by others such as Hering's three reversible chemical substance theory of vision, Ebbinghaus' work on memory, the conscious processes begun by Lotze, and the psychophysicalism of Fechner, developing axioms that were to eventuate in isomorphism of the gestaltists Wertheimer and Köhler. Notwithstanding his *Die Gesichtspunkte und die Tatsachen der psychophysischen Methodik* (The Viewpoints and Data of Psychophysical Methodology, 1903), the ultimate in accomplishments in psychophysics, it served merely as a *summa* rather than contributing any new advancement to that field.

Jost's Law. Utilizing Ebbinghaus' method of complete mastery *(Erlernungsmethode),* Müller undertook experiments in this area, publishing the results in 1893 before working on the method of right associates *(Treffermethode).* At this time a student of his at Göttingen, *Adolph Jost* (c. 1870-1920), established in 1897 that of two associations of equal strength commmitted to memory, the fresher one will lose strength with the passage of time more quickly than the older one so that repetition strengthens the older association more so than the younger. Thus the older association maintains its strength more effectively than the younger.

ERICH RUDOLF JAENSCH (1883-1940): Eidetic Imagery

The Breslau-born German phenomenological psychologist, Jaensch, attended, the universities of Tübingen, Jena, and Breslau before obtaining his doctorate under Müller at Göttingen in 1908. The two years that he was at the University of Göttingen saw the publication of *Zur Analyse der Gesichtswahrnehmungen*, a work dedicated to both Ebbinghaus and Müller. In 1913 he left for Marburg after a year at the University of Halle as *Privatdozent*.

The experimental research of Jaensch dealt with space perception and sight, and of course with the discovery of *eidetics* for which he is best known in psychology. He also sought to effect a closer relationship between psychology and philosophy.

Eidetic, (eidetic imagery or percept-image), a term coined by Jaensch, is defined in Warren's *Dictionary of Psychology* as "a clear image (usually visual) which possesses an external or perceptual character, though generally recognized as subjective. Commonly found among children; rarely after adolescence. Distinguished from imagination by its strong sensory character, and from hallucination by its non-illusory character, it is a perception-like image of hallucinary clearness." Developing his view in *Eidetik und die typologische Forschungsmethode* (The Eidetic and Typological Method of Investigation) in 1925, Jaensch saw his eidetics as "the first systematic application of typological methods of investigation" (1930, p. 1). Investigating two psychophysical reaction systems, the B-type or Basedow syndrome of over activity of the thyroid gland (integrate type) and T-type or tetany type of fixated attention (disintegrate type), Jaensch connected them with endocrine functioning, and related the B-type to hyperthyroid activity, and the T-type to hypoparathyroid activity. The former type experiences vivid memory imagery and the latter a type of involuntary afterimage.

> Optical perceptual (or eidetic) images are phenomena, that take up an intermediate position between sensations and images. Like ordinary physiological after-images, they are always *seen* in the literal sense. They have this property of necessity and under all conditions, and share it with sensations. In other respects they can also exhibit the properties of images *(Vorstellungen)*. In those cases in which the imagination has little influence, they are merely modified after-images, deviating from the norm in a definite way, and when that influence is nearly, or completely zero, we can look upon them as slightly intensified after-images. In the other limiting case, when the influence of the imagination is at its maximum, they are ideas that, like after-images, are projected outward and literally *seen* (1930, p. 1).

The work was continued at Marburg by Jaensch (1923) and his brother W. Jaensch (1926). Type psychology was important for Jung, Rorschach, Kretschmer, Sheldon, Ewald, and Birnbaum. The psychology became one concerned with types, genetically interpreting personality, especially so with the advent of nazism.

EDMUND HUSSERL (1859-1938):
Founder of the Phenomenological Movement

The German philosopher and phenomenological psychologist, Husserl, was born in Prossnitz, Moravia. Although initially trained as a mathematician, his friend, Thomas Masaryk, encouraged him to attend Brentano's classes. After attending Brentano's lectures from 1884 to 1886 in Vienna, he left mathematics for philosophy, obtaining his Ph.D. in 1881. Subsequent to lecturing as *Privatdozent* at Halle (1887-1901), he went to Göttingen for a decade and a half (1901-1916), and from there to a full professorship at Freiburg (1916-1929) for the remainder of his teaching career. Among Husserl's distinguished students are *Max Scheler* (1874-1928), who applied phenomenology and set the German base for the logotherapy of the Viennese Viktor E. Frankl (1905-   ), and the German *Martin Heidegger* (1889-   ), whose existentialism and *dasein* concept of man as a *being-in-the-world* laid the foundation of existential psychiatry of two Swiss psychiatrists: the *daseinsanalysis* of Medard Boss (1903-   ) and Ludwig Binswanger (1881-1966) as well as the existential psychotherapy of the American Rollo May (1909-   ). Heidegger dedicated his classic *Being and Time* (1962) to Edmund Husserl in friendship and admiration. Inspired by Heidegger, the French existentialist, Jean-Paul Sartre (1905-   ), developed an existential psychoanalysis in his *Being and Nothingness: An Essay on Phenomenological Ontology* (1925). Kurt Goldstein also came under the influence of Husserl's "phenomenological analysis," especially the Husserlian *Lebenswelt* (life-world).

Everyone who studied with Brentano had a passion for logical precision, and Husserl was no exception, nor did his close associate Carl Stumpf escape. Husserl required a correct point at which to begin, one with apodictic certainty and complete clarity as the firm foundation of human knowledge. With Brentano's encouragement, his attention turned to the philosophy of mathematics, its fruit being his first book, *Philosophie der Arithmetik* (Philosophy of Arithmetic) in 1891.

Some scholars see him as the precursor of Gestalt psychology because of his concern for the immediate apprehension of configural characters, e.g., a flock of birds or the formation of a group of soldiers. His life, marked by three major periods and their corresponding interests, includes: critique of *psychologism* as the first period (occupied the major portion of his time at Halle); descriptive phenomenology as the second period (included the first years at Göttingen); and transcendental phenomenology as the third or Freiburg period.

Psychologism and Intentionality. His first major work, *Logische Untersuchungen* (Logical Investigations) appeared in two volumes in 1900 and 1901. It was in the first volume, titled *Prolegomena to a Pure Logic* that he launched into "psychologism," the position reducing the fundamental principles and concepts of logic to psychology and the validity of logic contingent on the mind. He sought the emancipation of pure logic from psychology. Psychologism is exemplified by the views of John Stuart Mill and Theodor Lipps.

In the second volume of his work, he endorsed Brentano's view of *intentionality*, that mental acts are intentional, that is they have their counterpart in the objective world. Every act of cogitation *(noesis)* has its external referent or intentional object termed *cogitata* or *noema* (Greek term for "that which is perceived"). Every thought corresponds to that which is thought about; every perception has that which is imagined; every intention its referent object (be it idea or physical object).

Phenomenology. The bulk of his phenomenology, his 1907 lectures, resulted in *Ideas: General Introduction to Pure Phenomenology* published in 1913. In this work intentional acts are discussed and his introduction of "transcendental-phenomenological reduction," a methodological technique leading to *pure consciousness* or the *transcendental ego* and the discovery of all that exists in an object.

Inasmuch as all psychology assumes the attitude and approach of the natural sciences, it therefore becomes a science of fact, i.e., a psychophysics. But phenomenology, as the science of pure consciousness, is liberated from naturalistic presuppositions and biases as well as physical involvements, and as such is a science of essence grounded on the method of immanent inspection or the contemplation of essence. Consequently, psychology as the science of mental facts, deals with experiences, while physics treats facts and nonexperiences, that is, with the intended objects of acts to which experiences refer.

A preliminary stage, *epoché*, i.e., the methodological suspension of beliefs and judgments so as to ascertain the pure contents of consciousness, is required.

> Our comprehensive ἐποχή (epoché) puts, as we say, the world between brackets, excludes the world which is simply there! from the subject's field, presenting in its stead the so-and-so-experienced-perceived-remembered-judged-thought-valued-etc. world, as such, the "bracketed" world. (1944, p. 700).

The *phenomenological attitude* (as opposed to a natural attitude) was important to Husserl for through it phenomena are obtained by eliminating "natural or systematic connections" by utilizing the method of *phenomenological reduction*. The antinaturalism of Husserl required placing into brackets or parentheses the object's natural connections by suspending judgment *(epoché)* so as to be enabled to grasp the actually given phenomenon uncluttered by scientific bias, theories, and explanations. Accordingly the phenomenologically real is a fact of immediate or immanent inspection *(Anschauung)* that examines not red per se but its essence. Phenomenologically speaking, red is neither a vibration, sensation, nor a physiological cortical process but a phenomenological experience acquired from an immanent-psychological analysis. Rather than being a science of facts, phenomenology is a science of essences. Not explanations but meanings are important.

Phenomenology, the study of essences, is defined as a descriptive analysis of subjective processes, and is distinguished by (1) its search for essences, which are the ideal intelligible structure of phenomena, and (2) the procedure of attending or grasping that which is itself immediately presented to consciousness without bias of any kind, including the biases of scientific method, philosophical preconceptions, and religious dogmas. One considers only that which is in immediate consciousness by bracketing out (a term adopted from mathematics) all else by holding all judgment in suspension or *epoché* (a term and concept borrowed from the Greek skeptics signifying the suspension of judgment). Following Descartes, Husserl was seeking those absolutely certain facts flowing in one's stream of consciousness. Thus the facts of consciousness intuitively given are the only indubitable and authentic data. Only the given content of consciousness is pure phenomena and has priority over theory and scientific or philosophical interpretation.

Concerning phenomenology as the universal science, Husserl asserted: "For phenomenology as the science of all concrete phenomena proper to subjectivity and inter-subjectivity, is *eo ipso* an a priori science of all possible existence and existences. Phenomenology is universal in its scope, because there is no a priori which does not depend upon its intentional constitution" (1944, p. 702). To Husserl philosophy was a serious, sacred business and calling of emancipating one from bias. Of it he wrote:

> But when all is said, this work of mine can help no one who has already fixed his philosophy and his philosophical method, who has thus never learnt to know the despair of one who has the misfortune to be in love with philosophy, and who at the very outset of his studies, placed amid the chaos of philosophies, with his choice to make, realizes that he has really no choice at all, since no one of these has taken care to free itself from presupposition, and none has sprung from the radical attitude of autonomous self-responsibility which the meaning of a philosophy demands (1962, p. 21).

Phenomenology has influenced a number of psychologists, including Pfänder, Messer, Külpe, Geiger, Linke, Brunswig, Rogers, Frankl, and a number of psychiatrists. Philosophical psychologists such as Max Scheler (1874-1928) in his *Der Formalismus in der Ethik und die materiale Wertethik* (Formalism in Ethics and the Material Ethic of Value, 1913-1916) and *The Nature of Sympathy* (1913) have applied it successfully and influenced a number of psychologists. Scheler was born in 1874, the year Brentano's *Psychologie vom empirischen Standpunkt* (Psychology from an Empirical Standpoint) appeared.

The phenomenological movement was underway with the publication of its organ, *Jahrbuch für Philosophie und Phänomenologische Forschung* (Yearbook for Philosophy and Phenomenological Research) in 1913 with Husserl its chief editor. Heidegger's classic *Being and Time* was published in this journal in 1927, three years before the last issue appeared. Although Husserl terminated the journal in 1930, its English equivalent continued under Marvin Farber at the University of Buffalo (now the State University of New York at Buffalo) and is currently in publication as *Philosophy and Phenomenological Research.*

DAVID KATZ (1884-1953): Phenomenology of Color

After obtaining his Ph.D. from the University of Göttingen under Müller in 1884, Katz remained there as Müller's assistant at the psychological institute until 1919 when he left for the University of Rostock as *Ordentlicher Professor* (assistant professor) of psychology and pedagogy. From there he went to the University of Stockholm as Professor of Psychology. He felt that his student days at Göttingen were during the "golden age" at the Göttingen Institute because at that time a dozen doctoral candidates were pursuing their degrees, among them being: N. Ach, E. R. Jaensch, O. Külpe, William McDougall, Edgar Rubin, Schumann, and Charles Spearman, as well as himself.

The year he left the institute in 1919, Katz married another student who received her Ph.D. under Müller at Göttingen, Rosa Heine (1885-   ). In 1929 Katz went to the University of Maine in Orono as a visiting professor, and from 1933 to 1937 he spent time at the University of Manchester, and at London with Cyril Burt. Owing to the Nazi persecution, he left for the University of Stockholm where he became its first professor of psychology, shaping the "youngest laboratory in Sweden." In 1950 he delivered the Hitchcock Lectures at the University of California (Berkeley Campus). His close friends include Edgar Rubin and William Stern.

Color Theory. Katz made a phenomenological research of modes of the appearance of colors and reported it in his classic *Die Erscheinungsweisen der Farben und ihre Beeinflussung durch die individuelle Erfahrung* (Modes of Appearance of Colors and Their Modification through Individual Experience) in 1911, later developing and expanding the theory in his *The World of Color* (1930). The study, which sought to demonstrate the inseparable relationship between space and color, postulated three color modes: (1) surface colors, (2) film colors, and (3) volumic colors. The first, bidimensional colors, are those perceived on objects; the second lack localization and are spectroscopically observed; and the third, tridimensional colors, are exemplified by a translucent object of three dimensions such as a glass containing red liquid.

By looking through a spectroscope, Katz discovered different modes of appearance than those found on colored paper with which one is so familiar, for spectral color is not localized. By viewing colored surfaces through the hole on a "reduction screen," colored surfaces are reduced to a film-like effect owing to the elimination of perceptual position, relation, etc. He explained his findings accordingly:

> The spongy texture of the spectral colour is not of such a nature that it could be referred to as a *voluminousness* or as a colour-*transparency*. Rather, a spectral colour has this much in common with the colour of a paper, that *it is extended through space in the form of a bidimensional plane, and functions as a rear boundary for it*. The delimitation of space takes place differently for the two types of colour. A spectral colour never loses an essentially frontal-parallel character. When the colour fixated is directly before the eyes and projected on the fovea, the plane in which it is seen always presents an orientation essentially perpendicular to the direction of vision. The colour of a paper, on the other hand, can assume *any orientation whatsoever with reference to the direction of vision,* for its plane is always that of the surface of the coloured paper. If it appears in frontal-parallel orientation, this is to be considered simply as a special case. We shall distinguish between these two opposed types of colour-impression on the basis of their common and differentiating factors by characterizing spectral colours, and all the colours

which share their mode of appearance, as *film colours* and the opposite type as *surface colours*. Surface colours are seen almost solely on objects so that it might not be out of place to speak of them as "object colours." In some cases, however, this term might be misleading. Thus we tend to consider the redness of a red glass or of a red liquid as an object colour, belonging to the object, whereas this red does not possess the character of a surface colour, but presents rather the mode of appearance which we shall characterize below as *voluminousness* (1935, pp. 8-9).

The experiment successfully proved the inadequacy of the established orientation to psychology. By 1925 when Katz published his *Der Aufbau der Tastwelt* (Construction of a World of Sense), it was quite apparent that he repudiated atomistic views, preferring the gestalt viewpoint despite its limitations. His interest in gestalt psychology culminated with the publication of *Gestalt Psychology: Its Nature and Significance* in 1943.

EDGAR RUBIN (1886-1951): Visual Perception of Figure-Ground Phenomena

Prior to the appearance of Wertheimer's classic paper on gestalt theory, Rubin, a Danish psychologist who was the protégé of the distinguished psychologist Harald Höffding of the University of Copenhagen, was conducting research in experimental phenomenology at Göttingen under Müller. Experimental investigation at that institution in phenomenology was well under way by 1910 when Wertheimer was just beginning his research.

Born in Copenhagen, Rubin studied philosophy and psychology at the University of Copenhagen under Höffding and Alfred Lehmann from 1904 to 1911 when he went to the Institute of Psychology at the University of Göttingen. Here he studied under G. E. Müller and conducted his classic experiments on figure and ground. His doctor of philosophy degree was conferred in 1915. He returned the following year to Copenhagen as *dozent*, and finally as Lehmann's successor as professor of experimental psychology, directing the laboratory of psychology there. Rubin, who served as president of the Tenth International Congress for Psychology in 1932, remained at Copenhagen for the remainder of his life, except for a couple of years as a visiting professor at the University of Lund in Sweden.

By 1915 Rubin published his findings in Danish, but wide attention was not accorded until they appeared in German in 1921. Rubin's experimental findings are so close to those of the gestalt movement that the gestaltists have adopted him as one of their own, and with the gestaltists he remained in close proximity.

Figure-Background Phenomena. Rubin's work produced the famous vase-profile and claw-finger figure-background phenomena, that is, the dichotomous divison of a visual field of perception so that the object of attention becomes the field and the remainder the background. Attention may then be reversed resulting in the ground becoming the figure, and the previous figure becoming the new background as illustrated in Fig. I below.

Fig. I.

The black surface alternates with the white to function
first as figure and then as ground.

Explaining the difference between figure and ground in perception, Rubin asserted:

In relation to the ground, the figure is more impressive and more dominant. Everything about the figure is remembered better, and the figure brings forth more associations than the ground (1958, p. 199).

Furthermore he provided rules regulating the probability that a surface is perceived as the figure, that is, the characteristic qualities rendering one field as figure and the other field as ground.

If one of the two homogeneous, different colored fields is larger than and encloses the other, there is a great likelihood that the small, surrounded field will be seen as figure. . . .

Conscious intent can also play an important role. . . .

Further, there is a certain tendency to uniformity. In a design in which the same motifs are repeated, there is a tendency to see the repetition in the same way. There is a tendency to experience a cohesive, homogeneously colored field either entirely as figure or entirely as ground (1958, pp. 202-3).

Obviously a field cannot simultaneously be perceived both as figure and ground. Colors too play a factor so that one color appears to dominate another. Figures of contours also depend upon a background field.

Figural After-Effect. Rubin also spoke of figural after-effect, the phenomenon occurring following repeated experiments on figure-ground distinctions. In the majority of subjects, once a reaction is established (so that in the vase-profile figure-ground experiment a person responds to the vase as figure first each time it is presented), the subject will respond in the same manner in subsequent presentations, as if it were retained in memory.

Despite Wertheimer's classic publication in 1912 antedating Rubin's by three years, the two men worked completely independently of each other and without the knowledge of each other's efforts. Rubin returned to Copenhagen from the University of Göttingen to emerge as Denmark's foremost psychologist. At that time Denmark had but few psychologists, *The Psychological Register* for 1929 listing only 17, and failing to list Rubin!

The End of an Era

With the passing of Müller in 1934, the era of the psychological titans in Germany came to an end; only Stumpf outlived him by a couple of years. It was not Husserl but Narziss Ach that succeeded Müller; Husserl left for Freiburg. David Katz who left Germany for Sweden put it succinctly when he wrote:

> With the destruction of German psychology, America has assumed leadership in all fields of our science, and my desire to renew contact with American psychology was fulfilled in 1950 when I was invited to give the Hitchcock Lectures at the University of California at Berkeley. I must leave to fate whether I shall be able to take advantage of the great incentive received from this renewed acquaintance with an extremely productive science (1952, p. 211).

In sheer numbers alone there are more registered American psychologists in the American Psychological Association than the rest of the entire world combined if one can judge from the 20,000 questionnaires sent out to psychologists the world over in order to compile the 8,000 included in the 1966 edition of the *International Directory of Psychologists* (excludes the United States) compared to the over 30,000 psychologists who were actual members of the American Psychological Association in 1970. But more than sheer numbers, American psychologists have made most of the major contributions in psychology at the present time. Not only did Germany concede the leadership of psychology to the United States but the flavor of psychology was becoming *ganz Amerikanisch* (entirely American) as Wundt would say.

CHAPTER 8

The Austrian School of Act Psychology: Psychology at the Universities of Vienna, Graz, Prague

Psychology of Act

In sharp contrast and opposition to content psychology (chiefly epitomized by Wundt and his disciples), the Austrian school of psychologists were proponents of act psychology or *intentionalism* depicted by Brentano and his psychological heirs. Whereas content psychology emphasizes the elemental contents of the mental life, the *psychology of act (Aktpsychologie* as the Germans termed it) stresses the act of intending or reference to objects as characterizing psychical processes or data as psychic activities. For the content psychologists or the structuralists, experience is regarded as a structure but for act psychologists it is a way of acting.

Act psychology, originally initiated by Aristotle and revived by the scholastic psychologists of the Medieval period, was introduced to contemporary psychology by Brentano in 1874 and perpetuated by Meinong and the students of both of these psychologists. The group came to be known as the Austrian school because their principal connections were at the University of Vienna (founded in 1365), University of Graz (founded in 1585), and the University of Prague (founded in 1348). Prague, currently the capitol of Czechoslovakia, was under Austrian governance during the advent of act psychology, and was virtually a German city since the beginning of the nineteenth century. Full independence for Czechoslovakia was achieved subsequent to World War I. Vienna, well known as a city of culture and learning, rivals Paris, for its name is associated with musicians and composers such as Mozart, Strauss, Beethoven, Haydn, and Schubert; while in psychology it may boast of Freud, Adler, Frankl, and Moreno, just to name the heads of the four leading schools of Viennese psychiatry.

Act psychology was not the sole possession of those stemming from the scholastic tradition, for the German psychologists from Leibniz to Kant to Herbart were developing theories of the activity of the human mind: Leibniz speaking of nothing present in the mind which was not first in the senses except the intellect or mind itself, and Kant speaking of the synthetic machinery of the mind responsible for intuitive processes. But the Austrian school psychologists responded more to Kantian positivism, i.e., de-emphasizing the thing-in-itself *(ding-an-sich)* in favor of the act of experiencing, e.g., the act of seeing red is mental rather than the color itself which is a physical quality. Instead of being concerned with the transcendent or noumenal object, they were interested in the transcendental activity of the human mind.

While the content psychologists were experimenting in the field of sense physiology, those elements of sensation, the Austrian school treated *perception* as of major experimental consideration, investigating space-perception and its related issues, especially esthetics. Form-qualities *(Gestaltqualitäten)* and their perception (which was to become the prime consideration of the gestalt psychologists) emerged as the important work in experimental perception. Thus act psychology is one of mental arrangement.

The Composition of the Austrian School. The universities of the Austrian school were named as Vienna, Graz, and Prague but the University of Munich in southern Germany not far from the Austrian border could properly be included in this group, for Stumpf, Lipps, and Cornelius were there, Lipps succeeding Stumpf at Munich. The University of Munich, probably Germany's largest with approximately 14,000 students in the late fifties (the Free University of Berlin with almost 10,600 at that time) was founded in 1472. Traditionally a Roman Catholic college from its inception, it was moved to Landshut in 1800 and from there to Munich in 1826.

A roll call of the Austrian school would produce among its important figures: *Franz Brentano* (1838-1917) of the University of Vienna; *Alexius Meinong* (1853-1920) of the University of Graz; *Ernst Mach* (1838-1916) of the universities of Prague and Vienna; *Christian Ehrenfels* (1859-1932) of the universities of Vienna and Prague; *Theodor Lipps* (1851-1914) of the University of Munich; *Carl Stumpf* (1848-1936) of the University of Munich (later Berlin); *Hans Cornelius* (1863-   ) of the University of Munich; and two of Meinong's students: *Stephen Witasek* (1870-1915) at the University of Graz and *Vittorio Benussi* (1878-1927) (the Italian psychologist whose investigations of respiratory change occurring during emotion eventuated in lie detector research) also of the University of Graz.

Form quality *(Gestaltqualität)* as a school is a movement of the 1890   the decade Ehrenfels wrote his *Über Gestaltqualitäten* (On Form-qualities, 1890), Meinong his *Zur Psychologie der Komplexionen und Relationen* (Complexions and Relations, 1891), and Cornelius *Über Verschmelzung und Analyse* (Fusion and Analysis, 1892). The following decade two of Meinong's students at the University of Graz assumed the cudgels in a number of their writings. While defending Meinong, Cornelius modified the "consolidated" or "founded content" of Meinong to a "consolidated" or "founded attribute" as indicative of form-quality. Both positions rested on the perception of the *Fundamente* or related elements of Ehrenfels, e.g., the perception of a square as a square instead of four lines, the square being a new quality formed rather than a mere combination or sum of the four lines. Witasek, who reasoned that perception is based on an effect resulting from the psychical act of producing, conducted experiments grounded on the Austrian school's presuppositions. But it remained for the gestalt movement from 1912 on to inaugurate gestalt psychology on its important mission in the history of psychology. Whether the gestalt movement is a continuation of the school of act psychology is a debatable issue. But for the new school of gestalt psychology one must leave Austria for Germany to the University of Frankfurt and also to Berlin.

Moreover it is interesting to note that some attempts were made at synthesizing act and content psychology, one such attempt being undertaken by *August Messer* (1867-1937), both student and professor at the University of Giessen in his *Empfindung und Denken* (Sensation and Thinking) in 1908. Messer is the familiar figure from the Würzburg school, and was closely associated with Külpe, spending the summer semester with him there in 1905. Messer's views have been largely shaped by Husserl and Külpe, and Külpe's thinking colored by Husserl.

(A) BRENTANO AND HIS INFLUENCE

FRANZ BRENTANO (1838-1917):
Father of Phenomenology and Act Psychology

The German philosopher, psychologist, and Roman Catholic priest, Brentano, was born in Marienburg. After becoming a priest he joined the University of Würzburg as a lecturer *(Habilitation)* in philosophy in 1866, being appointed a professor in 1872. His inability to accept the new doctrine of papal infallibility together with the controversies, in which he engaged, attendant upon the doctrine obliged him to resign both his university position and the priesthood in 1873. The following year he accepted a full professorship at the University of Vienna, holding that post until 1880 when he married and felt constrained to relinquish his position in a state university of a Catholic nation. Thus he was reduced to the status of an unsalaried lecturer of a *Privatdozent* for another decade and a half. Freud himself confronted a similar predicament in Vienna where his promotions were not forthcoming owing to his being a Jew. Because his expected permanent appointment was withheld, Brentano left for the life of a private scholar in Florence, Italy, and subsequently to Zurich where he died of appendicitis at almost eighty years of age.

Brentano's Place in the History of Psychology. Brentano exerted a profound influence upon his students, many of them distinguishing themselves in psychology. He can number among them Carl Stumpf, who changed from the profession of law to philosophy under the influence of Brentano at Würzburg (later to become a professor of philosophy there); Anton Marty, who was so impressed by him that he had actually proceeded with priestly orders; Edmund Husserl, who founded the phenomenological movement; and Alexius Meinong. Although Brentano's psychology was empirical, it was not experimental. Others, however, such as the Würzburg school, proceeded to undertake experiments on his theory of meaning.

Act Psychology

Known principally for his *Psychologie vom empirischen Standpunkt* (Psychology from an Empirical Standpoint) that appeared in 1874, Brentano advanced the thesis that the content of psychology derives directly from observing the mental processes rather than theorizing out of a mere abstract mind. He defined psychology as the science of psychical phenomena, regarding phenomena as active rather than static, the acts of a person. Hence he introduced act psychology by stating that mental processes are acts, the three prime acts being: (1) sensing (ideating), (2) judging, and (3) feeling (loving and hating). On the one hand, he divided the knowing process into sensing and judging, on the other he joined acting and feeling as did Aristotle before him because they felt that action follows feeling.

> Every presentation *(Vorstellung)* of sensation or imagination offers an example of the mental phenomenon; and here I understand by presentation not that which is presented, but the act of presentation. Thus, hearing a sound, seeing a colored object, sensing warm or cold, and the comparable states of imagination as well, are examples of what I mean. . . . Furthermore, every judgment, every recollection, every expectation, every inference, every conviction or opinion, every doubt is a mental phenomenon. And again, every emotion, joy, sorrow, fear, hope, pride, despair, anger, love, hate, desire, choice, intention, astonishment, wonder, contempt, etc., is such a phenomenon (1960, p. 41).

Consequently for purposes of defining psychology, it is necessary to broaden it so as to encompass phenomenological data. "It is only mental phenomena in the sense of actual states which we shall have to regard as the true object of psychology. And it is exclusively with reference to them that we say psychology is the science of mental phenomena" (1960, p. 61). Intentionality is an important factor, for there is no thinking without the object thought, and no desire without the object of desire. In the act of loving something is loved, in the act of hating something hated, in the act of desiring something desired. But it is *intentional inexistence* that characterizes mental phenomena, distinguishing it from the physical. Intentional inexistence is the subjective experience of the objective referent. "Intentional inexistence is exclusively characteristic of mental phenomena," for in the physical it is lacking. The mental is characterized by "direction upon something," "reference to a content," "direction upon an object" as well as "intentional inexistence." Mental activities and their intention take precedence over the mental content psychology of Wundt.

> Every mental [psychical] phenomenon is characterized by what the scholastics of the Middle Ages have termed the intentional (as well as mental) inexistence of an object, and what we should term (although the terms are not completely free from ambiguity) reference to a content, a direction upon an object (not meaning a reality in this case), or an immanent objectivity. Each contains within itself something as its object, though not always in the same way. In idea something is ideated, in judgment something is affirmed or denied, in love something is loved, in hate hated, in desire desired, etc.
>
> The intentional inexistence is the exclusive property of mental phenomena. No physical phenomenon exhibits anything like it. Accordingly we may define mental phenomena by saying that they are phenomena which contain an object intentionally (1874, 1, p. 195).

Theory of Meaning. The principal role that meaning held for the Würzburg school and its importance to phenomenology and subsequent psychology derives from Brentano. Whereas mental processes are not important for what they are but for what they mean, objects on the other hand are significant for what they are.

Not only did Brentano give the impetus to the Würzburg school of imageless thought, but he drew Külpe away from the content psychology of Wundt and closer to act psychology. His influence reached beyond individuals such as Stumpf, Meinong, and Husserl; it extended to the range of schools, including the gestalt and phenomenological movements. Furthermore, his influence was more than local, it not only encompassed the Germanic speaking world, it reached the British psychologists with whom he was rather close, having corresponded with John Stuart Mill and no less a man than Freud (in his youth) translating the letters. Freud also came within the orbit of Brentano, attending his lectures.

The able logician Brentano conveyed to his students the need and technique of incisive thought, and in some cases he did too well, his own student, Husserl, charging him with "psychologism," of reducing logic to psychology. The distinguished mathematician and logician, Gottlob Frege (1848-1925) also accused him of the same.

• **Brentano's Influence.** The influence of Brentano extended in a dual direction, fructifying into what was to become known as the phenomenological and gestalt movements. This fact is especially evident as seen through his students, Meinong and Ehrenfels, the latter's *Gestaltqualität* (form quality) that subsequently found its way into gestalt psychology, and the phenomenological ideas that fecundated into Husserl's phenomenological movement.

ALEXIUS MEINONG (1853-1920): Act Psychology

The distinguished Austrian psychologist and philosopher Meinong was professor at the University of Graz from 1882 until his death and in 1894 established Austria's first psychological institute. Known for developing a general theory of value based on psychology, Meinong who studied under Brentano at Vienna from 1875 to 1878, developed a theory of objects, theory of assumptions, and theory of evidence as well as a theory of value.

His chief contribution to psychology, however, is his *theory of objects (Gegenstandstheorie)* that initially appeared in his article *Über Gegenstandstheorie* in 1904, and later in virtually all of his writings. Here he theorized the presence of objects that do not exist, and yet in a fashion they are constituted, hence valid predications may be made of them. Everything is an object with its peculiar characteristics whether or not it possesses some kind of being. Consequently the "character" *(Sosein)* of an object which they all possess is independent of its "being" *(Sein)*. The entire body of objects is not restricted to the merely real. An example of a statement pertaining to a nonexistent object *(Sosein)* is: "The mountain of which I am thinking is golden." Thus it is a true statement about a nonexistent object. A *Sosein* statement is not existential, and though it is devoid of existence it nevertheless does possess *Sosein* (a meaningful character). He referred to this independence of the objects' characters *(Sosein)* and to their actual being *(Sein)* as the doctrine of *Aussersein*. Plato's ideal objects may subsist, other objects exist, but there is a third entity of objects that are meaningful, a *tertium quid,* that must be accounted for. Although it is *Nichtsein* (nonexisting), it does possess *Sosein* (characteristics), but both are objective. Explaining his position, Meinong wrote:

> There is thus not the slightest doubt that what is supposed to be the Object of knowledge need not exist at all. But our account up to now may seem to leave room for the conjecture that wherever existence is absent, it not only *can* be but *must* be replaced by subsistence. But even this restriction is inadmissable, as may be seen by contrasting the characteristic functions of judging and assuming, a distinction I have attempted to maintain by contrasting the "thetic and synthetic function" of thought. In the former case, the act of thought grasps a *Sein,* in the latter a *"Sosein."* In each case, naturally, it is an Objective that is grasped (1960, p. 81).

In his theory of emotional presentation, Meinong distinguished between knowing that the temperature is hot and knowing that it is agreeable, the latter being known by a subjective feeling, and the former by a subjective sensation. In both cases it is a subjective experience of a presented object.

One may speak of a correct or incorrect emotion as he does with respect to judgments, as well as their being justified or unjustified, and worthy of merit or unworthy. According to his psychologically based theory of value, Meinong imputed objective reference to value feelings, that is, value feelings have objects. His psychological value theory is found in his *Psychologischethische Unter-suchungen zur Werttheorie* (Psychological-ethical Investigations of Value Theory, 1894) and the posthumously published *Zur Grundlegung der al-legemeinen Werttheorie* (Foundation of a General Theory of Value, 1923).

Brentanŏ's distinguished disciple, Meinong, emerged as the head of the Graz school, and in 1894 established Austria's first laboratory of experimental psychology. Such an important force was he that some psychologists (Mary W. Calkins, 1914) referred to him as the Meinong school.

CHRISTIAN FREIHERR EHRENFELS (1859-1932): *Gestaltqualtäten*

Born in Rodaun (proximity of Vienna), the psychologist and philosopher, Ehrenfels, studied under Brentano and Meinong at the University of Vienna, receiving his doctorate in 1885 from the University of Graz. After teaching as *Privatdozent* at the University of Vienna from 1888 to 1896, he left for the German University of Prague as extraordinary professor before being elevated to full professor in 1900, his tenure lasting to 1929.

The movement of act psychology as it developed its notion of form qualities in the last two decades of the nineteenth century stems from the publication in 1890 of the classic paper, "Über Gestaltqualitäten," (Gestalt Qualities) by Ehrenfels. Inasmuch as Ehrenfels based his premises upon the Machian thesis of *form qualities* and *space qualities* as explained in his *Analysis of Sensations* (1886) four years earlier, it is advisable that Mach's ideas be examined first.

Ernst Mach (1838-1916): Analysis of Sensations. One of the founders of "empiriocriticism," Ernst Mach was a physicist, philosopher, and psychologist who attempted a realistic philosophy grounded on the analysis of sensations. The Austrian Mach was born in Turas, Moravia (currently Czechoslovakia). After his student years at the University of Vienna where he was also *Dozent*, he accepted a professorship of mathematics at Graz in 1864, leaving three years later for a professorship of physics at Prague in 1867. At Prague, where his tenure lasted 28 years, he accomplished much, including his more important books and work. While Rector Magnificus there from 1869 to 1880, he resisted the introduction of Czech to replace German at the University of Prague. In 1895 he returned to Vienna as professor of physics but by that time Brentano had left. In 1901 when he has resigned from the University of Vienna, he was elected to membership in the Austrian house of peers.

Fusing physics with psychology, Mach concluded that all existence is sensation. Fechner's *Psychophysics* led him to Kantian noumenalism, a pivotal point he used to espouse a physical phenomenalism. What is ego (self) and nonego (external world) is virtually indistinguishable so that one appears to be the continuation of the other. Indebted to Berkeley and Hume for his sensationalism, Mach also depended upon Kant, Helmholtz, and *Richard Heinrich Ludwig Avenarius* (1843-1896), the Paris-born German philosopher who became professor of philosophy at Zurich after studying at Zurich, Berlin, and Leipzig and obtaining his degree at Leipzig in 1876. Independently, he and Mach arrived at the same ideas of *empiriocriticism*, he in his *Kritik der reinen Erfahrung* (Critique of Pure Experience, 1888-1890), and Mach in his *Beiträge zur Analyse der Empfindungen* (Contributions to the Analysis of Sensations, 1886); by the time the fifth edition appeared the title was abbreviated to *Analysis of Sensations* (1906).

Empiriocriticism of Avenarius seeks to establish a philosophy of *pure experience,* "cleansed of all adulterating additions," grounded on a "natural concept of the world" ("sum total of the constituents of the environment"), and on the "economy of thought." The antimetaphysical positions of these two men resulted in the elimination of metaphysical reality. It was with the denial of reality by these two men that Lenin took such severe objection, addressing his work, *Materialism and Empirio-Criticism* (1909), to that issue.

However, it was the concept of the Machian "space form" and "time form" that led to Ehrenfels' "form quality" (*Gestaltqualität*) as the perceiver's own activity that was to become the basis of gestalt psychology. The description of objects is through their analysis into shapes, colors, and textures, an element being a simple, uniform color covering one's visual field. To describe the world economically entails those elements which are gained through sense experience, for "the world consists only of our sensations. In which case we have knowledge only of sensations" (1897, p. 10). Both physics and psychology have as their elementary data sensations (the equivalent of experience). One also has sensations of "space form" and "time form." In the case of a space form, one may alter the color and size of a geometrical figure such as the letter "N" and yet its form remains recognizable.

In examining two figures which are alike but differently colored (for example, two letters of the same size and shape, but of different colors), we recognize their sameness of form at the first glance, in spite of the difference of color-sensation. The sight-perceptions, therefore, must contain some identical sensation-components. These are the space-sensations — which are the same in the two cases (1897, p. 44).

The same holds true for time form, objects occurring sequentially, such as note of a melody.

That a definite, specific time-sensation exists, appears to me beyond all doubt. The rhythmical identity of the two adjoined measures, which vary utterly in the order of their tones, is immediately recognised. We have not to do here with a matter of the understanding or of reflexion, but with one of sensation. In the same manner that bodies of different colors may possess the same spatial form, so here we have two tonal entities which, acoustically, are differently colored, but possess the same temporal form. As in the one case we pick out by an immediate act of feeling the identical spatial components, so here we immediately detect the identical temporal components, or the sameness of the rhythm (1897, p. 110).

Ehrenfels' Form Quality

The sensationalist Mach failed to carry his elements any further toward the concept of gestalt. Actually he was "gestalt-blind" according to Bühler, only lightly touching the issue of organization in sensation and perception. It remained for Ehrenfels to recognize the supreme importance of form quality and develop the gestalt notion that space forms and time forms are new qualities or syntheses rather than mere combinations of other qualities because the gestalt remains the same despite the sum of its component elements varying. Qualities of form are genuine perceptual contents. A complex of elements must be like one similar to itself to the extent that its elements are alike. Yet the same melody is perceptible though heard in various keys and despite every tone differing, that is, it is perceived more as the same tune than as tones constructed with the same elements but in a different sequence, the same notes in another arrangement.

The same melody may be made up of quite different groups of notes, as happens when the self-same melody is transposed into different keys. If the melody were nothing else than the sum of the notes, different melodies would have to be produced, because different groups of notes are here involved (1937, p. 521).

Form qualities are defined by Ehrenfels as positive ideational or representational contents or complexes comprised of separable *Fundamente* or foundation elements (related elements). He defined gestalt-quality as:

> When the memory-images of successive notes are present as a simultaneous complex in consciousness, then an idea *(Vorstellung)*, belonging to a new category, can arise in consciousness, a unitary idea, which is connected in a manner peculiar to itself with the ideas *(Vorstellungen)* of the complex of notes involved. The idea of this whole belongs to a new category, for which the name 'founded contents' *(fundierte Inhalte)* came into use. Not all founded contents are perceptual in character and allied to the idea of melody. There are also founded contents which are not perceptual, as for example relations. The essence of the connection between the founded content and its base *(Fundament)* is the irreversible conditioning of the former by the latter. Every founded content necessarily requires a base. A certain complex of base ideas can support only a certain founded content. But not every case need be crowned, so to speak, and held together, by a founded content (1937, pp. 521-2).

Whereas Meinong and his student Benussi agreed with this interpretation of gestalt, Wertheimer and Köhler held that the gestalt quality is given together with its base, and the individual's perception of the gestalt in a melody is due to his observation rather than what is produced by the "founded content."

The necessary ideational, (perceived) complex producing a gestalt or form quality, he termed *Grundlage* (ground or basis) of form qualities. A mental phase of the complex is a necessary factor; it is termed the "positive ideational (perceptual) content" and is the "form quality," that which remains the same despite each element being changed. The proof of this is seen in substituting every element yet retaining the same form as in a melody. "Melody is more than a sum of sensations and, therefore, contains a new conscious quality which we will call a quality of form." Thus ideational components are necessary and are the form qualities coupled to sensations so as adequately to explain the perception of melodies, forms, and dynamic temporal events. A gestalt or form quality is therefore something added to the sum of sense data not originally given in sense elements.

Two criteria must be met in order for structures to qualify as form qualities *(Gestaltqualitäten):* (1) the inability of comprising them out of elements, and (2) the ability of transposing them like melodies.

Meinong's Modification of Form Quality. Developing Ehrenfels' gestalt qualities further, Meinong coined new terminology so that the *Fundamente* were called by Meinong founding contents *(fundierende Inhalte)*, and the *Gestaltqualität* (form quality) was termed founded contents *(fudierte Inhalte)*. In a later paper on gestalt qualities (Über Gestaltqualitäten) published in 1932, Ehrenfels adopted Meinong's terminology. The term *form quality* (gestalt quality) acquired a number of synonyms: "complexion," "members," "funded contents," and "founded contents," so that the complexion such as a melody may be said to be built upon its members (tones).

Revision by Cornelius of Form Quality. As Meinong supported Ehrenfels, Cornelius (1892, 1897) came to the defense of Meinong. His starting point was the complex (rather than simple contents) which he termed the fusion, and regarded the primary mental structure as a whole. Form quality was modified from a founded content to a founded attribute, so that the founded content being a ''sensation-whole'' is merely an unanalyzed fusion rather than an addition to the sum of the parts as Ehrenfels held. Whereas for Ehrenfels the founded contents are intact provided the relationship of the parts remains intact (e.g., a founded melody is not ruined by transportation) for Cornelius (and Meinong) the founded contents can be changed without altering the elements merely by refocusing attention. Raw experience confronts the individual as an unanalyzed whole, and shifting attention from the whole to parts damages and obliterates the founded attributes. While Ehrenfels regarded founding as dependent upon external conditions, Cornelius and Meinong treated it as a subjective process.

Witasek's Contribution. Meinong's student at Graz, Stephen Witasek (1897), worked out a system in which Ehrenfels' gestalt qualities were built upon other gestalt qualities, resulting in ''complexions of higher order,'' such as a polyphonic composition constructed of diverse voices wherein each voice is a complexion. In a counterpoint arrangement that is contrapuntal, each voice may be funding by itself or unite with others forming a complexion of a higher order. The intensity of the voice of the soloist may be greater than the accompaniment as well as with its own distinctive sound color (clang).

Content acquires importance for Witasek (1908) since without content there is no act, and without act there is no content. The distinction is a psychological one inasmuch as content and act are both mental. ''My ideating, thinking, feeling, and willing are always in their own peculiar manner aimed at something. I ideate something'' (1908, p. 73). Consequently a psychical phenomenon has two parts: the content and the act; a determinate object is brought to consciousness by the former, and the latter renders an object one of perception, imagination, or judgment.

Schumann's Opposition to Form Quality. Opposition to the school came from *Friedrich Schumann* (1863-1940) in 1900 and later. Schumann, Stumpf's assistant at the University of Berlin, was fortified to assume the cudgels against the proponents of form quality with G. E. Müller's unpublished lecture notes. Schumann found it unnecessary to resort to form quality as new ideational contents in his analysis of visual forms and illusions. Laws of attention could account for perception of form. Color clang was eliminated by Stumpf by tracing it to tonal color found in the elements. Schumann accounted for the funded aspect of complexion in terms of feelings and concomitant ideas. Factors, e.g., contours, nearness, and the properties of figures contribute to combining units into groups.

(B) ACT PSYCHOLOGY IN MUNICH

Theodor Lipps (1851-1914): Theory of Empathy. Although he is often identified with phenomenologists and the act psychologists, which his psychology favors over content psychology, Lipps is a peripheral member of the Austrian school. His education was at the universities of Erlangen, Tübingen, Utrecht, and

Bonn; and his university appointments at Bonn (1877-1890), Breslau (1890-1894), and Munich (1894-1914), where in 1896 he founded the Psychological Institute. But Munich, in southern Germany, became infiltrated with Austrian act psychology. With his predecessor at Munich, Stumpf, he was joint president of the International Congress of Psychology in 1896.

(Einfühlung) Empathy Theory. According to the theory of empathy *(Einfühlung)*, a person projects himself into the perceived object. The theory, which first appeared in *Raumästhetik* (Esthetics of Space, 1893-1897), holds that the act of sympathetic projection is to be distinguished from the perceiving person but it may be projected into other persons or objects.

He regarded empathy as "the objectivated enjoyment of the self" so that an indentification is established between oneself and another person or object of esthetic perception or contemplation. Esthetic feeling is grounded in empathy. He distinguished four types of empathy: (1) general apperceptive empathy, (2) empirical empathy, (3) mood empathy, and (4) empathy for the sensible appearance of living beings.

Psychology as the Science of Consciousness. Psychology is defined by Lipps as the science of consciousness and of the experiences of consciousness, the essence of consciousness being to "reach out" to a transcendent world beyond itself. Of the four classes of "conscious contents or conscious experiences," he listed: (1) "the directly experienced I with its determinations, the feelings;" (2) "the contents of sensation and sense-perception;" (3) "the directly experienced relations of the I to what is objective, and the relations of the I in general;" and (4) "the indeational contents corresponding with all these conscious contents."

Whereas sensation is simply possessing some sense content, he regarded experiences as acts of thought, the image content of these thoughts being adequate to their objects. Experiences turn into an activity when the "mind's eye" inspects the sense content acquired by the "eye of sense." Activity is always a conscious act of conation. Consciousness is an activity, the two classes of conscious experience being: (1) feelings proper, and (2) experienced relations.

CARL STUMPF (1848-1936):
Stumpfian Act Psychology and Phenomenology

The German philosopher and psychologist, Stumpf, was born in Wiesentheid, Bavaria. He held chairs in philosophy at Würzburg (1873-1879) at the age of 25, then went on to Prague (1879-1884), Halle (1884-1889), and Munich (1889-1893) before going to the University of Berlin in 1894 at the age of 46, where he remained until mandatory retirement after a quarter of a century of service. But he continued until 1923, when he was succeeded by Wolfgang Köhler. Two profound influences on his life occurred when he studied under Brentano at Würzburg (also in the province of his birth, Bavaria) and Lotze at Göttingen. Owing to Brentano's recommendation, Husserl left the University of Vienna to become Stumpf's associate at Halle as *Privatdozent*. Apparently Stumpf came under the contagion of Husserl's phenomenology, for he employed the term noticeably throughout his writings. Not that Husserl possessed any special monopoly on the term, for it was in fair use even in America by such men as Charles Sanders Peirce at the turn of the century.

It was through the efforts of Brentano and Lotze that the Würzburg professorship opened to Stumpf, and again through Brentano, when he was at Vienna, that Stumpf was called to Prague to succeed Volkmann because they wanted ''to gain in Austria a firmer hold for our theories'' (act psychology). A longing for the German fatherland prompted his acceptance of a call to Halle in 1884, and it was here that he met Husserl in 1886. ''Husserl, recommended by Brentano, was my first student, later an instructor, and became intimately associated with me scientifically and as a friend'' (1930, p. 400). The first volume of *Tonpsychologie* (Psychology of Tone) appeared in 1883, which antedates his association with Husserl, but the second volume was published in 1890 from Munich where he was called in 1889 to succeed Prantl, thus bringing him nearer to his ''old home'' and ''beloved Munich.'' After five years he yielded to the temptation of accepting the coveted chair at the University of Berlin to succeed Zeller and become associated with Dilthey who at the time was representing the historical approach. At Munich he was discouraged because it was impossible for him to found an institute of psychology at Munich. Yet when he left, Lipps was granted a seminary and Külpe a sizable institute. At Berlin a psychological seminary of three ''dark back rooms'' emerged into a large institute of 25 rooms in a former imperial castle, where his assistants *Friedrich Schumann* (1863-1940) and *Hans Rupp* (1880-   ) became active. Here in the world's foremost musical city he associated one semester with Helmholtz and established cordial relations with Dilthey and Paulsen, two distinguished philosophers.

In 1896 Stumpf (with Lipps) was in charge of the Third International Congress of Psychology in Munich; in 1900 he established the Archive for Phonograms, a 10,000 phonograph record collection of primitive music as well as founding the *Gesellschaft für Kinderpsychologie* (Society for Child Psychology); from 1907 to 1908 he served as Rector of the University of Berlin, a one-year appointment as head of the university, resulting ordinarily by faculty vote.

Stumpf's Phenomenology and Act Psychology

According to Stumpf, phenomenology, a neutral prescience or propaedeutic science *(Vorwissenschaft)*, has primary and secondary phenomena as its content or subject matter. It is a descriptive science, a discipline suitable for every established science. Whereas Brentano and Husserl spoke of facts, Stumpf and Külpe preferred the term ''function,'' the psychical functions for Stumpf being perceiving, willing, desiring, conceiving, and grouping.

The proper subject matter or contents of psychology are psychical functions, phenomenology being a neutral, propaedeutic, or prescience. Psychical functions (also termed acts, states, and experiences) are connected with phenomena, each function with its specific content. Three fundamental classes of experience or the three irreducibles of the ''immediately given,'' each with its respective science

(Vorwissenschaft), are cited by Stumpf (1907a, b): (1) *phenomena,* the subject of the science of phenomenology (such as sensory or imaginal contents); (2) *psychical functions* such as perceiving, conceiving, desiring, willing, and grouping; and (3) *immanent relations* between functions and phenomena that fall under the propaedeutic science of logology. Each function has its correlate or contents (forms, values, objectives, concepts) which collectively constitute formations. Structural laws, not grounded on induction, do actually exist. Thus a special class was introduced to account for the immanent object of the functions, terming such objects *formations,* and assigning them to another propaedeutic science, *eidology.* An example of an immanent object formation is "I like red," the problem being whether red is a genuine phenomenon such as that encountered when looking at a red object. Agreeing with Meinong and Husserl, Stumpf drew a distinction between the object of an act and content, an object being a conceptual formation. But an act is without an object if it is not up to the level of conceptions. There is no object in perceiving per se, but only relational or phenomenal contents. Content and object coincide when thought is directed toward a universal.

The two major classes of psychical functions are the *intellectual* and *emotive* (affective). The intellectual function includes (1) perceiving (embraces sensing and ideating), (2) *conceiving,* and (3) *judging.* Paired bipolarities of joy and sorrow, willing and rejecting, search and avoidance constitute the emotive.

Whereas for Stumpf the act of sensation is psychical and the content phenomenological; for Brentano the act is psychical but the content physical. For Witasek both act and content are psychical.

Feelings as Sensations. A theory of feelings as sensations, offered by Stumpf in 1907 and defended in 1916, espoused the existence of "feel-sensations" *(Gefühlsempfindungen),* a new type of sensation with its content being feelings. Distinguishing between psychological and physical (or independent) parts, he regarded the former as dependent or as attributes, and the latter as capable of spatial segmentation.

Husserl felt that Stumpf employed the term phenomenology with a "completely different meaning," resulting in confusion. He said:

> Stumpf, in his important Berlin Academy Essays (1906a,b), uses the word "function" in the connexion "psychical function" in opposition to that which he calls "appearance." The distinction is intended as a psychological one, and as such fits in with the opposition we have set up (and applied in a psychological sense only) between "acts" and "primary contents." It should be noted that the terms in question bear a completely different meaning in our expositions from that which the distinguished scientist has given them. With superficial readers of the writings on both sides it has already frequently happened that they have confused Stumpf's concept of phenomenology (as doctrine of "appearances") with my own (1962, p. 233).

Husserl dedicated his *Logische Untersuchungen* (Logical Investigations, 1900-1901) to his one-time professor, Stumpf, "in honor and friendship."

Psychology of Tone: Tonal Fusion

Consonance of tone is identified as the degree of fusion of tones. "The fundamental phenomenon of music, namely, consonance, I defined in terms of fusion'' (1930, p. 427). Fusion of tones is defined as a plurality of tones that form a unity or a whole in consciousness. Consonance then is a unit of several tones, a unity or homogeneity of tones. Several individual tones vanish by merging into one. While consonance is a ''sounding together,'' dissonance is a severance, an individuation. Consonance, as an immediate given in consciousness, is fusion. Fusion is a gestalt.

> We term fusion that relation of two contents, especially sensation-contents, in which they form not a mere sum, but a whole. The consequence of this relation is, that in its higher degrees the total impression under otherwise like conditions approaches more and more that of a single unified sensation, and becomes more and more difficult to analyze (1890, Bd. II, ¶19, sect. 1).

In addition to the degrees of fusion or degrees of differences from high to low, there are laws of fusion. The degrees of fusion are contingent on the ratio of vibrations as the principal law of tonal fusion. Other laws of fusion are:

1. The degree of fusion is independent of the tonal region.
2. The degree of fusion is independent of the strength [of different tones].
3. The degree of fusion of two given tones is in no way influenced by the addition at pleasure of a third and fourth tone.
4. As in general the changes of stimulus below a certain degree effect no perceptible changes of sensation, so likewise very minute deviations of the number of vibrations from the above mentioned ratios create no perceptible change of the degree of fusion.
5. The fusion remains and retains its degree when both tones do not affect the same ear, but one is presented exclusively to the right, the other exclusively to the left.
6. Fusion remains also in the mere representation of the imagination.
7. If we proceed above an octave, the same degrees of fusion recur with the rates of vibration increased one or more octaves (1890, Bd. II, ¶19, sect. 3).

Stumpf later revised his position so that fusion and consonance of simultaneous tones are consequences rather than causes of the relation.

Stumpf's Influence

While Stumpf held important positions, especially the chair at the University of Berlin, and despite his having such distinguished students as Schumann, Köhler, and Koffka, he was not as successful as Meinong, Wundt, and others in wielding much influence over his students. But it seems incredible that he did not influence the gestaltists. Moreover he was heading the laboratory at Berlin at a time when many of the American psychologists were turning to the universities in the United States for their Ph.D.s, such as G. Stanley Hall, the first to obtain his Ph.D. in the ''new psychology'' under James in 1878. Americans were studying with professors trained at Leipzig, at Wundt's laboratory of psychology, because it had been publicized as an unphilosophical laboratory.

CHAPTER 9

Gestalt Psychology at Frankfurt-am-Main and the Berlin School

(A) GESTALT AT FRANKFURT

The gestalt movement was spawned at Frankfurt-am-Main and transported to the University of Berlin. Frankfurt-on-the-Main River enters the gestalt story because of Wertheimer's stopping there en route to the Rhineland while vacationing during the summer of 1910. Wertheimer alighted from his train in Frankfurt in order to obtain a toy stroboscope for experiments which he conducted at his hotel. His interest was in producing the conditions of optimal movement. While at Frankfurt he established contact with Schumann, who had only that summer arrived at the Institute of Psychology as professor.

The University of Frankfurt. Frankfurt was not a university town as was the case with respect to the other universities discussed. Although one of the oldest German cities, with its share of celebrities such as Wolfgang Goethe (his birthplace), Arthur Schopenhauer, Martin Luther, and Meyer Amschel Rothschild (of banking fame) taking up residence there, it had no university until 1912, but did have the Royal Institute for Experimental Therapeutics that was moved to Frankfurt in 1899. Its university today however is of respectable size, numbering over seven thousand students in the late fifties, thus making it larger than most German universities including those at Göttingen, Marburg, and Würzburg. It was, however, at the Psychological Institute in Frankfurt a/M that gestalt psychology had its birth. The Academy of this Institute is today the University of Frankfurt.

The Phi Phenomenon: Birth of Gestalt Psychology at Frankfurt-am-Main.

While at the Institute of Psychology at Frankfurt-am-Main during the fall and winter of 1910, Wertheimer was offered space by Schumann at the Psychological Institute and a tachistoscope, enabling him to experiment with this as well as his new found apparatus, a toy stroboscope, that he had purchased at a store and taken to his hotel to experiment on the phenomenon of movement that eventuated in the phi phenomenon (visual movement) and its concomitants. It constituted the birth of gestalt psychology and the gestalt movement. In 1910 Kurt Koffka, who was serving as an assistant at the Psychological Institute, joined in Wertheimer's efforts, with Wolfgang Köhler joining Koffka as second assistant in the fall. His mind pregnant with ideas, Wertheimer opened his suitcase containing his primitive stroboscope. It resulted in the three, who knew but little concerning each other, collaborating as the first three gestalt psychologists in an age of "cheerful revolt in German psychology. . . . Some believed that the founding fathers of experimental psychology had done grave injustice to every higher form of mental life. Others suspected that at the very bottom of the new science there were some premises which tended to make its work sterile" (Köhler, 1942, p. 97). Köhler and Koffka served as experimental subjects.

The birth of gestalt psychology is traced to 1912, the date of the publication of Wertheimer's classic paper that initiated the movement, *Experimentelle Studien über das Sehen von Bewegungen* (Experimental Studies on the Seeing of Motion). It served as his dissertation for *Habilitation* at the Psychological Institute of the Academy at Frankfurt-am-Main. The paper, containing his famous experiment on the phi phenomenon (apparent movement), established the perception of motion as a gestalt, a unique property that is not present in the sense elements. The phenomenon is that witnessed in motion pictures; still pictures flashed on a screen in rapid succession produce the phi phenomenon. Wertheimer's apparent movement experiment was accomplished by flashing light at short intervals through a small aperture on a screen with the room in darkness. To do the same with a second aperture with its light flashed to the right of the first with carefully spaced or timed intervals produces an oscillation or the lights jumping to and fro from side to side, rather than the experience of two distinct lines. Thus two light flashes appear as a single one in motion (stroboscopic movement). It is the apparent movement perceived in flashing neon signs giving the appearance of movement. Explaining his (phi) phenomenon, Wertheimer stated:

> Two objects were successively given as stimuli. These were perceived. First *a* was seen, then *b*; between, a "motion from *a* to *b* was seen," without the corresponding motion or the spatially and temporally continuous positions between *a* and *b* actually being exposed as stimuli.
>
> The psychic state of affairs can be called—without prejudice—*a ∅ b*. ∅ designates something that exists outside the perceptions of *a* and *b*; what happens between *a* and *b*, in the space interval between *a* and *b*; what is added to *a* and *b*. . . .
>
> ∅ is something which uniformly concerns *a* and *b*, something which is built on them, which both embraces and unites them (1961, pp. 1049-50).

When the time interval flashes between *a* and *b* are over 200 milliseconds the phenomenal appearance is one of succession, but when it is less than 30 milliseconds simultaneity is the resulting phenomenal perception. Pure movement (the phi phenomenon or apparent movement) is perceived between these intervals, optimally at 60 milliseconds, the point at which one perceives a single object moving. In pure *phi* no trace of an object is left; only pure motion is perceived.

Interpretation "from Above:" The Theory of Wholes

Wundt, Fechner, and the other elementists restricted themselves to interpreting components "from below" because the components under their consideration were mutually independent. But gestalt findings call for an interpretation "from above" (to use Wertheimer's dictum) because the component "parts exhibit characteristics which they owe to their position within the larger entity . . . They have to be interpreted 'from above'; because with this type it is a situation as a whole which determines the behavior of its parts" (Köhler, 1944, p. 143).

KURT GOLDSTEIN (1878-1965):
His Gestalt Psychopathology and Satellites

The German neuropsychiatrist, Goldstein, was born in Kattowitz, Germany (currently Poland) and died in 1965 in New York City. His medical degree was earned at Breslau in 1903. From 1906 to his appointment in 1916 at the Neurological Institute at the University of Frankfurt-am-Main, he spent at the University of Königsburg on the staff of its psychiatric clinic. At Frankfurt as Professor *(Ordinarius)* of Neurology and as Director of the Neurological Institute and of the Institute for Brain-Injured Solders, Goldstein remained until his appointment as a professor of neurology at the University of Berlin in 1930. It was during his stay at the University of Frankfurt that his orientation assumed the gestalt stance, and with other gestaltists (Wertheimer, Köhler, Koffka, and Hans W. Gruhle (1880-1958) the *Psychologische Forschung* (Psychological Investigation) the organ of the gestalt movement, was founded in 1921.

With the advent of Nazism in 1933, he was among the first to be forced from his University of Berlin post and exiled to Amsterdam where in 1934 he wrote his classic *The Organism: A Holistic Approach to Biology Derived from Pathological Data in Man.* The thesis of the book is that

> one evaluates any aspect of the human organism in relation to the condition of the organism in its totality. On this understanding is based what I have called self-realization. The trend toward self-realization is not merely a stimulus but a driving force that puts the organism into action. What one usually calls the influence of the environment is the coming to terms between the organism and the world in "adequacy" (1967, pp. 150-1).

Goldstein spoke of "only one drive, the drive of self actualization" (1963, p. 197). "Preferred behavior" is one of "good gestalt," or the "coming to terms of the organism with the world." Good gestalt is a "form of coming to terms of the organism with the world, that form in which the organism actualizes itself, according to its nature, in the best way" (1963, p. 197). Failure in coming to terms with the world or failure in adequacy results in anxiety or a catastrophic situation. Except in catastrophe, one lives in adequacy.

His study with aphasics and brain-injured persons over the years led him to the foregoing conclusions and to the fact that aphasics lack the ability to name objects as class symbols rather than experiencing the loss of words and word images. Concepts and symbols, the dedifferentiation of language, are lost. While defects can be localized, functions cannot. Abstraction impaired restricts self-realization, rendering one a victim of the "catastrophic reaction," keynoted by anxiety accompanied by a sense of "losing existence" or the feeling that one is unable "to be.'' The goal of well and ill persons alike is self-actualization, but tension characterizes a pathological state.

The tendency to discharge any tension whatsoever is a characteristic expression of a defective organism, of disease. . . . Since the tendency to actualize itself as fully as possible is the basic drive, the only drive by which the sick organism is moved, and since the life of the normal organism is determined in the same way, it is clear that the goal of the drive is not a discharge of tension, and that we have to assume only one drive, the drive of self-actualization (1963, pp..141-2).

These views were summarized in Goldstein's William James Lectures *(Human Nature in the Light of Psychopathology)* delivered at Harvard University in 1940.

In 1935 Goldstein arrived in New York City where until 1940 he was at the Psychiatric Institute of Columbia University and concurrently headed the neurophysiological laboratory at Montefiore Hospital. The next five years (1940-1945) were spent at the Medical School of Tufts University in a similar capacity before returning to New York, teaching at the College of the City of New York, Columbia University, the New School for Social Research, and intermittently appearing as guest professor at Brandeis University in Waltham, Massachusetts, where Abraham H. Maslow, who had fallen under the spell of Goldstein's holism, had been heading the department of psychology since 1951.

Abraham H. Maslow (1908-1970): Self-Actualizationism. The Brooklyn-born Maslow was taught gestalt psychology by Max Wertheimer and Kurt Koffka at the New School for Social Research. His degrees, however, were conferred by the University of Wisconsin (B.A., 1930; M.A., 1931; Ph.D., 1934). Maslow, along with Kurt Goldstein, Charlotte Buhler, Rollo May, Carl Rogers, and others, became a founder in 1962 of the American Association for Humanistic Psychology whose organ, *The Journal of Humanistic Psychology,* enunciates its four major tenets:

(1) Centering of attention on the experiencing person, and thus a focus on experience as the primary phenomenon in the study of man.

(2) Emphasis on such distinctively human qualities as choice, creativity, valuation, and self-realization, as opposed to thinking about human beings in mechanistic and reductionistic terms.

(3) Allegiance to meaningfulness in the selection of problems for study; opposition to a primary emphasis on objectivity at the expense of significance.

(4) An ultimate concern with and valueing of the dignity and worth of man and an interest in the development of the potential inherent in every person (Brochure prepared by Charlotte Buhler and James F. T. Bugental).

Some of the members of this organization have left, joining with the recently created Division 32 of the American Psychological Association, the Division of Humanistic Psychology founded in 1971 with 374 charter members.

Maslow, one of the leading forces in humanistic psychology and a president of the American Psychological Association shortly before his death in 1970, became known in humanistic psychology for his holistic-dynamic theory of motivation articulated in his *Motivation and Personality* in 1954 and revised in 1970. His self-actualization theory derived from Goldstein was elaborated in 1962 in his *Toward a Psychology of Being*. Studying healthy people, Maslow was pursuing the nature of "full humanness," a state attained by self-actualization and epitomized by "peak experiences"—religious-like experiences. Investigating the psychology of religious experience in the vein of William James' *Varieties of Religious Experience*, Maslow found that " 'revelations' or mystical illuminations can be subsumed under the head of the 'peak-experiences' or 'ecstasies' or 'transcendent' experiences" (1964, pp. 19-20). But the peak experiences need not be limited to religious or mystical settings for they are common to a number of sensitive persons. A psychological utopia comprised of psychologically healthy individuals, he term a *eupsychia*. Optimistic in his outlook, Maslow held that a person's instinctoid needs or basic needs are fundamentally good, calling for actualization, i.e., resulting in "full-humanness." Growth then is normal; its inhibition leads to neurosis, for neurosis is a failure of personal growth. Healthy people are self-actualizing persons. In this normative orientation to psychology, "superior people" are "self-actualizers." According to Maslow's "Third Force" (humanistic) psychology, a "high synergic relationship" (a concept borrowed from Ruth Benedict) exists in a culture providing for the mutual reinforcement of the actions of its members; it is "one in which virtue pays."

His *Motivation and Personality* had its sequel in *The Psychology of Science* in 1966 in which he examined the psychology of scientists as well as science. Viewing science as a product of human nature, Maslow offered the thesis that

> the model of science in general, inherited from the impersonal sciences of things, objects, animals, and part-processes, is limited and inadequate when we attempt to know and to understand whole and individual persons and cultures. . . . But only recently has it been demonstrated just how and where this impersonal model failed with the personal, the unique, the holistic (1966, p. xiii).

Scientists in vain have attempted to "deal impersonally with the personal." Normative psychologies are necessary, one "humanizing science."

Maslow's papers, summarizing his position, were collected by his wife and posthumously published as *The Farther Reaches of Human Nature* in 1971. The title expresses his objectives with respect to humanistic psychology. Prior to his coming to Brandeis where he was tenured until his death, Maslow taught at Brooklyn College from 1937 to 1951.

Fritz S. Perls (1893-1970): Gestalt Psychotherapy. The Berlin-born and educated Fritz (Frederick) S. Perls acquired the gestalt orientation when he was assistant to Kurt Goldstein in 1926 at the Institute for Brain-Injured Soldiers. Educated at the universities of Freiburg and Berlin (receiving his M.D. from the latter institution), Perls studied and underwent psychoanalysis with Wilhelm Reich, Karen Horney, and Otto Fenichel, but gestalt to him was "inherent in nature." Other than working with Goldstein, the gestaltists never accepted him, nor was he a "pure gestaltist."

With the advent of Hitler, Perls left for Holland in 1933, and in 1934 for South Africa as a training analyst in Johannesburg, a job obtained through Freud's friend and biographer, Ernest Jones. There in 1942 in South Africa he wrote his first book, *Ego, Hunger, and Aggression*. This gestalt approach to psychotherapy was published at Durbin in 1945, and dedicated to the memory of Max Wertheimer. It was a "holistic-semantic" orientation, holism being a "field conception," and "semantics" the meaning of meaning. Viewing the "organism-as-a-whole," i.e., the "organism-environment unity," he addressed himself to the "human organism within its environment. The central conception is the theory that the organism is striving for the maintenance of a balance which is continuously disturbed by its needs, and regained through their gratification or elimination" (1966, p. 7).

After the close of World War II, Perls came to the United States in 1946, founding the New York Institute of Gestalt Therapy and publishing *Gestalt Therapy* with his collaborators Ralph E. Hefferline, a Columbia University psychologist, and Paul Goodman, who earned his Ph.D. in humanities. In this work gestalt concepts of figure/ground and unfinished situations become important. The authors explained their position accordingly:

> In neurosis, and much more in psychosis, the elasticity of figure/ground formation is disturbed. We often find either a rigidity (fixation) or a lack of figure formation (repression). Both interfere with the habitual completion of an adequate Gestalt.
>
> In health the relation between figure and ground is a process of permanent but meaningful emerging and receding. Thus the interplay of figure and background becomes the center of the theory as presented in this book: attention, concentration, interest, concern, excitement and grace are representative of healthy figure-ground formation, while confusion, boredom, compulsions, fixations, anxiety, amnesias, stagnation and self-consciousness are indicative of figure/ground formation which is disturbed (1951, p. ix).

In his autobiography published the year before he died, *In and Out the Garbage Pail* (1969), Perls made a journal-like entry: "1966 Gestalt Theory is on the map. I finally find a community, a place of being: Esalen" (p. 62). Esalen Institute at Big Sur, California was founded for gestalt therapy; later he founded and directed the Gestalt Therapy Institute of Canada at Lake Cowichan, British Columbia. His final book on the subject, *Gestalt Therapy Verbatim* (1969), appeared just before he died. By this time Perls was thoroughly humanistic in outlook and completely disenchanted with psychoanalysis, for "it took a long time to debunk the whole Freudian crap" (p. 1). Now he characterizes gestalt therapy as making "the person whole and complete again," as promoting the "growth process," as developing the "human potential," as "existential," and as discovering "the meaning of life is that it is to be lived, and it is not to be traded and conceptualized and squeezed into a pattern of systems" (p. 3). Elsewhere (1966) he wrote that the aim of gestalt therapy "is to increase human potential through the process of integration," the gaining of maturity.

By the time Perls died in 1970, a number of centers for gestalt therapy were flourishing in America (including Canada). His popularity among American psychotherapists was on the increase.

(B) GESTALT MOVES TO BERLIN

With the publication of his classic phi phenomenon in 1912, Wertheimer became *Privatdozent* at Frankfurt, leaving after four years for the University of Berlin with the same status, but elevated to assistant professor in 1922, the year after Köhler arrived there to succeed to the chair left vacant by Stumpf's retirement. In 1929 Wertheimer returned once again to Frankfurt to assume Schumann's chair, but eventually all three migrated to the United States with the ominous advent of Hitlerism, Köhler and Koffka both received their doctorates from Berlin, while Wertheimer earned his under Külpe at Würzburg. Koffka never joined them at Berlin except in the capacity of a fellow student with Köhler in pursuit of his Ph.D.

Tenets of Gestalt Psychology

To the German term *Gestalt,* signifying "form," "shape," "configuration," the gestaltists have added the meanings: structure, organic whole, and organization. Wertheimer defined its fundamental thesis accordingly:

> There are contexts in which what is happening in the whole cannot be deduced from the characteristics of the separate pieces, but conversely; what happens to a part of the whole is, in clear-cut cases, determined by the laws of the inner structure of its whole (1944, p. 84).

Koffka defined gestalt as "the attempt to find within the mass of phenomena coherent functional wholes, to treat them as full primary realities and to understand the behavior of these wholes as well as of their parts, from whole rather than from part laws" (194 b, p. 654).

The gestalt approach is phenomenologically oriented, and is antipositivistic. Defending the role of meaning and value that was rejected by the positivists, Köhler asserted:

> Never, I believe, shall we be able to solve any problems of ultimate principle until we go back to the sources of our concepts,—in other words, until we use the phenomenological method, the qualitative analysis of experience. In this our Positivists show scarcely any interest (1938, p. vii).

There are situations in which only a phenomenological analysis will lend clarity to certain notions.

Although the gestalt movement began from 1910 to 1912, gestalt in psychology antedates that period by at least three decades. It is indebted to Ernst Mach's *Analysis of Sensations* (1886) in which he spoke of space forms and time forms, and to Christian von Ehrenfels' *Über Gestaltqualitäten* (On Gestalt-qualities, 1890) in which he demonstrated gestalt by a melody changing its key and notes without losing its structural recognition. The Dane, Edgar Rubin, also contributed the gestalt figure-ground concept from Göttingen but not until 1915. Moreover, the Austrian school (Mach and Ehrenfels), which transpired approximately from 1886 to 1900, and the Würzburg school with their theory of *Bewusstheit* (awareness), which lasted approximately from 1901 to 1908, were treating their new data as novel elements. It was not until the Göttingen laboratory of psychology with Jaensch, Katz, and Rubin during the period of 1909 to 1915 that the phenomenological character of gestalt became recognized as was the case with the experimentalists at Frankfurt-am-Main whose movement may be said to date from their first publication of gestalt in 1912.

Nevertheless the three founders of the gestalt movement contributed considerably, among their offerings being: *Prägnanz,* closure, proximity, similarity, symmetry, psychophysical isomorphism, trace theory, insight learning, productive thinking, isolation effect, and relational theory as well as those ideas treated such as the phi phenomenon and gestalt. The primary data of perception of these theorists being specific structures or gestalts, it is therefore inaccurate to correlate stimuli with sensations. Instead one must correlate patterns of stimuli with specific structures as the primary content of the field of perception.

Gute Gestalten (**Good Gestalts**). For Wertheimer, *gute Gestalten* were unique configurations that have attained a maximum of balance so that no further improvement would be attained by any local change. According to Wertheimer's theory of perception, a perceptual field is one in which part characteristics derive from their larger structures. According to Köhler, Wertheimer utilized

> the term 'good' in order to indicate that the dynamics of perception are fundamentally the same as those of motivation and of thought. . . . Those who try to exclude value from the field of perception merely refuse to face facts. After all, when referring to *gute Gestalten* and their fitting parts we only acknowledge that the subject matter of aesthetics on its most elementary level is perception; and aesthetics deals with value (1944, p. 145).

The expression *gute Gestalten* yielded to *Prägnanz,* defined by the gestalt social psychologist Solomon Asch as ''grouping tends toward maximal simplicity and balance, or toward the formation of 'good form' '' (1968, p. 160).

Prägnanz. The term Prägnanz was employed by Wertheimer to express organization in its most typical form and toward which structures tend. Its corresponding word in English is *precision* (rather than pregnancy). Koffka defined it in Wertheimerian terms: ''Psychological organization will always be as 'good' as the prevailing conditions allow'' (1935, p. 110). Elsewhere he said:

> According to a very general law of Gestalt theory, called the law of Prägnanz, the best possible equilibrium will be achieved, the actual organization will be as ''good'' as the conditions allow, with regard to closedness, articulation, consistency of the particular wholes on the one hand and of the total field on the other (1931b, p. 644).

Prägnanz plays an important role in motivation, *good form* being motivational. ''Meaningful behavior remains meaningful in theory'' (1931b, p. 644). Moreover, ''if one sees an 'attractive' object one is actually attracted by it and tends to approach it, i.e. the organization of the psychophysical field contains a pull which is relieved by the movement of the body'' (1931b, p. 644). *Prägnanz* most typifies gestalt theory, conveying the notion that experienced perceptual wholes will (under existing conditions) tend in the direction of maximum regularity, clarity, and simplicity.

Closure, Proximity, and Similarity. Also gestalt laws of mental organization are closure, proximity, and similarity. *Closure,* a term introduced by Wertheimer, is the principle by which segregated or imperfect wholes tend toward complete, closed, or perfect forms. A dynamic variation of *Prägnanz,* closure is the tendency of perceptions, thoughts, action, and memories to assume a closed form, a symmetrical form, or a good definition. Lewin and Zeigarnik found that tension impels one toward completing incomplete tasks; incompletion motivates toward completion.

According to the law of *proximity*, objects are perceived as a unity when they are observed in close proximity, as in figure 1.

Fig. 1.

The gestalt law of *similarity* states that objects observed in like form or color will be perceived as assuming a grouped formation. This gestalt law is applicable to memory recall.

Psychophysical Isomorphism. Gestaltists have replaced psychophysical parallelism (a psychic element has its corresponding physical element) with their doctrine of psychophysical isomorphism, the view that brain functions tend to take the form of specific molar events corresponding to those structures that are found in experience. It stemmed from Köhler's interest in field physics derived from his professor, the Nobel prize winning *Max Planck* (1857-1947), who developed quantum theory in 1901 when he was a professor at the University of Berlin. Köhler, who was most particularly interested in the doctrine and feeling that it was the physical background of psychological gestalt, spoke of it as psychophysiology under the foreboding title of *Die physischen Gestalten in Ruhe und im stationären Zustand* (Static and Stationary Physical Configurations) in 1920.

Koffka defined isomorphism: "If similar experienced qualities find as their correlates similar cerebral processes, then at least as far as the similarity relations go consciousness and the cerebral processes are comparable." He added:

> Wertheimer has propounded the idea, which was not alien to Fechner's mind, that isomorphism refers not only to the abstract principles of order and classification but to the concrete dynamic aspects of the events themselves, an idea which has been elaborated by Köhler. Where I experience a movement, the underlying physiological processes will also have the character of a movement; when I see a symmetrical, clear and self-contained form, the underlying process will also be symmetrical, well segregated from the rest of the field and relatively self-subsistent (1944a, p. 216).

Köhler defined isomorphism as "the thesis that our experiences and the processes which underlie these experiences have the same structure" (1947, p. 201). Thus for Köhler isomorphism is a psychoneural correspondence in which the phenomenal field of perception comports with the brain field. His psychoneural isomorphism provoked criticism from physiologists and psychologists, the former viewing the brain as a network of connections, and the positivistic psychologists wishing to ascertain precisely how one affects the other rather than resting content with a mere declaration that the mind and body correspond.

Learning by Insight. Learning according to gestalt theory is the acquisition of insight, grasping relations, perceiving the meaningful whole. Köhler, who introduced the term *insight,* defined it as referring

> to the fact that, when we are aware of a relation, of any relation, this relation is not experienced as a fact by itself, but rather as something that follows from the characteristics of the objects under consideration. Now when primates try to solve a problem, their behavior often shows that they are aware of a certain important relation (1959, p. 729).

When one gains insight, he learns not by chance but by genuinely solving the problematic situation. It was with his experiments with chimpanzees that Köhler hit upon insightful learning, reporting it in *The Mentality of Apes* in 1917. There he cited the criterion of insight as "the appearance of a complete solution with reference to the whole lay-out of the field" (1927, p. 190). Unlike hens, chimpanzees assess a situation, taking inventory as it were, before resorting to the necessary behavior required for the solution. A suddenness of grasping relations often attends solution by insight. Learning by insight is "learning of one kind or another which gives the right relation and corresponding insight their chance to operate" (1959, p. 730).

Köhler reported his experiment with Sultan who telescoped two bamboo rods in order to retrieve a banana outside of his cage.

> His sticks are two hollow, but firm, bamboo rods. . . . The one is so much smaller than the other, that it can be pushed in at either end of the other quite easily. Beyond the bars lies the objective, just so far away that the animal cannot reach it with either rod. . . . Sultan first squats indifferently on the box, which has been left standing a little back from the railings; then he gets up, picks up the two sticks, sits down again on the box and plays carelessly with them. While doing this, it happens that he finds himself holding one rod in either hand in such a way that they lie in a straight line; he pushes the thinner one a little way into the opening of the thicker, jumps up and is already on the run towards the railings, to which he has up to now half turned his back, and begins to draw a banana towards him with the double stick (1956, pp. 113-4).

It was on the basis of this experiment (which did not occur within a single day) and comparable ones that Köhler reached his learning by insight theory.

Relational Theory of Learning. The gestaltists discovered from experimenting with chickens that animals learn structures and relations rather than responding to positive or absolute stimuli. Köhler (1918) found that an animal which has learned to respond to the lighter of two greys has learned the relation and not the positive or absolute value of the stimulus so that if the animal were presented with another pair of two greys (one including the lighter grey to which it was trained to respond and another still lighter) the animal will respond not to the grey to which it is accustomed but to the lighter shade because a relation has been learned (a gestalt or structure) rather than a positive stimulus. The animal has not learned an independence of colors but a togetherness of both. Köhler recounted his experiment with chickens:

> The animal is trained to choose, say, the lighter of two greys, $\overset{+}{g}r$ and avoid the darker one, $\overline{g}r$. After this training is completed there is suddenly presented, in a "critical experiment", $\overset{+}{g}r$ and the still lighter grey, $\overset{\circ}{g}r$. If it is true that the positive value of $\overset{+}{g}r$ is attached to the unaltered grey sensation experienced by the animal, then there is no reason why $\overset{+}{g}r$ should lose this value under the new circumstances. The new grey, if sufficiently different from $\overset{+}{g}r$, can have no positive value, for it will then fall outside the range of substitutions of $\overset{+}{g}r$; and it can have no negative value, for it is even farther removed from $\overline{g}r$ than $\overset{+}{g}r$ is. Therefore $\overset{\circ}{g}r$ must be "neutral". . . . The "neutral" colour . . . was chosen over twice as often as the "positive" one (1938, pp. 217-9).

Kenneth Spence (1907-1967) took issue with Köhler's relational theory, arguing that "the Gestalt theories have failed to furnish either a satisfactory explanation of these phenomena or an adequate experimental formulation of the problem" (1960, p. 306). Spence began championing the position of the absolute stimulus theory in 1937, arguing that a person learns specific stimulus-response connections so that a positive response is established to a given value of the rewarded stimulus.

Productive Thinking. In a posthumous book titled *Productive Thinking* (1945), Wertheimer drew a distinction between laws of logic and laws of thought, the former being habitual or imitative behavior and the latter creative or productive acts of thinking. Wertheimer (1934) regarded truth as "structural truth," and experience as dynamic. By grasping "wholes," one exerts minimal energy in the production of work. Citing a case of productive thinking and good gestalt in a young child, Wertheimer related:

> A child to whom I had given the parallelogram, a long one cut out of paper . . . , remarked in the beginning, "The whole middle part is all right, but the ends—" She continued to look at the form, clearly interested in the ends, suddenly took the paper figure, and, with a smile, made it into a ring, bringing the two ends together. Asked what this meant, she answered, holding the two ends together with her little fingers: "Why, I can cut it now, this way" and indicated a vertical somewhere in the middle, "Then it is all right" (1959, pp. 48-9).

Memory Traces and Isolation Effect or Restorff Effect. According to trace theory, there exist memory traces of forms that at one time were perceived and subsequently recalled. Memory traces are related to the Restorff effect (1933) or the isolation effect, i.e., a distinctive item on a list is more readily recalled than similar ones that merge into each other as is the case with nonsense syllables. The homogeneity of nonsense syllables renders them more difficult to recall as Koffka explained:

A series of nonsense syllables are not only nonsensical but also homogeneous, i.e., they consist of elements which are all of the same *kind*. Restorff has proved that this second aspect of theirs, their homogeneity, and not, as previously thought, their nonsense character, is chiefly responsible for their refractoriness, and that the effect of the homogeneity results from processes in the traces, the formation of larger trace systems in which the individual traces become absorbed and lose their independence and individuality. . . . Nothing could be more complete than Restorff's proof that homogeneity of material is of itself a factor that interferes with memory functions (1935, p. 482).

Retroactive inhibition and proactive inhibition are accounted for by the merging or crowding of similar memory traces. Isolated items such as those at the beginning or end of a list, or distinctive ones that stand out or are meaningful are learned better and recalled easier.

Biographical Perspective of the Founders of Gestalt

Max Wertheimer (1880-1943). Born in Prague, Wertheimer attended the universities of Prague (three semesters), Berlin (three semesters), and Würzburg (two semesters), receiving his Ph.D. under Külpe at Würzburg in 1904. It was the practice in the Germany of that day for students to migrate from university to university, remaining for but a few semesters. His university professional connections included: Frankfurt (1912-1916, with an additional three-year leave of absence), Berlin (1916-1929), Frankfurt (1929-1934), New School for Social Research (1934-1943).

Wolfgang Köhler (1887-1967) was born in Reval (currently Tallinn), Estonia, and studied from 1905 to 1909 at Tübingen, Bonn, and Berlin universities, receiving his doctorate in 1909 from Berlin. In 1909 he went to Frankfurt as assistant in the psychological laboratory, becoming *Privatdozent* in 1911. At the recommendation of Stumpf, who was at Berlin University, he was appointed Director of the Anthropoid Station of the Prussian Academy of Science on Tenerife Island from 1913 to 1920. Tenerife, largest of the Canary Islands, is a Spanish province in the Atlantic Ocean. From his gestalt psychological studies there on apes and their insight-learning emerged *The Mentality of Apes* in 1917.

On returning Köhler accepted a professorship at the University of Göttingen for the 1921-1922 school year before accepting the chair of psychology and philosophy at Berlin where he remained until 1935 when he was forced out of nazi Germany and came to Swarthmore College in the United States. He left Swarthmore for Dartmouth College as a research professor, remaining there until his death. He was a visiting professor at Clark University (1925-1926) and at the University of Chicago (1935) as well as the William James Lecturer at Harvard (1934-1935), the lectures published as *The Place of Value in a World of Facts* (1938). In addition to delivering the distinguished Gifford Lectures in Edinburgh in 1958, he gave the Herbert Langfeld Lectures at Princeton in 1966, publishing them as *The Task of Gestalt Psychology* (1969). His first book in English, *Gestalt Psychology* (1929), was published "for America," and dedicated to Max Wertheimer with the words: "I should like to dedicate something of which I could be prouder than these ten chapters. I hope he will accept them, however, as a testimony of my good will and of our friendship" (pp. ix-x). His *Selected Papers* appeared posthumously in a volume edited by Mary Henle in 1971; they were planned as an eightieth birthday gift.

Kurt Koffka (1887-1941). The Berlin-born Koffka received his doctorate from his home town University of Berlin in 1908, but studied at the University of Edinburgh during the 1904-1905 school season. He served assistantships at the universities of Würzburg and Frankfurt before joining the University of Giesen, initially as *Privatdozent,* and left as professor in 1927. Visiting professorships in the United States included Cornell (1924-1925) and Wisconsin (1926-1927) before his professorship in 1927 at Smith College in Northampton, Massachusets, where he died on November 22, 1941.

At Würzburg, Koffka served under Külpe and then assisted Marbe when Külpe left. At Frankfurt he assisted Schumann. In 1921 Wertheimer, Köhler, Koffka, Kurt Goldstein (1878-1965, who was at the University of Frankfurt a/M), and Hans W. Gruhle (1880-1958) founded the *Psychologische Forschung* (Psychological Investigation), the organ of the gestalt movement. After running through 22 volumes it ceased publication in 1938 with Köhler editing it from Swarthmore. Koffka's *summa* on gestalt psychology in English appeared in 1935 under the title *Principles of Gestalt Psychology,* a book dedicated to his colleagues Köhler and Wertheimer. Koffka was perhaps the first to win Americans to gestalt with his *Perception: An Introduction to Gestalt-Theorie,* written in 1922 for the *Psychological Bulletin* in order to acquaint American psychologists with gestalt. Prior to this publication, he was known to psychologists for his application of gestalt to developmental and child psychology in the book, *The Growth of Mind* (1921).

Gestalt Applied to Social Psychology

Fritz Heider (1896-   ): Gestalt in Interpersonal Relationships. At Smith College, Koffka had a colleague who applied gestalt to the field of social psychology, Fritz Heider. The Viennese Heider, who obtained his Ph.D. from the University of Graz (Austria) in 1920, joined Koffka at Smith College in 1930, remaining there a half dozen years after Koffka's demise. Since 1947 he has been at the University of Kansas.

In 1946 Heider developed a gestalt theory of interpersonal relations and elaborated on it in his *The Psychology of Interpersonal Relations* (1958), a book that would more appropriately have been titled the theory of interpersonal perceptions. Accordingly Heider had taken the perception psychology of gestalt and applied it to interpersonal relations, relations between two people. A relationship between two persons is a gestalt.

> Generally, a person reacts to what he thinks the other person is perceiving, feeling, and thinking, in addition to what the other person may be doing. In other words, the

presumed events inside the other person's skin usually enter as essential features of the relation (1958, p. 1).

In his "cognitive" social psychology, Heider sought the "cognitive matrix" that underlies an individual's interpretation of another's behavior. He argued for a tendency toward balance. His basic hypothesis is:

Attitudes towards persons and causal unit formations influence each other. An attitude towards an event can alter the attitude towards the person who caused the event, and if the attitudes towards a person and an event are similar, the event is easily ascribed to the person. A balanced configuration exists if the attitudes towards the parts of a causal unit are similar (1946, p. 107).

Sentiment (liking or disliking) relationships between persons (or person and object) are relationships of belonging, hence are unit relations. Unit relations belonging together are in a "state of balance." Heider's is referred to as the p-o-x theory of cognitive balance: p (reference person) and o (other person) form U (unit relation such as possession or belonging); x standing for an impersonal entity such as situations, events, ideas, things, etc. In humans there is a proclivity toward balance. Summarizing his position, Heider wrote:

This theory of balance deals mainly with configurations consisting of a number of entities between which exist certain relations. The entities can be persons—their own person or other persons—and other entities, as for instance, things, situations, or groups. The relations considered are mainly of two sorts: on the one hand attitudes of liking or disliking, and on the other hand unit relations of belonging. The main idea is that certain of these configurations are preferred, and that, if circumstances allow, they will be realized by the person either in such a mental reorganization as wishful thinking, or in actual change through action (1960, p. 167).

In American social psychology, Heider proved influential. The psychologist Dorwin Cartwright and the mathematician Frank Harary (both at the University of Michigan in 1956) almost immediately seized upon the theory by formalizing and generalizing it into a structural balance in a graph-theoretic context. They were successful in arriving at a degree of balance.

Two years after Cartwright and Harary's paper, Robert P. Abelson and Milton J. Rosenberg (both at that time at Yale University), inspired by Cartwright and Harary's structural balance theory and Heider's cognitive balance theory, developed their own balance model of attitude change, a "symbolic psycho-logic" model of attitudinal cognition. Other theories in the vein of cognitive consistency flourished, such as an acquaintance process theory by Theodore M. Newcomb (1953, 1961) of the University of Wisconsin, whose theory of communicative acts assumed the form of an A-B-X system and Leon Festinger's theory of cognitive dissonance (concerning which more will be said later).

Solomon E. Asch (1907-   ): Minority of One Experiment. A colleague of Maslow at Brooklyn College in the middle forties, and an associate professor at the New School for Social Research (where the gestaltists were concentrated) in the later forties, the Warsaw-born Asch received his Ph.D. from Columbia University in 1932 and a score of years later wrote an entire text, *Social Psychology* (1952), oriented from the gestaltist stance.

Acknowledging his indebtedness to von Ehrenfels and Wertheimer for his appreciation of gestalt psychology, Asch became known in psychology owing to his transporting gestalt into social psychology and for experiments on group pressure.

> To understand a person we must see him in his setting, in the context of his situation and the problems he is facing. If we wish to understand a given quality in a person we must see it in relation to his other qualities. For this reason also, the "same" quality in two persons is often not the same psychologically. . . . When the phenomena being observed have order and structure, it is dangerous to concentrate on the parts and to lose sight of their relations. It becomes necessary instead to look at facts, as Wertheimer stated, "from above to below" (1952, p. 60).

To apply gestalt tenets to social psychology means to view data as structured; to structure an issue results in a patterning of values so that true differences become apparent. One must structure the social field so that people, events, and ideas can be seen and evaluated from one standpoint. Man tends to be as good as the prevailing conditions permit according to the gestalt principle of *Prägnanz*.

In an influential experiment on group pressure in which a person, a minority of one, confronts the pressures exerted by a unanimous majority, Asch (1951, 1956) found that a person will yield to the opinion of the majority despite his own senses providing him with contradictory information. With an increase in the size of the majority (levelling off at three), pressure toward conformity is intensified. Some persons, however, maintain their autonomy.

Harry Helson (1898-   ): Adaptation Level Theory. Though not a "100 percent" gestaltist as he phrased it, Helson (born in Chelsea, Massachusetts) became infected with *"Gestalttheorie"* as a young instructor at Cornell when Koffka came there as a visiting professor during the 1924-1925 school season. Attending Koffka's seminar along with Karl M. Dallenbach (1887-   ), Joy Paul Guilford (1897-   ), and three or four others, Helson became fired up, especially during his weekly visits to Koffka's home where the history and psychology of gestalt was discussed. Helson then proceeded to prepare a series of four articles on gestalt psychology for the *American Journal of Psychology* (1925-1926). But it was through Edwin G. Boring (1886-1968) at Harvard that Helson's acquaintance with gestalt initiated and where a Ph.D. dissertation on gestalt and its history was written for his degree (granted in 1924), the thesis being the four articles mentioned above for journal publication.

Known for his *adaptation level (AL) theory,* Helson regarded it as an extension of gestalt. The Helson law of the visual adaptation-level states that "an adaptation-level is a certain function of intensities from the figure and ground of a visual field" (1951, p. 19). At the adaptation level, which is a subjective point of equality, stimuli are neutral or indifferent, stimuli above and below the adaptation level (e.g., pleasant and unpleasant stimuli) being complementary to each other. Adaptation level theory

> furnishes a quantitative basis for the study of interaction effects by specifying the neutral or indifferent response as a weighted log mean of focal contextual and residual stimuli. Quality and magnitude of responses (including sensory and perceptual responses) are shown to be a function of their distance above or below level (distance being used here in the sense of interval, ratio, or any other suitable type of scaling) (1972, p. 104).

Adaptation level theory was first introduced in journal form in 1947 and reached its culmination in a volume, *Adaptation-Level Theory: An Experimental and Systematic Approach to Behavior,* in 1964. After subjects responded to numerous stimuli, they could determine the stimulus that was "in the middle" from the "big" and "small" ones. Each dimension of perception has these neutral points or reference points so that a person's perceptual apparatus, adapting to situations, provides constant and sensitive perception. Adaptation level serves as a frame of reference so that the observed colors are determined in terms of differing light stimuli.

Although the quantitative theory appeared in 1947, adaptation theory occurred to Helson when he (with Deane B. Judd) constructed a sphere covering the subject's head and containing a light source for investigating total chromatic adaptation with constant light flux extending to every portion of the retina.

> By taking the level of adaptation as a fulcrum or origin with respect to which behavior is organized, an analytical approach to problems of patterning or Gestalt becomes possible. Thus, if we know the brightness, loudness, or weight that is judged medium or indifferent in a series of stimuli then we can order all other members of the series with respect to these qualities. The relation of any stimulus to prevailing level determines its perceived magnitude and quality. By defining adaptation level as a weighted mean of all stimuli affecting behavior, past as well as present, it becomes a quantitative, operational concept for handling the varied adaptations and adjustments of organisms to the conditions confronting them (1964, p. xvi).

(C)   THE LEWINIAN TRADITION

KURT LEWIN (1890-1947):
Field Theory and Topological Psychology

Born in Mogilno, Germany, Kurt Lewin spent a distasteful semester at the University of Freiburg in 1909 and another semester at Munich the end of that year before going to the University of Berlin, where he received his Ph.D. in 1916. He developed a serious interest in psychology when an instructor challenged him regarding a statement he made on a scientific concept. When the instructor queried whether Lewin's contention would hold true for psychology, Lewin's defense led him in 1910 to the University of Berlin's Psychological Institute where Carl Stumpf, the director, was eventually to become his dissertation director ("thesis father"). Here he met the philosopher Ernst Cassirer, who left a lasting influence on him with respect to philosophy of science. Here also he joined a lively group of students engaged in discussing and challenging conventional theories.

In 1921 Lewin became an assistant in the Psychological Institute at the University of Berlin, and began teaching courses as a *Privatdozent*. At the Psychological Institute he established associations with Köhler and Wertheimer, who were establishing formulations for the new gestalt psychology, a holistic psychology that Lewin found appealing. While Lewin never fully became an orthodox gestaltist, its holistic orientation impressed him, and he became a vital factor in the development of gestalt because he felt that it provided the best psychological explanation of actual experience.

Applied Psychology. In the late teens, Lewin was engrossed in applied or industrial psychology, writing two papers on the subject in 1919 and 1920 in which he contended that a person produces to live and not vice versa. The worker's well-being is enhanced, not simply by reducing his man hours on the job, but through the improvement of his psychological components, the important factor being the enhancement of the "inner value" afforded by working.

Dynamic Theory and the Field Approach in Psychology. In 1922 his philosophy of science began to crystallize, and he developed it in his *Der Begriff der Genese in Physik, Biologie und Entwicklungsgeschichte* (The Concept of Genesis in Physics, Biology and Evolutionary History, 1922), with additional formulations in a paper titled "The Conflict between Aristotelian and Galileian Modes of Thought in Contemporary Psychology" (1931a). According to Lewin, psychology had arrived at a "Galileian turning point," the point at which a psychologist must no longer think in Aristotelian terms of absolute contrasting pairs such as black and white but in terms of *dynamic sequences* along a continuum in a unified field as Galileo introduced. Black and white are not opposites separated from each other but component parts of the same continuum in an uninterrupted sequence. Psychology must follow the example of Galileian physics.

> As in physics, the grouping of events and objects into paired opposites and similar logical dichotomies is being replaced by groupings with the aid of serial concepts which permit of continuous variation, partly owing simply to wider experience and the recognition that transition stages are always present (1935, p. 22).

Psychology, like physics, must adopt the dynamic concept of sequence, and abandon static concepts such as disjunctive pairs.

The whole, an object studied in its totality, acquires significance. *"Only by the concrete whole which comprises the object and the situation are the vectors which determine the dynamics of the event defined* (1935, p. 30). Grasping the totality requires a description of the concrete single case, involving the totality of forces operative at any one time which entails both external or environmental forces and internal forces such as needs.

> Thus in the psychological fields most fundamental to the whole behavior of living things the transition seems inevitable to a Galileian view of dynamics, which derives all its vectors not from single isolated objects, but from the mutual relations of the factors in the concrete whole situation, that is, essentially, from the momentary condition of the

individual and the structure of the psychological situation. *The dynamics of the processes is always to be derived from the relation of the concrete individual to the concrete situation,* and, so far as internal forces are concerned, from the mutual relations of the various functional systems that make up the individual (1935, p. 41).

Without the total psychological field (life space) in view at a given time, human behavior cannot be predicted. Consequently a large number of cases of a given phenomenon are not as valuable as a single case known in its totality (the wholeness of the person and his psychological field). Hence not numerous repetitions of phenomena of a specific type, but the totality of the concrete whole situation assumes precedence. Behavior is a function of the total situation.

Field Theory. Lewin listed a half dozen major characteristics of his field theory:

(1) The use of a constructive rather than a classificatory method.
(2) An interest in the dynamic aspects of events.
(3) A psychological rather than a physical approach.
(4) An analysis which starts with the situation as a whole.
(5) Behavior as a function of the field at the time it occurs.
(6) A mathematical representation of the field (1942, p. 215).

In the constructive method, an individual case is represented by elements of construction such as "psychological position" and "psychological forces." The dynamic approach calls for scientific constructs dealing methodologically with the underlying forces of behavior, dynamics signifying psychological forces. A psychological approach treats the "behavioral environment" as Koffka put it, or the field or "life space" by which the individual is influenced. As a rule it is advantageous to proceed with an analysis of the total situation. Behavior is a function of the present psychological field of forces that are in effect, the past possessing only an indirect effect inasmuch as past events no longer exist hence are currently ineffective. Mathematical representations of psychological situations are necessary tools for logical strictness and for the employment of constructive techniques of topological and vectorial concepts in order to produce conceptual precision in psychology.

Psychical Tension as Energy Sources: The Tension Systems

At the University of Berlin's Institute of Psychology, Lewin's students associated informally in a *Quasselstrippe* (quassel = "ramble on;" strippe = "string"), that is, chatting freely at their meetings in the Schwedische Cafe located opposite the Institute. Freud, at the Cafe Arkadan in Vienna, and Adler, at Vienna's Cafe Siller, did the same. The custom was to talk over coffee and cake sometimes as long as three hours. MacKinnon, recalling one of these events with Lewin, reported it to Marrow (1969):

On one such occasion, somebody called for the bill and the waiter knew just what everyone had ordered. Although he hadn't kept a written reckoning, he presented an exact tally to everyone when the bill was called for. About a half hour later Lewin called the waiter over and asked him to write the check again. The waiter was indignant. 'I don't know any longer what you people ordered,' he said, 'You paid your bill.' In psychological terms, this indicated that a tension system had been building up in the waiter as we were ordering and that upon payment of the bill the tension system was discharged (1969, p. 27).

Lewin held that important problems of everyday living must be observed and translated into the language of psychology and then quantitatively investigated in the laboratory. "Nothing is as practical as a good theory," he exclaimed. It was this theory that his student Zeigarnik experimented upon with her classic results in 1927.

Tension, that state of readiness or that state in which one is prepared for action, Lewin regarded as a "reservoir of energy." It is not habits that are motivating, but tension systems, those "psychical energies, that is, tense psychical systems which derive, as a rule, from the pressure of will or of a need, are always the necessary condition of the occurrence—in whatever way—of the psychical event" (1935, p. 44). Psychical tensions are the sources of energy. "System" he defined as a region with respect to its state (particularly a state of tension), and "tension" he defined as "a state of a region relative to surrounding regions. It involves forces at the boundary of the region which tends to produce changes such that differences of tension are diminished" (1936, p. 218).

The Women in Lewin's Life

While Lewin was at Berlin, the most significant experimental contributions fortifying his theories were contributed mostly by women, students pursuing their Ph.D.'s from the university.

Bluma Zeigarnik (1900-   ): Zeigarnik Effect. The most significant contribution to his field theory was that of the Russian-born Zeigarnik, currently a professor at Moscow University and chief of laboratory at the Institute of Psychiatry. Born in Prenay, Zeigarnik received her Ph.D. under Lewin at the University of Berlin in 1927.

Her intent was to experiment with respect to Lewin's thesis that a system of psychological tension is motivating until the intended task is executed fully. Goal directed activity left unfulfilled keeps the psychological system pent up with undischarged tension.

The *Zeigarnik effect*, unfulfilled tasks are retained better than completed ones, was the first experimental confirmation of Lewin's thesis on tension systems. Publishing her findings in 1927 in a paper titled "Über das Behalten von erledigten und unerledigten Handlungen" (On the Retention of Finished and Unfinished Tasks), Zeigarnik reported that

a quasi-need persists if the task has not been completed *to the subject's own* satisfaction regardless of whether this is equivalent to what may seem from another's inspection to constitute "finished" or "unfinished". Tasks with whose solution the subject is not content will function in his memory as "unfinished" even though the experimenter may have classified them as completed tasks, and vice versa (1968, p. 443).

A quasi-need operates as a state of tension. Lewin defined a *need* as corresponding to a "tension system of the inner-personal region," and a *quasi-need* as intention. "Both needs and quasi-needs reveal themselves in the fact that certain things or events assume, by virtue of these needs or quasi-needs, *valences* calling for certain activities" (1967, p. 293). A valence corresponds to a field of force, the structure of which is a central field.

Maria Ovsiankina: Need Satisfaction and Tension Release. A year after Zeigarnik published her findings, Maria Ovsiankina, another Russian female student studying under Lewin at Berlin, continued research in the vein of Zeigarnik, but her concern was the quantification of the spontaneous resumption of the once interrupted tasks. In her paper "Die Wiederaufnahme von interbrochenen Handlungen" (The Resumption of Interrupted Activities), she corroborated Lewin's thesis by establishing a definite correlation between tension release and need satisfaction.

Vera Mahler (1899-   ): Degrees of Substitute Activity. A third female student, born in Hamburg, Germany, received her Ph.D. from the University of Berlin in 1933, the year in which she published her finding on substitute activity. This student of Lewin (currently a lecturer at the University of Tel-Aviv, Israel) explored the possibility of substitute activity functioning as a release of those tensions produced by interrupted tasks. Substitution, a form of sublimation, consisted of talking, thinking regarding the activity, and the like. Her paper "Ersatzhandlungen verscheidenen Realitätsgrades" (Substitute Activities of Different Degrees of Reality, 1933) supported Lewin's contention by establishing that quasi-need tensions can be satisfied by resorting to substitutes when the ordinary vehicle for their satisfaction is unavailable. Provided the inner goal or intention is sufficiently satisfied through substitute activity, satisfaction ensues with a concomitant decrement in tension. Mere talking, without some form of goal attainment, is insufficient. Lewin noted that "substitution occurs only when this inner goal is in sufficient degree attained by the substitute activity" (1935, p. 249).

Kate Lissner: Substitute Value. Still another female student of Lewin published her experimental finding in 1933 on "Die Entspannung von Bedürfnissen durch Erstazhandlungen" (The Discharge of Needs by Substitute Activities) in which a difficult performance serving as the substitute value was found of considerably higher worth than a relatively easy one. Moreover, the greater the similarity of the substitute activity then the greater its value, the degree of relationship being a vital factor.

Environmental Forces and Topological Psychology

When Lewin speaks of a person's environment, he is referring to his psychological environment, and when he talks of a person's *life space,* it is the totality of facts or events by which one's behavior is determined at any given moment. Describing behavior in terms of life space is topological psychology, life space being the larger concept engulfing both the person and his environment. Consequently behavior *(B)* becomes a function of life space *(L)* and in turn is a function of the person *(P)* and his environment *(E)* , hence

$$B = f(L) = f(P,E)$$

Psychological environmental forces apply equally to a person's momentary situation and to his permanent environment.

Other constructs representing the Lewinian psychological field include (1) force, (2) the position of the person within the total psychological field, (3) position of other parts of the field in relation to each other, and (4) potency. *Force* is a tendency to act in a specific direction and is more than a drive or excitatory tendency, for it is a cause of change with properties of strength, direction, and point of application. Both strength and direction are *vectoral forces,* that is, they can be represented by a vector. A field of forces with a central field for its structure is a *valence* (attraction), a valence attracting being a positive one, and a negative one repelling (comparable to Freud's concept of cathexis and anticathexis). Retaining the notion that environment is psychological, it follows that when a person (psychologically) moves (locomotes) from one psychological region (a part of life space) to another, *locomotion* of a change in structure has occurred. But in so doing he may encounter a *barrier,* a boundary or boundary zone that resists locomotion. The barrier may be outer, hence encircling the individual, or inhomogeneous with differing resistance at varying points, or impassable, completely inhibiting locomotion. Even *gestalt* for Lewin is defined dynamically (rather than perceptually) as "a system whose parts are dynamically connected in such a way that a change of one part results in a change of all other parts" (1936, p. 218).

Conflict. Defining conflict "psychologically as the opposition of approximately equally strong field forces" (1933, p. 605), Lewin's analysis uncovered three major types: (1) two positive valences (approach-approach conflict); (2) a positive and a negative valence (approach-avoidance conflict); and (3) two negative valences (avoidance-avoidance conflict). An example of the first is a child desirous of both going on a picnic and remaining at home with his friends. The second is exemplified by a child who would like to climb a tree yet is fearful. The third is illustrated by the child who is required to do a distasteful task and faces punishment if failing to do so. The various forces exerted on a person constitute a field.

Field Theory in Social Science

In 1951 Lewin's papers were collected and published under the title *Field Theory in Social Science,* a fitting title because of Lewin's continuous interest in social psychology. Three years earlier another posthumous publication similar to it was issued under the title *Resolving Social Conflicts.* Both were suitable titles because Lewin in his later career became deeply interested in group dynamics.

In 1921 Lewin began his career as *Privatdozent* at the University of Berlin and left with Hitler's advent in 1933 as Professor of Philosophy and Psychology.

Though he officially severed with Berlin in 1933, he left for Stanford University a year earlier. After a year at Stanford and a couple following at Cornell, his investigations went into high gear at the Child Welfare Research Station of the State University of Iowa beginning in 1935. It was here that some of his students, who went on to distinguish themselves, received their Ph.D.'s, including *Leon Festinger* (1919-   ), who obtained his in 1942, and *Ronald Lippitt* (1914-   ), whose degree was conferred in 1940.

Social Space. Lippitt went to Iowa on a graduate assistantship where he was assigned to assist in frustration-regression experiments with *Tamara Dembo* (1902-   ), another Russian female student of Lewin whose Ph.D. came from the University of Berlin in 1930. But the experiments in social space resulted from an "autocracy-democracy" study listed by Lewin in a memorandum he sent to incoming graduate students. Carrying Lewin's theories into his field experiment, Lippitt's research fructified into his doctoral thesis in 1940, titled "An Experimental Study of Authoritarian and Democratic Group Atmospheres." Lewin and Lippitt were joined by a Stanford Ph.D., Ralph K. White (1907-   ), a post doctoral research fellow who came to Iowa in 1937. In 1939 the three published one of their first reports on social space, "Patterns of Aggressive Behavior in Experimentally Created 'Social Climates.'" This publication grew out of Lippitt and White's work with small groups of boys from Iowa City in 1938, and the findings of these two men expanded into a book-length report in 1960 under the title *Autocracy and Democracy: An Experimental Inquiry*.

The researchers, concerned with the nature of leadership and the relative efficiency of a democratic social climate compared to an authoritarian one, reported that while the autocratic group existed in a social atmosphere of high tension and directed concerted aggression against a single individual, the democratic group displayed a greater expression of cooperative endeavor, objective attitude, constructiveness, feeling of "we'ness," group stability and unity, and feeling for group property (Lewin & Lippitt, 1938).

Believing in social space, Lewin professed: "I am persuaded that there exists a social space which has all the essential properties of a real empirical space" (1939, p. 21). Explaining his method of investigating social space he wrote: "Instead of observing the properties of individuals, the properties of the group as such were observed" (1939, p. 23).

According to Lewin, even reality is social. " 'Reality' for the individual is, to a high degree, determined by what is socially accepted as reality. . . . 'Reality,' therefore, is not an absolute. It differs with the group to which the individual belongs" (1948, p. 57).

Group Dynamics. By the time of his death, Lewin was deeply intrenched in group dynamics, publishing "Frontiers in Group Dynamics" (1947), the year of his death. By 1945 he had founded the Research Center for Group Dynamics at Massachusetts Institute of Technology and attracted notable social psychologists as its directors, among them being Dorwin Cartwright (1915-   ), Ronald Lippitt, John R. P. French (1913-   ), and Leon Festinger. With Lewin's death, the center (under the directorship of Cartwright) moved to the University of Michigan in 1947.

The last decade of his life Lewin was virtually through with developing concepts related to personality theory and had turned his attention toward social psychology, particularly group dynamics and social space, applicable to community, religion, family, and work groups. Group behavior now became regarded as a function of not only the person but the social situation as well, both variables being necessary and studied. His perception of social space left him believing that groups effect a significant change upon their constituent members so that reciprocal relations have an effect on each other. While attractive groups exert considerable pressure, weaker ones have considerably less. As the opportunities for achieving objectives of the individual members of the group are augmented, then group cohesiveness is concomitantly increased. Conformity likewise has a direct ratio to the degree of group cohesiveness. Provided a group is a *gestalt* (a whole comprised of unlike elements), it need not be similar to any considerable extent. "The whole is different from the sum of its parts: it has definite properties of its own." In "Field Theory and Experiment in Social Psychology" (1939), Lewin noted this fact is evident in family life where man, wife, and child can be more dissimilar than the man is with respect to other men of his social class and age. "Not similarity, but a certain interdependence of members constitutes a group."

The Research Center for Group Dynamics at M.I.T. had as its principal objective the development of group experiments, especially the changes that occur in group life, and developmental concepts and theories of group dynamics. In conjunction with the Research Center, Lewin undertook the Commission on Community Interrelations for the American Jewish Congress. He served visiting professorships at the University of California (Berkeley) during the summer of 1939, and at Harvard during the spring terms of 1938 and 1939.

Leon Festinger (1919-): Cognitive Dissonance

Festinger, who obtained his Ph.D. under Lewin in 1942 at the State University of Iowa, was a friend of Lippitt. Both men were there working with Lewin and also with the rats of the distinguished Kenneth W. Spence, a Yale Ph.D., who headed the department of psychology at Iowa in the early forties. Festinger, Lewin's most distinguished American student, was a research associate at Iowa in 1943 when he became an instructor at the University of Rochester. It was in 1945 that Lewin took Festinger along with him to M.I.T. as associate professor. When the Research Center moved to the University of Michigan after Lewin's death in 1947, Festinger went along the following year as director. From there he went to Stanford before settling in 1968 at the gestaltist's stronghold at the New School for Social Research.

Dissonance theory came about in consequence of studies stemming from the Indian earthquake of 1934 when numerous rumors arose in its wake with respect to still worse disasters. The curious question it evoked was: Why are anxiety-provoking rumors arising and why are they widely accepted? Could it be that anxiety-provoking rumors provide people with information that accords with their feelings? Dissonance theory was the result. People were seeking information consonant with their behavior, a fact that extends to information-seeking processes.

According to dissonance theory, a person has a proclivity for internal harmony and congruity, resembling a need-state. The unpleasantness of cognitive dissonance functions as motivation, impelling an individual to its reduction.

> The basic background of the theory consists of the notion that the human organism tries to establish internal harmony, consistency, or congruity among his opinions, attitudes, knowledge, and values. That is, there is a drive toward consonance among cognitions. . . . . Dissonance almost always exists after an attempt has been made, by offering rewards or threatening punishment, to elicit overt behavior that is at variance with private opinion. . . . Post decision dissonance may be reduced by increasing the attractiveness of the chosen alternative, decreasing the attractiveness of the unchosen alternatives, or both (1957, pp. 260-1, 264).

Mental unpleasantness results from the failure of a relation among cognitions to cohere harmoniously, resulting in psychological discomfort driving one to restructure his cognition in order to diminish stridency. A concomitant relation exists between a person's inner harmony and the manner in which he structures his world. Dissonance is the result of a person's behavior being discrepant with his cognitions. Festinger found that "insufficient reward does lead to the development of extra preference. . . . Rats and people come to love things for which they have suffered" (1961, p. 11). When considerable effort is expended to achieve a goal and the reward is found wanting then dissonance results. In order to reduce dissonance, it is necessary either to restructure one's cognitions or his behavior so that they comport with each other.

Gestalt Migrates to America

Although great schools or movements of psychology are not the order of the day, gestalt in psychology is still prevalent, especially in social psychology where the tradition is carried on by S. E. Asch, M. Deutsch, F. Heider, J. R. P. French, L. Festinger, R. Lippitt, D. Cartwright, and many associated with the Research Center for Group Dynamics.

But these psychologists are Americans, evidence that gestalt has been transplanted to the United States. The perceptive reader will have noted that gestalt became an American psychology owing to nazi intolerance. So much so did it become American that Lewin during his first days in the United States was not only determined to learn English immediately, but by the time of the World's Fair in New York in 1939, where he was visiting, he remarked as Marrow reported: " 'Let's have a couple of hot dogs,' Lewin said. 'That's what we Americans eat on Sunday evenings in the summer!' Five minutes later that's what we were doing" (1969, p. 171).

PART FOUR

PARIS AND VIENNA: RISE OF CLINICAL PSYCHOLOGY

Psychotherapy as it is known today was sired in Paris, growing out of the phenomenon of hypnosis. Although hypnotism had its birth in Vienna by the Viennese, Friedrich (Franz) Anton Mesmer (1734-1815), it was repudiated by the Austrians. Not until Mesmer arrived at Paris, where subsequent espousers of his views developed and perpetuated his notion of hypnotism, did this phenomenon find its way into psychotherapy, including the psychoanalysis of Freud. Freud learned of hypnosis when he went to Paris to continue his education with Charcot. "In the distance glimmered the great name of Charcot," reminisced Freud, who planned on "going to Paris to continue my studies" (1963, p. 19). Freud continued:

> What impressed me most of all while I was with Charcot were his latest investigations upon hysteria, some of which were carried out under my own eyes. He had proved, for instance, the genuineness of hysterical phenomena and their conformity to laws . . . , the frequent occurrence of hysteria in men, the production of hysteria paralyses and contractures by hypnotic suggestion and the fact that such artificial products showed, down to their smallest details, the same features as spontaneous attacks, which were often brought on traumatically (1963, p. 22).

Having satisfied the curious that psychotherapy, including the roots of Freudian psychoanalysis, finds its inception in Paris, it behooves us to examine more closely psychotherapy as it unfolded in Paris and its Viennese offshoot. Before that undertaking, however, it should prove profitable to review psychotherapy from its meager beginnings in antiquity to the period of its great enlightenment in Paris, where such notables as *Philippe Pinel* (1745-1826), *Jean Esquirol* (1772-1840), *Friedrich (Franz) Anton Mesmer* (1734-1815), *Jean-Martin Charcot* (1825-1893), and *Pierre Janet* (1859-1947) gave birth to clinical psychology. From Paris (and Nancy) the development of psychotherapy transfers to Vienna for its maturing years, where the great luminaries are *Sigmund Freud* (1856-1939), *Alfred Adler* (1870-1937), *Viktor E. Frankl* (1905-   ), *J. L. Moreno* (1892-1974), and the neurophysiological psychotherapists *Manfred J. Sakel* (1900-1957) and *Julius Ritter Wagner von Jauregg* (1857-1940).

Origins of Psychotherapy

Psychotherapy can be traced to inchoate beginnings in the twentieth century BC where, in the *Code of Hammurabi* (*c.* 1950 BC), opium and olive oil are prescribed as the recommended cures for demonism. In ancient Mesapotamia, medical practice was essentially psychosomatic, owing to psychotherapy in the form of incantation being administered in conjunction with drugs. Moreover they were the first therapists to examine the life history of the patient. Egypt's first therapist, *Imhotep* (fl. *c.* 2980-2950 BC), was deified when Egypt became a Persian province in 525 BC. His Memphian temple with time became a hospital (and medical school) where incubation sleep was prescribed as psychotherapy. Hysteria is also of Egyptian origin where it was viewed as of emotional origin. The term itself, of Greek origin, is a later derivative. The Greeks, attributing emotional disorder to a disrupted uterine position, sought to restore the uterus to its proper position. The "father of medicine," *Hippocrates* (*c*. 460-377 BC), the first to administer a medical code of ethics to his disciples, developed a humoral behavior theory together with a three-fold classification of mental disorder: mania, melancholia, and dementia. The humoral theory of psychopathology was expanded by *Galen* (fl. 2nd cen. AD), a Greek physician who settled in Rome. The term *insanity* is attributed to the Roman writer *Aulus Cornelius Celsus* (25 BC-50 AD).

Almost contemporary in his outlook, *Asclepiades of Bithynia* (fl. 100 BC), a Greek physician, identified mental disorder with emotional disturbances (passions of sensations). Furthermore, centuries before Esquirol, he anticipated him by differentiating between hallucinations and delusions. He also utilized music and baths as therapeutic measures. A stoic type of philosophical psychotherapy was suggested by the Roman philosopher *Marcus Tullius Cicero* (106-43BC). One of the first to appreciate mental disorders as psychogenic, Cicero was aware of the characteristics of the neurotic and psychopathic personalities. Rather than physical factors, he traced ailments to emotional ones, hence initiated psychosomatic medicine. Originally from Rome, the physician *Caelius Aurelianus* (fl. 5th century AD or earlier) translated the works of his teacher, *Soranus* of Ephesus, in a volume titled *On Acute Disease and on Chronic Disease*. These philosophical methodists, concerned with the methods of treatment, were reformers who opposed the harsh treatment of the mentally ill. Thus they anticipated Pinel's eighteenth century reforms in Paris. While Celsus chained and starved his patients, Soranus relieved mental discomfort through talking, thus anticipating modern psychotherapeutic techniques.

Although in 429 the *Codex Theodosianus* eschewed magic as an evil, psychotherapy in the medieval era was reduced to demonology, the devil being the causative agent of mental disorder such as melancholy. The German humanist *Johannes Tritheim* (1462-1516), an abbot at Sponheim and author of *Antipalus Maleficiorum*, attributed mental illness to witches leaving human beings possessed. Two other Germans, brothers of the Dominican order, *Johann Sprenger* and *Heinrich Kraemer*, published the *Malleus Maleficarum* (Witches' Hammer) in 1487 dealing with psychopathology and witchcraft. Their mission was the extermination of witches, a movement that gained the support of the scientific community of their time. They theorized that an ailment that does not respond to drugs is caused by the devil's witchcraft. An insatiable carnal lust in women accounts for all witchcraft. For two centuries the *Malleus Maleficarum* dominated the law.

It remained for the Belgian physician *Johann Weyer* (1515-1588), regarded by Zilboorg (1967, p. 165) as "the founder of modern psychiatry," to challenge, ridicule, and repudiate witchcraft as superstition, as articulated in his classic *De Praestigiis Daemonum* (The Deception of Demons) in 1563. Weyer's older contemporary, the Spaniard *Juan Luis Vives* (1492-1540), was dubbed by Foster Watson as "the father of modern psychology" (1915, p. 333). In one of the first modern works on psychology, *De Anima et Vita* (1538), Vives initiated psychodynamics by calling attention to the "logic of emotions," maintaining that emotional experience (passion) holds primacy over reason in mental processes.

This same century, the sixteenth, saw the establishment of the first hospitals for the mentally ill, among them being the Bethlehem Royal Hospital (nicknamed "Bedlam") at London in 1547; the following year Italy's first hospital for psychiatric care, the Santa Maria della Pieta, was established at Rome; and the first in the Americas was established by Bernardino Alvares in Mexico.

The next century, the seventeenth, experienced the anticipations of some modern psychotherapeutic techniques, including the beginnings of electrotherapy and experiments in magnetism by the "father of electricity," *William Gilbert* (1540-1603), an English physician and physicist known for his *De Magnete, Magneticisque Corporibus* (1600). In 1679 the English physician William Maxwell published his *De Medicina Magnetica* in which he mentioned a vital magnetic force residing inside and outside of the body. It was developed from his interest in Maxwell's theory of magnetic medicine and from ideas of the Swiss *Philippus Aureolus Paracelsus* (1493-1541; his real name is *Theophrastus Bombastus von Hohenheim*). A professor of medicine at Basel, Paracelsus, who regarded mental disorders as a spiritual disease, anticipated Freud in postulating hysteria as sexual in character as well as citing the unconscious motivation operative in neurosis. His major work, *Von den Krankheiten so die Vernunfft Berauben,* written in 1526, appeared in 1567. Owing to his defiance of tradition, he was expunged from the university, settling in Salzburg after practicing medicine in a number of places in Germany.

Contributions to psychotherapy during the eighteenth century include the "near-shock" therapy of the Dutch professor of medicine at the University of Leiden, *Hermann Boerhaave* (1668-1738), who drenched his patients in extremely cold water as well as resorting to purgatives. Three of his students, *George Cheyne* (1671-1743), *Robert Whytt* (1714-1766), and *William Cullen* (1710-1790), also distinguished themselves in medical psychology. A Scottish physician who settled in London around 1700, Cheyne was among the first to recognize the widespread nature and common prevalence of the neurosis, publishing his views on the matter in his *The English Malady: Or, a Treatise of Nervous Diseases of All Kinds, as Spleen, Vapours, Lowness of Spirits, Hypochondriacal, and Hysterical Distempers* (1733). Another Scott, Whytt, a professor of medicine at the University of Edinburgh, made a three-fold division of neuroses: (1) hysteria, (2) hypochondriasis, and (3) nervous exhaustion, a term that was subsequently superseded by *George Miller Beard's* (1839-1883), *neurasthenia* and *Pierre Janet's* (1859-1947), *psychasthenia*. While both men were neurologists, Beard, author of *Nervous Exhaustion* (1880) and *American Nervousness* (1881) was an American, and Janet, whose fame stems from his research on hysteria and other neuroses, was French. The third, a Scot, Cullen, who was a professor at the universities of Glasgow (1751-1755) and later at Edinburgh (from 1756 on), was the first to employ the concept neurosis as an ailment that was fever-free. Moreover his nosology was adopted by Philippe Pinel. Boerhaave's influence was widespread, reaching the American shores through "the founder of American psychiatry," *Benjamin Rush* (1745-1813), author of the first textbook on mental disorders, *Medical Inquiries and Observations upon the Diseases of the Mind* (1812). Rush, a professor of chemistry at the University of Pennsylvania (then the College of Philadelphia), attributed mental illness to pathology of the cerebral arteries. Consequently his therapy called for circulation of the blood, cold showers, and a gyrating chair to relieve the congested blood. His efforts resulted in the addition of a wing on the Pennsylvania Hospital in 1796 for the mentally ill.

Parisian Clinical Psychology

(A) THE NOSOLOGISTS

PHILIPPE PINEL (1745-1826): Reformer and Nosographer

The revolution in the treatment of mental patients and consequently of the progress of clinical psychology was through the singular efforts of the French physician Pinel, who called for the humanitarian treatment of the mentally ill. As a result he made the Parisian hospitals, Bicêtre and Salpêtrière, famous in the history and progress of medical psychology. While Bicêtre, which became affiliated with the General Hospital in 1660, housed "madmen," Salpêtrière, constructed as a hospital by edict of Louis XIV in 1656, was intended as a place "to lock up mad men and women." The mental patients at these institutions were actually chained, until Pinel, who attributed much of the "vast pandemonium" to their confinement, had their chains and fetters removed because he felt that liberty and fresh air were necessary factors in restoring health. In his *Treatise on Insanity* (1801), he shared his experiences:

> The Asylum de Bicêtre, which was confided to my care during the second and third years of the republic [1793-1795], widened to a vast extent the field of enquiry into this subject, which I had entered upon at Paris. . . . In lunatic hospitals, as in despotic governments, it is no doubt possible to maintain, by unlimited confinement and barbarous treatment, the appearance of order and loyalty. . . . A degree of liberty, sufficient to maintain order, dictated not by weak but enlightened humanity, and calculated to spread a few charms over the unhappy existence of maniacs, contributes, in most instances, to diminish the violence of the symptoms, and in some, to remove the complaint altogether. . . . Cruel treatment of every description, and in all departments of the institution, was unequivocally proscribed. No man was allowed to strike a maniac even in his own defence (1806, pp. 9, 89-90).

Two years after Pinel undertook the administration of the Bicêtre in 1793, he headed Salpêtrière, reforming it comparably. Although currently an immense hospital, Salpêtrière (saltpeter) owes its name to its origin as the Petit-Arsenal, the place where gunpowder was manufactured for the Royal Army. Saltpeter is an essential ingredient of gunpowder.

After studying at the universities of Toulouse and Montpellier, receiving his degree in medicine in 1773, Pinel left for Paris in 1778 where he devoted himself to psychiatry. His work in psychopathology began when individuals throughout Europe were critical of the unsanitary conditions prevalent in hospitals and were moving toward reform. Furthermore one of the consequences of the French Revolution was to guarantee all individuals protection against enslavement, including the insane. Pinel promoted the attitude that the insane were ill mentally, rather than demon-possessed.

Pinel's (1798) interest turned toward nosology (identifying mental disorder by name) and etiology (identifying mental disorder by cause), believing that proper treatment was contingent on the nature and etiology of the mental ailment. Warm, comfortable, and sleep-inducing baths replaced the dousings of ice water; other unnecessary measures, such as bleedings, were abolished. Moreover he recommended half-way houses, a place for the patient to convalesce in his transition from the hospital environment to the world at large.

Jean Esquirol (1772-1840): Founder of French Psychiatry

Pinel's distinguished pupil, *Jean Étienne Dominique Esquirol*, developed further his mentor's diagnostic and nosological techniques at Salpêtrière, where he initiated formal instruction in psychiatry for the first time. On Pinel's death, Esquirol became physician-in-chief at the Salpêtrière. As early as 1805 he based mental disorder in emotions. Working with patients at the Bicêtre and at the Salpêtrière, Esquirol was also the first to differentiate illusions from hallucinations, coining the latter term. Though most of his terminology is antiquated, his classic *Des maladies mentales considérées sous les rapports médical, hygiénique et médico-légal* (1838) served for over half a century as a basic text, providing novel and accepted definitions in clinical psychology. It was he who furnished the first accurate description of idiocy as well as the current use of the term hallucination. Having equated insanity with "mental alienation," he defined it as "a cerebral affection, ordinarily chronic, and without fever; characterized by disorders of sensibility, understanding, intelligence, and will" ([1838] 1945, ch. 1, no. 1). Esquirol went on to illustrate hallucination:

> A lady aged twenty-seven in the last stage of phthisis, becomes exceedingly annoyed by the odor of burning charcoal. She believes that they wish to suffocate her; accuses the proprietor of the house, and hastens to denounce him to her friends. This odor follows her everywhere. Everywhere she is assailed by the fumes of charcoal. She quits her lodgings, changing them many times in a month. The principal disease continues to make progress, and the patient dies, tormented to the last by her hallucination ([1838] 1845, ch. 1, no. 1).

Monomania, one of Esquirol's concepts, anticipated the current view of one form of schizophrenia.

Jean Pierre Falret (1794-1870): Folie à Deux. Esquirol's pupil, Falret, exerted influence on legal authorities to discard terms such as "furor," "imbecility," and "dementia," for *mental alienation.* His profound interest in suicide contributed to the cultivation of mental hygiene. Having observed the existence of a psychological or emotional contagion in which two individuals reciprocally induce mental symptoms in one another, he (with E. C. Lasègue) identified it in 1877 as *folie à deux* or *folie communiquée.* Moreover Falret developed an interrogative method of investigating patients (another viable idea of his) as well as involving himself in issues of legislation, public health, and hospital reform.

Benedict Augustin Morel (1809-1873): **Dementia Praecox.** Falret's pupil, Morel, influenced by Darwin's evolutionary theory, sought a hereditary explanation of mental disorder. By 1860 he advanced a degeneration theory of mental illness articulated in his *Traité des maladies mentales.* It was Morel who coined the term *dementia praecox* that was renamed *schizophrenia* by the University of Zurich professor, **(Paul) Eugen Bleuler (1859-1939)** in a monograph titled *Dementia Praecox: or the Group of Schizophrenias* (1911). Bleuler, who studied with Charcot at the Salpêtrière, actually introduced the term as early as 1908 in his paper "Die Prognose der Dementia Praecox (Schizophreniegruppe)." Also credited· with the concept *autism,* noting that "schizophrenics lose contact with reality" ·([1916] 1951, p. 384), Bleuler observed that

> the most severe schizophrenics, who have no more contact with the outside world, live in a world of their own. They have encased themselves with their desires and wishes (which they consider fulfilled) or occupy themselves with the trials and tribulations of their persecutory ideas; they have cut themselves off as much as possible from any contact with the external world.
>
> This detachment from reality, together with the relative and absolute predominance of the inner life, we term autism ([1911] 1950, ch. 1, #B).

Bleuler, who obtained his M.D. from the University of Bern, directed the Cantonial Hospital at Burgholzli (the psychiatric hospital at Zurich) from 1898, remaining there as director and as Professor of Psychiatry at the University of Zurich until his retirement in 1927.

Kahlbaum, Hecker, and Kraepelin: German Nosologists. Nosology and the delineation of mental disorders continued in Germany with *Karl Ludwig Kahlbaum* (1828-1899). Noting from investigations on general paresis that symptoms could be organized into clusters, Kahlbaum introduced new terminology, including "catatonia," a classificatory term still in use to identify the schizophrenic who remains mute with rigidly, curious postures. The term is found for the first time in his *Die Katatonie oder das Spannungsirresein* (1874). "Symptom complex" and "cyclothymia" are also credited to him, the latter term (like hebephrenia) is still currently used to designate oscillating periods of mild moods of cheerfulness and depression.

Also interested in schizophrenic symptomology was Kahlbaum's student, *Ewald Hecker* (1843-1909), who introduced "hebephrenia" (a psychosis terminating in rapid mental deterioration) in his "Die Hebephrenie" (1871).

Nosology climaxed with the classification of *Emil Kraepelin* (1856-1926), Professor of Psychiatry at Munich, and director of its psychiatric clinic. Much of the classification in use currently resembles essentially that of Kraepelin in his *Compendium der Psychiatrie* (1883), a work that appeared in its eighth edition in four volumes by 1915. In 1899 Kraepelin observed that dementia praecox and manic-depressive psychoses stood in opposition, the former being incurable and the latter remedial. Kraepelin, whose predecessors opened the way for his elaborate classification of psychiatric nomenclature, is regarded by some as having established a new era in psychiatry.

(B) THE DISCOVERY OF PSYCHOTHERAPY

The emergence of psychotherapy was in consequence of the discovery of hypnosis. In fact the discovery of neurosis is likewise attributable to hypnosis (Zilboorg, 1967, ch. 9), hypnosis being the first genuine form of psychotherapy. That being the case, it appears then that not only did psychotherapy stem indirectly from Mesmer who first hit upon hypnotism, but so did neurosis.

FRANZ ANTON MESMER (1734-1815): Animal Magnetism

The Viennese who took Paris by storm with his *animal magnetism* (later termed *mesmerism,* and still later, *hypnosis*) was Franz Anton Mesmer, holder of three earned doctorates from the University of Vienna: one in philosophy, a second in law, and a third in medicine (1776).

According to Mesmer's animal magnetism theory, the curative force of the magnet, which he purportedly established through experimentation, was believed also to reside in himself. His doctrine of animal magnetism emanates from his doctoral dissertation, *De Planetarum Influxu,* dealing with the planetary influence on the physical body of humans. He theorized that a universal fluid, in a constant state of flux and reflux, permeates everything. It is the medium through which human beings are influenced by planets.

It was later, however, in 1774 that the notion of magnetism was associated with therapy. By applying magnets to an individual, he effected an astounding cure. The experiment, repeated several times with success, led him to hypothesize qualities other than physical as the curative agent. When Mesmer witnessed cures effected merely through touch by the popular healer Johann Gassner, he concluded that the universal fluid must be in living beings. Carrying his analogy of the magnet further, he surmised that animal magnetic poles exist, health being contingent on the proper balance of like and unlike poles. He reasoned that some humans, similar to physical agents (like magnets), are potent poles of animal magnetism. These select individuals effect a cure by altering the ill person's inadequate distribution or lack of animal magnetism, thus bringing it into balance. Explaining his theory of animal magnetism, Mesmer stated:

> Considering that the reciprocal influence is general between bodies; that the *magnet* represents that model of that universal law, and that the animal body is susceptible to properties analogous to those of the magnet, I feel sufficiently justified in using the name *animal magnetism,* which I have adopted to designate the system or doctrine of influences in general, giving it suitability to the animal body, as well as to the remedy and method of cure ([1799] 1957, pp. 26-7).

Mesmer observed that a crisis situation is crucial in effecting animal magnetism successfully.

Charged with malpractice, Mesmer was forced to leave Vienna for Paris in 1778, where his popularity swelled, but so did controversy. The final humiliation occurred in 1784 when the Faculty of Medicine of the Académie des Sciences appointed a committee of five (headed by the American ambassador to France,

Benjamin Franklin) who issued a finding denying the existence of animal magnetism. They dismissed the cures Mesmer effected as the consequences of unknown physiological causes. Notwithstanding their failure to charge Mesmer with charlatanism, he was nevertheless forced to flee Paris for Switzerland, owing to abuse hurled upon him by the medical profession.

The Development of Hypnotism: Puységur; Quimby; Eddy; Elliotson; Esdaile; Braid

In a letter written to Desfontaines (November 27, 1784), Pinel wrote that "magnetism . . . is already on the decline," but four decades after this letter was written, all Europe was obsessed with animal magnetism. By the 1880s hypnotism was permanently established. However, the transition from Mesmer's concept of animal magnetism to hypnosis as it is currently understood was an evolutionary process.

The first stage of develpoment of animal magnetism began in 1774 when two of Mesmer's students, the *Marquis de Puységur* (1751-1825) and his brother, undertook experiments with the gardener as their subject. However, they did not employ magnets of Mesmer's ritual (assuming that electric power was supplied through universal fluid). Their subjects were lulled into an artificial somnambulism in which an intelligent conversation ensued. The outcome was the discovery of post-hypnotic suggestion, for they instructed their subjects that on awakening their symptoms would vanish. Hence the convulsive crises and much of the occult mystery of Mesmer were eliminated, for they had reduced hypnotism to mere suggestion, a practice currently employed.

It was *Charles Poyen,* the Marquis de Puységur's student, who imported hypnosis to America in 1836, demonstrating magnetism publically in Maine where he converted *Phineas Parkhurst Quimby* (1802-1866) to its validity. Like others, Quimby, a watchmaker, accounted for hypnosis in mesmeric terms of electricity, until he inadvertently mesmerized his student, Louis Burkmar, during an electric storm. Owing to the electrical element in animal magnetism, mesmerizing during lightening storms was avoided. It was now obvious that electricity was absent in hypnosis. Quimby discovered a still higher level of sophistication in hypnosis when he observed that uncritical faith played an important factor. He found that when a patient protested against taking an expensive drug and a cheap drug was substituted with success, that psychological faith was a causative agent.

Quimby, who from 1847 had practiced mental healing through hypnosis from his office in Portland, Maine, eventually developed a science of health based on the religious philosophy of mental healing. In 1862 and again in 1864, one of his clients was a forty year old school teacher, *Mary Baker Eddy* (1821-1910), later to become the founder of the Christian Science Church. Having dramatically recovered from her neurotic symptom of hysterical paralysis through Quimby's mental healing, she subsequently turned to the Bible where she discovered her system, which came to be termed Christian Science. There are those who claim that Eddy's views on Christian Science derive from Quimby.

From Continental Europe, the influence of Marquis de Puységur reached Britain where mesmerism was pursued by *John Elliotson* (1791-1868) in 1837 to alleviate pain during surgery, by *James Esdaile* (1808-1859) in the latter 1840s to perform painless operations on Hindu convicts, and by *James Braid* (1795-1860) who replaced mesmerism with the term *hypnosis,* the Greek word for sleep. The Cantabridgian Elliotson, a professor of the practice of medicine at University College, London, was a founder of the Phrenological Society. The German anatomist and physician, Franz Joseph Gall (1758-1828), the older contemporary of Mesmer and founder of *phrenology,* also like Mesmer studied medicine at Vienna and his teachings were banned in Vienna. In 1807 Gall left for Paris with Johann Kaspar Spurzheim (1776-1832), cofounder of· phrenology, which he dubbed *cranioscopy.* Their major work was the four volume *Anatomie et physiologie du système nerveux en général* (1810-1819). Spurzheim collaborated in only the first two volumes. While phrenology is of negligible import at present, it played a major role in the nineteenth century by influencing social reforms, brain dissection, and promoting cerebral localization despite its absence of any specific contribution to that field of research.

It was the British surgeon Braid whose experiments established the subjective character of hypnotism, proving the absence of magnetic forces. The influence passing from hypnotist to subject he termed neurohypnotism, abbreviating it later to *hypnotism.* After introducing his findings on June 29, 1842 to the British Association in Manchester where he practiced (titling his paper a "Practical Essay on the Curative Agency of Neuro-Hypnotism"), Braid published his major work the following year under the title *Neurypnology or the Rationale of Nervous Sleep Considered in Relation to Animal Magnetism of Mesmerism and Illustrated by Numerous Cases of Its Successful Application in the Relief and Cure of Disease* (1843). His technique, still used by some hypnotists, employed a bright object held a foot from the subject's eyes. Let Braid relate the rest for himself:

The patient must be made to understand that he is to keep the eyes fixed on the object, and the mind riveted on the idea of that one object. It will be observed, that owing to the consensual adjustment of the eyes, the pupils will be at first contracted: they will shortly begin to dilate, and after they have done so to a considerable extent, and have assumed a wavy motion, if the fore and middle fingers of the right hand, extended and a little separated, are carried from the object toward the eyes, most probably the eyelids will close involuntarily, with a vibratory motion. If this is not the case, or the patient allows the *eyeballs* to *move,* desire him to begin anew, giving him to understand that he is to allow the eyelids to close when the fingers are again carried towards the eyes, but that the *eyeballs must be kept fixed in the same position,* and the *mind riveted to the one idea of the object held above the eyes.* It will generally be found, that the eyelids close with a vibratory motion, or become spasmodically closed. After ten or fifteen seconds have elapsed, by gently elevating the arms and legs, it will be found that the patient has a disposition to retain them in the situation in which they have been placed, if *he is intensely affected.* If this is not the case, in a soft tone of voice desire him to retain the limbs in the extended position, and thus the pulse will speedily become greatly accelerated, and the limbs, in process of time, will become quite rigid and involuntarily fixed (1843, ch. 2).

Notwithstanding Braid's demonstrations of hypnotism, the British medical association, among many other negative reactions to hypnotism, refused to countenance his essay. Widespread hostility toward hypnosis by the medical community continued until the neurologist Jean-Martin Charcot, by according it serious attention at the Salpêtrière, lent it the respectability it subsequently acquired. The reputation and fame of Charcot as a distinguished neurologist was established beyond question, consequently despite hypnosis being held in jaundiced repute by the majority of the medical profession. Charcot could afford to become involved in hypnotism without danger of disgrace. By the 1880's hypnotism was deeply entrenched as an established and respected method of research and technique of treatment. *Thus it was that through hypnosis neurosis was discovered as a psychogenic disturbance and it was through hypnosis as well that psychotherapy came into existence.*

THE NANCY SCHOOL:
Ambrose-August Liébault (1823-1904) and
Hippolyte-Marie Bernheim (1840-1919)

Mesmerism was imported from Paris to Britain, underwent modifications by Braid, and shipped back to France in 1859, the year Darwin published his *Origin of Species*. The following year Prof. Azam of Bordeaux popularized Braidism in a publication in the *Archives de médecine*. However, the work that contributed the most to the early establishment of Braid's hypnosis in France was Liébault's *Du sommeil et des états analogues considérés surtout au point de vue de l'action du moral sur le physique* (1866). Liébault, a country physician who took up residence in Nancy (northeast of France) in 1864, studied hypnotic phenomena for twenty years by administering to poor, simple peasants without charging a fee. As a medical student he was introduced to mesmerism, and his serious investigations preceded his major publication by a matter of years.

Explaining the nature of Liébault's hypnosis, Bernheim wrote:

> The concentration of the mind on a single idea, the idea of sleep, facilitated by the fixation of the gaze, brings about the repose of the body, the deadening of the senses, their isolation from the external world, and finally the arrest of thought, and an unvarying condition of consciousness. . . . His thoughts concentrated, the subject remains in relationship with the person who has put him to sleep. . . . Being incapable of passing from one idea to another by himself, his mind remains fixed on the idea which has been last suggested to him. If, for example, this idea is that of extension of the arms, he keeps them extended.
>
> Ordinary sleep does not differ from hypnotic sleep. . . .
>
> The *hypnotized subject* falls asleep, with his thought fixed, *in relationship with the hypnotizer;* hence the possibility of the suggestion of dreams, ideas and acts, by this foreign will.
>
> The loss of memory on waking from deep hypnosis, comes from the fact that all the nervous force collected in the brain during sleep, diffuses itself anew throughout the whole organism when the subject wakes (1887, pp. 117-8).

With Liébault's pronouncements, the Nancy school of hypnosis was underway, and contradicted the Paris school (the Salpêtrière school of hypnosis) inaugurated by Charcot in 1878. The point of contention between the two schools was that while the Nancy school held that hypnosis is ordinary sleep induced by heightened suggestibility, the Paris school viewed it as pathological, a morbid condition —hysteria neurosis.

While Charcot's prize pupil was Janet, Liébault's was Bernheim. The latter two were both connected with Nancy, Bernheim being Professor in the Faculty of Medicine there. The Faculty of Medicine is a university's school of medicine, the most celebrated being the French Faculty of Medicine at the University of Paris (Sorbonne). French Faculties of Medicine function in close relationship with hospitals, serving comparably to the American teaching hospitals, except that the Chief of Clinic is in the Faculty of Medicine, appointed and serving under a professor.

In the 1880s Bernheim championed Liébault's efforts, having been his disciple when Liébault was Doctor of Medicine at the University of Nancy. They held that: (1) the primary factor in inducing hypnosis is expectation, (2) heightened suggestion is its characteristic symptom, and (3) the hypnotist exerts mental influences upon his subject. Thus with suggestion as the basis of hypnotism, and posthypnotic suggestion its phenomenon, the way was revealed for Freud to postulate the existence of and explore the nature of the unconscious.

Emile Coué (1857-1926): Autosuggestion. It was at Nancy that Coué established his free clinic in 1910, after being a pharmacist in the town of his birth, Troyes, from 1882 to 1910. Having studied hypnotism and suggestion from the opening of the twentieth century, Coué introduced his own psychotherapeutic technique of autosuggestion, which came to be called Couéism.

According to Coué, neurosis being "nothing but the result of unconscious autosuggestion," it follows that autosuggestion can remedy it. Inasmuch as "every thought entirely filling our mind becomes true for us and tends to transform itself into action" 1961, p. 17), therefore thoughts can be used for one's good or ill. Consequently a person must be instructed that

> he carries within him the instrument by which he can cure himself, and that you are, as it were, only a professor teaching him to use this instrument, and that he must help you in your task. Thus, every morning before rising, and every night on getting into bed, he must shut his eyes and in thought transport himself into your presence, and then repeat twenty times consecutively in a monotonous voice, counting by means of a string with twenty knots in it, this little phrase:—"Every day, in every way, I am getting better and better" (1961, pp. 22-3).

As surmised, Coué studied with Liébault and Bernheim at Nancy, acquiring his psychology of suggestion and hypnotic psychotherapy from them beginning in 1901, with his self-help clinic opening less than a decade later. He became widely known through his *Self-Mastery through Conscious Autosuggestion* and by lecturing in the United States and in Britain. He firmly believed in self-mastery through autosuggestion, healing disease through the directed use of the imagination as opposed to the will.

Gustave Le Bon (1841-1931): **A Social Psychology Based on Hypnosis.** A French M.D., who devoted his life to social psychology, *Gustave Le Bon*, is principally known for his work *La psychologie des foules* (1895) translated the following year as *The Crowd: A Study of the Popular Mind.* Le Bon theorized that the mentality of crowds, couched in sentiment and emotion, diffuses its ideas through a contagion grounded in hypnotism. "Contagion," asserted Le Bon, "is a phenomenon of which it is easy to establish the presence, but that it is not easy to explain. It must be classed among those phenomena of a hypnotic order, which we shall shortly study" (1896, p. 33). The cause of hypnotic contagion is *suggestibility.* Inasmuch as a crowd is an anonymous entity, the individual in a crowd becomes irresponsible, yielding to the dictates of the crowd. The crowd is characterized by (1) unanimity, termed the law of mental unity of crowds; (2) emotionality; and (3) credulousness and infralogicality, crowds being credulous, their logic infrarational, and their minds ignoring the principle of contradiction.

Just as Freud was inspired by Charcot's application of hypnosis to hysteria, he was influenced by Le Bon's hypothesis that the individual in a crowd regresses to a state of primitive mentality. While an individual is capable of a cultivated and rational disposition, in a crowd he can be reduced to barbarous, emotional, and violent behavior, with complete abandonment of his moral, critical, and logical sensitivities. Lacking inhibitions, his uniquely individual characteristics vanish, and he becomes dominated by the unconscious laden with a common ancestral heritage of a prelogical and premoral stage. The regressive characteristics of the crowd, adopted by Freud in his *Group Psychology and the Analysis of the Ego* (1921), were used to explain social anxiety (conscience) as diminishing in crowds inasmuch as social anxiety (conscience) is essentially a fear of public opinion. Freud also accepted Le Bon's comparison of individuals in a group as in a state of hypnosis or a heightened state of suggestibility.

Gabriel Tarde (1843-1904): **Laws of Imitation.** The decade in which Le Bon wrote his classic *The Crowd*, his compatriot, Tarde, issued his *Les lois de l'imitation* (1890), translated in 1903 as *The Laws of Imitation.* The French sociologist and criminologist Tarde was appointed to the chair of modern philosophy at the Collège de France at the turn of the twentieth century. He predicated his social psychology on imitation, with invention and opposition also being among the three fundamental processes of social interaction. As "the elementary social phenomenon," imitation is the "fundamental social fact" (1899, p. 56). Tarde, like Le Bon, likened group behavior to that of hypnotic phenomena, viewing society as "imitation and imitation is a kind of somnambulism" (1903, p. 87).

Historians mistakenly credit William McDougall and Edward A. Ross as the first to publish books with social psychology in the title, for they published theirs in 1908 while Tarde published his *Études de psychologie sociale* (Studies in Social Psychology) in 1898.

Independent of Le Bon, the Italian *Scipio Sighele* (1868-1913) also developed a social psychology based on "suggestion" as a pernicious factor. Sighele (1891, 1893, 1895) viewed the subconscious as a criminal mind. So much so did the views of Le Bon and Sighele resemble one another, that the two engaged in controversy with respect to originality.

THE PARIS SCHOOL:
Jean Martin Charcot (1825-1893) and
Pierre Janet (1859-1947)

Having traced the course of hypnotism from Paris to England and the United States, we find that it brings one back to Paris again where it is pursued by the celebrated father of clinical neurology, Jean Martin Charcot, and subsequently by his distinguished student and successor, Pierre Janet. A second eminent pupil, Sigmund Freud, was to transport hypnotism from Paris to Vienna, where he made his home city world renowned for psychotherapy, triggering a number of Viennese schools of psychotherapy. Thus distinction at the University of Paris and at the Salpêtrière was perpetuated from the days of Pinel to Charcot who brought them to their height of distinction in the field of medical psychology.

The Parisian born Charcot obtained his degree from the University of Paris in 1853, becoming Professor of Pathologic Anatomy in 1860. In recognition of his achievements he was appointed in 1882 to the newly created chair of Professor of Clinical Diseases of the Nervous System. The latter appointment, *Professeur de la Chaire* (Full Professor or Professor and Head of Department) is an extraordinary achievement that Charcot first attained in 1872. The first academic appointment, *Professeur Agrégé à la Faculté de Médecine* (Professor of Agregation in the Faculty of Medicine), a medical school appointment, is granted on successfully passing a competitive examination. The majority of candidates fail. Charcot passed on his second attempt in 1860, having failed in 1857. Prior to his elevation to professor, he had a nonteaching appointment as physician to the Hospitals of Paris in 1856, and in 1862 physician to the Salpêtrière, where he remained throughout life. Here he established a neurological clinic, subsequently to become known as the founder of the clinical-anatomical or clinicopathologic approach to the investigation of neurological disorders.

Charcot as Neurologist

The major contributions of Charcot to neurology came in the first decade of his career, from 1862 to 1870, when he for the first time offered an accurate classification of nervous diseases. Prior to this time only a spotty knowledge and an inaccurate classification were available. His biographer, Georges Guillain, reported:

> By the time of Charcot's death, however, the entire framework of modern neuropathology had been structured and carefully illustrated. The major categories of neurologic disease had been distinctly identified and exquisitely correlated with their anatomic and pathologic substrata; the clinicoanatomic approach to the nervous system, designed and developed by Charcot, is what created the foundations of neurology; and it was Charcot who was the first to establish neurology as an independent discipline at the Faculty of Medicine and at the Salpêtrière (1959, p. 83).

Employing the method prevalent in psychiatry of clinically studying symptoms, and eventually integrating them into syndromes, Charcot was able successfully to identify diseases of the nervous system, including multiple sclerosis.

The decade of the 1870s carried his investigations into the cerebrum, inspiring psychologists, neurologists, and physiologists (a number of whom were his students) to pursue this phase of viable research. Productive results issued especially from the British neurophysiologists in London.

British Neurological Psychology. Continuing the lead received from Charcot were the Queen Square neurologists at London: **Charles Édouard Brown-Séquard (1817-1894), John Hughlings Jackson (1835-1911), H. Charlton Bastian (1837-1915), David Ferrier (1843-1928),** and **Victor Horsley (1857-1916).** The National Hospital at Queen Square, London, became a world center in the field of neurology. Investigating speech defects in diseases of the brain, the neurologist Jackson related them to defects in the left cerebral hemisphere; motor spasms (convulsions limited to a single limb), currently termed Jacksonian epilepsy, he attributed to local brain irritation. The anatomist and neurologist Ferrier distinguished himself by his investigations on localization of brain functions. Bastian coined the term *kinaesthesis,* the muscle, tendon, or joint sense.

The Cambridge school of physiology, dates from 1870 when **Michael Foster (1836-1907),** a founder of the Physiological Society in 1876 and the *Journal of Physiology* two years later, arrived at the University of Cambridge where he devised a practical laboratory technique. Other Cambridge physiologists include **W. H. Gaskell (1847-1914),** who established that muscular heart contraction was independent of nerves, and that there were no branches from each spinal nerve to the sympathetic nervous system. Foster's successor both to the chair of physiology at Cambridge and as editor of the *Journal of Physiology,* **John Newport Langley (1852-1925),** extended Gaskell's researches into the sympathetic nervous system further from 1890 to 1906. Known for his *Autonomic Nervous System* (1921), Langley coined the term *autonomic* (suggesting a "local autonomy of function") in 1898 to identify what Gaskell termed the "visceral" or "involuntary" nervous system. In 1903 he offered the term "parasympathetic." The autonomic nervous system, comprised of the sympathetic and parasympathetic nervous system, and partially self-regulating, is a system of nerves (ganglia and plexuses) innervating the viscera, glands, heart, smooth muscles and blood vessels. A subdivision of the autonomic nervous system, the parasympathetic nervous system stimulates selectively a variety of visceral organs, producing the opposite effect of that of the sympathetic nervous system. Also a component of the autonomic nervous system, the sympathetic nervous system stems from chains of ganglia running from either side of the spinal cord, innervating bodily organs and connecting with many sympathetic ganglia. During emergency conditions the sympathetic nervous system brings about intense physical changes, such as the discharge of adrenalin, acceleration of heart beats, elevation of blood pressure, etc. It was Langley who saw that the influence of adrenalin was limited to effects resulting from the stimulation of sympathetic fibres.

Influenced by Gaskell was **Henry Head (1861-1940),** a disciple of Jackson and an associate of Rivers. Trained at Cambridge, and later appointed to the London Hospital, Head was editor of the journal *Brain* from 1910 to 1925. His investigations of lesions in peripheral sensory nerves (with Rivers) resulted in distinguishing between protopathic and epicritic cutaneous sensibility as reported in his *Studies in Neurology* (1920). His second major field of success included speech disorders as contained in his two volume *Aphasia and Kindred Disorders of Speech* (1926) which he dedicated to Jackson, Gaskell, and Hering. At Prague he studied under Hering.

The vanguard in aphasia was not Head, but the French surgeon and anthropologist **Paul Broca (1824-1880),** a pioneer in craniology. In 1861 he discovered the area of articulate speech in the brain, locating aphasia (aphemia) in a unilateral lesion in the left cerebral hemisphere (termed Broca's area). Aphasia, the partial or complete inability to speak or otherwise use language, is due to brain damage.

Another Cambridge graduate, **Charles Scott Sherrington (1857-1952),** was (along with Gaskell and Langley) one of the most distinguished pupils of Foster. The major portion of his career was spent as Professor of Physiology at the University of Liverpool (1895 to 1913) where his major discoveries were made, and at the University of Oxford (1913 to 1936). From its inception Liverpool was outstanding in physiology, its first physiologist being **Richard Caton (1842-1926)** followed by Sherrington's predecessor **Francis Gotch (1853-1913).** Sherrington, who coined the term *synapse* in his classic *The Integrative Action of the Nervous System* (1906), explained it:

> the nexus between neurone and neurone in the reflex-arc, at least in the spinal arc of the vertebrate, involves a surface of separation between neurone and neurone; and this as a transverse membrane across the conductor must be an important element in intercellular conduction. The characters distinguishing reflex-arc conduction from nerve-trunk conduction may therefore be largely due to intercellular barriers, delicate transverse membranes, in the former.
>
> In view, therefore, of the probable importance physiologically of this mode of nexus between neurone and neurone it is convenient to have a term for it. The term introduced has been *synapse* (p. 18).

For his discovery of the function of the neurone, Sherrington was awarded the Nobel prize. He is also known for his *Man and His Nature* (1941) and *Mammalian Physiology* (1919). The former work more than contributed to psychology, it lent support to its development.

Charcot's Investigations of Hysteria Neurosis and Hypnosis

The third and last phase of Charcot's career coped with hysteria and hypnosis. By training and disposition a clinical neurologist, Charcot assumed that hypnosis was rooted in pathology as a nerve disorder. In neurologically grounding hypnosis, he rescued it from the occult, hence won approval for it from the medical community, a feat that was heretofore unsuccessful by his predecessors. This together with his prestige accorded hypnosis respectibility. Hypnosis, like hysteria, was symptomatic of a morbid condition that he viewed as hystero-epilepsy. Thus he assumed that only hysteria neurotics could be hypnotized and that fact alone was symptomatic of morbidity. His tracing hysteria to the uterus meant that a disorder of the womb was responsible for both neurosis and hypnosis, a premise that contributed to Freud's pansexual psychology. As it turned out, not only did Freud abandon hypnosis in therapy, but the Nancy school proved accurate in its view of hypnosis rather than Charcot and the Paris school. Hysteria did not prove to be a female sexual disorder, nor did hypnosis come to be considered pathological. By the time Charcot wrote the third volume of his *Leçons sur les maladies du système nerveux* (Lectures on the Diseases of the Nervous System) in 1887, he was deeply convinced of male hysteria neurosis.

According to Charcot, a person in a hypnotic trance is undergoing a genuine neurosis, comprised of three states or phases: (1) a lethargic stage (a state of relaxation or sleep in which suggestion is impossible); (2) a cataleptic condition in which the subject retains the position in which he is placed; and (3) somnambulism, a state of anaesthesis, hypersensibility, and susceptibility to suggestion. The three states comprise *le grand hypnotisme*, i.e., the great hypnotic neurosis.

JANET: Last of the Distinguished Saltpêtrière Psychiatrists

When *Pierre Marie Felix Janet* (1859-1947), Charcot's pupil and successor, died, it seemed as if the great line of French medical psychologists had come to an end. It is true that there was psychology other than psychotherapy or medical psychology, but much of it was from the French speaking Swiss (Claparède and Piaget) rather than France.

At the University of Paris, Janet studied with both the Faculty of Letters and the Faculty of Medicine, receiving a doctorate on the dissertation *L'autotisme psychologique* (Psychology of Automatic Activities) in 1889. He had already been appointed by Charcot to be in charge of the psychological laboratory at the Saltpêtrière before receiving this degree. In 1892, owing to his efforts at the Salpêtrière, he obtained a doctorate in medicine on *L'état mental des hystériques* (The Mental State of Hystericals). While directing the Salpêtrière psychological laboratory he was on the faculty of the Sorbonne until 1902 when he succeeded *Théodule Armand Ribot* (1839-1916), the French pioneer in experimental psychology as well as in psychopathology, to the chair of psychology at the Collège de France, his tenure lasting until his retirement in 1936. In 1904 Janet, with *Georges Dumas* (1866-1946), founded the *Journal de psychologie normale et pathologique* (Journal of Normal and Pathological Psychology), which he edited until 1937.

The Dissociation School of Psychopathology. Janet, who sought a reconciliation or a synthesis of psychiatry and psychology, founded the dissociation school of psychopathology. Like Charcot, his mentor, Janet reduced hysteria to mental disintegration caused by cerebral exhaustion of a weak constitution. *Psychasthenia,* resulting in a split personality, was his term for the weak psychic constitution yielding to shock or excessive fatigue. Characterizing psychasthenia as deteriorative, degenerative, or as "stigmata," a hangover term from the dark ages when mental disorder was seen as "witch" oriented, Janet wrote in *The Mental State of Hystericals:*

> The diagnosis of hysteria . . . teaches us, then, that in the definition of hysteria we must add one more element—duration,—namely, the permanency for a considerable length of time of the undoubling (dédoublement) of consciousness. . . . We shall just call them psychasthenics (1901, p. 519).

Thus a dissociation or splitting of consciousness accounts for neurosis with its obsessions and phobias. While consciousness in normal life is an integrated, coherent stream, in the neurotic it is dissociative. Hysteria is defined by Janet as "a form of mental depression characterized by the retraction of the field of personal consciousness and a tendency to the dissociation and emancipation of the systems of ideas and functions that constitute personality" (1920, p. 332). Suggestibility is the hysterical stigmata, for suggestibility is the sign of hysteria. Mental stigmata include anaesthesias, amnesias, abulias (diminution of will), and motor disturbances.

During Janet's lifetime neurosis as psychogenic (not neurogenic) began to dominate, becoming a psychoneurosis. Hypnosis as psychological prevailed over the view earlier held by Charcot and Janet. With time hypnosis itself began to vanish with the emergence of psychotherapy with its probing into the unconscious mind. Whereas Janet was ahead of Freud in postulating the unconscious, it was Freud who penetrated into its various dimensions. Actually Freud claimed credit for introducing the unconscious in psychotherapy, contending that Janet's use was but a *"façon de parler"* (manner of speaking). Unlike Freud, Janet was left without any disciples to perpetuate his psychology. Consequently when he died in 1947, a great tradition in French medical psychology at Paris and at the Saltpêtrière came to a close. Also in Janet's lifetime, clinical psychology had moved away from neurogenic or physiogenic to the psychogenic, the great psychogenic era opening with the psychoanalytical psychology of Freud. Before considering Freudian psychology, however, Binet and the French Swiss psychologists (Claparède and Piaget) deserve consideration.

Alfred Binet (1857-1911): Intelligence Testing

The French psychologist Binet studied at the Salpêtrière with Charcot's pupil, *Charles Féré* (1852-1907). While Féré was Assistant Physician at the Salpêtrière, Binet collaborated with him in writing a volume titled *Animal Magnetism* (1887). The book purports to be a study of hypnosis "made in accordance with the method inaugurated by M. Charcot, the chief of the school of the Salpêtrière. that is, in accordance with the experimental method" (1888, p. v). When Binet was attracted to the Salpêtrière, Charcot was exceedingly popular, attracting enormous audiences, a member of his audience being *Théodule Armand Ribot* (1823-1891) who in 1877 won Binet from law to psychology. On Ribot's advice Binet studied psychopathology, observing that while Germans study psychophysics, and English comparative psychology, the French investigate pathological psychology. In 1894 he earned his D.Sc. from the Sorbonne, and the following year founded (with Beaunis) the journal *L'année psychologique.*

Binet eventually rose to the position of director of the laboratory of physiological psychology at the Sorbonne of the University of Paris, where he remained until his death in 1911. Earlier he had competed unsuccessfully with Janet for the chair at the Collège de France, a chair vacated by Ribot. He also competed unsuccessfully with George Dumas (1866-1946) for the chair at the Sorbonne. Though Binet received but an honorarium for his position as director, he nevertheless did in effect found experimental psychology in France during the last decade of the nineteenth century, and actually published *An Introduction to Experimental Psychology* in 1894.

For the remainder of his life Binet was to devote himself to the experimental investigation of the psychology of individual differences or differential psychology. In this respect Binet left the tradition of French psychology which was essentially psychopathology and psychotherapy for the British individual psychology in the tradition of Galton. He published in 1903 what some authorities consider his best work, *Étude expérimentale de l'intelligence,* a differential psychological study of his two daughters Madeleine and Alice. With his contrasting intellectual types (objective and subjective) he was anticipating Jung's extrovert and introvert types. His attention had been turning from the psychological laboratory toward studies in schools with children, resulting in 1905 in the work for which he is best known *Méthodes nouvelles pour le diagnostic du niveau intellectuel des anormaux,* with his collaborator *Théodore Simon* (1873-1961). The result was the famous Binet-Simon intelligence tests for children which measured degrees of intelligence according to a standard devised by them. Binet and Simon explain their method as

> one by which the intelligence of a child may be estimated. The method consists in asking the child some precise questions and having him perform some simple experiments; these questions and experiments are called tests. As much research has revealed which of these tests a normal child passes successfully at a given age, it is easy to ascertain whether the child under examination gives results equal to the normal child of his age, or whether he is advanced or retarded in relation to this norm (1913, p. 7).

The following are some examples that Binet and Simon used in their intelligence test:

THREE YEARS
Shows nose, eyes and mouth.
Repeats two digits.
Enumerates objects in a picture.
Gives family name.
Repeats a sentence of six syllables.

SIX YEARS

Distinguishes between morning and afternoon
Defines in terms of use.
Copies a lozenge.
Counts thirteen pennies.
Compares faces from the aesthetic point of view.

TEN YEARS

Arranges five weights.
Copies drawings from memory.
Criticizes absurd questions.
Understands difficult questions.
Uses three given words in two sentences.

The tests were in response to Binet's being appointed to a special commission in 1904 by the Minister of Public Education of Paris to ascertain a way of distinguishing between normal and subnormal children.

The influence of Binet was immense, extending child psychology and the psychology of individual differences (intelligence testing) throughout the world. In England, his ideas were pursued by Cyril Burt (1909, 1911); in Germany, Stern (1911) extended them from a "mental age" to a "mental quotient" by dividing the mental age by the chronological; Terman (1916) at Stanford University extended them still further in his Stanford Revision of the Binet Scale by coining Stern's ratio (MA/CA) the "intelligence quotient" (IQ); H. H. Goddard extended the ideas of Binet to the dimension of feeble-mindedness. His classic *The Kallikak Family* (1912) sought to establish feeble-mindedness as hereditary, the strain extending through a number of generations. In Switzerland the whole idea of child psychology was developed by Claparède, and later by Piaget. Claparède, who dubbed Binet the "Paganini of psychology," actually studied in Paris, where he spent a year at the Salpêtriére engaged in clinical and experimental psychology. Thus it becomes clear why the line of French psychology at the University of Paris and the Salpêtrière was imported just across the border into French Switzerland, Geneva.

(C) THE FRENCH SWISS PSYCHOLOGISTS
Theodore Flournoy (1854-1920), Édouard Claparède (1873-1940), and Jean Piaget (1896-   ): Swiss Child Psychology

Flournoy: Founder of French Swiss Psychology. After receiving his baccalaurete from the University of Geneva in the field of mathematics, Flournoy went on for his doctorate in medicine at the universities of Freiburg and Strasbourg. The Genevan Flournoy, whose family fled France owing to religious persecution, studied with Wundt at Leipzig in 1878 before going to Paris. From Paris he returned to Geneva where he went from philosophy to psychology, becoming the first to occupy the chair of physiological and experimental psychology at the University of Geneva in 1891. The following year Flournoy, at whose insistence psychology was affiliated with science rather than philosophy, founded a laboratory of psychology in which he experimented on reaction time, ideation, and sensation, as well as parapsychology.

In 1901, Flournoy, with his cousin Claparède, who worked in his psychological laboratory and taught as *Privatdozent,* founded the first Swiss psychological journal, the *Archives de psychologie,* which was later edited by Piaget. When the Congress of Psychology was held in Geneva in 1906, Flournoy was its President.

Claparède: Founder of Swiss Child Psychology. Influenced by his cousin Flournoy to become a psychologist, Édouard Claparède studied medicine at the University of Geneva, obtaining his doctorate in medicine in 1897. Thus Claparède followed the route of the French toward a career in psychology. The 1892-1893 academic year found him at the University of Leipzig. Before the conclusion of that decade (1898-1899), Claparède spent a year at Paris working in neurology with *Joseph Jules Déjerine* (1849-1917), who coauthored *Anatomie du système nerveux* (Anatomy of the Nervous System) with his wife Augusta Klumpke Déjerine (1859-1927). It was while working with Déjerine at Paris that Claparède became acquainted with Binet for whom he developed the profoundest respect.

Claparède left for the city of his birth, Geneva, where he remained throughout the rest of his life. His career opened as *Privatdozent,* working in the laboratory of psychology that Flournoy directed and teaching a course on sensation. At the turn of the century (1901), he founded the *Archives de psychologie* (with Flournoy) and edited them for almost four decades.

Claparède's profound and lasting interest in child psychology became apparent with the publication in 1905 of his *Psychologie de l'enfant et pédagogie expérimentale* (translated as *Experimental Pedagogy and the Psychology of the Child,* 1911). The work, the one for which he is best known, underwent at least four editions and ten translations. Experimental pedagogy, he defined as "the knowledge of, or the inquiry into, the circumstances favourable to the development of the child, and the means of educating him towards a given end" (1911, p. 41). The book, which laid heavy stress on child development, influenced Jean Piaget in his experimental studies on the development of the child.

In 1912 Claparède founded the Institut J. J. Rousseau for the purpose of developing child psychology in the light of its padagogical applications. The institute in 1947 became an affiliate of the University of Geneva, falling under its educational division of the Institut des Sciences de l'Education. He joined the Faculty of Sciences at the University of Geneva in 1909, succeeding to the chair of experimental psychology in 1919 left vacant by Flournoy's retirement.

Jean Piaget: Child Developmental Psychology. Also profoundly and permanently influenced by Binet's psychology and at the Salpêtrière was Piaget, successor to Flournoy and Claparède at the University of Geneva. After receiving his doctorate in science at the University of Neuchâtel, Switzerland (city of his birth), in the field of zoology (studying mollusks), he went on to Zurich, studying under

Jung, and working with Bleuler and in Lipps' laboratory. At the University of Zurich, *Gottlob Friedrich Lipps* (b. 1865), a Leipzig Ph.D. (1887), was professor and director of the psychological laboratory (institut) from 1911. Piaget's interest in abnormal psychology, acquired from Bleuler and Jung, followed him to Paris, where from 1919 to 1921 he became acquainted with Binet's collaborator, Simon. Binet had died in 1911, but Simon was on the faculty of the Sorbonne. Here Piaget administered Binet's reading tests to the children of Paris. As a consequence of these studies, Piaget turned permanently to the study of child psychology. In addition he complemented his findings with data obtained from children confined at the Salpêtrière with mental disorders. When he began publishing his findings in 1921 in the Parisian *Journal de psychologie,* Claparède appointed him director of studies at the J. J. Rousseau Institut. The same year he was awarded a doctorate of natural science from the University of Paris. A professorship in philosophy was granted him in 1925 at the University of Neuchâtel, his alma mater. He left that post in 1929 for the University of Geneva as professor of the history of scientific thought, where in 1940 his title was changed to professor of experimental psychology and director of its laboratory of psychology. In 1955 he accepted the post of professor of child psychology at the Sorbonne.

Piaget's findings in his research with children at the Maison des Petits of the Institut J. J. Rousseau and pupils at the primary school of Geneva were issued sequentially as progress reports in his *The Language and Thought of the Child* (1923); *Judgment and Reasoning in the Child* (1924); *The Child's Conception of the World* (1926); *The Child's Conception of Physical Causality* (1930); and *The Moral Judgment of the Child* (1932). The common theme throughout each of these books is that of a developmental principle, an evolutionary process in which a person progresses from the mentality of a child to that of an adult.

Despite their interpersonal activity, children are much more egocentric and much less social in thought and speech than are adults. "The adult thinks socially, even when he is alone, and the child under 7 thinks ego-centrically, even in the society of others" (1959, p. 40). Only a spurious social life is found among children under seven. Rather than reasoning in universal terms, children's thoughts deal with individual instances. Rather than thinking in terms of abstract generalizations, "they form a logic of action but not yet a logic of thought" (1928, p. 56). The inability of the child to generalize is due to his mind being locked in a realism. The child's egocentrism does not permit him to think in relative, but only in absolute terms so that an enemy is an absolute entity instead of being a relation to oneself. Self-contradictions are not avoided, owing to the transductive reasoning of the child, that is, reasoning from one particular instance to another rather than reasoning from deduction or induction. The animistic thinking of a seven year old child assumes that the sun moves because it is alive, but his thinking ends there rather than generalizing to "All things that move are alive." The child's conception of the world is animistic, inputing spontaneous movement to bodies.

Piaget observed four stages of moral development in his *Moral Judgment of the Child* (1932): (1) a motor or individual stage in which motor habits assume a ritual character or he responds according to his own desires; (2) egocentric stage (two to five years of age) in which the child's play is with a disregard for rules; (3) cooperative stage (seven to eight years of age) in which rules are respected though the notion of them is vague; and (4) codification of rules stage (eleven to twelve years of age) in which society's rules are observed and known. The child proceeds from the motor stage (mechanical) to individual (egocentric) to social (cooperative). While rules for the very young are sacred realities, they are matters of mutual agreement for older youth. Important to the moral judgments of children are social facts (constraint and unilateral respect) and moral facts (cooperation and mutual respect). "The sense of justice, though naturally capable of being reinforced by the precepts and the practical example of the adult, is largely independent of these influences, and requires nothing more for its development than the mutual respect and solidarity which holds among children themselves" (1932, pp. 195-6).

Later, Piaget, relating logic to psychology, structured four stages of cognitive development in his *Logic and Epistemology* (1953). The four include: (1) the sensori-motor period (from birth to 2 years of age) in which the child performs motor actions devoid of thought; (2) the pre-operational thought period (from 2 to 7 years) characterized by symbolic function, e.g., language, fictional invention, and symbolic play; (3) concrete operations period (7 to 11 years) keynoted by thought activity, logic, and reversibility; and (4) propositional or formal operations period (from 11-13 to 14-15 years of age) marked by reasoning by hypothesis or hypothetical-deductive reasoning. These four periods, extending from birth to maturity, are stages in the construction of, or the psychological development of, operations. "Operations are actions which are internalizable, reversible, and coordinated into systems characterized by laws which apply to the system as a whole" (1953, p. 8).

Influenced by the gestaltists in his *The Child's Conception of Space* (with Bärbel Inhelder, 1948), Piaget observed that the child views space topologically rather than geometrically. Spatial relationships are qualitative rather than metric, a conception that the child later develops. Thus the genetic orientation runs consistently throughout the psychology of Piaget.

Although Piaget devoted over half a century to his psychological research, his basic ideas appear within the first decade of his research. Widely read, he has stimulated considerable experimental research throughout the world as well as provoking criticism. The Harvard psychologist Roger Brown, who has a high regard for Freud, remarked that "after Freud, it is Jean Piaget, I think, who has made the greatest contribution to modern psychology" (1965, p. 197).

CHAPTER 11

Viennese Clinical Psychology

(A) THE DEPTH PSYCHOTHERAPISTS

The enormous strides and the position as frontrunner enjoyed by the Parisians yielded to the Viennese with the advent of Freud. At Paris the trunkline of psychopathology began to branch off in two major directions: that of the dissociation psychology of Janet and the psychoanalytic psychology of Freud. The two shared many points of resemblance: each was a student of and developed from Charcot; each was interested in hypnosis though both subsequently abandoned it; each was intensely involved in hysteria neurosis; each discovered the clinical significance of the unconscious; and each discovered catharsis (although Freud derived his in a sense from the Austrian physician *Josef Breuer* (1842-1925). Several other comparisons are possible such as both being physicians. Thus in a sense Parisian clinical psychology was transported to Vienna by Freud, or at least a branch of it was. However, as the great tradition of abnormal psychology came to an almost total eclipse in Paris with the advent of Freud, it not only grew in magnificent proportions in Vienna to a degree exceeding the fondest dreams of the psychotherapists at Paris, but fructified into at least a half dozen major systems of psychotherapy. Lamentably while Janet was left without successors, happily Freud was progenitor of systems, schools, and ideas that are still flourishing.

Not that either Freud or Janet discovered the unconscious or catharsis, for Socrates and Plato knew of it and dealt with it in antiquity; Plato even knew of dream interpretation, and Aristotle had much to say concerning dreams and catharsis. In more modern times, Leibniz offered a psychological explanation of the unconscious, and Schopenhauer plumbed deep into it. Schopenhauer's disciple, Eduard von Hartmann (1842-1906) developed an entire philosophy out of it. However, Freud and Janet moved the unconscious into the realm of clinical psychology.

SIGMUND FREUD (1856-1939): Psychoanalysis

The psychiatrist and neurologist Freud, who founded psychoanalysis, was born of Jewish parents in Freiberg, Moravia. After obtaining his M.D. degree from the University of Vienna in 1881, he continued there in 1883 as *Privatdozent,* rising to Professor of Neuropathology in 1902. His long tenure at the University of Vienna came to a close a year before his death in 1938 when he was compelled to abandon Nazi-ridden Vienna for London. From the age of four to the year prior to his death, Freud lived in Vienna.

The great influences on his professional life contributing toward his astronomical achievements in psychology originated from two sources: (1) his studies with Charcot in Paris (1885-1886) involving hypnosis, hysteria, and the sexual basis of mental disturbances; and (2) his work with the Viennese *Josef Breuer* (1842-1925) entailing the treatment of hysteria neurosis by hypnotic techniques that led to catharsis. At the Salpêtrière, Freud attended Charcot's celebrated lectures, *Leçons du Mardi* from October 20, 1885 to February 23, 1886, translating them later into German. In 1889, Freud, in order to improve his hypnotic technique, visited Bernheim and Liébault in Nancy. From Bernheim he learned posthypnotic suggestion, hence the existence of unconscious motivation.

Among the immense psychoanalytic contributions of Freud to psychology are: a new orientation to psychology and mental disorder; a theory of personality (id, ego, and superego); libidinal stages of personality development; subconscious defense mechanisms; infantile sexuality; sexuality as polymorphous; unconscious motivation; psychopathological characteristics of "normal" everyday living; the rationale of irrational behavior; a theory of social psychology; psychological interpretations of religious behavior and thought; psychic energy and its transformations into physical disorder (psychosomatic medicine); psychogenic interpretation of mental and physical disorders; interpretation of instincts (eros and thanatos) and their sublimations; topography of the mind with its unconscious, preconscious, and conscious dimensions; and dream interpretation.

Development of Psychoanalysis

On learning of male hysteria (uterus in Greek) as a mental disturbance from Charcot, Freud thereupon lectured publicly in Vienna concerning the subject on October 15, 1866, the year he returned to Paris. When he was met with ridicule and scorn for it, he sought to vindicate himself with an actual case study. It was not that particular case, however, but another that launched psychoanalysis on its way, the case of Anna O. (Bertha Pappenheim), a patient of *Josef Breuer* (1842-1925). A personal friend of Ernst Mach and Freud, Breuer, who worked on the vestibular sense with Ewald Hering, obtained his M.D. in 1881 after beginning studies as early as 1859 at the University of Vienna. In consequence of his developing friendship with Freud, Breuer shared with him his remarkable hysteria patient. On the data gleaned from this patient, the two emerged with their own theory of hysteria, which they published jointly in 1893 as "On the Psychical Mechanism of Hysterical Phenomena: Preliminary Communication." In 1895 their findings and theory appeared in the coauthored work *Studies in Hysteria,* marking the founding of psychoanalysis. Of the 800 copies printed, only 625 copies were sold thirteen years later. The book was the first and only collaborated effort of the two men, intellectual and emotional differences disrupting their friendship.

This work marked the birth of psychoanalysis because it offered (1) a theory of hysteria neurosis, (2) a theory of therapy: catharsis (abreaction) and the talking cure (free association), and (3) a theory of unconscious motivation. Explaining these features, Freud wrote:

> We found, at first to our greatest surprise, that the individual hysterical symptoms immediately disappeared without returning if we succeeded in thoroughly awakening the memories of the causal process with its accompanying affect, and if the patient circumstantially discussed the process in the most detailed manner and gave verbal expression to the affect.

We furthermore attempted to explain how our psychotherapeutic method acts: It abrogates the efficacy of the original non-abreacted ideas by affording an outlet to their strangulated affects through speech. It brings them to associative correction by drawing them into normal consciousness (in mild hypnosis) or by eliminating them through medical suggestion in the same way as in somnambulism with amnesia ([1895] 1937, p. 190).

Breuer's patient (Anna O.), a young girl suffering from hysterical symptoms of disturbances of vision and speech as well as paralysis of limbs and anaesthesia, developed them while nursing her ill father. Cognizant that the girl acquired the symptoms through self-induced hypnosis, Breuer sought to alleviate the symptoms through hypnosis and through her talking freely of herself. The "talking cure" (as the patient phrased free association) together with a surging upheaval of emotional ejaculation (abreaction) resulted in the vanishing of her symptoms. The repressed hostility that she harbored because of her father's illness combined with the attendant guilt feelings owing to her resentment toward her helpless father were revealed through hypnosis. His patient's gratitude, which assumed the form of falling in love with him (transference), intimidated Breuer to such an extent that he terminated the case.

Among their many conclusions, Breuer and Freud found that hypnosis is an artificial hysteria; "the hysteric suffers mostly from reminiscences" (1937, p. 4). A reaction that is repressed remains indelibly in memory. Repressed and forgotten experiences serve as unconscious motivations, while normal people dissipate emotions consciously, that is, "the reason why the pathogenically formed ideas retain their freshness and affective force is because they are not subject to the normal fading through abreaction and through reproduction in states of uninhibited association" (1937, pp. 7-8). Freud's theory of repression arose from patients' "forgettings" or repeated blockings of memory.

The free association of ideas (freely allowing one idea to suggest another without conscious direction) superseded hypnosis, for the repressed experiences (complexes) are not effectually abreacted in hypnosis so as to produce a catharsis. Inhibited and repressed thoughts function as unconscious motivations unless surfaced to consciousness, where their mere awareness often is curative. Though Freud early knew of the role played by sex in mental disturbances, the emphatic and central position of a pansexualism came later. The term psychoanalysis itself probably was coined by him in 1896 in a paper on "Further Remarks on the Defence Neuro-Psychoses" in which he referred to the method employed in *Studies in Hysteria* as psychoanalysis. He spoke of a "reliable method of psychoanalysis which I use in making these investigations and by which at the same time the investigations serve a therapeutic purpose" ([1896] 1959, p. 155).

At the turn of the century Freud's first major monograph, *The Interpretation of Dreams* (1900), appeared. When he wrote it, his theory of sexuality was still in the future, but he referred to dreams as "the first member of a class of abnormal psychical phenomena of which further members, such as hysterical phobias, obsessions and delusions, are . . . of concern to physicians" ([1900] 1953,

Preface). Considered by Alexander and Selesnick (1966, p. 248) as Freud's most important contribution, *The Interpretation of Dreams* expresses the view that dreams serve to relieve emotional tensions, tensions disruptive to perfect rest (sleep). Among the variety of mechanisms active in dreams are condensation, censorship, displacement, representation, distortion, and repression. Freud defined condensation as "an inclination to form fresh unities out of elements which in our waking thoughts we should certainly have kept separate" (1940, p. 47). Condensation and displacement are the "craftsmen" structuring dreams. By the latter mechanism, highly charged psychical intensities are distorted by the accompaniment of another psychic mechanism, the censor.

> The consequence of the displacement is that the dream-content no longer resembles the core of the dream-thoughts and that the dream gives no more than a distortion of the dream-wish which exists in the unconscious. We traced it back to the censorship which is exercised by one psychical agency in the mind over another. Dream-displacement is one of the chief methods by which that distortion is achieved. . . . We may assume then, that dream-displacement comes about through the influence of the same censorship—that is, the censorship of endopsychic defence ([1900] 1955, p. 343).

Dreams, as wish-fulfillments, are sometimes distorted, displaced, and condensed, owing often to the activity of the censor. In "Two Encyclopaedia Articles" (1922, p. 115) Freud asserted that the "dream-censorship" is a manifestation of the same mental forces as the mechanism of repression. Dreams are either wish-fulfillments or wishes to sleep.

The year following the *The Interpretation of Dreams,* Freud published his *The Psychopathology of Everyday Life* (1901) in which he cited commonplace errors that all people experience daily as being unconscious motivations of an abnormal character. These included slips of the tongue (Freudian slips), purposive accidents, errors of memory such as inability to recall the name of a disliked person, and a variety of other errors. An example of a Freudian slip is inadvertently to say the word "orgasm" for "organism." A purposive accident, one he related about himself, is to break an inkwell for the unconscious purpose of having an excuse to purchase a desired new one.

Five years after the appearance of his *The Interpretation of Dreams,* Freud published his *Three Essays on the Theory of Sexuality* (1905), considered by some authorities as his most "momentous and original" contribution, second only to *The Interpretation of Dreams*. He saw sex as the underlying causative factor in anxiety neurosis and neurasthenia. These findings led him to the extensive investigation of the important and preponderant role of sex in psychic life.

The Founding of the Vienna Psychoanalytical Society

By this time, Freud, who had been a professor at the University of Vienna since 1902 and had written four major books, was gaining international fame. In 1906 he began his international correspondence with *Carl G. Jung* (1875-1961), his "son and heir;" (in previous years *Alfred Adler* (1870-1937), *Wilhelm Stekel* (1868-1940), and *Otto Rank* (1884-1939) became associated with him). The following year he was joined by *Karl Abraham* (1877-1925) and *Max Eitengen* (1881-1943). Another year (1908) brought *Sandor Ferenczi* (1873-1932) and *Ernest Jones* (1879-1958), the same year in which the Vienna Psychoanalytical Society was founded and held its first congress, which was to be the first of many to come, in Salzburg. The First International Psycho-Analytical Congress, held in Nuremberg in 1910, elected Jung its first president, while the Vienna Psycho-analytical Society, already eight years old, elected Adler as president.

Acrimonious dissension did not permit the group to fare well, resulting in four major and influential members seceding, with Adler leaving in 1911 to found his own individual school of psychology; *Wilhelm Stekel* (1868-1940), who was psychoanalyzed by Freud in 1901, followed Adler's example a year later; Jung, in 1913, left to found his analytical school of psychology; and Rank did likewise in 1926 with a system called will therapy in his *Technik der Psychoanalyse* (1926-1931). While Adler objected to Freud's oedipal complex as fabrication, and thus alienated himself, Rank's *The Trauma of Birth* (1924) offended Freud. Freud regarded Stekel as a case of "moral insanity" devoid of an "ego-ideal" (Jones, 1963, p. 309). Thus the three were forced out of the Vienna Society, while Jung found Freud's pansexualism repugnant.

No reliable knowledge exists as to the inception of the Vienna Psychoanalytical Society, except that Stekel and Freud probably founded it in 1902 when Freud sent postcards to Adler, Stekel, Kahane, and Reitler inviting them to his home for discussions, which habituated into Wednesday evening discussions in Freud's waiting-room. Accordingly the meetings were called the "Psychological Wednesday Society." By 1908 it acquired the "Vienna Psycho-Analytical Society" as its name, retaining it until destroyed by the Nazis in 1938. Early guests and members of the group, other than those previously mentioned, include *Paul Federn* (1872-1950), *Hanns Sachs* (1881-1947), and the Swiss *Ludwig Binswanger* (1881-1966).

The Clark Lectures and Introductory Lectures on Psychoanalysis

One of the happiest moments in Freud's life was when he, joined by Jung, Jones and Ferenczi, went to Clark University in Worcester, Massachusetts in 1909 at the invitation of its President, G. Stanley Hall, to deliver a series of lectures and receive an honorary doctorate. Hall, disturbed with a neurosis of his own, developed an increasing interest in Freud and clinical psychology. The event was in effect Freud's first major recognition of his achievements, a recognition of international proportion, and one that spread his distinction throughout America.

The Clark University Lectures, for which Freud received travel expenses of 3,000 marks ($714.60), consisted of five lectures delivered extemporaneously for five days beginning on Monday, September 6, 1909. These conversational-type lectures, subsequently published in a variety of forms, were as follows: (1) Symptoms Have Psychological Meaning; (2) Repression and Sympton Formation; (3) Psychic Determinism, Dreams, and Parapraxes; (4) Infantile Sexuality and Neurosis; (5) Transference and Resistance. Having established friendships with

Morton Prince, J. J. Putnam, and William James (all of Harvard), Freud left pleased with James' words of parting with his arms around Freud's shoulder, "the future of psychology belongs to your work." Freud's biographer, Ernest Jones, commented as he reminisced concerning the Clark conference:

> A particularly affecting moment was when Freud stood up to thank the University for the Doctorate that was conferred on him at the close of the ceremonies. To be treated with honor after so many years of ostracism and contempt seemed like a dream, and he was visibly moved when he uttered the first words of his little speech: "This is the first official recognition of our endeavors" (1963, p. 260).

The most elaborate and systematic expression of the Clark University lectures appeared in print as *Introductory Lectures on Psycho-Analysis (1916-1917)*. These latter lectures, however, were delivered at the Vienna Psychiatric Clinic during two Winter Terms (1915-1916 and 1916-1917) before an audience gathered from the combined faculties of the University of Vienna. In all there were 28 lectures which were followed up with an additional seven lectures in a volume titled *New Introductory Lectures on Psychoanalysis* in 1933. Unlike the former lectures, the latter, owing to Freud's terminal ailment, were never actually delivered. With the exception of Freud's social psychology and psychology of religion, these two books together with one written the year before he died (but left unfinished), *An Outline of Psychoanalysis* (1940), provide an adequate systematic view of Freudian psychoanalysis.

TENETS OF PSYCHOANALYSIS

Having introduced concepts of repression, abreaction, catharsis, unconscious motivation, and free association in his work with Breuer, *Studies on Hysteria*, and other views such as dream interpretation with the various mechanisms of censor, condensation, displacement, and the like in his *Interpretation of Dreams*, Freud had reached the point of integrating his ideas into a system with a complete theory of personality, motivation theory, libidinal theory of development, topography of mind, and psychical apparatus (id, ego, and superego) as well as a social psychology.

Structure of the Personality: Id, Ego, and Superego

The psychical apparatus, or the mental components, Freud term *id, ego,* and *superego*. The oldest, the id, comprises all that is inherited or present at birth. These innate qualities are essentially unconscious, with their most important being instincts. The id, governed by the primary process, is dominated by the pleasure principle. The id, unaware of the demands of reality or society, responds only to pleasure and the alleviation of tensions (sex and hunger). "Everything that happens in the id," said Freud, "is and remains unconscious" (1964, p. 22). There are no conflicts within the id because contradictions and illogicalities, as in dreams, exist there.

Instincts: Their Pressure, Aim, Object, Source, Classes, and Sublimation.
Instincts, the essential make-up of the id are comprised of two major classes: (1)

eros or the productive and life giving instincts, such as sex; and (2) thanatos (death) or destructive instincts whose aims are reducing living things to an inanimate or inorganic state. Inhibited destructive instincts, such as in the case of aggressiveness, contribute to ill health, but an aggressive rage can invert itself to self-destructiveness (suicide).

Instincts, namely those tensions arising from the id's needs, are characterized by their pressure, aim, object, and source. The pressure is the force exerted by instincts, their sole aim is to gain satisfaction, their object is the vehicle or instrument providing the wherewithal to acquire satisfaction of the aim, and the source is the somatic process (physical organ mentally stimulated).

While the energy source of eros instincts is the *libido,* there is no comparable counterpart for thanatos. Libidinal energy stored within the ego makes for *narcissism,* typical of young children, but the narcissistic libido transfers to *object libido* as the person matures and loves another rather than self. When another person is the object cathexis, one's psychic energy is directed toward or invested in that person.

Instinctual impulses that for some reason cannot be satisfied (such as sex inhibited by society's restrictions) can be *sublimated.* Freud defined sublimation as

a process that concerns the object-libido and consists in the instinct's directing itself towards an aim other than, and remote from, that of sexual gratification; in this process the accent falls upon the deflection from the sexual aim ([1914] 1959, p. 51).

Unlike instinctual gratification, sublimation always leaves some residual tension. Sublimated energy, as desexualized libido, transpires through the ego's mediation, libido being the entire energy available to eros. Unless sublimated, repressed sexual instincts take a circuitous route in the personality's subconscious and assume the form of some insidious expression.

The Ego as the Conscious Executor of the Personality. As an offshoot of the id, owing to the influence of the external world of reality, the ego, which is basically an organization, is defined by Freud as

a mental organization which is interpolated between their sensory stimuli and the perception of their somatic needs on the one hand and their motor acts on the other, and which mediates between them (1964, pp. 17-18).

The ego is characterized by external and internal functions, external being self-preservation, storing experiences from external stimuli into the memory, avoiding overly intense stimuli through flight, coping with moderate stimuli through adaptation; while the internal are acquiring control over the demands of the instincts; permitting postponing, or sublimating instinctual gratification, and coping with tensions. "Life is not easy," Freud commented:

If the ego is obliged to admit its weakness, it breaks out in anxiety—realistic anxiety regarding the external world, moral anxiety regarding the super-ego and neurotic anxiety regarding the strength of the passions in the id ([1923] 1964, p. 78).

Whereas the primary process governs the id, the ego is regulated by laws of a secondary process, the ego being developed out of the id's "cortical layer," and acquiring the character of its surroundings as well as those of the id. Dealing with the external world, the ego responds to the "reality principle," for the ego must attend to the organism's self-preservation. Adaptation and self-preservation is grounded on the ego's "testing the reality of things." The ego, as organizer of the personality, must cope with excessive external as well as internal demands, those of the real world as well as the instinctual. As executor of the personality, the ego must mediate among three forces making demands upon it: (1) those of the world of reality, (2) those of the id, and (3) those of the superego. In doing so, the ego must preserve its own autonomy by maintaining its own integrated organization.

The Superego and Conscience. Whereas the determinations of the ego are those acquired from an individual's experience, and the id the influences of heredity, the superego is essentially the influence acquired from other persons (parent and society). Moreover, it serves as the vehicle producing the phenomenon of *conscience*, and is "heir of the Oedipus complex." *In Moses and Monotheism*, published the year in which he died, Freud explained the superego.

> In the course of individual development a part of the inhibiting forces in the outer world becomes internalized; a standard is created in the Ego which opposes the other faculties by observation, criticism, and prohibition. We call this new standard the *Super-ego* .
> . . . The Super-ego is the successor and representative of the parents (and educators) who superintended the actions of the individual in his first years of life; it perpetuates their functions almost without a change (1939, p. 149).

Thus the supereago, while it is not present at birth, occurs early in the child's life.

Via the mechanism of *identification* the superego comes into existence. "The superego arises," wrote Freud, "from an identification with the father regarded as a model. Every such identification is in the nature of a desexualization or even of a sublimation" ([1923] 1962, p. 44).

Psychodynamics of Neurosis and Psychosis. *Neurosis* results when the ego is weakened by the intensity of demand exerted upon it owing to lowering the instinctual pressures of the id, thus dissipating enormous expenditures of energy on anticathexes (processes whereby repression is maintained and sustained by the preconscious preventing unconscious ideas from intruding). The moral demands of a remorseless superego are also a source of conflict contributing to neurosis. Energy sapped from these two conflicts cripples the ego's energy for other tasks. An overpowering id and superego can reduce the ego's organization to such a state of disorganization that its relation to the world of reality is disrupted or annihilated (such as occurs in dreams). "When the ego is detached from the reality of the external world," wrote Freud, "then, under the influence of the internal world, it slips down into psychosis" (1940, p. 51). Thus an integrated personality is one with a potent and organized ego maintaining harmonious balance among its three forces (reality, id, and superego).

Psychoanalytic Therapy. Therapy is merely the mediation of the therapist in the weakened ego's gaining strength through education, insight, catharsis, and becoming conscious of repressed experiences lodged in the unconscious. The ego thereby copes with the moral demands of the superego and the instinctual pressures of the id by employing judgments based on the facts of reality (social and physical). The analyst and patient achieve their objective by observing "the fundamental rule of analysis," namely free association. The patient, said Freud,

must tell us not only what he can say intentionally and willingly, what will give him relief like a confession, but everything else besides that his self-observation presents him with—everything that comes into his head, even if it is *disagreeable* to say it, even if it seems *unimportant* or positively *meaningless* (1940, p. 53).

Repressed material in the unconscious is met by resistance which must be penetrated, until a transference occurs.

Transference, an intense rapport, attraction, or love for the analyst, can be either positive or negative. A positive transference is desirable because it lends itself to the analyst's exercising power over the superego of the neurotic in order to re-educate it as if the analyst were the parent who originally indoctrinated the superego with its social and moral idealistic demands. In a negative transference, the patient exhibits a hostile attitude toward his analyst, creating problems, whereas the positive transference, claimed Freud,

becomes the true motive-force for the patient's collaboration; the weak ego becomes strong; under the influence of this aim the patient achieves things that would otherwise be beyond his power; his symptoms disappear and he seems to have recovered—all of this simply out of love for his analyst (1940, p. 53-4).

Topography of the Mind: Conscious, Preconscious, and Unconscious. Mapping the human mind topographically, Freud attributed three qualities to its mental processes: conscious, preconscious, and unconscious (subconscious processes). While Freud viewed the mind like an iceberg with most of it submerged (unconscious), the simile belongs to the British psychologist F. C. Meyers. Even considerable portions of the ego and superego are unconscious. While the id is totally unconscious, reality testing (perception of the external world of reality) entails consciousness. Unlike the preconscious, the unconscious is incapable of consciousness. Between the conscious and unconscious stands the preconscious, screening the one from the other. Defining the term Freud stated that "everything unconscious that can easily exchange the unconscious condition for the conscious one, is better described as 'capable of entering consciousness,' or as *preconscious*" (1940, p. 40). Neurotic maladjustment is in part the repression of preconscious material into the unconscious. The id reaches the ego through the preconscious.

Libidinal Development: Psychosexual Stages of Mental Development. The phases or stages of psychosexual development Freud listed as (1) *oral stage,* (2) *anal stage,* (3) *phallic stage* with its oedipus phase (for boys) or electra phase (for girls), (4) *latency stage* and (5) *genital stage.* The stages of human development represent libidinal development, libido being a term employed in "the theory of the instincts for describing the dynamic manifestations of sexuality" ([1923] 1963, p. 180).

While the entire body is erogenous, at various stages of human development there is special attention paid to particular areas. The erotogenic zone of the oral stage is the mouth, the first center of the child's mental activity, representing the vehicle of self-preservation. The anal phase, occurring with the appearance of teeth, is characterized by aggression and pleasurable attentiveness to the excretory function. The third or phallic phase (from age three to seven) anticipates the genital stage by a preoccupation with pleasure derived from stimulation of the genital organs. During the phallic stage the male child experiences a conflict owing to incestuous wishes for his mother with an attendant sense of guilt and fear of castration by his father. Out of this conflict neurosis arises. During the latency stage, from age six to eleven, the child identifies with the parent of his own sex, associates with members of his own sex, and represses the aggressive and incestuous wishes of the oedipal phase. In the final stage of psychosexual or mental development (the genital), affectionate, sexual relationships are formed with members of the opposite sex.

Freud, who initially introduced libidinal development in 1905 in his *Three Essays on the Theory of Sexuality,* viewed it as normal development. To be fixated or arrested at any stage contributes to later or adult mental maladjustment. Successful or normal infant and childhood development is critical to adult mental health, for "the child is father to the man" (1940, p. 64), according to Freud's dictum. Problems in adult life tend to cause a person to regress to a period of life in which he was fixated or arrested in development.

Psychoanalytic Social Psychology

From 1913 when he wrote *Totem and Taboo* to 1930 when he published *Civilization and Its Discontents,* Freud turned his attention to socio-psychological phenomena. Stimulated by Wundt's social psychology *(Völkerpsychologie,* 1900-1909) and Jung's *Psychology of the Unconscious* (1912), Freud was desirous of deriving phenomena from social psychology to resolve problems in the psychology of the individual. The outcome was four essays published in the first two volumes of the psychoanalytical journal *Imago* (in 1912 and 1913) ''On Some Points of Agreement between the Mental Lives of Savages and Neurotics,'' which became the subtitle of *Totem and Taboo* (1913). The book, based on the findings of anthropologists, especially James George Frazer's (1854-1941) *The Golden Bough* (1890), concluded that the savage's dread of incest accounts for totemism and its attendant exogamous practice resembling symptoms of a compulsion neurosis. Freud remarked that

> the facts of folk-psychology can be seen in a new light through the application of the psychoanalytic point of view, for the incest dread of savages had long been known as such, and is in need of no further interpretation. What we can add to the further appreciation of incest dread is the statement that it is a subtle infantile trait and is in striking agreement with the psychic life of the neurotic ([1913] 1946, p. 24).

Killing the primal father and the resulting guilt feelings played a role in the early history of mankind as well as in the neurotic's suppressed wishes. Accordingly totemism and taboo are rooted in the oedipus complex, the root of neurosis, as are the beginnings of religion, society, and morality. Freud reasoned that

a process like the removal of the primal father by the band of brothers must have left ineradicable traces in the history of mankind and must have expressed itself the more frequently in numerous substitutive formations the less it itself was to be remembered. . . .

I want to state the conclusion that the beginnings of religion, ethics, society, and art meet in the Oedipus complex. This is in entire accord with the findings of psychoanalysis, namely, that the nucleus of all neuroses as far as our present knowledge of them goes is the Oedipus complex. It comes as a great surprise to me that these problems of racial psychology can also be solved through a single concrete instance, such as the relation to the father ([1913] 1946, pp. 200, 202).

Group Psychology. Influenced by William McDougall and especially by Le Bon's *The Crowd* (1895), Freud continued his social psychology in *Group Psychology and the Analysis of the Ego* (1921), agreeing with Le Bon's theory that a person in a crowd regresses to a primitive and unconscious level of behavior. In this condition he is in a heightened suggestible state resembling hypnosis. At this point Freud extended Le Bon's thesis by explaining conscience in terms of *social anxiety*, i.e. fear of public opinion. The hypnotic spell is cast by the group leader, the group's ego ideal. The libidinal attachment of the group to the leader is through an "aim inhibited libido" (desexualized libido). Comparable to Nietzsche's superman of the future, the primal father of the horde was an individual who loved himself only. Group members, however, needed to fancy that they were equally loved by him. Identification with the leader, as the group's ego-ideal, as well as the desexualized libido is the binding force cementing individuals together as a group. Social feeling is inverted hostility. In identifying with the leader, the group's father image, a protective defense is established containing the individual's hostile feelings.

Freudian Psychology of Religion. With the publication of *The Future of an Illusion* (1927) Freud, whose psychoanalytic interest expanded pervasively into social psychology, offered his psychology of religion. The individual, in conflict with a society founded on instinctual renunciation and compulsory labor, has no choice but to accept it for the sake of his security. In order to cope with nature or his environment, the individual takes refuge in religion. "Religious ideas have sprung from the same need as all the other achievements of culture," wrote Freud, "from the necessity for defending oneself against the crushingly superior force of nature. To this a second motive was added—the urge to rectify the shortcomings of civilization which made themselves painfully felt" ([1927] 1964, p. 30). Appealing to ideas in his *Totem and Tabu,* Freud saw the longing for the father as the basis of the need for religion, God serving as the exalted father. God, essentially a father complex, serves the individual's need for protection and is a guard against helplessness.

When the growing individual finds that he is destined to remain a child forever, that he can never do without protection against strange superior powers, he lends those powers the features belonging to the figure of his father; he creates for himself the gods whom he dreads, whom he seeks to propitiate, and whom he nevertheless entrusts with his own protection. Thus his longing for a father is a motive identical with his need for protection against the consequences of his human weakness ([1927] 1964, p. 35).

Thus out of childish dependency needs, a religion arising out of a father complex manufactures a God. Religion is an illusion, with the dogma of a future life a wish-fulfillment. However, an illusion is not to be equated with an error. When the principal motivating factor is wish-fulfillment, then the belief in question is an illusion.

In *The Future of an Illusion*, Freud, unlike his previous work, was deep into the area of philosophy, notwithstanding his contention that he was approaching it as a scientist. God had become a father complex, religious values illusions, and religion an obsessional neurosis or at least comparable to a childhood neurosis. Freud argued that people do not need the "consolation of religious illusion" in order to "bear the troubles of life and the cruelties of reality." Furthermore the probability is that "those who do not suffer from the neurosis will need no intoxicant to deaden it" ([1927] 1964, p. 81). The sole contention of his book was to point out that adults cannot remain children permanently, and that they should undergo "education to reality." Unlike religion, science is not an illusion. The book was a source of polemic lasting at least into the mid-twentieth century.

In the last work of this general character, *Moses and Monotheism* (1939), Freud, wandering in a field in which he lacked expertise, hypothesized that Moses was an Egyptian rather than a Jew. The Egyptian trend toward monotheism was the impetus for his monotheistic view, and the explanation for the Jewish conversion toward this doctrine. The leadership of the irate, dominant Moses was terminated by his rebellious people murdering him, an act resulting in the Jew's unconscious sense of guilt from which he was never able to escape. Freud related:

> It would be worth while to understand why the monotheistic idea should make such a deep impression on just the Jewish people, and why they adhered to it so tenaciously . . . The great deed and misdeed of primeval times, the murder of the father, was brought home to the Jews, for fate decreed that they should repeat it on the person of Moses, an eminent father substitute (1939, p. 113).

Freud analyzed this action as comparable to neurotic behavior, with the mechanism of denial displacing memory for action. He continued:

> In the religion of Moses itself there was no room for direct expression of the murderous father-hate. Only a powerful reaction to it could make its appearance: the consciousness of guilt because of that hostility, the bad conscience because one had sinned against God and continued to sin. This feeling of guiltness, which the Prophets incessantly kept alive and which soon became an integral part of the religious system itself, had another, superficial motivation which cleverly veiled the true origin of the feeling. . . . If they wished to keep happiness, then the consciousness of guilt because they themselves were such sinners offered a welcome excuse for God's severity (1939, pp. 172-3).

In this work Freud was still the analyst seeking to enlighten people to unconsciously hidden motivations and to the fact that people in reality are not what they appear on the surface to be. Needless to comment, the book evoked intense opposition among the Jews.

Concluding Comments on Psychoanalysis. Freud never sensed the enormity of the extent of his accomplishments in psychology. How ironic that he had to remark concerning Einstein:

> The lucky fellow has had a much easier time than I have. He had the support of a long series of predecessors from Newton onward, while I have had to hack every step of my way through a tangled jungle alone. No wonder that my path is not a very broad one, and that I have not got far on it (Jones, 1957, vol. 3, p. 131).

Freud is probably better known to the masses than Einstein, at least with respect to his views, that is, the general public is aware of terms such as frustration and psychoanalysis, while few know Einstein's $E = mc^2$. Instead of the proper term, psychotherapy, the average person seems to confuse it with psychoanalysis, unaware that psychoanalysis is one of the many psychotherapies in existence.

In 1933 the Nazis in burning Freud's books fancied they were exterminating his ideas, and another half dozen years later his body was cremated, but neither action succeeded in annihilating the phoenix Freud whose ideas were perpetuated not only by a variety of intellectual successors (if that term be permissive) but by a horde of people and by a diversity of disciplines, inasmuch as his views permeated religion, art, literature, sociology, and the list goes on and on.

Who were those individuals who perpetuated Freud's ideas? The more influential ones paradoxically were those who established an antithetical stand to his, including Jung, Adler, Fromm, Horney, and Sullivan. These individuals tended to desexualize Freudianism. While Adler, Fromm, Horney, and Sullivan humanized and socialized psychoanalysis, Jung imputed a will to live as the energizing or driving force of Freud's libido rather than sexual instinctual urges. Comparable to Henri Bergson's (1907) *élan vital* and Arthur Schopenhauer's (1818) *will,* Jung viewed the libido as psychic energy, later broadening the concept to include a general life instinct. "In my book, *The Psychology of the Unconscious*" (1917), he wrote, "I called attention to my notion of a general life instinct, termed libido, which replaces the concept 'psychic energy' that I used in the *Psychology of Dementia Praecox* [1907]" (1928, p. 32). Jung was also in disagreement with Freud respecting the understanding and psychotherapy of neurosis. While Freud delved into the unconscious and the patient's past fixations and conflicts, Jung analyzed present problems and maladjustments. Both shared the intensive use of dream analysis as an important psychotherapeutic tool.

CARL GUSTAV JUNG (1875-1961): Analytical Psychology

Born in Kesswil, Switzerland, Jung was reared in Basel from the age of four, receiving his doctorate in medicine from its university in 1902 with the dissertation *On the Psychology and Pathology of So-called Occult Phenomena.* In it he theorized that each person is predisposed toward a "totality of the psyche." The dissertation, evidence of his early interest in depth psychology, resulted from his patient's somnambulism during the 1898-1899 season. The personality, splitting-off consciousness, was its anticipation of a more mature, future self. The year 1902 also found him in Paris, attending the lectures of Janet.

In 1900 he had joined the staff of the Burghölzli Hospital as assistant to Eugen Bleuler at a time when hypnotism was in vogue there. It must be remembered that August Forel, the celebrated psychiatrist and authority on hypnotism, was Bleuler's predecessor. Thus Jung was deeply involved in hypnotism, knowing of unconscious motivation from post-hypnotic suggestion. But he, like Freud, abandoned the practice for analytic techniques which placed the initiative upon the patient.

In 1905 he became a lecturer at the University of Zurich, and the following year became acquainted with Freud, but severed relations with both Freud and the university in 1913. A founder of the International Psychoanalytical Society and its first president, Jung severed (owing to Freud's pansexualism) in order to found his own analytical psychology. From 1913 on he travelled and wrote extensively, the 1920s finding him in Tunis, Algiers, New Mexico, and Arizona. He studied the religions of India and China as well as Greek mythology and Christian mysticism. His contributions to psychology include the word association test; the collective unconscious and its archetypes; a theory of personality together with its concepts of self, ego, persona, individuation process, and mandala; psychological types and functions; a new theory of psychic energy and libido; and a new approach to dreams and analysis.

The Founding of Analytical Psychology

If Freud's psychoanalysis can be regarded as pansexualism, then Jung's is a panunconsciousness. Like Freud before him, Jung also made a sojourn in 1902 to Paris to sit at the feet of the great Janet and listen to his lectures. It must not be thought that Jung obtained his concept of the unconscious directly and solely from Freud, because he, like Freud, knew of posthypnotic suggestion and its implication of the unconscious. Furthermore Jung (1904) began experimenting in psychopathology, utilizing the mental association methods of Wundt that led to his famous *word association test*. Reminiscing, he said:

> I studied the experimental association methods of Wundt. . . . I made use of the association tests, and I found out that the important thing in them has been missed, because it is not interesting to see that there is a reaction—a certain reaction—to a stimulus word. . . . The interesting thing is why people could *not* react to certain stimulus words, or only react in an entirely inadequate way.
>
> . . . I soon found out that it was a matter of intimate personal affairs people were thinking of, or which were in them, even if they momentarily did not think of them when they were unconscious with other words; that the inhibition came from the unconscious and hindered the expression in speech (1964, pp. 27-8).

Thus did Jung become fascinated and permanently fixated on the unconscious mind. Jung's introduction to Freud was through his review of Freud's

Interpretation of Dreams in 1900. This coupled with his own experiments on word association convinced him of Freud's theory of repression and symbolization, the latter concept remaining with Jung indelibly. In 1903 he published on hysteria, the following year (with Franz Riklin) on experiments in association. When he, with Freud, attended the twentieth anniversary celebration at Clark University, he lectured on "The Association Method," publishing it the following year.

The Word Association Test. Jung's word association test was comprised of one hundred common terms (e.g., head, book, angry, anxiety) which were stimulus words given to an individual. The response to these terms was an immediate reply to the first word entering a person's mind, but those delayed responses, responding with the same word, or those for which no response was forthcoming were emotionally charged groups of ideas for which Jung coined the term *complex*, i.e., a repressed "feeling-toned" content imbedded in the unconscious. Like some prejudices, they can become *autonomous complexes*, dominating and motivating the personality.

Word association was not new, nor were stimulus terms. Galton pioneered experimentally in it in 1879, Wundt had experimental association methods, and the Munich psychiatric clinic had applied Wundtian methods. However, its emotional significance, its implication for complexes and unconscious motivation, belongs to Jung. At Wundt's laboratory, the American psychologist Cattell undertook mental tests (and even coined the term in 1890).

The Collective and Personal Unconscious. Jung was even more convinced than Freud of the presence, depth, expansiveness, and all-pervasiveness of the unconscious mind. Whereas Freud divided the mind into a triune conscious, preconscious, and unconscious state, Jung dichotomized the unconscious into personal and collective unconscious, the latter being a racial or transpersonal unconsciousness shared by the group that is inherited in terms of Lamarackian theory of inherited acquired characteristics. "While the personal unconscious is made up essentially of contents which have at one time been conscious but which have disappeared from consciousness through having been forgotten or repressed," asserted Jung, "the contents of the collective unconscious have never been in consciousness, and therefore have never been individually acquired, but owe their existence exclusively to heredity" (1959, p. 42). He defined the collective consciousness as that portion of the consciousness that is "not individual but universal" (1959, p. 3). Conscious and unconscious compensate each other.

The Collective Unconscious and Its Archetypes. Both Freud and Jung knew from posthypnotic suggestions that the unconscious was motivating, but unlike their predecessors these two psychiatrists were intent on discerning precisely the motivating activity of the unconscious. Freud was aware of it because of repressed elements in the unconscious, and Jung through complexes that he uncovered by his hundred word association test.

However, Jung exceeded Freud by claiming sources of unconscious motivation that were never in the conscious. Rather they were archetypes acquired by inheritance (Lamarckian theory), whereas Freud contended that the contents of the unconscious (other than id instincts) arrived there through conscious experience, and for that reason (repression) were giving the individual maladjustive problems. Jung maintained that archetypes were autonomously motivating despite an individual's personal experiences.

These dynamic archetypes that comprise the structure of the collective unconscious are the images of instincts with an autonomous motivating force, notwithstanding their remaining completely unconscious. Among the numerous archetypes (primordial images) are syzygy (anima and animus) shadow, mandala, and even the Freudian oedipus complex. Unlike repressed complexes, certain complexes have never been conscious at any time, but are contents or constructs of a real unconscious, not merely one that is furnished by conscious experiences. While instincts exist where the conscious plays a role in complexes, the majority of them are unconscious. "That was my first point of difference with Freud," remarked Jung,

I saw in the association experiment that certain complexes are quite certainly not repressed. They simply won't appear. This is because, you see, the unconscious is real; it is an entity; it works by itself; it is autonomous (1964, p. 100).

Whereas the unconscious was a product of the conscious to Freud, it was a reality in its own right to Jung.

Mandala (Including the Concepts: Self, Ego, Persona, and Individuation Process). "Mandala," the archetype of inner order, is the self's wholeness, the *ego* being a mere fragment of the entire personality. It has a compensatory function during periods of personality disorder, tending to restore order, bringing about a wholeness termed by Jung the *self*. The ego, the empirical aspect of the self, comprises that of which a person is conscious. While the ego represents the genuine person, the *persona*, partially dictated by societal expectations, is not the real personality but a masked one, e.g., one personality might be displayed at home with family and quite another at work with colleagues.

The persona is a complicated system of relations between individual consciousness and society, fittingly enough a kind of mask, designed on the one hand to make a definite impression upon others, and, on the other, to conceal the true nature of the individual (Jung, [1945] 1953, p. 190).

The goal of development, *individuation,* is the psychological process of becoming an "in-dividual, that is, a separate, indivisible unity or 'whole' " (1959b, p. 275). It is a "coming to selfhood" or "self-realization." Unity into perfect wholeness is achieved through the transcendent function synthesizing opposites into perfect selfhood, an indestructible whole (an individual).

Other Archetypes: Syzygy (Anima and Animus). Jung observed a number of completely unconscious motivating forces, and referred to two of them as *syzygy* (a joining together), namely the *anima* (feminine primordial types found in men) and *animus* (the male counterpart in women). When a man asserts that he has fallen in love with a particular woman at first sight, that *femme fatale* is merely the objectification or stimulation of his anima. Comparable to a man's having a minority of female genes, he has its psychological counterpart in the archetypal form of the completely unconscious anima. The corresponding masculine image in the female mind, the animus, is an unconscious primordial image that occasionally becomes conscious. The woman who believes that she has finally met the perfect man for her has actually found one stimulating and corresponding to her animus. Explaining the matter for himself, Jung wrote:

> No man is so entirely masculine that he has nothing feminine in him. . . . A man counts it a virtue to repress his feminine traits as much as possible. . . . The repression of feminine traits and inclinations naturally causes these contrasexual demands to accumulate in the unconscious. No less naturally, the imago of woman (the soul-image) becomes a receptacle for these demands, which is why a man, in his love-choice, is strongly tempted to win the woman who best corresponds to his own unconscious femininity— a woman in short, who can unhesitatingly receive the projection of his soul. Altogether such a choice is often regarded as felt as altogether ideal, it may turn out that the man has manifestly married his own worst weakness ([1945] 1953, p. 187).

The Shadow. There exists a ''shadow-side'' of psyche presenting itself to the entire ego-personality as a challenging moral problem. It arises when an individual becomes aware of the ''dark aspects of the personality as present and real,'' and as an emotional inferiority. The shadow aspect of his personality is joined to him ''like a shadow.''

> With a little self-criticism one can see through the shadow—so far as its nature is personal. But when it appears as an archetype, one encounters the same difficulties as with anima and animus. In other words, it is quite within the bounds of possibility for a man to recognize the relative evil of his nature, but it is a rare and shattering experience for him to gaze into the face of absolute evil (1968, p. 10).

In denying the darkness cast by the shadow as being in oneself, there is a feeling that it is another and that ''the other is always guilty.'' The shadow archetype, comprised of animal instincts, characterizes a person's animal nature, but it can be in the personal unconscious or in the conscious.

Psychological Types: Introversion and Extroversion

Jung's system of typology began when he observed certain individuals with either introverted or extroverted attitudes, each of these in turn manifesting one of four functions: sensing, thinking, feeling, or intuiting. The extrovert, with his ''outward-turning of the libido,'' is outgoing, whereas the introvert, with his ''turning inwards of the libido,'' views the world from within. When the introverted attitude becomes habitual, the individual is known as an introverted type. For compensatory reasons, the introvert will marry an extrovert, and vice versa.

The Four Functions: Sensing, Thinking, Feeling, and Intuiting. Of the four ways of functioning or responding to work (sensation, thought, feeling, and intuition), one of them predominates in each individual. Thus when thinking predominates in an extrovert, he is termed an extroverted thinking type. Either introvert or extrovert can be characterized by any one of the four functions. There are people who respond to the world with their senses preponderate, others by thoughts prevailing, still others by feeling, and even some by intuition.

Jung's *Psychological Types* (1921) had a profound effect on the American psychologist William H. Sheldon as did Ernst Kretschmer's *Physique and Character* that was published the same year. With the German Jaensch brothers also publishing on typology in the decade of the 1920s *(Eidetic Imagery and Typological Methods of Investigation* by Erich Jaensch in 1925, and *Grundzüge einer Physiologie und Klinik der psychophysischen Persönlichkeit* in 1926), the investigation of psychological types became an important area of psychology between the two world wars, for Sheldon's "Morphological Types and Mental Ability" appeared in 1927 and his *Varieties of Temperament* in 1942.

Ernst Kretschmer (1888-1964): Constitutional Types. The German psychologist and psychiatrist Kretschmer, under the influence of Emil Kraepelin, developed a correlation between physique and character. Having studied medicine at the University of Munich where Kraepelin was professor of psychiatry, he had learned from his mentor that mental disorder was organically grounded. He had also become strikingly aware that his mother was what he characterized as a pyknic-cyclothymic and his father by contrast was a schizothyme. His objective was to draw a correlation between body types and mental disorders. Before going to the University of Marburg as professor of psychiatry and neurology, he was on the faculty of Tübingen where he published his views in *Physique and Character* in 1921.

In the work for which he is best known, *Physique and Character,* Kretschmer postulated three constitutional types: (1) asthenic type; (2) athletic type; and (3) pyknic type. Prone to schizophrenia is the asthenic type with his long lanky body. The well-built middle to tall sized individual with projecting shoulders and superb chest is the athletic type. The third, or pyknic type, is the roly-poly or rotund built person who is predisposed to manic-depression or cycloid disturbance. He reported that he called

> the members of that large constitution-class from which the schizophrenes are recruited, "*schizothymes,*" and those corresponding to the circular psychotics are called "*cyclothymes.*" One may for convenience call the transitional stages between illness and health, or the abortive pathological forms, "schizoid" and "cycloid" ([1921] 1936, p. 30).

Robert Gaupp, a professor of psychiatry at the University of Tübingen where Kretschmer once studied, acclaimed the book with enthusiasm and the Nazis used it to their own advantage. The book proved a source of considerable polemic, but a constructive influence inspired by it was the constitutional psychology of William Sheldon into which the book was to fructify.

William H. Sheldon (1899-   ): Constitutional Psychology. A Rhode Islander who had taken his Ph.D. (1926) and M.D. (1933) from the University of Chicago, Sheldon had developed a complete personality theory based on constitutional psychology during the decades of the 1940s. The basis of his research was completed during his years at Harvard University where he joined the faculty in

1938, leaving in 1947 for the Constitutional Laboratory at Columbia University. While at Harvard, Sheldon met S. S. Stevens; together they collaborated to produce the first of his volumes on physique and temperament, *The Varieties of Human Physique* (with W. B. Rucker, 1940) and *The Varieties of Temperament* (1942). At Columbia he collaborated with E. M. Hartl and E. McDermott to produce *Varieties of Delinquent Youth: An Introduction to Constitutional Psychiatry* (1949), and then in 1954 *Atlas of Men: A Guide for Somato-typing the Adult Male at All Ages* (with C. W. Dupertuis and E. McDermott).

The three-fold typology that Sheldon developed had its predecessors in L. Rostan (1828) and almost a century later in Kretschmer (1921). Rostan's digestive type and Kretschmer's pyknic type became Sheldon's endomorphs; Rostan's muscular and Kretschmer's athletic type became Sheldon's mesomorphs; Rostan's respiratory-cerebral type and Kretschmer's asthenic type became Sheldon's ectomorph. The refinement Sheldon brought to the study was a more scientific approach complete with measurements along a seven point scale. Describing his system, Sheldon explained:

> The somatotype is a series of three numerals, each expressing the approximate strength of one of the primary components in a physique. The first numeral always refers to *endomorphy*. . . , the second to *mesomorphy,* and the third to *ectomorphy.* Thus when a 7-point scale is used, a 7-1-1 is the most extreme endomorph, a 1-7-1 is the most extreme mesomorph, and 1-1-7 the most extreme ectomorph. The 4-4-4 falls at the mid-point . . . with respect to all three components (1944, p. 539).

In the *Varieties of Human Physique,* seventy-six varieties of somatotypes have been described.

For each physique type, Sheldon had its corresponding temperament: *visceratonia, somatotonia,* and *cerebrotonia.* Each is explained in the *Varieties of Temperament:*

> *Viscerotonia* . . . is characterized by general relaxation, love of comfort, sociability, conviviality, gluttony for food, for people, and for affection. . . .
>
> *Somatotonia* . . . is roughly a predominance of muscular activity and of vigorous bodily assertiveness. . . . These people have vigor and push. . . .
>
> *Cerebrotonia* . . . is roughly a predominance of the element of restraint, inhibition, and of the desire for concealment. Cerebrotonic people shrink away from sociality as from too strong a light (1942, p. 23).

Throughout the history of psychology, typology held the interest of a number of psychologists with quite different outlooks, all the way from the typology of Pavlov to the typing of Freud, for Freud would see people as anal-sadistic types, oral types, etc., depending upon one's arrested development or point of fixation. *Erik H. Erikson* (1902-   ) built upon Freud's stages of libidinal or psychosexual development with his own psychosocial identity encompassing eight stages of an individual in his *Childhood and Society* (1950). Each stage with its attendant crisis is (1) oral-sensory stage (trust vs. mistrust); (2) muscular-anal stage (autonomy vs. shame and doubt); (3) locomotor-genital stage (initiative vs. guilt); (4)

latency stage (industry vs. inferiority); (5) puberty and adolescence stage (identity vs. role confusion); (6) young adulthood stage (intimacy vs. isolation); (7) adulthood stage (generativity vs. stagnation); (8) maturity stage (ego integrity vs. despair). The Dane Erikson was trained in psychoanalysis under Anna Freud in the 1920s, and lectured at Harvard and Yale, before retiring in California.

Also interested in typing was Alfred Adler, who typed according to the relative position a child holds in his family (first-born, middle, or last). He also typed them according to inferiority or superiority striving.

(B) NEO-FREUDIAN CULTURAL ANALYSTS

ALFRED ADLER (1870-1937) and the Cultural Analysts

The names of Freud, Jung, and Adler have long been linked together, as the following incident recorded by Jung's biographer, E. A. Bennett, attests:

> During this visit to London, Jung had occasion to look up some references, and he went to the Reading Room of the British Museum. He was asked if he had a reader's ticket. 'No,' he replied, 'I'm afraid I haven't. . . . 'Who are you?' he was asked. 'What is your name?' 'I am a Swiss doctor on a visit to London. My name is Jung—Dr. Jung.' 'Not, Freud, Jung, and Adler?' exclaimed the assistant. 'Oh, no,' he replied. 'Only Jung!' (1962, p. 6).

The Vienna-born Adler received his degree in medicine from the University of Vienna Medical School in 1895. At the turn of the century he became interested in psychopathology, becoming acquainted with Freud in 1906 (the same year Jung began his correspondence with Freud). The following year it became evident that Adler differed sharply from Freud when his *Study of Organ Inferiority and Its Psychical Compensation* (1907) appeared. Neither Freud's interpretation of dreams nor his theory of sex trauma as the cause of mental disorder agreed with Adler , who made his rift with Freud in 1911 when nine of his followers deserted Freud with Adler out of a group of probably less than three dozen. The two men never again met. The following year he proclaimed his position in *The Neurotic Constitution* (1912) and dubbed his system "Individual Psychology" *(Individual-psychologie)*. The organ of his school, *Zeitschrift für Individualpsychologie (Journal for Individual Psychology)*, was also founded in 1912, currently named the *Journal of Individual Psychology* (U.S.).

Returning from World War I, Adler, a lecturer at the Pedagogical Institute, founded the first child-guidance clinic in Vienna in 1921. In 1926 he was appointed a lecturer at Columbia University, and in 1935 moved to the United States. In Scotland, at the University of Aberdeen during a lecture series, Adler died on the street of a heart attack.

Adler's Individual Psychology

While Freud dug beneath the surface of consciousness to the unconscious repression to uncover the source of motivation in the unconscious, and Jung peered even deeper into a layer below the personal unconscious to find a motivation common to the entire race in a racial or collective unconscious, Adler went in the opposite direction and found it on the surface, the physical body of a person. Adler traced motivation from an uncomfortable irritation that he recognized as a feeling of inferiority stemming from an inferior member of some part of the body. First calling attention to it in 1907 in his *Study of Organ Inferiority and Its Psychical Compensation,* Adler asserted that the purpose of that book was to prove that children suffer from hereditary organic weakness, which they attempt to compensate for physically, and even to overcompensate for it. The inferiority has its attendant psychological effect, causing peculiar exaggerations and overemphases to the point of producing individual personality traits. Hence the degree of physical perfection is a factor of successful or unsuccessful psychological development. "Every neurosis," asserted Adler, "can be understood as an attempt to free oneself from a feeling of inferiority in order to gain a feeling of superiority" ([1913] 1959, p. 23), but the causal factor is not sexual.

Inferiority and Superiority Feelings. One of the psychological traits arising from a sense of organ inferiority is agressiveness. "We will always discover in fighting, aggressive children," observed Adler, "an inferiority complex and a desire to overcome it. It is as if they were trying to lift themselves on their toes in order to appear greater and to gain by this easy method success, pride and superiority" (1969, p. 29). Thus an inferiority feeling might become a complex that is autonomously motivating, the superiority complex being no more than an expression of insidious inferiority. Inferiority drives a person to impertinence, arrogance, and pugnaciousness as if he were superior. Inferiority compensates for itself in a variety of ways and mechanisms. It was Adler who coined *inferiority feeling* and the mechanism of compensation (and overcompensation), which arises from inferiority. The striving for perfection can be overcompensation for inferiority feelings. In *The Neurotic Constitution: Outlines of a Comparative Individualistic Psychology and Psychotherapy* (1907), Adler postulated

> a remarkable relationship between somatic inferiority and psychic overcompensation, so that I gained a fundamental viewpoint, namely, that the realization of somatic inferiority by the individual becomes for him a permanent impelling force for the development of his psyche (1926, p. 1).

He observed that pampered children and hated children tend to develop an abnormal sense of inferiority. Also he postulated that all drives are subordinate to the agressive drive.

Striving for Superiority. With time Adler came to the growing realization that in every psychological phenomenon there is a striving for superiority. "Life (and all psychic expressions as part of life)," asserted Adler, "moves ever toward perfection, toward superiority, toward success" (1935, p. 6). Accordingly while Freud's basic motivation was a drive toward pleasure (the pleasure principle), Adler's was a drive toward superiority. Adler concluded:

> This, now appeared to me as the fundamental law of all spiritual expression: that the total melody is to be found again in every one of its parts, as a greatest common measure— in every individual craving for power, for victory over the difficulties of life (1930, p. 339).

The mode assumed by the drive of superiority characterizes the personality. The characteristic form taken by the drive, appearing early in life, is contingent on what Adler called the "life style."

The Life Style. Quite early in life, even at two, and at least by his fifth year, the life style is quite perceptible in the goal that the child sets for the need and drive of his psychological development, a goal toward which all ancillary currents of his mental life contribute. One's style of life is in consequence of the approach taken by a person in his struggle to overcome his inferiority feelings. A person's style of life may be ascertained by taking "into account the meaning of the individual about his goal of superiority, the strength of his feeling of inferiority, and the degree of his social feeling" (Adler, 1964, p. 39). To detect the style of life, it is necessary to view the personality of the individual not as a battlefield of ego, superego, and id in perennial and irreconcilable conflict but as a unity or totality. "Very early in my work," observed Adler concerning the personality,

I found him to be a *unity!* The foremost task of Individual Psychology is to prove this unity in each individual—in his thinking, feeling, acting; in his so-called conscious and unconscious—in every expression of his personality. This unity we call the "Life-Style" of the individual. What is frequently labeled "the ego" is nothing more that the style of the individual (1935a, p.7).

The life style is each individual personality's form of creative activity.

While there is one principal life style that is wholesome (the socially useful), three major types are undesirable or neurotic life styles: (1) the ruling type, (2) the getting type, and (3) the avoiding type. Their undesirablity lies in their inability to resolve life's problems which are essentially social problems. The female's "masculine protest" falls into a neurotic life style, a style that appears "as if the patient wished to change from a woman to a man" (Adler, 1926, p. 100). The masculine protest is essentially a form of overcompensation, one with its attendant errors. "Womanliness," asserted Adler, "is experienced like an inferior organ from which there grows a strong compensatory striving" (1970, p. 47). Certain women, fearing the feminine role, react with a masculine protest.

Finalism and Fictional Finalism. An important tenet of individual psychology is that of finalism, a person's seeking goals, being motivated by them in his search for a meaningful life. The final goal of an individual, established early in childhood, is an integral part of his style of life. While the final goals of a normal person are realistically within reach, those of the neurotic are fictional.

The neurotic keeps before his eye his God, his idol, his ideal of personality and clings to his guiding principle, losing sight in the meanwhile of reality, whereas the normal person is always ready to dispense with this crutch, this aid, and reckon unhampered with reality (1926, p. 66).

Receiving his cue from Hans Vaihinger's *Philosophy of 'As If'* (1911), Adler found that many individuals guide their lives by fictions, fictional finals (goals). A person is teleologically oriented; he is a goal striving personality. The more desirable goals are those consonant with a social feeling or social interest.

Social Feeling or Social Interest. Personality problems arise from lack of social usefulness, whereas the wholesome personality, a cooperative one, contributes to the benefit of others. The degree of social feeling in a person can be gauged when his social situation is altered. For example, "when we send a child to school," said Adler, "we may observe his social interest there just as in general social life. We can see whether he mixes with his fellows or avoids them" (1969, pp. 25-6). One can detect whether he is sly, clever, or hyperactive, thus noting his style of life and whether or not it is one of social feeling. Innate social instincts account for socialization.

Adlerian Psychotherapy. Social feeling plays an important role in the psychotherapeutic technique of individual psychology because successful therapy calls for inducing social interest within a person. Inasmuch as a neurosis arises from a life-style lacking in social interest, a socially useful one rich in social feeling tends to resolve life's problems. Social interest along with self-transcendence and reason characterize mental health.

> Individual psychology considers the essence of therapy to lie in making the patient aware of his lack of cooperative power, and to convince him of the origin of this lack in early childhood maladjustments. What passes during this process is no small matter; his power of cooperation is enhanced by collaboration with the doctor. His "inferiority complex" is revealed as erroneous. Courage and optimism are awakened. And the "meaning of life" dawns upon him as the fact that proper meaning must be given to life (1930, p. 404).

Another aid in Adlerian therapy is to ascertain a person's early memories, for these are important indications of his style of life.

Early Memories. An individual's old remembrances are vital in ascertaining his personality, motivations, life style, and problems. Memories are reminders that follow him about; as such there are no "chance memories." Adler observed that

> early recollections have especial significance. To begin with, they show the style of life in its origins and in its simplest expressions. . . . The first memory will show the individual's fundamental view of life; his first satisfactory crystallization of his attitude (1931, pp. 74-5).

Once early memories are detected, and the style of life or the "law-of-movement" of the individual ascertained, one must work toward enhancing social interest and social cooperation, for in such will a person find his salvation.

> Only he who carries within himself, in his "law-of-movement," a sufficient degree of the community ideal, and lives according to it as easily as he breathes, will be in a position to solve, in the meaning of the community, those conflicts which are inevitably his (1935b, p. 12).

The Trend toward Cultural Explanations of Personality Development
Ruth Benedict (1887-1948) and Margaret Mead (1901-   ): Cultural Determinants of Personality. Adler's move toward the social as a factor in

personality development was the start of a wave of competing theories challenging psychoanalysis. Three women, *Ruth Benedict* (1887-1948), *Margaret Mead* (1901-   ), and *Karen Horney* (1885-1952) turned their attention from a person's evolutionary past to the present cultural environment with the resulting effect of reducing some of Freud's sacred ideas to chauvinistic influence. In her anthropological investigations reported in her *Patterns of Culture* (1934), Benedict found that a person is a "creature of his culture," with social determinants responsible for traits such as honesty and leadership. Not instinct, but custom molds. Freud erred when he held that society and the individual were at odds. Mead, who carried Benedict's views still further in her *Male and Female* (1949), found that male and female types rather than being innate as Freud contended were the result of cultural factors. Not physiology, but society accounts for sex roles. Mead (1967) found that normal and abnormal were norms prescribed by society rather than a disorder of nature.

Both Benedict and Mead were Columbia Ph.D.s in anthropology who gathered data from primitive tribes. Their data so impressed a female psychoanalyst from Berlin, Karen Horney, that she adapted their findings to psychoanalysis, resulting in her expulsion from the New York Psychoanalytic Institute.

Karen (Danielsen) Horney (1885-1952): Neo-Freudianism and the Sociological School. With ideas resembling Adler's to such an extent that she has been thought of as revising Adlerian psychology, Horney utilized the findings of Benedict and Mead. An M.D. trained in psychoanalysis under Freud's close friend, *Karl Abraham* (1877-1925), the German Horney spent a dozen years (1920-1932) as instructor at the Berlin Institute for Psychoanalysis before coming to the United States at the invitation of *Franz Alexander* (1891-1964) as associate director of the Chicago Institute for Psychoanalysis. In 1934 she left for New York, where, in addition to private practice, she taught at the New School for Social Research.

With her publications, *The Neurotic Personality of Our Time* (1937) followed two years later by *New Ways in Psychoanalysis* (1939), it became quite evident that she departed radically from orthodox psychoanalysis. The New York Psychoanalytic Society responded with her ejection from the society, and she rebutted with the founding of the American Institute for Psychoanalysis, which she headed until her death.

Freud's libido theory, death instinct, and penis envy complex were equally objectionable to her, but more especially the psychic determinism of the libido theory or accounting for personality in terms of erotic instinctual energy, thus reducing human relationships to sexual ones. The death instinct could be adequately explained as an intense and provocative reaction against one's social environment. Orthodox Freudians considered a person who fails to direct his hostile, aggressive "death instinct" feelings toward others to be suicidal, the victim of possible self-destruction. Freud's ethnocentrism victimized him into explaining in terms of a penis envy complex what could more adequately be accounted for by cultural or social conditions and their effect on the psychology of women. Accordingly feminine psychology is not to be explained as the mere offshoot of masculine psychology.

Excessive anxiety suffered as a result of interpersonal relations during the early period of family life accounts for neurosis. Owing to the child's complete dependence upon parents, hostility toward them that is repressed is experienced as *basic anxiety,* a childhood sense of loss of love and respect.

> I first saw the core of neurosis in human relations. Generally, I pointed out, these were brought about by cultural conditions; specifically, through environmental factors which obstructed the child's unhampered psychic growth. Instead of developing a basic confidence in self and others the child developed basic anxiety, which I defined as a feeling of being isolated and helpless toward a world potentially hostile. In order to keep this basic anxiety at a minimum the spontaneous moves toward, against, and away from others became compulsive. While the spontaneous moves were compatible, each with the others, the compulsive ones collided. The conflicts generated in this way, which I called basic conflicts, were therefore the result of conflicting needs and conflicting attitudes with regard to other people (Horney, 1950, pp. 366-7).

Thus anxiety, the source of neurosis, and neurosis are culturally based.

To anxiety, Horney added the concept of *alienation* to identify the condition of a person who finds himself divorced from his true or real self and from others. In the process of neurosis, an individual abandons his real self for an idealized one; neurosis is a "disturbance in one's relation to self and to others" (Horney, 1950, p. 368). The basic conflicts of neurotics manifest themselves as (1) "moving toward people" (compliant type); (2) "moving against people" (aggressive type); or (3) "moving away from people" (detached type).

In western civilization a person is threatened with mental disturbance unless he capitulates his genuine identity for the less acceptable psychological activity of his neurotic culture. In this state of abnormal social conditions, neurosis is regarded as normalcy. What then is one to do? Either he can turn to social reform or preferably to *self analysis* (1942), utilizing the latter to reintegrate the personality through desirable interpersonal relationships as well as through his own inner resources. Psychic growth in which the real self develops requires warm and cordial interpersonal relations out of which the real self can emerge.

Psychotherapy, considered in the light of these factors, is therefore personality reorganization through analysis, rather than the Freudian surfacing of unconscious conflicts to consciousness. Her former associate, Alexander, inspired her psychotherapeutic insights.

Erich Fromm (1900-   ): Humanistic Psychoanalysis. Born in Frankfurt am Main with a Ph.D. from the University of Heidelberg in 1922, Fromm like Horney studied at the Psychoanalytic Institute in Berlin. Also like her he migrated to the United States, but two years later (1934) he began teaching at Columbia University (1934-1941) and Bennington College in Vermont (1941-1950). In 1952 he became a professor at the National University of Mexico, and concurrently joined the faculty at Michigan State (1957-1961). In 1962 he was appointed professor of psychiatry at Columbia University.

The cultural psychoanalyst Fromm, like Horney, took issue with Freudianism's failure to see the social factor's role in human psychology. He sought to humanize psychoanalysis by replacing individual as animal with the person as human, his personality being a product of culture rather than biology. Unlike the animal a person's needs are more than instinctual, they are singularly human. Five major human needs are (1) relatedness, (2) transcendence, (3) rootedness, (4) identity, and (5) orientation. The thesis of his *Escape from Freedom* (1941) is that

> man, the more he gains freedom in the sense of emerging from the original oneness with man and nature and the more he becomes an "individual," has no choice but to unite himself with the world in the spontaneity of love and productive work or else to seek a kind of security by such ties with the world as destroy his freedom and the integrity of his individual self (pp. 22-3).

Fromm viewed the person as a social being in a social situation, the individual being a member of a sane society by successfully adjusting and contributing by the sublimation of Freudian instincts. In the *Sane Society* (1955), a society in which a person can successfully fulfill his human needs, he depicted one

> in which man relates to man lovingly, in which he is rooted in bonds of brotherliness and solidarity, rather than in the ties of blood and soil; a society which gives him the possibility of transcending nature by creating rather than by destroying, in which everyone gains a sense of self by experiencing himself as the subject of his powers rather than by conformity, in which a system of orientation and devotion exists without man's needing to distort reality and to worship idols (p. 362).

The sane society Fromm termed a *humanistic communitarian socialism*.

Harry Stack Sullivan (1892-1949): Interpersonal Theory of Psychiatry. Extending psychology, personality, and mental disorders into the realm of social psychology reached its climax in the American psychiatrist Harry Stack Sullivan who equated psychiatry with social psychology. According to Sullivan,

> psychiatry as it is—the preoccupation of extant psychiatric specialists—is not science nor art but confusion. In defining it as the study of interpersonal relations, I sought to segregate from everything else a disciplinary field in which operational methods could be applied with great practical benefits. This made psychiatry the probable locus of another evolving discipline, one of the social sciences, namely, *social psychology* (1947, p.x.).

An M.D. from the Chicago College of Medicine and Surgery in 1917, Sullivan, a specialist with schizophrenics, especially with respect to *empathy* or emotional communication he established in interpersonal processes with them, defined personality to comport with that experience as "the relatively enduring pattern of recurrent interpersonal situations which characterize a human life" (1947, p. xi). The person as an individual is a myth.

While at St. Elizabeth's Hospital in Washington, D.C., he encountered Freudian psychoanalytic theory but in innovated form through the influence of William Alanson White. In 1936 he helped found the Washington School of Psychiatry. Like Horney, he emphasized the role of anxiety in behavioral disorder, holding anxiety to be empathetically induced from mother to child. "The tension of anxiety, when present in the mothering one, induces anxiety in the infant" (1953, p. 41), resulting in insecurity. Thus psychiatric disorders are interpersonal phenomena. The "dynamism of the self-system" is developed by the child to ward off increasing degrees of anxiety related to the educative process arising from interpersonal relations.

Psychiatry accordingly is viewed by Sullivan as the interpersonal process of alleviating anxiety (absolute tension) with the assistance of the psychiatrist as a participant observer, the results of psychotherapy being homeostasis or equilibrium (security) and a feeling of euphoria. The pursuit of satisfaction, being the goal of behavior, is in consequence of biological needs (sleep, food, and sex) fulfilled.

(C) PHENOMENOLOGISTS AND EXISTENTIALISTS

VIKTOR E. FRANKL (1905-   ): Logotherapy: The Will to Meaning

Contrary to Sullivan, Frankl does not espouse the Sullivanian theory of tension-reduction, homeostasis, tranquility, and euphoria. Rather, tension interspersed with respite is indicated. The healthy individual, argued Frankl, does not seek homeostasis but the challenge of life. "The homeostasis principle," he asserted, "is by no means a normal phenomenon but rather a neurotic one. It is the neurotic individual who cannot abide the normal tension of life—whether physical, psychic, or moral" (1967, pp. 47-8).

Frankl, whose logotherapy is considered the third Viennese school of psychotherapy (Freud and Adler being the first two), notes that while Freud's system was founded on a drive to pleasure and Adler's on a drive to power, his is on a *will* to meaning. Will signifies that a person is not driven but pulled because a drive requires a consummatory response (eating, sex activity) as relief, whereas will implies teleological motivation issuing in fulfillment.

Frankl's initiation into medical psychology was in 1924 when at the invitation of Freud he wrote a paper for the *International Journal of Psychoanalysis* at the youthful age of nineteen. The Vienna-born Frankl, who spent his career at the University of Vienna, obtained his M.D. there in 1930 and his Ph.D. in 1949. Prior to his rising to Professor of Neurology and Psychiatry at its medical school while serving as head of the department of neurology at Vienna's Poliklinik Hospital, Frankl nobly endured three years in Hitler's concentration camps, including Auschwitz and Dachau. Well known to America where he has lectured extensively and taught as a visiting professor (e.g., Harvard, Southern Methodist, U.S. International University), Frankl is a leading force for humanistic psychology and innovator of new techniques in psychotherapy. At the U.S. International University Frankl founded the Institute of Logotherapy in the decade of the 1960s.

Tenets of Logotherapy

Logotherapy by definition means a psychotherapy through a meaningful life.

However, it, like Freudian psychoanalysis, has branched out into a personality theory as well. Logotherapeutic techniques include (1) paradoxical intention, (2) dereflection, (3) self-detachment, (4) the acquisition of meaning in life, (5) altering one's attitude toward the unchangeable vicissitudes of life, (6) humor, (7) medical ministry, (8) logodrama, (9) the technique of the common denominator.

Since much of a person's mental anguish arises from mental stress contributing to his emotional and behavioral disturbances, one manner of reversing the situation is by *paradoxical intention* which undercuts anticipatory anxiety. For example, to be concerned about trembling or stuttering simply contributes to intensifying it, but willingly and with a good sense of humor and self-detachment mentally embracing that concerning which one senses anxiety will diminish both the anxiety and the behavioral consequence be it either emotional such as trembling or behavioral such as stuttering. The psychodynamics of paradoxical intention is best understood in the light of "anticipatory anxiety." Commented Frankl:

> it is commonly observed that such anxiety often produces precisely that situation of which the patient is afraid. The erythrophobic individual, for example, who is afraid of blushing when he enters a room and faces a group of people, will actually blush at precisely that moment. A symptom evokes a psychic response in terms of anticipatory anxiety which provokes the symptom to reappear. The reoccurrence of the symptom in turn reinforces the anticipatory anxiety, and thus a vicious circle is completed (1965, p. 221).

Implementing reinforcement is Frankl's synthesizing of neobehaviorism or learning theory psychology with psychodynamics or depth psychology into logotherapy.

Also playing a role in anticipatory anxiety is the technique of *dereflection,* seen best in the hyperreflective attitude of some insomniacs. Sleep comes by not forcing it, by not attempting to sleep, the same being true of many sexual failures or inadequacies.

Will to Meaning

A large percentage of current neuroses, rather than being of a sexual origin, is existentially rooted, growing out of an existential frustration and existential boredom, thus leading to a *noogenic neurosis.* All of this is due to the singularly human character of people. Viewing the human being as three-dimensional, Frankl cited him as physical, psychological, and *noological* (human). In the *humanistic psychology* of Frankl it is this third dimension of the individual that is emphasized.

Rather than many drives as espoused by his predecessors, Frankl held that human motivation is neither driven nor comprised of a plurality of drives. A person is pulled by the meaningful phenomenological qualities that surround him in life. Thus the *phenomenologist* Frankl contends that there is only one motivational force, a pulling rather than a driving one, a will to meaning. An individual whose life is meaningful escapes neurosis. The object of logotherapy is to assist the patient in finding for himself those phenomenological entities that are meaningful for him.

Defining a person as a "unity in spite of multiplicity" (1969, p. 22) in the tradition of Aquinas and William Stern, Frankl is confident that meanings exist for him as a genuine phenomenological reality, an insight inspired by Max Scheler (1916). They cannot be concocted or fabricated, they must be discovered as genuine. The drug LSD, for example, furnishes only a counterfeit meaningful experience. Meanings that are shared by everyone, Frankl termed values.

Meanings abound everywhere, especially in suffering. Frankl referred to pain, death, and guilt as the tragic triad, especial targets of logotherapy. Transforming any of the elements of the tragic triad into a meaningful experience results in a suitable adjustment toward them. Fond of citing Nietzsche's (1889) maxim that anyone who has a reason for living will overcome almost any obstacle, Frankl held that any element of the tragic triad can become meaningful by an attitudinal change, if no other option is available. Thus attitudinal values become one of a triad along with creative and experiential values. These inferences are predicated on the premises of logotherapy: (1) freedom of will, (2) will to meaning, and (3) meaning of life, each premise standing firmly opposed to its respective antithesis: (1) the pandeterminism of Freud, (2) the homeostasis theory of Sullivan, and (3) the reductionism of behaviorism and psychoanalysis. In response to Freudian reductionism, that of reducing values to defense mechanism, reaction formation, and instinctual drives, Frankl lashed out with "I would not be willing to live for the sake of my 'defense mechanisms,' much less to die for the sake of my 'reaction formations'" (1967, pp. 10-11).

Existential Analysis: Ludwig Binswanger (1881-1966) and Medard Boss (1903-   ). Although Frankl regards himself as an existential psychiatrist, having been the first to use the term in reference to psychiatry, his system is much more consonant with the phenomenology of Max Scheler. Scheler's associate, *Martin Heidegger* (1889-   ), was the philosopher through whose ideas existentialism entered psychology. It was Heideggerian existentialism that Binswanger and Boss, and subsequently the American psychologist *Rollo May* (1909-   ) embraced. None of these individuals coined the term; that credit belongs to the French philosopher *Jean Wahl* (1888-   ).

Notwithstanding Binswanger and Boss being Swiss, their existential psychiatry represents an abrupt break from the tradition of Jung. Referring to their orientation in psychology as *existential analysis,* they share only the concept of analysis with Jung, despite their training at the University of Zurich. Educated at the universities of Lausanne, Heidelberg, and Zurich, Binswanger spent a year each at Burgholzli (Zurich) and at Jena (under Bleuler) before settling a lifetime (from 1910) at the Sanatorium Bellevue in Kreuzlingen. Boss spent almost all of his life in Zurich where he was educated before becoming Professor of Psychotherapy at the University of Zurich.

The German Heidegger's *Being and Time* (1927) provided the base upon which existential psychologists construct their position. With a humanistic view of an individual, Heidegger saw him as a being-in-the-world or an in-the-world type of being, which he termed *dasein* (being-there). A person, if he is to be properly understood, must be viewed in the light of his own world, his phenomenological world. All traditional existentialists think of themselves as phenomenologists in methodology in the tradition established by *Edmund Husserl* (1859-1938). This fact holds true for the *existential psychoanalysis* of Jean-Paul Sartre (1905-   ) as well. While Sartre subtitled his classic *Being and Nothingness* (1943) *An Essay on Phenomenological Ontology,* Heidegger dedicated his magnum opus *Being and Time* (1972) to Edmund Husserl.

Taking its lead from Heidegger, the book containing the selected papers of Binswanger is appropriately titled *Being-in-the-World* (1963). The principal work of Boss, *Psychoanalysis and Daseinsanalysis* (1963), seeks to stress the kinship to psychoanalysis while emphasizing the analysis of *dasein,* the being of an individual as human—a person. Analysis of dasein reveals him to be an existential being in the continual process of development with his unlimited possibilites. Through freedom of choice the personality is chosen into whatever mode suits one. Authentic selfhood is sought through the exercise of responsible choice. Through the psychotherapeutic encounter of therapist entering into the world of the patient, a decisive inner experience is effected whereby the patient achieves a new weltanschauung and personality reconstruction. It is the moment of *kairos,* the moment of decision, wherein decisive personality changes occur. The therapist-patient encounter is a personal one of an "I-thou" (Martin Buber, 1923) relationship in which a genuine human "presence" is experienced. Inasmuch as each patient is a being-in-the-world, possessing his personal subjective world, it follows that no two individuals are the same nor can they be treated alike.

The strongest force for existential psychology in America, Rollo May, is a New York psychotherapist who obtained his Ph.D. from Columbia University in 1949. He is known best for introducing existential psychology in the United States through his edited books *Existence: A New Dimension in Psychiatry and Psychology* (1958) and *Existential Psychology* (1961), and through his collected papers *Psychology and the Human Dilemma* (1967).

CARL R. ROGERS (1902-   ): Client-Centered Therapy

It is difficult to categorize Carl Rogers, a third generation graduate from Columbia University, who obtained his Ph.D. from Teachers College in 1931. What makes Rogers an exception to the rule is that he is a pioneer abandoning everything Teachers College, Columbia University stood for, by creatively developing a new psychotherapeutic approach without any roots whatever at Columbia. Actually his client-centered therapy for which he is celebrated was developed in his post-doctoral years. An early influence, if indeed there was any, could have been Alfred Adler, who impressed him in a lecture by contending that "an elaborate case history was not necessary" (1967, p. 357). Otto Rank's description of his therapy also made an impression. However, the real birth of client-centered therapy came during Rogers' twelve years at Rochester as Director of the Child Study Department and later as first Director of the Rochester Guidance Center. At the Child Study Department, Rogers' flash of insight came when he counseled one of his first adult *clients*, as he termed his patients (partly because it accords them a status of equality desirable for successful therapy). The realization was that "it is the *client* who knows what hurts, what directions to go, what problems are crucial, what experiences have been deeply buried" (1967, p. 359). Thus it was imperative to be guided by the client for the direction of movement that the process of therapy was to assume, hence the inception of *client-centered therapy.*

Nondirective Psychotherapy. It was not at Rochester, but when he was professor of clinical psychology and executive secretary of the Counseling Center at Ohio State University that Rogers issued his first, and in some respects his most important, book on *Counseling and Psychotherapy: Newer Concepts in Practice* (1942). The nondirective approach, a Socratic one in which questions are answered by questions, aims at the feelings rather than intellect of the client.

> The individual and not the problem is the focus. The aim is not to solve one particular problem, but to assist the individual to *grow*, so that he can cope with the present problem and with later problems in a better-integrated fashion. If he can gain enough integration to handle one problem in more independent, more responsible, less confused, better-organized ways, then he will also handle new problems in that manner (1942, pp. 28-9).

Not the individual's past but his immediate situation is accorded emphasis. Therapy transpires despite the therapist's ignorance of the patient's past history. The four major characteristics of client-centered therapy are: (1) the individual rather than the problem as the focus, (2) emphasis upon feelings and emotions rather than intellectual aspects, (3) emphasis on the individual's immediate rather than his past situation, and (4) emphasis upon the therapeutic relationship as a growth experience.

Phenomenological Theory of Personality. Inasmuch as Rogers' entire system of psychotherapy is one of personality change and growth, it was inevitable for him to be led to the psychology of personality. Identifying himself, he said: "I am a psychologist; a clinical psychologist I believe, a humanistically oriented psychologist certainly; a psychotherapist, deeply interested in the dynamics of personality change" (1967, p. 343). While his theory was earlier presented in his *Client-Centered Therapy* (1951), a more definitive statement was outlined in "A Theory of Therapy, Personality, and Interpersonal Relationships, as Developed in the Client-Centered Framework" (1959).

The self, according to Rogers, develops through an awareness of *self-experience*, stemming from an awareness of being and of functioning. Through interaction with one's enrivonment (especially significant other persons), awareness of being and functioning elaborates into a concept of self, i.e., "a perceptual object in his *experiential field*" (1959, p. 233). Personality development, arising from a tendency toward actualizing the self, results ideally in the *fully functioning person.* Conditions necessary to effect this ideal state include the satisfaction of certain needs, such as the need for a *positive self-regard.*

If for no other reason, Rogers is important in the history of psychology owing to his client-centered therapy being more widely used in the United States during the decades of the 1950s and 1960s than any other psychotherapeutic system with the exception of psychoanalysis.

J. L. MORENO (1892-1974) Psychodrama and Group Psychotherapy

Frankl's logotherapy has come to be called the third Viennese school of psychotherapy, Freud's psychoanalysis and Adler's individual psychology being the predecessors. While this is true to a considerable extent, it may possibly be challenged by J. L. Moreno's psychodrama and group psychotherapy, for Moreno too was Viennese prior to his coming to the United States in 1927. After obtaining his M.D. from the University of Vienna in 1917, Moreno founded the Spontaneity Theatre in 1921, and the "living newspaper" in 1923 as the emergence of psychodrama. In 1929 he founded the Impromptu Theatre, followed two years later by the *Impromptu Magazine*. A lasting contribution, sociometry, he established in 1933 and published it in his major work *Who Shall Survive?* (1934), subtitled in a 1953 revision as *Foundations of Sociometry, Group Psychotherapy, and Sociograms*. He began publication of *Sociometry: A Journal of Interpersonal Relations* in 1937. His three volume *Psychodrama* saw its first volume in 1946, undergoing its fourth edition in 1972.

Unlike his Viennese predecessors, Moreno was predominantly interested in social psychology and social psychotherapy. His contributions in this area have been shamefully underestimated almost to the point of neglect by psychologists. Not only has he developed a system of group psychotherapy, but he has contributed a personality theory and a methodology for experiments in social psychology as well. *Sociometry* is the study of interpersonal relationships in the light of individuals choosing and rejecting relations with members of their own group. Sociometry is predicated on *spontaneity* and *creativity,* the former a catalyzer of interpersonal relationships and the latter functioning as a cultural conserve. Spontaneity-creativity is the personality's fundamental dimension, an insight inspired by Bergson (1907).

Moreno's Psychotherapy. The fundamental categories through which all psychological phenomena are understood, spontaneity and creativity, also become an integral part of Moreno's psychotherapy. As spontaneity is augmented, anxiety diminishes. Participants in a "spontaneity theatre" by enacting scenes arising out of their personal worlds evince an emotional catharsis. Where patient-therapist transference fails, spontaneity role playing succeeds. Psychodrama calls for the person's expressing his past experiences (true or fancied) with real or imaginary persons. Those people assisting in the patient's drama, termed "auxiliary egos," aid by functioning as a "double" (playing the role of the patient enabling the patient better to see himself) or as a variation of the double called the "mirror technique," where the patient observes while someone else plays his role for him. A variety of psychodramatic forms currently exist, one being where two hostile groups (police and the ghetto blacks) play each other's role (reverse role playing). Essentially a form of social psychotherapy, psychodrama contributes toward enhancing community feeling by intensifying catharsis owing to acting's being a superior vehicle to Freud's talking cure. Furthermore, therapy being effected in a social setting is closer to real life situations than is individual therapy. Contrasting Psychodrama with Freud's psychoanalysis, Moreno observed:

Psychoanalysis was constructed to permit words and their associations. . . . Psychodrama was constructed to permit action and production. . . . The psychoanalytic therapist has to "interpret" because he has no other alternative. . . . In the psychodrama the behavior and the acting of the patient interprets for the therapist. . . . When in psychodrama the chief therapist feels a need to play a specific role towards a patient, the role of a father or of an employer, there is an alternative: he may use another person as a helper to fullfill this task, an auxiliary ego (1959, p. 231).

Moreno's psychodrama and group psychotherapy have developed into a formidable movement. After World War II the American Society of Group Psychotherapy and Psychodrama began publishing their organ, *Group Psychotherapy and Psychodrama,* and by 1966 *The International Handbook of Group Psychotherapy* appeared.

(D) NEUROPHYSIOLOGICAL PSYCHOTHERAPISTS

JULIUS WAGNER-JAUREGG (1857-1940) and MANFRED J. SAKEL (1900-1957): The Birth of Shock Therapy in Vienna

When the Viennese psychiatrist and neurologist Wagner-Jauregg treated the organic psychosis, general paresis (caused by Syphilitic infection), with malarial fever, he introduced shock therapy into psychiatry. For subjecting this once fatal disease to control in 1917, he was awarded the Nobel Prize in 1927. Early aware of the possibility of fever therapy, Wagner-Jauregg reported on the matter in 1887, when he accidentally observed marked improvement in a case of general paresis following an attack of malaria. However, it was not until 1918 that his classic paper on "The Effect of Malaria on Progressive Paralysis" was published, and elaborated upon in 1927 in his Nobel Prize lecture. Explaining his procedure, he asserted:

In July, 1917, I inoculated three paralytics with the blood of a patient with tertian malaria who had already had several typical attacks and in whose blood the presence of tertian plasmodia had been microscopically proved. The inoculation was made by taking blood from a vein in the arm during an attack of fever and spreading it on small scarifications in the arm of the paralytic. . . . In only two cases was there no trace of remission; the patients had to be placed in insane asylums ([1918] 1968, pp. 360-1).

It was not, however, until *Alexander Fleming's* (1881-1955) discovery in 1928 of penicillin as an antibiotic that infectious diseases such as general paresis were safely cured without inducing infection. Wagner-Jauregg controlled malaria by quinine.

From the ancient Greek philosopher of Elea, *Parmenides* (c. 540-470 BC), Wagner-Jauregg had learned: "Give me the power to produce fever and I'll cure all disease," as well as being aware of Hippocrates mentioning the salutary effect fever produced on epilepsy.

After obtaining his M.D. degree from the University of Vienna in the early 1880s, Wagner-Jauregg remained with his alma mater until he was appointed professor of psychiatry and neurology at the University of Graz (1889-1893). He returned to the University of Vienna as professor of psychiatry and neurology, directing the university's hospital for nervous and mental diseases until his retirement in 1928.

Sakel's Insulin Shock Therapy for Schizophrenia. Like Wagner-Jauregg before him, Sakel's discovery of insulin shock therapy for schizophrenics in 1933 was also accidental. Also an M.D. (1925) from the Medical School of the University of Vienna, Sakel spent a few years at the Vienna Hospital before going to Berlin to the Urban Hospital and then as psychiatrist-in-chief of the Lichterfeld Hospital. In 1933, when he made his celebrated discovery in Vienna, until 1936 he served as associate in the Neuropsychiatric University Clinic in Vienna. With the rise of nazism in the 1930s, Sakel left for the United States in 1936, administering his insulin shock treatment to patients at the Harlem Valley State Hospital in New York.

When one of Sakel's Viennese patients following an accidental overdose of insulin recovered from the insulin coma with some indication of symptom remission, he applied it intentionally in 1927 in precoma doses to addicts and then to schizophrenics in convulsion-producing doses. The patient, who remains in a coma for about one-half hour to an hour, is brought to consciousness by dextrose solution. Allowing for the length and onset of schizophrenia, Sakel reported an almost 88% recovery rate. Other mitigating factors, such as the patient's age and prepsychotic stability, played a role.

Reporting his findings in a series of articles in the *Wiener medizinische Wochenschrift* in 1934 to 1935, Sakel offered an expanded version in *The Pharmacological Shock Treatment of Schizophrenia* (1938). Four phases of the treatment are reported by him accordingly:

> In Phase I they are pacified. . . . The pacification is particularly marked in cases of catatonic excitement. . . . Phase II constitutes the actual assault on the illness. . . . Within this phase doses must be varied from time to time in accordance with the changing reaction of the patient. . . . Phase III allows the patient to recuperate and affords the physician an opportunity to register the effect of the shocks. . . . In Phase IV the insulin doses are only allowed to produce a "prehypoglycemic" reaction. . . . Phase IV should stabilize and compose the patient's mental condition. When the patient seems and feels both lucid and adequate the doses are then gradually diminished (1938, pp. 10-12).

Insulin itself, however, was discovered by two University of Toronto professors, *Frederick Grant Banting* (1891-1941) and *Charles Herbert Best* (1899-) in 1921, when Best, an undergraduate, was Banting's laboratory assistant at Toronto.

Lazlo Joseph Meduna (1896-1964): Metrazol Convulsive Shock Therapy. While Sakel was pursuing insulin shock treatment in Vienna, a Budapest professor, Meduna, was administering convulsive treatment with metrazol, seeking to obtain similar results with schizophrenics. Meduna's insight was inspired by Nyirö and Jablonszky, who, working in 1929 at the Budapest-Lipótmezö Mental Hospital, noted that when epileptics became schizophrenics, the epileptic convulsions became rare and subsequently ceased. This biological antagonism between schizophrenia and epilepsy led Meduna to induce epileptoid seizures pharmacologically. The limited success with the drug camphor prompted him to turn to injections of metrazol, a camphor derivative, with success. First publishing his finding in German in 1934, Meduna two years later reported it in English:

> It is possible to establish the existence between the schizophrenic and the epileptic process. . . .
>
> I endeavored to produce epileptiform convulsions in patients with schizophrenia and to observe the effect on the schizophrenic process. There are several ways of producing epileptiform convulsions. First I used a 25 per cent oily solution of camphor in intramuscular injections, raising the dose from 8 to 30 cc. Later I used metrazol in a 10 per cent solution, injecting it intravenously in doses of from 3 to 6 or 7 cc. The difference between the ways in which these substances act is that after the administration of camphor the epileptiform convulsions appear in from one to two hours, while after the administration of metrazol they appear immediately. Of the two, metrazol is the more suitable for the production of epileptic convulsions (1936a, p. 362).

Born in Budapest, Meduna, after receiving his degree in medicine from the Royal University of Sciences there in 1921, went to the Budapest Interacademic Institute for Neurological Research in 1924 before becoming associate professor in the psychiatric department of the Royal University of Sciences in 1927. In 1933 he directed Budapest's Leopold Field Hospital, leaving for the United States in 1939 as associate professor of psychiatry and neurology at Loyola University in Chicago. Four years later he accepted the position as professor of psychiatry at the University of Illinois College of Medicine. A naturalized American citizen, Meduna reported his findings in depth in his *Die Konvulsionstherapie der Schizophrenie* (1936b), and *Carbon Dioxide Therapy* (1950) expressed a later interest.

Ugo Cerletti (1877-1963): Electroshock Therapy. A University of Rome professor of neuropathology and psychiatry, Cerletti, learned of insulin convulsive treatment directly from Sakel in Vienna and briefed himself on Meduna's cardiazol shock treatment. Aware of the availability of convulsivant drugs, Cerletti, in seeking a purely physical means of obtaining the same results, turned to the application of electric current in collaboration with Lucio Bini, his assistant. He was able to induce in dogs the same seizures obtained from cardiazol. After attempting it with animals, he tried it on a 39 year-old engineer from Milan who was sent to him from Rome's police commissioner because he was wandering aimlessly at the railroad station. The patient, who arrived on April 15, 1938 for observation, was diagnosed as schizophrenic. Cerletti related:

> Two large electrodes were applied to the frontoparietal regions, and I decided to start cautiously with a low-intensity current of 80 volts for 1.5 seconds. As soon as the current was introduced, the patient reacted with a jolt and his body muscles stiffened; then he fell back on the bed without loss of consciousness. He started to sing abruptly at the top of his voice, then he quieted down.
>
> . . . It was proposed that we should allow the patient to have some rest and repeat the experiment the next day. All at once, the patient, who evidently had been following our conversation, said clearly and solemnly, without his usual gibberish: "Not another one! It's deadly!" (1954, p. 193).

Cerletti's discovery of electric shock therapy was of durable value, inasmuch as it is currently in use.

Born in Conegliano, Italy in 1877, Cerletti received his medical training at Rome and Turin with postgraduate work in neuropsychiatry at Paris, Munich, and Heidelberg (where he studied under Kraepelin). Prior to his tenure at the University of Rome in 1935, Cerletti directed the Neurobiologic Institute of Milan Mental Diseases Hospital after World War I. In 1924 he accepted the directorship of neuropsychiatry at the University of Bari, leaving four years later for the University of Genoa as professor of neuropsychiatry. The last years of his life were spent in the United States.

Egas Moniz (1874-1955): Prefrontal Leucotomy. Although psychosurgery began in ancient Rome and Greece with *trephination* (perforating the skull) in order to release vapors or humors considered the cause of personality disorders, its modern sophisticated form is attributable to the Portuguese neuropsychiatrist, Egas Moniz. His work was anticipated by *Roger Frugardi,* who in the twelfth century at the medical center in Salerno suggested trephination of manic and melancholic patients in order to release noxious poisons.

Moniz set to work when he learned of psychosurgery at the Second International Neurological Congress in London in 1935. At the congress two Americans, *John J. Fulton* and *C. E. Jacobsen* (1935), reported that removal of the frontal lobes of chimpanzees eliminated anxiety and frustration in their once high-strung subjects. His organic theory of thought he derived from *Santiago Ramon y Cajal* (1852-1934), a Spanish professor of anatomy and later histology at the universities of Valencia (1881-1886), Barcelona (1886-1892), and Madrid (1892-1922), who is known for isolating the neuron and the discovery of laws pertaining to cranial nerve cells, and neuron changes as functional units.

On his return to Portugal from the London congress in 1935, having received his cue from the Fulton-Jacobsen experiments, Moniz, with his colleague *Almeida Lima,* developed the psychosurgical technique of *bilateral prefrontal leucotomy* by introducing an extended instrument above the eyeball into the white matter of the brain thereby destroying some neural pathways. Moniz reasoned that "these synaptic relations must be altered, and the paths in which the impulses revolve in constant passage must be modified, so that the ideas which are connected with them will be modified and the thought will take another course" (1954, p. 378). On November 12, 1935, Moniz alcoholized the white substance of the prefrontal lobe, and on December 27, 1935, he performed his first surgical operation with the leucotome. Explaining his first prefrontal leucotomy, Moniz wrote:

> I came to the decision that I would undertake to cut the fibers joining the active neurons. Inasmuch as I was convinced of the importance of prefrontal lobes in mental activity, I chose this region for the experiments. . . . By breaking up these relationships and bringing other fibrillo-synaptic complexes into action, I could not help but transform the patient's psychic reaction and bring him benefit. Since my objective was to inactivate an advantageous number of associations, we decided in favor of attacking en masse the fibers of the cellular connections of the anterior portion of both frontal lobes. . . .

Pursuant to the destructive process, alcohol injections were first given, and immediately thereafter incisions were made with the leukotome, a small apparatus we devised especially for this purpose. Inasmuch as the white substance of the brain has a very limited circulation, our surgical operation had to be free of danger (1954, p. 378).

Educated at the universities of Coimbra, Bordeaux, and Paris, Moniz, prior to occupying the chair of neurology at Lisbon's Faculty of Medicine, was professor of neurology at the University of Coimbra until 1911. His medical practice was at Lisbon's Hospital of Santa Marta.

Walter Freeman (1895-   ) and James W. Watts (1904-   ): Prefrontal Lobotomy. The technique of Moniz was soon adopted and revised by two American surgeons at the George Washington University Hospital in Washington, D.C. Their modification of prefrontal leucotomy resulted in prefrontal lobotomy, which they first performed in 1942. Their technique called for the cutting of the white matter in the frontal lobes

in the plane of the coronal suture. S burr hole is made through or near the suture line and with a long cannula the sphenoidal ridge is identified. With the coronal suture and the sphenoidal ridge as landmarks, the nerve pathways can be sectioned in the desired plane. The lobotomy may be performed with a blunt knife-life instrument or with a special leucotome—this is a matter of individual preference. However, accuracy in the placement of the incisions in the frontal lobes is of paramount importance if one is to compare clinical results and draw conclusions about frontal lobe function (1950, p. 33).

For a period of time prefrontal lobotomy, the most commonly practiced form of psychosurgery, was used to a considerable extent. Other techniques of psychosurgery included cerebral topectomy, cortical undercutting, and one developed in Italy in 1937 by A. M. Fiamberti (1939) called *transorbital lobotomy*.

Clinical psychology in recent times has branched out into a large variety of fields, encompassing psychopharmacology and a sizeable number of newer forms of psychotherapy, especially diverse forms of behavior therapy. The latter half of the twentieth century has seen academic psychology (which at one time far outdistanced all other psychology) being rivalled by nonacademic psychology.

PART FIVE

FUNCTIONALISM IN AMERICA

(A) DEVELOPMENT OF EARLY
AMERICAN PSYCHOLOGY

Subsequent to the Civil War, psychology in America became dominated by *functionalism,* that is to say, the first generation of American psychologists who sought to establish psychology as a science (William James, George Trumbull Ladd, and G. Stanley Hall) were inclined toward functional psychology as were succeeding generations of American psychologists.

Functional psychology was never precisely defined nor was the term coined until 1898. German *structural psychology,* originating with the opening of Wundt's laboratory in Germany in 1879, keynoted sensation. The term was coined and concisely defined in America in 1898. Although functionalism best characterizes American psychology, there were at least variations of it, if not deviations to the point of diverse psychologies. Functional psychology in the limited sense of the word stems from Dewey and his Chicago school, with Angell championing the cause in the footsteps of Dewey. Other schools of American psychology during the late nineteenth and the first part of the twentieth century include: (1) the *capacity psychology* of Cattell with its emphasis on mental testing and psychology of individual differences; (2) the *evolutionary psychology* of Hall and Baldwin with its genetic and developmental character; (3) the *comparative psychology* of Thorndike with its concern with animal psychology and animal intelligence; and (4) the *behaviorism* of Watson with its deemphasis of consciousness and stress on behavior (or motor processes), which led to psychology becoming defined as the study of behavior. Current experimental psychology in the United States is weighted in favor of what may be called neobehaviorism, learning theory, or behavior theory. Its parentage, stimulus-response psychology, stems from the old British school of associationism with its concentration on learning and memory, but its rebirth in the United States dates to 1898. All of these schools have been regarded as forms of functionalism in the broad sense of that term.

Four Stages of American Psychology Since 1640

In the three centuries that transpired in the United States since 1640, American psychology underwent at least four stages of development: (1) the first period, lasting 136 years from 1640 to 1776, was dominated by moral philosophy and mental philosophy. This stage may be subdivided into the period of English scholastic education (1640-1714) and the American Enlightenment (1714-1776). (2) The second stage, one of 110 years running from 1776 to 1886, was dominated by intellectual philosophy. This period may likewise be subdivided into that of Scottish philosophy (1776-1827) and the American textbook era (1827-1886). The third stage, the American Renaissance of psychology, lasting a decade (1886-1896), was a transitional one to American functional psychology. The fourth stage, beginning with 1896 and continuing to the present, is one of decisive American functionalism.

According to J. McK. Cattell, there was no history of American psychology prior to 1880, a chapter on it being comparable to the wealth of information on a chapter on "Snakes in a certain natural history of Iceland— 'There are no snakes in Iceland' " (1898, p. 536). Prior to that time, theologians or educators (often the same person) taught psychology. When the American Psychological Association was founded in 1892 with 31 members, they comprised physicians, educators, theologians, and philosophers as well as psychologists. In fact, over a third of the original members would be unable to qualify for full membership in the American Psychological Association today. The attitude is often assumed by historians of psychology that prior to the publication of James' *Principles of Psychology* in 1890, American psychology did not exist.

American Psychology: Stage One (1640-1776); Period of Moral Philosophy and Mental Philosophy. The birth of psychology in the United States was so inauspicious that it even lacked a name in 1640, the year Henry Dunster became Harvard's president. Psychology was lost in philosophy as an aspect of it, and could be found somewhere in those ethics, divinity, and philosophy courses that Dunster instituted by using their counterparts in the British universities as his paradigm. This first and earliest period of American psychology was one of theology and moral philosophy, for it was in such courses that psychology was taught. The nature of the psychology taught was in the tradition of British scholasticism.

English scholastic education in the United States ran from 1640 with courses introduced by Harvard's president Dunster and closed with the appearance of John Locke's *Essay concerning Human Understanding* (1690) in 1714. Locke's *Essay* opened the period of the enlightenment, and when it arrived in this country, it inaugurated the period of the American enlightenment, a period that saw contributions indirectly made to psychology by Samuel Johnson at King's College, William Brattle at Harvard, Thomas Clap at Yale, and also by Jonathan Edwards. Inasmuch as the three colleges: Harvard (1636), Yale (1701), and Princeton (1746) did not suffice, others soon sprang into existence, including the University of Pennsylvania (1740), King's College (Columbia University, 1754), Brown (1764), Dartmouth (1769), College of Charleston (1770), and Salem (at Winston-Salem, 1772). Other colleges, coming into existence in the eighteenth century in the United States subsequent to the Revolutionary War, include: Georgia (1785), Georgetown (1789), Washington (Maryland, 1782), North Carolina (Chapel Hill, 1789), Vermont (1791), Williams (1793), and Tusculum (Tennessee, 1794).

A sampling of texts utilized in instruction in psychology during the first period (stage of moral philosophy and theology) include: (1) English scholastic education period (1640-1714): Hobbes' *Human Nature* (1650), Berkeley's *New Theory of Vision* (1709) and *Principles of Human Knowledge* (1710), Descartes' *Discourse on Method* (1637), and Leibniz's *Philosophical Works* (1695); (2) period of the American enlightenment (1714-1776): Locke's *Essay concerning Human Understanding* (published in 1690 but arrived in the United States in 1714), Hume's *Treatise of Human Nature* (1739) and his *Enquiry concerning the Human Understanding* (1748), Hartley's *Observations on Man* (1749), Samuel Johnson's *Elementa Philosophica* (1752), Jonathan Edwards' *Freedom of the Will* (1754),

Condillac's *Treatise on the Sensations* (1754), and Thomas Reid's *Enquiry into the Human Mind* (1764).

While Johnson's book was used at King's College and the University of Pennsylvania, Edwards' was the text at Yale. Samuel Johnson (1696-1772) (not biographed by Boswell), who once taught at Yale while only 18 years of age, became the first president of King's College (now Columbia University). Johnson's psychology, like that of Aristotle,   reduced psychology to physics. Studying this period, Jay Wharton Fay observed:

> The conclusions drawn by Berkeley and Hume from the premises of Locke, the materialistic psychology of Hartley, the evolution of the Cartesian philosophy into the sensationalsim of Condillac and Bonnet and the materialism of d'Holbach and la Mettrie, and the work of Christian Wolff in Germany, all had a repercussion, favorable or unfavorable in the writings and thought of American philosophers. The revolt of Thomas Reid from the idealism of Berkeley and the skepticism of Hume reached this country at the end of the period, and proved to be of immense importance in shaping future developments on American soil (1939, p. 17).

The first period of the next stage, that of intellectual philosophy, was dominated by the Scottish psychologists.

American Psychology: Stage Two (1776-1886); Period of Intellectual Philosophy. Not long following the American Revolutionary War, the Scottish psychology of Thomas Reid and Dugald Stewart was imported into the United States where its dominating influence in psychology continued until the time of the "first generation" American psychologists (James, Ladd, and Hall). During the first period, the Scottish philosophy stage (1776-1827) of the period of intellectual philosophy (1776-1886), the texts of Stewart and Reid were either imported from abroad or reprinted in the United States and used as texts, but during the second period, that of the American textbook stage (1827-1886), American texts began to appear.

The attraction of Scottish philosophy and psychology was its reaction to the phenomenalism of Berkeley and Hume. James McCosh, Thomas Reid, William Hamilton, Dugald Stewart, and other Scotish psychologists offered a realism, a naive realism to be precise, in place of idealism and phenomenalism. Stewart, who was professor of moral philosophy at the University of Edinburgh, included the following chapters in his *Elements of the Philosophy of the Human Mind* (1792; American edition, 1821) which was used as a text in psychology at Yale University in 1824:

1. Perception
2. Attention
3. Conception
4. Abstraction (thinking, language, etc.)
5. Association of Ideas
6. Memory
7. Imagination

Reid, who was professor of moral philosophy at the University of Glasgow, published his *Essays on the Intellectual Powers of Man* in 1785, and his *Essays on the Active Powers of the Human Mind* in 1788. The *Intellectual Powers* treated topics such as: sensation, perception, conception (thinking), memory, and the like; while *Active Powers* dealt with: emotions, instinct, habit, will, moral sense, and the like.

With the arrival of the period of American textbooks (1827-1886) replacing the Scottish, there appeared James Rush's (1786-1869) *Analysis of the Human Intellect* (1865), Noah Porter's *The Human Intellect with an Introduction upon Psychology and the Soul* (1868), and John Fiske's *Mental Philosophy* (1842). James Rush is the son of the distinguished Benjamin Rush (1745-1813), author of *Medical Inquiries and Observations upon the Diseases of the Mind* (1812). Noah Porter (1811-1892), editor of *Webster's International Dictionary,* was President of Yale as well as Professor of Moral Philosophy and a Congregational clergyman, which was not unusual for the time. Similarly, James McCosh (1811-1894), author of the two volume *Psychology* (1886-1887), was president and taught psychology at Princeton.

The texts by Rush and Porter shed light on the transitional stage through which American psychology was tending from mental philosophy to psychology proper. In his "Preface" to *The Human Intellect*, Porter stated that his work "was prepared primarily and directly as a text-book for colleges and higher schools. It was also designed secondarily, though not less really, as a manual for more advanced students of psychology"(p. v). The chapters in the book include topics on: definition of psychology (as the science of the human soul); psychology as a branch of physics; faculties of the soul; psychology as a science; sense perception; consciousness; function, development and faculties of the human intellect; representation; association of ideas (as the condition and laws of representation); memory; and reason.

American Psychology: Stage Three (1886-1896); The American Renaissance. With the publication of McCosh's *Psychology* in 1886, psychology as mental philosophy was brought to a close, and with the publication of William James' two volume *Principles of Psychology* in 1890, a new era of American psychology as an independent science was born. McCosh's psychology, as he taught it during his tenure as president of Princeton, was an empirical psychology in contrast to the prevailing rational psychology of the day. The year 1886 saw psychology texts published by two other Americans, the first edition of John Dewey's *Psychology* (1886) when he was Assistant Professor of Philosophy at the University of Michigan, and Borden Parker Bowne's *Introduction to Psychological Theory* (1886) when he was Professor of Philosophy at Boston University. According to Bowne, "psychology deals with mental facts and processes. It aims to describe and classify those facts and processes, to discover and state their laws, and to form some theory concerning their origin and cause" (1886, p. 1).

By 1891 Dewey produced his third revised edition in which he defined psychology as "the science of facts or phenomena of self" (1891, p. 1). Although Dewey prefaced his work with the statement that he sought "to avoid all material not strictly psychology," he was receptive to philosophy, devoting chapters to moral control and will as the source of ideals. However, he abandoned Porter's view of psychology as the science of the soul; for Dewey the self is that which "acts or reacts." Thus the first signs of functionalism begin to appear in psychology.

The following year saw the publication of the first text in the "new psychology," George Trumbull Ladd's *Elements of Physiological Psychology* (1887), written when Ladd was Professor of Philosophy at Yale University. It was a tentative account of the functional orientation that was to find its way into the psychology of America. When James received a copy of Ladd's work, he wrote a letter to him saying: "What with Dewey's, Bowne's, and your books, all published within three months, and Hall's Journal announced, American psychology need not hang its head, and may look, methinks, to a rather brilliant future" (1910-1912, p. 696). In 1887 the first issue of G. Stanley Hall's *American Journal of Psychology* appeared. The year 1889 saw the first volume of James Mark Baldwin's *Hand-Book of Psychology* (1889-1891). Accordingly from 1886 to the publication of James' *Psychology*, which was rich in originality, American psychology was launched.

Prior to James' functional approach to psychology, American psychology was heavily entrenched in German and English psychology. James gave American psychology an originality that it had heretofore not yet known.

American Psychology: Stage Four (1896 to the Present); American Functionalism. At the age of thirty-five, John Dewey went to the University of Chicago to head its department of philosophy; two years later he published his classic paper "The Reflex Arc Concept in Psychology" (1896), thus marking the founding of functional psychology in the United States. Although the formal founding of functional psychology as a school is traced to the Chicago school under Dewey and his colleagues, the character of American psychology since the decade of the 1880s has been functionalistic in the broad sense of that term, and would include the orientation of the pioneers of American psychology, such as James, Ladd, Scripture, Hall, Baldwin, and Cattell.

American Psychology is the confluence of two major streams, the German tradition of experimentalism alluded to as the new psychology and the English tradition of testing arising chiefly from the work of Galton together with the evolutionary approach (which came to be called genetic psychology by G. S. Hall) that was fostered by Charles Darwin and Herbert Spencer.

The formation of the modern university as it is known was an evolutionary product, emerging in the 1880s, the first Ph.D. being granted by Yale in 1861, but the first in psychology about a quarter of a century later—in 1878 by Harvard to G. S. Hall. The second degree, conferred in 1884 by Johns Hopkins, was to John Dewey, who studied under Hall. The leading American universities granting Ph.D.s in psychology until World War II in 1918 are listed in order of date of granting their first Ph.D. degree in psychology.

Harvard; 53 Ph.D.s in psychology from 1878 to 1918

Johns Hopkins; 18 Ph.D.s in psychology from 1891 to 1918
Yale; 19 Ph.D.s in psychology from 1893 to 1918
Pennsylvania; 28 Ph.D.s in psychology from 1893 to 1918
Cornell; 37 Ph.D.s in psychology from 1894 to 1918
Columbia; 55 Ph.D.s in psychology from 1895 to 1918
Chicago; 51 Ph.D.s in psychology from 1899 to 1918
Ph.D.s gradually became recognized as professionals, responsible only to themselves and the standards of their professions rather than to their employers.

(B) THE FIRST GENERATION OF AMERICAN PSYCHOLOGISTS: JAMES, LADD, HALL

The first generation of American psychologists, James, Ladd, and Hall, were found at Harvard, Yale, and Johns Hopkins respectively, Hall later going to Clark University in Worcester, Massachusetts. The second generation of American psychologists included James McKeen Cattell, James Mark Baldwin, Joseph Jastrow, Edmund C. Sanford, Edward Wheeler Scripture, John Dewey, the German-born Hugo Münsterberg, and the British-born Edward Bradford Titchener. While Hall was at Johns Hopkins, he had such distinguished students studying under him as: Dewey, Cattell, Sanford, Jastrow, Donaldson, and Yujiro Motora, a founder of Japanese psychology. Hall in turn was James' student, the first to receive a degree in the new psychology (in 1878 from Harvard).

Both James and Hall were armchair psychologists, despite their founding the first psychological laboratories in the United States. Even Ladd turned his psychological laboratory over to Scripture. How amazing! The founders of the new experimental psychology (including Wundt) were *not* laboratory men.

Hall and James locked horns when the former boasted in the *American Journal of Psychology,* a periodical he founded in 1887:

> When the American Journal of Psychology was founded in 1887, it was a pioneer in its field. It represented the department of psychology at the Johns Hopkins University, was for years the only one of its kind in the country, and the establishment of which, as its subsequent history shows, was one of the boldest and most sagacious as well as one of the most successful and beneficent steps ever taken by this leader of the new academic movement (1895, p. 3).

Hall alienated himself still more by claiming that the men under him at Johns Hopkins and Clark were responsible for founding psychological laboratories even at Harvard and Yale by asserting that "under the influence of these men departments of experimental psychology and laboratories were founded at Harvard, Yale, Philadelphia, Columbia, Toronto, Wisconsin and many other higher institutions of learning." Immediately on the heels of the publication of the journal in October, 1895, James composed a lengthy letter on October 12, 1895 in which he stated:

> As an arm-chair professor, I frankly admit my great inferiority as a laboratory-teacher and investigator. But some little regard should be paid to the good will with which I have

tried to force my nature, and to the actual things I have done. One of them, for example, was inducting YOU into experimental investigation, with very naive methods, it is true, but you may remember that there was no other place but Harvard where during those years you could get even that. I remember also giving a short course of psychological lectures at the Johns Hopkins years before you went there [in 1878] (Perry, vol. 2, p. 9).

It was the contention of James that he founded the first psychological laboratory (at Harvard) when he offered courses such as ''The Relations between Physiology and Psychology'' in 1875. James remonstrated:

I, myself, ''founded'' the instruction in experimental psychology at Harvard in 1874-5, or 1876, I forget which. For a long series of years the laboratory was in two rooms of the Scientific School building, which at last became choked with apparatus, so that a change was necessary. I then, in 1890, resolved on an altogether new departure, raised several thousand dollars, fitted up Dane Hall, and introduced laboratory exercises as a regular part of the undergraduate psychology-course (1895, p. 626).

Not only had Hall undertaken the majority of his courses in psychology with James at Harvard, he utilized experimental room and equipment of James as well as accompanying him to Boston where he studied physiology with Bowditch at the Harvard Medical School.

Although James had a de facto laboratory of psychology as early as 1875, the de jure founding or formal laboratory at Harvard did not occur until 1891. When Hall studied with James, James' psychological laboratory comprised a small room beneath a stairway of Agassiz Museum, containing a horopter chart, a device for whirling a frog, and a few other pieces of apparatus. Harper, in a careful research of the evolution of the Harvard psychological laboratory, reported:

The history of the migration of experimental psychology at Harvard is now clear. James first gave instruction in Boylston Hall in 1872-73 and 1874-75. He established what may be called his first laboratory in Lawrence Hall in 1875 and it was continued there until 1891. This is really the world's first psychological laboratory. Certainly it is ahead of Leipzig's, founded in 1879. James also had additional laboratory space in the period 1877-81 in the Museum of Comparative Zoology and had students doing physiological experiments there as early as 1875. In 1891 James, with a few thousand dollars he had collected, formally ''founded'' the Psychological Laboratory in Dane Hall, and it stayed there until 1905, when Emerson Hall was ready. Emerson Hall was actually planned by the architects to contain a psychological laboratory on its third floor, and the Laboratory remained there from 1906 to 1946, forty years altogether, with adjuncts in Boylston Hall, in the Biological Laboratories, and the Psychological Clinic during the latter twenty of the forty years. Since 1946 the Laboratory has been in its newly-outfitted quarters in the basement of Memorial Hall (1949, p. 173).

Harper's research, reporting the matter, was published too early to report that the psychological laboratories today are in the recently constructed high rise building named in honor of William James. Though James had a psychological laboratory of sorts in 1875, it can hardly be regarded as founded, whereas ''the commonly accepted opinion,'' as Boring correctly explained, ''is that Wundt founded the world's first psychological laboratory in Leipzig in 1879 and G. Stanley Hall the first in America at Hopkins in 1883'' (1965, p. 5). The early laboratory of James was not founded, it simply came into existence.

CHAPTER 12

Harvard's Functionalism
From the Time of William James

(A) HARVARD DURING THE TENURE OF JAMES

WILLIAM JAMES (1842-1910): HARVARD'S LUMINARY

The American psychologist, physiologist, and philosopher, William James (1842-1910), was born at Astor House in New York City. He did not experience the usual formal precollege education although he was tutored throughout Europe, including England, France, Switzerland, and Germany. After his family returned from a European trip in 1843-1844, he attended school in New York from 1852 to 1855. From 1855 to 1860 he was tutored in Europe. James returned in 1860 to study painting with William Morris Hunt at Newport, but the following year entered Lawrence Scientific School of Harvard University. Regarding himself as physically disabled to enter the Civil War, he entered Harvard Medical School in 1864. His medical studies were interrupted from 1856 to 1866 because of an opportunity to join Louis Agassiz (1807-1873), the distinguished naturalist at the Lawrence Scientific School, on a scientific expedition to Brazil. On returning he resumed his career in medicine, serving a hospital internship for a brief period. In consequence of "neurasthenia," he left for Germany in 1867 and remained a year to improve both his health and his studies in psychology and philosophy. While at Berlin, he sent a letter in 1867 to Thomas W. Ward in which he said:

> I have blocked out some reading in physiology and psychology which I hope to execute this winter—though reading German is still disgustingly slow. . . . It seems to me that perhaps the time has come for psychology to begin to be a science—some measurements have already been made. . . . Helmholtz and a man named Wundt at Heidelberg are working at it. . . . The fact is, this sickness takes all the spring, physical and mental, out of a man (1920, vol. 1, pp. 118-9).

It appears that from "a man named Wundt," who was James' senior by a decade, James grasped an appreciation of the new experimental psychology.

James, who never received a bachelor's degree, did obtain his M.D. in 1869 from Harvard Medical School when he returned to the United States, but his plans never called for the practice of medicine.

For three long years following graduation the "neurasthenia" suffered by James deteriorated steadily to the point of extreme depression, coupled with an incidence of hallucination. He sensed some relief in 1872, and the following year was appointed as Instructor in Anatomy and Physiology at Harvard, being elevated to assistant professor in 1876. When his interests turned from physiology to psychology and philosophy, he accepted an offer from Holt to write his *Principles of Psychology* in 1878, the year he married Alice Howe Gibbens. It took James all of a dozen years to complete the book, which appeared in 1890 when he was 48 years old. James began teaching philosophy in 1879, and was appointed Assistant Professor of Philosophy the following year, his full professorship coming a half decade later in 1885.

In 1898 he suffered a heart ailment, his career at this time being deeply intrenched in philosophy. The 1901-1902 school year found him delivering the Gifford Lectures at Edinburgh; in 1906 he was an acting professor at Stanford; the 1906-1907 school year found him lecturing on pragmatism at the Lowell Institute and at Columbia University; and the 1908-1909 school year saw him delivering the Hibbert Lectures at Oxford. His retirement from Harvard was in 1907, his death occurring three years later in 1910 at his summer home in New Hampshire.

The Principles of Psychology

James' fame in psychology was assured with the publication in 1890 of his first book, *The Principles of Psychology*. The work, which gave a new slant to psychology, namely functionalism, was to keynote the approach American psychology was to assume thereafter. Angell received his functionalism from James and Dewey. The *Principles* also anticipated James' philosophy of pragmatism, as well as purporting to be an application of the theory of evolution in explaining human psychology.

Although James used Spencer's *Principles of Psychology* (1855) as a text in his courses, he repudiated Spencer's definition of life as "the continuous adjustment of internal relations to external relations (Vol. I, sect. 131)," preferring instead "the knower as an actor," that is, Spencer neglected to impute to the mind its spontaneous productivity and active originality. "Mental interests, hypotheses, postulates, so far as they are bases for human action," said James, "help to *make* the truth which they declare." Such was the fundamental premise of James' psychology.

Functionalism. James viewed the mind pragmatically or functionally, serving the individual as an instrument enabling his suitable adjustment to his environment as well as effecting changes enhansive to his well-being. "The mental life is for the sake of action of a preservative sort" (1892, p. 4). Rather than mental elements, mental operations hold the functionalist's interest. Man's feeling and thought life function as an aid to behavior, for consciousness, the characteristics of which are understood in the light of their practicality or utility, serve the end of conduct. "Mental life is primarily teleological; that is to say, that our various ways of feeling and thinking have grown to be what they are because of their utility in shaping our *reactions* on the outer world" (1892, p. 4). The criterion of mentality is the "pursuance of future ends and the choice of means for their attainment" (1890, vol. 1, p. 8). Thus action, entailing both purpose and the choice of means to the desired end, implies the activity of mind. "All mental states are followed by bodily activity of some sort" (1892, p. 5). Distinguishing between normal and abnormal behavior, James regarded the former as adaptive.

The Stream of Consciousness. James' functionalism becomes quite apparent in his concept of consciousness, which he postulated was not comprised of elements as the Wundtian structuralists contended but was a stream. To segment it into elements is to cause it to lose its primary qualities, its flowing character.

> Consciousness, then, does not appear to itself chopped up in bits. Such words as 'chain' or 'train' do not describe it fitly as it presents itself in the first instance. It is nothing jointed; it flows. A 'river' or a 'stream' are the metaphors by which it is most naturally described. *In talking of it hereafter, let us call it the stream of thought, of consciousness, or of subjective life* (1890, vol. 1, p. 239).

In assuming this position, James challenged structuralism by claiming that no person ever had experienced a simple sensation because consciousness is a "teeming multiplicity of objects and relations," the primary mental fact being the activity of the thought process. "Within each personal consciousness, thought is sensibly continuous" (1890, vol. 1, p. 237). Personal consciousness, being continuous, finds experience remolding a person constantly so that his mental reaction is the resultant of his total experience to date, a concept reminiscent of Herbart's apperceptive mass and Hamilton's redintegration.

Accordingly, consciousness is personal (belongs to an individual), permanently changing, continuous, and is selective (capable of executing choices).

Theory of the Self

For over a score of years after James offered his self theory, it seemed to command little interest despite its classic stature. Distinguishing between *me* and *I,* James regarded the former as "the self as known, or the *me,* the 'empirical ego' as it is sometimes called;" and the latter as "the self as knower, or the I, the 'pure ego' of certain authors" (1892, p. 176). He listed the constituents of the self as: (a) the material self; (b) the social self; (c) the spiritual self; and (d) the pure ego. The material self is comprised of the body; the social self is the recognition which one derives from his "mates," a person possessing as many social selves as "there are individuals who recognize him and carry an image of him in their mind;" the spiritual self, an empirical me, is the inner subjective self of psychic faculties and dispositions, a person's most intimate aspect, including his will, moral sensibility, and discriminative abilities or self as thinker. The self as pure ego was deleted two years later when James published the briefer version of his *Psychology.*

Psychology of Temperament: Tender-minded and Tough-minded. By 1907 when James had published his *Pragmatism,* a book in which James expressed his intellectual indebtedness to Mill, he reasoned that a person's psychological temperament accounts for his intellectual outlook or philosophical *Weltanschauung.* He dichotomized temperaments into tender-minded and tough-minded, each with corresponding opposing characteristics as follows:

Tender-minded Personality	*Tough-minded Personality*
1. rationalistic (going by principles)	1. empiricist (going by facts)
2. intellectualistic	2. sensationalistic
3. idealistic	3. materialistic

4. optimistic	4. pessimistic
5. religious	5. irreligious
6. free-willist	6. fatalistic
7. monistic	7. pluralistic
8. dogmatical	8. sceptical

James saw the pragmatic orientation as mediating between these two. It is not the only instance in which he assumed a middle or mediating stance, for with respect to optimism and pessimism of nature, he took the position of meliorism, the view that the world is getting better. Explaining his position, he asserted:

> Nevertheless there are unhappy men who think the salvation of the world impossible. Theirs is the doctrine known as pessimism.
> Optimism in turn would be the doctrine that thinks the world's salvation inevitable.
> Midway between the two there stands what may be called the doctrine of meliorism. . . . Meliorism treats salvation as neither necessary nor impossible. It treats it as a possibility, which becomes more and more of a probability the more numerous the actual conditions of salvation become.
> It is clear that pragmatism must incline towards meliorism (1907, pp. 285-6).

By working for ideals they become realized; they become actual things, and in that manner one's actions creates the world's salvation.

James-Lange Theory of Emotions

Another quite original contribution of James is his theory of emotions, which he and the Danish physician and psychologist *Carl Georg Lange* (1834-1900) arrived at independently of each other. James, who introduced the theory in 1884, a year ahead of Lange, viewed causes of emotions as physiological. He theorized that "the bodily changes follow directly the PERCEPTION of the exciting fact, and that our feeling of the same changes as they occur IS the emotion" (1884, pp. 189-90), a theory diametrically opposed to traditional theory of a mental perception of an event exciting the mental affection termed emotion.

The hypothesis that James proposed to defend reverses the sequence so that

> the bodily manifestations must first be interposed between, and that the more rational statement is that we feel sorry because we cry, angry because we strike, afraid because we tremble, and not that we cry, strike, or tremble, because we are sorry, angry, or fearful, as the case may be. Without the bodily states following on the perception, the latter would be purely cognitive in form, pale, colourless, destitute of emotional warmth. We might then see the bear, and judge it best to run, receive the insult and deem it right to strike, but we could not actually *feel* afraid or angry (1884, p. 190).

Lange, who was Professor of Pathological Anatomy at the University of Copenhagen from 1877 until his death, viewed emotions as life's most important factor and powerful force. He restricted the term emotion to sorrow, joy, fear, anger, etc., but love, hate, scorn, admiration and the like were passions. The cause of emotion is the stimulation of the vasomotor center. Lange, who was influenced by Darwin, stated his theory as follows:

If we fancy some strong emotion, and then try to abstract from our consciousness of it all the feelings of its bodily symptoms, we find we have nothing left behind, no "mind-stuff" out of which the emotion can be constituted, and that a cold and neutral state of intellectual perception is all that remains (1922, p. 102).

Though Lange agreed with James, he explained the theory on a considerably more limited foundation, restricting his explanation solely to the circulatory system. While felt-emotion to sensations was explained by James as stemming from the viscera, Lange saw these sensations as proceeding from the circulatory system. Sharing thoughts even more closely to James, Lange went on to assert:

In all cases of intellectual or moral rapture we find that, unless there be coupled a bodily reverberation of some kind with the mere thought of the object and cognition of its quality; unless we actually laugh at the neatness of the demonstration or witticism; unless we thrill at the case of justice, or tingle at the act of magnanimity; our state of mind can hardly be called emotional at all. It is in fact a mere intellectual perception of how certain things are to be called—neat, right, witty, generous, and the like. Such a judicial state of mind as this is to be classed among awareness of truth; it is a *cognitive* act (1922, p. 120).

Three years following Lange's publication of his theory, an Australian, Alexander Sutherland, published his version in the *Origin and Growth of the Moral Instinct* in 1898, though his formulation of the theory apparently occurred earlier and independently of James and Lange.

The James-Lange theory met with severe opposition from James' colleague at Harvard, Walter B. Cannon, who objected to James' theory that the perception of sensations accounts for emotional expression because he found that visceral changes are not fast enough to be considered an emotional source nor is their artificial induction by changes in the viscera typifying emotions capable of producing it. Furthermore, emotional experience is not changed by eliminating viscera from cortical connections. In whatever emotions occur, the visceral changes are the same, and though visceral nerves ceased to occur from brain excitation owing to the transection of the vagus nerve and spinal cord, emotion was still present. Moreover, visceral changes artifically induced by adrenaline injection produce experiences like emotion (fear).

Cannon's Thalamic Theory of Emotion

The behavior theory of emotion advanced by James and Lange encountered a strong contender in 1915 in a theory formulated by the Harvard physiologist *Walter Bradford Cannon* (1871-1945). He taught at Harvard Medical School from 1899 until his death. An M.D. from Harvard in 1900, Cannon, known in psychology for his thalamic theory of emotion, found that the "total separation of the viscera from the central nervous system does not alter emotional behavior" (1963, p. 348). Furthermore, Cannon found that identical visceral changes take place in quite different emotional states as well as in emotionless states. It is not the case that sensitivity increases the deeper the body is penetrated. Viscera are, relatively speaking, insensitive structures, their changes being much too slow to be considered as a source of emotional feeling. "Artificial induction of the visceral changes typical of strong emotions does not produce them" (1963, p. 355). Accordingly the James-Lange theory is not warranted by these findings.

Offering his own thalamic theory of emotions, Cannon viewed emotion as the function of the optic thalamus, thalamic processes being the source of emotion.

An external situation stimulates receptors and the consequent excitation starts impulses toward the cortex. Arrival of the impulses in the cortex is associated with conditioned processes which determine the direction of the response. Either because the response is initiated in a certain mode or figure and the cortical neurones therefore stimulate the thalamic processes, or because on their inward course the impulses from the receptors excite thalamic processes, they are roused and ready for discharge. . . . Within and near the thalamus the neurones concerned in an emotional expression lie close to the relay in the sensory path from periphery to cortex. We may assume that when these neurones discharge in a particular combination, they not only innervate muscles and viscera but also excite afferent paths to the cortex by direct connection or by irradiation. The theory which naturally presents itself is that *the peculiar quality of the emotion is added to simple sensation when the thalamic processes are roused* (1963, pp. 268-9).

Cannon's thalamic theory, the first formulated in which a mechanism of the brain serves as the explanation of emotional expression and experience, saw the thalamus as producing emotions and the cortex as their inhibitor. For the time it was developed, it was a remarkable achievement. As an emergency theory of emotion, it was an extension of Darwin's theory of biological utility in which the adaptation principle is extended internally into the human organism, producing emotional changes conducive to adaptation.

Cannon's Homeostasis Theory. Not only did Cannon contribute to psychological theory by way of his thalamic theory of emotions but it was he who coined the term *homeostasis*, the tendency of complex organisms to maintain constancy or strive to restore equilibrium when constancy is disrupted. As a protective device bodily homeostasis frees the nervous system

from the necessity of paying routine attention to the management of the details of bare existence. Without homeostatic devices we should be in constant danger of disaster, unless we were always on the alert to correct voluntarily what normally is corrected automatically. With homeostatic devices, however, that keep essential bodily processes steady, we as individuals, are free from such slavery—free to enter into agreeable relations with our fellows, to enjoy beautiful things, to explore and understand the wonders of the world about us, to develop new ideas and interests, and to work and play untrammeled by anxieties concerning our bodily affairs (1939, p. 323).

Cannon regarded fear and anger as two emergency emotions, emotion being indicative of disturbance requiring the restoration of equilibrium immediately following the cessation of emergency.

Evaluation of Cannon's Theory. In accord with Cannon's theory of emotion, the consensus of critics favors the entire autonomic nervous system (rather than merely the sympathetic) as the more adequate explanation of emotion. The autonomic nervous system more than functions defensively in times of danger; it serves also to maintain homeostasis. The fight and flight reaction was accounted for by Cannon by the hormone epinephrine alone, but currently psychologists use it to account for fear and anxiety, and norepinephrine secretion for hostile states, the independent secretion of the two hormones occurring. Whereas the utility of physical changes occurring in emotion was underscored by Cannon, it is known that numerous maladaptive changes also occur that prove disruptive and disintegrating to the organism.

Selye's General Adaptation Syndrome (G.A.S.)

Since 1936 Cannon's doctrine of homeostasis was extended by Hans Selye's (1907-   ) general adaptation syndrome (G.A.S.) theory. It hypothesizes organized or structured patterns of biological reactions to stress. The Vienna-born Selye, who obtained his M.D. and Ph.D. from the German University at Prague in 1929 and 1931 respectively and who has been at the University of Montreal since 1945, found that when he exposed animals to different kinds of stress they increased secretions both of adrenaline and corticoids (adrenal cortical hormones), the latter counteracting the damage of the former.

Defining stress as *"the state manifested by a specific syndrome which consists of all the nonspecifically induced changes within a biologic system"* (1956, p. 423), Selye identified its manifestations as: "adrenocortical enlargement with histologic signs of hyperactivity, thymicolymphatic involution with certain concomitant changes in the blood count (eosinopenia, lymphopenia, polynucleosis) and gastrointestinal ulcers, often accompanied by other manifestations of damage or shock" (1973, p. 2). The three evolutionary stages of the *general adaptation syndrome* are: (1) *alarm reaction phase* (exposure to noxious stimuli) with its two phases: *(a) shock phase* (reactions such as tachycardia, loss of muscle tone, temperature and blood pressure depressed) and *(b) countershock phase* (defense forces mobilized such as the beginning of the enlargement of the adrenal cortex and increase of secretion of adrenocorticoid hormones); (2) *stage of resistance* (full adaptation to stressor with improvement or disappearance of symptoms and decreasing resistance to other stimuli); and (3) *stage of exhaustion,* owing to the inability of interminable adaptability. Without abatement of stress, symptoms recur with ensuing death.

Inasmuch as "man's ultimate aim is *to express himself as fully as possible, according to his own lights,"* Selye observed:

> The goal is certainly not to avoid stress. Stress is part of life. It is a natural by-product of all our activities; there is no more justification for avoiding stress than for shunning food, exercise, or love. But, in order to express yourself fully, you must first find your optimum stress-level, and then, use your adaptation energy at a rate and in a direction adjusted to the innate structure of your mind and body.
> The study of stress has shown that complete rest is not good, either for the body as a whole, or even for any organ within the body. Stress, applied in moderation, is necessary for life. Besides, enforced inactivity may be very harmful and cause more stress than normal activity (1956, pp. 299-300).

Thus the general adaptation syndrome is so-called because stress reaction is general, adaptive, and a syndrome. Stress is a condition disruptive to normal functioning.

HUGO MÜNSTERBERG (1863-1916): Psychology Applied and Harvard's Laboratory

The first of the great pioneers of applied psychology, Münsterberg, was Assistant Professor of Psychology at the University of Freiburg at Baden when William James called him to be in charge of Harvard's laboratory of psychology in 1892. The same year Titchener arrived to assume his duties in the United States, the two directing rival psychological laboratories in America. Both men received their Ph.D.s under Wundt at the University of Leipzig, and the two were introspectionists, but while Titchener remained a Wundtian structuralist, Münsterberg early separated from Wundtianism. The Danzig-born Münsterberg, after obtaining his Ph.D. in 1885, also earned a degree in medicine from Heidelberg in 1887 before coming to Harvard as professor of psychology and director of the laboratory of psychology.

However, Münsterberg increasingly came to neglect his laboratory, eventually leaving the duties to his assistant, *Herbert Sidney Langfeld* (1879-1958), who came to Harvard in 1910. Langfeld assumed directorship of the laboratory from 1917 until he left for Princeton to undertake the same duties there in 1924. A Berlin Ph.D. (1909), Langfeld was one of Stumpf's pupils, who turned his attention increasingly to the study of emotions in esthetics.

Though his ideas failed to command lasting attention, Münsterberg was considered by some authorities as the foremost psychologist of his day next to Wundt! His place in the history of psychology is assured due to his being the first applied psychologist, applying psychology in 1908 to law, and thereafter to industry, medicine, and education. The first applied psychology text to appear was his *Psychology: General and Applied* (1914). A year earlier, however, he published the first book on industrial or applied psychology, *Psychology and Industrial Efficiency* (1913). Münsterberg sought to establish that psychology is of practical benefit to the society at large and that applied psychology is a legitimate endeavor of the psychologist. Psychology applied to law found its expression in his little book, *On the Witness Stand* (1908), applied to education in his *Psychology and the Teacher* (1910), applied to medicine in *Psychotherapy* (1909), and applied to society in *Psychology and Social Sanity* (1914). He regarded them as "practical applications of modern psychology." As early as the 1890s, he introduced the notion that blood pressure might be correlated to one's truthfulness in testimony, thus being the precursor to the modern polygraph for lie detection.

A vice-president of the International Psychological Congress in Paris in 1900, and vice-president and organizer of the International Congress of Arts and Sciences at the Saint Louis World's Fair in 1904, Münsterberg was known in Germany for his *Die Willenshandlung* (*Voluntary Action*, 1889), a work critical of Wundt and mechanistic in its orientation. He treated the physical as spatial and the mental as nonspatial. His *actionistic psychology,* popular during his lifetime, was a psychomotor explanation of sensation dependent upon specific nerve stimulus and intensity as well as the quality of stimulus, but the vividness of sensation was contingent on an induced motor response.

A German who repudiated American citizenship, Münsterberg died at the age of 53 from a heart attack while delivering a lecture at Radcliffe in 1916 as the World War I clouds were intensifying.

(B) HARVARD DURING BORING'S TENURE

The long tenure of *Edwin Garrigues Boring* (1886-1968) lasted from 1922 when he arrived at Harvard from Clark University up until his death in 1968, but technically to the time of his retirement from Harvard in 1957. Though Boring was a product of Titchener, the structuralist and introspectionist, and though he felt (like Freud with respect to his father) that he was not free until the death of Titchener, Boring was nevertheless an eclectic rather than a Titchenerian. He did, however, trace his intellectual heritage to Wundt through Titchener, and considered Ernest G. Wever (1902-   ) and Stanley Smith Stevens (1906-1973) his intellectual heirs. Boring felt that he "inveigled" Stevens into producing his monumental *Handbook of Experimental Psychology* (1951). However, Stevens' greatest contribution to psychology is his *power law* or what some psychologists have termed the *Stevens' law.*

When Boring arrived at Harvard, he found *Herbert Sidney Langfeld* (1879-1958) there in care of Harvard's psychological laboratory since Münsterberg's death. Also at Harvard, Boring found *William McDougall* (1871-1938), who had come from Oxford (studied at London, Cambridge, Oxford, and Göttingen) to Harvard in 1920 but left in 1927 for Duke University.

The mission Boring assigned himself at Harvard was more than embellishing a psychological laboratory; he was intent on establishing a psychology department that was liberated from the aegis of philosophy. Despite the ultimate realization of his objective, it proved to be a long evolving process stemming from the twenties. One major decision of the twenties was for his psychology department to enter the area of dynamic, clinical or abnormal psychology, a choice forced upon him when the distinguished Boston psychiatrist Morton Prince, M.D. arranged for Harvard's psychology department to receive an endowment of $125,000 in order to bring abnormal psychology closer to normal psychology.

Murray and the Harvard Psychological Clinic

The outcome of the Prince-arranged endowment was the institution of the Harvard Psychological Clinic, with Prince appointed an associate professor for a couple of years and *Henry Alexander Murray* (1893-   ) as second in command. It was not the world's first clinic, however, for that honor goes to the University of Pennsylvania where one was supposed to have come into existence as early as 1896, or at least that institution celebrated the fiftieth anniversary of the clinic in 1946.

The fruits of the clinic produced Murray's *Explorations in Personality* (1938) and *Assessment of Men* (1948), as well as (with Christiana D. Morgan) his classic TAT (Thematic Apperception Test) in 1935. Murray, known for his personality theory termed *personology,* defined the term as the "science of men, taken in gross units" (1938, p. 4) and personality as the "temporal integrate of mutually dependent processes (variables) developing in time." His long tenure at Harvard began in 1926, roughly a half dozen years after he received his M.D. from Columbia in 1919; he later went on to earn a Ph.D. from the University of Cambridge in 1929.

Harvard's Psychological Laboratory

While Harvard had a psychology laboratory in operation by James since the mid 1870s, Boring wanted one liberated from philosophy. A dozen years had passed by since Boring had come to Harvard, and his de jure Laboratory of Psychology was in a de facto Department of Psychology, which in turn was in a de jure Department of Philosophy and Psychology under the Division of Philosophy in the Faculty of Arts and Sciences. In 1934 the two departments, psychology and philosophy, were divided, becoming autonomous.

From 1924 to 1949 Boring directed the psychological laboratory, and headed the department for a dozen years (from 1924 to 1936), two years after the Department of Psychology came into existence as autonomous. He resumed the chairmanship again when the department split, fissioning off into a Department of Social Relations in 1945.

Boring's Star Pupil: Skinner (and His Operant Behavior Theory). Two years before Stevens received his Ph.D., *Burrhus Frederic Skinner* (1904-   ) earned his under Boring in 1931 at Harvard. Skinner too claims an important protégé when he was teaching at the University of Minnesota, *William Kaye Estes* (1919-   ). Estes, known for his stimulus sampling theory, developed a statistical theory of learning in 1950 and subsequently expanded it with E. D. Neimark in *Stimulus Sampling Theory* (1967).

Skinner's doctoral dissertation on the reflex with its behavioristic orientation keynoted his future intellectual course. He remained at Harvard as a Junior Fellow before making a twelve-year circuit to Minnesota, then to Indiana, and back again to Harvard in 1948 where he has been for over a quarter of a century. Skinner's claim to a niche in the history of psychology is his *operant behavior theory* as elaborated in his *Behavior of Organisms* in 1938 and in his *Science and Human Behavior* (1953), designed as a textbook for his students in psychology at Harvard. As a result of the former book, annual conferences commenced in 1946 at Indiana on the Experimental Analysis of Behavior, eventuating a decade later in the founding of the organ of that group, the *Journal of the Experimental Analysis of Behavior* as well as a division of the American Psychological Association, the Division for the Experimental Analysis of Behavior. Before the decade of the 1930s closed, his attention turned to *programmed instruction,* producing a teaching machine, which he demonstrated at the University of Pittsburgh in 1954, and explained in a 1958 article, "Teaching Machines." His collected papers appeared in a third edition in 1972 under the appropriate title *Cumulative Record.*

Tracing his insight of experimental method to Pavlov's belief that if the environment is controlled then behavior is ordered, Skinner, in response to two Polish physiologists (Konorski and Miller), introduced the term *operant behavior.* The term was employed "to identify behavior traceable to reinforcing contingencies rather than to eliciting stimuli" (1967, p. 400), reinforcement being that which heightens the probability or frequency of a given mode of behavior occurring. Tolman, while teaching summer school at Harvard in 1931, also had a bearing on Skinner's thinking. Whereas operant behavior is emitted, respondent is merely a stimulus reaction, i.e., behavior that is reflexly elicited. "If the occurrence of an operant is followed by presentation of a reinforcing stimulus, the strength is increased" (1938, p. 21), Skinner proposed as his primary law of operant conditioning.

The expansion of Skinner's operant behavior theory (notwithstanding his objection to his system being termed a theory) was extended to encompass: (1) verbal behavior, i.e., "behavior reinforced through the mediation of other persons" (1957, p. 2), including: mand, echoic behavior, textual behavior, intraverbal behavior, and tact; (2) contingencies of reinforcement ("the class of responses upon which a reinforcer is contingent is called an operant" [1963, p. 7]) with their (3) schedules of reinforcement such as: fixed interval, fixed ratio, variable interval or ratio, multiple schedules, differential reinforcement of rate of responding; (4) operant behavior applied to psychotherapy as behavior therapy; and (5) an operant behavior theory of social psychology.

In recent years Skinner's attention has extended to philosophical issues based on his psychology, the result being the volume *Beyond Freedom and Dignity* in which he subscribes to determinism and other ideas earlier articulated. He believes that societies as well as individuals can be controlled. Skinner, with little concern for his critics' comments, arrogantly remarked that people "do not think at all." Consequently he claimed that he never read Chomsky's classic review of his *Verbal Behavior,* except for a half dozen pages or less.

Stevens and Harvard's Psycho-Acoustic Laboratory

In the early forties Boring, Stevens, and other psychologists at Harvard were in the process of setting up a new 108-room Psychological Laboratory in the cellar in what was in James' time the commons of Memorial Hall. The task of planning fell to Stevens whose interests in experimental psychology focused on psycho-acoustics. The Navy, interested in the field, granted $100,000 toward the project, (with an additional $150,000 spent by Harvard after the war). The psychological laboratory was now in respectable shape, but the Psycho-Acoustic Laboratory was actually operational in 1940 under Boring's favored student and disciple, S. S. Stevens. Furthermore, it was Stevens who went to Budapest in 1937 to attract Békésy to his psycho-acoustic laboratory, and in 1953 R. J. Herrnstein was hired as Stevens' assistant. In the latter half of the 1960s, the entire department complete with laboratory (including the social relations department with its laboratory in Emerson Hall) was moved to its new white-stoned high rise building, William James Hall.

The "power law" or "Stevens' law," articulated in 1959, deals with the quantification of sensations, stating that the magnitude of sensation that the stimulus produces grows as a function of some power of the intensity of that stimulus. Or, as stated by Stevens: "The sensation magnitude Ψ grows as a power function of the stimulus magnitude $\emptyset$" (1959, p. 614).

Born in Ogden, Utah, Stevens earned his Ph.D. from Harvard in 1933. From 1949 to 1962, succeeding Boring, he directed the Psychological Laboratory at Harvard which was originally founded by James. In 1962 he became Professor of Psychophysics and Director of the Laboratory of Psychophysics.

Allport and the Department of Social Relations

The repercussions of World War II had an effect on psychology at Harvard. Social psychologists with cultural anthropologists and empirical sociologists came to the realization that they shared the study of human nature socially oriented. Consequently they proposed to fuse clinical psychology, social psychology, sociology, and cultural anthropology into a single unity termed the Department of Social Relations in 1946, with its own Laboratory of Social Relations on the top floor of Emerson Hall.

The Department of Social Relations was spearheaded by its chairman *Gordon W. Allport* (1897-1967), a Harvard Ph.D. (1922) in the tradition of William James via his mentor *Edwin Bissell Holt* (1873-1946). Holt, a pupil and admirer of James, lent behaviorism philosophical strength in his *The Freudian Wish* (1915) in which he attacked the Cartesian view of consciousness or mind as an unextended substance. The Harvard Ph.D. (1901) Holt was Münsterberg's adjunct in the psychological laboratory, leaving Harvard in 1918, and in 1926 spending a decade at Princeton. Holt not only supported behaviorism but dynamic psychology, modifying and adapting the Freudian wish concept in terms of drive, thus playing a considerable role in the development of dynamic psychology.

Another Harvard psychologist in the tradition of James via Holt was *Edward Chace Tolman* (1886-1959), a Harvard Ph.D. (1915) who studied under McDougall and Ralph Barton Perry. Acquiring from these men an interest in motivation, Tolman was also influenced by Holt's course in Experimental Psychology, Langfeld's general psychology, and Yerkes' Comparative Psychology course (in which Watson's book *Behavior: An Introduction to Comparative Psychology* was the text used). At the University of Geissen Tolman came under the influence of Koffka's gestalt psychology. His long tenure at the University of California (Berkeley Campus) extended from 1918 until his becoming Professor Emeritus in 1954. As early as 1922, Tolman espoused a *purposive behaviorism* in order to set his psychological stance apart from Watson's "muscle twitch psychology," a term coined by Tolman. Tolman's is a *cognitive psychology* in which he explained that a stimulus-response psychology could be significant provided "intervening variables" were employed, the intervening variables being that interposed between an environmental stimulus and observable response such as "cognitions," purposes, and "expectancies." As an experimental psychologist, Tolman was a "rat" psychologist. His sign-learning or sign gestalt theory holds that an organism learns when pursuing a sign to its goal by mapping his way to his goal with a cognitive map as it were. His views, elaborated in his classic *Purposive Behavior in Animals and Men,* appeared in 1932.

However, *Gordon W. Allport* was far from being a behaviorist, rather he followed in the spirit of William James. Even his concept of *functional autonomy* was James' idea in modern garb. Always with a deep and abiding interest in the psychology of personality and social psychology, Allport wrote his doctoral dissertation on "An Experimental Study of the Traits of Personality: With Special Reference to the Problem of Social Diagnosis." This trait theory of personality fructified into his *Personality: A Psychological Interpretation* in 1937, and revised as *Patterns and Growth in Personality* in 1961, in which a person is regarded as individual and unique. His long tenure at Harvard spanned over two score years from 1924 to the time of his death in 1967, the only interruption being a four year period at Dartmouth.

The baton of social psychology at Harvard was passed from McDougall to Pitirim A. Sorokin (who became Harvard's first head of the Department of Sociology, which replaced Social Ethics) and Allport, the two becoming members of the same department when the Department of Social Relations was founded in January, 1946. Within a few years approximately 200 candidates were purs ing their Ph.D.s in the department. The distinguished names in the department included David McClelland, Clyde Kluckhohn, Robert White, George Homans, Frederick Mosteller, Robert F. Bales, Talcott Parsons, and, for a period of time, Edward Tolman.

Social psychology prospered through the individual members of the department: George Caspar Homans (1910-   ) contributing an elementary social behavior theory (based on B. F. Skinner's behavior theory) in his *The Human Group* (1950) and *Social Behavior: Its Elementary Forms* (1961); and David McClelland (1917-   ) offering a key hypothesis of the achieving society based on Max Weber's *The Protestant Ethic and the Spirit of Capitalism* (1904-1905). McClelland's views are developed in his *The Achieving Society* (1961). Robert Freed Bales (1916-   ) contributed his interaction process analysis initially in 1950 and in developed form in his *Personality and Interpersonal Behavior* in 1970.

Fritz J. Roethlisberger (1898-1974) and Field Studies. The era of field work in social psychology was underway at Harvard when three professors from the Harvard Univ. rsity Graduate School of Business Administration (Fritz J. Roethlisberger, Elton Mayo, and Thomas North Whitehead) undertook socio-psychological experiments in the mid 1920s at the Western Electric Company, Hawthorne Works, Chicago. Later they were assisted by members of Harvard's Department of Social Relations, the results of their efforts appearing in Roethlisberger and Dickson's *Management and the Worker* (1939). Initially investigating fatigue in workers, the researchers found that individuals participating in an experiment, become an active part — affecting the experiment itself. Not the physical, but the social environment became the critical factor. Roethlisberger reasoned that

> if one experiments on a stone, the stone does not know it is being experimented upon—all of which makes it simple for people experimenting on stones. But if a human being is being experimented upon, he is likely to know it. Therefore, his attitudes toward the experiment and toward the experimenters become very important factors in determining his responses to the situation (1941, p. 14).

These researches continued for at least three dozen years, yielding a series of elaborate hypotheses as reported in *The Motivation, Productivity, and Satisfaction of Workers* (1958) by Zaleznik, Christensen, and Roethlisberger.

After the lapse of approximately a quarter of a century, the Department of Social Relations and the Department of Psychology at Harvard wedded into the Department of Psychology and Social Relations in 1972, the first catalogue listing courses in the joint department appearing the following year.

CHAPTER 13

Functionalism at Johns Hopkins and Clark Universities from Its Inception with G. Stanley Hall

GRANVILLE STANLEY HALL (1844-1924)

Hall's Early Life and Education. The Massachusetts-born Granville Stanley Hall (1844-1924) descended from a line of Congregational Protestants stemming from John Alden. Born in the small farming town of Ashfield, Hall came from a family of limited means who found the Congregational Church their social pivotal point. He graduated from Williams in 1867 and sought graduate study in philosophy in one of the main avenues available at the time—the clerical profession at Union Theological Seminary. It was at Union that his thoughts turned to a career as a professor of philosophy.

In New York, Hall developed an association with a distinguished Congregational minister of the Plymouth Church of Brooklyn, Henry Ward Beecher, who, on learning of Hall's financial need, provided him with a letter to be presented to Henry W. Sage, a merchant who was one of Cornell University's principal benefactors. It was in the spring of 1869 that Hall, a second-year student at Union delivered the note to Sage, who after grumbling concerning liberties ministers presume with another's wealth, wrote a check for $500 and presented it to the dumbfounded Hall, who left with it for Germany in June. With the money a year's study in Germany was assured.

Though Hall left for Bonn, he soon thereafter settled in Berlin, enrolling in the philosophy faculty of its university. Here, he decided to become a philosopher. When his money ran out, he had no option but to return to Union for his degree. However, his intentions were to utilize it to teach philosophy. During these years his fascination for evolutionary theory developed, having returned an eclectic Hegelian from Berlin, the stronghold of the evolutionist Hegel. Darwinian evolution was the scientific counterpart of Hegelian evolutionary philosophy.

Blaming his unorthodoxy or the *odium theologicum* for his numerous rejections for the philosophical posts to which he applied at various universities, Hall did not begin a university career until James K. Hosmer, a scholar of literature with whom Hall established an acquaintance in Berlin, contacted him in New York to arrange for Hall to assume his duties in rhetoric and English literature at Antioch College where Hosmer's father was the president. Hall seized the opportunity, leaving for western Ohio in 1872 at twenty-eight years of age, where he remained for four years, attaining a full professorship in mental philosophy and English literature. The 1870s also saw him departing from Hegelianism (with which he had a love-hate relationship throughout life) for positivism and the outlook of Charles Darwin, Herbert Spencer, and G. H. Lewes.

Hall at Harvard

With the growing realization that his career at Antioch was not materializing in the direction of philosophy as he desired, Hall left in 1876 for the nation's intellectual center, Cambridge, Massachusetts and for Harvard University. Here he attended lectures and found the philosophy department's assistant professor of physiology, William James, offering the new scientific psychology. Only a year earlier, James, who was Hall's elder by only two years, had prevailed upon the college's authorities to permit him to offer physiological psychology for the first time in the United States. James, who offered it as an undergraduate course, had made arrangements with Henry P. Bowditch (1840-1911) of Harvard Medical School to use his physiological laboratory. Bowditch is credited with having established the first physiological laboratory in America. As early as 1872 Harvard provided for the Ph.D. degree in the new psychology, and Hall was the first in the United States to receive such a degree, which was conferred on him in 1878. The first Ph.D. ever granted at Harvard was only five years earlier, and was a doctorate in chemistry. The first Ph.D. awarded in America was by Yale in 1861. In order to finance his graduate studies, Hall taught English at Harvard while candidating in the department of philosophy for his Ph.D. in the new psychology.

Hall's appointment on the Harvard faculty was not renewed for a second year, but out of his savings from his Antioch years he was able to continue his course of study. While most of his courses were with James, some were with Bowditch in physiology, and some of his time was spent with the experimental equipment in James' room. Utilizing psychology to resolve his philosophical or epistemological perplexities, Hall settled on the study of the muscular perception of space and offered it as his doctoral dissertation. Hall (1878a) believed that through muscular sense he had uncovered the mind-matter relationship. His theory was grounded on the doctrine of evolution, for he argued that the psychic evolvement from muscle to nerve fibers is due to the organic evolution of life. He felt that Friedrich Adolf Trendelenburg's (1802-1872) theory, "movement explains all things," was demonstrated by him. The German Trendelenburg, an Aristotelian who opposed Hegel, was a professor of philosophy at the University of Berlin, where Hegel's fame was without peer. Nevertheless Hall was never able to extricate himself from Hegel, and his functional psychology bore an indelible genetic or developmental character permeated with the Hegelian notion "that we may be said to know a thing, even the mind itself, most truly when our thought has followed all its changes in time, or has traced all its processes above" (1878b, p. 100). The developmental point of view remained Hall's orientation throughout his psychological career.

At Harvard, Hall was introduced to Charles Sanders Peirce's (1839-1914) pragmatism by James so that by the time he left Harvard, Hall was indoctrinated with a functional and pragmatic approach to psychology that remained permanently with him. Mind for him was an activity, and its functions those of willing, choosing, and acting. His psychology was developmental or genetic, functional, and dynamic with a hint of behaviorism. In adhering to atomistic sensationalism, Hall departed from James: He also differed in his monistic universe with its material base which James found repugnant, substituting in its stead a pluralistic universe with a mind possessing genuine freedom.

Hall's Second Sojourn to Germany. Having received the first Ph.D. in psychology in 1878, Hall found that there was little call for it so he yielded to an old yearning to return to Germany for post-doctoral work, planning to study at Berlin with Helmholtz and the physiologist Du Bois-Reymond, and at Leipzig with Wundt and the physiologist Ludwig. He began more and more to believe that philosophy was grounded on psychology, and psychology in turn on physiology. Viewing psychology as a natural science led him to abandon metaphysics. While in Germany, Hall encountered Cornelia Fisher, a young lady a couple of years his junior, who was studying art in Europe, and married her in the fall of 1879 in Berlin at the age of thirty-five.

Hall at Johns Hopkins

At thirty-six Hall returned to the United States in 1880 to become one of the country's most influential psychologists in the decade to follow. After spending the 1880-1881 school season lecturing in psychology at his alma maters, Williams and Harvard, he left for Johns Hopkins for an eight-year tenure before accepting the presidency of the newly found Clark University in 1888. Johns Hopkins was newly founded in 1876 as a graduate school with its first president, Daniel Coit Gilman (1831-1908). The place of eminence that it soon acquired as a graduate school was the envy of President Charles W. Eliot of Harvard who by the 1890s regained it for Harvard. Graduate study with its emphasis on research as it is known today in Ph.D. studies actually began in this country at Johns Hopkins University by Gilman whose indoctrination in it derives from his familiarity with German universities. A little over a dozen years later, Hall carried the idea of graduate education that was research oriented to Clark. Graduate study at other institutions prior to Hopkins was merely advanced undergraduate work, rather than research centered.

Several times Hall approached Gilman for a faculty appointment but in vain, even though once with the support of James' recommendation. Hall was unfortunately a man with a new degree for which there was no demand, accordingly Hall turned to a new subject acquired from Germany, pedagogy. He lectured on it at Harvard, Boston, and its surrounding towns with remarkable success, acquiring his first taste of its sweetness. Hall replaced moral character as the aim of education with *man's development to a higher evolutionary level of progress.* Success in the field of education was unfulfilling to this man, dedicated to psychology, who viewed pedagogy as merely one phase of applied psychology.

However, success in pedagogy did obtain a lectureship for him at the coveted Johns Hopkins University in the spring of 1881, and subsequently led to lectures in his beloved new psychology in 1882. The psychology lectures fructified into a three-year appointment as a lecturer in psychology and pedagogics in the department of philosophy. With him in the department were two other lecturers: Charles Sanders Peirce, coiner and father of pragmatism, and George S. Morris, a cherished friend. The department was without a full professor owing to the university's inability to find one of sufficient distinction. The three men vied for the position, but Peirce was not reappointed in 1884 because of his alienating personality. Writing President Gilman of a possible appointment, Hall requested permission to break his contract if necessary. Apparently Hall's strategy worked, for Gilman announced Hall's appointment in the spring of 1884 as the Professor of Psychology and Pedagogy. Not Hall's but Gilman's pressuring resulted in pedagogy being yoked with psychology in Hall's appointment. This did not make Hall the first professor of psychology, that honor going to James McKeen Cattell who became the first Professor of Psychology in 1888 at the University of Pennsylvania, but Hall was the first professor with psychology in his title. Psychology up to this time was an adjunct of philosophy, physiology, or pedagogy. Thus Hall at forty, a father of two young children, obtained his first permanent professorial appointment with the more than adequate salary of $4,000 (since $500 saw him through Germany for a year). The appointment was significant inasmuch as it was a landmark for psychology as a science in the United States.

During his tenure at Johns Hopkins, Hall had several students who distinguished themselves in psychology, among them being James McKeen Cattell and John Dewey, who were at the university when Hall began lecturing in January, 1883. His students and some of his friends and associates never benefited from him with respect to recommendations for appointments. When President Gilman was considering Hall's friend and associate, Morris, for a post in 1885, Hall wrote that Morris ''never can touch our best students.'' When Cattell's and John Dewey's fellowships came up for renewal, it was Hall who took Cattell's fellowship and gave it to Dewey, and then opposed Dewey's being renewed. Could it have been professional jealousy since Dewey informed Hall of his plan to write a text in psychology? The text materialized in 1886, two years after Dewey's Johns Hopkins Ph.D. was granted. He was twenty-seven at the time. Joseph Jastrow held the fellowship for the 1885-1886 school year. The Warsaw-born *Joseph Jastrow* (1863-1944) received his Ph.D. from Johns Hopkins in 1886, the year Dewey published his text *Psychology*. The first to receive a Ph.D. in psychology, Jastrow went on to the University of Wisconsin in 1888 where he spent his career, retiring in 1927. Reminiscing with pride at receiving the first Ph.D. in psychology, Jastrow reported in his *Autobiography,* ''the first Ph.D. given specifically in psychology was conferred upon me in 1886, as Cattell had left, and the other degrees that preceded my own were conferred in philosophy'' (1930, p. 139). Apparently, at Wisconsin he founded the second chair of psychology in 1888; the first was Cattell's at the University of Pennsylvania. Such chairs ordinarily included a laboratory of psychology. Known at best as a popularizer in psychology and at worst as given to occult phenomena, Jastrow wrote a number of books. An early one, inspired by the Society for Psychical Research, which was inaugurated in 1882, he titled *Fact and Fable in Psychology* (1900). When he wrote his *The Subconscious* in 1905, it was not Freudianism that he was talking about but normal phenomena of the personality with respect to possible survival. Jastrow's most outstanding pupil was *Clark L. Hull,* who received his Ph.D. under Jastrow at the University of Wisconsin in 1918 and went on to distinguish himself in learning theory at Yale's Institute of Human Relations.

Returning to Cattell's plight, he is found, disappointed and discouraged, leaving for Leipzig to study with Wundt, reporting in 1884 to his parents that "Dr. Hall has not acted honorably towards me." A few years after Dewey left Hopkins, President Gilman recommended to Hall that either James Mark Baldwin or Dewey be offered an appointment, but Hall reported both of them incompetent! It appeared that Hall would recommend only those of whom there would be virtually no chance of accepting the position. Hall's biographer, Dorothy Ross, observed:

> The best that can be said for Hall in this affair is that still insecure in his position and driven to appease all around him, he praised Cattell when with Cattell and agreed to Dewey's superiority when with Morris and Gilman, even though he secretly had come to doubt Dewey's merit. . . . The worst that can be said is that at a time when he himself had not yet produced very much in his field, he felt safer without strong intellectual challengers around him and set about to eliminate them (1972, p. 146).

In the wake of Hall's deserting Hopkins for Clark, he denuded the Hopkins' faculty by transplanting its department of psychology, and consequently the only remains Hopkins had left was a feeble philosophy department and no department of psychology whatever!

When Hall's little laboratory of psychology was instituted at Johns Hopkins in 1883, he had Dewey, Jastrow, and Cattell actively involved with him in experimental work. Edmund C. Sanford joined them later as a student as did Yujiro Motora, a pioneer in Japanese psychology at Kyoto University. The following year the laboratory was moved from a small building adjacent to the university's main complex to a room designed for psychophysiological research in the new biology building. By the opening of the school year in 1886, Hall had four rooms in the newly opened physics building.

Requiring an organ for the publication of the findings of his psychological laboratory, Hall initially utilized the British publication *Mind,* but in 1886 set for himself the task of planning for a journal of psychology for Americans. He realized that he needed one inasmuch as Hopkins was the only university in the United States with a department for the exclusive use of psychology, other psychologists finding themselves and their specialties as ancillary to philosophy. In 1887 his *American Journal of Psychology* came into existence as the first in the country devoted solely to psychology due to a $500 grant from a virtual stranger, R. Pearsall Smith. Smith, a spiritualist and member of the American Society for Psychical Research, expected a journal in psychical research or at least favorable to it. The overly enthusiastic Hall printed approximately 1500 copies, resulting in such debt that it required five years in order to recoup his losses. His disappointed benefactor gave him no further financial support nor did his university subsidize the *Journal*.

When the journal appeared, its personality was obviously that of Hall's, the editor, who contributed better than two thirds of the reviews, with articles and reviews contributed only by him or his students and colleagues at Johns Hopkins. It was keynoted by Hall's characteristic exclusivism. After denigrating the psychological texts of McCosh of Princeton and Bowne of Boston University, he dismissed Dewey's text as Hegelian, describing it with epithets such as "naive" and "pathetic." Only Ladd's *Psychology*, which Hall had a chance of reviewing and correcting before its publication, escaped his scurrilous attacks, but he went on to assert that Ladd lacked understanding of psychology as a laboratory science. Unless one shared Hall's psychological bent, the journal lacked appeal. Hall sought out James to write a review of the first issue of the *Journal* for the *Nation*, but James, with his objections to (and reservations of) the *Journal*, recommended that the task be offered to Jastrow. Hall used the journal to gain leadership for himself in the new psychology and saw it as a rallying point in polarizing the adherents of the new psychology.

Hall as President of Clark University

Hall had been successful at Hopkins, attracting approximately a half dozen students a year to graduate study in psychology, but he left for the presidency of Clark University in Worcester, Massachusetts in order to realize his ambitions for psychology. The emphasis that he lent the discipline in its formative years contributed considerably to its development as a science. Not Harvard, but Clark and Hopkins were the closest institutions in the United States to the German universities. Harvard did not have the freedom for research of which Hall at Clark could boast. When Hall moved out of Hopkins, he took with him his finest students: Sanford to direct the Clark laboratory of psychology, William Burnham to undertake educational psychology, Donaldson for physiological psychology as well as the major portion of the apparatus at the Hopkins laboratory of psychology. Left in a condition of practically no department of psychology, much less a laboratory of psychology, the laboratory at Johns Hopkins closed from 1887 until 1903, when it reopened under James Mark Baldwin.

Clark University, like Hopkins, was a graduate school, posing as a severe competitor to Harvard, being in Harvard's "backyard." Clark was actually a scientific institute dominated by the psychology department. It appeared as if the two universities would have to vie for the same graduate students in psychology. Clark University appointed the noted German-born American anthropologist and ethnologist *Franz Boas* (1858-1942) to the department of anthropology and aimed for the most prestigious department of the new psychology in the country. Hall's ambitions moved James to enlarge Harvard's psychological laboratory in 1890 (the opening year of actual operations at Clark), and within two years to appoint as its director, Hugo Münsterberg of Freiburg, considered by some at the time to be the foremost psychologist in the world. Hall established the psychological laboratory at Clark in 1889 with E. C. Sanford as its director, and began publications from the laboratory within two years. Hall sent feelers to James hoping "to regard the departments of both institutions as if they were in one University" (1890), but this proposition never materialized. Instead, when James accumulated $4,300, he approached Münsterberg saying that Harvard must lead in psychology as America's best university.

Hall attracted men of distinction to Clark but did so by bargaining and cutting the salaries they were currently earning at their former employment. For example, Boas was earning $2,000 when Hall appointed him to Clark for half that amount. Hall saw to it that he himself earned the desirable sum of $6,000 annually. As a professor at Hopkins he earned $4,000 but his professors at Clark earned from $3,500 down. In 1889 he opened his university with a better than two to one ratio of faculty to students, 34 students and 18 faculty members. Of the university community, fifteen were either students or faculty at Johns Hopkins, twelve of the nonfaculty were holders of the Ph.D. By the turn of the century, Hall's Ph.D.s had and were still outnumbering the rest.

After a 31-year occupancy of the presidency of Clark, Hall retired in 1920, leaving behind a vast void. Hall, succeeded by the Harvard geographer, Wallace W. Atwood, whose sense of academic freedom was far from his predecessor's, saw several of his finest faculty members leave, among them *Edwin G. Boring* (1886-1968), who came to Clark fresh from World War I in 1919 to assume the post of professor of experimental psychology. Due to a controversy in 1923 over freedom of speech with Hall's successor, Atwood, he left that fall for Harvard where his tenure lasted until his death. More than an experimental psychologist, Boring went on to become the dean of American historians of psychology. Like Hall before him, Boring likewise never completely extricated himself from Hegelianism as his *History of Psychology* (1950) testifies. Throughout that work Boring lays heavy stress upon the *Zeitgeist* (spirit of the times), which is simply Hegel's *Weltgeist* (world-spirit) operative sometimes in terms of the Hegelian dialectic and other times in terms of nondialectic evolution.

In order to vindicate himself, especially his life and years at Clark, Hall undertook to publish his autobiography in 1923 for the purpose of ventilating a "long-repressed impulse to tell the inside story of the early days of Clark University and to correct, so far as I could before I die, the long injustice done me" (1923, p. 5).

Founding of the American Psychological Association

In spearheading the founding of the American Psychological Association, Hall contributed significantly to the new psychology by establishing an institutional base for it. While president of Clark, he mailed at least twenty-six invitations to psychologists to assemble at a preliminary meeting at Clark University at Worcester, Massachusetts to organize an association of psychologists on July 8, 1892. The men invited were to an extent representative of American psychology, rather than merely his own bias, but most were his friends and former students. However, the nation's most distinguished psychologists failed to attend, including the authors of the best psychology texts of the time such as: James, Ladd, Dewey, and Bowne. Albrecht opined:

> In all probability, the actual founders were Hall, Sanford, Jastrow, two interested alienists from nearby McClean Asylum, Fullerton, several students at Clark, and one student from Harvard. All save the student from Harvard were Hall's personal friends, and most of them were or had been his friends (1960, pp. 189-190).

Charter members, however, comprised those who returned "letters of approval and accepted membership." Consequently only Bowne from Boston University was not a charter member among the textbook authors mentioned. James was in Switzerland, and Dewey was too far away to break from his duties at the University of Michigan. With the exception of Fullerton, those who attended could reach Clark University within an hour.

Of the twenty-six charter members, six (or almost 25%) came from Clark (Burnham, Gilman, Griffin, Hall, Krohn, and Sanford); three from Harvard (James, Nichols, and Royce); two from each of the following: Columbia (Cattell, and Hyslop); McLean Hospital in a Boston suburb (Cowles and Noyes); University of Pennsylvania (Fullerton and Witmer); the University of Toronto (Baldwin and Hume); Yale (Ladd and Scripture); and one each from Brown (Delabarre); Indiana (Bryan); Iowa (Patrick); Michigan (Dewey); Nebraska (Wolfe); Stanford (F. Angell); and Wisconsin (Jastrow who became the group's first secretary). Thus the association's members were from the east to the west coast.

At this organizational meeting in July, 1892, it was decided to hold the First Annual Meeting the following December at the University of Pennsylvania where Hall became the association's first president. At this meeting Münsterberg from Harvard, Titchener from Cornell, Ormond from Princeton, Mills from McGill, and Pace from Catholic University were elected into membership. Hall delivered a paper on the "History and Prospects of Experimental Psychology in America," with Ladd and Baldwin discussants. Thus nearly all influential American psychologists were in attendance except Bowne and James. From twenty-six charter members (or thirty-one its first year), the American Psychological Association grew to 530 in 1930, and to over 30,000 in 1970. It has an imposing modern building in Washington, D.C., and over thirty divisions with specialties ranging from the experimental analysis of behavior and psychopharmacology to hypnosis and humanistic psychology.

Hall enters the annals of the history of psychology with many firsts to his credit: the first in the United States to receive a Ph.D. in psychology (Harvard's philosophy faculty in 1878 had called a special meeting for the granting of a degree in psychology); the first to publish a journal of psychology in the United States, the *American Journal of Psychology* in 1887; the first to open a formally recognized laboratory of psychology in the United States (in 1884 at Johns Hopkins); the first in America to award a Ph.D. from a department of psychology (to Joseph Jastrow at Johns Hopkins in 1886); and the first to introduce the psychology of adolescence (1904) and senescence (1922).

Adolf Meyer (1886-1950) and G. S. Hall

Hall's interest in abnormal psychology continued to grow from his days in Europe to Hopkins to Clark. Observing psychiatry on the horizon of psychology, he became increasingly involved with the study. At Hopkins he sent out leads hoping to obtain an honorary M.D. because he wanted to work more closely with clinical psychology. His students at Clark were exposed to the lectures of Swiss-born *Adolf Meyer* who came to the Worcester State Hospital (near Clark University) as its director from the post of neuropathologist at the Kankakee State Hospital in Illinois. In 1908 when Johns Hopkins opened its department of psychiatry, he was appointed professor, a post he held until his retirement in 1941. It was Meyer who coined the term "mental hygiene." One of the first functionalists in psychiatry, Meyer's holistic or psychobiological approach (which he termed *ergasiology*) held that a man's thinking affects his functioning pervasively even to the point of the cellular and biochemical dimension. Viewing psychiatric disorders as exaggerated forms of reaction patterns, Meyer regarded schizophrenia as the product of deteriorated habit patterns. American psychiatry found itself under his dominance in the first two score years of the twentieth century.

The efforts of Hall and the attraction of Clark University contributed to Meyer's coming to Worcester. In Hall, Meyer found support for his own objectives. At Clark University, Hall had actually appointed him docent in psychiatry.

Hall and Freud

Clark University celebrated its decennial in 1899 with Auguste Henri Forel (1848-1931), the distinguished Swiss psychiatrist who was known for his work in hypnotism, forensic psychiatry, and the anatomy of the brain, as its principal speaker. It was becoming more obvious that the interest in psychiatry exhibited by Hall was becoming increasingly profound. He was beginning to lecture on the theories of Janet and Hughlings Jackson as well as on Freud as early as 1903. The prominent role granted sex by Freud also fascinated Hall, who was urging sex education in 1907.

Accordingly, when Hall saw an opportunity for a vigentennial celebration, he began in 1908 to plan for distinguished Europeans to lecture at Clark. Although his faculty recommended that the psychologists Herman Ebbinghaus and Ernst Meumann be presented to the trustees, the autocrat Hall, on his own initiative, invited Freud as well, and along with him, Carl G. Jung. On September 5, 1909, Jung and Freud arrived with Sandor Ferenczi accompanying them at Freud's invitation. Jung and Freud lectured in German, Freud delivering five psychoanalytic lectures from Tuesday through Saturday at eleven in the morning. Jung, offering at least three on his association method, was granted an honorary doctorate. Also participating were Wilhelm Stern, Franz Boas, E. B. Titchener, and Adolf Meyer. Freud testified that the event was the first recognition accorded him anywhere in the world.

Hall's Genetic Psychology

Among American psychologists, Hall was the greatest "founder" of them all. It was mentioned that he founded America's first psychological laboratory, first journal of psychology, the first and only American Psychological Association, but he also was the founder of the *Pedagogical Seminary* (renamed the *Journal of Genetic Psychology*) in 1891 which was the second psychological journal in the United States; in 1904 he founded the *Journal of Religious Psychology* (which survived only a decade); and in 1915 the *Journal of Applied Psychology*.

Hall's is an *evolutionary psychology*, a *genetic psychology* as he preferred to call it. He drew from the evolutionary thinkers (Darwin and Spencer), from the British associationists, and from Wundt, under whom he studied. Hence he had an eclectic or *synthetic psychology* as he termed it, taking his lead from Spencer. His devotion to genetic psychology was so complete that when he died he left a legacy to Clark University for the establishment of a chair of genetic psychology, which is presently named for him.

A genetic psychologist is interested in human (and animal) development with its attendant questions of adaptation. It was his genetic psychology that introduced him to child psychology and pedagogy or child development, and then to adolescent development, and eventually to development of the aging, i.e., senescence. Out of it came his magnum opus, *Adolescence: Its Psychology, and Its Relations to Physiology, Anthropology, Sociology, Sex, Crime, Religion, and Education* in 1904, which is currently in a 1969 reprint. As he was aging he sought to understand himself, and the result was his book *Senescence* in 1922.

Hall's Influential Students: Terman and Gesell

At the opening of the twentieth century while Hall was at Clark, he produced two remarkable Ph.D.s, *Lewis Madison Terman* (1877-1956) and *Arnold Lucius Gesell* (1880-1961), both originally from the midwest. Terman, a pioneer in mental testing in the United States was from Indiana (near Indianapolis) and Gesell, dubbed the father of scientific child study, was from Alma, Wisconsin. Both were influenced by Hall, especially his child or genetic psychology, the former receiving his doctorate under him in 1905 and the latter his a year later. Terman went to Stanford in 1910 and made it a stronghold of child psychology and the mental measurement of children, while Gesell went to Yale in 1911 where he founded the Clinic of Child Development. Before arriving at their life tenured positions, both of them (along with another Clark Ph.D., Edmund B. Huey who went to Johns Hopkins) went to posts at Los Angeles State Normal School because of the influence of Hall who enlisted them in the "new faith" of psychology revolutionizing education, a factor that caused a considerable number of Hall's students to accept positions at normal schools and high schools.

Terman at Stanford. When Terman arrived at Stanford University in 1910, Frank Angell (1857-1939), a Wundtian Ph.D. from Leipzig (1891), had been the executive head there from 1892 to 1923, but on his retirement Terman assumed the responsibility. Terman was already a full professor of education, acquiring that on the publication of his classic *The Measurement of Intelligence: An Explanation of and a Complete Guide for the use of the Stanford Revision and Extension of the Binet-Simon Scale* in 1916. On Angell's retirement he became professor of psychology.

On Huey's advice in 1908, Terman developed further the Binet-Simon intelligence tests, the result being the Stanford-Binet Intelligence Scale published in 1916 as *The Measurement of Intelligence,* which became one of the most important tests of the first half of the twentieth century. It was found that intelligence in children increases rapidly in the early years, with a leveling off effect at age 16. Stern's IQ (intelligence quotient) was used. The mental age, being a percentage of the chronological, was obtained by dividing the mental by the actual age and multiplying that figure by 100. E.g., if a ten year old child's mental age is 14, then his IQ is 140, considered by Terman to be on the threshold of "genius."

In 1921 Terman turned to genetic studies of genius, and from 1925 to 1959 he published five volumes of his *Genetic Studies of Genius.* It comprised studies of 1,528 "gifted children" with an IQ of 140 or better who were investigated for 35 years with regular follow-up studies appearing in 1930, 1947, and another in 1959 after Terman died, the subjects being 17, 35, and 45 years of age at each report. Repudiating Galton's assertion that genius is characterized by eminence, Terman found that some gifted people such as a number of women employed their genius toward achieving private contentment, hence genius is not necessarily eminence, for it may assume the form of capacity for contentment.

Gesell at the Yale Clinic of Child Development. In 1910 Gesell left the Los Angeles State Normal School and went the following year to Yale as Assistant Professor of Education, the same year establishing and directing the Yale Psycho-Clinic which subsequently became the Yale Clinic of Child Development. Studying medicine concurrently, Gesell obtained his M.D. in 1915 when he was appointed Professor of Child Hygiene at Yale's graduate school. After 33 years at Yale he retired only to find himself still occupied in research at Harvard Pediatric Study and at the Gesell Institute of Child Development.

Combining clinical studies with scientific observation, Gesell investigated children by employing photography and one-way mirrors, reporting these studies in *The First Five Years of Life* (1940), and in the two-part study of *Child Development* (1943, 1946). Gesell's approach, a genetic one which held to a universality in the child's constitutional development, was criticized as too dogmatic, neglecting the cultural influence in which the child is developing. "It has taken Nature," wrote Gesell, "a billion years to fashion the structure and the potentialities of the human infant. Each newborn baby is a focal end product of aeons of evolution. . . . The genes initiate the mental as well as the physical products of growth. From the earliest stage the child develops as a unit" (1949, pp. vii-viii). Thus in Gesell's system, which is a constitutional psychology, development is seen as a mechanical necessity without room for variation or change, as if the child is predetermined or predestined. He was charged as being a mere recorder of rigid norms, of labeling without providing psychological explanations. The wide influence of his studies resulted in great numbers of children being denied adoption because they did not measure up to his *Developmental Quotients,* and the quotients of these children became lower owing to their institutional rearing. The samples used in his studies were criticized as being too small and highly restricted. This once giant of child development investigations of the thirties and forties, the heyday of his achievement, yielded considerable ground in the second half of the twentieth century.

Triplett: First Experimental Social Psychologist

Another of Hall's students, Norman Triplett (b. 1861), received his Ph.D. from Clark in 1900. He is noteworthy in the history of psychology because of his being the first experimental social psychologist. While studying for his master's degree at the University of Illinois, Triplett successfully conducted experiments in 1897 on pacemaking and competition in which he found that bicyclists tend to increase speed when pacing with other cyclists, and gain still greater speed in competition. Triplett's experiment led to *social facilitation,* a term coined by Floyd Allport (1924), which currently has gained considerable attention in social psychology. The term connotes increased efficiency in response owing to social stimulus (stimulus from others).

The Golden Era of psychology at Clark University was coterminus with Hall, similar to that at Cornell with Titchener. It was not the colleges that made the men great, but great men who lent stature to their respective institutions.

CHAPTER 14

The Tentative Functionalist Ladd
at Yale and His Heirs

(A) LADD'S YALE

A product of Western Reserve, *George Trumbull Ladd* (1842-1921) was born in Plainsville, Ohio, and graduated from Western Reserve University in 1842 before receiving his theological degree from Andover Theological Seminary (Massachusetts) in 1869. After spending a decade in the Congregational ministry, he accepted an appointment in the philosophy department at Bowdoin College in 1879. Two years later he went to Yale University where he remained for the rest of his career, a quarter of a century tenure lasting from 1881 to 1905. He also lectured in Japan and India, loving the people of the former place to such an extent that he had half of his cremated remains buried near Yokohama; etched in the stone marker the words read:

IN MEMORY OF
GEORGE TRUMBULL LADD
1842-1921
AMERICAN
GENTLEMAN, SCHOLAR
EDUCATOR, FRIEND OF JAPAN
"I HAVE LIVED, AND LOVED,
AND LABORED, ALL IS WELL."
ERECTED BY HIS
FRIENDS AND ADMIRERS

The second president of the American Psychological Association, Ladd was also honored as a delegate to the World's Congress of Psychologists (Paris, 1900), and to the International Congress of Arts and Sciences meeting held in conjunction with the St. Louis Exposition in 1904. In addition to a number of articles, he published thirty-five books.

Whereas in the 1880s, there were only three prominent psychologists in the United States (James, Hall, and Ladd), by 1900 *Who's Who in America* listed at least seven more: Frank Angell at Stanford, J. M. Baldwin at Princeton, B. P. Bowne at Boston University, J. McK. Cattell at Columbia, J. Jastrow at Wisconsin, E. W. Scripture at Yale, and E. B. Titchener at Cornell. Münsterberg's name was not included but he did not regard himself as an American; however, the absence of Dewey's name must have been an oversight, for he was heading Chicago's department at the time.

The Rise and Fall of Yale's Psychology Department: 1887-1905

After six years of preparation, Ladd published his impressive *Elements of*

Physiological Psychology in 1887, according him immediate eminence as a scientist in the new psychology. From 1887, the date of the publication of this work, until his forced retirement (dismissal) from Yale in 1905, his more important psychological contributions were made, including his *Psychology: Descriptive and Explanatory* in 1894, and his abridgement of it in 1898, *Primer of Psychology*.

Though he fought for the new experimental psychology, seeking to establish it as a science, he, preferring the theoretical, was (like James and Hall) not an experimentalist, despite his coining the disparaging term "arm-chair psychologist." He chose the life of a "speaking teacher" over that of experimentalist. Also like James and Hall (for that matter, virtually all of the American psychologists), he assumed a functional approach in psychology, stressing the mind as active and purposeful with the function of resolving life's everyday problems. His *Elements of Physiological Psychology,* wrote his biographer, Eugene S. Mills, was "an American interpretation of psychological problems. It was a restrained and somewhat tentative statement of the functional perspective that was to infuse itself into American psychology" (1969, p. 103).

He opened his *Elements* considering "psychology as that science which has for its primary subject of investigation all the phenomena of human consciousness" (1887, p. 3), and concluded that

> *the subject of all states of consciousness is a real unit-being, called Mind; which is of non-material nature, and acts and develops according to laws of its own, but is specially correlated with certain material molecules and masses forming the substance of the Brain* (1887, p. 613).

Remarkably the book survived ten printings and in 1911 was revised by Robert S. Woodworth. As could be expected, Ladd's *Elements of Physiological Psychology* relied heavily upon Wundt's *Grundzüge* for data but also upon Hermann Lotze's orientation, despite Ladd's denial of being a Lotzian.

By the time he wrote his *Psychology: Descriptive and Explanatory* in 1895, he defined the field of psychology (in his subtitle) as "a treatise of the phenomena, laws, and development of human mental life," thus viewing the matter genetically. He remained faithful to his definition of psychology as *"the science which describes and explains the phenomena of consciousness, as such"* (1894, p. 1). By the time the *Outlines of Descriptive Psychology* appeared in 1898, he added the term "systematic," defining psychology as "the systematic description and explanation of the phenomena of consciousness, as such" (1898, p. 1). This work he designed as a text, subtitling it "a text-book of mental science for colleges and normal schools." Psychology was regarded as "propaedeutic to philosophy."

Edward Wheeler Scripture (1864-1945): Yale's Psychological Laboratory. In the fall of 1892 Ladd founded a laboratory of psychology at Yale. E. W. Scripture, who left Clark to join the Yale faculty that year as Instructor of Experimental Psychology, became its director. Scripture, a University of Leipzig Ph.D. (1891) and a University of Munich M:D. (1906), remained at Yale until 1903 when he was fired during the period of upheaval at Yale's department of psychology. The university informed Scripture in 1903 that his appointment would not be continued following a year's leave of absence. Ladd, who had built the department, had to stand by and observe his department becoming "disintegrated and disgraced."

Departmental members were feuding among themselves, claiming that Ladd was dictatorial, especially regarding the laboratory. Departmental members Duncan, Sneath, Scripture, and Judd were disputing with Ladd and with each other concerning what part the laboratory should play in a department of psychology. In a private paper quoted by the biographer Mills, Ladd wrote:

> Dr. Scripture and Prof. Duncan were in constant communication, it plainly appeared, with the President, both by letter and by way of visits to his office. I was forced to remain powerless while I saw the Laboratory which I had founded, and with which my name and reputation were peculiarly connected, going to pieces as an effective branch of the Department service. Dr. Scripture was boasting openly that he had "a pull" upon the President (1969, pp. 219-220).

It's strange that Ladd should feel so strongly about the laboratory because he was not a laboratory psychologist, especially at that particular time.

Another Leipzig Ph.D. who received his degree in 1896, Charles Hubbard Judd (1873-1946), only an instructor in psychology at that time at Yale, took charge of the laboratory, informing Ladd that the laboratory was open to him *"only by courtesy."* In 1909 Judd left for the University of Chicago and became Director of the Psychological Laboratory. The upshot of the matter was that on May 17, 1904, Ladd was fired, as was Duncan. Scripture had already been dismissed, and Sneath was transferred to another department. Reviewing the matter, Mills reported:

> A once flourishing department had died. The demoralizing effect upon students and faculty and the loss of continuity in teaching and research were serious matters for the university, as well as for individuals. It would be a long time before psychology and philosophy could be properly revived at Yale. With the revival, however, there would be a new style and a new spirit in these academic disciplines. The tattered department of 1905 was more a symbol of the pain of birth than of the agony of death (1969, p. 224).

Ladd went into retirement, while Scripture went to Columbia University (1909 to 1914) before entering the field of phonetics at King's College, London, and later at the University of Vienna, founding a laboratory of speech neurology in a London hospital in the meantime.

When Scripture published his version of *The New Psychology* in 1897, he dedicated it to Wilhelm Wundt as the founder of the first psychological laboratory, to Hall as founder of the first one in the United States, and to Ladd as founder of the laboratory at Yale, "in recognition of their invaluable services in establishing a new science."

Carl E. Seashore (1866-1949): The Product of Yale's Laboratory. The most distinguished psychologist to come out of Ladd and Scripture's psychological laboratory at Yale was the Swedish-born Carl Emil Seashore, who took his Ph.D. from Yale in 1895. Seashore, who was introduced to experimental psychology by Ladd, became Scripture's assistant. Both Scripture and Seashore were almost the same age. Scripture, whose orientation was Darwinian, became distinguished after leaving for the University of Iowa in 1897, rising to head of the Department of Philosophy and Psychology before becoming Dean of the Graduate School in 1908.

When he arrived at Iowa, the philosopher George T. W. Patrick, who had studied psychology with Hall at Hopkins, was desirous of building a strong psychology department with funds already provided for a laboratory. Under Seashore the Iowa psychology laboratory soon became prominent, Seashore himself initiating the experimental psychology of music. Seashore's "pioneering in psychology" is reported in a book under that title published by him in 1942.

(B)   YALE'S INSTITUTE OF HUMAN RELATIONS:
Hull; Spence; Dollard; Miller; Mowrer; Sears; Doob

It was a University of Chicago man, James Rowland Angell, who infused life back into psychology at Yale. Coming to Yale in 1921 as its president, Angell had established the Institute of Psychology in 1924. The plan was to integrate research in three major fields of study: psychobiology, anthropology, and biology. Research in psychobiology and primate biology fell to *Robert Mearns Yerkes* (1876-1956); racial psychology to Clark Wissler, a 1901 Columbia Ph. D. under Cattell; and physiological psychology to Raymond Dodge, an 1896 University of Halle Ph.D.

The institute, failing to satisfy Angell's ambition for the progress of psychology, proposed a still more comprehensive approach to human behavior by envisioning an Institute of Human Relations. The Institute, which was underway by the fall of 1931 (though planned as early as 1929), included psychology, social science, research and clinical psychiatry, primate biology, and child development. Arnold Gesell assumed a major role in the Child Development Clinic which was a part of the institute, and Yale's School of Medicine was expanded and strengthened with the inclusion of psychiatry. Writing in the Bulletin of Yale University, Angell stated: "The Institute is designed to achieve two principal ends: first, to carry on research upon the basic problems of human nature and the social order; and second, to train a skilled personnel for work in these fields" (1930, p. 5). Within a decade the Institute could boast of such important names as Clark L. Hull (1884-1952), Neal E. Miller (1909-   ), O. Hobart Mowrer (1907-   ), John Dollard (1900-   ), Kenneth W. Spence (1907-1967), Leonard W. Doob (1909-   ), Robert R. Sears (1908-   ), Clelland S. Ford (1909-   ), Carl Iver Hovland (1912-1961), and John W. M. Whiting (1908-   ). This environment produced notable research in two important areas of psychology: learning theory and social psychology. In addition to Hull, Spence, and Mowrer in learning theory, the Yale group produced Ernest R. Hilgard (1906-   ), Arthur W. Melton (1906-   ), and Donald G. Marquis (1908-   ·). The social psychologists, spearheaded by the founder and director of the Yale Communication Research Program, C. I. Hovland, included Irving L.

Janis (1918-   ), Harold H. Kelley (1921-   ), William J. McGuire (1925-   ), and Fred(erick) D. Sheffield (1914-   ), who is better known in learning theory.

Yale as a Stronghold of Learning Theory

The moving spirit of learning theory at Yale during the thirties and the decade that followed, Clark L. Hull began in 1936 to run open seminars that attracted many of the distinguished names mentioned above. The seminars, undertaken in association with Miller, Dollard, and Mowrer, treated learning theory, i.e., reflexes, behavioral laws, and Freudian phenomena. Hull, a University of Wisconsin Ph.D. (1918), who had earned his degree under Joseph Jastrow, joined Yale University's Institute of Human Relations in 1929. A year later he came to the realization that psychology as a valid natural science has its own quantitatively expressible laws which can be stated in ordinary equations. Complex behavior as derivatives of secondary laws proceeds from primary laws and the conditions on which behavior rests. Social behavior is likewise derived from quantitative laws based on primary equations.

Enchanted with Newton's *Principia* (1686) and the *Principia Mathematica* (1913) of Alfred North Whitehead and Bertrand Russell, Hull went on with his colleagues to develop a hypothetico-deductive method, which was published in 1940 as *Mathematico-Deductive Theory of Rote Learning: A Study in Scientific Methodology*. Viewing his approach as a logical-deductive method, he sought to (1) structure postulates, (2) deduce experimentally testable conclusions from the postulates, (3) perform tests, (4) revise the postulates if the tests failed, and (5) add the postulates tentatively to the body of science if they proved successful.

Clark L. Hull (1884-1952): Drive Reduction Theory of Learning. Three years later the hypothetico-deductive method was applied to learning theory, yielding the publication *Principles of Behavior* (1943). The result, a neobehavioral learning theory, explained behavior in stimulus-response terms, learning being the bonding of stimulus with response through the mediation of intervening variables (symbolic constructs or activity occurring within the organism). Contrary to Watson's behaviorism which is reduced to the barest form of reflex behavior, Hull introduced purpose, ideas, insights, knowledge, and other constructs that cannot be objectively observed. Hull offered a drive reduction theory, that is, learning transpires when responses are reinforced owing to a reduction in drive strength. The drive's diminishing serves as reinforcement, reward, or Thorndike's law of effect. Also like Thorndike, Hull's is a connectionism in which he termed *habit strength* the bonding of stimulus with response. His fundamental law of learning or law of acquisition is that habit strength is the function of the number of reinforcements, the greater the number of reinforcements the greater the tenacity of the bonding. In the absence of either habit strength or drive then performance drops to zero, with no learning possible at all. Noting that animals perform much more readily when hungry than when sated, he expressed this fact by the formula: excitatory potential or the potential for response ($_SE_R$) equals drive *(D)* times habit strength ($_SH_R$). Satiation lowers response and the absence of reinforcement results in inhibition or the extinction of learning (habit). The excitatory potential eliciting the strongest attraction accounts for choice, while discrimination is accounted for by differing stimuli. The greater the dissimilarity of two stimuli, the simpler it is to discriminate because the less chance there is of generalization occurring, i.e., the less the two stimuli will be fused together and therefore confused in the mind of the individual.

The year Hull died, his *A Behavior System* (1952) appeared in which he revised his earlier position. Whereas his earlier learning theory allowed only for primary reinforcement, his revision incorporated secondary reinforcement as well. Rather than drive reduction occurring through stimulus alleviation (such as eating food) accounting for learning or habit, it is drive-stimulus reduction or a mere craving that is relieved. Habit strength depends on the frequency of occurrence of contiguous bonding of stimulus with response, rather than the amount of reinforcement. Provided there is at least some quantity of reinforcement present, learning becomes a matter of how often (rather than how much) contiguous stimulus-response occurs. The Hullian hypothesis read:

> When a stimulus (S) or a stimulus trace (s) acts at the same time that a hitherto unrelated response (R) occurs and this coincidence is accompanied by an antedating goal reaction (r_G), the secondary reinforcing powers of the stimulus evoked by the latter (S_G) will reinforce S to R, giving rise to a new S—R dynamic connection (1952, p. 14).

Fred D. Sheffield (1914-   ) and Thornton B. Roby (1924-   ): Sheffield-Roby Experiment. Why did Hull yield, making this concession to secondary reinforcement? His premises called for only consummatory responses of hunger or sex satisfaction (as Freud would have it) or survival as Darwin would have it. The compromise was induced by the experiments of two of his colleagues, Fred D. Sheffield and Thornton B. Roby (1924-   ), a young Yale Ph.D. (1950) working with Sheffield. These two researchers established that secondary reinforcement was effective for instrumental learning. Up to this time Hull was arguing with I. P. Pavlov in favor of classical conditioning (primary reinforcement of consummatory responses). In an experiment titled the "Reward Value of a Non-nutritive Sweet Taste" (1950), Sheffield and Roby adduced data supporting the contention

> that a non-nourishing but sweet-tasting substance served as a reinforcement for instrumental learning. Hunger was presumably in no way reduced by the saccharine solution, yet hungry animals clearly demonstrated acquisition in the three different learning situations in which the reward was a saccharine solution (p. 479).

Thus Sheffield and Roby disproved the theory that for anything to qualify as a reinforcer it must be able to reduce a physical need. What is of consequence is not drive reduction, but what an individual does with respect to goal activity. Not drive reduction per se, but the *act* of consuming the goal object was of consequence, argued Sheffield and Roby. However, these two researchers in concluding that it was the "drinking activity" failed to show it was not the "sweet taste" per se that was the explanation.

Edwin R. Guthrie (1886-1959): Contiguous Conditioning Learning Theory. What Sheffield and Roby had succeeded in was establishing the learning theory of Edwin Ray Guthrie (1886-1959), a University of Pennsylvania Ph.D. who spent his career at the University of Washington. Guthrie's contiguity theory of learning purports that "a combination of stimuli which has accompanied a movement will on its recurrence tend to be followed by that movement" (1952, p. 23). Note that it is the act or movement that is the critical factor in learning. A person learns immediately on doing, on taking action, for "a stimulus pattern gains its full associative strength on the occasion of its first pairing with a response" (1942, p. 30). The initial association is bonding. Guthrie's final statement on the matter was that "what is being noticed becomes a signal for what is being done" (1959, p. 186). In arguing for association by contiguity. Guthrie was to a large extent returning to the contentions of the early British associationists Hume and Locke.

Wiliam K. Estes (1919-   ): Stimulus Sampling Theory of Learning. The one-time student of B. F. Skinner, *William Kaye Estes* (1919-   ), came to the support of Guthrie's learning theory with his own *statistical theory of learning* in 1950 which was grounded on stimulus sampling. A 1943 Ph.D. from the University of Minnesota, Estes sought to establish (as Guthrie did before him) that learning or conditioning is on an all-or-none-basis once it occurs, and that repeated reinforcements simply give "repeated opportunities for the formation of an association between a stimulus pattern and the reinforced response" (Estes, Hopkins, and Crothers, 1960, p. 338). Thus learning is complete on a single trial. His stimulus sampling theory holds that the response learned is the one being conditioned and that one is a representative sample of all possible stimulus elements that the individual may subsequently encounter in future trials. His stimulus sampling theory of learning is based on the premise that "each response has some fixed probability of being reinforced . . . on any trial, regardless of the S's present or past choices" (1964, p. 89). With E. D. Niemark, Estes presented his theory in a volume titled *Stimulus Sampling Theory* (1967).

Kenneth W. Spence (1907-1967): Hull's Intellectual Successor. Hull's influence reached a number of influential learning theorists associated with Yale's Institute of Human Relations, including Mowrer, Dollard, Miller, and Spence. But it was *Kenneth Wartinbee Spence* (1907-1967), a Yale Ph.D. (1933), whose learning theories remained considerably faithful to that of Hull. Nevertheless Spence severed from his mentor in one important respect. Whereas Hull multiplied drive and incentive motivation in order to obtain the total level of motivation, Spence simply added the two. Both Drive (D) and incentive motivation (K) are motivational variables, the former being an internal state (e.g., physical need of hunger), and the latter an external one. Spence's formula is $E = H \times (D+K)$, that is, the excitatory strength (E) or learning potential (strength of inclination capable of eliciting a given response of a particular stimulus) equals habit strength (H) derived from the number of trial times the two motivational variables of drive

(D) and incentive motivation (K) added together. Incentive functions as an anticipated reinforcer.

Because drive (D) and incentive motivation (K) are motivational variables, Spence emerged with not just a learning theory but a theory of behavior also. D is the primary motivation, a drive, a need, or an emotion. Spence, the neobehaviorist, is an S-R associationist who sees the strength of habit level as the number of instances joining a response to its stimulus. Reward, rather than being linked to habit, is tied to incentive motivation (K). His views, delivered as the Silliman Lectures at Yale University, were published as *Behavior Theory and Conditioning* in 1956.

John Dollard (1900-   ) and Neal E. Miller (1909-   ): Social Learning Theory. At the Institute of Human Relations, Yale University, John Dollard and Neal E. Miller advanced a drive-response-cue-reward theory of learning, articulated in two major books: *Social Learning and Imitation* (1941), which was dedicated to Hull and William F. Ogburn, and *Personality and Psychotherapy* (1950), dedicated to Pavlov and Freud. For their social learning theory Miller and Dollard drew upon the ideas of the men to whom the books were dedicated, thus theirs is a synthetic psychology, amalgamating the behavior theory of Hull, the psychoanalysis of Freud, and culture theory from sociologists such as Ogburn. Behavior is viewed as being produced from a combination of psychological principles and social conditions. For example, neurosis results from social learning. Essentially drive-reduction theorists, Dollard and Miller view reinforcement as a reduction of drive-strength so that with the absence of a drive, stimulation would be at a zero level of strength; at which level no reinforcement (and therefore no learning) is possible. Fear too can function as drive, but in the case of fear (an aversive drive) reinforcement would be its reduction. Culture enters this theory as a secondary drive, for secondary drives are culturally learned through personal experiences. Whereas drives stimulate behavior, learning is that mode of behavior that most effectively serves to reduce the strength of drive. While the principles of learning are provided by psychology, social sciences prescribe the conditions of learning. The four factors of learning include: (1) drive (motivation), (2) response (drive impels subjects to respond), (3) cues (tips or random behavior leading toward one's goal), and (4) reward (satisfaction).

> The drive impels responses, which are usually also determined by cues from other stimuli not strong enough to act as drives but more specifically distinctive than the drive. If the first response is not rewarded by an event reducing the drive, this response tends to drop out and others to appear. The extinction of successive nonrewarded responses produces so-called random behavior. If some one response is followed by reward, the connection between the cue and this response is strengthened, so that the next time that the same drive and other cues are present, this response is more likely to occur. This strengthening of the cue-response connection is the essence of learning (Miller & Dollard, 1941, p. 17).

What Miller (1959) sought to accomplish was the liberalization of the basic S-R concepts so as to extend them to account for conflict behavior, motivation, and social learning. His postulates treating conflict behavior follow:

1. The tendency to approach a goal is stronger the nearer the subject is to it.
2. The tendency to avoid a feared stimulus is stronger the nearer the subject is to it.
3. The strength of avoidance increases more rapidly with nearness than does that of approach.
4. The strength of tendencies to approach or avoid varies directly with the strength of the drive upon which they are based.
5. Below the asymptote of learning, increasing the number of reinforced trials will increase the strength of the response tendency that is reinforced.
6. When two incompatible responses are in conflict, the stronger one will occur (pp. 205-6).

Over the years Miller (1972) carried extensions of his S-R theory so as even to include the control of blood pressure within the scope of his learning theory.

Dollard, a University of Chicago Ph.D. (1931), was already at Yale's Institute of Human Relations when Miller arrived there for his Ph.D. studies, receiving his degree in 1935. While Dollard remained with Yale, Miller left in 1966 for Rockefeller University.

O. Hobart Mowrer (1907-   ): Two-Factor Learning Theory. A Johns Hopkins Ph.D. (1932), O(rval) Hobart Mowrer (1907-   ) became affiliated with Yale's Institute of Human Relations in 1934, where he remained until the middle of World War II. Known for his two-factor theory of learning that he offered in 1947, Mowrer cited the two different processes of learning as (1) solution learning and (2) sign learning. The first is Thorndike's law of effect that Hull elaborated upon, and the second is Pavlov's classical conditioning or associative learning. The first has learning contingent upon reward or reinforcement and the second is learned by association or contiguity (Guthrie). Mowrer's two-factor theory differed from Thorndike's law of effect

in holding that punishment, rather than directly weakening or "stamping-out" a neural connection, or "bond," achieves its action by causing fear to become conditioned to response-correlated stimuli, so that when the organism subsequently starts to repeat the punished response, fear is aroused, which causes conflict and response inhibition, or at least modification (1956, p. 128).

By the mid-fifties Mowrer revised his two-factor theory in order to account adequately for avoidance behavior which entails both sign learning and solution learning.

Habit formation is likewise dependent upon feedback, just as punishment is. If fear becomes conditioned to stimuli which are associated with a response that has been followed by punishment (drive increment), then *hope* (secondary reinforcement) becomes likewise connected to stimuli which are associated with a response that has been followed by reward (drive decrement). "Positive" feedback, rather than motive-behavior "bond," is thus hypothesized as the essence of habit (1956, p. 128).

By the end of that decade Mowrer (1960) was talking about a third version of the two-factor theory, being two factored because of the two types of reinforcement involved: (1) incremental (punishment) and (2) decremental (reward). While all learning is conditioning, the drives are dual (incremental and decremental).

The second version of two-factor theory was "two-factored" in two different ways: it distinguished between sign learning and solution learning *and* between incremental reinforcement and decremental reinforcement, sign learning being associated, presumably, with incremental reinforcement and solution learning with decremental reinforcement. Now the present version of the theory is two-factored in only *one* way: namely, with respect to the *two types of reinforcement,* incremental and decremental. With respect to the other principle of classification employed in the second version, the theory is now decidedly one-factored; that is, it assumes that all learning is sign learning and that solution learning (as well as response inhibition) is a derivative thereof (1960, pp. 256-7).

Thus the new version is one-factored with respect to types of learning, but two-factored concerning types of reinforcement. Currently Mowrer is a research professor of psychology at the University of Illinois, a position he assumed in 1948.

The Institute of Human Relations at Yale University was at its peak of influence in the latter 1930s and the early forties when such notables as Hull, Dollard, Miller, Doob, Mowrer, Spence, Sears, Hilgard, Marquis, Hovland, and other notables graced its halls. But psychology at Yale had a resurgence with social psychology in the forefront, a social psychology undergirded with learning theory as its support and point of orientation. Social psychology at Yale became primarily interested in communications and propaganda, with the Yale Communication Program getting underway spearheaded by Carl I. Hovland.

(C)   YALE COMMUNICATION RESEARCH PROGRAM: *Hovland; Janis; Kelley; McGuire*

It was money from the Rockefeller family that helped launch Yale's Institute, and financial support from the Rockefeller Foundation aided the Yale Communication Research Program. The *tour de force* in this program was *Carl I. Hovland* (1912-1961), its director. Hovland shared as a collaborator with Hull and others in the publication of the *Mathematico-Deductive Theory of Rote Learning* (1940) and was well intrenched in learning theory, being in the environment of the Yale Institute of Human Relations. On receiving his Ph.D. from Yale in 1936, he remained as instructor, and in less than a decade he became full professor and department chairman.

In 1942 he became interested in social psychology, deeply involved in research on the effects of social communication, which he pursued until his life was claimed by cancer even before he was fifty. Hovland is credited with carrying experimental psychology into the field of social communication, interpreting social psychological phenomena in the light of the learning theory that he was nurtured on at the Institute of Human Relations. With his colleagues, he accounted for the facts of social psychology in terms of the instrumental learning model, couched in terms of the learning theory of Hull, Miller, and Dollard. Attitudes or opinions are explained as habitual owing to their positive reinforcement value or incentive value (anticipatory reinforcement value). The Yale communication group sought the formulation of socio-psychological laws governing human behavior, especially those responsible for the strengthening and weakening of habits. Such laws provided the grounds on which to explain phenomena of social psychology, e.g., the displacement of hostility, propaganda, attitude change, and other concerns of social psychology.

Wartime Studies on Mass Communication. Interest in research on mass communication deepened when Hovland took a leave of absence from his duties at Yale in 1942 and undertook problems of a social psychological nature for the United States War Department. As chief psychologist in charge of directing experimental studies and research, Hovland devoted four years to investigating factors in the social psychology of military morale. The research branch of the information and education division of the War Department that experimental studies fell under was headed by Director of Professional Staff, Samuel Stouffer, the sociologist, who was Hovland's superior. A number of volumes by Stouffer and his colleagues (1950), containing the findings of Hovland's research, were published in the *American Soldier* series. The principal responsibility assigned to Hovland was an investigation of what influences the motivation of fighting men in the United States armed services. To assist him Hovland chose a half dozen graduate students of psychology: *Iriving L. Janis* (1918-   ), currently at Yale continuing the work started by Hovland; *Nathan Maccoby* (1912-   ), who is continuing communications research at Stanford University; *M. Brewster Smith* (1919-   ), currently Vice-Chancellor of Social Sciences at the University of California, Santa Cruz; *John L. Finan* (1911-   ), who is presently a consultant specializing in motivation and crisis theory; *Arthur A. Lumsdaine* (1913-   ), who currently chairs the department of psychology at the University of Washington; and *Fred D. Sheffield* (1914-   ), who is still involved in learning theory at Yale. Notwithstanding the military atmosphere in which these investigations were undertaken, they provided remarkable advances in the field of social psychology.

Seeking to investigate social psychological phenomena in a living situation, Hovland (1949) structured hypotheses relevant to the effectiveness of mass communication. Patterning this research after that of his earlier experience at Yale, Hovland became a distinguished pioneer in communications psychology, entailing the psychology of influence and attitude change. His wartime research provided the material for his (with Lumsdaine and Sheffield) *Experiments on Mass Communication* (1949), published in volume two of *Studies in Social Psychology in World War II* (Stouffer *et al.*), that the Social Science Research Council sponsored in conjunction with the War Department.

The Yale Communication and Attitude Change Program. From 1942 to 1945 Hovland served as Director of Experimental Studies at the Office of the Chief of Staff of the War Department. When he returned to Yale in the mid-forties he brought with him the wealth of information gathered in these wartime investigations and carried them further, especially through the decade of the 1950s with the assistance of Janis, Sheffield, Lumsdaine, and some new colleagues, including *Harold H. Kelley* (1921-   ), *William J. McGuire* (1925-   ), *Milton J.*

Rosenberg (1925-   ), *Robert P. Abelson* (1928-   ), *Muzafer Sherif* (1906-   ), *Jack W. Brehm* (1928-   ), and *Arthur R. Cohen* (1927-1963), all serving on the faculty at Yale under Hovland and researching in social psychology.

From time to time Hovland and his associates issued reports from the Yale Communication and Attitude Change Program which followed through with investigations initiated with the Research Branch, Information and Education Division, United States Army. The first, *Experiments on Mass Communication* (1949), dealt with the effects of presenting one side of the question (propaganda or opinion) as against offering individuals both sides of an issue in attempting to alter their opinions on a controversial issue. To the question: When the weight of evidence supports the main thesis being presented, is it more effective to present only the materials supporting the point being made, or is it better to introduce also the arguments of those opposed to the point being made? the researchers found that

> presenting the arguments on both sides of an issue was found to be more effective than giving only the arguments supporting the point being made, in the case of individuals who were *initially opposed* to the point of view being presented (1949, pp. 224-5).

However, for those individuals already favoring the viewpoint propagandized, arguments supporting both sides prove less effective. With educated persons it proved advisable to present both sides of the issue, but with the less educated exposure only to the side advocated (with which they already shared an opinion) was advisable. Propaganda information (containing data supporting both sides of an issue) proved least effective with the poorly educated who already shared the viewpoint being advocated.

In the second continuing report *(Communication and Persuasion)* issued in 1953, Hovland and his Yale group reported further findings on their investigations on how opinions and beliefs are actually modified by persuasive communications. With respect to the source or person (communicator) from whom the information is derived, it was found that "communications attributed to low credibility sources tended to be considered more biased and unfair in presentation than identical ones attributed to high credibility sources" (1953, p. 269). Consequently it is advisable to convey information through individuals who are esteemed for their credibility. A greater immediate effect is exerted upon the opinions of individuals by sources regarded as credible than from low credibility sources. However, after a period of several weeks, the effect (either positive from sources of high credibility or negative from low credibility sources) had a tendency to disappear.

From the standpoint of the communication itself, it was found effective to appeal to fear, but it must be followed up with providing reassurance for alleviating the emotional tension aroused. Group norms also proved incentives for either acceptance or rejection of opinions presented. The two-sided version (pro and con) was more effective in producing a sustained opinion change than offering only one side of the issue. It seemed to *inoculate* the individual against succumbing to an opposing view should he encounter one later. Later McGuire (with Demetrios Papageorgis) continued research on this matter, developing it into an inoculation theory, believing that individuals can be immunized against an opposing view by "pre-exposure to counterarguments (in a weakened form that stimulates, without overcoming, the receiver's defenses)" (1961, p. 336).

With respect to the individuals at whom the propaganda is directed, i.e., the people who are the target of opinion change, it was found that "persons who are most strongly motivated to retain their membership in a group will be most resistant to communications contrary to the standards of that group" (1953, p. 277). Susceptibility to persuasion is also contingent upon a person's level of intelligence. Those with low self-esteem have a predisposition toward being highly influenced by persuasive propaganda (communication), and yet there is a resistancy to persuasive communication by individuals with neurotic symptoms.

Response factors also played a part with respect to active participation and to the duration of effects. Role playing, referred to as the improvisation hypothesis (such as participating in a debate supporting a given conclusion), heightens the effectiveness of the persuasive communication. While wide variability was found with respect to the duration of effects of persuasive communication, an interesting phenomenon was uncovered, termed the *sleeper effect*. Hovland and Weiss (1951) found that although individuals initially tend to resist information provided by a source of low credibility, with the lapse of time they fail to associate the data received with the source that provided it, hence tend toward favorable attitudes respecting the communication. When individuals are reminded of the source, they revert to their negative attitudes.

In 1957 Hovland and his colleagues produced a volume on *The Order of Presentation in Persuasion* treating the effects of communications on opinions and attitudes when they are presented in different sequences. It was found that neither *primacy* (the side presented first) nor *recency* (the opposing side presented second) in a controversial issue necessarily had the advantage. A second finding was: "If, after hearing only one side of a controversial issue, a response is made which publicly indicates one's position on the issue, the effectiveness of a subsequent presentation of the second side of the issue is reduced, thus entailing a primacy effect" (1957, p. 131). However, the mere anonymous mentioning of one's opinion on a questionnaire following exposure to only one side of a controversial issue has no significant effect on reducing the potency of the second side. If one and the same person presents two sides of an issue in a single communication, the tendency is for the side presented first to leave the greater impression. Other findings were:

The primacy effect found in presenting contradictory information in the same communication was reduced by interpolating other activities between the two blocks of information and by warning the subjects against the fallibility of first impressions. . . .

Presentation of information relevant to the satisfaction of needs after these needs have been aroused brings about greater acceptance than an order which presents the information first and the need-arousal second. . . .

Order of presentation is a more significant factor in influencing opinion for subjects with relatively weak desire for understanding, than for those with "high cognitive need". . . .

Placing communications highly desirable to the recipient first, followed by those less desirable, produces more opinion change than the reverse order. . . .

When an authoritative communicator plans to mention pro arguments and also nonsalient con arguments, the pro-first order is superior to the con-first order (1957, pp. 134-7).

Two years later the Yale group published a volume on *Personality and Persuasibility* (Janis et al., 1959) treating "general persuasibility," that is "a person's readiness to accept social influence from others irrespective of what he knows about the communicator or what it is that the communicator is advocating" (1959, p. v). The researchers found evidence of persuasibility as a personality trait in some individuals. They were able to score persons with respect to their susceptibility to persuasiveness.

Hovland's final report appeared posthumously the year he died. The study, *Social Judgment: Assimilation and Contrast Effects in Communication and Attitude Change* (Sherif & Hovland, 1961), dealt with judgmental factors which underlie attitude change. From 1947 to 1949 Sherif was Research Fellow at Yale. When he left Yale for the University of Oklahoma, his work continued with grants from the Yale Communication and Attitude Change Program. Hovland and Sherif concluded that "an individual confronted with a series of stimuli tends to form a psychological scale for judgment, even when the stimulus series is not well graded and when explicit standards for judgment are lacking" (1961, p. 177). Many of the findings relate to Sherif's earlier work on the psychology of social norms.

Charge of research work at Yale passed at Hovland's death to Janis whose attention in the 1970s led him to the *groupthink hypothesis*. Discussing his views in *Victims of Groupthink: A Psychological Study of Foreign-Policy Decisions and Fiascoes*, Janis defined groupthink as "a quick and easy way to refer to a mode of thinking that people engage in when they are deeply involved in a cohesive in-group, when the members' strivings for unanimity override their motivation to realistically appraise alternative courses of action" (1972, p. 9). He added that "members of any small cohesive group tend to maintain esprit de corps by unconsciously developing a number of shared illusions and related norms that interfere with critical thinking and reality testing" (1972, p. 36). Thus it is vital for intelligent living that persons be fully aware of shared illusions so as not to become victimized by the groupthink predicament.

CHAPTER 15

Functionalism at Columbia:
Cattell and His Successors

The Columbia University that Cattell knew when he first arrived in 1891 was a small school with roughly 2,000 students, but by the time Thorndike graduated in 1898 it had approximately doubled in size under its then President Seth Low. While the make-up of its trustees had a Yale-conservatism about it, Columbia was considered on the "libertine-side" by other Ivy League college graduates, one reason being that its professors were readily visible in the smart restaurants of Manhattan. Partly in consequence of this, the feeling grew that undergraduates should be moved away from the Madison Avenue campus.

In competition with other universities, Columbia emphasized its graduate programs, adding two new graduate divisions in 1890 and 1892, Philosophy and Science. Political Science had already been in existence. Thus the college had now become a university. Although the psychology department profited much in this new development, it remained a small department with three men in 1907: J. McKeen Cattell, Robert S. Woodworth, and Albert Theodore Poffenberger. Notwithstanding that it was not until the first World War that the university began producing Ph.D.s in abundance, the psychology department was considered an important center for research. By 1917 fifty Ph.D.s in psychology were granted to individuals studying under Cattell. When Cattell founded the psychological laboratory at Columbia in 1890, the Madison Avenue campus had a number of private dwellings that it occupied across Forty-ninth Street. It was into one on Forty-fifth Street that he moved his psychological laboratory, the one occupied by President Low. Cattell's laboratory was located on the top floor and an electrical laboratory in the basement.

By the time Thorndike arrived at Columbia in 1897, the university moved from downtown Manhattan to Morningside Heights into a half dozen new buildings. Psychology always had a favored place at Columbia so that when Schermerhorn Hall, one of the new buildings, was opened psychology occupied nine of the rooms. The department's potency was so established that when President Nicholas Murray Butler in 1911 decided to share some of its space with the department of botany, Cattell fought back claiming that psychology was the largest and strongest department at Columbia, and consequently should retain its primacy.

Friction among psychologists and philosophers was negligible. Woodworth observed that

> during these years there was no more than a minimum of hostility between the philosophers and psychologists and a minimum of resistance was offered to the independent development of psychology. The philosophers never sought to control the affairs of the laboratory, its teaching or research. Cattell was for some years (1902-05) the

executive head of the joint department and was instrumental in calling to Columbia such eminent philosophers as Dewey and Montague (1942, p. 2).

Whereas in the early years of Columbia, the senior professor headed the department, the trustees of the university often appointed another departmental member as the executive head. Cattell headed the department from 1891 to 1912, followed by Woodworth (1912-1926), who was succeeded by Poffenberger (1926-1941), Garrett being his successor.

Functional psychology at Columbia differed from other American universities chiefly in its concern in attributing to data meaning and use in its broadest sense rather than accumulating data for the sake of data. Thus applied psychology is functional psychology. A 1924 graduate of Columbia who earned her Ph.D in psychology under Woodworth, *Edna Frances Heidbreder* (1890-   ), described the character of psychology at Columbia accordingly:

> A graduate student in psychology cannot spend many weeks at Columbia without becoming aware of the immense importance in that atmosphere of curves of distribution, of individual differences, of the measurement of intelligence and other human capacities, of experimental procedures and statistical devices, and of the undercurrent of physiological thought. He discovers immediately that psychology does not lead a sheltered life; that it rubs elbows with biology, statistics, education, commerce, industry, and the world of affairs. . . . The separate strands of teaching are not knit together for him into a firm and patterned fabric. No one cares how he arranges the threads that are placed in his hands; certainly there is no model which he is urged to copy (1933, pp. 191-2).

The atmosphere of individual differences, the measurement of intelligence and other human capacities, were brought to Columbia by Cattell. Even the character of his seminars differed from most of those with which the average graduate student of today is familiar. "Cattell's seminar," remarked Woodworth, "well remembered by the older alumni, was an occasion for presenting one's research work for the criticism of staff and fellow students; and such the Seminar has remained ever since" (1942, p. 7). Some students regarded it as a waste of time to listen to a mere student's report. Attempts to avoid the seminar were countered with the seminar being mandatory, but that practice changed to one of restricting it to students working on research problems.

(A) JAMES McKEEN CATTELL (1860-1944): THE FOUNDING OF COLUMBIA'S PSYCHOLOGY DEPARTMENT

In 1890 the Faculty of Philosophy was founded at the Graduate School of Columbia University, followed two years later by the Faculty of Pure Science. It was as part of the former faculty that psychology was nutured until 1947 when it became affiliated with the Faculty of Pure Science. Psychology found its way into Columbia in 1881 with the appointment of Archibald Alexander as Professor of Philosophy, Ethics, and Psychology. The first Ph.D. from this confluence of studies was granted in 1884 to Nicholas Murray Butler (1862-1947), who joined the Columbia philosophy faculty in 1890 and for almost the first half of the twentieth century was its president. The year 1881 marks the date that mental philosophy yielded to psychology (and moral philosophy to ethics).

Comparable to the German universities, the faculty at Columbia did not begin with departments but with chairs and courses so that in the case of psychology it was yoked with the faculty of philosophy and ethics. It was in 1891, however, that a chair was established in experimental psychology which was occupied by *James McKeen Cattell* (1860-1944), who had been at Columbia for a year as lecturer but now had a separate department for experimental psychology. In 1890 Cattell left Pennsylvania for Columbia as Lecturer in Experimental Psychology, becoming professor in 1891. Cattell, a second generation American psychologist, was a Leipzig Ph.D. (1886), who studied under Wundt and also under Hall at Johns Hopkins previous to going to the University of Leipzig where he approached Wundt declaring: "Herr Professor, you need an assistant and I shall be yours" (1928, p. 545). Thus for his last year at Leipzig he became Wundt's laboratory assistant, the first such appointment anywhere in the world. Prior to coming to Columbia, Cattell was at the University of Pennsylvania where he served as the world's first professor of psychology, whereas up to this time a person teaching psychology was a member of a department other than psychology, that is, psychology was an ancillary discipline yoked to another department. Here he not only founded a laboratory of psychology in 1889, but laboratory courses for students were offered for the first time in psychology proper, whereas the laboratories at Johns Hopkins (Hall's laboratory of psychology) and at Leipzig were research laboratories in which psychology was not the only subject treated by the professor.

During Cattell's tenure at Columbia from 1891 to 1917, included among the fifty persons earning their doctorates under him were E. L. Thorndike, an 1898 graduate; Robert S. Woodworth, who graduated a year later; Harry L. Hollingworth, a 1909 graduate; Edward Kellogg Strong, the industrial psychologist who graduated in 1911; Albert T. Poffenberger, a 1912 graduate who became Woodworth's successor at Columbia; John Frederick Dashiell, a 1913 graduate; the statistician Truman Lee Kelley of the class of 1914; and the educational psychologist Arthur I. Gates of the final class in 1917.

Cattell, who coined the term "mental tests," established (with James Mark Baldwin of Princeton University) the *Psychological Review* in 1894, America's second journal of psychology. Thus began his long career of producing journals, including *Science* in 1894 (which had suspended publication); *Popular Science Monthly* (acquired in 1900), which he renamed *Scientific Monthly; School and Society* (in 1915); and in 1923 he established the Science Press Printing Company for the publication of scientific journals and books, such as: *American Men of Science, Directory of American Scholars,* and *Leaders in Education;* as well as founding the Psychological Corporation in 1921 which provided the public and industry with psychological services. His unhappy severance from Columbia arose from his pacifistic position during World War I, resulting in his discharge on grounds of disloyalty to country.

Note that Cattell's contributions are to a movement, to an organization in psychology, rather than to founding a school, for he neither developed a system nor did he author a textbook in psychology. He did, on the other hand, participate in the founding of the American Psychological Association in 1892 (its president in 1895), and represented American psychologists by presiding over the Ninth International Congress of Psychology when it was held in 1929 at New Haven. Unlike the first generation psychologists (James, Hall, and Ladd), each of whom merely founded laboratories of psychology at their respective universities, Cattell was the only one who was engaged in experimental work, hence the only experimental psychologist among them.

Cattell's Capacity Psychology

During the 1890s in the United States, Cattell was the motivating force in the psychology of mental testing. He broke with Wundt's introspectionism, by promoting objective psychology, which became noticeable in his investigations of individual differences in reaction time, for such experiments on the capacities of individuals could be conducted without resorting to introspection. This fact also led him to his studies on reading in which his experiments indicated that the eyes, with grasshopper like juhps, leap during reading, words being perceptible during those moments when the eyes are at rest.

When Cattell introduced the objective study of individual differences into his experimental research at Leipzig's Laboratory of Psychology, Wundt pronounced it as *ganz Amerikanisch* (typically American). Rather than abandoning this approach, he carried it into his laboratory at Columbia University, having been reinforced by Galtonian methods during his contact with Galton in England when he lectured for a year at the University of Cambridge. Cattell's interest was testing a subject by measuring his separate capacities individually rather than lumping them together in the form of general intelligence as Binet did or the general factor (G) in intelligence as opposed to individual or specific factors as was the case with the British psychologist Charles Spearman. He was wroth with his students who presented a perfect experiment and did not adequately account for probable error, so much so that Titchener called "Probable Error" Cattell's god, and his student Woodworth commented that Cattell "was skeptical of any result that did not come out with a small 'probable error'" (1930, p. 369).

Declaring that "psychology is what good psychologists do," Cattell encouraged psychologists to venture wherever their minds dictated. Even his students were expected to rely on their own resources rather than expecting to be "spoonfed" by lectures, consequently his classes had the overtones of an oral examination for the doctorate. His contributions to psychology were those arising from the laboratory, including experiments on reaction time, association, mental abilities, psychophysics, individual differences, order of merit (ranking method), and perception in reading.

Reaction Time Experiments. Cattell's work on reaction time was under way as early as his student years at Johns Hopkins under Hall, when he and others assisted

Hall in setting up that university's laboratory of psychology at a private house adjacent to the university. The investigations were carried with him to Leipzig and became the basis of his doctoral dissertation under Wundt. Defining reaction time, Cattell explained: ''If one lifts one's hand as soon as possible after the sudden appearance of a light, the interval between the application of the stimulus and the beginning of the muscular contraction is a reaction time'' (1885, p. 512). Reaction time was introduced by Cattell to Wundt, for it was unknown to the Leipzig laboratory.

However, significant contributions to the field were made by Cattell who established that the time required for the reading of a short word and a single letter was comparable, lending support to the pedagogical technique of teaching children whole words rather than single letters. Though his research at Leipzig pivoted about time, he did not limit himself to reaction time, reserving reaction time technique for the more important research and for his later Columbia students.

Psychophysics. Not long after leaving Leipzig, Cattell experimented with psychophysics, but not in the traditional manner of the measurement of consciousness. Interested in objectivity and an operational approach, he conceived psychophysics as the investigation of the accuracy of observation conducted under varied conditions. He found that fusing reaction time and psychophysics produced a novel psychophysical method, i.e., the discrimination time method for indicating differences between qualities or magnitudes so that as the effective difference is increased, the more quickly one discriminates.

Mental Tests and Measurements. When Cattell returned to the United States from Leipzig with his newly won Ph.D., he came via Cambridge, England. In 1888 he returned briefly to lecture at the University of Cambridge as a Fellow Commoner at St. John's where he conducted experiments at Clerk Maxwell's laboratory (physics). In England Cattell became personally acquainted with Francis Galton, working in Galton's Anthropometric Laboratory in London, and regarding him as ''the greatest man whom I have known.'' Association with Galton confirmed his conviction that individual differences are measurable; consequently he set out to do so, publishing his views in 1890 in the British journal, *Mind,* in which he coined the term ''mental tests.'' He explained his objective:

> Psychology cannot attain the certainty and exactness of the physical sciences, unless it rests on a foundation of experiment and measurement. A step in this direction could be made by applying a series of mental tests and measurements to a large number of individuals. The results would be of considerable scientific value in discovering the constancy of mental processes, their interdependence, and their variation under different circumstances (1890, p. 373).

Ten tests, accumulated while he was at the University of Pennsylvania, were as follows:
1. Dynamometer pressure
2. Rate of movement
3. Sensation-areas
4. Pressure causing pain
5. Least noticeable difference in weight

6. Reaction-time for sound
7. Time for naming colors
8. Bi-section of a 50 cm. line
9. Judgment of 10 seconds time
10. Number of letters remembered on once hearing

While he was at Columbia, his list became more extensive, and the study contributed significantly to psychological development in respect to the method of correlation.

Order of Merit or Ranking Method. Mental tests, reaction time experiments, and psychophysics were the principal interests of Cattell in his early career along with a lesser interest in errors of observation. A later important contribution was the order of merit or the ranking method that was utilized in psychophysics and in value judgments. He asked subjects to arrange 200 varying shades of grey from the darkest black to the brightest white. The same technique was employed to rank American men of science, such as psychologists rating other psychologists, the average being the norm. At seven year intervals repetition of the research would shed light on interesting trends and changes in value judgments.

(B) CATTELL'S LUMINARIES AT COLUMBIA: THORNDIKE AND WOODWORTH

Just prior to the turn of the century, Cattell's two most distinguished students received their Ph.D.s, *Edward Lee Thorndike* (1874-1949) in 1898, and *Robert Sessions Woodworth* (1869-1962) the following year.

EDWARD LEE THORNDIKE (1874-1949): Connectionism

Thorndike was introduced to psychology in his junior year of undergraduate study at Wesleyan University (1893-1894), but his interest in the subject was fired when he read James' *Principles of Psychology* as a candidate for a prize. The Williamsburg, Massachusetts-born Thorndike left for graduate school at Harvard where he pursued the Ph.D. under James (Münsterberg was in Germany), but remained long enough only to acquire a master's degree. When James was refused space in Agassiz Museum for Thorndike to experiment with his chickens, Thorndike (at the courtesy of James) repaired to the cellar of James' home for his laboratory.

Thorndike left for Columbia owing to financial reasons. At Harvard he earned his way by tutoring a boy, but at Columbia a fellowship was in the offing, as well as Cattell's permission to pursue the Ph.D. on the mental life of animals. Consequently Thorndike, leaving for New York with his "two most educated chickens" in a basket, continued his research in the attic of Schermerhorn Hall at Columbia. The results of his research encompassed more than a Ph.D.; in 1898, they produced his dissertation which was a classic in psychology, *Animal Intelligence: An Experimental Study of the Associative Processes in Animals,* the same year, and in book form in 1911. With the exception of a year at Western Reserve University, Thorndike's career was spent at Teachers College, Columbia University where he became an institution. Though suspect owing to his dealing with animals, he was nevertheless appointed by Dean Russell because the dean was "satisfied that he was worth trying out on humans." It was at the young age of 25 that Thorndike joined Teachers College, rising to full professor and head of the Department of Educational Psychology within five years.

Animal Intelligence

Thorndike initially chose "Association in Animals" as the title of his thesis, reminiscent of British association psychology, but prior to submitting his dissertation he retitled it *Animal Intelligence*. Adaptive changes in animal behavior he regarded as "learning," i.e., the formation and reinforcement of associations that served to strengthen bonds of association. These associations came to be termed *connections, bonds,* and his system *connectionism,* a neo-associationism in the tradition of the British. He was greatly influenced by James and Hall. Notwithstanding James' version of associationism, Thorndike's was markedly more mechanical as well as being deterministic—an abhorrent thought for the free-willist James. The associationism found in Thorndike is closer to the tradition of Darwinism in which only quantitative differences rather than differences in kind distinguish man from animal, the human being just another mammalian form. Human and animal learning or behavior are alike despite man's higher mental processes, for qualitative distinctions do not exist. Also exerting influence on Thorndike was Galton, who laid great stress on heredity while refuting environmental explanations of behavior. Individual differences he treated as quantitative and innate (in preference to their being qualitative), accounting for differences by amount and complexity. Achievement and success he explained in terms of inherited qualities such as native intelligence and individual differences.

Only twenty-four years of age when the classic *Animal Intelligence* was first published in 1898, Thorndike, who was the first to advance a systematic investigation of animal intelligence from experiments arising out of a laboratory of psychology, had developed a learning theory in which animal behavior is accounted for by the "stamping in" (and "stamping out") of neural connections of a response to stimulus rather than cognition entailing the association of ideas. Learning is a matter of certain bonds being fixed and strengthened while others are weakened or eliminated, resulting in behavior formation. The mind is a connected system of physiological and biological cells capable of forming bonds between stimuli (situations).

Two Laws of Learning: Exercise and Effect. By 1911, Thorndike, convinced that behavior is predictable, formulated two major behavioral laws. He held that like situations will produce like responses in the same organism, and "that *if the same situation produces on two occasions two different responses, the animal must have changed*" (1911, p. 241). Thus he held that the same cause produces the same effect. The two principal laws: (1) the law of effect, and (2) the law of exercise are formulated by him accordingly:

> The Law of Effect is that: *Of several responses made to the same situation, those which are accompanied or closely followed by satisfaction to the animal will, other things being equal, be more firmly connected with the situation, so that, when it recurs, they will be*

more likely to recur; those which are accompanied or closely followed by discomfort to the animal will, other things being equal, have their connections with that situation weakened, so that, when it recurs, they will be less likely to occur. The greater the satisfaction or discomfort, the greater the strengthening or weakening of the bond.

The Law of Exercise is that: *Any response to a situation will, other things being equal, be more strongly connected with the situation in proportion to the number of times it has been connected with that situation and to the average vigor and duration of the connections* (1911, p. 244).

While the first law states that satisfying experiences tend to be retained and annoying ones eliminated, the second holds that the more frequent, recent, and vigorous bond exercised is the one most effectively stamped in the organism. Thus learning is not mental or ideational but mechanistic, a response to a stimulus. His two laws served as explanatory of the connection process, a learning process in which connections are formed between situations (stimuli) so that a person's feelings, wants, knowledge, and behavior are grounded on the connections established between stimuli.

Satisfiers and Annoyers. The effectualness of the law of effect is contingent on satisfying or unsatisfying consequences, and in turn the satisfying tend to be repeated.

The original basis of the wants which so truly do and should rule the world is the original satisfyingness of some states of affairs and annoyingness of others. Out of such original satisfiers and annoyers grow all desires and aversions; and in such are found the first guides of learning.

By a satisfying state of affairs is meant roughly one which the animal does nothing to avoid, often doing such things as attain to preserve it. By an annoying state of affairs is meant roughly one which the animal avoids or changes (1913, vol. 2, p. 123).

"Satisfying" is not to be equated with sensory pleasure nor is "annoy" equivalent to pain, pain being merely one of a number of annoyers—nor does it necessarily annoy inevitably.

Belongingness. Though Thorndike's experiments were limited to animals, he extended his theory to account for human intelligence as well. With time he acknowledged diverse dimensions and types of intelligence as well as a principle he termed "belongingness," i.e., one learns more readily when things are viewed as connected or as seeming "to go together."

Certain responses become connected with certain situations because of sequence in time, provided the response is treated by the mind (or brain) as "belonging" to the situation and provided the connection of the two has a certain acceptableness or freedom from disfavor (1931, p. 101).

Hence the law of exercise is insufficient, belongingness must be present. During the 1930s Thorndike repealed his law of exercise remarking that "if a certain state of affairs acts upon a man a thousand times a week for a year, he will, so far as the mere repetition of that state of affairs is concerned, probably respond no better the last week than the first" (1932a, pp. 62-3). He also modified his law of effect saying that "rewarding a connection always strengthened it substantially; punishing it weakened it little or not at all" (1932b, p. 311).

Spread or Scatter of Effect (Reward). Also in the 1930s Thorndike was led to the scatter of effect in which rewards are diffused, according benefit to proximate responses found in the immediate vicinity of the correct one. For example, it was found that when incorrect responses were made they were the ones nearest to those that were correct.

> The punished connections do not behave alike, but that the ones that are nearest to a reward are strengthened most. The strengthening influence of a reward spreads to influence positively not only the connection which it directly follows and to which it may be said to belong, but also any connections which are near enough to it (1933, p. 174).

Transfer of Training. Not only were Thorndike and Woodworth colleagues pursuing their Ph.D.s together at Columbia and teaching at the same university (except that Thorndike was at Teachers College while Woodworth was at Columbia proper), the two collaborated in 1901 (just two to three years after graduation) on an important paper dealing with the "transfer of training." They titled it "The Influence of Improvement in One Mental Function upon the Efficiency of Other Functions."

Transfer occurs when elements in one function learned are identical to those necessary in another function that is to be learned. Finding an inconsistency in carry-over from learning one function to utilizing that training for the performance of another function, they found that:

> Improvement in any single mental function need not improve the ability in functions commonly called by the same name. It may injure it.
>
> Improvement in any single mental function rarely brings about equal improvement in any other function, no matter how similar, for the working of every mental function-group is conditioned by the nature of the data in each particular case. . . .
>
> The loss in the efficiency of a function trained with certain data, as we pass to data more and more unlike the first, makes it fair to infer that there is always a point where the loss is complete. . . .
>
> The general consideration of the cases of retention or of loss practice effect seems to make it likely that spread of practice occurs only where identical elements are concerned in the influencing and influenced function (1901, p. 250).

Consequently training in one subject does not improve the mind so that it can generalize to a training of other subjects, that is, one cannot train the mind in general, for the mind is "on its dynamic side a machine for making particular reactions to particular situations" (1901, p. 249). These findings corroborated Thorndike's learning theory, learning being comprised of changes in specific bonds.

Albert T. Poffenberger (1885-) and Harry L. Hollingworth (1880-1956): Applied Psychology at Columbia

Another Cattell Ph.D., *Albert Theodore Poffenberger* (1885-), graduated from Columbia in 1912. Like many other psychologists from Columbia, Poffenberger entered the field of applied psychology. In 1915 he established that should the second task differ considerably from the first that has been learned then no transfer occurs. However, learned responses that are applicable to the new situation or function result in positive transfer of training, but negative transfer occurs if the new function requires a change in the formation of previously learned habits.

Poffenberger and another Columbia graduate under Cattell, who was Poffenberger's collaborator, *Harry Levi Hollingworth* (1880-1956), were among the first vocational psychologists, applying psychology particularly to advertising. The former published The *Psychology in Advertising* (1925) and *Applied Psychology* (1927), while the latter authored *Vocational Psychology* (1916) and a paper on "The Psychology of Advertising" (1912). Notwithstanding the fillip applied or vocational psychology received from the Columbia graduates during the era of Cattell, nevertheless the posture of the university was not one of applied psychology. Both Poffenberger and Hollingworth remained at Columbia as faculty members following graduation. While the latter was at Teachers College, Columbia University, the former was at the university proper.

Robert S. Woodworth (1869-1962): Dynamic Psychology

Like Thorndike, Robert Sessions Woodworth (1869-1962) was also born in Massachusetts but was Thorndike's senior by half a decade. Also like Thorndike, he attended a nearby college. Whereas Thorndike went to Wesleyan in the adjoining state of Connecticut, Woodworth graduated from Amherst in his native state of Massachusetts. Again like Thorndike, he attended the graduate school at Harvard prior to pursuing his Ph.D. at Columbia under Cattell. Thus both men studied together at Harvard under James, and later at Columbia under Cattell. The similarity continues still further, for both men spent their careers on the faculty at Columbia: Thorndike in educational psychology at Teachers College, and Woodworth at the Department of Psychology. The resemblance can be carried a stage further by pointing out that both were presidents of the American Psychological Association, Thorndike in 1912 and Woodworth in 1914.

Woodworth's influences were Hall, and four men with whom he studied: James, Cattell, Sherrington, and Külpe, spending time in 1912 at Külpe's laboratory in Bonn during a leave of absence from Columbia. Before settling at Columbia from 1903 on, Woodworth was an assistant in physiology at Harvard Medical School (1897-1898) and served as Sherrington's assistant in physiology at the University of Liverpool (1902-1903).

Unlike his mentor, Cattell, Woodworth published a number of textbooks in psychology, beginning with the revision of Ladd's *Elements of Physiological Psychology* (1911), followed by his *Dynamic Psychology* in 1918 which was prepared for his Monday night course, and three years later with his popular *Psychology* (1921), which by 1947 had undergone five editions. A book still in use is his *Contemporary Schools of Psychology* (1931, 3rd ed. 1964) planned for the second semester of his Wednesday night course titled "A Survey of Contemporary Psychology." His *magnum opus, Experimental Psychology* (1938, 1960), grew out of material gleaned in 1910 and put in mimeographed form for his college course in experimental psychology. A decade later the material evolved into the mimeographed *Textbook of Experimental Psychology*, and eventually appeared in print in 1938, revised with Harold Schlosberg in 1954, and again posthumously in 1971 with nineteen participants. His final book, *Dynamics of Behavior* (1958), remained true to his first text on *Dynamic Psychology* by maintaining the same basic viewpoint of a dynamic psychology.

Tenets of Dynamic Psychology

Though Woodworth never founded a school of psychology, he nevertheless did develop a system that he termed dynamic psychology. Dynamic psychology was intended to designate the entire Woodworthian psychology, but because he was interested in his *Dynamic Psychology* (1918) with the *how* and *why* of behavior, it came to signify "a study of motivation almost exclusively and is sometimes further restricted to the 'unconscious springs of human behavior' and the maladjustments resulting from unconscious conflicts" (1958, p. 1). Motivation, an important consideration for Woodworth, was inextricably interwoven with perception, learning, and thinking.

Woodworth and Thorndike shared interests in motivation. Woodworth postulated that an activity when aroused becomes motivating, consequently a mechanism can become a drive, a view anticipatory of Allport's theory of *functional autonomy*. "Any mechanism . . . once it is aroused, is capable of furnishing its own drive and also of lending drive to other connected mechanisms" (1918, p. 67).

Imageless Thought and Voluntary Action. Early interested in voluntary movement (in fact so much so that his doctoral dissertation on *The Accuracy of Voluntary Movement* (1899) dealt with this theme). Woodworth, investigating voluntary action, was led to "imageless thought," concluding that images and sensations were not to be found in actual experiences. On the matter of imageless thought, or as he also referred to it: "nonsensory recall" and "imageless recall," Woodworth concluded:

First, that vague and fleeting images, especially of the kinesthetic sort, are often present without being detected except by very fine introspection, some image being pretty sure to come up every few seconds when we are engaged in silent recall; but second, that images are not present every second of the time, and that at the instant when a non-sensory fact is recalled it is apt to be alone (1921, pp. 374-5).

With respect to the imageless thought controversy, Woodworth allied himself with Külpe's forces.

Functional Approach to Behavior: Woodworth's Behavior Primacy Theory of Motivation. Between the organism and the environment there is an interrelationship that Woodworth referred to as "dealing with the environment." It means that in addition to making muscular responses to received stimuli, the organism utilizes stimuli as indicators and muscles as adaptive movements. "This direction of receptive and motor activity toward the environment is the fundamental tendency of animal and human behavior and . . . it is the all-pervasive primary motivation of behavior" (1958, pp. 124-5). While purposive behavior is goal oriented so that the means adopted are directed to the desired end, incidental behavior is devoid of any aim or goal.

Situation-and-Goal-Set. "Preparatory set" or "preset" is the meaning of situation-and-goal-set in the sense that an organism can be preadjusted to meeting his anticipated demands comparable to an alarm clock that is set to awaken a person at a prescribed time. Preset implies adjustment toward that which is about to occur, accordingly "preparatory set is a state of readiness to receive a stimulus that has not yet arrived or a state of readiness to make a movement" (1958, p. 41; see 1937).

The S-O-R Formula. Rather than accepting the stimulus-response formula, Woodworth introduced an intervening process of the organism (O) that is active between stimulus and response. Consequently response is a function of both the stimulus and organism, hence S-O-R. Thus $R = f(S, O)$. An organism is more than merely responding to a stimulus, it is adjusting to the world around it.

Cognitive Theory of Learning. Developed in consequence of his functional approach to behavior is the cognitive theory of learning according to which a person is learning his environment. Defining behavior as "dealing with the environment," Woodworth spoke of "learning the environment." "Learning a person or thing or place," said Woodworth, "has an unfamiliar, awkward sound, though the awkwardness is gone if we say 'getting acquainted with' instead of 'learning.' No one can deny that getting acquainted with the environment and with the objects in it is a form of learning and should be included in any general investigation of the learning process" (1958, p. 221).

The process of sequence learning he explained, using Pavlov's dog as his example, occurs in two steps: (1) "a readiness for *something* to follow"; (2) "a readiness for meat powder to follow. The investigatory response was a behavioral index of the first step, the advance salivation an index of the second step," (1958, p. 229), the dog learning an environmental sequence of a signal that was followed by food.

(C) GARDNER MURPHY (1895-   ) AND THE THIRD GENERATION COLUMBIA PSYCHOLOGISTS: THE TREND TOWARD SOCIAL PSYCHOLOGY

The third generation of Columbia University psychologists began to appear in the 1920s, the most influential among them being Gardner Murphy (1895-   ), who traveled the same route as did his predecessors Woodworth and Thorndike, i.e., from Harvard's graduate school with a master's degree (1917) to Columbia for a Ph.D. (1923). However, Murphy did not study with the distinguished James at Harvard, for he entered that institution the year Josiah Royce (1855-1916) died and a half dozen years after the death of James. Nevertheless he was able to study under Yerkes, Münsterberg, Langfeld, Holt, and Troland, who were at Harvard during that school year.

It was Woodworth who guided Murphy into Columbia in 1919 where he was to remain for the next twenty-one years, studying and teaching. At Columbia he had

Hollingworth as instructor and the friendship of Poffenberger, Otto Klineberg, Ruth Benedict, Margaret Mead, Robert Lynd, and his wife Helen Lynd, the majority of them being social psychologists who played an influential role in his life.

The Emergence of History of Psychology as a Basic Course. Teaching for Murphy began in 1920 with some "extension courses," one course important to him being History of Modern Psychology, which materialized into a book in 1929 as *An Historical Introduction to Modern Psychology*, the first publication of its type outside of Brett's classic three volume *A History of Psychology* that appeared in 1921. Professor George Sidney Brett, who earned his M.A. at Oxford, was at the time Professor of Philosophy in the University of Toronto. It was only a matter of months before Boring's *A History of Experimental Psychology* was published. These two single-volume works helped entrench History of Psychology as a basic course in the psychology curriculum. Today no self-respecting psychology major would obtain his bachelor's degree without the course. History of Psychology also spawned another closely related course, Systems of Psychology or Systematic Psychology, sometimes offered as History and Systems of Psychology.

The Emergence of Social Psychology as a Science.

Teaching fellowships were exchanged for a bona fide instructorship at Columbia in 1925, and before the decade was over, Murphy found himself deeply preoccupied with Ph.D. dissertations in social psychology. His classmate at the graduate school at Harvard, *Floyd H. Allport* (1890-), was deeply entrenched in social psychology, having published his *Social Psychology* text in 1924. However, Murphy was not satisfied with Allport's behavioristic orientation to social psychology, which showed the influence of Wundt in its individualistic approach together with overtones of Harvard's Münsterberg.

As early as 1924 Murphy was teaching social psychology, a course left vacant by Woodworth, and in 1924 he taught Floyd Allport's course for him at Syracuse University during the summer session. These courses deepened Murphy's interest in social psychology to the extent that it became his major concern for the remainder of his tenure at Columbia (World War II).

The Likert Technique of Attitude Measurement. Social psychology as an experimental science received a potent upsurge in 1928 when Murphy at Columbia and *Louis Leon Thurstone* (1887-1955) at the University of Chicago designed methods for the study of social attitudes. As early as 1925 a sociologist from the University of Southern California, who received his Ph.D. in 1911 from the University of Chicago, Emory Stephen Bogardus (1882-), began measuring social distance. Influenced by the Chicago school (Ellwood, Ross, and even McDougall), Bogardus, taking advantage of the investigatory techniques of Robert E. Park and Ernest W. Burgess, constructed his social distance measurement scale. The year previous to Bogardus' publication in 1925 of "Social Distance and Its Origins" and "Measuring Social Distance," Park spoke of social distance and its measurement, noting that "we are clearly conscious, in all our personal relationships, of degree of intimacy. A is closer to B than C and the *degree of this intimacy measures the influence which each has over the other"* (1924, p. 340). Defining social distance as "a measure of actual or potential social conflict" (1955, p. 469), Bogardus observed that another person closely related to oneself on the social distance scale has distinct identifying characteristics while a person at a social distance acquires indistinguishable traits of group-like characteristics so that "all Chinese look alike" attitudes result.

Beginning with the 1928-1929 school year, Murphy designed a method for the study of social attitudes concerning liberalism and conservativism. With the assistance of his Ph.D. candidate, *Rensis Likert* (1903-   ), Murphy developed a method for scaling attitudes, termed the Likert Technique for Determining Attitudes. Likert, who was at that time an assistant in C. J. Warden's animal laboratory at Columbia, wrote up the technique and experiment as his doctoral dissertation under the title, "A Technique for the Measurement of Attitudes" (1932), the work appearing in book form as a follow-up study in 1938 by Murphy and Likert as *Public Opinion and the Individual.*

Likert's opinion questionnaire depicted the subject's intensity and direction of feeling with respect to his attitude. On a five point continuum from "strongly approve" to "strongly disapprove," the subject was asked to state his preference, with values from one to five assigned to the points along the continuum, one being at the negative end and five the positive, while the mid-point was a neutral position.

Thurstone's Equal Appearing Interval Method of Attitude Measurement. Likert's method, which came to be called the method of summated ratings, was similar to Thurstone's similar attributes or method of equal appearing intervals. Thurstone, not only obtained his Ph.D. from the University of Chicago but remained there on the faculty from 1924 to his retirement in 1952, establishing a Psychometric Laboratory, founding the Psychometric Society, and its organ, *Psychometrica.* Concerned with the issue of measurement, Thurstone applied it to attitudes and intelligence, defining the latter as a mental trait or *"the capacity to make impulses focal at their early, unfinished stage of formation"* (1924, p. 159). Holding that attitudes are measurable, he argued that equal appearing intervals can be subjectively measured. On this basis he (with Chave who assisted him by compiling the data) adapted it in developing an attitude scale. He explained the underlying fundamental concept of the scale: "The scale is so constructed that two opinions separated by a unit distance in the base line seem to differ as much in the attitude variable involved as any other two opinions on the scale which are also separated by a unit distance" (1929, pp. xi-xii). The individual's attitude is pinpointed along a continuum from one extreme (favorable) to another (unfavorable). Thurstone (1931, 1947) later turned his attention to *multiple factor analysis.*

Guttman's Cumulative Scaling Method in Attitude Measurement. It was not long before others were quickly caught up in the spirit of attitude measurement and soon there followed an era of attitude measurement. A University of Minnesota Ph.D. (1924), Louis Guttman (1916-   ), developed his cumulative scaling method for attitude measurement while on Cornell's faculty. His technique for scalogram analysis (as he termed it), appearing in 1947, was based on matrix algebra. Guttman's method differed from his predecessors in that his was a cumulative method in which individuals were asked to rank their attitudes subjectively with the highest figure cumulatively encompassing any figure less than it so that a response: "All of them" to the question: "How many officers are you content to serve as a subordinate?" would cumulatively include:

1. All of them
2. Most of them
3. Half of them
4. Few of them
5. None of them

The Congruity Principle of Attitude Change. The congruity principle was initiated in early 1952 and 1953 by *Charles E. Osgood* (1916-) at the University of Illinois and developed by a Ph.D. candidate at the same institution, *Percy H. Tannenbaum* (1927-), who exploited it as a doctoral dissertation in 1953, publishing it in 1956. These two with another Illinois Ph.D., *George J. Suci* (1925-), who received his degree in 1952, published a book on *The Measurement of Meaning* (1957), elaborating on the congruity principle which they based on the *semantic differential,* a measurement technique. The congruity model was grounded in the factor analysis of another Illinois professor, *Raymond B. Cattell* (1905-), a leader in the factor analytic movement and developer of a factor analytic theory of personality (1950). According to the congruity principle, *"changes in evaluation are always in the direction of increased congruity with the existing frame of reference"* (Osgood & Tannenbaum, 1955, p. 43). Tannenbaum devised a formula for calculating attitude change: "The total available pressure towards change between the source and concept" is "in inverse proportion to their respective degrees of polarization" (1968, p. 55) together with a hypothesis governing susceptibility to attitude change: "The amount of attitude change toward an object is inversely proportional to the intensity of the original attitude toward that object" (1965, pp. 414-5).

Other Theories of Attitude Change. There were a number of other theories of attitude measurement, among them being a *theory of data* and an *unfolding technique* of psychological scaling by *Clyde H. Coombs* (1912-), a University of Chicago Ph.D., who developed his *Theory of Data* in 1960 (expanding it in 1964) and his unfolding technique in 1950 and 1952. *Hadley Cantril* (1906-), who taught at Columbia for a brief period (currently with UNESCO), developed a self-anchoring scale in 1965. The founder of sociometry in 1934 together with its journal in 1937, *Sociometry: A Journal of Inter-Personal Relations,* J. L. Moreno (1892-1974) is deserving of mention. Sociometry, the measurement of social relations, engulfs a person's entire interpersonal relationships.

Sherif's Psychology of Social Norms. Social psychology advanced a stage higher when another of Murphy's Ph.D. candidates at Columbia University, *Muzafer Sherif* (1905-), developed his psychology of social norms, publishing his theory during his year of graduation in 1935, and in expanded book form a year later as the *Psychology of Social Norms*.

With Murphy's encouragement and Woodworth's permission to utilize the Columbia psychological laboratory for his experiments, Sherif experimented on the autokinetic movement phenomenon, illusory movement produced by a tiny light in a totally dark room. The light appears to move irregularly and slowly, the reason being the subject is without an objective standard of comparison or point of reference. Under these conditions, a subject seeks anchorage, a reference point. The same holds true in a social situation, in an unstructured group. Sherif observed:

> When individuals face the same unstable, unstructured situation as members of a group *for the first time,* a range and a norm (standard) within that range are established which are peculiar to the group. When a member of a group faces the same situation subsequently *alone,* after once the range and norm of his group have been established, he perceives the situation in terms of the range and norm that he brings from the group situation (1939, p. 91).

Thus people seek social norms as anchorages or reference points. In 1947, Sherif, in collaboration with Hadley Cantril, applied his social norm theory to personality theory or to attitudes and the self-system, the outcome being their book *The Psychology of Ego-Involvements: Social Attitudes and Identifications.*

Gardner Murphy's Role in the Development of Social Psychology. Murphy remained committed to social psychology throughout his entire career, launching its course as an experimental science with his huge handbook, *Experimental Social Psychology,* that he published in 1931. Even when he developed his personality theory in 1947, it was oriented from a social psychological standpoint, naming that tome *Personality: A Biosocial Approach to Origins and Structure.*

CHAPTER 16

Cornell: Titchener's Stronghold of Structuralism

EDWARD BRADFORD TITCHENER (1867-1927)

Once called the dean of experimental psychology in America, *Edward Bradford Titchener* (1867-1927) spent his long career in psychology at Cornell University, arriving there in 1892. Born in Chichester, England, Titchener studied four years at Malvern College (in Worcestershire, near Wales) before attending Oxford in 1885, where he received his A.B. in 1890. Philosophy in conjunction with physiology led the Germans to physiological psychology. Perhaps the same experience at Oxford where Titchener studied both disciplines captured his imagination. At any rate it led him to Wundt's laboratory of psychology at Leipzig at a time when Cattell was returning to the United States from there and Hall had newly founded his laboratory of psychology at Hopkins. However, F. Angell, Scripture, and Pace were still at Leipzig, where he made the beginnings of a lasting friendship with Angell. Only the previous year the International Congress of Psychology held its first meeting at Paris.

After two years of research for his doctorate, Titchener was awarded his Ph.D. in 1892 after submitting his dissertation on the binocular effects of monocular stimulation and a study on the chronometry of cognition. By the time he left the University of Leipzig, he was deeply influenced by Külpe (who was *Dozent* there and whose *Grundriss* Titchener translated and published in 1895), by Wundt, and by the positivism of Mach and Avenarius.

On returning to England, Titchener found no experimental psychology at his alma mater Oxford, so he left at the beckoning of Frank Angell for Cornell where Angell had opened a psychological laboratory a year earlier. Angell then departed for Stanford, recommending Titchener for the Cornell appointment. In 1892 Titchener went to Cornell, never to leave this initial appointment with a school where in the history of psychology the two words, Titchener and Cornell, are practically interchangeable terms.

Titchener's Cornell

During at least the last quarter of the nineteenth and the first quarter of the twentieth century, departments at universities were quite independent, and chairmen acquired immense importance and power at the large universities, many of them becoming *de facto* dictators who demanded allegiance to their ideals and philosophy. This was especially true of Titchener who (like George Holmes Howison) demanded from his departmental members a personal loyalty and (like Ladd) controlled psychology with an iron hand.

Cornell, partly a land-grant college chartered by the New York legislature in

1865, was named for Ezra Cornell, the principal stockholder for Western Union, who bestowed a half million dollars on his namesake because he wanted to "found an institution where any person can find instruction in any study." With this philosophical outlook, Cornell was among the first universities in diverse disciplines, while many of the other institutions remained traditional colleges offering a classical or liberal education rather than a practical one. By the time Cornell accepted its third class of freshmen, it was the largest college in America, numbering 250 in 1871.

Titchener: Wundt in America

It was never necessary for Wundt to go to the United States to promote his psychology, for Titchener in a very real way epitomized Wundtian psychology in America. He had translated several of Wundt's major publications even while his attention was on his own works, publishing his *Outline of Psychology* in 1896, with his *Primer of Psychology* following two years later when he was involved in writing his four volume *Experimental Psychology,* which appeared from 1901 to 1905. Titchener was so completely influenced by Wundt that he more than emulated him; he wrote concerning Wundt seemingly as if writing of himself, even to the point of employing phrases in defense of Wundt that he utilized to vindicate himself. Even Wundt's journals, the *Archiv* and the *Zeitschrift,* found their American counterpart in his eyes in the *American Journal of Psychology* and the *Psychological Review.* His Cornell series were probably an emulation of Wundt's *Psychologische Studien.*

Titchener represented *structural psychology,* a term James coined; it was employed in contrast to functional psychology, or as it was later substituted by Titchener, *introspectionism.* Woodworth referred to Titchener's system as "existential psychology," but that appellation has come to mean another psychological viewpoint. As such it stands in sharp contrast to the entire tradition in America, as did the personality Titchener himself, who was a "loner" and had little to do with the American Psychological Association. His own group, *The Experimentalists,* established by himself met annually, becoming the Society of Experimental Psychologists at his death. Titchener's demise was accompanied by that of his structural psychology, which collapsed when it no longer had the support of the sustaining personality of the man who nurtured it over the years.

Tenets of Structuralism and Introspectionism

Having defined mind as "the sum-total of human experience considered as dependent upon the experiencing person," Titchener went on to identify the scope of "psychology with the whole world of human experience" (1910, p. 25). Psychology is accordingly defined as the "science of mind." The mind, characterized by its memories, thoughts, imaginations, and feelings, in actuality "*is,* not *has*, thoughts and feelings; as the chair *is,* not *has,* seat and back, etc." (1899a, pp. 5-6). The objects with which science copes are things and processes, mind being a sum of processes. "Mind, then, as the sum of thoughts and feelings and the rest, is a sum of processes. The objects of the 'science of mind' are the processes of mind; the objects of 'mental science' are mental processes" (1899a, p. 7).

Introspectionism. Inasmuch as mental processes transpire within the body, "inside of us," they are knowable only by the person in question. The brain is the mind's organ. While the mind is not the brain's function, the body is, however, the condition of the mind. "Bodily processes . . . are the conditions of mental processes; and the statement of them furnishes us with the scientific explanation of the mental processes" (1899a, p. 18). The mind's consciousness is comprised of concrete processes, including: ideas, feelings, wishes, resolutions, and the like that form conscious experience.

Structuralism. According to Titchener the psychologist studies mental elements.

> No concrete mental process, no idea of feeling that we actually experience as part of a consciousness, is a simple process, but that all alike are made up of a number of really simple processes blended together. These simple processes are called *mental elements*. They are very numerous: there are probably some 50,000 of them: but they may all be grouped into two great classes, as *sensations* and *affections* (1899a, p. 21).

Qualities of sensation are: red, cold, bitter, etc., and those of affections are pleasant and unpleasant, the psychologist's task being that of rendering an exact accounting of the elementary processes of sensation and affection.

Experimental Introspection. Psychological observation encounters difficulties in rendering a careful, accurate, and impartial account of oneself.

> Psychological observation is observation by each man of his own experience, of mental processes which lie open to him but to no one else. Hence while all other scientific observation may be called *inspection*, the looking *at* things or processes, psychological observation is *introspection*, the looking *inward* into oneself (1899a, p. 27).

The act of observing oneself is also a mental process. The method of psychology, experimental introspection, is looking inward in order to acquire knowledge of mental processes. The general rules governing experimental introspection are: (1) be impartial; (2) be attentive; (3) be comfortable; and (4) be perfectly fresh. *"Live impartially, attentively, comfortably, freshly, the part of your mental life that you wish to understand. As soon as it is past, call it back and describe it"* (1899a, p. 35). There are also a number of special rules such as maintaining the same illumination when distinguishing all possible tints of blue.

Relation of Structuralism to Functionalism

Distinguishing structuralism from functionalism, Titchener explained that "introspection, from the structural standpoint, is observation of an Is; introspection, from the functional standpoint, is observation of an Is-for" (1899b, p. 291). According to Titchener, for every function there should be a structure, the aim of experimental psychology being the analysis of the mind's structure, that is, isolating elemental processes from the complexity of consciousness. In addition to a psychology of structure, a functional psychology may exist.

The primary aim of the experimental psychologist has been to analyze the structure of mind; to ravel out the elemental processes. . . . There is, however, a functional psychology, over and above this psychology of structure. We may regard mind, on the one hand, as a complex of processes, shaped and moulded under the conditions of the physical organism. We may regard it, on the other hand, as the collective name for a system of functions of the psychophysical organism (1898, p.451).

Titchener never abandoned his structuralism or experimental introspectionism, nor his one and only appointment at Cornell notwithstanding his being offered the presidency of Clark University in 1909. He even turned Harvard down in 1917 though he regarded Münsterberg's position at Harvard as the most coveted one in the nation. In the United States, Titchener and his associates stood virtually as the only exception to the great current of functionalism that was rapidly gaining momentum, and which was to remain the hallmark of American psychology. However, as has doubtless been surmised, even Titchener yielded some ground to the functionalists.

Titchener's Heirs: Washburn; Pillsbury; Dallenbach; Boring; and Guilford

Titchener produced his first Ph.D., *Margaret Floy Washburn* (1871-1939) in 1894, even before he attained to full professorship. During his tenure at Cornell, he graduated at least 56 doctorates, including: *Walter Bowers Pillsbury* (in 1896), *Karl M. Dallenbach* (1913), *Edwin G. Boring* (1914), and *Joy Paul Guilford* in his last graduating class in 1927.

While Boring (1886-1968) did not introduce the history of psychology, he did much to establish it as an important course at universities, whereas Guilford (1897-   ) contributed to experimental, differential, and statistical psychology, producing a book on *Psychometric Methods* in 1936. The same year Boring's *History of Experimental Psychology* (1929) appeared (which incidentally was dedicated to his teacher, Edward Bradford Titchener), Pillsbury (1872-1960) published his *The History of Psychology* (1929) also.

Washburn was probably the first woman to receive a Ph.D. in psychology in the United States, and the only notable American female in the nineteenth century with a Ph.D. in psychology. She is best known for her work in animal psychology, publishing *The Animal Mind* in 1908. Born in New York City, Washburn in 1903 returned to her alma mater, Vassar, where she received her baccalaureate. There she remained until her death, instituting a psychological laboratory in 1903, and publishing *Movement and Mental Imagery* in 1916, a work in which she sought to reconcile behaviorism with introspectionism, a situation that she regarded as the American psychological dilemma.

A Parting Note. As was the case with Hall at Clark University, so it was with Titchener at Cornell. Having carried their schools by their overpowering personalities, they found themselves without peers to succeed them. To say the least their successors were hardly their equals. Consequently the glory that was Clark (with Hall) and Cornell (with Titchener) was lost to their institutions and to psychology in these strongholds when the institutions lost these men.

In the case of Titchener, Boring observed:

Somehow Titchnerism in America had been sustained by his magnificent personality. With his death it suddenly collapsed, dwindling rapidly from the status of a vital faith in the importance of consciousness to the equally essential but wholly inglorious state of having been an unavoidable phase of historical development (1950, p. 420).

The structuralist Titchener, quite out of step with American functionalism, knew it. He fought bitterly against functionalism, and seemed to have an aversion for other things American. In a letter to the psychologist A. A. Roback (dated Feb. 1, 1923), Titchener wrote: "I am myself very decidedly an English psychologist, if the adjective means nationality; and I hope I am the same thing if it means type of thinking" (Roback, 1964, p. 237).

CHAPTER 17

University of Chicago: Functionalism's Bastion

(A) FUNCTIONALISM AT CHICAGO

Relative to the other universities discussed, the University of Chicago is but a youngster, its founding being in 1891. In order to capture the scene prevailing at that time, one need only realize that the following year Münsterberg came to Harvard and Titchener arrived for duties at Cornell University. A decade later when *Harvey A. Carr* (1873-1954) arrived at Chicago as a graduate student, he was appalled at what he found. On approaching the laboratory of psychology, he remarked, "imagine my surprise in encountering a small weatherbeaten dilapidated frame structure that had evidently been discarded as unfit for human habitation" (1930a, p. 74). As if that indignity were not enough, he discovered that the department of psychology and the department of education were lumped into the department of philosophy. Humiliations continued when he learned that he had been assigned to the department of education (and coerced to take courses in education) because students were apportioned among the three departments. When the opportunity finally fell to him to take a year's work in experimental psychology, he found to his dismay that it was taught by only an assistant professor, *James Rowland Angell* (1869-1949). Sharing his experience, Carr reported:

> I joined a couple of graduate students seated on the front steps and was told that the Professor had not yet arrived. Shortly there appeared a young man with an erect posture, a jaunty walk, a semiquizzical smile, and a hat slightly atilt over one eye. He entered the building and was mentally labelled as another graduate student not socially inclined. On entering the building, I found my graduate student at the lecturer's desk ready for business. Apparently erudition was associated in my mind with age and some degree of pompous dignity. There was nothing to do but make the best of the situation (1930a, pp. 74-5).

By the end of Carr's first year, *John Dewey* (1859-1952) left Chicago for Columbia, *John Broadus Watson* (1878-1958) received an appointment as instructor at Chicago and psychology was made a separate department headed by Angell. When Carr matriculated at Chicago, only Dewey was a name of which anyone was aware, but as destiny would have it, all four played major roles in the history of psychology.

JOHN DEWEY (1859-1952): Birth of Functionalism at Chicago

1896 marks the formal date of the birth of functionalism in psychology in the United States, owing to the publication of Dewey's classic critique of the reflex arc theory in psychology. In his "The Reflex Arc Concept in Psychology" (1896), Dewey initiated a new trend in psychology by his protestation against elementism that dominated psychology. The Hegelian Dewey was interested in the whole organism in its adaptation to its environment, and objected to the atomistic approach reducing psychological life to reflexism. "What is wanted," wrote Dewey, "is that sensory stimulus, central connections and motor responses shall be viewed, not as separate and complete entities in themselves, but as divisions of labor, functioning factors, within the single concrete whole, now designated the reflex arc" (1896, p. 358). *Coordination* is the key. It is wrong to view the reflex arc as a stimulus-response mechanical sequence with a sensation interposed between the stimulus and response. Or as Dewey phrased the matter:

> What shall we term that which is not sensation-followed-by-idea-followed-by-movement, but which is primary; which is, as it were, the psychical organism of which sensation, idea and movement are the chief organs? Stated on the physiological side, this reality may most conveniently be termed coordination (1896, p. 358).

A stimulus does not necessarily produce a response, inasmuch as a person may be inattentive to the stimulus, and hence not respond. If the organism does not respond then it has not been stimulated; it is not a mere motor activity; it is an act. Mere movement is but a spurious response, not a genuine one. For an individual to fall through a weakened floor is not to respond to a stimulus though movement is present. Dewey continued:

> The reflex arc idea, as commonly employed, is defective in that it assumes sensory stimulus and motor response as distinct psychical existences, while in reality they are always inside a coördination and have their significance purely from the part played in maintaining or reconstituting the coördination; and (secondly) in assuming that the quale of experience which precedes the 'motor' phase and that which succeeds it are two different states, instead of the last being always the first reconstituted, the motor phase coming in only for the sake of such mediation (1896, p. 360).

The instrumentalist Dewey contends that the reflex arc is an instrument, its purpose being that of "effecting a successful coördination." The reflex arc must be appreciated in terms of its utilitarian or purposeful character. "The fact is," argued Dewey, "that stimulus and response are not distinctions of existence, but teleological distinctions, that is, distinctions of function, or part played, with reference to reaching or maintaining an end" (1895, p. 365). In advancing his Hegelian attitude that the total organism must be viewed in the light of adapting successfully to its environment, the entire considered as a totality, Dewey was forecasting gestalt psychology. Dynamic psychology is also present in Dewey's explanation, inasmuch as his coördination concept is adaptive and teleological. Dewey concluded: "The reflex arc theory, by neglecting, by abstracting from, this genesis and this function gives us one disjointed part of a process as if it were the whole. It gives us literally an arc, instead of the circuit. . . . The circle is a coördination" (1896, p. 370).

This was not Dewey's first summons to functional psychology, for his first call came a dozen years earlier in his article "The New Psychology" (1884). Psychologists did not heed him, probably because he was writing in a journal that few if any of them read, the *Andover Review*, or possibly owing to the fact that he was little more than a youth at the tender age of twenty-five. Referring to his position as the new psychology, he declared that

> it insists upon the unity and solidarity of psychical life against abstract theories which would break it up into atomic elements or independent powers. It lays large stress upon the will; not as an abstract power of unmotivated choice, nor as an executive power to obey the behests of the understanding, the legislative branch of the psychical government, but as a living bond connecting and conditioning *all* mental activity. It emphasizes the teleological element, not in any mechanical or external sense, but regarding life as an organism in which immanent ideas or purposes are realizing themselves through the development of experience (1969, p. 60).

Thus from the beginning Dewey was attacking atomism in psychology.

The *instrumentalist* Dewey, for that is what functionalism actually was (and the term Dewey later employed as the designation of his position), thought of the reflex arc and all elements and qualities of persons as more effective means of living. The reflex arc and other human properties are instruments functioning for better adaptation or adjustment to life.

A Biographical Look at Dewey. The Vermonter John Dewey was born in Burlington the year that Charles Darwin published his classic *Origin of Species* (1859). In his home town he attended one of the oldest colleges in the United States, the University of Vermont, founded in 1791. For graduate school he chose Johns Hopkins where he studied under G. Stanley Hall and the founder and coiner of the term *pragmatism,* Charles Sanders Peirce (1839-1914). It was Peirce's pragmatism that inspired Dewey's functionalism. Peirce's pragmatism concludes that "the whole function of thought is to produce habits of action," and that to determine "what a thing means is simply what habits it involves" (1878, sect. 2). President Gilman of Johns Hopkins University stimulated him to think independently. In his autobiography (edited by his daughter Jane), Dewey said that "President Gilman constantly urged upon the students the feasibility and importance of original research" (1939, p. 15). Here he developed a close friendship with *Joseph Jastrow* (1863-1944) and *James McKeen Cattell,* through whose efforts Dewey obtained a faculty appointment at Columbia University when he abruptly resigned from the University of Chicago with no place to go. Dewey quit Chicago in 1904 because during his absence the college president merged his famous Laboratory School with the Chicago Institute (a training school for teachers). Owing to the merger, the Laboratory School was for all practical purposes obliterated. Except for a peripheral interest, once Dewey settled at Columbia, his attention was turned increasingly toward philosophy.

In one of these marginal works, *How We Think* (1910), Dewey analyzed a complete act of thought in five steps: "*(i)* a felt difficulty; *(ii)* its location and definition; *(iii)* suggestion of possible solution; *(iv)* development by reasoning of the bearings of the suggestion; *(v)* further observation and experiment leading to its acceptance or rejection, that is, the conclusion of belief or disbelief'' (1910, p. 72).

Dewey's functionalism even found its way into his social psychology titled *Human Nature and Conduct: An Introduction to Social Psychology* (1922). Explaining his approach, he wrote:

> it seriously sets forth a belief that an understanding of habit and of different types of habit is the key to social psychology, while the operation of impulse and intelligence gives the key to individualized mental activity. But they are secondary to habit so that mind can be understood in the concrete only as a system of beliefs, desires and purposes which are formed in the interaction of biological aptitudes with a social environment (Preface).

In both of these books Dewey's functionalism is evident, for thinking to Dewey was a human instrument for adapting to life situations and its problems.

The Structural-Functional Controversy

After Dewey lashed out against the elementism or atomism of his period, it was not long before he heard from the structuralist Titchener. By attacking, Titchener helped focus attention by psychologists, thereby imputing importance to this position and its adherents. The term *functionalism* was not as yet coined until Titchener came up with the appellation. Harrison noted that

> what Titchener was attacking was in fact nameless until he named it; hence he thrust the movement into high relief and did more than anyone else to get the term *functionalism* into psychological currency. Titchener interpreted the American writings as direct consequences of German *Akt* and *Funktion*, although in point of fact the American movement differed fundamentally from the German schools (1963, p. 395).

Not Titchener, but James is credited with coining the term *structuralism*. In opposing functionalism, Titchener believed that he was protecting psychology from lapsing from an independent science into the province of philosophy. By 1925, though Titchener's protestations continued, the then chairman of the department of psychology at Chicago, Harvey Carr, neither mentioned the structural-functional controversy nor the term functionalism in his *Psychology* (1925). Functionalism itself was undergoing transition from an emphasis on mental functions to a concern for the study of behavior. Some psychologists view behaviorism as an offshoot of functionalism. Its American founder, John Watson, received his Ph.D. under Angell at Chicago when functionalism was at its height. While Dewey initiated functionalism at Chicago, it was extended into social psychology by *George Herbert Mead* (1863-1931), climaxed by Angell, who unintentionally founded it as a school, and consummated by Carr.

GEORGE HERBERT MEAD (1863-1931):
Functionalism as a Social Psychology: Social Behaviorism

Dewey's University of Chicago associate and lifetime friend, George Herbert Mead, joined Chicago's Department of Philosophy the same year Dewey joined (1894) and at his invitation, remaining at his position until he died. Born in South

Hadley, Massachusetts, Mead was educated at Harvard University where he was first exposed to the functionalism of James as well as the teaching of Josiah Royce. Oddly enough, he never actually wrote a book; his collected notes by students and published papers constitute the several books of his that were posthumously published.

It was the functionalism of Dewey that Mead pursued in his social psychology of the act. Dewey's repudiation of atomism, his insistence on activity as a continuous whole, that stimulus and response are essentially function, that coordination is the key to understanding psychological phenomena, and that attention is the center of consciousness provided Mead's springboard for his functionalistic social psychology. Incorporating the values of behaviorism (for Watson was a student and later a faculty member at Chicago) into Dewey's functionalism produced Mead's social behaviorism. Thus Mead's *psychology of the act* is functionalism introduced into social psychology. As early as 1900 he introduced social psychology as a course in the University of Chicago, probably the first to be taught in the United States. Consequently once an act is initiated, it proceeds toward consummation.

The Process of Reflection. Closely paralleling Dewey's psychology of the thinking process, Mead offered his own five-stage analysis of reflection which is inherent in the experimental method: (1) the presence of a problem; (2) the statement of the problem in terms of the conditions of its possible solution; (3) the formation of hypotheses, the getting of ideas; (4) the mental testing of the hypothesis; and (5) the experimental or observational test of the hypothesis. Reflective thinking he observed as arising "in testing the means which are presented for carrying out some hypothetical way of continuing an action which has been checked" (1938, p. 79).

Social Behaviorism. Relying on evolutionary theory, especially the concept of emergent evolution, Mead emphasized the emergence of social relations. Among his many social psychological concepts are the *social self,* the *generalized other,* *vocal gesture,* and the *mind as the emergence of social acts.* In his "Social Psychology as Counterpart to Physiological Psychology" (1908), Mead argued that without social psychology, physiological psychology is unable to account for mind or consciousness. Even the *self* is produced by a social process; thus a self is a social self. "The growth of self," claimed Mead, "arises out of a partial disintegration,—the appearance of the different interests in the forum of reflection, the reconstruction of the social world, and the consequent appearance of the new self that answers to the new object" (1913, pp. 379-80). Selfhood is attributed to the *vocal gesture,* a concept inspired by Wundt's *Völkerpsychologie* (1900). While Wundt regarded language as the outgrowth of the vocal gesture, Mead added that "the language process is essential for the development of the self" (1964a, p. 199). He added: "The self, as that which can be an object to itself, is essentially a social structure, and it arises in social experience" (p. 204). The self finds its genesis in the vocal gesture. *Reflexivity,* the ability of self-reflection, is the condition necessary for the mind's emergence in the social process.

The Nature of the Consciousness. In his "The Definition of the Psychical"

(1903), Mead, criticizing Wundt, regarded only functional concepts as valid. Consciousness is psychical, psychical being an evolutionary emergent. In accord with Dewey, he held that consciousness (mind) comes into being when a problem disrupts the flow of activity of an intelligent organism. Consciousness or mind therefore is viewed as an instrument enabling an intelligent being to cope with life's problems by discovering a solution restoring the ongoing process of activity. Thus Mead, with respect to his process psychology, has come under the influence of Alfred North Whitehead's (1929) process philosophy.

Psychology of the Act. The concept *act* is Mead's peculiar way of identifying the phenomenon that the functionalists view as the transpiring between stimulus and response, what later came to be termed by psychologists, the intervening variable or psychological construct. The relation between the individual and his environment is determined by action (act). "The unit of existence," he wrote "is the act" (1938, p. 65). He identified attention as the epitome of consciousness, regarding it as an evolutionary evolvement as are all human qualities. Psychology itself is the evolved product of the act of the organism. Adaptation is achieved through the act.

> Our primary adjustment to an environment lies in the act which determines the relation between the individual and the environment. An act is an ongoing event that consists of stimulation and response and the results of the response (Mead, 1938, p. 364).

The three stages of the act he listed in "Concerning Animal Perception" (1907) as (1) perception, (2) manipulation, and (3) consummation. Perception Mead defined as "a relation between a highly developed physical organism and an object, or an environment in which selection emphasizes certain elements" (1938, p. 8). The relation entails both duration and process, process being action through media affecting the sense organs. Explaining the second and third stages of the act, Mead asserted:

> There is . . . a certain area implied in sense perception, within which contact, the immediate outcome of the act, takes place, while we still see it, or have distance experience of it. It is a mediate area, for consummation lies beyond it—for example, eating, rest, or warmth. I will call it the manipulatory area, for physical things are plainly things that we handle, but the handling is normally under the control of vision (1938, p. 141).

Although influenced by Watson's behaviorism, Mead took issue with it, superseding it with his own brand which he termed *social behaviorism*. "Behaviorism in this wider sense," claimed Mead, "is simply an approach to the study of the experience of the individual from the point of view of his conduct, particularly, but not exclusively, the conduct as it is observable by others" (1934, p. 2). Whereas Watsonism repudiates consciousness, Mead's social behaviorism regards the development of the individual's self-consciousness as of special interest to the social psychologist. Explaining his position, Mead asserted:

> While minds and selves are essentially social products, products or phenomena of the

social side of human experience, the physiological mechanism underlying experience is far from irrelevant—indeed is indispensable—to their genesis and existence; for individual experience and behavior is, of course, physiologically basic to social experience and behavior: the processes and mechanisms of the latter (including those which are essential to the origin and existence of minds and selves) are dependent physiologically upon the processes and mechanisms of the former, and upon the social functioning of these (1934, pp. 1-2).

Thus there is room for consciousness in Mead's social behaviorism which sees consciousness as an emergent, with the social act its precondition. Watson was also mistaken in limiting psychological study to individuals, i.e., in failing to accept social psychology.

A *gesture,* essentially social in character, and as "beginnings of social acts which are stimuli for the response of other forms" (1934, p. 43), serves as a stimulus of one individual to another. Thus it is a social stimulus. The mind originates with the presence of gestures, both being social. Gestures in the form of significant symbols (words) provide the fundamental elements of language. "The significant symbol is then the gesture, the sign, the word which is addressed to the self when it is addressed to another individual, and is addressed to another, in form to all other individuals, when it is addressed to the self" (1922, p. 160). Not that the mind is equated with linguistic behavior because mind contains more, such as imagery. Yet mind, for Mead, is a social process.

Well-known for his term the *generalized other,* Mead viewed it as the representative of society within the individual (i.e., the reference group). This attitude, acquired in childhood, Mead explained:

> The child must not only take the role of the other, as he does in the play, but he must assume the various roles of all the participants in the game, and govern his action accordingly. If he plays first base, it is as the one to whom the ball will be thrown from the field or from the catcher. Their organized reactions to him he has embedded in his own playing of the different positions, and this organized reaction becomes what I have called the "generalized other" that accompanies and controls his conduct. And it is this generalized other in his experience which provides him with a self (1924-1925, p. 269).

Known also for his distinction between the "I" and the "me," Mead held that the *I* never existed as an object of consciousness, whereas the "self-conscious, actual self in social intercourse is the objective 'me' or 'me's' with the process of response continually going on and implying a fictitious 'I' always out of sight of himself" (1964b, p. 141). He concluded that the "inner consciousness is socially organized by the importation of the social organization of the outer world" (1964b, p. 141). Consciousness, as a subvocal linguistic communication, i.e., inner communication, is social in character, mind being an internal symbolic communication. Notwithstanding the privacy of the experience of thinking, it is behavior whose orientation is the generalized other, for it is based on significant symbols, i.e., language that is basically social. Thinking is behavior resulting from interrupted activity, particularly when the act is inhibited, for such is the pragmatic theory of the thinking process. As a perceptual object, the self pertains to phases of activity, the "me" being the social self formed through role taking, and the "I" the individual as unique in the light of his perceived historical situation. At any rate a person is without a mind at birth, autonomy emerging through feedback, and self-control a reflection of social control. To paraphrase Mead's biographer, Grace C. Lee (1945), he is a psychologist of the social individual par excellence.

JAMES ROWLAND ANGELL (1869-1949): Postulates of Functionalism

Already prepped for Chicago's school of functional psychology by his exposure to James while a graduate student at Harvard (where he received his A.M. in 1892), James Rowland Angell, who never obtained an earned doctorate, went on to join Dewey at Chicago in 1894, where he rose to the presidency of the University of Chicago after heading its department of psychology. From 1921 to retirement he was Yale's president. More than being tutored by James, Angell, who was born in the same town (Burlington, Vermont) as Dewey a decade later, went on to study under Dewey at the University of Michigan, receiving both A.B. (1890) and A.M. (1891) degrees there while his father was president of the university. At Dewey's invitation, Angell joined the faculty of Chicago the same year Dewey and Mead arrived, three years after the founding of the university. The neurologist Henry Herbet Donaldson (1857-1938) was already there, appointed the previous year. Angell's responsibilities there included directing the psychological laboratory as well as teaching courses in psychology. Although receiving training in psychological research by pursuing his doctorate at the University of Berlin, he left before completion.

Articulating the functionalist's credo as early as 1903 in an article on "The Relations of Structural and Functional Psychology to Philosophy," Angell the following year published his *Psychology: An Introductory Study of the Structure and Function of Human Relations* (1904) in which he was still on the theme of structuralism and functionalism. Alerting his reader to his functionalist orientation, he prefaced his book:

> Psychologists have hitherto devoted the larger part of their energy to investigating the *structure* of the mind. Of late, however, there has been manifest a disposition to deal more fully with its functional and genetic phases. To determine how consciousness develops and how it operates is felt to be quite as important as the discovery of its constituent elements (p. iii).

He went on to explain its method as one of introspection supplemented by "objective observation of other individuals" (1904, p. 4). Operations of consciousness are regarded as "expressions of organic adaptations to our environment, an environment which we must remember is social as well as physical" (1904, p. 7). The appearance of consciousness resulted because reflexes and automatic acts were incompetent to aid the organism in coping with life.

As surmised from the foregoing, functionalism is emphatically Darwinian. Attributing functional and genetic psychology to Darwin, Angell saw as Darwin's contributions: "(1) his doctrine of the evolution of instinct and the part played by intelligence in the process; (2) the evolution of mind from the lowest animal to the highest man; and (3) the expressions of emotion" (1909, p. 154).

By the time he wrote his *An Introduction to Psychology* in 1918, intended initially as a briefer volume of the earlier *Psychology,* he felt that although "the structure-function distinction still seems to me significant, . . . it is no longer of acute controversy and so requires a less militant treatment" (1918, p. iv). Concerning the earlier work, the one in which functional psychology made its debut in book form for use in college courses, he asserted:

> It emphasized for the first time, so far as I am aware, the distinction between structural and functional methods in psychology. It adopted and consistently utilized an essentially biological point of view in its interpretation of the mental life, this position being reflected in part in the arrangement of the topics to exhibit the progressive stages of adjustment (1918, p. iii).

On the whole, however, the books were not very different from the structuralists. By the close of World War I, the dispute turned from structuralism to Watson's behaviorism. While Angell and other functionalists incorporated whatever they deemed worthwhile in behaviorism, he and his colleagues looked askance at the new found psychology of the "baby" member of their psychology department, Watson. Concerning the matter, Angell stated that the "polemic is now centered about the 'behavioristic' movement, which, with its gospel of objective methods and its crusade against introspection, presents an interesting blend of solid contribution and adolescent exaggeration" (1918, p. iv). Unlike his other books, Angell's *Chapters from Modern Psychology* (1912) contained a chapter on social psychology, perhaps Mead's influence (1930, p. 12).

The Functionalist's Platform. When Angell was elected president of the American Psychological Association in 1906, his presidential address published as "The Province of Functional Psychology" the following year was a detailed articulation of the platform of the functionalists. Recognizing functional psychology as originating with Aristotle, Angell traced its modern garb to Spencer's *Principles of Psychology* (1855) and to Darwin's *Origin of Species by Means of Natural Selection* (1859).

Above all, "functional psychology is synonymous with descriptions and theories of mental action as distinct from the materials of mental constitution" (1907, p. 63). Primarily one must identify "functional psychology with the effort to discern and portray the typical operations of consciousness under actual life conditions, as over against the attempt to analyze and describe its elementary and complex contents" (1907, pp. 62-3). While structural psychology deals with a description of elements of sensation, functional psychology is concerned with activities of sensation, their modus operandi. Mental process in actual living experience interests the functionalist, not the postmortem analysis of elements holding the attention of the structuralists.

> You cannot get a fixed and definite color sensation, for example, without keeping perfectly constant the external and internal conditions in which it appears. The particular

sense quality is in short functionally determined by the necessities of the existing situation which it emerges to meet. If you inquire then deeply enough what particular sensation you have in a given case, you always find it necessary to take account of the manner in which, and the reasons why, it was experienced at all.

. . . That is to say, the very description itself is functionalistic and must be so (1907, p. 67).

In addition to operations of mental process, the functionalist is concerned with mental activity in reference to biological forces and the environmental conditions of life. In the light of this approach, the functional psychologist studies mind as judging, mind as feeling, and the like. As a form of psychophysics, functional psychology is interested in ascertaining the physical and mental relations of the organism. In sum, the Chicago school stands for:

(1) functionalism conceived as the psychology of mental operations in contrast to the psychology of mental elements; or, expressed otherwise, the psychology of the how and why of consciousness as distinguished from the psychology of the what of consciousness. We have (2) the functionalism which deals with the problem of mind conceived as primarily engaged in mediating between the environment and the needs of the organism. This is the psychology of the fundamental utilities of consciousness; (3) and lastly we have functionalism described as psychophysical psychology, that is the psychology which constantly recognizes and insists upon the essential significance of the mind-body relationship for any just and comprehensive appreciation of mental life itself (1907, pp. 85-6).

In the sense that behavior is the control phenomenon of the biologist, so consciousness is the control phenomenon of the functional psychologist, control being the fundamental category in functional psychology.

HARVEY A. CARR (1873-1954): Angell's Successor

The product of Chicago's department of psychology, Harvey Carr, joined the faculty three years after receiving his Ph.D. in 1905, remaining there for the rest of his career and rising to become the head of the department by 1926. Although he wrote a chapter on "Functionalism" for the volume *Psychologies of 1930* as late as the third decade of the twentieth century, functionalism had by that time lost all of its fervor. From his book, *An Introduction to Space Perception* (1935), one could no longer discern that he was a Chicago functionalist.

His chapter, "Functionalism," is more a summary than an original contribution, synopsizing the views expressed earlier by Titchener and Angell, the former designating Ladd, Judd, Angell, James Baldwin, and Dewey as functionalists. To these names that of G. F. Stout is also added. Angell's three major features of functionalism are listed, noting that (1) functionalism deals with the whys and hows of contents in the light of their relation to their surrounding context; (2) the context includes the biological process of adjustment; and (3) functionalism translates mental processes into physiological ones and vice versa. Titchener's four characteristics of functional psychology are also listed:

1) Functional psychologies distinguish between activity or function of consciousness and its content or structure. . . .
2) Consciousness, especially in its active phase, has a value for organic survival. . . .
3) A functional psychology is teleological. . . .
4) Functional psychologies are written as a preface to philosophy. . . . Their spirit is primarily that of an applied science (1930, p. 61).

Products of the Chicago School: McGeoch and Robinson

The functional tradition at the University of Chicago was sustained by some of its graduates carrying functionalism into learning theory, two notables being *John Alexander McGeoch* (1897-1942) and *Edward S. Robinson* (1893-1937). McGeoch, a 1926 Ph.D., is known for his retroactive inhibition, differential forgetting, or interference theory, developed as early as 1932 and expanded in his *The Psychology of Human Learning* (1942). According to McGeoch, once an association is learned it is stored permanently, its inaccessibility (forgetting) is owing to inhibiting or competing associations. His differential forgetting theory holds that

during the course of practice a subject learns not only the correct responses, but also incorrect and conflicting ones which retard the fixation and interfere with the performance. Since these conflicting associations may be expected to be less well fixed than the correct ones, it is assumed that they should be forgotten at a faster rate during rest intervals. . . . Poorly learned associations are forgotten at a more rapid rate than well learned ones. It follows, then, that learning should be faster under distributed practice than under massed practice because the rest intervals give opportunity for this differential forgetting to occur (McGeoch & Irion, 1952, p. 183).

Edward S. Robinson, a 1920 Ph.D. from the University of Chicago, sought laws of associative learning, as did Harvey Carr (1931). In his *Association Theory Today: An Essay in Systematic Psychology* (1932), Robinson assembled a number of laws of association, including: contiguity, assimilation, frequency, intensity, duration, context, acquaintance, composition, and individual differences. In contemporary learning theory the laws are currently of little import.

As functionalism waned, behaviorism grew. But behaviorism is merely the offspring of functionalism, a form of functionalism. Its American founder and staunchest adherent, John Watson, was a product of the Chicago school, both as student and on its faculty. In Watson, functionalism has taken on the form of behaviorism.

(B) FUNCTIONALISM ASSUMES THE FORM OF BEHAVIORISM

JOHN B. WATSON (1878-1958): Behaviorism

Of the second generation psychologists at Chicago (first to attend the university), it was not Harvey Carr who received the first degree in psychology but John Broadus Watson in 1903, who founded American behaviorism in 1912. Subsequent to receiving their Ph.D.s, both men taught at their alma maters, but Watson left in 1908 for the attractive position of full professor at Johns Hopkins, where he remained for a little over a decade. Watson's final year at Johns Hopkins was 1919, a forced departure owing to his impending divorce. Life in academia came to a close for Watson, who joined the business world as vice-president of the J. Walter Thompson Company (1924-1936) and in the same capacity at William Esty and Company since 1936.

The Spawning of Behaviorism. Not at Johns Hopkins, but at the University of Chicago is where behaviorism was spawning, despite its being at the former institution that Watson's classic paper on the declaration of behaviorism, "Psychology as the Behaviorist Views It" (1913), was published. It was because of his preoccupation with animal psychology at Chicago that his fundamental conceptions of behaviorism began to unfold. While Watson objected to linking his behaviorism to functionalism, it is nevertheless a functional psychology, and the whole spirit of functionalism contributed to his rebellious attitude toward the established psychology of his day. It was not the stifling intellectual atmosphere of German universities, one which permitted no renegades, that gave functionalism its enthusiastic reception, but the American free spirit. Moreover, Watson admitted that "*behaviorism* is the only consistent and logical functionalism" (1914, p. 8).

The natural growth of behaviorism is its emergence out of animal psychology. Experimental work in animal behavior conduced to behavioristic interpretations of psychological phenomena. Studies in animal behavior facilitated objectivity. In eliminating the subjective factor, behavioral studies with the animal at the same time erased consciousness, since the introspective approach to contents of consciousness was infeasible. With the animal therefore only the study of behavior remained.

While all of Watson's psychological research at Chicago (from the time of his student days) was in animal behavior (his doctoral dissertation being *Animal Education,* 1903), he was neither the first to work on animals nor to see the relationship of animal behavior to a behavioristic psychology. Both of these achievements antedated him, the former by Thorndike at Columbia, and the latter as well as the former by the Russian reflex psychologists, Ivan Sechenov (1829-1905) and Ivan Pavlov (1849-1936). What then distinguished Watsonian behaviorism in the United States? In addition to his being (for all practical purposes) the first American behaviorist, he was both militant and extreme, insisting that behaviorism is the only valid scientific psychology, that no other form of psychology exists, and that consciousness is a nonentity. Thus, having weaned himself from the functionalism that saw him to maturity as a psychologist, he turned violently on the parent that reared him and dealt it a devastating blow by repudiating all forms of consciousness. In so doing, Watson offended the structuralist Titchener even more than he did his own functionalist colleagues at Chicago. While many of the Chicago functionalists assimilated aspects of behaviorism into their own systems of psychology, Titchener, who at one time rose vehemently in protestation against functionalism, was even readier to assail behaviorism. In effect he repeated the service he had rendered functionalism. By attacking he dignified behaviorism by centering the attention of the entire community of psychologists on this budding school of thought, instead of permitting it to go unnoticed.

If Darwinism proved a viable philosophy to functionalism, it was of even greater service to behaviorism. Watson was not interested in extrapolating his findings in animal psychology for application to the human; his adamant position was that no distinction whatever existed between animal and human psychology. Darwin's evolutionary theory supported him on this contention by holding that no qualitative distinctions existed between man and brute. Consequently whatever finding results from psychological investigation of animals holds equally valid for humans. Those features of functionalism adopted from Darwinism would ordinarily apply to behaviorism, such as the functionalist's consideration of a person (comparable to his animal counterpart) reacting to his environment, i.e., adaptation. Watson, in his "Autobiography" (1930, p. 276) also expressed his indebtedness to his intellectual predecessors in animal psychology, Thorndike and the British comparative psychologist C. Lloyd Morgan (1852-1936).

Tenets of Behaviorism

After declaring his views at Columbia University in 1912 in a series of lectures delivered there, Watson issued his first published statement the following year in his history-making paper, "Psychology as the Behaviorist Views It" (1913). The follow-up of the paper was a full length book a year later, *Behavior: An Introduction to Comparative Psychology* (1914), a work in which he argued for an independent place for comparative (animal) psychology among the recognized sciences. His classic paper opened with the claim that "psychology as the behaviorist views it is a purely objective experimental branch of natural science." Watson continued, "its theoretical goal is the prediction and control of behavior. Introspection forms no essential part of its methods" (1913, p. 158). Claiming that the behaviorist does not recognize any "dividing line" between humans and infrahumans, Watson held that all reference to consciousness must be discarded, the proper study of psychology being the science of behavior. Arriving at five conclusions, he stated them as:

1. Human psychology has failed to make good its claim as a natural science. . . .
2. Psychology, as the behaviorist views it, is a purely objective, experimental branch of natural science which needs introspection as little as do the sciences of chemistry and physics. . . .
3. From the viewpoint here suggested the facts on the behavior of amoeba have value in and for themselves without reference to the behavior of man. . . .
4. This suggested elimination of states of consciousness as proper objects of investigation in themselves will remove the barrier from psychology which exists between it and the other sciences. . . .
5. Psychology as behavior. . . . (1913, pp. 176-7).

His book *Behavior* (1914) reiterated and elaborated on the premises advanced in his celebrated 1913 journal article, as well as adducing experimental data supporting his contentions.

The extension of the principles gleaned from animal psychology to the province of human psychology was reserved for his *Psychology from the Standpoint of a Behaviorist* (1919). The book's thesis, that stimulus-response accounts for all psychological phenomena, serves to explain human as well as animal behavior. In this work, he dealt with human, especially child, psychology. He admonishes that the psychologist must not study his own behavior (introspectionism), but that of others. The book, prefaced with his primary bias, reads with italic emphasis:

> *If its facts were all at hand the behaviorist would be able to tell after watching an individual perform an act what the situation is that caused his action (prediction), whereas if organized society decreed that the individual or group should act in a definite, specific way the behaviorist could arrange the situation or stimulus which would bring about such action (control).* In other words, Psychology from the Standpoint of the Behaviorist is concerned with the prediction and control of human action and not with an analysis of 'consciousness' (1919, p. viii-ix).

Note that it is a Titchenerian who tended toward functionalism, Walter Bowers Pillsbury (1872-1957), who provided Watson with his definition of psychology as the study of behavior. In his *Essentials of Psychology* (1911), Pillsbury stated that "psychology may be most satisfactorily defined as the science of human behavior. Man may be treated as objectively as any physical phenomenon." By psychology as the science of behavior, Watson meant that

> the goal of psychological study is the ascertaining of such data and laws that, given the stimulus, psychology can predict what the response will be; or, on the other hand, given the response, it can specify the nature of the effective stimulus (1919, p. 10).

A popular version of Watsonism was issued in 1925, *Behaviorism*. Two interesting additions to his standpoint were his conciliatory attitude toward applied psychology, granting it his approval; and his negative attitude toward native intelligence, native talents or abilities, and instincts. His jaundiced view of heredity lent critical import to environmental factors and training, especially that of the formative stage of human life—infancy and early childhood.

At Johns Hopkins, Watson found a disciple in his most distinguished student, Karl S. Lashley, for whom Watson's behavioristic orientation held enormous appeal. Owing to Watson, Lashley pursued postdoctoral research in the field of vertebrate behavior, working with Watson on a number of issues. His investigations led to the conclusion that there exists an equipotentiality rather than a rigid localization of function in the cortex, and that a concomitant relationship exists between the amount of destruction of the cortical area and degree of behavior deterioration. Ironically, comparable to what Watson did earlier with respect to his intellectual parents, severing himself from their functionalism and then attacking it, Lashley discredited Watson's assumptions concerning neural activity. Lashley's investigations repudiated Watson's conditioned-reflex theory of behavior. Heidbreder observed:

The relation of Lashley's work to behaviorism is interesting from several points of view. First of all it definitely discredits the particular conception of neural activity that Watson assumes throughout his thinking; it denies that behavior is "built in" or constructed bit by bit on the conditioned-reflex plan. . . . From this point of view, Lashley's relation to behaviorism is somewhat like that of Külpe to the doctrines of Wundt, for both Lashley and Külpe, by using the distinctive methods of their respective schools, came upon facts contrary to the teachings of those schools (1933, p. 226).

Something quite similar, to be sure, transpired between Watson and the proprietors of functionalism.

KARL S. LASHLEY (1890-1958): Watson's Intellectual Successor

While Murray was at the Harvard Clinic near Charles River, and Boring at the Psychological Laboratory in Emerson Hall, Karl Spencer Lashley (1890-1958) was provided space at Harvard's Biological Laboratories with the title of Professor of Psychology in 1935, and Professor of Neuropsychology from 1937 to his death. A descendent of Jonathan Edwards, Lashley, a Johns Hopkins Ph.D. (1914), found his intellectual heritage in John Watson, having studied at Johns Hopkins with Watson and Adolf Meyer. Lashley sought to establish that a physiological psychologist does not require the concept of consciousnsss.

Mass Action and Equipotentiality. Although at first enamoured with the connectionist theory of conditioned reflex espoused by Watson, Lashley came to drift toward a field theory of brain function because of his doctrines of *mass action* and *equipotentiality* enunciated in his *Brain Mechanisms and Intelligence* (1929). According to the theory of equipotentiality, there is an ability of one part of the brain to assume functions of another part, a theory reminiscent of Kurt Goldstein's, but Lashley's influence stems from Shepherd Ivory Franz (1874-1933) when the two worked together,Lashley at Johns Hopkins and Franz at St. Elizabeth's Hospital (then named The Government Hospital for the Insane) at Washington.

Franz, strongly influenced by John B. Watson, Charles S. Sherrington, Henry Head, and J. McKeen Cattell (his professor at Columbia University where he received his Ph.D. in 1899), became an assistant in physiology on graduation at the Harvard Medical School, working under and influenced by Henry P. Bowditch, who was regarded as dean of American physiologists. Later he went to Dartmouth Medical School, McLean Hospital, and then to St. Elizabeth's Hospital for eighteen years (1904-1924) before terminating his career at the University of California (Los Angeles) up until his death in 1933. Franz's fame stems from his publication of "On the Functions of the Cerebrum: The Frontal Lobes in Relation to the Production and Retention of Simple Sensory Habits" in 1902. Experimenting on cats and monkeys, Franz found that a lobectomy of the frontal lobes that destroyed brain tissue resulted in the loss of recent but not earlier habits, with relearning of the habits lost despite the presence of the destroyed tissue remaining unregenerated.

In considering the functions of the cerebrum, therefore, we must rid ourselves of any preconceived notions regarding the fixity or definiteness of connections. Fixity or definiteness of an anatomical nature there undoubtedly is, but this fixity or definiteness is on the physiological side a multiplicity of fixities and definitenesses. One cell undoubtedly communicates with many others, and while this is an anatomical fixity it does not result in a physiological definiteness since at one time such a cell may be conceived to discharge in one direction along one collateral and at another time in another direction along another collateral (1915, p. 160).

While the findings of Franz favored those of Flourens and Jackson, they proved deleterious to Ferrier, as well as Fritsch and Hitzig.

By 1917 Lashley and Franz were coauthoring papers such as "The Retention of Habits by the Rat after Destruction of the Frontal Portion of the Cerebrum," papers that turned out to be Franz's final and Lashley's initial contribution to this area. The findings led to Lashley's doctrine of equipotentiality, and mass action, the latter implying that certain forms of learning are mediated through the cerebral cortex as a whole, and the former "used to designate the apparent capacity of any intact part of a functional area to carry out, with or without reduction in efficiency, the functions which are lost by destruction of the whole" (1929, p. 24).

Though an inspiring teacher, Lashley regarded "all teaching as useless," remarking that "those who need to be taught can't learn, and those who learn don't need to be taught" (Beach, 1961, pp. 163, 192).

Cerebral Localization: Descartes; Gall; Flourens; Broca; Fritsch and Hitzig; Ferrier; Munk; and Goltz. Lashley and Franz were contributing to a tradition that dated at least a century to the time of Gall in 1825, and probably to the time of Plato and Pythagoras, who over two and a half millennia ago traced mental functions to the brain. The influential Greek physician who flourished in the second century AD, *Galen* (*c*. 129-199), also corroborated the position of Plato and Pythagoras.

Little was contributed in this respect until 1650 when the Frenchman, *René Descartes* (1596-1650), a dualist, held that reality comprised things that were extended as well as that which was thought, i.e., mind and matter, the body interacting with the mind by virtue of the pineal gland in the brain, calling the gland the seat of the soul. "Let us conceive, then," he wrote in his treatise on *Passions of the Soul* in 1650,

> that the soul has its principal seat in this little gland in the middle of the brain, whence it radiates to all the rest of the body by means of the spirits, the nerves, and even the blood, which, participating in the impressions of the mind, can carry them by means of the arteries into the members (1892, art. 34).

Almost two centuries later the German physician, anatomist, and founder of phenology *Franz Joseph Gall* (1758-1828) reopened discussions on cerebral localization that lasted to the present time. In 1825 appeared his famous work *On Phrenology: The Localization of the Functions of the Brain* in which he advanced an anatomical theory of personality that located various sentiments and propensities in the brain. Over thirty mental properties, including the sentiment of property, propensity to theft, and instinct of providing and covetousness were relegated to specific areas of the brain and cranial protrusions or locations. The location or organ of property, he explained,

> is formed by certain convolutions . . . When these cerebral parts are very much developed, they produce a prominence on the head and skull, extending in a longitudinal direction . . . from the organ of cunning . . . nearly to the outer angle of the superior superciliary arch (1835, vol. 4).

Gall, adopting Reid's faculty psychology, reasoned that a faculty is found in a corresponding area of the brain, consequently the more developed faculties are larger in size and measurable by cranial contours. Accordingly a person's character is assessable simply by measuring his cranial contours.

Popular as Gall's phrenology was, it was dealt a crippling effect in 1824 by the French physiologist *Pierre Jean Marie Flourens* (1794-1867), who observed the behavior of pigeons following the removal of sections of their brains. Cortical localization doctrines reached a climax with Flourens' *Recherches expérimentales sur les propriétés et les fonctions du système nerveux dans les animaux vertébrés* (Experimental Researches on the Properties and Functions of the Nervous System in Animal Vertebrates) in 1824. Vehemently repudiating Gall's phrenology, Flourens held that both common action and specific action are traceable to various portions of the brain.

> The function of the cerebral lobes is to will, to judge, to remember, to see, to hear, or — in a word — to feel. The cerebellum directs and coordinates the movements of locomotion and grasping and the medulla oblongata those of conservation. The spinal cord links muscular contractions immediately excited by the nerves into whole movements.
>
> Yet, independently of this proper and exclusive action of each part, each part has its common action, that is to say, an action of each upon the others and of the others upon each.
>
> Thus, the cerebral lobes wish and feel; that is their proper action. The suppression of these lobes weakens the activity of the entire nervous system; that is their common action. The proper action of the cerebellum coordinates the movements of locomotion; its common action is to affect the activity of the entire system, and so forth and so on.
>
> Each part of the nervous system — the cerebral lobes, the corpora quadrigemina, the medulla oblongata, the nerves — thus has a proper function; and that is what makes it a distinct part: but the activity of each of these parts affects the activities of all the others; and that is what makes them parts of a particular system ([1824] 1965, p. 221).

Localization, Flourens found, is gross while function is common. In rejecting exact location, Flourens' theory became the precursor of views preferred by Lashley, Franz, J. H. Jackson, and H. Head.

Close to four decades later, another Frenchman, the surgeon and anthropologist *Paul Broca* (1824-1880), distinguished himself in the field of aphasia by successfully localizing the seat of articulate speech in the brain in 1861. He found aphasia, the loss of memory for words as he regarded it, due to the third convolution of the left frontal lobe, known as Broca's area. Broca concluded that the individual who is rendered aphasic by a deep and extensive lesion of the left hemisphere is in general only deprived of the faculty of reproducing the articulate sounds of language. He continues to understand what is being said to him, and consequently he knows perfectly the relation between words and ideas. In other words, the faculty of conceiving these relations belongs at the same time to the two hemispheres which can, in case of disease, replace each other; but the faculty to express them by coordinated movements, practice which is learned only after a well-established habit, seems to belong to only one hemisphere which is almost always the left one. . . .

It follows from this that a subject whose third *left* frontal convolution, the ordinary seat of articulate speech, happened to be emaciated since birth will learn to speak and will speak with the third *right* frontal convolution as a child born without a right hand becomes as able with his left hand ([1822]1968, p. 313).

Thus the theory of equipotentiality is continued in the findings of Broca since another portion of the brain is capable of functioning in the capacity of the damaged area. However, inasmuch as Broca was able to locate the speech center specifically, he caused the tide to drift away from the position of Flourens.

Facts seem to swing further away from Flourens with the findings of a couple of lecturers at the University of Berlin, the German anthropologist and naturalist *Gustav Theodor Fritsch* (1838-1927) and *Eduard Hitzig* (1838-1907), the principal investigator. These two experimentalists in 1870 found that contrary to the opinion prevalent at their time, it was possible to excite brain tissues directly, accomplishing the feat by electrically stimulating the cortex in order to produce movements of the eye. Their experiments on dogs and other animals favored cerebral localization theory because they had established motor centers in the cerebral cortex, localizing them in the precentral region. "By using very weak current," they explained,

one can localize these contractions exactly in narrowly delimited groups of muscle. . . .The possibility of isolated stimulation of a limited group of muscles is therefore limited to weak current on very small areas. For brevity's sake, we call these areas ''centers.'' Minute shifting of the electrodes, to be sure, generally sets the same extremities in movement" ([1870]1966, p. 231).

Cerebral localization theory was stimulated by the experimental findings of Fritsch and Hitzig. A half dozen years later the Scottish neurologist and cerebral anatomist *David Ferrier* (1843-1928), working with monkeys, in addition to localizing motor functions, localized sensory as well, articulating his findings in his *The Functions of the Brain* (1876). The removing of the occipital lobe resulted in blindness in the eye opposite to the side of the brain in which the ablation occurred. *Hermann Munk* (1839-1912), though favoring Ferrier's contentions, nevertheless did report (1890) that hemianopsia rather than blindness resulted, that is, each eye lost half its field of vision. Another researcher of that period, *Friedrich Leopold Goltz* (1834-1902), took issue with Munk, favoring Flourens' position that localizing is merely gross while function approaches the common.

Consensus among scientists moved away for the tradition of Gall, Fritsch and

Hitzig, Ferrier, and Munk in the direction of Flourens and Goltz, receiving its strongest fillip from Franz and Lashley.

DECLINING INFLUENCE OF UNIVERSITIES AND SCHOOLS OF PSYCHOLOGY

By the close of World War II, not only had the great schools of psychological thought seen a decline, but something comparable held true for the universities as well. The major schools such as functionalism, behaviorism, structuralism, psychoanalysis, gestalt, and the like gave way to theories and models in psychology. System builders were replaced by models or miniature systems as it were. An age of theories began to dominate areas of psychology, such as personality theories, learning theories, theories of development, of social psychology, of psychopathology, and the like. Experimentation was on the increase, contributing more to the decline of schools and the proliferation of theories and models. The major universities no longer had a monopoly on psychology, for many influential psychologists trained at these prestigious universities and at other institutions found careers elsewhere, many of them not even in academia.

Professionalism also contributed to post World War II psychological atmosphere. Whereas psychologists associated with academic institutions dominated the field of psychology prior to the war, the post war period witnessed a change to a majority of clinical psychologists, industrial and personnel psychologists, school and guidance psychologists, social psychologists, military psychologists, engineering (human factors) and space psychologists. Psychology was no longer an academic matter; it became an applied science as well as joining the ranks of professionalism. Most states in America presently license their psychologists, and the American Board of Examiners in Professional Psychology, established in 1946, certifies psychologists. The American Psychological Association, the largest in the World, lists over thirty classifications or divisions of psychology. Its Consolidated Roster for Psychology for 1973 listed 46,000 psychologists.

PART SIX

SOVIET PSYCHOLOGY

CHAPTER 18

Russian Behaviorism and Soviet Dialectical Psychology: Moscow and Leningrad

In contemporary Soviet Russia, psychologists are conscious of their scholarly heritage and remind themselves of it by tracing their historical accomplishments in psychology. Not only do they acknowledge contemporary dialectical psychology but predialectical psychology even prior to the communist era, i.e., the October Revolution in 1917. Although the communists like to fancy their psychological and philosophical history as a "solid materialist tradition" as Lenin phrased it and others reiterated, Russian psychology and philosophy has always been one of a thesis of materialism clashing with its antithesis, idealism. Early Russian psychology, as was true of its philosophy, was heavily indebted to Western thought. Soviet psychology still remains based upon philosophy, the premise of which is the philosophy of dialectical materialism.

The Moscow Psychological Society, founded in 1885, included such members as N. Ja. Grot (1852-1899), L. M. Lopatin (1855-1920), and G. I. Chelpanov (1862-1936). Calling for the investigation of "psychology proper," Chelpanov studied the "basic laws of the soul." The psychic was regarded as a manifestation of the soul and the brain its instrument through which its manifestations are conveyed. Without a soul the brain cannot think. Not the mind, but the soul aided by the brain perceives the external world. Kornilov regarded this group as the metaphysical school. The society's organ, *Problems of Philosophy and Psychology*, was founded in 1890 by Grot, but ceased publication after the October Revolution in 1918. The society's most distinguished member, Chelpanov, founded the Moscow Psychological Institute in 1912. Regarding the phenomenon of the spirit as independent and distinct from matter, he developed experimental techniques toward this end, and thus initiated the experimental method in psychology in Russia. The school's demise, and with it introspectionist psychology, gave way to the rise of mechanistic psychology when Kornilov replaced Chelpanov as Director of the Moscow Psychological Institute in 1924. Both Kornilov and Blonsky were students of Chelpanov.

The mechanistic period in Russian psychology came to a close by 1930 when the dialectical period assumed predominance. It held that position for a score of years, its height being from 1936 to 1950 when renewed discussion of Pavlov's psychology arose with the Pavlov Conference. The Conference, held from June 28 to July 4, 1950, was comprised of the Academy of Sciences of the U.S.S.R. Under Stalin's influence the conference stipulated a reconstruction of science along

Pavlovian lines. Though Soviet psychology was at stake due to the impending Pavlovization of psychology, the conference was addressed by only three psychologists: B. M. Teplov, V. M. Kolbanovskij, and S. L. Rubinstein. A. R. Luria's paper, while not presented at the conference, was contained in the published report. Relief to psychology came with Stalin's death in 1953.

Pavlovian psychology was built upon Sechenov's physiology, which in the early 1860s ushered in the reflex that was to play an important and lasting role in Soviet Russia. Sechenov's "reflex" theory was adopted by Pavlov, who discovered the conditioned reflex, and by Pavlov's contemporary, Bekhterev, who developed a system of "reflexology" that was to become the paradigm in 1913 for Watson's behaviorism. The reflex, and with it behavioristic psychology, was relayed to Kornilov, who transformed it into a "reactology" and Blonsky, who carried it into "pedological" theory. Russian psychology moved closer to Marxism with Vygotsky's "cultural historical developmental theory" of the human personality in which the human psyche was seen as the product of human development. By the mid-thirties, Rubinstein was contributing his extensive experimental material to foster dialectical psychology.

The decade from 1906 to 1916 saw five All-Russian Psychological Congresses held. It was the same period that Chelpanov founded the Psychological Institute, which was to play a lasting and important role in Soviet Psychology, as well as the period that N. N. Lange, founder of one of the first psychological laboratories in Russia (at the University of Odessa), published his *Psychology* (1914). It was as early as 1889 that a journal for psychology appeared, *Problems of Philosophy and Psychology,* founded by N. Ya. Grot.

The early thirties (from approximately 1930 to 1932) experienced a rapid exchange of views and criticisms. "Bourgeoise" psychology of the west was prevalent in the writings of Soviet authors. When Lenin's *Philosophical Notebooks* was published in 1929, it became possible to delineate a Marxist psychology. Behaviorism in all of its guises was repudiated and consequently signalled the demise of reactology and reflexology. Ananiev, who had affiliated himself with the Bekhterev school, wrote a "self-critical" article. In the immediately subsequent years, psychologists turned their attention to psychological methodology or the methodological basis of science. Rubinstein and Blonsky published major works during this period. In the thirties, Marxism was taking hold of psychology. Mind was regarded as a function of highly organized matter and was a reflection of external reality. These views arose in consequence of the publication of Lenin's *Philosophical Notebooks* which, although written from 1914 to 1916, was posthumously published in 1929. Lenin stressed the "self-movement of matter" as the ground of all change and viewed it as the essence of all dialectics. "Dialectics is the study of contradiction in the very essence of objects." Furthermore, he asserted in opposition to Mach, "sensation is the subjective image of the objective world."

A new stage of development was initiated when a devasting blow was dealt to pedology on July 4, 1936 by the Central Committee of the All-Union Communist

Party when it issued its decree "On Pedological Distortions in the System of the People's Commissariat of Education." The decree, denouncing the pedologists who were at the time engaged in Western type testing of individual differences, had wide reaching effects. The mid-thirties saw psychological journals liquidated one after the other. "Criticism and self-criticism" became the vogue. The thirties and forties witnessed the Russians reduced to an armchair psychology.

Rapid developments in psychology in consequence of Stalin's death began in 1955 with the publication of the journal, *Problems of Psychology (Voprosy Psikhologii)*. In 1959 the Society of Psychologists was established as an affiliate of the RSFSR Academy of Pedagogical Sciences with Smirnov its first president. By 1959 the Soviet Society of Psychologists held their first congress at Moscow, and by 1966 psychology departments at the universities of Moscow and Leningrad became separate schools or faculties of psychology, the world's first. The same year the Eighteenth International Congress of Psychology met in Moscow. The high point of that decade occurred in 1968 when there was issued a decree from the Council of Ministers of the U.S.S.R. granting doctoral degrees in psychology, thus marking psychology's coming to maturity in Soviet Russia.

(A) PRECURSORS OF RUSSIAN PSYCHOLOGY

M. V. LOMONOSOV (1711-1765): THE RUSSIAN ENLIGHTENMENT

The materialistic strain in Russian psychology stems from *M. V. Lomonosov* (1711-1765) who was not only the founder of the Russian philosophical materialism in the eighteenth century but also the founder of Moscow University in 1755. Interpreting sensations (especially visual perception) mechanistically and materialistically, Lomonosov reduced sensations to a combination of physical or physiological particles, viewing them ordered according to mechanical laws. He developed a tricomponent theory of color vision. Like Kant, he was interested in unifying rational and empirical cognition, seeing the cognitive process as a movement from appearances to essence, ideas being the reflection in a person's consciousness of objects in the world of reality. Hence he was a realist.

The Russian Enlightenment having started with the work of Lomonosov, some, such as *Ya. P. Kozel'skiy* (c. 1728-1754), came under his sway while others, such as *D. 'S. Anichkov* (1733-1788), expressed ideas consonant with his. The materialist Anichkov reduced the soul to an organic state, and cognitive activity to the brain or nerves, ideas that were adopted by *F. F. Keresturi* (1735-1811) and *M. I. Skiadana* (d. 1802). While Skiadana is regarded as the first to have identified the cerebral cortex as the organ responsible for higher psychic processes, Keresturi uncovered conduction paths for sensory and motor stimuli as well as tracing sense development phylogenetically. Another Russian of this period, *A. A. Antonskiy,* theorized human development as influenced by one's social and natural environment, an idea resembling contemporary dialectical psychology.

A product of the Russian Enlightenment, *N. I. Novikov* (1744-1818) published and edited the first journals related to Russian psychology. His pedagogical psychology emphasized the importance of an individual's psychological peculiarities, capacities, and "properties." Repudiating the Cartesian theory of innate ideas, *G. S. Skovoroda* (1722-1794) imputed the source of all knowledge to the external world, isolating ideas from an object's essence. Sensations are formed during the course of need satisfaction, hence sensations are contingent on a person's activity.

During the eighteenth century, Russian psychology climaxed with the efforts of *A. N. Radishchev* (1749-1802), who viewed psychic phenomena or the activity of the soul as a property that was brain produced. Man, comparable to the animal except for his intellect, articulate speech, and agile use of hands, could think owing to sensations. His theory of "coparticipation," his major contribution, was grounded on the spiritual kinship of people and the higher human feelings found in human beings.

Ananiev attributed the "motivational-dynamic trend" to *A. I. Galich,* a representative of the school of natural-philosophical idealism that was prevalent in the first half of the nineteenth century. A disciple of Schelling, Galich offered a theory of the phasic nature of human perception. According to the theory, "free" perception (which changes concomitantly with a person's mental development) proceeds from a base of "constrained" sense perception to the form of imagination and sense representation (idea). "Semi-thought" (plausible explanations, hypotheses, opinions, etc.) is the transition from "constrained" to "free" perception. Moral feelings and actions characterize a person's spiritual development. Motivation, passion, inclination, and habit constitute the internal conditions of practical activity.

P. M. LYUBOVSKY: Russian Associational Psychology.   A group of psychologists of the same period, following Wolff's dichotomization of psychology into rational and empirical, pursued the latter with their experimental attempts at psychology. One of them, who was a master of Kharkov University, *P. M. Lyubovsky,* published *A Short Handbook of Experimental Soul-Science* in 1815, hoping that it would become the nation's principle text in psychology. Texts up to this time in Russia were translations. One of the first Russians to promulgate the "association of ideas" as the explanation of mental processes, Lyubovsky developed a theory of human inclination, dividing it into mental inclinations (such as patriotism) and corporeal inclinations (e.g. temperament). Though the latter are derived from nature, they alter subject to living conditions.

Following the associational psychology of Lyubovsky was a professor at the Pedagogic Institute and the University of St. Petersburg, *P. D. Lodiy* (1764-1829), author of *Lectures in Logic,* a work which contained a course in psychology and appeared in the same year of Lyubovsky's publication. Interested in the psychology of language, he underscored the relationship of perception of speech, being the first to note the utilization of speech when one thinks to himself and traced individual differences to one's social situation.

The first half of the nineteenth century also had its share of physiologists interested in psychology. Three major ones, professors at Moscow University, were *Ye. O. Mukhin* (1766-1850), *I. Ye. Dyad'kovskiy* (1784-1841) and *A. M. Filomafitsky* (1807-1849). The three, interested in stimuli, regarded the nervous system as that which integrates the organism and by which contact is established with the outside world. The Russians credit Mukhin as the first to call attention to inhibition as the nonconduction of nerve fibers and association as a material process, a connection of neural paths. The anti-functionalist Dyad'kovskiy attempted to trace sense to nonsensing matter, holding that at higher or more complicated levels of development matter acquires the property of irritability. Not merely involuntary reactions, but the voluntary ones also were traced to the brain. The antivitalist Filomafitsky contributed the notion that every voluntary action is reflective, hence coined the term *reflective movements,* which came to be called reflex actions. His experiments on frogs concluded that an inhibiting effect is exerted by the brain on reflex actions.

THE REVOLUTIONARY DEMOCRATS: Materialistic Psychology

Considered important precursors of Soviet psychology were *Vissarion Grigorvevich Belinskiy* (1811-1848), *A. I. Gertsen* (1812-1870), *Nicholas Gavrilovich Chernyshevskiy* (1828-1889), and *N. A. Dobrolyubov* (1836-1861). These four *revolutionary democrats* of the 1860s as they are called, were materialistically grounded in psychology, which had close ties with philosophy at that time. Principally interested in personality theory, *Belinskiy* espoused a social nature theory of personality in which circumstances, rearing, and class consciousness play a role. Another principle contribution pertinent to his theory of the cognitive significance of the senses is the process of perception entailing reason and emotions in a unity. The metaphysical monist *Gertsen* acknowledged psychic reality as a peculiar qualitative property of the human being that is not reducible to other properties. This view countenanced psychology as an independent science rather than an adjunct to another science such as physiology despite its inseparable relationship to physiology. He did, however, view personality as the product of physiological and historical necessity, and repudiated freedom of the will while endorsing scientific necessity. The great Russian physiologist, I. M. Sechenov, was directly influenced by *N. G. Chernyshevskiy's* "pure philosophical materialism." In addition to his materialistic theory of aesthetic emotions *a la* Feuerbach, Chernyshevskiy, the leader of radical socialism in Russia and a principal Russian nihilist, held that sensations constitute genuine knowledge of objects which had their own objective existence, defining human thought in terms of a complex integrated process consisting of a mediated reflection occurring in a person's consciousness of those common regularities found in the external world. Viewing psychic processes or activity as impressions gained from objects existing in the external world, *Dobrolyubov* regarded these processes as produced by the cerebral hemisphere's activity. Yet he accorded historical factors a primacy over biological ones in explaining human development, viewing a person's mental qualities as being acquired. The debate of these materialists with the idealists was continued by a student of Chernyshevskiy and Dobrolyubov, *M. A. Antonovich* (1835-1918), who carried the debate in *The Contemporary,* an important journal that served as the organ of radical opinion during the period of the 1860s.

NIKOLAY NIKOLAYEVICH LANGE (1858-1921): Early Experimental Psychology

One of the first psychological laboratories in Russia was founded by *Nikolay Nikolayevich Lange* (1858-1921) at the Novorossiyskiy (Odessa) University. Approaching psychological questions dualistically, Lange developed the phasic character of perceptual processes and studied attention as a motor phenomenon. One of the first to investigate attention fluctuations, Lange compiled his findings in *Psychological Investigations: The Law of Perception; the Theory of Voluntary Attention* in 1893.

Another Russian psychologist whose life span extended into the twentieth century, *Mikhail Yakovlevich Basov* (1892-1931), was interested in child psychology and the psychology of personality as well as general psychology. His specialty, personality development and techniques for the psychological observation of children, made him one of the more distinguished pedagogues in Russia. *Methods of Psychological Observation,* published in 1923, is one of his more important works.

A still more recent psychologist, *Nadezhda Nikolayevna Ladygina-Kots* (1889-1963), specialized in comparative psychology. Utilizing her original technique of "matching to example," she studied the cognitive abilities of chimpanzees. Employing puzzle boxes, she investigated habit formation in monkeys. She also studied higher forms of adaptive activity in them. Two of her important books include *Investigation of the Cognitive Abilities of the Chimpanzee* (1923) and *Adaptive Motor Habits of the Macaque in Experimental Situations* (1928).

(B)   THE REFLEX PERIOD OF RUSSIAN PSYCHOLOGY

From the middle of the last century to the rise of dialectical psychology, Russian psychology has been essentially physiological, mechanistic, and rooted in reflex theory. Emphasis has been placed virtually exclusively on the objective with consciousness and subjective considerations relegated either to one side or entirely repudiated. The trend, essentially one of reductionism in which the psychic is explained in terms of (and reduced to) physiology, produced a conception of the human being that was radically monistic, i.e., a physical substance devoid of any psychic element that can be regarded as *sui generis.*

A portion of extreme or radical monism was moderated with the rise of dialectical psychology, which rejected reflexology as "vulgarly mechanistic." It regarded consciousness as the legitimate study of psychology despite its contingency upon physiology; and human psychology must be understood in the light of historical and social factors.

IVAN MIKHAILOVICH SECHENOV (1829-1905):
Reflex Theory of Mental Activity

Born in the village of Tyoply Stan (currently Sechenovo), Sechenov studied at the Military Engineering School in Petersburg, but a distaste for the subject soon had him graduating from the Faculty of Medicine at Moscow University. Sechenov, who was dubbed the "father of Russian physiology" by his successor Pavlov, abandoned his interest in Hegelian idealism for naturalism and mechanism. He is cited as the founder of objective physiological psychology in Russia.

The main currents of his life according to his *Biographical Notes* (1965), written approximately the year prior to his death, cite the years from 1843 to 1850 as training in engineering; from 1850 to 1856 studying medicine and physiology at Moscow University; from 1856 to 1860 studying abroad with associations with Johannes Müller, Hermann von Helmholtz, Brücke, and other notables; from 1860 to 1870 returning to Russia and accepting a professorship at the Petersburg Medical Academy; from 1870 to 1876 accepting a professorship in Odessa University; from 1876 to 1888 moving to a professorship at Petersburg University where he remained a dozen years; on November 2, 1905 he died of pneumonia.

His classic *Reflexes of the Brain,* written in the summer of 1863 in Petersburg, elaborated on two theses found in his doctoral dissertation. They were:

1. All the movements known in physiology as voluntary movements are reflex movements in the strict sense of the word.
2. The most general feature of the normal activity of the brain (expressed in the form of movement) is the disproportion between the excitation and the effect (movement) engendered by it *(Autobiographical Notes,* 1965, p. 108).

In 1863 he published *Mechanisms in the Brain of the Frog which Inhibit the Reflexes of the Spinal Cord* in which he initially established the action of localized inhibitory centers in the brain.

When it came time to publish his more general work *Reflexes of the Brain,* he offered it under the title *An Attempt to Bring Physiological Bases into Mental Processes,* but the censor rejected the title, and Sechenov was viewed as the "Champion of undisciplined temper," and a "nihilist philosopher." The manuscript, appearing in 1863 in a medical newspaper *(Medical Herald)* because the censors banned it from publication in *The Contemporary,* developed the thesis that the psychic is synonymous with reflex actions of the brain.

> *All psychical acts without exception, if they are not complicated by elements of emotion . . . develop by way of reflex. Hence, all conscious movements resulting from these acts and usually described as voluntary, are reflex movements in the strict sense of the term* (1965, p. 80).

His objective in writing the monograph was to establish that "all acts of conscious and unconscious life are reflexes by origin" (1965, p. 106). Thus psychic processes are inseparable from neural ones. "Pure psychology," one based merely on the data of consciousness, he repudiated in his *How and By Whom Shall Psychology Be Studied?* (1873). He chose the term "reflex" because "excitation of the sensory nerve is reflected in the motor nerve" (1965, p. 7), and held that *"all external manifestations of the functioning of the brain can be reduced to muscular movement"* (1965, pp. 3-4). A basic postulate of his was the organism's inability to exist without support from the external environment. As early as 1861, in *Vegetative Processes in Animal Life,* he asserted: "The organism cannot exist without the external environment which supports it, hence, the scientific definition of the organism must also include the environment" (quoted in I. P. Pavlov, *Selected Works,* 1955, p. 30).

Reviewing the contributions that originated with Sechenov, the following should be included: (1) reflex actions encompass both psychical and physiological reactions; (2) association is the reflex mechanism; and (3) the psychic arises from association and is mediated by the central nervous system, that is, ideas stem from the association of reflexes entailing the mechanism of the central nervous system. He was also radically environmentalistic, holding that ideas arise virtually from training and only minimally from heredity. His thoroughgoing "physical monism" reduced the psyche to neural and muscular action so that psychical phenomena are explicable in terms of bodily nervous acts.

Other contributions of Sechenov include: (1) the theory of the summation of stimulations, the discovery that nerve centers are able to summarize sensory stimulations which when applied singly prove ineffective, a theory that first appeared in 1868 in his *Electrical and Chemical Stimulation of Sensory Spinal Nerves in the Frog.* Others developed Sechenov's discovery of the nervous system's ability to summarize subthreshold stimulations. (2) The theory of central inhibition arose from the discovery that there are special apparatuses in the central nervous system that when stimulated produce the suppression of spinal reflexes. Four decades later Pavlov, who was enormously influenced by Sechenov's *Reflexes of the Brain* during his student days, undertook experimental work that supported the findings of Sechenov's reflex theory. It was not a Russian, but the Frenchman, Descartes, who first introduced the notion of reflexes into psychology or physiology. The Russian physiologists, Sechenov and Pavlov, underscored its adaptive character.

Sechenov influenced a number of disciples in addition to Pavlov, the most distinguished being *Nikolay Yevgen'yevich Vvedenskiy* (1852-1922), a physiologist known for his theory of parabiosis. His views on the unitary nature of inhibition and excitation processes are found in his *Excitation, Inhibition, and Narcosis* (1901).

IVAN PETROVICH PAVLOV (1849-1936):
Conditioned Reflex or Classical Conditioning

Sechenov's intellectual successor, I. V. Pavlov, was born during the year that A. M. Filomafitsky (1807-1849), Russia's founder of experimental physiology, died. Born in Ryazan and educated at its theological seminary before entering

Petersburg University in 1870, he went on to the Medical-Surgical Academy (Military Medical Academy) in 1875. He graduated from the latter in 1879 with his doctoral dissertation, *Efferent Nerves of the Heart*, published in 1883. Married with one son, Pavlov lived frugally owing to a meagre income, which was spent in part for experimental work until his appointment to a chair and two posts at the age of 41 when he became Professor of Pharmacology (subsequently physiology) at the Military Medical Academy in 1890, and headed the department of physiology at the Institute of Experimental Medicine in 1891.

From 1888 Pavlov occupied himself with the physiology of digestion, the fruits of which led to his famous discovery of the ''conditioned reflex'' that was first given to the world in 1903 at the International Congress of Medicine at Madrid in a paper titled: ''Experimental Psychology and Psychopathology of Animals,'' and the following year was awarded the Nobel Prize. From this time on he devoted virtually all his research to the conditioned reflex, or ''higher nervous activity,'' a term synonymous with his system. In 1923 his experiments were presented in a work, *Twenty Years of Objective Experimental Study of the Higher Nervous Activity of Animals*, and five years later published in English as *Lectures on Conditioned Reflexes: Twenty-five Years of Objective Study on the Higher Nervous Activity (Behaviour) of Animals*. A second volume of the English translation appeared in 1941 as *Conditioned Reflexes and Psychiatry*. Pavlov's experimental activity spanned a sixty-year period. His principal contributions to science included areas of digestion, establishing laws of coordination of various portions of the digestive tract and the digestive activity's dependence on ingestion (winning him the Nobel Prize in 1904); blood circulation; conditioned reflexes; and the trophic role of the nervous system. Pre-Pavlovian physiology differs from that of Pavlov in that it is segmented, treating organs and tissues in isolation, while Pavlov studied the organism and its activity as a whole.

Conditioned Reflexes. Classical learning theory is to be traced to Pavlov's celebrated experiments with dogs in which he caused salivation by reflex action by introducing acid solution into the mouth of a dog. Saliva functioned as a diluting and cleansing agent, cleansing the mucous membrane by diluting the acid. Utilizing such reflex action, Pavlov found it possible for the dog to learn by association, which he termed *objective association*. Prior to injecting acid into the dog's mouth, one may sound a bell or some other neutral stimulus. After several of these episodes, Pavlov found that the dog had established an association of the bell with the acid, and the animal would salivate at the sound of the signal only.

Let us take one of these unconditioned reflexes, a most common one, of daily occurrence, the food reflex. A definite motor and secretory reaction to food as a stimulus occurs when it is placed before the dog or when it gets into his mouth. If a few seconds before the food is in the mouth of the dog, there acts, for example, on his ear, the sound of a metronome, and if such coincidence takes place one or more times, then the metronome will call out the same reaction as the food, *i.e.*, there will appear the same movements and the same salivary and other digestive secretions. This new food reaction can become as exact as if the food actually were in the mouth, and it may exist for an indefinitely long time.

These reactions are what I call *unconditioned reflexes* (1928, p. 354).

Unconditioned reflexes are inborn, and generic, whereas the conditioned are acquired and temporary. Pavlov believed that a *Bahnung* had been established, that is, a path had been formed in the nervous system, facilitating reflex reaction owing to its frequent repetition. The reflex act, Pavlov termed the *unconditioned reflex* and it served to account for instinctive reactions as well, while the temporary connection evoked was called a *conditioned reflex*.

First and Second Signal Systems. The conditioned reflex differed from the unconditioned with respect to its "psychical" characteristics. Since it served as a sign for signalling action, he termed it the *first signal system* or *first signal conditioning*. The cerebral cortex acts as a connecting, combining, or coupling function when it operates mechanically, and as a signalling function when it functions in terms of "significance." "Distant reflexes" or "signalling reflexes," Pavlov later identified as "conditioned reflexes." Pavlov stressed the coupling nature of conditioned reflexes as a temporary coupling, connecting two foci of excitation transpiring in the brain; their temporal nature is obvious when one realizes that they disappear (extinction) under certain conditions. The adaptive quality of the conditioned reflex augments the organism's equilibrium with its environment. By heredity it is possible for conditioned reflexes to be transformed into unconditioned ones. Adaptive orientation stems from the *orienting reflex*, a basic energizer producing the "what-is-it-reactions" such as the pricking up of the ears to listen for danger signals.

While sensation characterizes the first signal system, speech is the hallmark of the second signal system. Through human speech a person gains a reflection of reality as well as abstract or scientific knowledge.

> If our sensations and notions caused by the surrounding world are for us the first signals of reality, concrete signals, then speech, especially and primarily the kinesthetic stimuli which proceed from the speech organs to the cortex, constitute a second set of signals, the signals of signals. They represent an abstraction from reality and make possible the forming of generalizations; this constitutes our extra *specially human, higher mentality* creating an empiricism general to all men and then, in the end, science, the instrument of higher orientation of man in the surrounding world and in himself (1932a, p. 271).

Unlike the American psychologists: Tolman, Hull, and Skinner who developed behavioral systems, Pavlov's objective psychology is a *nervism* derived from S. P. Botkin. "By nervism," Pavlov said, "I mean the tendency in physiology which tries to extend the influence of the nervous system on the greatest possible number of functions of the organism" (1904). In Pavlov's neurobehavioral system, the S-R is replaced with S-N-R (stimulus-neural process-response). Conditioning, in the objective associationism of Pavlov, calls for the unconditioned stimulus (US), (e.g., food) that produces an unconditioned response (UR), (e.g., salivation) being paired with a neutral stimulus (e.g., bell) several times so that its results in a conditioned reflex.

Among the psychological laws that Pavlov established are: (1) *irradiation* or *generalization;* (2) *concentration;* (3) *inhibition* and *disinhibition;* (4) *spontaneous recovery;* (5) *high order conditioning;* (6) *dynamic stereotypy;* and (7) *reciprocal induction.* *Irradiation* is that process of excitation or inhibition spreading or *generalizing* to adjacent cortical regions irradiating neighboring cells of the hemisphere, the result being that a conditioned reflex that has been established with a tone of 14,000 c.p.s. can generalize so that the same results may be obtained with a tone of 12,000 cycles per second. The opposite of generalization, *concentration* or *discrimination,* arises when the excitation of a given cortical area is established but adjacent regions are inhibited and responses to them extinguished so that the dog is fed only for responding to the tone of 14,000 c.p.s. Thus the 14,000 c.p.s. tone is reinforced and the others become neutral stimuli.

Pavlov identified *external inhibition (retroactive inhibition)* as a new reflex inhibiting or competing with an active, existing one. *Internal inhibition (extinction)* results when the stimulus of a given conditioned reflex is no longer accompanied by the desired result. *Spontaneous recovery* of the conditioned reflex is proof that the conditioned reflex is not destroyed but merely temporarily inhibited because a conditioned reflex can be restored completely in a spontaneous manner. *Disinhibition* he explained as the irradiation of an accessory weak stimulus transforming "the effect of a certain acting negative conditioned stimulus into the opposite, positive effect" (1934, p. 256). Hypnosis is the irradiation of a weak inhibitory process. Pavlov spoke of three phases: (1) the *equalization phase,* (2) the *paradoxical phase,* and (3) the *ultraparadoxical phase,* and described them accordingly:

> Contrary to the rule of a more or less parallel change in the size of the salivary effect of the conditioned alimentary reflexes, corresponding to the physical intensity of the stimuli, all stimuli become equal in effect (the equalization phase). Then the weak stimuli provoke a more abundant secretion of saliva than the strong (paradoxical phase). And finally there takes place a distortion of effects: the conditioned positive stimulus remains fully ineffective, whereas the negative stimulus produces a secretion of saliva (the ultra-paradoxical phase) (1934, p. 256).

According to the *law of reciprocal induction,* "the effect of the positive conditioned stimulus becomes stronger when the latter is applied immediately or shortly after the concentrated inhibitory stimulus" (1934, p. 258). The laws of reciprocal induction, concentration, and irradiation are so interrelated that they limit, balance, and reinforce each other. Reciprocal induction results when opposite processes are induced by the concentration of excitatory and inhibitory processes.

Dynamic Stereotype Theory. By dynamic stereotype theory Pavlov meant a system of coordination processes and equilibrium of the internal processes so that stimuli converge and interact systematically. The system consists of positive and negative stimuli of varying intensities acting on different receptors.

Countless stimuli, different in nature and intensity, reach the cerebral hemispheres both from the external world and the internal medium of the organism itself. Whereas some of them are merely investigated (the orienting reflex), others evoke highly diverse conditioned and unconditioned effects. They all meet, come together, interact, and they must, finally, become systematized, equilibrated, and form, so to speak, a dynamic stereotype (1932b, p. 454).

Dynamic stereotype is the particular position or order each stimulus assumes in the entire pattern of conditioning rather than its character in determining its strength in the conditioned reflex process.

Theory of Analyzers. An analyzer, a complex nervous mechanism originating with the external receiving apparatus and ending within the brain, transforms external energy into a process of the nervous system. Comparable to physical analyzers such as the prism that decomposes white light into many hues, the nervous system with its analyzers detects oscillations of light by the retina or those of air by the ear's acoustical ability. By ear analyzers, tones are divided into wave lengths, amplitudes and forms. Accordingly the nervous system has another function: that of "analysing the external environment, in decomposing the different complexities of the world into their separate elements" (1916, pp. 404-5).

The Rule of the Summation of Conditioned Stimuli. Pavlov observed that the strength of stimuli has limits so that a limit exists beyond which a stronger stimulus actually tends to decrease the effect rather than strengthening it.

In combining a number of weak conditioned stimuli, one may often observe their exact arithmetical sum. In combining a weak stimulus with a strong one, one observes a certain increase in the resulting effect, within a certain limit; whereas in combining two strong stimuli the effect, passing the limit, becomes less than that of each of the components (the rule of the summation of conditioned stimuli) (1930, p. 210).

Theory of Types: Genotype and Phenotype. Typology or temperament became an intensified interest of Pavlov's near the end of his career. Influenced by the Lamarckian theory of inherited acquired characteristics, Pavlov believed that conditioned reflexes are hereditarily transformed into unconditioned reflexes. His interest in the genetics of the higher nervous system at the Koltushi Biological Station led to the belief in inborn reflexes or unconditioned reflexes arising from conditioned ones. His study of dogs produced the hypothesis of different nervous systems in different canines.

Type is a congenital, constitutional form of the nervous activity of the animal—the genotype. But since the animal is exposed from the very day of its birth to the most varied influences of the environment, to which it must inevitably respond by definite actions which often become more and more fixed and, finally, established for life, the ultimate nervous activity of the animal (phenotype, character) is an alloy of the characteristics of type and the changes produced by the external environment (1934, pp. 260-1).

He found three major types or temperaments in animals: (1) *excitatory types,* (2) *inhibitory type,* and (3) *central type.* But the central type (which were well balanced, equilibrated animals) he subdivided into *quiet* and *lively.* The first two are extreme types. Thus Pavlov concluded four types of temperament, each with its corresponding nervous system. The extent to which each type manifests itself in an organism depends upon the extent to which strength, balance and mobility are present. Before Pavlov could pursue his ideas on the matter any further, death had overtaken him. But his typology became a field of research in Soviet Russia with psychologists such as Teplov continuing experiments in typology.

BORIS MIKHAILOVICH TEPLOV (1896-1965): Typology

A member of the Presidium of the Academy of Pedagogical Sciences of the RSFSR, Teplov, the one-time editor of *Problems of Psychology (Voprosy Psikhologii)*, was born in Tula and educated at the University of Moscow. After the October Revolution he studied at the Higher School of War Camouflage, graduating in 1921 as Engineer of War Camouflage. From 1921 to 1933 he was chief of the Department of Experimental Stations of the Higher School of War Camouflage, working in the scientific research division of the Red Army as chief of the Scientific Laboratory of Visual Perception of the Scientific-Experimental Engineering-Technical Proving Ground. From 1929 he worked at the Institute of Psychology, heading it in 1933. His graduate school and later interest included auditory perception and the psychology of music as attested by his doctoral dissertation, *The Psychology of Musical Ability*. Later he became interested in the psychology of talent, abilities, and personality. He was widely known for publishing a psychology textbook for high school classes that was translated into 14 languages.

Influenced by Sechenov and Pavlov, he investigated the field of typology, studying human individual differences and founding a new school for research in this field. He distinguished himself as a result of his investigations of the typological differences of human higher nervous activity. He was one of the influential forces at the Pavlovian Sessions of the Academy of Science and the Academy of Medical Sciences in 1950. At the Institute of Psychology he directed the Laboratory of Higher Neural Dynamics.

Typology, the study of the psychological types, is treated by Teplov as types of nervous systems. The object is to ascertain those typological properties of the nervous system which account for the natural basis of psychological, individual differences among people with respect to their temperament, character, and capabilities. In order to accomplish this aim, the physiological content of the properties must be investigated. Teplov considered the determination of individual psychological differences in persons as one of psychology's most important tasks.

Defining *types* as "a complex of the basic properties of the nervous system" (1961, p. 31), Teplov adopted Pavlov's doctrine of types of higher nervous activity and applied it to human beings by proceeding from properties to types rather than vice versa. Strength and mobility are not psychological conceptions but properties of the nervous system. Defining *temperament* as "the individaul peculiarities of the individual as manifested in (1) emotional excitability . . . , (2) a more or less marked tendency to strong outward expression of feelings . . . , and (3) rapidity of the movements and general mobility" (1961, p. 41), Teplov felt that his definition contributed to the description of the traditional four temperaments such as the choleric, sanguine, etc. He was fond of his hypothesis: "If general typological properties determine the temperament of man, then particular properties will be of the greatest significance in the study of particular abilities" (1961, p. 46). Nevertheless the hypothesis was too restricted to suit him. The physiological basis for individual psychical properties (including aptitudes) is grounded in the typology of higher nervous activity.

With the exception of the physiological grounding of temperament and types in Pavlovian psychology, much of Soviet typology is essentially or closely allied to western psychology of individual differences and constitutional psychology of the Kretschmer tradition.

SOKOLOV (1920-   ): Orienting Reflex

With respect to Pavlov's "orienting reflex," it has stimulated research among Soviet psychologists, especially has it engaged the attention of Sokolov and his associates at Moscow State University. Concentrating on the reflex basis of attention, the *orienting reflex,* when he was employed at Kravkov's laboratory, Sokolov was occupied with the relation of extinction to the orienting reflex. Later he investigated the neural mechanisms of the orienting reflex, which he found resembled the neural basis of memory.

Sokolov cited the distinguishing properties of the orienting and adaptive reflexes with respect to their vascular, cutaneous galvanic, and cortical electrical responses accordingly:

Orienting reactions:
(a) develop only in response to a change of stimulus;
(b) in all cases the sign of reaction is the same, and is such as to increase sensory sensitivity;
(c) they disappear during the maintained action of the stimulus, to appear once more when it ceases;
(d) they develop in response to a wide range of stimuli;
(e) they include many components affecting many different organs;
(f) they may be divided into general and special orienting reactions;
(g) they become extinguished by repetitions;
(h) they are restored by the application of extraneous stimuli or by a change in the conditions of the experiment.

Adaptive reactions:
(a) the response is proportional to the strength and to the quality of the adequate stimulus;
(b) the sign of the reaction differs according to whether the stimulus is applied or withdrawn;
(c) they are maintained during the whole of the period of application of the stimulus;
(d) they represent special reactions which occur only in response to adequate stimuli;
(e) they are not extinguished by repetition;
(f) they may be inhibited by extraneous stimuli, being temporarily replaced by orienting reactions (1961, p. 193).

Notwithstanding their differences, the two (orienting and adaptive reflexes) are closely associated, and interact at the cortical level, thus indicating the reflex basis of perception.

Defining the orienting-exploratory reflex as "a system of reactions which is directed toward a contact of the organism and the object, and which facilitates the 'tuning in' of the analysers of the animal and man and insures the best conditions for the perception of the acting stimulus" (1965, p. 141), Sokolov viewed the orienting reflex as a system of reactions that tune the analyzer. But it must be distinguished from the "adaptational reflexes" that adapt the analyzer to the intensity level of the stimulus which acts upon the organism. As a system of reactions, the orienting reflex possesses afferent and efferent mechanisms. The efferent mechanisms, a complex of reactions, comprise the orienting reflex. Various stimuli can evoke the same complex of reactions in the orienting reflex. Orienting reflexes fall into two categories: the localized reflexes and the generalized reflexes. By repeatedly presenting a stimulus, one can change the generalized reflex into a localized orienting reaction. By repeatedly presenting a stimulus, one can also extinguish an orienting reflex. An orienting reflex can be evoked by a conditioned stimulus. Thus the orienting reflex serves to adapt the organism better to its environment as is seen in a dog pricking up its ears as if it had a "what-is-it reaction" as Pavlov put it.

According to his investigations, he found that "reflex activity is mediated through complex mechanisms in the central divisions of analyzers which function to reflect the external world" (1969, p. 702). A neural trace is detected when the scope of the orienting reflex is measured during the administration of controlled test stimuli. The trace, a neural model of the stimulus, registers intensity, duration, space location, rhythm, and qualitative characteristics of stimuli. The nervous system, by the creation of an internal model of its own environment, accurately reflects the external world. The accuracy of the internal neural model's being in accord with objective reality is contingent on the effectiveness of the organism's interaction with its environment. One may ascertain from practical activity how adequately or accurately the neural model in question has reflected its material.

VLADIMIR MIKHAILOVITCH BEKHTEREV (1867-1927): Reflexology

Pavlov's contemporary, V. M. Bekhterev, was a physiologist, psychologist, and psychiatrist trained in medicine at the Medical-Surgical Academy (Military Medical Academy) at Petersburg, graduating in 1878 at 21 years of age. But his doctoral degree came in 1881 with the dissertation *Results of Clincial Investigation of Body Temperature in Certain Forms of Psychic Disease.* In 1884 he researched abroad, studying under such notables as Wundt, Charcot, Meynert, and Du Bois Reymond. Having been appointed a professor of psychic diseases at the University of Kazan in 1885, he founded the first laboratory of experimental psychology in Russia the following year. A decade later, 1896, he founded the *Review of Psychiatry, Neuropathology and Experimental Psychology,* the first journal containing "experimental psychology" as part of its title. He returned to his alma mater in 1893 as professor, and two years later as director of the Military Medical Academy, founding the Russian Society for Normal and Pathological Psychology. His writings, which number close to 1000, include two classic texts in neurology: *Nerve Paths in the Brain and Spinal Cord* (1893) and the seven volume *Fundamentals of Brain Functions* (1903-1907); and three in psychology: *Objective Psychology* (1907), *General Principles of Human Reflexology* (1917), and *Collective Reflexology* (1921). He left the Academy under governmental pressure in 1913 but remained with the Psychoneurological Institute which he founded in 1907 in Petersburg. He founded at least seven other institutes, including the Pathologo-Reflexological Institute. After the October Revolution, he held the chair of psychiatry and reflexology at the University of Petrograd (with which the Psychoneurological Institute had merged) from 1918 until his death.

As early as 1904, Bekhterev was promoting *objective psychology* as a distinct study; he identified it as *psychoreflexology* in 1912, and abbreviated it to *reflexology* by 1917. Pavlov in 1903 had antedated Bekhterev by only a year with respect to the insistence of employing objective principles, and by only four or five years with respect to his conditioned reflexes as opposed to the latter's association reflexes. For Pavlov's "conditioned reflex," Bekhterev coined the term "association reflex." American publications on the matter did not appear until Watson's publications in 1913 and 1916 with "Psychology as a Behaviorist Views It" and "The Place of Conditioned-Reflex in Psychology." Though Watson was initially influenced by Bekhterev rather than Pavlov, it was Pavlov who all but eclipsed Bekhterev in influence both in Soviet Russia and abroad. Reflexology was denounced as "vulgar mechanism" by party ideologists in the 1930s and yielded all of its ground that it had gained and enjoyed for over a score of years to Pavlovian psychology. Reflexology, a dominant psychology during the decade following the October Revolution in 1917, had waned with the event of Bekhterev's death in 1927.

Reflexology as a Psychology

His desire to establish psychology as an objective science comparable to other natural sciences (such as physics) led Bekhterev to regard the method of introspection in psychology as invalid. Rather, he preferred the study of psychology from a "strictly objective, bio-social standpoint." Man must be investigated as if the psychologist arrived from another planet and did not share the same psychological characteristics. The approach would include phenomena of "psychic activity" or the "spiritual sphere" wherein is to be found feeling, knowing, and willing, as well as social activity. Psychic activity, objectively studied, includes the investigation of the activity of man's facial expressions, vocal expressions, gestures, etc. as signs. Such a study would be based on an investigation of innate reflex actions, i.e., the outer reaction ensuing from a given external stimulus.

Reflexology, the "antithesis of empirical psychology," studies both inherited and acquired reflexes. The phenomenon of conscious activity, however, is studied as a manifestation of energy. Both psychic and cerebral processes entail the same neural energy or neural electricity, the same energy manifested in heavenly bodies, animate and inanimate organisms as well as human individual and social life (collective reflexology). Bekhterev's radical monism is complete, integrated, and systematic; psychic phenomena are reduced to the laws not merely of physiology but of physics. Defining reflexology, Bekhterev said that it consisted

> in the study of the organism's correlative activity . . . , and by correlative activity we mean all the organism's inherited and individually acquired reactions, beginning from innate and complex-organic reflexes up to, and including, the most complex acquired reflexes, which in man go by the name of actions and conduct and comprise his characteristic behavior (1933, p. 171).

A person is not an object and subject but a unitary being both object and subject whose external aspects only are subject to scientific investigation by external observation. The external (reflexes) are the proper objective study, for the subjective cannot be directly investigated. The inner or latent reflexes are studied through an "objectively given verbal account" of them.

> Let us note in conclusion that man is an agent whose mechanism is set in motion by external and internal stimuli, for he is a product both of the past life of his ancestors (racial experience) and of his own past individual experience. In accordance with this, and in dependence on it, he develops reaction to certain external and internal influences, and these reactions take the form of various—sometimes complex, sometimes more simple—concatenated reflexes produced by external, as well as internal, stimuli not only present, but also past (1933, p. 173).

Psychical processes Bekhterev saw as resulting from tension from nervous energy or nervous current. Conscious phenomena accompany concentration which is bound to the detention of nervous current. Consciousness is weakened or absent when nervous current travels unimpeded. Whereas habitual actions are unconscious, those performed for the first time are predominantly conscious. Thought is an inhibited reflex.

KONSTANTIN NIKOLAYEVICH KORNILOV (1879-1957): Reactology

Behavioristic psychology received a fillip from K. N. Kornilov's *reactological psychology* and his influence in the 1920s when he assumed directorship at the Moscow Psychological Institute in 1924. His address at the All-Russian Psychological Congress in 1923 devasted the "idealistic" schools of Russian psychology together with their method of introspectionism. With the elimination of subjective factors, the question arose as to the validity of psychology as a distinct and independent discipline. Many Russian psychologists doubted that consciousness could exist in a materialistically based psychology. Later, however, it became apparent that consciousness was an indispensable entity in dialectical psychology.

The reflexological school of Bekhterev was severely challenged and criticized by psychologists at the Psychological Institute in Moscow under the leadership of Kornilov, a student of Chelpanov. From 1923 to 1927 in the journal, *Under the*

Banner of Marxism, mechanism in reflexology was attacked repeatedly by Kornilov, who sought a Marxist based psychology. That is, in order for psychology to qualify as Marxist, it must be: *(a)* materialistic; *(b)* deterministic, and *(c)* dialectical. While the first two points were well entrenched in Russian psychology, the third was unacceptable to a number of psychologists and scientists.

To fill the void, Kornilov tendered what he believed was a genuine Marxist psychology. He termed it *reactology,* the investigation of human reactions to stimuli and to the demands of human environment. Though Kornilov shared with Pavlov and Bekhterev the notion that psychology deals with a person's external reactions to his environment, he differed by concerning himself with the subjective factors of human behavior. "Reaction" is not equivalent with "reflex," for while the latter is a purely physiological concept, the former extends beyond the quantitative to the qualitative and ideological content which is foreign to the reflex concept. Nevertheless, reactology is behavioristic. Unless the subjective finding in psychology is validated by the objective, it is unacceptable. Authenticity rests with the objective.

> *Only the objective side of an experiment is a sufficient guarantee of its authenticity. As regards the subjective side, that is, the data of self-observation, these possess significance only in so far as they are corroborated by the objective facts* (1930, p. 270).

Dissociating himself from the objective school of psychology, Kornilov viewed psychical phenomena as one but not identical with the physiological process by which they are processed. With its own peculiar qualitative feature, the psychic is the other side of the physiological process and constitutes the peculiar qualitative characteristics of consciousness. He viewed psychology as a "unity of the subjective and objective, a *theory of behavior of a living, integral, concrete individual in concrete social conditions"* (1930, p. 264). Accordingly psychology is defined as the science of behavior and of individual development. Though biological elements are important, Marxian psychology finds a person more influenced by the social; hence an individual is the product and sum of social relations, a "conglomeration of social influences." Existence determines consciousness but consciousness reciprocally influences existence.

In the study of personality, Kornilov regarded "*reactions* as the responses of the living organism to the stimuli of its surroundings. Therefore from an analytical point of view we call psychology 'reactology,' that is, the science of the reactions of the individual" (1930, p. 268). Reactions are, however, biosociological. With respect to his social relations, a person's reactions acquire a social meaning. Consequently psychology is a social science, and not physiology or a natural science. The quantitative or scientific aspects of reaction involve the acquisition of four types of facts: (1) the rate at which the reaction occurs, (2) the intensity of reaction, (3) the form of movements transpiring in a reaction, and (4) the contents of the reaction of its social significance. By measuring these reactions, one is supposedly measuring mental energy.

Kornilov's reactology was not the only candidate for a "truly Marxist psychology,'' for there were a number of contenders including Bekhterev's reflexology and Blonsky's behavioral human psychology. But none of them was found satisfactory, and many of them were dismissed as "vulgarly materialistic" or mechanistic, including Kornilov's system which had the overtones of American behaviorism and thus was categorized as "bourgeoise" or capitalistic. Soviet psychology was in no small part based on Lenin's theory of reflection as enunciated in his *Materialism and Empirio-criticism* (1909) and *Philosophical Notebooks* (1929).

Kornilov's moment of glory was brief, for his psychology fell under the criticism that prevailed in the 1930s, and it was found unsuitable. His reactology was denounced as mechanistic and his hope of developing a Marxist psychology failed to measure up to expectation. It was damaged by Lenin's theory of reflection which imputed a distinct property to the psyche as well as characterizing it as actively directing human behavior and by viewing consciousness as a reflection of the world. Kornilov neglected to take this theory of Lenin's into account in his psychological system. Another important concept lacking in Kornilov's system was a theory of psychic development, one developed by L. S. Vygotsky and his associates in 1928 in which human psychic development is a concomitant of cultural historical development.

ALEKSEY ALEKSEYEVICH UKHTOMSKY (1884-1942):
Theory of the Dominant

A Soviet physiologist and academician, Ukhtomsky, exerted considerable influence with his theory of the dominant that he developed in 1923 in a book entitled *The Dominant as a Working Principle of Nervous Centers*. The concept of the dominant resulted from investigations on excitation and inhibition processes. The theory holds that a stable seat of excitation determines the organism's behavior during a prescribed period of time. At a given moment in time a focus of heightened excitation in the cortex dominates the rest of it. This dominance has the blocking effect of warding off irrelevant stimuli so that the organism is undistracted from performing its task.

London explained the theory of the dominant "as a seat of temporarily heightened neural excitation, deflecting to itself stimuli from other possible seats and thus dominating and determining the joint action of neural centers" (1949, p. 250). The theory was grounded on two observations: "(1) A cat, surprised in the act of micturition by a dog, seems rooted to the spot, paralyzed not by fear but by its momentary activity; (2) electrical stimulation of the motor cortex of an animal with a full rectum will not lead invariably to movement of the corresponding extremities but frequently to defecation. Only when the rectum has been emptied will electrical stimulation of the motor cortex always evoke the customary motor responses" (1949, p. 250).

Part of the attractiveness of the concept of the dominant was its tying-in goal-directed behavior with physiological psychology. Nevertheless, it did have the effect of spurring on experimental investigation.

Following the lead of Sechenov, Ukhtomsky likewise stressed that memory provides the organism with a guide to purposeful action. Devoid of memory, an animal would not be able to distinguish "a tree from an enemy" nor would it be able to orient itself within the objects of its surrounding environment.

(C)   THE PEDOLOGICAL PERIOD IN RUSSIAN PSYCHOLOGY

PAVEL PETROVICH BLONSKY (1884-1941): Pedological Theory

The pedological period in Russian psychology can be traced to the publication in 1925 of *Pedology* by *Pavel Petrovich Blonsky* (1884-1941). Pedology, based on the genetic investigation of child psychology, enjoyed its height at the time of the First Russian Congress of Pedologists in 1928. Characterized by tests and measurements, pedologists held that heredity and environment were the essential determining factors in child development. The pedologists fell into three camps: (1) the *biologists* such as Blonsky who emphasized that dominant factors affecting development were the inherited, biological ones; (2) the *sociologists* such as Vygotsky and Basov who stressed the social environmental factors; and (3) the *biosociologists* who treated both factors as of equal importance. Active in school reform, Blonsky, a pedagogue, psychologist, and student of Chelpanov, is known for his *Vocational Schools* (1919) as well as the above-mentioned *Pedology* (1925) and other works. *Vocational Schools,* containing a theory of vocational and polytechnical education, was an attempt to bring pedology within the scope of Marxism. Man's psyche is dynamically viewed by Blonsky as developing gradually from his biological processes. In man there coexists diverse processes belonging to varying states of development. A Watson-type behaviorist, Blonsky was criticized for his sway toward "idealism" as well as toward "vulgar materialism." In 1930 he wrote: "But when I refuse to understand consciousness without a neurological foundation for consciousness, when I say that without a knowledge of the brain one cannot understand psychology, I am not being a biologist but a materialist, demonstrating the *ABC*'s of pure materialism" (pp. 45-6).

From 1928 on when Kornilov severely attacked tests and measurements as a "game with jackstraws," pedology suffered from increased onslaughts, enduring them until 1936 when the Central Committee of the Communist Party of the Soviet Union issued its decree "On the Pedological Distortions in the Commissariat of Education." One consequence of the decree was the establishment of the *three-factor theory* as a tenet of psychology in Soviet Russia. Along with pedology, the *two-factor theory* was condemned, the theory attributing an equal role to heredity and environment. The new tenet lent emphasis to *social conditions* including living conditions and education as an important factor.

Charges brought against the pedologists were that testing tended to perpetuate class stratification; regarding failure in a negative sense as if nothing can be done to alleviate the situation; failing to give emphasis to the positive factors that mold children; and emphasizing the environmental factor to such an extent that determinism, fatalism, and pessimism resulted. Bauer (1952) enumerated the charges accordingly:

> The decree charged that the pedologists carried out their work "in complete isolation from the pedagogues and from scholastic studies." The work of the pedologists "amounted to pseudo-scientific experiments and numberless investigations on pupils and their parents in the form of senseless and harmful questionnaires, tests, et cetera, long since condemned by the Party." Pedologists were accused of attempting "to prove from the would-be 'scientific,' 'biosocial' point of view of modern pedology that the pupil's deficiency or the individual defects of his behavior are due to hereditary and social conditioning." Chief among the "pseudo-scientific" and "anti-Marxist theses" singled out for condemnation was the "principle 'law' of modern pedology—the 'law' of the fatalistic conditioning of children's fate by biological and social factors, by the influence of heredity and invariant milieu. This profoundly reactionary 'law'," the decree continued, "stands in flagrant contradiction to Marxism and to the whole practice of Socialist reconstruction which successfully reëducates men in the spirit of socialism and liquidates the survivals of capitalism in economics and in human consciousness." This "law," ordinarily referred to as the two-factor theory, was considered to be the heritage of bourgeois pedology, "which for the purpose of preserving the supremacy of the exploiting classes aims, on the one hand, at proving the special giftedness and the special right to existence of the exploiting classes and 'superior races,' and on the other hand, at proving that the working classes and 'inferior races' are physically and spiritually doomed." Psychological tests were formally characterized as instruments for perpetuating the class structure of bourgeois societies (1952, pp. 123-4).

The collapse of pedology owing to *the decree* terminated the hope of this school as a leading contender for official Soviet psychology.

(D) THE DIALECTICAL ERA OF RUSSIAN PSYCHOLOGY

As the door closed in 1936 to the transitional period of the thirties, another opened to dialectical psychology as the authoritative psychology in the Soviet Union. While the transitional period ran from 1930 to 1936, the dialectical period extended from 1930 to 1950. The duration of the mechanistic period was from the time of the October Revolution in 1917 to 1930. The late twenties and early thirties experienced a "battle for consciousness" as Luria and Leontiev phrased it. Psychologists sought to liberate themselves from "vulgar materialism" and introspectionism.

To the Soviets the *unity of consciousness and activity* became increasingly important and their efforts were devoted to the psychological analysis of concrete human activity. *Theory and practice* were also seen as a unity. Psychic development, especially social development and historical development became hallmarks of Soviet psychology. Western tests and measurements found in the psychology of individual differences were repudiated as fatalistic. The two-factor theory of explaining personality in terms of heredity and environment was superseded by the *three-factor theory* with education playing a major role. Consciousness became viewed as a mere reflection of the external world with social relations regarded as an important objective reality, so that psychology began to move from physiology to social psychology, that is, a social science.

Dialectical Materialism

Coined in 1908 by Plekhanov, dialectical materialism is the synthesis of two German philosophies: the Hegelian dialectic and the humanism of Feuerbach. The Marxists regarded Feuerbachian humanism as materialism. According to Plekhanov, "the philosophy of Marx and Engels is not only a materialist philosophy, it is a dialectical materialism" (1936, p. 112). In Lenin's estimation, one must be versed in Plekhanov's writings in order to appreciate the dialectical materialism of Marx and Engels.

In the *Filosofskaya Entsiklopediya* published in Moscow from 1960, A. G. Spirkin wrote an article titled "Dialectical Materialism," enunciating the major tenets of this school of thought. The basis of the universe is matter with consciousness regarded as its attribute in a highly organized state, brain function, and the reflection of the objective world. *Dialectical* characterizes the motion and development of the universe as it unfolds from the activity of internal contradictions. *Matter* is primary with consciousness its derivative. *Consciousness,* though a function of the brain, must be studied with its own peculiar properties. Knowledge, a dialectical process, is the reflection of the world in human consciousness, as Lenin taught. *Social practice,* a person's interaction with his surrounding world and interpersonal relations, transpires in historical and social situations. Organically connected with logical thought, sense knowledge arises from history. During the course of human historical development, both object and subject of perception alter qualitatively. As Marx asserted, the eye becomes a human eye the moment its object becomes a human and social being. Practice also is a social phenomenon. Human thought is a product of history, consequently theories are historically conditioned. As such theories are relative truths. Truth is not abstract, but concrete. Social practice, the ultimate·objective of man's knowledge, is the criterion of truth. Reality results from developmental processes as well as the processes of social life and of nature.

Connections among phenomena are by laws, those internal, indispensable connections or essential relationships. Though psychology like other concrete sciences has specific laws, there are *general laws* attesting to the unity of the world and pertaining to the existence, alteration, or development of individual things. Dialectical materialism's three most general laws are: (1) the *transition from quantity to quality,* (2) the *unity and struggle of opposites,* and (3) the *negation of negation.* These laws, the expression of universal forms, are the driving forces accounting for the world's development. *Development* is seen as the discontinous and continuous uniting, revolutionary changes occurring by leaps, and changes in phenomena occurring evolutionarily. According to the first law, a qualitative change can result from a number of quantitative ones. The second law, the unity and struggle of opposites, accounts for the driving force responsible for development. Since each entity contains its opposite, development results from the contradiction of the two, that is, the two actively interacting, colliding, or struggling in opposition to each other. Hence dialectics is the study of a contradiction that exists in the very essence of objects as Lenin asserted. The third law, negation of negation, signifies the synthesis arising from the negative of the thesis (i.e., its object or antithesis) being negated. The second law is the negation of the thesis or object. By the second law, to negate a thesis or object results in a clash, conflict, contradiction. But to negate the negation is to bring about a reconciliation or synthesis. Thus development occurs by the Hegelian dialectic of the thesis encountering conflict with its antithesis, and the two resulting in a higher development or synthesis.

Historical materialism results when dialectical materialism is applied to the social or society's development. According to dialectical materialism, social being determines social consciousness. Dialectical materialism is rooted in the primacy of matter over consciousness, i.e., the derivative nature of consciousness arising from matter. Social consciousness entails the theories, politics, culture, philosophy, art, morality, religion, and science of people. Consequently consciousness is produced socially as brain function, resulting from social conditions, social life, social activity, and human labor. According to dialectical materialism, all is in flux including social life.

LEV SEMYONOVICH VYGOTSKY (1896-1934),
ALEXANDER R. LURIA (1902-   ), and
ALEKSEI LEONTIEV (1903-   ):
Sociohistorical or Cultural Historical Development

A graduate of Moscow State University and Shanyavskiy University, Vygotsky majored in history and philosophy, but read widely in psychology, social science, and linguistics. His serious and systematic effort in psychology began when he went to Moscow in 1924 to work in the Institute of Psychology of the Krupskaya Academy of Communist Upbringing and in the Second Moscow State University. It was here that he developed his cutural-historical origin of man's higher mental functions as well as developing techniques for studying mental processes. A decade later he died at the youthful age of 38 of tuberculosis.

Vygotsky, with such able students and associates as Luria and Leontiev, led his school, beginning in 1928, in critical attacks on the issue of development. *Luria,* born in Kazan, received his Ph.D. in 1936 and his M.D. in 1943 from the University of Moscow. At the invitation of Kornilov he came to the Institute of Psychology during the 1920s. At the International Congress of Psychology in New Haven in 1929, he, with his colleague Vygotsky, delivered a paper and consequently became known to American psychologists. Owing to translations of his writings, such as *The Nature of Human Conflicts* published in English in 1932, he is one of the most familiar Russian psychologists to the west. Currently Professor of Psychology at the University of Moscow, Luria is also an editor of the journal *Problems of Psychology (Voprosi Psihologii) and Neuropsychologia Cortex* as well as chief of the diagnostic research section of the Burdenko Institute of Neurosurgery.

His associate, Leontiev, a Moscow product, was born and educated in Moscow where he received his Ed.D. His professional affiliation with the University of

Moscow began in 1924. In the thirties he was chairman of the psychology section of Kharkov Institute of Psychoneurology. Currently he is Professor and Head of the Department of Psychology at the University of Moscow. With over a hundred publications to his name, Leontiev is an editor of the journals *Problems of Psychology* and *Problems of Philosophy (Voprosi Filosofii)*. He was president of the 18th International Congress of Psychology held in Moscow in 1966. Leontiev and Luria were Vigotsky's most distinguished students.

Out of the joint efforts of these three arose the theory of socio-historical or cultural historical development. The theory was an attempt to utilize Marxian psychology as the basis underlying human development; to treat psychic development dialectically in terms of discrete qualitative stages; to offer a historical explanation of psychic development; and to seek the principle explanatory of higher psychic process, including: speech, logical memory, conceptual thought, active attention, and voluntary recall. According to the cultural historical development theory, activity that two persons share becomes internalized and serves to organize the behavior of a child. What was previously regarded as innate, Vygotsky claimed is mental activity formed in the process of the child's social development. Leontiev credited Vygotsky as the first Russian psychologist to offer the notion that the historical approach should be instituted as the fundamental principle for the construction of the psychology of man. In reference to the theory of the socio-historical condition of the human psyche, he wrote: "In addition to the theory of the psyche as a function of a material organ (the brain) manifested in the reflection of objective reality, the very earliest Soviet psychological investigations persistently advanced the theory of the role of the social environment—of the concrete-historical, class conditioning of the human psyche" (1959, p. 12).

Summarizing his position, Vigotsky stated:

> Thought development is determined by language, i.e., by the linguistic tools of thought and by the sociocultural experience of the child. Essentially, the development of inner speech depends on outside factors; the development of logic in the child . . . is a direct function of his socialized speech. The child's intellectual growth is contingent on his mastering the social means of thought, that is, language.
>
> . . . If we compare the early development of speech and of intellect . . . with the development of inner speech and of verbal thought, we must conclude that the later stage is not a simple continuation of the earlier. *The nature of the development itself changes,* from biological to sociohistorical. Verbal thought is not an innate, natural form of behavior but is determined by a historical-cultural process and has specific properties and laws that cannot be found in the natural forms of thought and speech. Once we acknowledge the historical character of verbal thought, we must consider it subject to all the premises of historical materialism, which are valid for any historical phenomenon in human society. It is only to be expected that on this level the development of behavior will be governed essentially by the general laws of the historical development of human society.
>
> The problem of thought and language thus extends beyond the limits of natural science and becomes the focal problem of historical human psychology, i.e., of social psychology (Vygotsky, 1962, p. 51).

Prior to Vygotsky, psychologists concerned themselves with isolated psychological functions, whereas Vygotsky sought to demonstrate higher mental processes (such as those mentioned earlier) as resulting developments of the interaction of children with adults. These processes were investigated by his "method of dual stimulation." The meeting of an abstract or general word alters during the development of a child and functions differently as a reflection of reality and as mediating mental activity at different developmental stages. These processes, treated as the products of interpersonal development, are gradually internalized in the child. Thought arises from the internalization of overt action; especially when external interpersonal dialogue is internalized does language become a potent tool within human thought. Thus the tools and instruments that a child uses shapes him. Cultural development is essentially adopting and assimilating behavior grounded on "sign-utilization," and employing it as a means of executing various actions. It is analogous to "tying a knot in order to remember." Natural or the organic development of memory differs from the cultural development which is an attempt to master various symbolic methods of recall.

Vygotsky, who held to the uniqueness of human mental life, employed the Vygotsky-Sakharov method to establish thought patterns characteristic of schizophrenia. He was the first to uncover semantic disorganization in schizophrenics.

Volitional behavior, according to Vygotsky, is mediated activity; it is not the unconscious that affects the normal person but his social conditioning. His major thesis is that the *"functional significance of a given region of the cerebral cortex for an entire system of mental processes varies for different stages of development"* (Luria, 1969, p. 284). Luria, explaining the volitional as the formation of a person's social history, asserted:

> For a long time psychology has tried to achieve a scientific analysis of the most complex—volitional—aspects of behavior. Investigations have shown, however, that such an analysis was impossible so long as such behavior was viewed as an inherent attribute of psychic life. Only when these complex aspects of psychic activity are considered as operations formed in the course of the individual's social history and embodied in the complex functional systems of the human cortex, can real strides be made towards a scientific analysis of the higher forms of psychic activity. This is why the role of verbal communication, and subsequently that of the individual verbal system, in the organization of complex pieces of behavior has become a model in the light of which the formation of the most complex aspects of psychic activity can be traced with particular clarity (1961, pp. 9-10).

A defectologist, Vygotsky advanced a mental development theory of the defective child, one with speech defects, a deaf-mute, or a retarded child. Defects, a secondary result of the abnormal development of a child, are not due to simple brain lesions. "If one or another prerequisite to this development is damaged, then the entire development of the child acquires an abnormal character and, therefore, comparatively small defects (for instance, a slight impairment of hearing) may have far-reaching consequences" (Luria, 1969b, p. 285). Subsequent Soviet defectology, based on this theory, accelerated. A decade after Vygotsky's death, psychopathologists in the Soviet concerned themselves with psychologically analyzing and characterizing defects arising from pathological conditions of the brain. The following decade found them moving from a psychological analysis to a Pavolovian physiological analysis entailing the higher nervous activity.

In his *The Nature of Human Conflicts* (1932), Luria argued that

> the complex forms of organisation and disorganisation of human behaviour can in nowise be explained as a simple play of neurophysiological processes, that no phenomena of elementary neurodynamics can elucidate those configurations of integrated behaviour specific for the human as a social subject. . . .
>
> The author does not believe that the problems of the most complicated forms of human behaviour can be solved by the laws of the dynamics of tendency nor by the analysis of the conditioned reflex connections playing a role in the nervous system; the solution of this problem will be attained only by a careful description of the specific systems of behaviour produced in the process of the social historical development, which are distinguished by the peculiarities of the human, and without which the organisation of the higher neurodynamics remains incomprehensible (pp. xii-xiii).

Luria's investigations led to the hypothesis that a person's direct attempts at controlling his own behavior produce negative results; only by indirect means is mastery acquired. The product of complex growth, adult behavior is not the mere accumulation of experiences, for a person is developed as a historical subject culturally. Out of this development novel mechanisms arise as the high points of historical evolution such as speech and signs which become infused in every aspect of human activity including "every movement of the fingers." Only by analyzing cultural mechanisms can one understand the simple processes of neurodynamics.

Recently Luria (1969) stated that

> Soviet psychology holds that higher forms of reflection, which are expressed in active, voluntary, and conscious forms of activity, are the result of the work of the brain as manifested *in social conditions,* and are not inherent properties of the mind. Soviet psychology conceives of mind as the product of social life and treats it as a form of *activity* which was earlier shared by two people (that is, orginated in communication), and which only later, as a result of mental development, became a form of behavior within one person (1969b, p. 143).

Reiterating much of what Luria had asserted, Leontiev dissociated psychology from biology. The point of orientation of Soviet psychologists is the Marxian thesis that "the consciousness of man is social and historical in its nature, that it is determined by social existence and that it changes qualitatively with changes in social and economic conditions" (1961a, p. 36). Objective living conditions of human beings in society (rather than human nature) account for peculiar mental factors. Personality characteristics are produced by human life and activity developing in a state of social relations. The inner contradictions of a person's life in society are the driving force in human development. The decisive force in the formation of a person intellectually is that exerted by the people in one's own society, and not forces spontaneously erupting. Consequently, education is a decisive factor. Psychology's primary objective is the investigation of those processes by which science and ideology are internalized into human consciousness, making themselves personality traits. Psychological theory must be closely connected with practice.

With the course of development, a child's psyche changes. One's memory capacity does not simply increase with age, his memory changes qualitatively. As memory is transformed, the way a person thinks actually becomes different. It improves with the instructor's influence.

> The conditions under which the Soviet children grow up are determined by the collective character of their society. They therefore escape such phenomena as self-doubt, loneliness, contrast between ideal and reality, which are characteristic of the life of children living under capitalism and which bourgeois psychology wrongly assumes to be universal (1961b, p. 58).

The stages of human development are contingent upon social conditions and are not innate products of heredity.

Leontiev's accomplishments include the following conclusions: (1) "a previously completely imperceptible stimulus becomes perceptible when it serves as signal for another stimulus which has positive or negative significance in the subject's investigatory activity" (1966, p. 8); (2) the reflex nature of sensation; (3) the classification of animal stages of mental development according to the animal's evolutionary stage of reflecting the features of his environment; and (4) the child's mental development.

The psychology of Vygotsky and the earlier writings of Luria suffered attack for uncritically borrowing from the *bourgeois* psychologists of the West. It was a common practice in the late twenties. Vygotsky devoted entire chapters in his book to men such as Piaget, Watson, and Stern, while Luria freely cited European and American psychologists.

SERGEY LEONIDOVICH RUBINSTEIN (1889-1960):Formation of Psyche as Activity

Born in Odessa, the Jewish Soviet psychologist, Rubinstein (Rubinshteyn), graduated from Richelieu Academy of his home town in 1908. The following year he went to Germany, studying at the University of Freiburg and then to Marburg where he came under the influence of neo-Kantians, Herman Cohen and Paul Natorp, under whose direction he obtained his doctorate in philosophy upon presenting his dissertation on a study of the problem of method in 1913. At Marburg he also acquired an interest in Hegel. The years from 1915 to 1930 were spent at Odessa in pedagogical activity; in 1919 he accepted a post as lecturer in philosophy and psychology at Novorossiskij University. By 1921 he was heading the department of psychology at the Institute for Public Education. From 1930 to 1950, his dialectical period, was spent in Leningrad and Moscow where his writing career began with a number of articles, the most important one being in 1934 on "Problems of Psychology in the Works of Karl Marx." The first edition of his *magnun opus, Fundamentals of General Psychology,* was published in 1940. His *Fundamentals of Psychology* appeared in 1935. For a dozen years beginning in 1930 he was head of the Kafedra of Psychology at Leningrad Institute of Pedagogy and then left for Moscow in 1942 where he founded the *Kafedra* (department) of Psychology at its University, concurrently heading the Institute of Psychology there. Although he did not leave as Director of the Kafedra until 1950, he undertook the post of head of the department of psychology at the Institute of Philosophy of the Academy of Sciences of the U.S.S.R. from 1945 to the time of his death in 1960. From 1950 to 1960, his Pavlovian period, his most productive, was spent in Moscow where they elected him Member of the Academy of Sciences of the U.S.S.R. in 1953.

With the publication of his *Fundamentals of General Psychology* in 1940, Rubinstein emerged as one of the foremost and authoritative exponents of Soviet psychology. But by the conclusion of the Pavlov Conference which was held a decade later, it was decided that his views required revision. Self-criticism prompted him to state that he failed to follow in Pavlov's footsteps, that Soviet psychologists were still under the influence of idealism, and that they had not yet acquired the "spirit of creative Marxism."

The major principles formulated in his *Fundamentals* are summarized by Payne accordingly:

(1) the principle of psycho-physical unity—the unity of the psychic with its organic substrate, the brain, of which it is a function, and with the external world, of which it is a reflection;

(2) the principle of psychic development—the psychic is a derived but specific component in the development of the organism; it develops along with the changes in the structure of the organism and of its mode of life;

(3) the principle of historicity—a determination of (2) — human consciousness changes with the development of man's social being;

(4) the principle of unity of theory and practice.

Rubinstein sees these four principles as the expression of one basic principle of Soviet psychology, i.e., the principle of the unity of consciousness and behaviour (1968, p. 52).

When in 1952 Rubinstein revised his position in an article "The Teachings of I. P. Pavlov and Some Problems of the Reconstruction of Psychology," he retained the last three points, revising only the first on psychophysical unity by reducing it to materialistic monism, i.e., the view that the psychic is a derivative of the material. These same four principles were enunciated by Rubinstein in 1943 in an article titled "Soviet Psychology in the Years of the Great Patriotic War," and translated the following year as "Soviet Psychology in Wartime." Here the four are summarized as follows:

Soviet psychology proceeds to their [problems of personality development] solution from several basic principles: the principle of psycho-physical unity and the principle of evolution, in its dialectical materialistic form; then, the historical principle as applied to the development of human consciousness; finally, the principle . . . of the unity of consciousness and activity, in its diverse theoretical and methodological connotations (1944, p. 183).

Repudiating the psychologies of mechanistic behaviorism (reflexology and reactology) that preceded him, Rubinstein sought to order Soviet psychology along Marxist-Leninist lines so that human behavior is not a mere complex of reactions severed from consciousness. He viewed the task as eliminating the pseudo dualism of separating consciousness and behavior by establishing consciousness as a "unity of subjective experience and objective knowledge," grounded on Lenin's theory of reflection. As Marx earlier had stated: Consciousness is consciousness of being, a unity of subjective and objective. The unity principle also encompasses the unity of the individual and the social. Consequently the starting point for psychology is the unity of a person's consciousness and activity.

Personality development occurs "in concrete activity, in work, in adult social practice, in child-training and education, mental characteristics do not only *appear,* but are *formed*" (1944, p. 182). Race psychology is rejected as fascistic; so-called racial psychological characteristics are explained by the socio-economic structure of society, i.e., by social psychology. One obtains the "deepest knowledge of the world in the process of changing it," hence the importance of the interaction of investigation and action as a fundamental premise of Soviet methodology in psychological research. A dictum from the methodological principle is: "Study the children, teaching them; teach the children, studying them." The premise requires the "investigation of phenomena in the process of modifying them." Thus the important relationship that exists between psychology and practice. Psychology must concern itself with investigating "consciousness in terms of the concrete conditions in which human activity is performed" (1944, p. 184).

Throughout his entire career, Rubinstein fought for consciousness, for mind as a definite form of activity, but stressed the deterministic character of mental processes. Behaviorism he eschewed as arising from the isolation or disappearance of consciousness. The mind as activity is not to be confused with mechanical behavior. Human activity and consciousness are inseparable; the unity of consciousness and behavior must not be abridged. In the light of the unity of consciousness and behavior, behavior is regarded as the external side of the internal (consciousness), the two in mutual interaction and interpenetration, hence the unity of subject and object. Not merely passive contemplation, consciousness is an active principle that determines, guides, and directs behavior. Thus behavior is inexplicable merely in terms of stimulus-response. Physiological laws are inadequate in explaining laws of human activity. By engaging in human activity, consciousness is more than internal. By virtue of human activity, a person alters the external world or nature by imputing to it that which is found in himself, i.e., his subjective world of goals, motives, and abilities. Consciousness changes activity. Objective reality is reflected in consciousness. Reflection is used in the sense of reaction as well as "mirroring." The psychic is comprised of its "connections and mediations" by which it is discovered. To the material world, the psychic is related by brain matter of the neurological system and to the external world of material reality.

According to Rubinstein, consciousness, the subjective element of a person, is an evolvement of an evolutionary process of the outer material world. It meets the organism's need for a form of activity to cope more effectively with changing environmental demands; it evolved to deal with needs for successful adaptation. By acting on his objective environment, a person is self-creating by creating new conditions. Consciousness both guides and directs a person's activity. In his ontogenetic course of development, social consciousness influences the development of individual consciousness through educational training and through its own activity. According to Rubinstein's *theory of aspects* of the psychic in which he delineates the qualities, properties, or aspects of consciousness, he cited two properties of the psychic: (1) higher nervous activity; and (2) an ideal reflection, i.e., ideally reflecting the external world of matter.

ANATOLI A. SMIRNOV (1894-   ) and P. I. ZINCHENKO (1903-   ): Involuntary Memory

A number of psychologists have conducted experiments and have developed theories in the Soviet Union that have not been treated here. But they are of lesser distinction than those that have been discussed with the possible exception of *Anatoli A. Smirnov,* the Moscow-born director of the Institute of Psychology who is one of the editors of the journal *Problems of Psychology (Voprosi Psikhologii).* Smirnov, holding a doctorate from the University of Leningrad, was the first president of the Society of Psychologists founded in 1957. His career opened at the Institute in 1918 and in 1945 he became its director.

One of Smirnov's major contributions was in collaboration with his colleague, the Ukrainian *P. I. Zinchenko,* born in Nicolayevsk. Zinchenko, with a doctorate from Moscow and Chairman of the Department of Psychology at the University of Kharkov, collaborated with Smirnov on experiments on voluntary and involuntary memory, a topic of Zinchenko's doctoral research. Since 1939 Zinchenko was publishing on involuntary memory which he viewed as the result of goal-oriented behavior. Involuntary memory, the function of activity, is achieved by committing to some activity the material that is to be memorized. Smirnov (1948) argued that the activity which is the base for involuntary memory is invariably aimed at some object, indicating the importance of intention in recall. Experiments were therefore constructed in order to ascertain the specific characteristics of activity providing the most favorable conditions for achieving the greatest success in involuntary remembering. They concluded that "material which is part of the content that forms the goal of an activity is recalled significantly better than the same material when it comprises the subject matter that serves as a means whereby a goal is achieved" (Smirnov & Zinchenko, 1969, p. 460). Involuntary recall is more successful when in a given activity both the position and content of the material are taken into consideration.

(E) PSYCHOLOGY IN ARMENIA AND GEORGIA

Numerous psychological experiments have been taking place in the Soviet Union, including Georgia and Armenia. In Soviet Armenia, M. A. Mazmanyan has been among the most active even to the extent of writing a history of Armenian psychology, in Armenian. A. A. Lalayan has also been active in the history of Armenian psychology.

In Georgia, psychology had its inception with the establishment of a department of psychology at Tbilisi University in 1918. The department consisted of only one professor who was one of its founders, *Dmitriy Nikolayevich Uznadze* (1886-1950). By 1922 a psychological laboratory was organized, and currently the department has over ten doctorates in the Uznadze Institute of Psychology. Uznadze, founder of the Georgian Psychological Society in 1927, also founded the Georgian Institute of Psychology which is presently named after him. He is credited with initiating the "psychology of set" in the Soviet Union, and as early as 1925 wrote his first volume on *Foundations of Experimental Psychology*. At Kiev in 1964, the Ukrainian Republic conference of psychologists met. Writings of the Georgian psychologists can be found in summary form in *Psychological Abstracts* published by the American Psychological Association.

PART SEVEN

ORIENTAL AND LATIN AMERICAN PSYCHOLOGY

Oriental psychology, currently in a transitional state, is found making its greatest progress in Japan. Therefore Japanese psychology is accorded greater treatment than psychology emanating from other Asiatic countries. While most of the progress in psychological studies arising out of the Orient occurred in the post World War II era, psychology in some form, ordinarily of a religious or philosophical nature, was transpiring earlier. Currently in the Orient, however, the psychology that found its roots in oriental religion or philosophy is making its way into systems and theories of the most prestigious psychologists of Asia.

Japanese Academic Degrees. While some of the most influential Japanese psychologists studied in Europe and the United States, acquiring their Western degrees that are recognizable and meaningful to Westerners, many of their psychologists received degrees from their own institutions. These degrees from their own universities, inasmuch as they are unfamiliar to many Westerners, are listed below:

I. Degree from the Faculty of Letters:
   1. *Bungakushi,* a title granted after three or four years of college education, bringing one's education to a total of sixteen or seventeen years. It is the closest academic degree in Japan to the B.A. (Bachelor of Arts) degree. A thesis and comprehensive examinations are required.
   2. *Bungakuhushi,* an intermediate degree, comparable to the M.A. (Master of Arts), is granted on the successful completion of two years of graduate study.
   3. *Bungakuhakushi,* the closest degree to the Western Ph.D., is earned after five years of graduate study, evidence of advanced scholarly achievement, and the presentation of a thesis to a faculty of letters to whom a special request has been presented in order to study for the degree.
II. Degrees from the Faculty of Science:
   4. *Rigakushi,* the first level degree, is comparable to the bachelor's degree.
   5. *Rigakuhakushi* is the highest degree in science.
III. Degrees from the Faculty of Medicine:
   6. *Igakushi,* from the Faculty of Medicine, is comparable to the M.D.
   7. *Igakuhakushi* is the advanced degree from the Faculty of Medicine.
IV. Degrees from the Faculty of Law;
   8. *Hogakushi* is the first level degree granted by the Faculty of Law.

It is not strange to find a person with a degree in one field engaged in what to the Western mind would be another. Occasionally what would normally be considered a discipline in science is under the aegis of the Faculty of Letters. Historically in Japan this has been the case with psychology, where the degree traditionally has been granted by the Faculty of Letters. Even in some European countries psychology has not made a clean break from other subjects. At the University of Cambridge, for example, psychology (should one pursue the Ph.D. degree) falls under the Faculty of Biology. In the embryonic years of psychology in the United States, psychology has been traditionally ancillary to the Department of Philosophy.

The degree, corresponding closest to the American Ph.D., the *Bungaku-hakushi,* literally means Doctor of Literature, and is granted by the Faculty of Literature. Ordinarily it is not granted until the candidate approaches fifty years of age. That the degree is a doctorate of literature and from the Faculty of Letters might strike the Westerner as strange, but one must keep in mind that the Ph.D. is a Doctor of Philosophy (whether in the field of psychology or any other science). Traditionally in the Western world a candidate took his degree in philosophy, minoring in the subject of his preference. Accordingly, at the beginning of the twentieth century, a Ph.D. candidate at Boston University, for example, was required to take his Ph.D. with philosophy as his major, his minor being physics, music, or whatever he choose as his professional objective.

Reporting on conditions in academia in the mid-fifties, and especially on psychology in Japan, Sato and Graham (1954) observed that Tokyo University had only recently acquired a second professorship. Another leading university, Kyoto, had but one. By contrast, Kyoto University had seven chairs allocated to philosophy, the ratio of philosophy professors to those in psychology being traditionally seven to one since 1906.

CHAPTER 19

Japanese Psychology at the Universities of Tokyo, Kyoto, and Kyushu

Japanese psychology can historically be sectioned into four major periods of development: (1) precursors of psychology, a period prior to the 1880s; (2) the introduction of psychology as a science, a period extending from the 1880s to 1926, and influenced by American functionalism (including behaviorism); (3) the period of gestalt influence, transpiring from 1926 to the end of World War II; and (4) the period of experimentation, an Americanization of Japanese psychology; and the revival of Zen as psychology.

After an extended period of philosophical psychology based on the religions of the orient (Buddhism, Shintoism, and Confucianism), experimental psychology found its way into Japan, principally through the efforts of two Japanese psychologists who were trained in the United States: *Yujiro Motora* (1858-1912), a Johns Hopkins graduate who was trained under G. Stanley Hall; and *Matataro Matsumoto* (1865-1943), a Yale Ph.D. trained by Edward Wheeler Scripture. While the former introduced experimental psychology into Japan and founded its first laboratory of psychology, the latter founded applied experimental psychology in Japan.

During Motora's era as the leading figure at Japan University where he became the first professor of psychology in Japan, the American psychology of functionalism prevailed, with some support for Wundt's psychology of structuralism. Within two years after Motora's death, Watson's behaviorism made a rapid rise, but was eclipsed in the later 1920s by the introduction of the German gestalt psychology by *Kanae Sakuma* (1888-1970), a pupil of Köhler and Lewin. Gestalt psychology maintained its strength at least until the close of World War II, the post war period being dominated by psychology prevalent in the United States, rather than by particular schools of psychology. Zen also returned to Japan in the form of psychology, especially through the efforts of *Koji Sato* (1905-1971), founder of the English language Japanese journal *Psychologia: An International Journal of Psychology in the Orient* in 1957. Prior to the efforts of Sato, a Japanese psychiatrist, *Shoma Morita* (1874-1938), founded psychotherapy based on Zen which came to be known as Morita therapy.

The year Morita founded his psychotherapeutic system, *Genji Kuroda* (1886-1957), a graduate and later professor at Kyoto University, founded a principal journal of psychology in Japan, named the *Japanese Journal of Psychology*. The journal, which lasted approximately four years, was referred to as the Kyoto Series, and was succeeded by the New Series in 1926. Japan's first journal of psychology, *Psychological Research (Shinri Kenkyu)*, lasted from 1911 to 1925. The opening of the Showa era (1926) was marked by a strong upsurge in interest in gestalt psychology; during this general period the Japanese Psychologi-cal Association was established with its first annual convention in 1927. By the 1930s, child psychologists and pedagogues in combined effort made clinical studies of normal and abnormal children, thus marking the opening of clinical psychology in Japan. While the term clinical psychology was not employed at that time, the psychologists did utilize diagnostic and other psychological testing techniques in clinics. Publication of journals peaked during the mid 1930s, with the various universities publishing a wide variety of periodicals, including the *Japanese Journal of Educational Psychology* and *Animal Psyche* out of Tokyo; the *Japanese Journal of Experimental Psychology* out of Kyoto; the *Japanese Journal of Applied Psychology* out of Hiroshima; the *Acta Psychologica Keijo* out of Seoul; and the *Tohoku Psychologica Folia* out of Sendai.

Social psychology in Japan was coterminous with that in the United States, for K. Higuchi wrote his *Social Psychology* in 1908, the same year that McDougall wrote his when he was at Oxford University, and E. A. Ross published one in the United States. The early years of social psychology in Japan had a Wundtian flavor, as evidenced by two books of *Yoshizo Kuwata* (1882-1967), *Group Psychology* (1917) and *Folk Psychology of Wundt* (1918). Although Kuwata obtained his Bungakuhakushi and undergraduate degrees from Tokyo University in 1905 and 1921 respectively, he did study under Wundt at the University of Leipzig from 1910 to 1912. His first work in social psychology appeared in 1916 as *Soul-Cult and Ancestor-Worship*. Kuwata spent his long academic career at Tokyo University where he began in 1906, and rose to full professor exactly twenty years later. However, social psychology in Japan lacked strength and originality until post World War II years, and even then it was saturated with ideas from the United States, e.g., theories of Lewin, Heider, Festinger, Osgood and the Berkeley Researchers (A. W. Adorno *et. al., The Authoritarian Personality,* 1950). The first Japanese book in this field after the war was *Social Psychology* (1949) by *Hiroshi Minami* (1914-   ), who happened to be in the United States during World War II. Minami, who received his Bungakuhakushi degree from Kyoto University in 1961, is Professor of Psychology at Hitotsubashi University, where he is editor of the *Japanese Annals of Social Psychology*. Reporting in 1959, *Kimiyoshi Hirota* (1924-   ) of Kansai University estimated that ten percent of the 2,000 members of the Japanese Psychological Association find their expertise in social psychology. In 1955 the social psychologists found their identity in the establishment of the Society for Social Psychological Study.

(A)   EARLY JAPANESE PSYCHOLOGY

Amane Nishi (1826-1894): Tanzan Hara (1819-1892): Shigeki Nishimura (1828-1902): Soho Takuan(1573-1645); Baigan Ishida (1685-1744); Toan Tejima (1718-1786);Ho Kamada (1753-1821); Mabuchi Kamo (1697-1769); Seisho Fujitani (1737-1778); Mitsue Fijitani (1767-1832); Norinaga Motoori (1725-1801): Pre-Twentieth Century Japanese Psychology

Western psychology was unknown to Japan until a decade after the opening of the Meiji era, a period extending from 1868 to 1912. Roughly around 1880 Western psychology, in a setting dominated by Indian and Chinese philosophy and psychology, found its way into Japan. Before the close of the nineteenth century, Japanese psychologists (Motora, Matsumoto, Nakajima, Okabe, and Kakise) introduced psychological experimentation and translations of works in psychology into their country, among these translations being books by Bain, Sully, Wundt, and Ladd.

The first Western work on psychology, Joseph Haven's *Mental Philosophy* (1869), appeared in translation as *Psychology*. The translation contributed importantly to psychology's becoming an independent science, rather than an ancillary of the philosophy of human nature. The translator, *Amane Nishi* (1826-1894), influenced by the French founder of sociology and positivism, August Comte (1798-1857), developed his own psychological theory in his *Hayku-ichi Shin-ron* (A New Theory on the Unity of Many Viewpoints, 1874). The work considers physics as the science of observation, and psychology as physics applied. Psychology and biology are subsumed under anthropology. Psychology applied entails the synthesis of numerous theories and consequently contributes to more effective human living.

Thus early psychology in Japan was oriented from a Comtean positivistic standpoint, as is evidenced by the psychology of *Tanzan Hara* (1819-1892), a Zen priest. In a publicized work, *Shinsei-Zikkenroku* (Experimental Records of Mind, 1873), Hara investigated human nature experimentally. His postivistic position was perpetuated by subsequent Japanese scholars.

The inroad psychology was making as a distinct science benefited from the efforts of *Shigeki Nishimura* (1828-1902), who distinguished the new psychology from the traditional by identifying the former with the study of acquiring knowledge or data pertinent to the mind rather than merely manipulating the mind. Factual knowledge, he held, is also utilitarian, useful in governing the mind. Rather than espousing a rational psychology, Nishimura proposed an empirical one in which the phenomena of consciousness are analyzed and described. The phenomena of consciousness, comprised of intellect, feeling, desire, and volition, are subdivided into a number of faculties of a phenomenal character. Owing to the mind's operations being more extensive than consciousness, some mental activities exist independent of consciousness.

Early Japanese Philosophical Psychology. Prior to these early Japanese psychologists, the character of psychology in Japan was of a religious or philosophical order, entrenched in Shintoism, Buddhism, and Confucianism. Early Japanese psychology, couched in the Buddhism of *Vijnaptimatrata siddhisastra* of *Vasubandhu* (420-500) and developed by *Dosho* (629-700) and *Genbo* (d. 763), was interested in a psychology of salvation in which a person attains freedom from passion, with consciousness an important issue. It then proceeds to a psychology of Confucianism developed by *Chu-tze* (1130-1120) and *Wang-Yangming* (1472-1528). While the former developed a theory of human nature, the latter was concerned with the problem of learning, theirs being a psychology of morality, inasmuch as they were interested in the acquisition of moral training techniques.

By the seventeenth century Japanese thinkers became active, imputing to their psychology a Japanese character. The first of these thinkers, *Soho Takuan* (1573-1645), developed a theory of human nature inspired by the theory of *Chu-tzu* in which he viewed the human being as a microcosmos, the individual being a small replica of the universe. A person is a manifestation of the principle active in the universe *(nous)*. Explaining this position, Mantaro Kido wrote:

> Takuan . . . regards human being as a microcosmos in contrast with the macrocosmos, assuming human nature as the nous, i.e. the principle of universe which manifests itself as a human figure, mind as regulation of body, temperament as a mind controlled by the body, consciousness as perception of the outer world by mind, conation as demand of mind on things, emotion as expression of the affection of mind on things, occasion as circumstance which mind manifests itself, and . . . deities as givers of occasion to mind to operate human conduct (1961, pp. 1-2).

According to Japanese thought, morality is conducive to a felicitous social life.

Like Takuan, *Baigan Ishida* (1685-1744) belonged to the Chu-tzu school, but his was an eclectic theory, synthesizing the views of this school with those of Shintoism, Buddhism, and the Wang-Yangming school. Formulating his psychology in his *Seiri-mondo* (Dialogue on Human Nature), he hypothesized behavior as a manifestation of the forms of mind, the mind being an aspect of the physical. Mental nature is the mind's shaping by human experiences. Mind does not exist detached from human physical and social intercourse, i.e., without reaction to things and social behavior. The human mind, altered by learning experiences, varies in its characteristic form, traits, or configuration owing to one's mode of existence. Consequently to alter a person's situation would cause his mind to function differently, hence change his personality.

Ishida's disciple, *Toan Tejima* (1718-1786), a realist and positivist, identified the mind with a physical thing. In his *Zendo Shuchi* (Knowing with Good Insight), he argued that people see with the things themselves rather than with the eyes. Inasmuch as it is only a thing in itself that can possibly know another thing, it follows that mind must be identified with thing.

Another advocate of the Chu-Tzu school, *Ho Kamada* (1753-1821), saw psychology as the natural science of mind with the function of issuing moral happiness to human life. His rational psychology included intellect, emotion, and desire as mental faculties, with the intellect comprised of perception and apperception. His work, *Kokoro no Kajitsu* (Fruits of Mind), listed fourteen emotions, and his *Shingaku Gosoku* (Five Axioms of the Mental Discipline) explained the acquisition of fear and anxiety as drives rooted in respect, love in benevolence, and pleasure by a conscious sense of destiny.

A national philosophy emerged out of Shintoism, with its attendant hermeneutic psychology, which seeks mental expression through poetry and psychological understanding through literature. Its votary, *Mabuchi Kamo* (1697-1769), constructed a psychology of language development in his *Goiko*, which investigated the meaning of words and phonetic symbolism. A psychological analysis of the Japanese language was attempted by *Seisho Fujitani* (1737-1778) in a work titled *Ayui-sho*. His son, *Mitsue Fujitani* (1767-1832), developed an inversion theory of hermeneutics in which the subject is regarded as latent in the object. Inasmuch as a person is an irrational being, language is the only access to his mind. Language per se, however, is not identical with mind. The outer form of a word is to be distinguished from its inner form (the meaning or soul of the word). By the inner form, meaning, or soul of the word, it is possible by employing language to comprehend another person's mind. By three expressive linguistic forms (explicit, implicit, and poetical), the state of mind is manifested and apprehended: Pursuing Fujitani's theory further, *Norinaga Motoori* (1725-1801) observed that personality development need not arise through personal experiences directly, it may occur by sublimative, cathartic, and other processes through poetry or literature. The oldest extant Japanese book published pertaining to psychology, *Kojikiden* (Records of Ancient Matters, 1764-1796), was by Norinaga.

(B) FOUNDERS OF JAPANESE EXPERIMENTAL PSYCHOLOGY

YUJIRO MOTORA (1858-1912): Japan's First Experimental Psychologist

Unlike their predecessors in Japan, Motora and Matsumoto were trained psychologists with the highest credentials even by Western standards. In fact their graduate work in psychology was at Johns Hopkins and Yale universities respectively. Motora received his Ph.D. in 1888 under G. Stanley Hall, when Hall was at Johns Hopkins. Born in Osaka, Japan, Motora studied at Boston University prior to attending Johns Hopkins. He returned to Japan whereupon he became that nation's first professor of psychology, a position he held at Tokyo University where he designed and founded Japan's first laboratory of psychology in 1888.

Motora's research on dermal sensitivity while at Johns Hopkins was reported (with Hall) as "Dermal Sensitiveness to Gradual Pressure Changes" in Hall's *American Journal of Psychology* in 1888, the second year of the journal's founding. His views are contained in his *Psychology* (1893) and *Essentials of Psychology* (1910) as well as the posthumous *Outline of Systematic Psychology* (1915). An interest in Zen developed not long after his return to Japan.

The pragmatic Motora was not content with restricting psychology to the laboratory, and sought to carry his investigations to living situations, into the world of society, where he hoped to discover pertinent psychological laws. Primarily an experimentalist, Motora is credited with introducing "mental physics" into Japan as well as instruments for psychological testing.

MATATARO MATSUMOTO (1865-1943): Psychocinematics.

Succeeding Motora at Tokyo University was Matataro Matsumoto, a second founder of experimental psychology in Japan. Like his predecessor, Matsumoto was American trained, receiving his Ph.D. under Scripture from Yale University where he studied from 1896 to 1898, and where he served as an assistant. He spent an academic year with Wundt at the University of Leipzig (1898-1899), returning to Japan in 1900 where he taught at a number of normal schools in Tokyo as well as serving at Tokyo University as a lecturer. While at Tokyo University, he is reputed to have designed a laboratory of psychology in 1903 along the German-American type. His first professorship was at Kyoto University from 1910 to 1915, where he founded both the department of psychology and a psychological laboratory. From 1920 he served as professor at Toyko University.

While at the Yale Psychological Laboratory, Matsumoto researched acoustic space, reporting on it in 1897. Referring to his system of psychology as *psychocinematics,* he began to publish a number of books on the subject from 1910 on. In his *Psychocinematics (Mental Works,* 1914) he is interested in controlled experimental conditions in which certain regularity of activities can be put in motion by mental powers. By siring his science of psychophysiological behavior (psychocinematics), Matsumoto fathered applied experimental psychology in Japan. His psychocinematics, the objective investigation of purposive bodily movements, shows a decided Wundtian influence.

Interest in applied psychology continued in several directions so that by 1925, Matsumoto produced a work of over eleven hundred pages on the *Psychology of Intelligence,* followed by *Psychology and Practical Life* (1926). His interest in the psychology of art, which found expression in his *Psychological Interpretation of Modern Japanese Paintings* in 1915 continued to 1926 with the publication of *Psychology of Esthetic Appreciation of Pictorial Arts,* the same year that another book on applied psychology appeared by him, *Psychology and Practical Life* (1926).

(C) BEHAVIORISM MAKES ITS DEBUT IN JAPAN

Matsumoto's Disciples: Asataro Narasaki (1882-   ) and Kwanichi Tanaka (1882-1962). Association with the Aeronautical Research Institute of Tokyo University exposed Matsumoto to human engineering psychology. One of his associates at the Institute, Kwanichi Tanaka, became affiliated with the Institute in 1920, the year after receiving his Bungakuhakushi degree from Tokyo University. Tanaka extended Matsumoto's "mental works" (psychocinematics) into the field of human engineering, publishing his *Human Engineering* in 1922. In 1924 he joined the faculty at Nihon University.

Unlike Tanaka, Asataro Narasaki received his Bungakuhakushi degree from Kyoto University in 1923, having completed his undergraduate work there (1907-1910) under Matsumoto. Narasaki (1922), who held a professorship at the Tokyo Higher Normal School, promoted Matsumoto's psychocinematics. Neither Tanaka nor Narasaki (1923) considered psychocinematics (mental dynamics) as traditional psychology because traditional psychology, being pure psychology, is attainable through introspective techniques rather than by objective methods.

Narasaki: Importer of Watsonian Behaviorism into Japan. Behavioristic tendencies of a pre-Watsonian mode were introduced into Japan by *Yoichi Ueno* (1883-1957), a Tokyo University graduate who received his Bungakushi degree in 1908. Ueno, who made a Japanese translation of Angell's *Psychology* in 1910, called for a Pillsbury-type definition of psychology as the study of behavior in his "Behavior Theory: A New Definition of Psychology" (1913). Notwithstanding his behavioristic tendencies, Ueno was not prepared to abandon consciousness as did Watson. In fact, he (with Noda, 1922) criticized Watsonian behaviorism.

The year following Watson's classic paper, "Psychology as the Behaviorist Views it," Narasaki and *Hiroshi Hayami* (1876-1943) introduced his behaviorism into Japanese psychology. Hayami, in addition to studying at Tokyo University where he received his Bungakuhakushi degree in 1921, invested the 1925-1926 academic year at the University of Berlin. After spending a year teaching psychology at Tokyo University (1912-1912), he subsequently left for Keijo University, becoming Professor and Dean of the Faculty of Letters in 1926. With Motora and R. Nakajima, he translated G. Stanley Hall's *Adolescence* in 1910. For a period he was charmed by Wundt, writing the *Psychology of Wundt* in 1915.

Narasaki (1914) saw no discrepancy between the psychocinematics of his mentor and Watson's behaviorism, inasmuch as both employ the objective method. Neither psychocinematics nor behaviorism classify as pure psychology, since both treat things rather than mind.

The phenomenological psychologist Hayami did not endorse Watsonian behaviorism despite his publicizing it in Japan. His intellectual sympathies were with Lipps, Husserl, and Natorp. Hayami accounted for the viability of behaviorism in its restrictiveness of not defining psychology traditionally, solely in terms of consciousness; traditional psychology failed to include animal (and child) psychology. Moreover, behavior is more than the mind's manifestations; it determines the mental function. Nevertheless the method of behaviorism, Hayami (1914b) contended, lacks a direct access to experience.

Behaviorism Meets with Opposition: Chiba and Kido. Both the behaviorism of Watson and the reflexology of Bekhterev met with opposition from 1915 to 1918 by *Tanenari Chiba* (1884-1972), a professor at Tohoku University, a post he assumed in 1923. A graduate of Kyoto University, Chiba obtained his Bungakushi degree in 1909. *Manatro Kido* (1893-   ), a graduate and professor at Tokyo University who favored Woodworth's purposive and dynamic psychology, scored behaviorism's inadequacy in accounting for the unifying principle of human experiences in his *Problems of Psychology* (1926) text.

Proposed Behavioristic Reconciliations: Masuda. In 1923 Koichi Masuda began a trend of harmonizing behaviorism and introspectionism. Because of his findings in experimental animal psychology in 1915, *Koreshige Masuda* (1883-1933) professed behaviorism, notwithstanding his accounting for animal behavior in terms of consciousness. Masuda (1926a,b) favored behaviorism because it contributed to the understanding of consciousness, for by it a psychologist can infer consciousness in animals and children, a deficiency of the introspective method. Moreover it may be considered at least as a symbol or as an aspect of consciousness. Nevertheless he yielded to acknowledging consciousness, and believed that Watson himself no doubt assumed it inasmuch as behavior is but a succession of physical movements if subjective consciousness is left out of account.

Kuroda: Japan's Prominent Animal Psychologist. Another conciliation between behaviorism and introspectionism was sought by *Ryo Kuroda* (1890-1947), a leading Japanese animal psychologist. Kuroda was Western trained in psychology, having studied in the United States at the universities of California and Chicago (1920-1921) before attending the University of Leipzig (1921). His undergraduate work was completed at Tokyo University, where he remained on the faculty. His *Animal Psychology* (1936) sees consciousness and behavior as two aspects of one and the same psychic phenomenon rather than mutually exclusive or contradictory entities. Concurring with others, he views behavior as the objective representation of consciousness which is the content of experience.

Although gestalt from Germany arrived in Japan by 1920, it crested during the 1930s. By that time, whatever thrust was left in behaviorism assumed the form of neobehaviorism amalgamated with gestalt theory of the order of Tolman and Lashley. Gestalt, the most dominant Western influence in Japanese psychology, was initiated by Kanae Sakuma in the 1920s.

(D) INTRODUCTION OF GESTALT PSYCHOLOGY INTO JAPAN

KANAE SAKUMA (1888-1970): Psycholinguistics

While the earliest form of psychology in Japan traces its beginnings to its religious philosophies of Buddhism, Confucianism, and Shintoism, the first indications of psychology as a science in the Western sense of that term appeared in the 1920s. The dominant influences, importations by Japanese scholars studying in the West, were the functionalism of William James and the gestalt of the Germans, such as Köhler. For example, a product of the Tokyo (Imperial) University, *Kanae Sakuma* (1888-1980), the first professor of psychology at Kyushu University (1925-1948), translated into Japanese *The Varieties of Religious Experience* in 1914, and later Köhler's *Gestalt Psychology*. After receiving his Bungakuhakushi degree in 1923, he left for the University of Berlin, studying with Lewin as well as Köhler.

It was Sakuma (1933, 1951) who introduced gestalt psychology into Japan on his return in 1925, bringing with him the works of Stumpf as well as other German psychologists. One of the first psychologists (if not the first) anywhere in the world to become involved in psycholinguistics, Sukuma, who devoted his life to the study of phonetics and philology of the Japanese language, published the first book on psycholinguistics in 1917, *Shinrikenkyuakai* (Accent of Japanese Language). Two years later it was followed by his *Dobunkan* (Pronounciation and Accent of Japanese Language, 1919). Explaining Sakuma's findings, Yoshiharu Akishige of Tokyo's Komazawa University wrote:

The rule of accent was based on his Gestalt theory and it influenced many philologists and phoneticians in Japan, and from those phonetic facts there developed many rules of the structure and phraseology of modern Japanese language, especially the systematic explanation of pronoun and demonstrative pronoun, also to point out the structural deficiency of subject-predicate relationship of traditional Japanese, and he used the special term of so-called "So-shu" (over-all subject) and tried the new interpretation which was highly appraised in and out of Japan as a revolutionary achievement (1970, p. 161).

Sakuma, who was born in Chiba Prefecture, majored in psychology, entering the Faculty of Literature of Tokyo University in 1910. As in the case of some other Japanese psychologists (e.g., Koji Sato), Sakuma, toward the latter part of his career, turned his attention from a gestalt oriented psychology to one based on Zen, indicative of his publication, *Science of Mystical Experience.*

(E) THE RETURN OF ZEN PSYCHOLOGY

SHOMA MORITA (1874-1938) and KOJI SATO (1905-1971): Zen Psychology

Psychotherapy in the form of Zen returned to Japanese psychiatry in the early 1920s, when *Shoma Morita,* Professor of Psychiatry at Tokyo Jikeikai School of Medicine, published his *Therapy of Nervosity and Neurasthenia* (1921a) and *Lectures on Psychotherapy* (1921b). It was after World War II, however, that the distinguished Japanese psychologist, *Koji Sato,* became interested in Zen as a psychology, summarizing his position in *Psychological Zen* (1961).

Morita Therapy: The Application of Zen Buddhism to Psychotherapy

For a score of years Morita developed his psychotherapy, which he accidently encountered in 1919 during a therapy session in his home with a few neurotic individuals. At his home he was caring for a certain female, a Miss Yatabe, who was disturbed with symptoms of obsessive neurosis. Her long stay at a hospital proved to no avail, but when Morita (in his own home) struck her during a momentary loss of temper, the girl was free from her neurotic symptoms.

Morita, who suffered neurotic symptoms himself from the age of sixteen, probably turned to psychiatry in consequence of his psychological problems. He was trained under *Shuzo Kure,* Japan's pioneer in psychiatry. At that time Kraepelin's system of psychiatry dominated Japanese psychiatry, hence Morita approached psychotherapy from the view of Kraepelin or an anti-Freudian orientation. Neither Freud nor Morita had any following in Japan for a number of years, the only notable exception being a devotee of Morita, *Mitsuzo Shimoda,* who has been Professor of Psychiatry at Kyushu University. With the successful application of Morita's therapy, his disciples began to increase, the most notable among them being the psychologist *Koji Sato.* Western psychotherapists did not incline toward Morita therapy (perhaps because they were not aware of it) until the 1950s, when Karen Horney and Erich Fromm were attracted toward it.

Shinkeishitsu and Arugamama. When Morita wrote his *Ways to the Therapy of Nervosity* (1935, 1937), he had in mind the German term *Nervosität*, and translated it into Japanese as *shinkeishitsu,* thinking of it as a hypochondriacal constitution. It is not the constitution per se that causes *shinkeishitsu* (neuroticism), but the undue attention paid to this disposition that tends to intensify the condition. Reacting to the condition calls attention to it, and attending to the condition increases reaction. This vicious circle of reaction and attention, Morita termed *toraware* ("to be caught"), i.e., to be overly preoccupied, or as H. Shinfuku rendered it, "to be bound with over-self-consciousness" (1954, p. 737).

The most effective means of dealing with neurotic symptoms is to employ *aru ga mama* ("to take things as they are"), that is, to gain an insight. *Arugamama* and the *satori* of Zen Buddhism are identical. In order to achieve this insight into nature, it is necessary to orient one's attitude so that it harmonizes with the universe, that is, not to challenge or fight with nature as the Western mind is predisposed to do but to accept it, living in peace with it. The Westerner's attitude on encountering a mountain that is blocking his way is to remove it or bore a hole through it, whereas the Oriental simply bypasses it. Accordingly in Morita therapy, nature is the therapist, the psychotherapist being merely a teacher assisting in acquiring insight.

In *arugamama,* a person is resigned to his fate (but not in the sense of fatalism). Rather he accepts his condition. Morita (1928, 1953) observed that the victim of *shinkeishitsu,* who believes that he is troubled with insomnia, is in fact disturbed with a "fear of insomnia" instead of insomnia per se. By letting nature take its course, the individual will fall asleep instinctively when sleep is indicated. Thus *arugamama* connotes "living with symptoms," "facing agony," "accepting things as they are," and the like.

Occupational therapy plays a role in Morita therapy. While it is not mandatory, it is viewed as natural and meaningful, being the natural vehicle provided the individual whereby he can unite with nature.

Four Stages of Morita Therapy. Four stages involved in Morita therapy include: (1) bed rest in isolation, (2) light manual tasks period, (3) heavier tasks period, and (4) preparatory period for returning to the world at large. During the first period (a week or so) when the individual's isolation intensifies his anxiety, the therapist's role is to see that he yields rather than fights his anxiety. During the second period a diary is kept; the therapist's duty is to offer suitable comments. In the third period the diary comments are continued. Worries are dispelled by calling attention to *toraware* (being caught in concern). The fourth period is one of interpersonal relations, the attainment of *arugamama* (to take things as they are), i.e., learning to be natural and at home or comfortable with oneself. Thus Morita therapy is rest therapy and work therapy integrated with insight.

Gradually Morita therapy came to be appreciated among Japanese psychologists and others, among them being *Takehisa Kora (1899-   ),* an M.D. (1924) from Kyushu University who succeeded to professor and chairman of the Department of Psychiatry and Neurology at the Jikeikai University School of Medicine in

Tokyo. Kora (1965) couched his Morita therapy in the light of Western ideas. *Yukiyoshi Koga* (1891-   ), Professor of Psychology at Nishogakuoha College and editor of the *Japanese Journal of Psychology*, developed Morita therapy with respect to psychosomatic medicine. *Koji Sato*, who employed it at Kyoto University in student counseling, developed it in conjunction with Lewin's theory of causality.

Koji Sato's Zen Psychology

The most celebrated Japanese psychologist during the mid-twentieth century, *Koji Sato* (1905-1971), was Professor of Psychology at Kyoto University. Born in Yamagata, Japan, Sato graduated from Kyoto University in 1928, where he obtained his Bungakuhakushi degree in 1956. His career saw him working as a psychologist from the Kyoto Prefectual Center for Youth Education (1929) and as Professor of Psychology at Otani University Preparatory Course, before becoming a professor at the Third National Junior College (1934-1950). From 1950 his career continued as Professor of Psychology at Kyoto University. He edited (or coedited) a number of journals, including *Psychologia* (which he founded in 1957); *Japanese Journal of Psychology; Japanese Psychological Research; Journal of Social Psychology;* and the *Indian Journal of Psychology.*

Sato, whose psychological interests grew progressively, was early interested in gestalt, having written his doctoral dissertation (Study of Apprehension of Relation) in 1955 based on Köhler's theories. During his early career he developed an interest in psychoanalysis and clinical psychology. The World War II years found him interested in the psychology of morale and human engineering psychology. The early 1950s found him interested in group dynamics and the *Psychology of Personality* (1951). Before that decade closed he was deeply involved with Morita therapy (1958a,b) and Zen psychology (1959a,b), the fascination for Zen remaining indelibly with him throughout the remainder of his life. Fifty percent of the almost one hundred articles written by Sato treated Zen.

Psychology of Zen. Zen psychology, essentially one of adjustment and personality development, consists in training for everyday life experiences. Zen training is comprised of (1) physical adjustment entailing posture and breathing, and (2) mental adjustment, enhancing serenity, flexibility, and clarity of mind through the realization that the self and the world are fundamentally interrelated, thereby having the true self quickened and a compassion cultivated for the well-being and happiness of living beings.

Initially emerging out of Buddhism in India and reaching Japan via China, Zen blossomed in Japan. It is the Taoist synthesis of Chinese Zen that distinguishes it from Yoga or Buddhism. Thus Zen Buddhism is a Chinese importation of the twelfth and thirteenth centuries into Japan. Four great objectives of New World Zen according to Sato are equivalent to the four great vows of Zen Buddhism: "1) To help *Shujo* (all beings, living and non-living) to become happy; 2) to eradicate our evil passions; 3) to learn all teachings; and 4) to realize the Ways of the Buddha (i.e., of the Enlightened and the Compassionate)" (1969, p. 20).

Zazen, or sitting Zen, promotes psychophysiological adjustment through posture, breathing, and the proper employment of mind, one resultant value being the coping with psychosomatic ailments. One begins Zen training by undertaking the psychophysiological adjustment before undertaking an environmental adjustment, a state of being stimulus-free or stimulusless. Posture adjustment, a lotus-posture seated position, calls for a straight spine, a relaxed neck, shoulders, and arms, with a natural increment of pressure on the lower abdomen. Breathing adjustment is one that is calm, slow, and deep (striving to achieve from five down to two times per minute). While the average person breathes with his throat, the Zen veteran breathes with his heels as it were. In order to adjust the mind, a person should concentrate first on counting breathing, and then proceed to breathing itself. Let irrelevant ideas vanish by a concentration on counting one's breathing.

Koan, like Zazen, a method for Zen training, is a problem derived from the experiences of Zen masters for guiding Zen students. These paradoxes (koans) are instrumental in achieving meditation through sudden intuitive enlightenment by forsaking reason. Two koans include *mu* or *nothingness* and the "sound of a single hand."

Satori, the essence of Zen, is the seeing of one's own nature or the awakening of the true self, i.e., enlightenment. Closely related to satori is *kensho* (the phenomenal experience), satori being the realization of its meaning. Kensho therefore is the phenomenological investigation of the subjective self, in the sense that one is looking through his own nature. Eventually there is an extinguishing between inner and outer, and the true self emerges. Kensho is characterized by *narikiru* (to become one with oneself completely) and *nukekiru* (getting completely rid of oneself or completely out of the way of oneself). Kensho is the experience of *todatsu,* experiencing the self as transparent, for such a self is the true self, one resulting in peace of mind. By stripping off layers (complexes) of the overt self, one approaches the true self.

At least ten benefits derive from Zen training, including: (1) vitality and the alleviation of chronic disorders; (2) cure of neurosis; (3) personality or temperament change; (4) increased will control; (5) work efficiency; (6) heightening intellectual functions; (7) integration of personality; (8) satori (awakening of the true self) through the realization of the oneness of the self and the universe; (9) a deep compassionate disposition; and (10) peace of mind.

Relation of Zen Psychology to Western Psychology. Sato, comparing his Zen psychology with Frankl's logotherapy, saw among the striking similarities that the two stress all levels of human existence, including the physical, the mental and the life of the spirit. Logotherapy and Morita therapy share a number of common notions, such as Frankl's paradoxical intention and Morita's paradox of thought, the former's dereflection and the latter's *arugamama* or *sonamama* (as it is)—lowering of the hyperattention and overpreoccupation. The *geistig* unconscious (spiritual unconscious) of Frankl and the *no-mind* of Zen are comparable. Rather than unconsciousness in the ordinary sense of the term, no-mind is a "polished" consciousness, being the ultimate result of personality development.

The no-mind concept of Zen, though devoid of images, ideas, and strain, maintains awareness, a consciousness of a highly practiced behavior.

The psychology of Jung and Zen share common ground also, such as the resemblance of Jung's collective unconscious with the Buddhistic notion of *alaya* consciousness. Atman, Hinduism's true self, is mentioned by Jung. The *autogenic training* of J. H. Schultz (with Luthe, 1959) compares with *zazen* training, especially with respect to breathing.

Carl R. Rogers, whose system of psychotherapy is widely accepted in Japan, is related to Zen psychology by Sato:

> Rogers discussed about that self which one truly is. Away from facades, Away from 'oughts,' Away from meeting expectations, Away from pleasing others, Toward self-direction, Toward being process, Toward being complexity, Toward openness to experience, Toward acceptance of others, Toward trust of self, are the directions toward his true self. These traits can be seen very well in Zen people: naturalness, freedom and depending on self, openness, flexibility, being process, etc. The True Self of Zen may be seen as the limit in this direction. But there must be a leap. The True Self of Zen is not a substantial self, but Void. It is so-to-say the Cosmic Self, but in this case also different from the substantial Prusha of Hinduism. The author would rather say: the Rogerian true self may develop very well on the basis of the bottomless bottom of the True Self of Zen (1968, pp. 17-18).

Other psychologists and psychiatrists share concepts with Zen, and still others have derived their own notions from Zen, as is the case with Erich Fromm (1959; with Suzuki, and DeMartino, 1960). Karen Horney, who visited Japan in 1952, probably would have made use of her knowledge of Zen psychology had it not been for her death the same year. Zen psychology and psychoanalysis have been compared, not only by Fromm, but others, such as Norma Haimes (1972).

CHAPTER 20

Psychology from the Orient: Southeast Asia

Psychology in Asian countries has neither the roots nor the development that is enjoyed by the Western world. Outside of Japan, psychology in universities and in professional life is a post World War II manifestation, typified by the growth of psychology in the Republic of China.

(A) PSYCHOLOGY IN THE REPUBLIC OF CHINA

The birth of psychology as a science in China dates from 1950 when the State Council's recently instituted Chinese Academy of Sciences formed a committee for psychology. The Academy in 1951 established the Psychology Research Office, expanding it into the Institute of Psychology by the middle of the decade. Nanking University's physiology department (which offered courses in psychology) provided both equipment and personnel. The Institute of Psychology came under the aegis of the Department of Philosophy and Social Sciences, one of the Academy's five departments. The staff's chief members were well credentialed, its first director being *P'an Shu*, a University of Chicago Ph.D. (1926). Of the six known members of the Institute, four were trained in the United States, one in Canada, and one, its deputy director *Ts'ao Jih-c'ang*, at the University of Cambridge, where he received his Ph.D. in 1948. In the list of 78 distinguished Chinese psychologists prepared by the Director of the Institute of Psychology, 51 earned graduate degrees in American universities, and only fifteen from universities in China. Of the early Chinese psychologists, *The Psychological Register* (1929) lists only eleven of them, ten of whom did their graduate training in the United States, six of them studying at Columbia University. Members of the Institute founded the first Chinese Psychological Association in 1937.

By 1956, the Institute of Psychology was training graduates in psychology. Prior to this time, graduate instruction in psychology was offered at Hua-tung Normal University and at Peking University, where the first psychology course in China was offered before the close of the first decade of the twentieth century. A department of psychology existed in Peking University in the 1920s, but in 1952 it was placed under the aegis of the department of philosophy. Although a degree in psychology was issued by the Psychology Specialty of the Department of Philosophy, in the latter 1950s the faculty in the Psychology Specialty was comprised of ten psychologists. More than general, child, as well as history of psychology was offered by the Psychology Specialty; they also taught political theory, foreign languages, and even logic. Psychology in China always played a major role in education, especially through teacher training.

The 1950s also saw the translations of texts in psychology, particularly by

Russian psychologists, including Pavlov, Kornilov, and Teplov, the earliest text in Chinese being one by Yuan Kung-wei in 1953. The year 1955 saw the inauguration of the Chinese Psychological Association, with its first Annual Congress that summer. Within three years the Association's membership increased tenfold, numbering almost 600 psychologists. The Association almost immediately instituted an editorial committee, so that the following year (1956) the first issue of the journal *Acta Psychologicol Sinica* appeared. The same year the *Journal of Translations in Psychology* was published, but it was short-lived, lasting only two years (from 1956 to 1958).

Besides educational psychology, Chinese psychologists were interested in delineating the field of psychology, members of the Institute of Psychology regarding it as the study of reflection. They held that ''psychologists should concentrate on the origin, development, and laws of the process whereby the brain reflects objective reality'' (Chin & Chin, 1969, p. 54). While others wanted to isolate social consciousness from individual consciousness, they found their opposition from the Hua-tung Normal University faculty, which viewed psychological consciousness as class consciousness, the essence of mind being class mind. The Marxist orientation, man as the product of his social relations, was supported by the Peking Normal University faculty, who, having defined psychology as the study of consciousness, argued that a person is the sum of his social relations, one's consciousness arising from labor. Psychological consciousness finds its origin in social experience. Introspectionism of the West, however, was condemned.

Chinese Psychology Since the Cultural Revolution. In consequence of the Chinese Cultural Revolution in the mid-sixties, psychology suffered severe reverses. The Chinese Psychological Association, which was at one time responsible for the publication of four journals, was abolished. Currently the only psychological journals in China are from the United States, and a number of the new textbooks from England. Albert H. Yee, an American psychologist traveling through China in 1972 lamentably reported that ''little empirical research seems to have been conducted since the Cultural Revolution and methodology appears to be little understood'' (1973, p.4). He went on to report that ''Peking psychologists are members of the Philosophy Department and the Shanghai group resides in the Pedagogy Department'' (1973, p. 4). The bleak outlook for psychology in China leaves one with the impression that psychologists must start anew.

(B) PSYCHOLOGY IN INDIA

Outside of Japan, psychology in southeast Asia has not been as aggressively pursued. For example, there is only one universtiy in Ceylon, the University of Ceylon, and that was only relatively recently founded. Though established in 1942, it is still without a separate department of psychology. Psychology is taught by the Department of Education or the Department of Sociology.

The situation in India proper is appreciably better where psychology became an independent subject in 1916 at Calcutta University, with N.N. Sangupta the first professor in the Department of Psychology. Mysore University followed suit, with N.V. Gopalawswamy heading the department. When Sangupta left Calcutta to join Lucknow University, he founded a laboratory there in 1929.

Psychologists in India organized, forming the Indian Psychological Association in 1925, three years after the Indian Psycho-analytical Society was established. The organ of the psychological association, the *Indian Journal of Psychology*, is the oldest in Indian psychology. By 1945 the University of Calcutta was offering a Certificate Course in Applied Psychology. Child guidance clinics had been in progress since the one instituted in New Delhi in 1937. The National Institute of Sciences of India had made psychology (along with veterinary sciences and educational sciences) a subdivision of physiology. Udai Pareek believes that "the development of modern natural and social sciences in India can be traced back to the impact of European thought through the British system of education finally decided for this country about a hundred years back" (1957, p. 55).

In Indian psychological publications (Mitra, 1955; Pareek, 1957), psychology indigenous to the people of India is ordinarily ignored in treating the progress of psychology in that nation. In the present treatment, yoga psychology is analyzed.

Yoga Psychology

The author of *Yoga Sūtra,* Patañjali, who flourished during the second half of the second century, is the reputed founder of the Yoga school of thought. The term *yoga* derives from *yujir,* meaning to unite, the significance being the union of individual and universal soul. It is necessary to still the workings of the mind, otherwise it is impossible to know and unite that which transcends the mind. The mind is released from the dissolution of its hindrances and impairments. Yoga is a psychological technique for achieving physical and mental control of human nature by channeling the activity of consciousness. Oriented from the standpoint of psychological funtionalism, yoga, by the suppression of mental states, effects "a transformation of the psychic organism making it possible for the self to transcend and to dissolve the various planes of world experience" (Reyna, 1971, p. 159). According to yoga, life energies can be directed (or redirected) through physical organs as well as withdrawn. Through yoga peace of mind is achieved through concentration. Control and direction of the intellect are essential. *Yoga Sūtra* opens with "yoga consists in the stopping of the spontaneous activities of mind-stuff," an act which is intentionally effected.

The phenomenal aspect of mind, *citta,* entails the intellect and self-consciousness with states of mind, including cognitions, memory, imagination, and sleep. The mind, a battleground of conflicting forces, is laden with satisfaction-seeking desires, self-preservative and reproductive vital urges, and passions that are difficult to control. Only through self-restraint, the restraint of needs, is self-realization attained. Latent tendencies also must be annihilated if spiritual equilibrium is to be achieved. *Citta,* essentially an unconscious mind, reflects the consciousness of *purusa* (self or conscious mind). Mental states are subdued by concentration, enabling the self to find its true nature. The true self is unaffected by phenomenal existence; obstacles to its concentration are comprised of egoism, love of life, attachment, aversion, etc. Three qualities *(gunas)* possess the mind: (1) *tamas* (inertia), (2) *rajas* (activity or passion), and (3) *sattva* (harmony); a preponderance of tamas inclines a person toward dullness, resentfulness, or sluggishness; of the rajas toward aggressiveness, haughtiness, or heroics; and the sattva toward a state of enlightened repose (as such it is a state of perfect personality development). Yoga discipline extricates the personality from its entanglements with tamas and rajas. By removing tamas, citta (phenomenal mind) becomes transparent. By expurgating rajas (passion), mental agitation subsides and peace ensues. Thus is articulated a constitutional theory of personality.

Since emotional stress both colors and directs thought, considerable discipline and concentration are required before reason is isolated from emotional influence. Intense mental concentration by yoga suppresses mental activities.

CHAPTER 21
Psychology in Latin America

Development of Psychology in Mexico. Although psychology in Latin America is in a state of transition toward a science, it has nevertheless made strides since 1567, the date of the founding of its first mental hospital in Mexico City, the Hospital de San Hipólito, directed by Bernardine Alvarez. Mexico has other firsts, leading the way in psychology in South America, with the first publication of a work in psychology, the *Exposición Sumaria del Sistema Frenológico del Doctor Gall* in 1835 by Jesús R. Pacheo, a polemical work on Gall's phrenology. A psychiatric work, *Psiquiatría Optica* (1884), by Rafael Serrano of Puebla, Mexico, offered a nosology of psychosis as well as a psychophysical technique in psychiatric diagnosis. Mexico also distinguished itself with the first text in psychology in Latin America, the publication in 1902 of *La Psicología* by Enrique C. Alacrón. The following year Ezequiel A. Chávez, also of Mexico City, translated Titchener's *A Primer of Psychology*, the Spanish text being in use for over a quarter of a century. The first physiological psychology (encompassing the physical and social environment as well as psychopathology and therapy) appeared in Mexico in 1907 by Juan N. Cordero, titled *La Vida Psíquica*.

The National University of Mexico opened its Department of Psychology in 1945, though psychology as a career was founded in Mexico in 1937 under the leadership of Ezequiel A. Chávez at the National University of Mexico. Six years later in Mexico City, the Sociedad Interamericana de Psicología was founded in 1951.

Development of Psychology in Argentina. After Mexico made the initial start in psychology, the momentum was carried for a period of time by Argentina, where experimental psychology found its way in South America by the establishment of the first psychological laboratory in 1898 by Horacio C. Piñero at the Colegio Nacional of Buenos Aires. Three years later (in 1901), he founded a second at the Universidad de Buenos Aires. It appears that Latin America's first Ph.D. in psychology went to Carl Jesinghaus, who received his doctorate under Wundt at Leipzig in 1911. After two years at the University of Halle, he left in 1913 for Buenos Aires for the Instituto Nacional del Profesorado.

Buenos Aires also has the distinction of publishing Latin America's first journal expressly in the field of psychology proper, the *Anales del Instituto de Psicología de la Facultad de Filosofír y Letras de las Universidad de Buenos Aires*, founded in 1935 (terminated in 1941) under the editorial leadership of Enrique Mouchet. Latin America, where historically the interest has been in medical psychology, founded the journal of *Revista de Psiocoanálisis* in 1943 at Buenos Aires, and its most important journal of psychology, the *Revista Interamericana de Psicología*, the official organ of the Sociedad Interamericana de Psicología, in 1967.

Development of Psychology in Peru. Not counting *Revista de Filosofía*, a

433

philosophical journal that included a number of papers on psychology, which was founded in 1915, the first journal of a psychological nature was *El Psicoanálisis,* established by Honorio Delgado of Lima in 1919. Peru has long enjoyed being Latin America's birthplace of culture with its University of San Marcos in Lima. In 1551 Emperor Charles V. Delgado (with Mariano Ibérico) was responsible for another important psychological publication, *Psicología* (1933), which proved influential in Peru. The Binet-Simon test found its way in 1920 into research on Peruvian children by Felipe Chueca. When the German psychologist Walter Blumenfeld arrived in Lima in 1935, he organized the Instituto de Psicología Experimental y Psicotecnia at the Universidad de San Marcos.

Development of Psychology in Brazil. Brazil's role in Latin American psychology received its initial impetus from the Polish psychologist *Waclaw Radecki,* who arrived at Rio de Janeiro in 1923, establishing Brazil's first laboratory of psychology and developing the fields of general psychology as well as experimental psychology. There he founded the Instituto de Psicología de Assistancia a Psichopatas, which was to become part of the University of Rio de Janeiro.

The study of Blacks became an important interest in Brazilian psychology, spearheaded by *Arture Ramos,* author of *O Negro Brasileiro* in 1934. Ramos, whose doctorate was in medicine from the medical school in Bahía, distinguished himself in social psychology and psychiatry. Arriving in Rio de Janeiro in 1933, he lectured, the following year becoming head of the Mental Hygiene Service of the Institute of Educational Research of the Federal District. By 1935 he held the chair of social psychology at the University of Rio, publishing his Introduction to Social Psychology in 1936. Analyzing the book, Beebe-Center and McFarland wrote:

> The book besides constituting a thorough and up-to-date presentation of the subject as a whole, has several chapters devoted to the interrelation of thought processes in primitives, psychotics, neurotics, children, youths, and normal adults. The fundamental thesis of the author is that Lévy-Brühl's hypothesis of special primitive type of thinking is essentially correct, that such primitive thought is closely related to the thinking of children and of certain abnormal individuals, that all of these types of thinking are largely manifestations of Freudian unconscious mechanism, and that this same primitive-unconscious thinking is present to a greater or lesser degree in normal adults (1941, pp. 637-8).

Psychology in Cuba. In all of Latin America, only in Brazil and Cuba is psychology accorded legal recognition. In Cuba, where psychology is taught under the aegis of the Faculty of Sciences, a person may obtain a doctorate in psychology, specialties in psychology there being educational, clinical, industrial, and psychology of language. In 1958, Cuba opened its Escuela de Psicología at the Universidad de las Villas.

Concluding Observations. Psychology in Latin America has been reviewed by Ruben Ardila (1968, 1970), who sees psychology in Latin America as a unit. He assessed Latin American interest in psychology as follows:

> The first area of interest seems to be clinical psychology, mainly the dynamic (psychoanalytic) approach . . . .

The second area of active research is cross-cultural studies. This implies social psychology, value systems in different cultures, personality development, and the like . . . .

Psychometrics is also a favorite field of work. . . .

Operant conditioning is beginning to be studied seriously, including its applications to behavior therapy (1968, p. 570).

Henry P. David (1965) seems to corroborate Ardila's analysis.

EPILOGUE

Perhaps the most exasperating aspect of writing a history of psychology is its futility! It cannot be brought to a close inasmuch as progress in psychology continues even as the book is being written. Furthermore, it is difficult to assess the lasting or historical value of psychology currently transpiring. It is for this very reason that a number of historians of psychology conclude their treatises at some point in the past such as World War II. However, any cut-off point is fictitious because an important system may have begun before the cut-off point and continues at an intensive pace so that its progress and importance in psychology cannot be ignored.

Some daring historians have divined into the future, such as Gardner Murphy writing in 1963 on the psychology of 1975. Another problem is deciding not only the psychologists to treat but how extensively to deal with them and which ones to omit. An exhaustive history of psychology text is infeasible, and even if it were feasible, it would be unwieldly and unacceptable to the vast segment of the reading population. On the other hand, a book too skimpy would not provide the information necessary to span the subject. Hopefully, this work will be found to mediate these two extremes.

REFERENCES

Abelson, R. P., & Rosenberg, M. J. Symbolic psycho-logic: A model of attitudinal cognition. *Behavioral Science,* 1958, *3,* 1-13.

Ach, N. *Ueber die Willenstätigkeit und das Denken* (Volition and thought), 1905.

Adams, D. K. William McDougall. *Psychological Review,* 1939, *46,* 1-8.

Adler, A. *Study of organ inferiority and its psychical compensation: A contribution to clinical medicine,* 1907. New York: Nervous and Mental Disease Publishing, 1917.

Adler, A. *Practice and theory of individual psychology,* 1909-1920. Paterson, NJ: Littlefield, Adams, 1959.

Adler, A. *The neurotic constitution: Outlines of a comparative individualistic psychology and psychotherapy,* 1912. New York: Dodd, Mead, 1926.

Adler, A. Individual psychology. In C. Murchison (Ed.), *Psychologies of 1930.* Worcester, MA: Clark University Press, 1930. Pp. 395-405.

Adler, A. *What life should mean to you.* Boston: Little, Brown, 1931.

Adler, A. *Social interest: A challenge to mankind,* 1933. New York: Capricorn, 1964.

Adler, A. Introduction: The fundamental views of individual psychology. *International Journal of Individual Psychology,* 1935, *1,* 5-8. (a)

Adler, A. What is neurosis? *International Journal of Individual Psychology,* 1935, *1,* 9-17. (b)

Adler, A. *The science of living.* Garden City, NY: Doubleday, 1969.

Adorno, T. W., Frenkel-Brunswik, E., Levinson, D. J., & Sanford, R. N. *The authoritarian personality.* New York: Harper, 1950.

Akishige, Y. For the memory of the late Professor Kanae Sakuma. *Psychologia,* 1970, *13,* 161-162.

Albrecht, F. McA. The new psychology in America: 1880-1895. Unpublished doctoral dissertation, Johns Hopkins University, 1960.

Alexander, F. G., & Selesnick, S. T. *The History of psychiatry: An evaluation of psychiatric thought and practice from prehistoric times to the present.* New York: Harper & Row, 1966. Reprinted, New York: New American Library, 1968.

Alexander S. *Space, time and deity.* 2 Vols. London: Macmillan, 1920.

Allport, F. H. *Social psychology.* Boston: Houghton Mifflin, 1924.

Allport, G. W. A test for ascendance-submission. *Journal of Abnormal and Social Psychology,* 1928, *23,* 118-136.

Allport, G. W. *Personality: A psychological interpretation.* New York: Henry Holt, 1937.

Allport, G. W. *Pattern and growth in personality.* New York: Holt, Rinehart and Winston, 1961.

Allport, G. W., & Vernon, P. E. *Study of values: A scale for measuring the dominant interests in personality.* Boston: Houghton Mifflin, 1931.

Angell, J. R. The relations of structural and functional psychology to philosophy. *Philosophical Review,* 1903, *12,* 243-271.

Angell, J. R. *Psychology: An introductory study of the structure and function of human consciousness.* New York: Henry Holt, 1904.

Angell, J. R. The province of functional psychology. *Psychological Review,* 1907, *14,* 61-91.

Angell, J. R. The influence of Darwin on psychology. *Psychological Review,* 1909, *16,* 152-169.

Angell, J. R. *Chapters from modern psychology.* New York: Longmans, Green, 1912.

Angell, J. R. *An introduction to psychology.* New York: Henry Holt, 1918.

Angell, J. R. Autobiography. In C. Murchison (Ed.), *A history of psychology in autobiography.* Vol. 3. Worcester, MA: Clark University Press, 1930. Pp. 1-38.

Ardila, R. Psychology in Latin America. *American Psychologist,* 1968, *23,* 567-574.

Ardila, R. Landmarks in the history of Latin American psychology. *Journal of the History of the Behavioral Sciences,* 1970, *6,* 140-146.

Aristotle. *De anima.* In W. D. Ross (Ed.), *The works of Aristotle.* Vol. 3. Oxford: Clarendon Press, 1931.

Aristotle. *On memory and reminiscence.* In R. McKeon (Ed.), *The basic works of Aristotle.* New York: Random House, 1941. (a)

Aristotle. *Politics.* In R. McKeon (Ed.), *The basic works of Aristotle.* New York: Random House, 1941. (b)

Asch, S. E. Effects of group pressure upon the modification and distortion of judgments. In H. Guetskow (Ed.), *Groups, leadership, and men.* Pittsburgh, PA: Carnegie Press, 1951. Pp. 177-190.

Asch, S. E. *Social psychology.* Englewood Cliffs, NJ: Prentice-Hall, 1952.

Asch, S. E. Studies in independence and conformity. *Psychological Monographs,* 1956, *70,* 1-70.

Asch, S. E. Gestalt theory. *International Encyclopedia of the Social Sciences,* 1968, *6,* 159-174.

Aubert, H. Ueber die Grenzen der Farbenemfindung auf den seitlichen Theilen der Retina. *Arch. Ophthal. Berlin,* 1857, *3,* 38-67.

Aubert, H. Physiologie der Netzhaut (Physiology of the retina). Breslau: Morgenstern, 1865.

Avenarius, R. *Kritik der reinen Erfahrung* (Critique of pure experience). 2 Vols. 1888-1890.

Baer, K. E. *Über Entwicklungsgeschichte der Thiere.* 2 Vols. 1828-1837.

Baer, K. E. *Untersuchungen über die Entwicklung der Fische,* 1835.

Bagehot, W. *Physics and politics,* 1869. Reprinted, New York: Appleton, 1875; and New York: Knopf, 1948.

Bain, A. *The senses and the intellect,* 1855, 3rd ed., 1868. (a)

Bain, A. *Mental science; a compendium of psychology, and the history of philosophy. Designed as a text-book for high-schools and colleges,* 1868. (b)

Bain, A. *The emotions and the will,* 1859. 3rd ed., 1888.

Bain, A. *Logic: Deductive and inductive*, 1870.

Bain, A. *Mind and body*, 1872. 7th ed., 1883.

Bain, A. *James Mill: A biography*, 1882.

Bain, A. *Practical essays*, 1884.

Baldwin, J. M. *A hand-book of psychology*. 2 Vols. 1889-1891.

Baldwin, J. M. (Ed.) *Dictionary of philosophy and psychology*. 3 Vols. New York: Macmillan, 1901-1902. Third volume of bibliographical data compiled by B. Rand in 1905.

Baldwin, J. M. *Development and evolution: Including psychophysical evolution, evolution by orthoplasy, and the theory of genetic modes*. New York: Macmillan, 1902.

Bales, R. F. A set of categories for the analysis of small group interaction. *American Sociological Review*, 1950, *15*, 257-263. (a)

Bales, R. F. *Interaction process analysis: A method for the study of small groups*. Reading, MA: Addison-Wesley, 1950. (b)

Bales, R. F. *Personality and interpersonal behavior*. New York: Holt, Rinehart and Winston, 1970.

Bartlett, F. C. Some experiments on the reproduction of folk stories. *Folk Lore*, 1920, 30-70.

Bartlett, F. C. *Psychology and primitive culture*. New York: Macmillan. 1923.

Bartlett, F. C. *Remembering; A study in experimental and social psychology*. Cambridge: Cambridge University Press, 1932.

Bartlett, F. C. *Thinking: An experimental and social study*. New York: Basic Books, 1958.

Basov, M. Y. *Methods of psychological investigation*, 1923.

Bauer, R. A. *The new man in Soviet psychology*. Cambridge, MA: Harvard University Press, 1952.

Beach, F. A. Karl Spencer Lashley: June 7, 1890-August 7, 1958. *Biographical Memoirs*. Washington, DC: National Academy of Sciences, 1958.

Beard, G. M. *Nervous exhaustion*, 1880.

Beard, G. M. *American nervousness*, 1881.

Beebe-Center, J. G., & McFarland, R. A. Psychology in South America. *Psychological Bulletin*, 1941, *38*, 627-667.

Békésy, G. Current status of theories of hearing. *Science*, 1956, *123*, 779-783.

Békésy, G. *Experiments in hearing*. New York: McGraw-Hill, 1960.

Bekhterev, V. M. *Nerve paths in the brain and spinal cord*, 1893.

Bekhterev, V. M. *Fundamentals of brain functions*, 1903-1907.

Bekhterev, V. M. *Objective psychology*, 1907.

Bekhterev, V. M. *General principles of human reflexology*, 1917. London: Jarrolds Publishers, 1933.

Bekhterev, V. M. *Collective reflexology*, 1921.

Bell, C. *Anatomy of the human body*, 1809.

Bell, C. *Idea of a new anatomy of the brain*, 1811.

Bell, C. *An exposition of the natural system of the nerves of the human body with a republication of the papers delivered to the Royal Society, on the subject of nerves,* 1825.

Bell, C. *The nervous system of the human body,* 1830.

Bender, L. A visual motor gestalt test and its clinical use. *Research Monographs* No. 3. New York: American Orthopsychiatric Association, 1938.

Benedict, R. *Patterns of culture.* Boston: Houghton Mifflin, 1934.

Bennet, E. A. *C. G. Jung.* New York: Dutton, 1962.

Bennett, G. K. *Mechanical comprehension test.* New York: The Psychological Corporation, 1940.

Bergson, H. *L'évolution créatrice.* Paris, 1907. Translated, *Creative evolution.* New York: Holt, 1911.

Berkeley, G. *An essay towards a new theory of vision,* 1709. In G. Sampson (Ed.), *The works of George Berkeley, D. D. Bishop of Cloyne.* Vol. 1. London: George Bell, 1897.

Berkeley, G. *A treatise concerning the principles of human knowledge,* 1710. In G. Sampson (Ed.), *The works of George Berkeley, D.D. Bishop of Cloyne.* Vol. 1. London: George Bell, 1897.

Bernheim, H. *Suggestive therapeutics: A treatise on the nature and uses of hypnotism,* 1880. Rev. ed. New York: G. P. Putnam's Sons, 1902.

Bernoulli, D. Specimen theoriae novae de mensura sortis. Comment. *Acad. scient. imp Petropolit T.V.,* 1738.

Binet, A. *L'étude expérimentale de l'intelligence,* Paris: Schleicher, 1903.

Binet, A., & Simon, Th. Sur la nécessité d'établir un diagnostic scientifique des états inférieur de l'intelligence, *L'année psychologique,* 1905, *11,* 163-190. (a)

Binet, A., & Simon, Th. Méthodes nouvelles pour le diagnostic du niveau intellectual des anormaux, *L'année psychologique,* 1905, *11,* 191-244. (b)

Binet, A., & Simon, Th. Application des méthodes nouvelles au diagnostic du niveau intellectuel chez des enfants normaux et anormaux d'hospice et d'école primarire, *L'année psychologique,* 1905, *11,* 245-336. (c)

Binet, A., & Simon, Th. *A method of measuring the development of the intelligence of young children,* 1905, 1908, 1911. 3rd ed. Chicago: Chicago Medical Book, 1913.

Binet, A., & Simon, Th. Le développement de l'intelligence chez les enfants, *L'année psychologique,* 1908, *14,* 1-94.

Binswanger, L. *Being-in-the-world.* New York: Basic Books, 1963.

Bleuler, E. Die Prognose der Dementia Praecox (Schizophreniegruppe). *Allgemeine Zeitschrift für Psychiatrie und Physisch-gerichtliche Medizin,* 1908, *65,* 436-464.

Bleuler, E. *Dementia praecox: Or the group of schizophrenias,* 1911. New York: International Universities Press, 1950.

Bleuler, E. *Lehrbuch der Psychiatrie,* 1916. Translated as *Textbook of psychiatry.* New York: Dover, 1951.

Blix, M. Experimentela bidrag till lösning af fragan om hudnerveras specifika energies. (Experimental contributions on the solution of the question about specific energies). *Uppsala Läkfören. Förh.,* 1882, *18,* 87-102.

Blonsky, P. P. *Vocational schools*, 1919.

Blonsky, P. P. *Pedology*, 1925.

Blonsky, P. P. Certain errors which are encountered in pedology. *On the Way to a New School*, 1931, *6*, 41-50.

Bogardus, E. S. Social distance and its origins. *Journal of Applied Sociology*, 1925, *9*, 216-227. (a)

Bogardus, E. S. Measuring social distance. *Journal of Applied Sociology*, 1925, *9*, 299-308. (b)

Bogardus, E. S. *The development of social thought*. 3rd ed. New York: Longmans, Green, 1955.

Boole, G. *Mathematical analysis of logic*, 1847.

Boole, G. *An investigation of the laws of thought*, 1854. Reprinted, New York: Dover Publications, n.d.

Boring, E. G. *A history of experimental psychology*. New York: Appleton-Century-Crofts, 1929. 2nd ed., 1950.

Boring, E. G. On the subjectivity of important historical dates: Leipzig, 1879. *Journal of the History of the Behavioral Sciences*, 1965, *1*, 5-9.

Boss, M. *Psychoanalysis and daseinsanalysis*. New York: Basic Books, 1963.

Bowne, B. P. *Introduction to psychological theory*. New York: American Book, 1886.

Braid, J. *Practical essay on the curative agency of neuro-hypnotism*, 1842.

Braid, J. *Neurypnology or the rationale of nervous sleep considered in relation to animal magnetism or mesmerism and illustrated by numerous cases of its successful application in the relief and cure of disease*, 1843. London: George Redway, 1899.

Brentano, F. *Psychologie vom empirischen Standpunkt* (Psychology from an empirical standpoint), 1874. Portion reprinted in R. M. Chisholm (Ed.), *Realism and the background of phenomenology*. Glencoe, IL: Free Press, 1960.

Brett, G. S. *A history of psychology*. 3 Vols. New York: Macmillian, 1921.

Breuer, J., & Freud, S. *Ueber den psychischen Mechanismus hysterischer Phänomene*, 1893. Translated, On the psychical mechanism of hysterical phenomena. In S. Freud, *Collected Papers*. Vol. 1. New York: Basic Books, 1959. Pp. 24-41.

Breuer, J., & Freud, S. *Studien Ueber Hysterie*, 1895. Translated, *Studies in hysteria*. New York: Nervous and Mental Disease Publishing, 1937. Reprinted, Boston: Beacon Press, and in *The standard edition of the complete psychological works of Sigmund Freud*. Vol. 2. London: Hogarth, 1955.

Broca, P. Remarques sur le siège de la faculté du langage articulé, suivies d'une observation d'aphémie. *Bulletin de la Société Anatomique de Paris*, 1861, *6*, 343-357.

Broca, P. Sur le siège de la faculté du langage articulé. *Bulletins et Mémoires Société Anthropologie*, 1965, *6*, 377-393. In W. S. Sahakian (Ed.), *History of psychology: A source book in systematic psychology*. Itasca, IL: F. E. Peacock, 1968. Pp. 312-313.

Brown, R. *Social psychology*. New York: Macmillan (Free Press), 1965.

Brown, T. *Inquiry into the relation of cause and effect*, 1805.

Brown, T. *Lectures on the philosophy of the human mind,* 1820. 3 Vols.

Buber, M. *I and thou,* 1923. 2nd ed. New York: Scribner, 1958.

Buhler, K. Tatsachen und Probleme zu einer Psychologie der Denkvorgänge: I. Ueber Gedanken (Facts and problems of the psychology of thought processes: I. On thoughts). *Archiv gesamte Psychologie,* 1907, *9,* 297-305.

Buhler, K. *The mental development of the child: A summary of modern psychological theory.* London: Routledge & Kegan Paul, 1930.

Burt, C. Experimental tests of general intelligence. *British Journal of Psychology,* 1909, 3, 94-177.

Burt, C. Experimental study of general intelligence. *Child Studies,* 1911, *4,* 33-45, 77-89.

Burt, C. General and specific factors underlying the primary emotions. *British Association Ann. Rep.,* 1915.

Burt, C. *Mental and scholastic tests.* London: King & Son, 1921.

Burt, C. *The subnormal mind.* Oxford: Oxford University Press, 1935.

Burt, C. The analysis of temperament. *British Journal of Medical Psychology,* 1938, *17,* 158-188.

Burt, C. The factorial analysis of emotional traits. *Character and Personality,* 1939, *7,* 238-254, 285-299.

Burt, C. *The factors of the mind.* London: University of London Press, 1940.

Burt, C. Autobiography. In E. G. Boring et al. (Eds.), *A history of psychology in autobiography.* Vol. 4. Worcester, MA: Clark University Press, 1952, Pp. 53-73.

Burt, C. Factor analysis and the analysis of variance. In R. B. Cattell (Ed.), *Handbook of multivariate experimental psychology.* Chicago: Rand McNally, 1966. Pp. 267-287.

Byrne, D. The repression-sensitization scale: Rationale, reliability, and validity. *Journal of Personality,* 1961, *29,* 334-349.

Calkins, M. W. *A first book in psychology.* New York: Macmillian, 1909. Rev. ed., 1914.

Cannon, W. B. *Bodily changes in pain, hunger, fear and rage: An account of researches into the function of emotional excitement.* New York: Appleton-Century, 1915. Rev. ed., 1929. Reprinted, New York: Harper & Row, 1963.

Cannon, W. B. *The wisdom of the body.* New York: Norton, 1932. Rev. ed., 1939.

Cantril, H. *The pattern of human concerns.* New Brunswick, NJ: Rutgers University Press, 1965.

Carpenter, W. B. *The principles of general and comparative physiology,* 1839.

Carpenter, W. B. *Principles of human physiology,* 1846.

Carr, H. A. *Psychology.* New York: Longmans, Green, 1925.

Carr, H. A. Autobiography. In C. Murchison (Ed.), *A history of psychology in autobiography.* Vol. 3. Worcester, MA: Clark University Press, 1930. (a)

Carr, H. A. Functionalism. In C. Murchison (Ed.), *Psychologies of 1930.* Worcester, MA: Clark University Press, 1930 (b)

Carr, H. A. The laws of association. *Psychological Review,* 1931, *38,* 212-228.

Carr, H. A. *An introduction to space perception*. New York: Longmans, Green, 1935.

Cartwright, D. & Harary, F. Structural balance: A generalization of Heider's theory. *Psychological Review*. 1956, *63*, 277-293.

Cattell, J. McK. The influence of the intensity of the stimulus on the length of the reaction time. *Brain*, 1885, *8*, 512-515.

Cattell, J. McK. Mental tests and measurements. *Mind*, 1890, *15*, 373-381.

Cattell, J. McK. The advance of psychology. *Science*, 1898, *8*, 533-541.

Cattell, J. McK. Early psychological laboratories. *Science*, 1928, *67*, 543-548.

Cattell, R. B. *Psychology and the religious quest*. New York: Nelson, 1938.

Cattell, R. B. *An introduction to personality study*. London: Hutchison House, 1950. (a)

Cattell, R. B. *Personality: A systematic theoretical and factual study*. New York: McGraw-Hill, 1950. (b)

Cattell, R. B. The scientific ethics of "beyond." *Journal of Social Issues*, 1950, *6*, 21-27. (c)

Cattell, R. B. *Personality and motivation structure and measurement*. Yonkers-on-Hudson, NY: World, 1957.

Cattell, R. B. *The scientific analysis of personality*. Baltimore: Penguin, 1965.

Cattell, R. B. (Ed.) *Handbook of multivariate experimental psychology*. Chicago: Rand McNally, 1966.

Cerletti, U. Electroshock therapy. *Journal of Clinical and Experimental Psychopathology and Quarterly Review of Psychiatry and Neurology*, 1954, *15*, 191-217.

Charcot, J. M. *Leçons sur les maladies du système nerveux*, 1872-1887. Translated as *Clinical lectures on certain diseases of the nervous system*. 3 Vols. London: New Sydenham Society, 1877-1889.

Cheyne, G. *The English malady: Or, a treatise of nervous diseases of all kinds, as spleen, vapours, lowness of spirits, hypochondriacal, and hysterical distempers*. London, 1733.

Chiba, T. Experimental psychology cannot exist. [*Psychological Research*], 1915, *7*, 345-346.

Chiba, T. On objective psychology. *Philosophical Research (Testsugaku Kenkyu)*, 1918, *3*, 29-53.

Chin, R, & Chin, A. S. *Psychological research in Communist China: 1949-1966*. Cambridge, MA: Massachusetts Institute of Technology Press, 1969.

Claparède, É. *Psychologie de l'enfant et pédagogie expérimentale*. Geneva: Kündig, 1905. Translated as *Experimental pedagogy and the psychology of the child*. 4th ed. London: Edward Arnold, 1911.

Condillac, E. B. de *Essai sur l'origine des connaissances humaines* (Essay on the origin of human knowledge). 2 Vols. 1746.

Condillac, E.B. de *Traité des sensations*, 1754. Translated as *Condillac's treatise on the sensations*. Los Angeles: University of Southern California, 1930.

Coombs, C. H. Psychological scaling without a unit of measurement. *Psychological Review*, 1950, *57*, 145-158.

Coombs, C. H. *A theory of psychological scaling.* Ann Arbor, MI: Engineering Research Institute, University of Michigan, 1952.

Coombs, C. H. A theory of data. *Psychological Review,* 1960, *67,* 143-159.

Coombs, C. H. *A theory of data.* New York: Wiley, 1964.

Cornelius, H. Über Verschmelzung und Analyse. *Vierteljahrschrift für wissenschaftliche Philosophie,* 1892, *16,* 404-446.

Cornelius, H. *Psychologie als Erfahrungswissenschaft,* 1897.

Corti, A. Recherches sur l'organe de l'loïe des mammifères. *Z. wiss. Zool.,* 1851, *3,* 109-169.

Coué, E. *Self-mastery through conscious autosuggestion,* 1922. Reprinted in E. Coué and C. H. Brooks, *Better and better every day: Two classic texts on the healing power of the mind.* New York: Barnes & Noble, 1962.

Dalton, J. *Extraordinary facts relating to the vision of colours,* 1794.

Darwin, C. *Journal of researches into the geology and natural history of the various countries visited by H. M. S. Beagle,* 1839. Reprinted, New York: Hafner, 1952.

Darwin, C. *Origin of species by means of natural selection or the preservation of favored races in the struggle for life,* 1859. Reprinted, New York: Washington Square Press, 1963.

Darwin, C. *The descent of man and selection in relation to sex,* 1871. Reprinted, Chicago: University of Chicago Press, 1965.

Darwin, C. *The expression of emotions in man and animals,* 1872. Reprinted, University of Chicago Press, 1965.

Darwin, C. *Autobiography, 1809-1882.* Written in 1886; posthumously published, 1887. Reprinted in N. Barrow (Ed.), *The autobiography of Charles Darwin.* London: Collins, 1958.

Darwin, C. *Life and letters.* 2 Vols. New York: Appleton, 1889.

Darwin, C. R., & Wallace, A. R. *Evolution by natural selection,* 1842-1858. Cambridge: Cambridge University Press, 1958.

David, H. P. International trends in clinical psychology. In B. B. Wolman (Ed.), *Handbook of clinical psychology.* New York: McGraw-Hill, 1965. Pp. 1469-1506.

De Morgan, A. *Formal logic,* 1847.

Descartes, R. *Discourse on the method of rightly conducting the reason,* 1637. In *The philosophical works of Descartes.* Vol. 1. Cambridge: University Press, 1911.

Descartes, R. *Passions of the soul,* 1650. New York: Henry Holt, 1892.

Descartes, R. *Treatise of man,* 1662. Cambridge, MA: Harvard University Press, 1972.

Descartes, R. *Fourth set of objections.* In *The philosophical works of Descartes.* Vol. 2. Cambridge: University Press, 1911. Pp. 79-95.

Dewey, J. The new psychology. *Andover Review,* 1884, *2,* 278-289. Reprinted in John Dewey, *The early works, 1882-1898.* Vol. 1. 1882-1888. Carbondale, IL: Southern Illinois University Press, 1969. Pp. 48-60.

Dewey, J. *Psychology*. New York: American Book, 1886. 3rd ed., 1891.

Dewey, J. The reflex arc concept in psychology. *Psychological Review*, 1896, *3*, 357-370.

Dewey, J. *How we think*. Boston: D. C. Heath, 1910.

Dewey, J. *Human nature and conduct: An introduction to social psychology*. New York: Holt, 1922.

Dewey, J. Biography of John Dewey (edited by Jane M. Dewey). In P. A. Schilpp (Ed.), *The philosophy of John Dewey*, Evanston, IL: Northwestern University, 1939. Pp. 3-45.

Dollard, J., & Miller, N. E. *Personality and psychotherapy: An analysis in terms of learning, thinking, and culture*. New York: McGraw-Hill, 1950.

Donaldson, H. H. On the temperature of sense. *Mind*, 1885, *10*, 339-416.

Donders, F. C. Die Schnelligkeit psychischer Processe. *Archiv für Anatomie und Physiologie*, 1868, 657-681.

Donders, F. C. Ueber Farbensysteme. *Archiv Ophthal. Berlin*, 1881, *27*, 155-223.

Drever J. McDougall, William. *International Encyclopedia of the Social Sciences*, 1968, *9*, 502-505.

Drobisch, M. W. *Empirische Psychologie nach naturwissenschafticher Methode* (Empirical psychology according to the methods of natural science), 1842, 2nd. ed., 1898. Translated in part in B. Rand (Ed.), *The classical psychologists*. Boston: Houghton Mifflin, 1912.

Duijker, H. C. J., & Jacobson, E. H. *International directory of psychologists*. 2nd ed. Netherlands: Royal VanGorcum, 1966.

Ebbinghaus, H. *Memory: A contribution to experimental psychology*, 1885. New York: Teachers College Press, 1913.

Ebbinghaus, H. *Theorie des Farbensehens*, 1893.

Ebbinghaus, H. Ueber eine neue Methode zur Prüfung geistiger Fähigkeiten und ihre Anwendung bei Schulkindern. *Zeitschrift für Psychologie*, 1897, *13*, 401-459.

Ebbinghaus, H. *Psychology: An elementary text-book*, 1908. Boston: D. C. Heath, 1908.

Edgell, B. The British Psychological Society. *British Journal of Psychology*, 1937, *37*, 113-132.

Edgeworth, F. Y. On correlated averages. *Philosophical Magazine*, 1892, *34*, 190-204.

Edwards, J. *Freedom of the will*, 1754. In *The works of President Edwards*. Vol. 2. New York: Robert Carter, 1869. Pp. 1-190.

Ehrenfels, C. Über Gestaltqualitäten. *Vierteljahrsschrift für wissenschaftliche Philosophie*, 1890, *14*, 249-292.

Ehrenfels, C. Über Gestaltqualitäten, 1932. In C. Ehrenfels, *Gestalthaftes Sehen*. Darmstadt: Wissenschaftliche Buchgesellschaft, 1960.

Epictetus. *The enchiridion, or manual*. In *The works of Epictetus*. Boston: Little, Brown, 1865.

Epictetus. *Discourses*. In W. J. Oates (Ed.), *The stoic and epicurean philosophers: The complete extant writings of Epicurus, Epictetus, Lucretius, Marcus Aurelius*. New York: Random House, 1940.

Erikson, E. H. *Childhood and society*. New York: Norton, 1950, 2nd ed., 1963.

Esquirol, J. E. D. *Des maladies mentales considérées sous les rapports médical, hygiénique et médico-legal*, 1838. Translated as *Mental maladies: A treatise on insanity*, 1845.

Estes, W. K. Toward a statistical theory of learning. *Psychological Review*, 1950, *57*, 94-107.

Estes, W. K. Probability learning. In A. W. Melton (Ed.), *Categories of human learning*. New York: Academic Press, 1964.

Estes, W. K., Hopkins, B. L., & Crothers, E. J. All-or-none and the conservation effects in the learning and retention of paired associates. *Journal of Experimental Psychology*, 1960, *60*, 329-339.

Eustachi, B. *De auditu organis*, 1562.

Evans, R. I. *Conversations with Carl Jung and reactions from Ernest Jones*. Princeton, NJ: Van Nostrand, 1964.

Exner, S. Experimentalle Untersuchung der einfachsten psychischen Processe. *Pflüg der Archiv gesamte Physiologie*, 1873, *7*, 601-660.

Eysenck, H. J. *Dimensions of personality*. London: Routledge & Kegan Paul, 1947.

Eysenck, H. J. Criterion analysis—an application of the hypothetico-deductive method to factor analysis. *Psychological Review*, 1950, *57*, 38-53.

Eysenck, H. J. *The scientific study of personality*. London: Routledge & Kegan Paul, 1952.

Falret, J. P., & Lasègue, E. C. *Folie à deux ou folie communiquée*, 1877.

Fay, J. W. *American psychology before William James*. New Brunswick, NJ: Rutgers University Press, 1939. Reprinted, New York: Octagon Books, 1966.

Fechner, G. T. *Beweiss, dass der Mond aus Iodine bestehe* (A demonstration that the moon is made of iodine), 1821.

Fechner, G. T. *Das Büchlein vom Leben nach dem Tode*, 1836. Translated as *On life after death*. Chicago: Open Court Publishing, 1906.

Fechner, G. T. *Nanna, oder über das Seelenleben der Pflanzen* (Nanna, or the soul-life of plants), 1848. 3rd. ed., 1903. Abridgement in W. Lowrie (Ed.), *Religion of a scientist: Selections from Gustav Th. Fechner*. New York: Pantheon Books, 1946.

Fechner, G. T. *Zendavesta, oder über die Dinge des Himmel und des Jenseits* (Zend-Avesta, of the things of heaven and the hereafter), 1851. 2nd. ed., 1901.

Fechner, G. T. *Elemente der Psychophysik*, 1860. 2 Vols. Translated as *Elements of psychophysics*. New York: Holt, Rinehart and Winston, 1966. Selections containing the Fechner Law in W. S. Sahakian (Ed.), *History of psychology: A source book in systematic psychology*. Itasca, IL: F. E. Peacock, 1968.

Fechner, G. T. *Zur experimentalen Aesthetik*, 1871.

Fechner, G. T. *Einige Ideen sur Schöpfungs, und Untwickelungsgeschichte der Organismen* (Some ideas on the creation and evolution of organisms), 1873.

Fechner, G. T. *Vorschule der Aesthetik* (Introduction to esthetics), 1876.

Fechner, G. T. *Die Tagesansicht gegenüber der Nachtansicht* (The daylight-view versus the night-view). Abridgement in W. Lowrie (Ed.), *Religion of a scientist: Selections from Gustav Th. Fechner*. New York: Pantheon Books, 1946. (b)

Ferrier, D. *The functions of the brain*. London: Smith, Elder, 1876.

Festinger, L. *A theory of cognitive dissonance*. Stanford, CA: Stanford University Press, 1957.

Festinger, L. The psychological effects of insufficient rewards: *American Psychologist*, 1961, *16*, 1-11.

Fiamberti, A. M. Considerazioni sulla leucotomia prefrontale con il metodo transorbitario. *Giov. Psichiat. Neuropat.*, 1939, *67*, 291.

Fiske, J. *Mental philosophy*, 1842.

Flourens, M. J. P. *Recherches expérimentales sur les propriétés et les fonctions du systeme nerveux vetébrés*, 1824. In R. J. Herrnstein & E. G. Boring (Eds.), *A source book in the history of psychology*. Cambridge, MA: Harvard University Press, 1966. Pp. 220-223.

Flourens, M. J. P. *Expériences sur le système nerveaux*, 1825.

Flugel, J. C. *A hundred years of psychology: 1833-1933*. London: Duckworth, 1933. Revised with an additional part: *1933-1963* by D. J. West. New York: Basic Books, 1964.

Fourier, J. B. J. *Théorie analytique de la chaleur*, 1822.

Frankl, V. E. *The doctor and the soul: From psychotherapy to logotherapy*, 1946. New York: Knopf, 1955. 2nd ed., 1965.

Frankl, V. E. *Psychotherapy and existentialism: Selected papers on logotherapy*. New York: Washington Square Press, 1967.

Frankl, V. E. *The will to meaning*. New York: World Publishing, 1969.

Franz, S. I. Variations in the distribution of the motor centers. *Psychological Monographs*, 1915, *19*, 147-160.

Freeman, W., & Watts, J. W. *Psychosurgery: In the treatment of mental disorders and intractable pain*. 2nd. ed. Springfield, IL: Charles C. Thomas, 1950.

Freud, S. Further remarks on the defence of neuro-psychoses, 1896. Vol. 1. *Collected papers*. New York: Basic Books, 1959. Pp. 153-182.

Freud, S. *The interpretation of dreams*, 1900. New York: Basic Books, 1955. Reprinted, New York: Avon Books, 1965. Vols. 4-5. *The standard edition of the complete psychological works of Sigmund Freud*. London: Hogarth, 1953.

Freud, S. *The psychopathology of everyday life*, 1901. Vol. 6. *The standard edition of the complete psychological works of Sigmund Freud*. London: Hogarth, 1960.

Freud, S. Three essays on the theory of sexuality, 1905. Vol. 7. *The standard edition of the complete psychological works of Sigmund Freud*. London: Hogarth, 1953.

Freud, S. *Five lectures on psycho-analysis*, 1910. Vol. 11. *The standard edition of the complete psychological works of Sigmund Freud*. London, Hogarth, 1957.

Freud, S. *Totem and taboo,* 1913. New York: Random House, 1946. Vol. 13. *The standard edition of the complete psychological works of Sigmund Freud.* London: Hogarth, 1953.

Freud, S. On narcissism: An introduction, 1914. Vol. 4. *Collected papers.* New York: Basic Books, 1959. Pp. 30-59.

Freud, S. *Introductory lectures on psycho-analysis,* 1916-1917. Vols. 15-16. *The standard edition of the complete psychological works of Sigmund Freud.* London: Hogarth, 1963. Translated also as *A general introduction to psychoanalysis.* Garden City, NY: Garden City Publishing, 1943.

Freud, S. *Group psychology and the analysis of the ego,* 1921. Vol. 18. *The standard edition of the complete psychological works of Sigmund Freud.* London: Hogarth, 1959.

Freud, S. Two encyclopaedia articles, 1922. Vol. 5. *Collected papers.* New York: Basic Books, 1959. Pp. 107-135.

Freud, S. *The ego and the id,* 1923. Vol. 19. *The standard edition of the complete psychological works of Sigmund Freud.* London: Hogarth, 1962.

Freud, S. The libido theory, 1923. In S. Freud, *General psychological theory: Papers on metapsychology.* New York: Collier, 1963. Pp. 180-184.

Freud, S. *An autobiographical study,* 1925. New York: Norton, 1963

Freud, S. *The question of lay analysis,* 1926. New York: Norton, 1950. *Reprinted, Garden City: NY: Doubleday, 1964. Vol. 20. The standard edition of the complete psychological works of Sigmund Freud.* London: Hogarth, 1959.

Freud, S. *The future of an illusion,* 1927. Garden City, NY: Doubleday, 1961. Vol. 21.*The standard edition of the complete psychological works of Sigmund Freud.* London: Hogarth, 1961.

Freud, S. *New introductory lectures on psycho-analysis,* 1933. Vol. 22. *The standard edition of the complete psychological works of Sigmund Freud.* London: Hogarth, 1964. New York: Norton, 1933.

Freud, S. *Moses and monotheism,* 1937-1939. Vol. 23. *The standard edition of the complete psychological works of Sigmund Freud.* London: Hogarth, 1964. New York: Random House, 1939.

Freud, S. An outline of psycho-analysis. *International Journal of Psychoanalysis,* 1940, *21,* 27-84.

Frey, M. Beiträge zur Physiologie des Schmerzsinns (Contributions on the physiology of the sense of pain). *Ber. sächs. Ges. Wiss., Math-Phys. Cl.,* 1894, *46,* 185-196, 283-296.

Frey, M. Beiträge zur Sinnesphysiologie der Haut (Contributions on the physiology of the senses of the skin). *Ber sächs. Ges. Wiss., Math-Phys.,* 1895, *47,* 166-184.

Frey, M. Untersuchungen über die Sinnesfunctionen der menschlichen Haut; Druckempfindung und Schmerz. *Abhandl. säch. Ges. Wiss., Math-Phys.,* 1896, *23,* 175-266.

Frey, M. *Vorlesunger über Physiologie* (Lectures on physiology). Berlin: Springer, 1904. Portion translated in W. S. Sahakian (Ed.), *History of psychol-*

ogy: A source book in systematic psychology. Itasca, IL: F. E. Peacock, 1968. Pp. 151-155.

Fritsch, G., & Hitzig, E. Ueber die elektrische Erregbarkeit des Grosshirns. *Archiv für Anatomie, Physiologie, und wissenschaftliche Medicin,* 1870, pp. 300-332. In R. J. Herrnstein & E. G. Boring (Ed.), *A source book in the history of psychology.* Cambridge, MA: Harvard University Press, 1966. Pp. 229-233.

Fromm, E. *Escape from freedom.* New York: Holt, Rinehart and Winston, 1941.

Fromm, E. *The sane society.* New York: Rinehart, 1955.

Fromm, E. Psychoanalysis and Zen Buddhism. *Psychologia,* 1959, *2,* 79-99.

Fromm, E., Suzuki, D. T., & DeMartino, R. *Zen Buddhism and psychoanalysis.* New York: Harper, 1960.

Fulton, W., & Jacobsen, C. E. The function of the frontal lobes, a comparative study in monkeys, chimpanzees, and man. London: *Abstracts of the Second International Neurological Congress,* 1935.

Gall, F. J. *Gall's works: on the functions of the brain and each of its parts, with observations on the possibility of determining the instincts, propensities and talents, and the moral and intellectual dispositions of men and animals by the configuration of the brain and head,* 1825. 6 Vols. Boston, 1835.

Gall, F. J., & Spurzheim, J. K. *Anatomie et physiologie du système nerveux en général.* 4 Vols. Paris: Schoell, 1810-1819. Rev. ed., 6 Vols. 1825.

Galton, F. *Hereditary genius: An inquiry into its laws and consequences.* London: Macmillan, 1869.

Galton, F. Statistics by intercomparison, with remarks on the law of frequency of errors. *Philosophical Magazine,* 1875, *49,* 33-46.

Galton, F. Statistics of mental imagery. *Mind,* 1880, *5,* 301-318.

Galton, F. *Inquiries into the human faculty and its development,* 1883. Reprinted, London: J. M. Dent, n.d.

Galton, F. Co-relations and their measurement, chiefly from anthropological data. *Proceedings of the Royal Society,* 1888, *45,* 135-145.

Galton, F. *Natural inheritance.* London: Macmillan, 1889.

Galton, F. *Finger prints.* London: Macmillan, 1892. Reprinted, New York: DeCapo, 1965.

Galton, F. *Memories of my life.* London: Methuen, 1908.

Gay, J. *Dissertation concerning the fundamental principle of virtue or morality,* 1731. 5th ed., 1781.

Gesell, A. Early mental growth. In *Yale University, Clinic of Child Development, the first five years of life: A guide to the study of the preschool child.* New York: Harper, 1940.

Gesell, A., & Amatruda, C. S. The study of the individual child. In *Yale University, Clinic of Child Development, the first five years of life: A guide to the study of the preschool child.* New York: Harper, 1940.

Gesell, A., & Ilg, F. L. *Child development: An introduction to the study of human growth. Part 1: Infant and child in the culture of today,* 1943. New York: Harper, 1949.

Gesell, A., & Ilg, F. L. *Child Development: An introduction to the study of human growth. Part 2. The child from five to ten*, 1946. New York: Harper, 1949.

Gilbert, W. *De magnete, magneticisque corporibus*, 1600.

Goddard, H. H. The Binet and Simon tests of intellectual capacity. *The Training School*, 1908, *5*, 3-9.

Goddard, H. H. *The Kallikak family: A study in the heredity of feeble-mindedness*. New York: Macmillian, 1912.

Goethe, J. W. *Farbenlehre*, 1810.

Goldscheider, A. *Die spezifische Energie der Temperaturneven* (Specific energy of the temperature of nerves). *Monatschefte prak, Dermatol.*, 1884, *3*, 198-208.

Goldstein, K. *The organism: A holistic approach to biology derived from pathological data in man*, 1934. New York: American Book, 1939. Boston: Beacon Press, 1963.

Goldstein, K. *Human nature in the light of psychopathology*. Cambridge, MA: Harvard University Press, 1940, 1963.

Goldstein, K. Autobiography. In E. G. Boring & G. Lindzey (Eds.), *A history of psychology in autobiography*. Vol. 5. New York: Appleton-Century-Crofts, 1967. Pp. 147-166.

Goltz, F. L. *Ueber die Verrichtungen des Grosshirns*, 1881 (4 papers, 1876-1881).

Goodenough, F. L. *Measurement of intelligence by drawings*. Yonkers, NY: World Book, 1926.

Grimm, J. *Deutsche Grammatik* (German grammar), 1819-1837.

Grimm, J., & Grimm, W. *Grimm's fairy tales*, 1816-1818.

Guilford, J. P. *Psychometric methods*. New York: McGraw-Hill, 1936.

Guillain, G. *J. M. Charcot: 1825-1893; his life–his work*. New York: Paul B. Hoeber, 1959.

Guthrie, E. R. *The psychology of learning*. New York: Harper & Row, 1935. Rev. ed., 1952.

Guthrie, E. R. Conditioning: A theory of learning in terms of stimulus, response, and association. In N. B. Henry (Ed.), *The forty-first yearbook of the National Society for the Study of Education. Part II. The psychology of learning*. Chicago: The National Society for the Study of Education, University of Chicago Press, 1942. Pp. 17-60.

Guthrie, E. R. Association by contiguity. In S. Koch (Ed.), *Psychology: A study of a science*. Vol. 2. New York: McGraw-Hill, 1959. Pp. 158-195.

Guttman, L. The Cornell technique for scale and intensity analysis. *Educational and Psychological Measurement*, 1947, *7*, 247-279. (a)

Guttman, L. Suggestions for further research in scale and intensity analysis of attitudes and opinions. *International Journal of Opinion and Attitude Change*, 1947, *1*, 30-35. (b)

Guttman, L. On Festinger's evaluation of scale analysis. *Psychological Bulletin*, 1947, *44*, 451-465. (c)

Haimes, N. Zen Buddhism and psychoanalysis—a bibliographic essay. *Psychologia,* 1972, *15,* 22-30.

Hall, G. S. The muscular perception of space. *Mind,* 1878, *3,* 433-450. (a)

Hall, G. S. Notes on Hegel and his critics. *Journal of Speculative Philosophy,* 1878, *12,* 93-103. (b)

Hall, G. S. Letter of Granville Stanley Hall to William James, April 1, 1890. In *William James papers.* Cambridge, MA: Houghton Library, Harvard University.

Hall, G. S. *Adolescence: Its psychology and its relation to physiology, anthropology, sociology, sex, crime, religion and education.* 2 Vols. New York: Appleton, 1904.

Hall, G. S. *Senescence: The last half of life.* New York: Appleton, 1922.

Hall, G. S. *Life and confessions of a psychologist.* New York: Appleton, 1923.

Hall, G. S., & Motora, Y. Dermal sensitiveness to gradual pressure changes. *American Journal of Psychology,* 1888, *1,* 72-98.

Hall, M. On a particular function of the nervous system. *Proceedings of the Zoological Society,* 1832.

Hall, M. On the reflex action of the medulla oblongata and medulla spinalis. *Philosophical Transactions of the Royal Society,* 1833, *123,* 635-665.

Haller, A. *Primae linae physiologiae,* 1747. 3rd ed., 1764.

Haller, A. *Elementa physiologiae corporis humani.* 8 Vols. 1757-1766.

Hamilton, W. *Lectures on metaphysics,* 1858. 2 Vols. Boston: Gould and Lincoln, 1859.

Hara, T. *Shinsei-Zikkenroku* (Experimental records of mind), 1873.

Harman, H. H. *Some observations on factor analysis.* Santa Monica, CA: Rand Corporation, 1955.

Harper, R. S. The laboratory of William James. *Harvard Alumni Review,* 1949, *52,* 169-173.

Harrison, R. Functionalism and its historical significance. *Genetic Psychology Monographs,* 1963, *68,* 387-419.

Hartley, D. *Observations on man, his frame, his duty, and his expectations.* 2 Vols. London, 1749.

Hathaway, S. R., & McKinley, J. C. A multiphasic personality schedule (Minnesota): I. Construction of the schedule. *Journal of Psychology,* 1940, *10,* 249-254.

Hayami, H. Recent trends in psychology. *[Psychological Research],* 1914, *6,* 314-318. (a)

Hayami, H. *[Present-day psychology].* Tokyo: Furokaka, 1914. (b)

Hayami, H., Motora, Y., & Nakajima, R. Japanese translation of Hall's *Adolescence,* 1910.

Head, H. *Aphasia and kindred disorders of speech.* 2 Vols. Cambridge: Cambridge University Press, 1926.

Hearnshaw, L. S. *A short history of British psychology: 1840-1940.* New York: Barnes & Noble, 1964.

Hecker, E. Die Hebephrenie. *Archiv für pathologische Anatomie und Physiologie,* 1871, *52.*

Hegel, G. W. F. *The phenomenology of mind,* 1807. New York: Harper & Row, 1967.

Heidbreder, E. *Seven psychologies.* New York: Appleton-Century, 1933.

Heidegger, M. *Being and time,* 1927. New York: Harper & Row, 1962.

Heider, F. Attitudes and cognitive organization. *Journal of Psychology,* 1946, *21,* 107-112.

Heider, F. *The psychology of interpersonal relations.* New York: Wiley, 1958.

Heider, F. The gestalt theory of motivation. In M. R. Jones (Ed.), *Nebraska symposium on motivation.* Lincoln, NE: University of Nebraska Press, 1960. Pp. 145-172.

Helmholtz, H. *De Fabrica Systematis nervosi Evertebratorum.* Inaugural-Dissertation, 1842.

Helmholtz, H. On the conservation of force, 1847. In C. W. Eliot (Ed.), *Harvard Classics.* Vol. 30. New York: Collier, 1910. Pp. 181-220.

Helmholtz, H. *Description of an ophthalmoscope for the investigation of the retina in the living eye,* 1850. Chicago: Cleveland Press, 1916.

Helmholtz, H. Über die Methoden, kleinste Zeittheile zu messen, und ihre Anwendung für physiologische Zwecke (On the methods of measuring very small portions of time, and their application to physiological processes). *Philosophie Magazin,* 1853, s. 4, 6, 313-325.

Helmholtz, H. *Treatise on physiological optics,* 1856. 3 Vols. Rochester: Optical Society of America, 1924.

Helmholtz, H. *On the sensations of tone,* 1863. New York: Dover, 1885, 1954.

Helmholtz, H. *The mechanism of the ossicles of the ear,* 1869. New York: William Wood, 1873.

Helmholtz, H. The facts of perception, 1878. In R. Kahl (Ed.), *Selected writings of Hermann von Helmholtz.* Middletown, CT: Wesleyan University Press, 1971.

Helson, H. The psychology of *Gestalt. American Journal of Psychology,* 1925, *36,* 342-370, 494-526.

Helson, H. The psychology of *Gestalt. American Journal of Psychology,* 1926, *37,* 25-62, 189-223.

Helson, H. Adaptation-level as frame of reference for prediction of psychophysical data. *American Journal of Psychology,* 1947, *60,* 1-29.

Helson, H. *Theoretical foundations of psychology.* New York: Van Nostrand, 1951.

Helson, H. *Adaptation level theory: An experimental and systematic approach to behavior.* New York: Harper & Row, 1964.

Helson, H. Some highlights of an intellectual journey. In T. S. Krawiec (Ed.), *The psychologists.* Vol. 1. New York: Oxford University Press, 1972. Pp. 91-111.

Herbart, J. F. *A text-book in psychology: An attempt to found the science of psychology on experience, metaphysics, and mathematics,* 1816. New York: Appleton, 1891.

Herbart, J. F. *Psychologie als Wissenschaft, neu Gegründet auf Erfahrung, Metaphysik und Mathematik* (Psychology as a science, newly based upon experience, metaphysics, and mathematics). 2 Vols. 1824-1825. Portion translated in T. Thorne (Ed.), *Classics in psychology*. New York: Philosophical Library, 1961.

Hering, E. *Beiträge zur Physiologie: Zur Lehre vom Ortsinn der Netzhaut* (Contributions to physiology: theory of sense of locality of the retina), 1861-1864. Portion translated in R. J. Herrnstein & E. G. Boring (Eds.), *A source book in the history of psychology*. Cambridge, MA: Harvard University Press, 1966. Pp. 148-151.

Hering, E. *Zur Lehre vom Lichtsinne* (Theory of light sensation), 1878. Portion translated in W. S. Sahakian (Ed.), *History of psychology: A source book in systematic psychology*. Itasca, IL: F. E. Peacock, 1968. Pp. 144-148.

Hering, E. *Grundzüge der Lehre vom Lichtsinn*, 1920. Translated as *Outlines of a theory of light sense*. Cambridge, MA: Harvard University Press, 1964.

Higuchi, K. [Social psychology], 1908.

Hirota, K. Development of social psychology in Japan. *Psychologia*, 1959, *2*, 216-228.

Hobbes, T. *Human nature, or the fundamental elements of policy. Being a discovery of the faculties, acts, and passions, of the soul of man, from their original causes; according to such philosophical principles, as are not commonly known or asserted*. London: Fra Bowman of Oxon, 1650.

Hobbes, T. *Leviathan, or the matter, form, and power of a commonwealth ecclesiastical and civil*, 1651. Reprinted, Cambridge: University Press, 1904.

Hobhouse, L. T. *Mind in evolution*. London: Macmillan, 1901.

Hobhouse, L. T. Comparative psychology. *Encyclopaedia Britannica*, 1944, *6*, 167-170.

Hollingworth, H. L. The psychology of advertising. *Psychological Bulletin*, 1912, *9*, 204-206.

Hollingworth, H. L. *Vocational psychology*. New York: Appleton, 1916.

Holt, E. B. *The Freudian wish and its place in ethics*. New York: Macmillan, 1914.

Homans, G. C. *The human group*. New York: Harcourt, Brace & World, 1950.

Homans, G. C. *Social behavior: Its elementary forms*. New York: Harcourt, Brace & World, 1961.

Horney, K. *The neurotic personality of our time*. New York: Norton, 1937.

Horney, K. *New Ways in psychoanalysis*. New York: Norton, 1939.

Horney, K. *Self analysis*. New York: Norton, 1942.

Horney, K. Neurosis and human growth. New York: Norton, 1950.

Hovland, C. I. *The order of presentation in persuasion*. New Haven: Yale University Press, 1957.

Hovland, C. I., & Janis, I. L. *Personality and persuasibility*. New Haven: Yale University Press, 1959.

Hovland, C. I., Janis, I. L., & Kelley, H. H. *Communication and persuasion*. New Haven: Yale University Press, 1953.

Hovland, C. I., Lumsdaine, A. A., & Sheffield, F. D. *Experiments on mass communication. Vol. III. Studies in social psychology in World War II.* Princeton, NJ: Princeton University Press, 1949.

Hovland, C. I., & Weiss, W. The influence of source credibility on communication effectiveness. *Public Opinion Quarterly,* 1951, *15,* 635-650.

Hull, C. L. *Principles of behavior: An introduction to behavior theory.* New York: Appleton, 1943.

Hull, C. L. *A behavior system: An introduction to behavior theory concerning the individual organism.* New Haven: Yale University Press, 1952.

Hull, C. L., Hovland, C., Ross, R., Hall, M., Perkins, D. T., & Fitch, F. B. *Mathematico-deductive theory of rote learning: A study in scientific methodology.* New Haven: Yale University Press, 1940.

Hume, D. *A treatise of human nature: Being an Attempt to introduce the experimental method of reasoning into moral subjects,* 1739. Reprinted, Oxford: Clarendon Press, 1960.

Hume, D. *An enquiry concerning human understanding,* 1748. Rev. ed., 1777. Reprinted, Oxford: Clarendon Press, 1902.

Hume, D. *The life of David Hume,* 1777. In N. K. Smith (Ed.), *Hume's dialogues concerning natural religion.* New York: Social Sciences Publishers, 1948.

Hurvich, L. M., & Jameson, D. An opponent-process theory of color vision. *Psychological Review,* 1957, *64,* 384-404.

Husserl, E. *Logische Untersuchungen* (Logical investigations), 1900-1901.

Husserl, E. *Ideas: General introduction to phenomenology,* 1913. New York: Collier, 1962.

Husserl, E. Phenomenology. *Encyclopaedia Britannica,* 1944, *17,* 699-702.

Jaensch, E. R. Zur Analyse der Gesichtswahrnehmungen. *Zeitschrift für Psychologie,* 1909, Ergbd. *4,* 388 pp.

Jaensch, E. R. *Ueber den Aufbau der Wahrnehmungswelt und ihre Struktur im Jugendalter,* 1923.

Jaensch, E. R. *Eidetic imagery,* 1925. 2nd ed., 1927. London: Kegan Paul, Trench, Trubner, 1930.

Jaensch, W. *Grundzüge einer Physiologie und Klinik der psychophysischen Persönlichkeit,* 1926.

James, W. II.—What is an emotion? *Mind,* 1884, *9,* 188-205.

James, W. *The principles of psychology.* 2 Vols. New York: Henry Holt, 1890.

James, W. *Psychology: Briefer course.* New York: Henry Holt, 1892.

James, W. Experimental psychology in America. *Science,* 1895, *2,* 626.

James, W. *The varieties of religious experience: A study in human nature,* 1902. Reprinted, New York: Collier, 1961.

James, W. *Pragmatism: A new name for some old ways of thinking.* New York: Longmans, Green, 1907.

James, W. Letters of William James. In H. James (Ed.), *Letters of William James.* 2 Vols. Boston: Atlantic Monthly Press, 1920. Reprinted, New York: Kraus Reprint, 1969.

Janis, I. L. *Victims of groupthink: A psychological study of foreign-policy decisions and fiascoes.* Boston: Houghton Mifflin, 1972.

Jastrow, J. *Fact and fable in psychology.* Boston: Houghton Mifflin, 1900.

Jastrow, J. *The subconscious.* Boston: Houghton Mifflin, 1905.

Johnson, S. *Elementa philosophica,* 1752.

Jones, E. *The life and work of Sigmund Freud.* 3 Vols. New York: Basic Books, 1961. Reprinted in abridgement, Garden City, NY: Doubleday, 1963.

Jost, A. Die Associationsfestigkeit in ihrer Abhängigkeit von der Verteilung der Wiederholungen. *Zeitschrift für Psychologie,* 1897, *14,* 436-472.

Joule, J. P. *The calorific effects of magneto-electricity and the mechanical value of heat,* 1843.

Jung, C. G. *On the psychology and pathology of so-called occult phenomena.* Leipzig: Oswald Mutze, 1902. In C. G. Jung, *Collected works.* Vol. 1. *Psychiatric studies.* New York: Pantheon, 1957. Pp. 3-88.

Jung, C. G. *The psychology of dementia praecox,* 1907. In C. G. Jung, *Collected works.* Vol. 3. New York: Pantheon, 1960, Pp. 1-151.

Jung, C. G. The association method. *American Journal of Psychology,* 1910, *21,* 219-240.

Jung, C. G. *Psychology of the unconscious,* 1917. London: Kegan Paul, 1921. 2nd ed. 1927. In C. G. Jung, *Collected works.* Vol. 7. New York: Pantheon, 1953. Pp. 1-117.

Jung, C. G. *Psychological types,* 1920. London: Kegan Paul, 1923. In C. G. Jung, *Collected works.* Vol. 6. New York: Pantheon, 1953.

Jung, C. G. *Contributions to analytical psychology,* 1926. New York: Harcourt, Brace, 1928.

Jung, C. G. *The relations between the ego and the unconscious,* 1945. In C. G. Jung, *Collected works.* Vol. 7. New York: Pantheon, 1953. Pp. 121-292.

Jung, C. G. *Aion: Researches into the phenomenology of the self,* 1951. In C. G. Jung, *Collected works.* Vol. 9, pt. 2. Princeton, NJ: Princeton University Press, 1968.

Jung, C. G. *Archetypes and the collective unconscious,* 1954. In C. G. Jung, *Collected works.* Vol. 9, pt. 1. New York: Pantheon, 1959.

Jung, C. G. Conversations. In R. I. Evans, *Conversations with Carl Jung and reactions from Ernest Jones.* Princeton, NJ: Van Nostrand, 1964.

Jung, C. G., & Riklin, F. *Studies in word association: Experiments in the diagnosis of psychopathological conditions carried out at the psychiatric clinic of the University of Zurich, under the direction of C. G. Jung,* 1904. London: Heinemann, 1918.

Kahlbaum, K. L. *Die Katatonie oder das Spannungsirresein.* Berlin, 1874.

Kant, I. *Critique of pure reason,* 1781. New York: St. Martin's, 1929. John Watson's translation is used in the text.

Kant, I. *Prolegomena and metaphysical foundations of natural science,* 1786. London: George Bell, 1883.

Katz, D. Erscheinungsweisen der Farben und ihre Beeinflussung durch die individuelle Erfahrung (Modes of appearance of colors and their modification through individual experience). *Zeitschrift für Psychologie,* 1911, Ergbd. 7.

Katz, D. *Der Aufbau der Tastwelt* (Construction of a world of sense), 1925.

Katz, D. *The world of colour,* 1930. London: Kegan Paul, 1935.

Katz, D. *Gestalt psychology: Its nature and significance,* 1943. 2nd ed., 1948. New York: Ronald, 1950.

Katz, D. Edgar Rubin. *Psychological Review,* 1951, *48,* 387-388.

Katz, D. Autobiography. In E. G. Boring *et al.* (Eds.), *A history of psychology in autobiography.* Vol. 4. Worcester, MA: Clark University Press, 1952, Pp. 189-211.

Kido, M. [*Problems in psychology*]. Tokyo: Iwanami, 1926.

Kido, M. Origin of Japanese psychology and its development. *Psychologia,* 1961, *4,* 1-10.

Koffka, K. *The growth of mind,* 1921. London: Routledge & Kegan Paul, 1924. 2nd ed., 1928.

Koffka, K. Consciousness. *Encyclopaedia of the Social Sciences,* 1931, *4,* 212-220. (a)

Koffka, K. Gestalt. *Encyclopaedia of the Social Sciences,* 1931, *6,* 642-646. (b)

Koffka, K. *Principles of gestalt psychology.* New York: Harcourt, Brace, 1935.

Köhler, W. *The mentality of apes,* 1917. 2nd ed., 1924. New York: Harcourt, Brace, 1925. Rev. ed, 1927. Reprinted, New York: Random House, 1956.

Köhler, W. Nachweis einfacher Strukturfunktionen biem Schimpanses und beim Hauschuhn. Über eine neue Methode zur Üntersuchung des bunten Farbensystems. (Aus der Anthropoidenstation auf Teneriffa). *Abh. d. Preuss. Acad. d. Wissenschaft,* Phys.-Math. Klasse. 1918, *2,* 1-101. Portion translated in W. D. Ellis (Ed.), *A source book of gestalt psychology.* London: Kegan, Paul, Trench, Trubner, 1938. Pp. 217-227.

Köhler, W. *Die Physischen Gestalten in Ruhe und im stationären Zustand* (Static and stationary physical configurations), 1920. Portion translated in W. D. Ellis (Ed.), *A source book of gestalt psychology.* London: Routledge & Kegan Paul, 1938. Pp. 17-54.

Köhler, W. *Gestalt psychology.* New York: Liveright, 1929. Revised as *Gestalt psychology: An introduction to new concepts in modern psychology,* 1947.

Köhler, W. *The place of value in a world of facts.* New York: Liveright, 1938.

Köhler, W. Kurt Koffka. *Psychological Review,* 1942, *49,* 97-101.

Köhler, W. Max Wertheimer. *Psychological Review,* 1944, *51,* 143-146.

Köhler, W. Gestalt psychology today. *American Psychologist,* 1959, *14,* 727-734.

Köhler, W. *The task of gestalt psychology.* Princeton, NJ: Princeton University Press, 1969.

Köhler, W. Selected papers. In M. Henie (Ed.), *The selected papers of Wolfgang Köhler.* New York: Liveright, 1971.

Kölliker, R. A. Zur Anatomie und Physiologie der Retina. *Verh. phys.-med. Ges. Würzburg,* 1852, *3,* 316-336. (a)

Kölliker, R. A. *Mikroskopische Anatomie,* 1852. (b)

König, A. Ueber den menschlichen Sehpurpur und seine Bedeutung für das Sehen. *Sitzungsber. preuss. Akad. Wiss.*, 1894, 557-598.

Kora, T. Morita theory. *International Journal of Psychiatry*, 1965, *1*, 611-640.

Kornilov, K. N. Psychology in the light of dialectical materialism. In C. Murchison (Ed.), *Psychologies of 1930*. Worcester, MA: Clark University Press, 1930. Pp. 243-278.

Kraepelin, E. *Compendium der Psychiatrie*, 1883. 8th ed. revised as *Psychiatrie*. 4 Vols. Leipzig: Barth, 1909-1915. Translated as *Clinical psychiatry*. New York: Macmillan, 1907.

Kretschmer, E. *Physique and character: An investigation of the nature of constitution and the theory of temperament*, 1921. 2nd ed. New York: Harcourt, Brace & World, 1936.

Kries, J. Über die Funktion der Netzhautstäbehen. *Zeitschrift für Psychologie*, 1894, *9*, 81.

Kries, J. Theories of vision. In H. Helmholtz, *Physiological optics*, 1911. 3rd ed. Rochester: Optical Society of America, 1924. Pp. 426-454.

Külpe, O. *Zur Theorie der sinnlichen Gefühle*, 1887.

Külpe, O. *Outlines of psychology: Based upon the results of experimental investigation*, 1893. 3rd ed. New York: Macmillan, 1909.

Külpe, O. *Introduction to philosophy: A handbook for students of psychology, logic, ethics, aesthetics and general philosophy*, 1895. 4th ed. New York: Macmillan, 1915.

Külpe, O. *Grundlagen der Aesthetik* (Elements of esthetics), 1921.

Kuroda, R. [*Animal psychology*]. Tokyo: Sanseido, 1936.

Kuwata, Y. [*Soul-cult and ancestor-worship*], 1916.

Kuwata, Y. [*Group psychology*], 1917.

Kuwata, Y. [*Folk psychology of Wundt*], 1918.

Ladd, G. T. *Elements of physiological psychology: A treatise of the activities and nature of the mind from the physical and experimental point of view*. New York: Scribner, 1891.

Ladd, G. T. *Psychology: Descriptive and explanatory*. New York: Scribner, 1894.

Ladd, G. T. *Outlines of descriptive psychology*. New York: Scribner, 1898.

Ladd, G. T. Private paper. In Henry P. Wright collection of letters and papers, 1898-1911. Yale University Library.

Ladd, G. T. The autobiography of a teacher. Unpublished manuscript, 1910-1912.

Ladd-Franklin, C. The nature of the colour sensations: A new chapter on the subject. In H. Helmholtz, *Physiological optics*, 1911. 3rd ed. Rochester: Optical Society of America, 1924. Pp. 455-468.

Ladd-Franklin, C. *Colour and colour theories*. New York: Harcourt, Brace, 1929.

Ladygina-Kots, N. N. *Investigation of the cognitive abilities of the chimpanzee*, 1923.

Ladygina-Kots, N. N. *Adaptive motor habits of the macaque in experimental situations*, 1928.

Lamarck, J. B. P. A. de M. *Philosophie Zoologique,* 1809.

Lambert, J. H. *Neues Organon, oder Gedanken über die Erforschung und Bezeichnung des Wahren und dessen Unterscheidung von Irrtum und Schein* (New organon, or thoughts on the investigations and indication of truth and of the distinction between error and appearance), 2 Vols. 1864.

La Mettrie, J. O. de *Histoire naturelle de l' âme* (Natural history of the soul), 1745. Translated as *Man a machine.* LaSalle, IL: Open Court, 1912.

Lange, C. G. The emotions: A psychophysiological study. In C. G. Lange and W. James, *The emotions.* Baltimore: Williams & Wilkins, 1922. Pp. 33-135.

Lange, N. N. *Psychological investigations: The law of perception; the theory of voluntary attention,* 1893.

Langeley, J. N. *The autonomic nervous system.* Cambridge, Eng.: W. Heffer, 1921.

Laplace, P. A. *Théorie analytique des probabilités* (Analytic theory of probabilities), 1812-1820.

Lashley, K. S. *Brain mechanisms and intelligence: A quantitative study of injuries to the brain.* Chicago: University of Chicago Press, 1929.

Lazo, J. A. (Ed.) *American psychological association, 1970: Biographical directory.* Washington, DC: American Psychological Association, 1970.

Le Bon G. *La psychologie des foules,* 1895. Translated as *The crowd: A study of the popular mind.* London: T. Fisher, 1896.

Lee, G. C. *George Herbert Mead: Philosopher of the social individual.* New York: King's Crown Press, 1945.

Leibniz, G. W. *The principle of individuation,* 1663.

Leibniz, G. W. *Theodicy,* 1710. New Haven: Yale University Press, 1952.

Leibniz, G. W. *Monadology,* 1714. Oxford: Oxford University Press, 1898.

Leibniz, G. W. *Principles of nature and of grace, founded on reason,* 1714. In G. W. Leibniz, *Philosophical writings.* London: J. M. Dent, 1934.

Leibniz, G. W., *New essays concerning human understanding,* 1704. New York: Macmillan, 1896.

Lenin, V. I. *Materialism and empirio-criticism,* 1909. Moscow: Foreign Languages Publishing House, n.d.

Lenin, V. I. *Philosophical notebooks,* 1929. In V. I. Lenin, *Collected Works,* Vol. I. Moscow: Foreign Languages Publishing House, 1963.

Leontiev, A. N. The historical approach to the study of the psyche of man. In B. G. Ananiev *et al.* (Eds.), *Psychological science in the USSR.* Vol. 1. Moscow: Scientific Council of the Institute of Psychology, Academy of Pedagogical Sciences RSFSR, 1959.

Leontiev, A. N. The present tasks of Soviet psychology. In R. B. Winn (Ed.), *Soviet psychology.* New York: Philosophical Library, 1961. Pp. 31-47. (a)

Leontiev, A. N. The intellectual development of the child. In R. B. Winn (Ed.), *Soviet psychology.* New York: Philosophical Library, 1961. Pp. 55-78. (b)

Leontiev, A. N. In honor of the president of the congress. *Voprosy psikhologii,*

1963, *9*, 3-4. In D. I. Slobin (Ed.), *Handbook of Soviet psychology*, 1966, *4*, nos. 3-4.

Lewes, G. H. *Problems of life and mind*. 5 Vols. 1873-1879. London: Trubner, 1879.

Lewin, K. Die Sozialisierung des Taylorsystems. *Praktischer Sozialismus*, 1920, no. 4.

Lewin, K. *Der Begriff der Genese in Physik, Biologie, und Entwicklungsgeschichte*. Berlin: Julius Springer, 1922.

Lewin, K. Vorsatz, Wille, und Bedürfnis (Mit Vorbemerkungen über die psychischen Kräfte und Energien und die Struktur der Selle. *Psychologische Forschung*, 1926, *7*, 294-385. Portion translated as: Will and needs. In W. D. Ellis (Ed.), *A source book of gestalt psychology*. New York: Humanities Press, 1967. Pp. 283-299.

Lewin, K. The conflict between Aristotelian and Galileian modes of thought in contemporary psychology. *Journal of Genetic Psychology*, 1931, *5*, 141-177.

Lewin, K. Environmental forces in child behavior and development. In C. Murchison (Ed.), *A handbook of child psychology*. Worcester, MA: Clark University Press, 1931. Pp. 94-127. 2nd ed., 1933. Pp. 590-625.

Lewin, K. *A dynamic theory of personality*. New York: McGraw-Hill, 1935.

Lewin, K. *Principles of topological psychology*. New York: McGraw-Hill, 1936.

Lewin, K. Field theory and experiment in social psychology. *American Journal of Sociology*, 1939, *44*, 868-897.

Lewin, K. Field theory of learning. *Forty-first yearbook of the National Society for the Study of Education. Part II: The psychology of learning*. Chicago: University of Chicago Press, 1942. Pp. 215-242.

Lewin, K. *Resolving social conflicts*. New York: Harper, 1948.

Lewin, K. *Field theory in social science*. New York: Harper & Row, 1951.

Lewin, K., & Lippitt, R. An experimental approach to the study of autocracy and democracy: A preliminary note. *Sociometry*, 1938, *1*, 292-300.

Lewin, K., Lippitt, R., & White, R. Patterns of aggressive behavior in experimentally created "social climates." *Journal of Social Psychology*, 1939, *10*, 271-299.

Liébault, A. A. *Du sommeil et des états analogues considérés surtout au point de vue de l'action du moral sur le physique*, 1866.

Likert, R. A technique for the measurement of attitudes. *Archives of Psychology*, 1932, *#140*, 1-55, whole.

Lipps, T. *Raumästhetik und geometrisch-optische Täuschungen*, 1893-1897.

Lissner, K. Die Entspannung von Bedürfnissen durch Ersatzhandlungen. *Psychologische Forschung*, 1933, *18*, 218-250.

Locke, J. *An essay concerning human understanding*, 1st ed., 1690; 4th ed., 1700; 5th ed., 1706. London: J. M. Dent, 1961.

London, I. V. A historical survey of psychology in the Soviet Union. *Psychological Bulletin*, 1949, *46*, 241-277.

Lotze, R. H. *Metaphysik,* 1841.

Lotze, R. H. *Allgemeine Pathologie und Therapie als mechanische Naturwissenschaften* (General pathology and therapy as mechanistic natural science), 1842.

Lotze, R. .H. *Logik,* 1843.

Lotze, R. H. *Medizinische Psychologie oder Physiologie der Seele* (Medical psychology or physiology of the soul), 1852.

Lotze, R. H. *Grundzüge der Psychologie: Dictate aus den Vorlessungen,* 1881. *Outlines of psychology: Dictated portions of lectures.* Boston: Ginn, 1886.

Luria, A. R. *The nature of human conflicts or emotion, conflict and will: An objective study of disorganization and control of human behavior.* New York: Liveright, 1932.

Luria, A. R. *The role of speech in the regulation of normal and abnormal behavior.* New York: Liveright, 1961.

Luria, A. R. The neuropsychological study of brain lesions and restoration of damaged brain functions. In M. Cole & I. Maltzman (Eds.), *A Handbook of contemporary Soviet psychology.* New York: Basic Books, 1969. Pp. 277-301. (a)

Luria, A. R. Speech development and the formation of mental processes. In M. Cole & I. Maltzman (Eds.), *A handbook of contemporary Soviet psychology.* New York: Basic Books, 1969. Pp. 121-162. (b)

Lyell, C. *Principles of geology,* 1830-1835.

Lyubovsky, P. M. *A short handbook of experimental soul-science,* 1815.

McClelland, D. C. *The achieving society.* New York: Macmillan, 1961.

McCosh, J. *Psychology.* 2 Vols. 1886-1887.

McDougall, W. *Physiological psychology.* London: Dent, 1905.

McDougall, W. *An introduction to social psychology,* 1908. 23rd ed., London: Methuen, 1960.

McDougall, W. *Body and mind: A history and defense of animism.* London: Methuen, 1911.

McDougall, W. *The group mind: A sketch of the principles of collective psychology, with some attempt to apply them to the interpretation of national life and character.* New York: Putnam, 1920.

McDougall, W. *Outline of psychology.* New York: Scribner, 1923.

McDougall, W. An experiment for the testing of the hypothesis of Lamarck. *British Journal of Psychology,* 1927, *17,* 267-304.

McDougall, W. Autobiography. In C. Murchison (Ed.), *A history of psychology in autobiography.* Worcester, MA: Clark University Press, 1930.

McGeoch, J. A. Forgetting and the law of disuse. *Psychological Review,* 1932, *39,* 352-370.

McGeoch, J. A. *The psychology of human learning.* New York: Longmans, 1942.

McGeoch, J. A., & Irion, A. L. *The psychology of human learning.* 2nd ed. New York: Longmans, Green, 1952.

McGuire, W. J., & Papageorgis, D. The relative efficacy of various types of prior belief-defense in producing immunity against persuasion. *Journal of Abnormal and Social Psychology*, 1961, *62*, 327-337.

Mach, E. Ueber die Wirkung der räumlichen Vertheilung des Lichtreizes auf der Netzhaut. *Sitzunsber. Akad. Wien, math.-naturw.*, 1865, *52*, 303-322.

Mach. E. *Beiträge zur Analyse der Empfindungen*, 1886. 5th ed., *Die Analyse der Empfindungen* (Analysis of sensations), 1905. First edition translated as *Contributions to the analysis of sensations*. Chicago: Open Court, 1890. Fifth edition translated as *The analysis of sensations and the relation of the physical to the psychical*. Reprinted, New York: Dover, 1959.

Magendie, F. Expériences sur les fonctions des racines des nerfs rachidiens. *Journal de physiologie expérimentale et pathologique*, 1822, *2*, 276-279.

Mahler, V. Ersatzhandlungen verscheidenen Realitätsgrades. *Psychologische Forschung*, 1933, *18*, 26-29.

Malthus, T. H. *An essay on the principle of population*, 1798; 2nd ed., 1803.

Marbe, K. *Experimentellpsychologische Untersuchungen über das Urteil, eine Einleitung in die Logik* (Experimental investigations of the psychology of judgment), 1901.

Marrow, A. J. *The practical theorist: The life and work of Kurt Lewin*. New York: Basic Books, 1969.

Maslow, A. H. *Motivation and personality*. New York: Harper & Row, 1954. 2nd ed., 1970.

Maslow, A. H. *Toward a psychology of being*. Princeton, NJ: Van Nostrand, 1962. 2nd ed., 1968.

Maslow, A. H. *Religions, values, and peak-experiences*. Columbus: Ohio State Press, 1964.

Maslow, A. H. *The psychology of science*. New York: Harper & Row, 1966.

Maslow, A. H. *The farther reaches of human nature*. New York: Viking Press, 1971.

Masuda, Koichi. [Behaviorism versus introspectionism reconsidered]. [*Psychological Research*,] 1923, *24*, 79-95.

Masuda, Koreshige. [An experiment in learning with fish: V.]. [*Psychological Research*], 1915, *8*, 454-461.

Masuda, Koreshige. [*Introduction to experimental psychology*]. Vol. 1. Tokyo: Shinbundo, 1926. (a)

Masuda, Koreshige. [Four meanings of the study of behavior in psychology]. *Japanese Journal of Psychology*, 1926, *1*, 110-118. (b)

Matsumoto, M. Researches on acoustic space. *Studies of the Yale Psychological Laboratory*, 1897, *5*.

Matsumoto, M. [*Psychocinematics*]. Tokyo: Rikugokwan, 1914.

Matsumoto, M. [*Lectures on experimental psychology*]. Tokyo: Kodokan, 1914.

Matsumoto, M. [*Psychological interpretation of modern Japanese paintings*]. Tokyo: Hokubunkan, 1915.

Matsumoto, M. [*Psychology of intelligence*]. Tokyo: Kaizosha, 1925.

Matsumoto, M. [*Psychology and practical life*]. Tokyo: Jitsugyo Nipponsha, 1926.

Matsumoto, M. [*Psychology of esthetic appreciation of pictorial arts*]. Tokyo: Iwanami Shoten, 1926.

Maxwell, W. *De medicina magnetica*. London, 1679.

May, R. (Ed.) *Existential psychology*. New York: Random House, 1961. 2nd ed., 1969.

May, R. *Psychology and the human dilemma*. Princeton, NJ: Van Nostrand, 1967.

May, R., Angel, E, & Ellenberger, H. F. *Existence: A new dimension in psychiatry and psychology*. New York: Basic Books, 1958.

Mayer, A., & Orth, J. Zur qualitativen Untersuchung der Associationen (Qualitative investigation of associations). *Zeitschrift für Psychologie*, 1901, *26*, 1-13.

Mayer, J. R. *Bermerkungen über die Kräfte der unbelebten Natur*, 1842.

Mead, G. H. The definition of the psychical. *The Decennial Publications of the University of Chicago, First Series*. Vol. 3. Chicago: University of Chicago Press, 1903. Pp. 77-112.

Mead, G. H. Concerning animal perception. *Psychological Review*, 1907, *14*, 383-390.

Mead, G. H. Social psychology as counterpart to physiological psychology. *Psychological Bulletin*, 1909, *6*, 401-408.

Mead, G. H. The mechanism of social consciousness. *Journal of Philosophy, Psychology, and Scientific Methods*, 1912, *9*, 401-406. Reprinted in G. H. Mead, *Selected writings*. Indianapolis: Bobbs-Merrill, 1964. Pp. 134-141.

Mead, G. H. The social self. *Journal of Philosophy, Psychology, and Scientific Methods*, 1913, *10*, 374-380.

Mead, G. H. A behavioristic account of the significant symbol. *Journal of Philosophy*, 1922, *19*, 157-163.

Mead, G. H. The genesis of the self and social control. *International Journal of Ethics*, 1924-1925, *35*, 251-277.

Mead, G. H. *Mind, self and society from the standpoint of a social behaviorist*. Chicago: University of Chicago Press, 1934.

Mead, G. H. *The philosophy of the act*. Chicago: University of Chicago Press, 1938.

Mead, G. H. *On social psychology*. Rev. ed. Chicago: University of Chicago Press, 1964. (a)

Mead, G. H. *Selected writings*. Indianapolis: Bobbs-Merrill, 1964. (b)

Mead, M. *Male and female: A study of sexes in a changing world*. New York: William Morrow, 1949.

Mead, M. The changing world of living. *Diseases of the Nervous System*, 1967, *28*, suppl., 5-11.

Meduna, L. J. Über experimentelle Campherepilepsie. *Archiv für Psychologie*, 1934. *102*, 333-339.

Meduna, L. J. New methods of medical treatment of schizophrenia. *Archives of Neurology and Psychiatry*, 1936, *35*, 361-363. (a)

Meduna, L. J. *Die Konvulsionstherapie der Schizophrenie. Halle: Marhold, 1936. (b)*

Meduna, L. J. *Carbon dioxide therapy: A neurophysiological treatment of nervous disorders.* Springfield, IL: Charles C. Thomas, 1950. 2nd ed., 1958.

Meinong, A. *Psychologischethische Untersuchungen sur Werttheorie* (Psychological-ethical investigations of value theory), 1894.

Meinong A. Über Gegenstandstheorie, 1904. Reprinted in *Gesammelte Abhandlungen.* Vol. 2. Translated as *The theory of objects* in R. M. Chisholm (Ed.), *Realism and the background of phenomenology.* Glencoe, IL: Free Press, 1960.

Meinong, A. *Zur Grundlegung der allgemeinen Werttheorie* (Foundation of a general theory of value), 1923.

Mesmer, F. A. *Précis historique des faits relatifs au magnétisme-animal,* 1781.

Mesmer, A. A. *Memoir,* 1799. New York: Eden Press, 1957.

Messer, A. Experimentell-psychologische Untersuchungen über das Denken (Experimental investigations of the psychology of thought). *Archiv gesamte Psychologie,* 1906, *8,* 1-224.

Michotte, A. Autobiography. In E. G. Boring *et al.* (Eds.), *A history of psychology in autobiography.* Vol. 4. Worcester, MA: Clark University Press, 1952. Pp. 213-236.

Mill, J. *Analysis of the phenomena of the human mind,* 1829. Revised edition with notes by John Stuart Mill, 1869.

Mill, J. S. *A system of logic, ratiocinative and inductive,* 1843. New York: Harper, 1846.

Mill, J. S. *Essays on some unsettled questions of political economy,* 1844.

Mill, J. S. *Principles of political economy,* 1848. Reprinted, Baltimore: Penguin Books, 1970.

Mill, J. S. *Examination of Sir William Hamilton's philosophy.* London, 1865. Reprinted in M. Cohen (Ed.), *The philosophy of John Stuard Mill.* New York: Random House, 1961.

Miller, N. E. Liberalization of basic S-R concepts: Extensions to conflict behavior, motivation, and social learning. In S. Koch (Ed.), *Psychology: A study of a Science.* Vol. 2. New York: McGraw-Hill, 1959. Pp. 195-292.

Miller, N. E. Profiles: Viceral learning I, II. *New Yorker,* 1972, August 19, Pp. 34-57; August 26, Pp. 30-57.

Miller, N. E., & Dollard, J. *Social learning and imitation.* New Haven: Yale University Press, 1941.

Mills, E. S. *George Trumbull Ladd: Pioneer American psychologist.* Cleveland: Press of Case Western Reserve University, 1969.

Minami, H. [*Social psychology*]. Tokyo: Kobunsha, 1949.

Mitra, S. C. Progress of psychology in India. *Indian Journal of Psychology,* 1955, *30,* 1-21.

Moniz, E. How I succeeded in performing the prefrontal leukotomy. *Journal of Clinical and Experimental Psychopathology and Quarterly Review of Psychiatry and Neurology,* 1954, *15,* 373-379.

Morel, B. A. *Traité des maladies mentales,* 1860.

Moreno, J. L. *Who shall survive? A new approach to the problem of interrelations.* Washington, DC: Nervous and Mental Disease Publishing House, 1934. Revised as *Who shall survive? Foundations of sociometry, group psychotherapy and sociodrama.* Beacon, NY: Beacon House, 1953.

Moreno, J. L. *Psychodrama,* 1946-1972. 3 Vols. Beacon, NY: Beacon House, 1946-1969. Vol. 1. 1946, 4th ed., 1972. Vol. 2, 1959. Vol. 3, 1969.

Moreno, J. L. (Ed.) *The international handbook of psychotherapy.* New York: Philosophical Library, 1966.

Morgan, C. D., & Murray, H. A. A method for investigating fantasies: The thematic apperception test. *Archives of Neurology and Psychiatry,* 1935, *34,* 289-306.

Morgan, C. L. *An introduction to comparative psychology.* London: Walter Scott; New York: Scribner, 1898.

Morgan, C. L. *Emergent evolution.* New York: Holt, 1923.

Morita, S. [*Theory of nervosity and neurasthenia*]. Tokyo: Nihon Seishinigakukai, 1921. (a)

Morita, S. [*Lectures on psychotherapy*]. Tokyo: Nihon Seishinigakukai, 1921. (b)

Morita, S. [*Nature and therapy of nervosity*]. Tokyo: Tohodo, 1928.

Morita, S. [*Ways to the therapy of nervosity*]. Vol. 1. Koyoto: Jinbunshoin, 1935. Vols. 2 & 3. Tokyo: Shinkeishitsukenkyukai, 1937.

Morita, S. [*Nature and therapy of nervosity*]. New ed., Tokyo: Hakuyosha, 1956.

Motora, Y. [*Psychology*], 1893.

Motora, Y. [*Essentials of psychology*], 1910.

Motora, Y. [*Outline of systematic psychology*]. Tokyo: Hobunkwan, 1915.

Mowrer, O. H. On the dual nature of learning—a reinterpretation of "conditioning" and "problem solving." *Harvard Educational Review,* 1947, *17,* 102-148.

Mowrer, O. H. Two-factor learning theory reconsidered, with special reference to secondary reinforcement and the concept of habit. *Psychological Review,* 1956, *63,* 114-128.

Mowrer, O. H. *Learning theory and behavior.* New York: Wiley, 1960.

Müller, G. E. *Zur Theorie der sinnlichen Aufmerksamkeit,* 1873.

Müller, G. E. Die Gesichtspunkte und die Tatsachen der psychophysischen Methodik. In L. Asher & K. Spiro, *Ergenbnisse der Physiologie.* Jhrg. II, Abth. ii, 267-516. Reprinted in 1904.

Müller, G. E., & Schumann, F. Experimentelle Beiträge sur Untersuchungen des Gedächtniss. *Zeitschrift für Psychologie,* 1894, *6,* 301-303.

Müller, H. Zur Histologie der Netzhaut. *Z. wiss. Zool.,* 1851, *3,* 234-237.

Müller, J. *Zur vergleichenden Physiologie des Gesichtsinns,* 1826.

Müller, J. *Handbuch der Physiologie des Menschen,* 1833-1840. Translated as *Elements of physiology.* 2 Vols. London: Taylor and Walton, 1842.

Müller, J. Supplement to the second volume of Professor Müller's "Elements of physiology." In W. Baly & W. S. Kirkes, *Recent advances in the physiology of motion, the senses, generation, and development; being a supplement to the second volume of Professor Müller's "Elements of physiology,"* 1848.

Munk, H. *Ueber die Functionen der Grosshirnrinde,* 1890 (17 Papers, 1877-1898).

Münsterberg, H. *Die Willenshandlung,* 1889.

Münsterberg, H. *On the witness stand.* New York: McClure, 1908.

Münsterberg, H. *Psychotherapy.* New York: Moffat, Yard, 1909.

Münsterberg, H. *Psychology and the teacher.* New York: Appleton, 1910.

Münsterberg, H. *Psychology and industrial efficiency.* Boston: Houghton Mifflin, 1913.

Münsterberg, H. *Psychology and social sanity.* New York: Doubleday, Page, 1914. (a)

Münsterberg, H. *Psychology: General and applied.* New York: Appleton, 1914. (b)

Murchison, C. (Ed.) *The psychological register.* Worcester, MA: Clark University Press, 1929.

Murchison, C. *Psychologies of 1930.* Worcester, MA: Clark University Press, 1930.

Murphy, G. *Historical introduction to modern psychology.* New York: Harcourt, Brace & World, 1929. 3rd ed. (with J. K. Kovach) New York: Harcourt Brace Jovanovich, 1972.

Murphy, G. *Experimental social psychology.* New York: Harper & Row, 1931. Revised (with L. B. Murphy & T. M. Newcomb), 1937.

Murphy, G. *Personality: A biosocial approach to origins and structure.* New York: Harper & Row, 1947.

Murphy, G. The psychology of 1975: An extrapolation. *American Psychologist,* 1963, *18,* 689-695.

Murphy, G., & Likert, R. *Public opinion and the individual: A psychological study of student attitudes on public questions, with a retest five years later.* New York: Harper, 1938.

Murray, H. A. *Explorations in personality: A clinical and experimental study of fifty men of college age.* New York: Oxford University Press, 1938.

Murray, H. A. *et al. Assessment of men.* New York: Holt, Rinehart and Winston, 1948.

Myers, C. S. *A text-book of experimental psychology.* London: Arnold, 1909.

Myers, C. S. Autobiography. In C. Murchison (Ed.), *A history of psychology in autobiography.* Vol. 3. Worcester, MA: Clark University Press, 1930. Pp. 215-230.

Nagel, W. Adaptation, twilight vision, and the duplicity theory. In H. Helmholtz, *Physiological optics,* 1911. 3rd ed. Rochester: Optical Society of America, 1924.

Narasaki, A. [Some doubts in psychological studies]. [*Psychological Research*]. 1914, *5,* 296-297.

Narasaki, A. [*Mental dynamics in children and youth*]. Tokyo: Chubunkan, 1922.

Narasaki, A. [*Mental dynamics*], 1923.

Neimark, E. D., & Estes, W. K. *Stimulus sampling theory.* San Francisco: Holden-Day, 1967.

Newcomb, T. M. An approach to the study of communicative acts. *Psychological Review*, 1953, *60*, 393-404.

Newcomb, T. M. *The acquaintance process*. New York: Holt, Rinehart and Winston, 1961.

Newton, I. *New theory about light and colours*, 1672.

Newton, I. *Principia*, 1686. Reprinted, New York: Daniel Adee, 1846.

Newton, I. *Opticks or a treatise of the reflections, refractions, inflections and colours of light*, 1704. 4th (last) ed., 1730. Reprinted, New York: Dover, 1952.

Nietzsche, F. *Beyond good and evil*, 1886. Chicago: Henry Regnery, 1955.

Nietzsche, F. *A genealogy of morals*, 1887. In A. Tille (Ed.), *The works of Friedrich Nietzsche*. Vol. 10. New York: Macmillan, 1897.

Nietzsche, F. *The twilight of the idols*, 1889. Baltimore: Penguin, 1968.

Nietzsche, F. *The antichrist*, 1895. Rev. ed. New York: Knopf, 1931.

Nishi, A. *Hyaku-ichi Shin-ron* (A new theory on the unity of many viewpoints), 1874.

Ohm, G. S. Ueber die Definition des Tones, nebst daran geknüpfter Theorie der Sirene und ähnlicher tonbilder Vorrichtungen. *Ann. Phys. Chem.*, 1843, *135*, 497-565.

Origen. *On first principles*, c. 231. New York: Harper & Row, 1966.

Osgood, C. E. The nature and measurement of meaning. *Psychological Bulletin*, 1952, *49*, 197-237.

Osgood, C. E. *Method and theory in experimental psychology*. New York: Oxford University Press, 1953.

Osgood, C. E., Suci, G. J., & Tannenbaum, P. H. *The measurement of meaning*. Urbana, IL: University of Illinois Press, 1957.

Osgood, C. E. & Tannenbaum, P. H. The principle of congruity in the prediction of attitude change. *Psychological Review*, 1955, *62*, 42-55.

Ovsiankina, M. Die Wiederaufnahme von interbrochenen Handlungen. *Psychologische Forschung*, 1928, *2*, 302-389.

Paracelsus, P. A. *Von den Krankheiten so die Vernunft Berauben*, 1567.

Pareek, U. Psychology in India. *Psychologia*, 1957, *1*, 55-59.

Pavlov, I. P. Efferent nerves of the heart. *Arkhiv kliniki vnutrennykh boleznei*, 1883, *8*, 645-719.

Pavlov, I. P. Experimental psychology and psychopathology in animals, 1903. In I. P. Pavlov, *Lectures on conditioned reflexes*. New York: International Publishers, 1928, Pp. 47-60.

Pavlov, I. P. *Autobiography*. Moscow, 1904. In E. A. Asratyan, *I. P. Pavlov, his life and work*. Moscow, 1953. Also in I. P. Pavlov, *Selected works*. Moscow: Foreign Languages Publishing House, 1955. Pp. 41-44.

Pavlov, I. P. Physiology and psychology in the study of the higher nervous activity of animals, 1917. In I. P. Pavlov, *Selected works*. Moscow: Foreign Languages Publishing House, 1955. Pp. 395-413.

Pavlov, I. P. *Lectures on conditioned reflexes: Twenty-five years of objective study of the higher nervous activity (behaviour) of animals*. Vol. 1. New York: International Publishers, 1923.

Pavlov, I. P. *Lectures on conditioned reflexes: Conditioned reflexes and psychiatry.* Vol. 2. New York: International Publishers, 1928.

Pavlov, I. P. A brief outline of the higher nervous activity. In C. Murchison (Ed.) *Psychologies of 1930.* Worcester, MA: Clark University Press, 1930. Pp. 207-220.

Pavlov, I. P. Physiology of the higher nervous activity, 1932. In I. P. Pavlov, *Selected works.* Moscow: Foreign Languages Publishing House, 1955. Pp. 271-286. (a)

Pavlov, I. P. Dynamic stereotypy of the higher part of the brain, 1932. In I. P. Pavlov, *Selected works.* Moscow: Foreign Languages Publishing House, 1955. Pp. 454-459. (b)

Pavlov, I. P. The conditioned reflex, 1934. In I. P. Pavlov, *Selected works.* Moscow: Foreign Languages Publishing House, 1955. Pp. 245-270.

Pavlov, I. P. *Selected works.* Moscow: Foreign Languages Publishing House, 1955.

Payne, A. F. *Sentence completions.* New York: New York Guidance Clinic, 1928.

Payne, T. R. *S. L. Rubinštejn and the philosophical foundations of Soviet psychology.* Dordrecht, Holland: D. Reidel Publishing, 1968.

Pearson, E. S. *Karl Pearson: An appreciation of some aspects of his life and work.* Cambridge: Cambridge University Press, 1938.

Pearson, K. *The grammar of science.* London: Walter Scott, 1892. Reprinted, London: J. M. Dent, 1937.

Pearson, K. Contributions to the mathematical theory of evolution. *Philosophical Transactions of the Royal Society of London,* 1894, *185,* 71-110. Series A.

Pearson, K. On the criterion that a given system of deviations from the probable in the case of a correlated system of variables is such that it can be reasonably supposed to have arisen from random sampling. *The London, Edinburgh and Dublin Philosophical Magazine and Journal of Science,* 1900, *50,* 157-175. Fifth Series.

Pearson, K. Mathematical contributions to the theory of evolution. X. Supplement to a memoir on skew variation. *Philosophical Transactions of the Royal Society of London,* 1901, *197,* 443-459. Series A.

Pearson, K. Mathematical contributions to the theory of evolution. XIII. On the theory of contingency and its relations to association and normal correlation. *Drapers' Company Research Memoirs,* 1904, Biometric Series I.

Pearson, K. Mathematical contributions to the theory of evolution. XIV. On the general theory of skew correlations and non-linear regression. *Drapers' Company Research Memoirs,* 1905, Biometric Series II.

Pearson, K. *The letters and labours of Francis Galton.* 3 Vols. Cambridge: Cambridge University Press, 1924.

Pearson, K. *Early statistical papers.* Cambridge: Cambridge University Press, 1948.

Peirce, C. S. How to make our ideas clear. *Popular Science Monthly,* 1878, *12,* 286-302.

Perls, F. S. *Ego, hunger and aggression,* 1945. San Francisco: Orbit Graphic Arts, 1966.

Perls, F. S. Gestalt therapy and human potentialities. In H. A. Otto (Ed.), *Explorations in human potentialities.* Springfield, IL: Charles C. Thomas, 1966.

Perls, F. S. *Gestalt therapy verbatim.* Layfayette, CA: Real People Press, 1969. (a)

Perls, F. S. *In and out of the garbage pail.* Lafayette, CA: Real People Press, 1969 (b) Reprinted, New York: Dell, 1972.

Perls, F. S., Hefferline, R. F., & Goodman, P. *Gestalt therapy: Excitement and growth in the human personality.* New York: Julian Press, 1951. Reprinted, New York: Dell, 1966.

Perry, R. B. *The thought and character of William James: As revealed in unpublished correspondence and notes, together with his published writings.* 2 Vols. Boston: Little, Brown, 1935.

Piaget, J. Essai sur quelques aspects du developpement de la notion de partie chez l'enfant. *Journal de Psychologie,* 1921, *38,* 449-480.

Piaget, J. *The language and thought of the child,* 1923. 3rd ed. New York: Harcourt, Brace, 1959.

Piaget, J. *Judgment and reasoning in the child,* 1924. New York: Harcourt, Brace, 1928.

Piaget, J. *The child's conception of the world,* 1926. New York: Harcourt, Brace, 1929.

Piaget, J. *The child's conception of physical causality,* 1927. London: Kegan, Paul, 1930.

Piaget, J. *The moral judgment of the child.* London: Kegan, Paul, 1932.

Piaget, J. *The child's conception of number,* 1941. New York: Humanities, 1952.

Piaget, J. *Logic of Epistemology.* Manchester, England: Manchester University Press, 1953.

Pillsbury, W. B. *Essentials of psychology.* New York: Macmillan, 1911.

Pillsbury, W. B. *The history of psychology.* New York: Norton, 1929.

Pinel, P. *La nosographie philosophique: Ou, la méthode de l'analyse appliquée à la médecine,* 1798. 6th ed. Paris: Brosson, 1818.

Pinel, P. *Le traité médioc-philosophique sur l'aliénation mentale,* 1801. Translated as *A treatise on insanity, in which are contained the principles of a new and more practical nosology of maniacal disorders.* London: Cadell & Davis, 1806; and New York: Hafner, 1962.

Plato. *Phaedo.* In B. Jowett (trans.), *The dialogues of Plato.* Vol. 1 New York: Scribner, 1890. Pp. 361-447.

Plato. *Republic.* In B. Jowett (trans.), *The dialogues of Plato.* Vol. 2. New York: Scribner, 1901. Pp. 1-352.

Plekhanov. G. V. *Fundamental problems of Marxism,* 1908. New York: International Publishers, 1936.

Plotinus. *Enneades*. London, 1817. Recent edition translated by S. MacKenna. New York: Pantheon, 1957.

Poffenberger, A. T. The influence of improvement in one simple process upon other related processes. *Journal of Educational Psychology*, 1915,6, 459-474.

Poffenberger, A. T. *Psychology in advertising*. Chicago: Shaw, 1925.

Poffenberger, A. T. *Applied psychology: Its principles and methods*. New York: Appleton, 1927.

Porter, N. *The human intellect: With an introduction upon psychology and the soul*. New York: Scribner, 1868.

Priestley, J. *Essay on the first principles of government*, 1768.

Priestley, J. *Hartley's theory of the human mind on the principle of the association of ideas*, 1775.

Priestley, J. *The doctrine of philosophical necessity illustrated*, 1777.

Punch, or The London Charivari, September 22, 1894.

Rank, O. *The trauma of birth*, 1924. New York: Brunner, 1952.

Rank, O. *Technik der Psychoanalyse* (Technique of psychoanalysis). 3 Vols. Leipzig and Vienna: Deuticke. Vol. 1, *Die analytische Situation illustriert an der Traumdeutungstechnik*, 1926. Vol. 2, *Die analytische Reaktion in ihren konstrucktiven Elementen*, 1929. Vol. 3, *Die Analyse des Analytikers und seiner Rolle in der Gesamtsituation*, 1931.

Reid, T. *Inquiry into the human mind, on the principles of common sense*, 1764.

Reid, T. *Essays on the intellectual powers of man*, 1785. Charlestown, MA: Samuel Etheridge, 1814.

Reid, T. *Essays on the active powers of the human mind*, 1788. Charlestown, MA: Samuel Etheridge, 1815.

Restorff, H. Analyse von Vorgangen in Spurenfeld. I. Über die Wirkung von Bereichsbildungen im Spurenfeld. *Psychologische Forschung*, 1933,4, 57-71.

Révész, G. *Phänomenologie der Empfindungsreihen* (Phenomenology of the series of sensations). Budapest: Atheneum, 1907.

Révész, G. *Die Formenwelt des Tastsinnes* (The forms of the world of the sense of touch). 2 Vols. The Hague: Nijhoff, 1937.

Reyna, R. *Introduction to Indian philosophy*. Bombay: Tata McGraw-Hill, 1971.

Rivers, W. H. R. *Instinct and the unconscious*, 1920. 2nd ed. Cambridge: Cambridge University Press, 1922.

Rivers, W. H. R. *Conflict and dream*. London: Harcourt, 1923.

Rivers, W. H. R. *Medicine, magic, and religion*. London: Harcourt, 1924.

Roback, A. A. *A history of American psychology*. Rev. ed. New York: Collier, 1964.

Roback, A. A., & Kiernan, T. *Pictorial history of psychology and psychiatry*. New York: Philosophical Library, 1969.

Robinson, E. S. *Association theory today: An essay in systematic psychology*. New York: Appleton-Century-Crofts, 1932.

Roethlisberger, F. J., & Dickson, W. J. *Management and the worker: An account of a research program conducted by the Western Electric Company, Hawthorne Works, Chicago.* Cambridge, MA: Harvard University Press, 1939.

Rogers, C. R. *Counseling and psychotherapy: Newer concepts in practice.* Boston: Houghton Mifflin, 1942.

Rogers, C. R. *Client-centered therapy.* Boston: Houghton Mifflin, 1951.

Rogers, C. R. A theory of therapy, personality, and interpersonal relationships, as developed in the client-centered framework. In S. Koch (Ed.), *Psychology: A study of a science.* Vol. 3. New York: McGraw-Hill, 1959. Pp. 184-256.

Rogers, C. R. Autobiography. In E. G. Boring & G. Lindzey (Eds.), *A history of psychology in autobiography.* New York: Appleton-Century-Crofts, 1967. Pp. 343-384.

Romanes, G. J. *Animal intelligence.* London: Kegan Paul, Trench, 1882.

Romanes, G. J. *Mental evolution in animals.* New York: Appleton, 1884.

Romanes, G. J. *Mental evolution in man,* 1885. London: Kegan Paul, 1887.

Rorschach, H. *Psychodiagnostics,* 1921. 4th ed. New York: Grune and Stratton, 1942.

Ross, D. *G. Stanley Hall: The psychologist as prophet.* Chicago: University of Chicago Press, 1972.

Rostan, L. *Cours élémentaire d'hygiène.* 2 Vols. 2nd ed. Paris, 1828.

Rubin, E. *Synsoplevede Figurer,* 1915.

Rubin, E. *Visuell wahrgenonmene Figuren,* 1921. German translation of the 1915 Danish publication. A portion of the German translation in D. C. Beardslee & M. Wertheimer (Eds.), *Readings in perception.* Princeton: Van Nostrand, 1958.

Rubinstein, S. L. Problems of psychology in the works of K. Marx. *Sovetskaja psixotexnika,* 1934, *7,* 3-20.

Rubinstein, S. L. *Fundamentals of psychology,* 1935.

Rubinstein, S. L. *Fundamentals of general psychology,* 1940. 2nd ed., 1946.

Rubinstein, S. L. Soviet psychology in the years of the Great Patriotic War. *Pod znzmenem marksizma,* 1943, Nos. 9-10, 45-62.

Rubinstein, S. L. Soviet psychology in wartime. *Journal of Phenomenology and Phenomenological Research,* 1944, *5,* 181-198.

Rubinstein, S. L. The teachings of I. P. Pavlov and some problems of the reconstruction of psychology. *Voprosy filosofii (Questions of Philosophy),* 1952, *5,* 197-210.

Rush, B. *Medical inquiries and observations upon the diseases of the mind,* 1812. 4th ed. Philadelphia: Grigg, 1930.

Rush, J. *Analysis of the human intellect,* 1865.

Rutherford, W. A new theory of hearing. *Journal of Anatomy and Physiology,* 1886, *21,* 166-168.

Sahakian, W. S. (ed.) *History of psychology: A source book in systematic psychology* Itasca, IL: F. E. Peacock, 1968.

Sahakian, W. S. Psychology, History of. *Encyclopaedia Britannica,* 1974, *15,* 151-158.

St. Augustine, A. On the trinity. In P. Schaff (Ed.), *A select library of the Nicene and post-Nicene fathers.* Vol. 3. Buffalo: Christian Literature, 1887. Pp. 1-228.

St. Augustine, A. *The confessions.* c. 397. London: J. M. Dent, 1907.

St. Thomas Aquinas. *Summa theologica.* In *Basic writings of Saint Thomas Aquinas.* 2 Vols. New York: Random House, 1945.

Sakel, M. *The pharmacological shock treatment of schizophrenia.* New York: Nervous and Mental Disease Publishing, 1938.

Sakuma, K. *Shinrikenkyukai* (Accent of Japanese language), 1917.

Sakuma, K. *Dobunkan* (Pronunciation and accent of Japanese language), 1919.

Sukuma, K. [*Standpoint of gestalt psychology*]. Tokyo: Uchida-Rokakuho, 1933.

Sakuma, K. [Translation of W. Köhler, *Gestalt psychology*]. Tokyo: Kai Uchidarokakuho, 1938.

Sakuma, K. [*Gestalt psychology*]. Tokyo: Kobundo, 1951.

Sartre, J-P. *Being and nothingness: An essay on phenomenological ontology,* 1943. New York: Philosophical Library, 1956.

Sato, K. [*Psychology of personality*]. Tokyo: Sogensha, 1951.

Sato, K. Psychotherapeutic implications of Zen. *Psychologia,* 1958, *1,* 213-218. (a.)

Sato, K. Morita therapy — a kind of Zen psychotherapy. *Psychologia,* 1958, *1,* 219-225. (b)

Sato, K. How to get Zen enlightenment — on a five days' intensive course for its attainment. *Psychologia,* 1959, *2,* 107-113. (a)

Sato, K. [Zen and psychology]. *Japanese Journal of Psychology,* 1959, *30,* 286-295. (b)

Sato, K. Zen from a personological viewpoint. *Psychologia,* 1968, *11,* 3-24.

Sato, K., & Graham, C. H. Psychology in Japan. *Psychological Bulletin,* 1954, *51,* 443-464.

Schapp, W. *Beiträge zur Phänomenologie der Wahrnehmung* (Contributions to the phenomenology of perception). Göttingen: Kaestner, 1910. 2nd ed., Erlangen: Palm & Enke, 1925.

Scheler, M. *Zur Phänomenologie und Theorie der Sympathie-gefühle und vom Liebe und Hass,* 1913. Translated as *The nature of sympathy.* London: Routledge & Kegan Paul, 1954.

Scheler, M. *Der Formalismus in der Ethik und die materiale Wertethik,* 1913-1916. 2 Vols. Bern: A. Franke, 1966. Translated as *Formalism in ethics and non-formal ethics of value: A new attempt toward the foundation of an ethical personalism.* Evanston, IL: Northwestern University Press, 1973.

Schopenhauer, A. *Die Welt als Wille und Vorstellung,* 1818. Translated, *The world as will and idea.* London: K. Paul, Trench, Trübner, 1896.

Schultz, J. H., & Luthe, W. *Autogenic training.* New York: Grune & Stratton, 1959.

Schultz, M. Zur Anatomie und Physiologie der Retina. *Archiv für mikroscopische Anatomie,* 1866, *2,* 175-186, 247-261.

Schultz, M. Ueber Stäbchen und Zapfen der Retina. *Archiv für mikroscopische Anatomie,* 1867, *3,* 215-247. (a)

Schultz, M. Bemerkungen über Bau und Entwickelung der Retina. *Archiv für mikroscopische Anatomie,* 1867, *3,* 371-382. (b)

Schumann, F. Zeiträge zur Analyse der Gesichtswahrnehmungen. *Zeitschrift für Psychologie,* 1900, *23,* 1-32; 1900, *24,* 1-33.

Scripture, E. W. *The new psychology.* New York: Scribner, 1897.

Seashore, C. E. *Pioneering in psychology.* Iowa City, IA: University of Iowa Press, 1942.

Sechenov, I. M. Vegetative processes in animal life. *Medical Herald,* 1861.

Sechenov, I. M. *Reflexes of the brain,* 1863. Cambridge, MA: Massachusetts Institute of Technology, 1965. (a)

Sechenov, I. M. *Mechanisms of the frog which inhibit the reflexes of the spinal cord,* 1863. (b)

Sechenov, I. M. *Electrical and chemical stimulation of sensory spinal nerves in the frog,* 1868.

Sechenov, I. M. *How and by whom shall psychology be studied?* 1873.

Sechenov, I. M. *Autobiographical notes.* Washington, DC: American Institute of Biological Sciences and American Psychological Association, 1965.

Selye, H. Stress and psychiatry. *American Journal of Psychiatry,* 1956, *113,* 423-427.

Selye, H. *The stress of life.* New York: McGraw-Hill, 1956.

Selye, H. Stress and the general adaptation syndrome. Unpublished manuscript, 1973.

Selz, O. *Die Gesetze des geordneten Denkverlaufs.* 2 Vols. 1913-1922.

Sheffield, F. D., & Roby, T. B. Reward value of a non-nutritive sweet taste. *Journal of Comparative and Physiological Psychology,* 1950, *43,* 471-478.

Sheldon, W. H. Morphological types and mental ability. *Journal of Personality Research,* 1927, *5,* 447-451.

Sheldon, W. H. Constitutional factors in personality. In J. McV. Hunt (Ed.), *Personality and the behavior disorders.* Vol. 1. New York: Ronald, 1944, Pp. 526-549.

Sheldon, W. H. Dupertuis, C. W., & McDermott, E. *Atlas of men: A guide for somatotyping the adult male at all ages.* New York: Harper, 1954.

Sheldon, W. H., Hartl, E. M., & McDermott, E. *Varieties of delinquent youth: An introduction to constitutional psychiatry.* New York: Harper, 1949.

Sheldon, W. H., Stevens, S. S., & Tucker, W. B. *The varieties of human physique: An introduction to constitutional psychology.* New York: Harper, 1940.

Sherif, M. A study of some social factors in perception. *Archives of Psychology,* 1935, No. 187.

Sherif, M. *The psychology of social norms.* New York: Harper & Row, 1936.

Sherif, M. An experimental approach to the study of attitudes. *Sociometry,* 1937, *1,* 90-98.

Sherif, M., & Hovland, C. I. *Social judgment: Assimilation and contrast effects in communication and attitude change.* New Haven: Yale University Press, 1961.

Sherrington, C. S. *The integrative action of the nervous system.* New Haven: Yale University Press, 1906.

Sherrington, C. S. *Mammalian physiology: A course of practical exercises.* Oxford: Clarendon Press, 1919.

Sherrington, C. S. *Man and his nature,* 1940. Rev. ed. Cambridge: University Press, 1951.

Shinfuku, H. [Psychopathology of 'toraware (to be bound with over-self-consciousness)']. *Japanese Journal of Psychiatry and Neurology,* 1954, *55,* 737.

Sighele, S. *La foule criminelle,* 1891. French translation, Paris: F. Alcan, 1892.

Sighele, S. *Le crime à deux,* 1893. French translation, Lyon: A. Storck, 1893.

Sighele, S. *La delinquenza settaria* (The delinquency of sects), 1895. Retitled, *Morale private e morale politiche.* French translation, *Psychologie des sectes.* Paris: V. Giard & E. Brière, 1898.

Skinner, B. F. *Behavior of organisms.* New York: Appleton-Century-Crofts, 1938.

Skinner, B. F. *Science and human behavior.* New York: Macmillan, 1953.

Skinner, B. F. *Verbal behavior.* Appleton-Century-Crofts, 1957.

Skinner, B. F. *Cumulative record,* 1959. 3rd ed. New York: Appleton-Century-Crofts, 1972.

Skinner, B. F. *Beyond freedom and dignity.* New York: Knopf, 1971.

Smirnov, A. A. *The psychology of memory.* Moscow: Izd. Akad. Pedag. Nauk RSFSR, 1948.

Smirnov, A. A., & Zinchenko, P. I. Problems in the psychology of memory. In M. Cole, & I. Maltzman (Eds.), *A handbook of contemporary Soviet psychology.* New York: Basic Books, 1969. Pp. 452-502.

Sokolov, E. N. Reflex receptor mechanisms. In N. O'Connor (Ed.), *Recent Soviet psychology.* New York: Liveright, 1961. Pp. 186-194.

Sokolov, E. N. The orienting reflex, its structure and mechanisms. In L. G. Voronin, A. N. Leontiev, A. R. Luria, E. N. Sokolov, & O. S. Vinogradova (Eds.), *Orienting reflex and exploratory behavior.* Washington, DC: American Institute of Biological Sciences and American Psychological Association, 1965. Pp. 141-151.

Sokolov, E. N. The modeling properties of the nervous system. In M. Cole, & I. Maltzman (Eds.), *A handbook of contemporary Soviet psychology.* New York: Basic Books, 1969. Pp. 671-704.

Spearman, C. "General intelligence" objectively determined and measured; *American Journal of Psychology,* 1904, *15,* 201-293.

Spearman, C. *The nature of "intelligence" and the principle of cognition.* London: Macmillan, 1923.

Spearman, C. *The abilities of man: Their nature and measurement.* London: Macmillan, 1927.

Spearman, C. "G" and after—a school to end schools. In C. Murchison (Ed.) *Psychologies of 1930.* Worcester, MA: Clark University Press, 1930. Pp. 339-366.

Spence, K. W. The differential response in animals to stimuii varying within a single dimension. *Psychological Review, 1937, 44,* 430-444.

Spence, K. W. *Behavior theory and conditioning.* New Haven: Yale University Press, 1956.

Spence, K. W. *Behavior theory and learning.* Englewood Cliffs, NJ: Prentice-Hall, 1960.

Spencer, H. The development hypothesis. *Leader,* 1852. Reprinted in H. Spencer, *Essays: Scientific, political and speculative.* Vol. 1. New York: Appleton, 1951. Pp. 1-7.

Spencer, H. *The principles of psychology,* 1855. 2 Vols. 3rd ed., 1880. New York: Appleton, 1880, 1910.

Spencer, H. *The study of sociology,* 1873. Ann Arbor, MI: University of Michigan Press, 1961.

Spencer, H. *Descriptive sociology: Or, groups of sociological facts.* London: Richard Scheppig and James Collier, 1873-1934.

Spencer, H. *Data of ethics.* New York: A. L. Burt, 1879.

Spiegelberg, H. *Phenomenology in psychology and psychiatry.* Evanston, IL: Northwestern University Press, 1972.

Spinoza, B. *Ethics,* 1677. New York: Dover, 1951.

Spirkin, A. G. Dialectical materialism. *Filosofskaya Entsiklopediya, 1960, 1,* 479-495.

Spanger, E. *Types of men.* Halle: Max Niemeyer, 1928.

Sprenger, J., & Kraemer, H. *Malleus maleficarum* (Witches' hammer), 1487.

Stern, W. *Person und Sache* (Person and thing). 3 Vols. Leipzig, 1906-1924.

Stern, W. *Die differentielle Psychologie* (Differential psychology), 1911.

Stern, W. *Psychology of early childhood up to the sixth year of age,* 1914. New York: Henry Holt, 1930.

Stern, W. *General psychology from the personalistic standpoint,* 1935. New York: Macmillan, 1938.

Stern, W. Autobiography. In C. Murchison (Ed.), *A history of psychology in autobiography.* Worcester, MA: Clark University Press. Reprinted, New York: Russell & Russell, 1961.

Stevens, S. S. *Handbook of experimental psychology.* New York: Wiley, 1951.

Stevens, S. S. The quantification of sensation. *Daedalus,* 1959, *88,* 606-621.

Stewart, D. *Elements of the philosophy of the human mind,* 1782. Albany: Websters and Skinners, 1821.

Stouffer, S. A., Guttman, L., Suchman, E. A., Lazarsfeld, P. F., Star, S. A., & Clausen, J. A. *Measurement and prediction. Vol. IV, Studies in social psychology in World War II.* Princeton, NJ: Princeton University Press, 1950.

Stouffer, S. A., Lumsdaine, A. A., Lumsdaine, M. H., Williams, R. M., Smith, M. B., Janis, I. L., Star, S. A., & Cottrell, L. S. *The American soldier: Combat and its aftermath. Vol. II, Studies in social psychology in World War II.* Princeton, NJ: Princeton University Press, 1949.

Stouffer, S. A., Suchman, E. A., DeVinney, L. C., Star, S. A., & Williams, R. M. *The American soldier: Adjustment during army life. Vol. I, Studies in social pyschology in World War II.* Princeton, NJ: Princeton University Press, 1949.

Stout, G. F. *Analytic psychology,* 1896. 2 Vols. 2nd ed. London: Allen & Unwin, 1918.

Stout, G. F. *Manual of psychology,* 1899. 4th ed., 1932. 5th ed. London: University Tutorial Press, 1938.

Stout, G. F. *Studies in philosophy and psychology.* London: Macmillan, 1930.

Strong, E. K. A vocational interest test. *The Educational Record,* 1927, *8,* 107-121.

Stumpf, C. *Tonpsychologie* (Psychology of tone). 2 Vols. 1883-1890. Portion translated in W. S. Sahakian (Ed.), *History of psychology: A source book in systematic psychology.* Itasca, IL: F. E. Peacock, 1968. Pp. 486-490.

Stumpf, C. Erscheinungen und psychische Funktionen. *Abhl. preuss. Akad. Wiss. Berlin (philos.-hist. Kl.),* 1906, no. 4, 40 pp. (a)

Stumpf, C. Zur Einteilung der Wissenschaften. *Abhl. preuss. Akad Wiss. Berlin (philos.-hist. Kl.),* 1906, no. 5, 94 pp. (b)

Stumpf, C. Über Gefühlsempfindungen. *Zeitschrift für Psychologie,* 1907, *44,* 1-49.

Stumpf, C. Apologie der Gefühlsempfindungen. *Zeitschrift für Psychologie,* 1916, *75,* 1-38.

Stumpf, C. Autobiography. In C. Murchison (Ed.), *A history of psychology in autobiography.* Vol. 1. Worcester, MA: Clark University Press, 1930.

Sullivan, H. S. *Conceptions of modern psychiatry.* New York: Norton, 1947.

Sullivan, H. S. *The interpersonal theory of psychiatry,* New York: Norton, 1953.

Sully, J. *Sensation and intuition.* London: C. K. Paul, 1874. 2nd ed., 1880.

Sully, J. *Outlines of psychology.* London: Longmans, Green, 1884. 3rd ed., 1896.

Sully, J. *The human mind: A text-book of psychology.* New York: Appleton, 1892.

Sully, J. *Studies of childhood,* 1895. Rev. ed., New York: Appleton, 1903.

Sully, J. *An essay on laughter.* London: Longmans, Green, 1902.

Sutherland, A. *Origin and growth of the moral instinct,* 1898.

Tanaka, K. [*Human engineering*]. Tokyo: Yubunkan, 1922.

Tannenbaum, P. H. Attitudes toward source and concept as factors in attitude change through communications. Unpublished doctoral dissertation, University of Illinois, 1953.

Tannenbaum, P. H. Initial attitude toward source and concept as factors in attitude change through communication. *Public Opinion Quarterly,* 1956, *20,* 411-425.

Tannenbaum, P. H. The congruity principle: Retrospective reflections and recent research. In R. P. Abelson *et al.* (Eds.), *Theories of cognitive consistency: A sourcebook.* Chicago: Rand McNally, 1968. Pp. 52-72.

Tarde, G. *Social laws,* 1898. New York: Macmillan, 1899.

Tarde, G. *The laws of imitation,* 1901. New York: Henry Holt, 1903.

Taylor, J. A. A personality scale of manifest anxiety. *Journal of Abnormal and Social Psychology,* 1953, *48,* 285-290.

Teplov, B. M. Typological properties of the nervous system and their psychological manifestations. In N. O'Connor (Ed.), *Recent Soviet psychology.* New York: Liveright, 1961. Pp. 21-51.

Terman, L. M. *The measurement of intelligence.* Boston: Houghton Mifflin, 1916.

Terman, L. M. *Genetic studies of genius.* Stanford, CA: Stanford University Press, 1925-1959.

Theophrastus *Physikon Doxai* (Doctrines of natural philosophers). In H. Diels (Ed.), *Doxographi Graeci,* 1879.

Thomson, G. H. *The factorial analysis of human ability.* Boston: Houghton Mifflin, 1951.

Thorndike, E. L. Animal intelligence. *Psychological Review Monograph,* 1898, supplement # 2.

Thorndike, E. L. *Animal intelligence: Experimental studies.* New York: Macmillan, 1911.

Thorndike, E. L. *Human learning.* New York: Century, 1931.

Thorndike, E. L. *Fundamentals of learning.* New York: Columbia University Teachers College, 1932. (a)

Thorndike, E. L. Reward and punishment in animal learning. *Comparative Psychology Monographs,* 1932, *8,* 58-61. (b)

Thorndike, E. L. A proof of the law of effect. *Science,* 1933, *77,* 173-175.

Thorndike, E. L. *The psychology of wants, interest, and attitudes.* New York: Appleton-Century, 1935.

Thorndike, E. L., & Woodworth, R. S. The influence of improvement in one mental function upon the efficiency of other functions. *Psychological Review,* 1901, *8,* 247-261, 384-395, 553-564.

Thorpe, W. H. & Zangwill, O. L. *Current problems in animal behaviour.* Cambridge: Cambridge University Press, 1961.

Thurstone, L. L. *The nature of intelligence.* London: Routledge & Kegan Paul, 1924.

Thurstone, L. L. Attitudes can be measured. *American Journal of Sociology,* 1928, *33,* 529-554.

Thurstone, L. L. *The reliability and validity of tests.* Ann Arbor, MI: Edwards, 1931. (a)

Thurstone, L. L. Multiple factor analysis. *Psychological Review,* 1931, *38,* 406-427. (b)

Thurstone, L. L. *Multiple factor analysis: A development and expression of the vectors of the mind.* Chicago: University of Chicago Press, 1947.

Thurstone, L. L. Psychological implication of factor analysis. *American Psychologist,* 1948. *3.* 402-408.

Thurstone, L. L., & Chave, E. J. *The measurement of attitude: A psychological method and some experiments with a scale for measuring attitude toward the church.* Chicago: University of Chicago Press, 1929.

Titchener, E. B. *An outline of psychology.* New York: Macmillan, 1896. 2nd ed., 1902.

Titchener, E. B. *A primer of psychology.* New York: Macmillan, 1898. Rev. ed., 1925. (a)

Titchener, E. B. The postulates of a structural psychology. *Philosophical Review,* 1898, *7,* 449-465. (b)

Titchener, E. B. Discussion: Structural and functional psychology. *Philosophical Review,* 1899, *8,* 290-299.

Titchener, E. B. *Experimental psychology: A manual of laboratory practice.* 2 Vols. New York: Macmillan. Vol. I: Qualitative experiments, 2 parts, 1901. Vol. II: Quantitative experiments, 2 parts, 1905.

Titchener, E. B. *Lectures on the elementary psychology of feeling and attention.* New York: Macmillan, 1908.

Tichener, E. B. *Lectures on the experimental psychology of thought-processes.* New York: Macmillan, 1909.

Titchener, E. B. *A text-book of psychology.* New York: Macmillan, 1910. Revision of *An outline of psychology.*

Titchener, E. B. *Systematic psychology: Prolegomena.* New York: Macmillan, 1929.

Tolman, E. C. A new formula for behaviorism. *Psychological Review,* 1922, *29,* 44-53. Reprinted in E. C. Tolman, *Collected papers in psychology.* Berkeley, CA: University of California Press, 1951.

Tolman, E. C. *Purposive behavior in animals and men.* New York: Appleton-Century-Crofts, 1932.

Tripplett, N. The dynamogenic factors in pacemaking. *American Journal of Psychology,* 1897, *9,* 507-533.

Ueno, Y. Japanese translation of Angell's *Psychology,* 1910.

Ueno, Y. [Behavior theory: A new definition of psychology]. [*Psychological Research*], 1913, *4,* 289-292.

Ueno, Y., & Noda, N. [*A modern history of psychology*]. Tokyo: Dubunkan, 1922.

Uznadze, D. M. *Foundations of experimental psychology,* 1925.

Uznadze, D. M. *Experimental basis of the psychology of set,* 1949.

Vaihinger, H. *The philosophy of 'as if,'* 1911. London: Routledge & Kegan Paul, 1924, 2nd ed., 1935.

Vierordt, K. Neue Methode der Quantitativen Mikroskopischen Analyse des Blutes. *Archiv für Physiologie Heilkunde,* 1852, *11,* 26-46.

Villa, G. *Contemporary psychology,* 1899. London: Swan Sonnenschein, 1903.

Vives, J. L. *De anima et vita.* Basel, 1538.

Vvedenskiy, N. Y. *Excitation, inhibition, and narcosis,* 1901.

Vygotsky, L. S. *Thought and language,* 1934. Cambridge, MA: Massachusetts Institute of Technology Press, 1962.

Wagner-Jauregg, J. The effect of malaria on progressive paralysis. *Psychiat. Neuro. Wochenschr.,* 1918, *20,* 132-134, 251-255. Translated in W. S. Sahakian (Ed.), *History of psychology: A source book in systematic psychology.* Itasca, IL: F. E. Peacock, 1968. Pp. 360-361.

Walker, H. M. *Studies in the history of statistical method.* Baltimore: Williams & Wilkins, 1929.

Wallace, A. R. *On the tendency of varieties to depart indefinitely from the original type,* 1858.

Wallas, G. *Human nature in politics.* London: Archibald Constable, 1908.

Wallas, G. *The great society.* New York: Macmillan, 1914.

Wallas, G. *Our social heritage.* New Haven: Yale University Press,, 1921.

Ward, J. Psychology. *Encyclopaedia Britannica.* 9th ed., 1886. 11th ed., 1911.

Ward, J. *Psychological principles,* 1918. 2nd. ed. Cambridge: Cambridge University Press, 1920.

Ward, L. *Outlines of sociology.* New York: Macmillan, 1897.

Washburn, M. F. *The animal mind: A text-book of comparative psychology.* New York: Macmillan, 1908.

Washburn, M. F. *Movement and mental imagery: Outlines of a motor theory of the complexer mental processes.* Boston: Houghton Mifflin, 1916.

Watson, F. The father of psychology. *Psychological Review,* 1915, *22,* 333-353.

Watson, J. B. *American education,* 1903.

Watson, J. B. Psychology as a behaviorist views it. *Psychological Review,* 1913, *20,* 158-177.

Watson, J. B. *Behavior: An introduction to comparative psychology.* New York: Holt, Rinehart and Winston, 1914.

Watson, J. B. The place of conditioned-reflex in psychology. *Psychological Review,* 1916, *23,* 89-117.

Watson, J. B. *Psychology from the standpoint of a behaviorist.* Philadelphia: Lippincott, 1919. 3rd ed., 1929.

Watson, J. B. *Behaviorism.* New York: People's Institute Publishing, 1924. Rev. ed. New York: Norton, 1930.

Watson, J. B. Autobiography. In C. Murchison (Ed.), *A history of psychology in autobiography.* Vol. 3. Worcester, MA: Clark University Press, 1930. Pp. 271-281.

Watt, H. J. Experimentelle Beiträge zur einer Theorie des Denkens (Experimental contributions to a theory of thought). *Archiv gesamte Psychologie,* 1905, *4,* 289-436.

Watt, H. J. *The psychology of sound,* 1917.

Weber, E. H. *De tactu: annotationes anatomicae et physiologicae,* 1834. Translated in W. S. Sahakian (Ed.), *History of psychology: A source book in systematic psychology.* Itasca, IL: F. E. Peacock, 1968. Pp. 108-110.

Weber, E. H. *Der Tastsinn und das Gemeingefühl* (The sense of touch and the common feeling), 1846.

Weber, M. Die protestantische Ethik und der Geist des Kapitalismus. *Archiv für Sozialwissenschaft und Sozialpolitik,* 1904, *20;* 1905, *21.*

Wechsler, D. *The measurement of adult inteligence,* 1939. 4th ed. titled *The measurement and appraisal of adult intelligence.* Baltimore: Williams & Wilkins, 1958. 5th ed. by J. D. Matarazzo, *Wechsler's measurement and appraisal of adult inteligence.* Baltimore: Williams & Wilkins, 1972.

Wertheimer, M. Experimentelle Studien über das Sehen von Bewegung. *Zeitschrift für Psychologie,* 1912, *61,* 161-265. Published separately as a *Habilitationsschrift* at Leipzig: Johann Ambrosius Barth, 1912. Translated as *Experimental studies on the seeing of motion.* In T. Shipley (ed.), *Classics in psychology.* New York: Philosophical Library, 1961. Pp. 1032-1089.

Wertheimer, M. On truth. *Social Research,* 1934, *1,* 135-146.

Wertheimer, M. Gestalt theory. *Social Research,* 1944, *11,* 78-99.

Wertheimer, M. *Productive thinking.* New York: Harper, 1945; enlarged ed., 1959.

Wever, E. G., & Bray, C. W. The nature of acoustic response: The relations between sound frequency of impulses in the auditory nerve. *Journal of Experimental Psychology.* 1930, *13,* 376-380.

Wever, E. G., & Lawrence, M. *Physiological acoustics.* Princeton, NJ: Princeton University Press, 1954.

Weyer, J. *De praestigiis daemonum* (Deception of demons), 1563.

Whitehead, A. N. *Process and Reality.* New York: Macmillan, 1929.

Whitehead, A. N., & Russell, B. *Principia mathematica.* Cambridge: Cambridge University Press, 1913.

Whytt, R. *An essay on the vital and other involuntary motions of animals.* 2nd ed., 1763. (Introduction dated October 1, 1751).

Witasek, S. Beiträge zur Psychologie der Komplexionem. *Zeitschrift für Psychologie,* 1897, *14,* 401-435.

Witasek, S. *Grundlinien der Psychologie,* 1908.

Woodworth, R. S. The accuracy of voluntary movement. *Psychological Review.* Monographs Supplement, 1899, #13. Pp. 114.

Woodworth, R. S. *Dynamic psychology.* New York: Columbia University Press, 1918.

Woodworth, R. S. *Psychology.* New York: Henry Holt, 1921. Fifth revised edition with D. G. Marquis, 1947.

Woodworth, R. S. Autobiography. In C. Murchison (Ed.), *A history of psychology in autobiography.* Vol. 2. Worcester, MA: Clark University Press, 1930.

Woodworth, R. S. *Contemporary schools of psychology.* New York: Ronald, 1931. Third edition with M. R. Sheehan, 1964.

Woodworth, R. S. Situation-and-goal-set. *American Journal of Psychology.* 1937, *50,* 130-140.

Woodworth, R. S. *Experimental psychology.* New York: Henry Holt, 1938. Second edition with H. Schlosberg, 1954. Third edition with J. M. Kling, L. A. Riggs and 17 contributors, 1971.

Woodworth, R. S. *The Columbia University psychological laboratory: A fifty-year retrospect.* New York, 1942.

Woodworth, R. S. *Dynamics of psychology.* New York: Holt, Rinehart and Winston, 1958.

Wundt, W. M. *Lectures on human and animal psychology,* 1863. 2nd ed., 1892 New York: Macmillan, 1894.

Wundt, W. M. *Principles of physiological psychology*, 1873-1874. 5th ed., 1902. London: Swan Sonnenschein, 1904.

Wundt, W. M. *Logik*, 1880-1883.

Wundt, W. M. *Ethik*, 1886.

Wundt, W. M. *System der philosophie*, 1889.

Wundt, W. M. *Hypnotismus und Suggestion*. 1892.

Wundt, W. M. *Outlines of psychology*, 1896. New York: G. E. Stechert, 1897, 1907.

Wundt, W. M. *Völkerpsychologie: Eine Untersuchung der Entwicklungsgesetze von Sprache, Mythus and Sitte*. 2 Vols. Leipzig: W. Engelmann, 1900-1909. Translated as *Elements of folk psychology*. New York: Macmillan, 1916.

Wundt, W. M. *An introduction to psychology*, 1911. London: George Allen, 1912.

Wundt, W. *Erlebtes und Erkanntes*, 1920.

Yale University, Clinic of Child Development. *The first five years of life: A guide to the study of preschool child*. New York: Harper, 1940.

Yee, A. H. Psychology in China bows to the Cultural Revolution. *APA Monitor*, 1973, *4*, 1, 4.

Yerkes, R. M. (Ed.) *Psychological examining in the army*. In *Memoirs of the National Academy of Sciences*. Vol. 15. Washington, DC: U.S. Government Printing Office, 1921.

Young, T. *A course of lectures on natural philosophy*. London, 1807.

Zaleznik, A., Christensen, C. R., & Roethlisberger, F. J. *The motivation, productivity, and statisfaction of workers: A prediction study*. Boston: Division of Research, Harvard University Graduate School of Business Administration, 1958.

Zangwill, O. L. *Cerebral dominance and its relation to psychological function*. Springfield, IL: Charles C. Thomas, 1960.

Zeigarnik, B. Über das Behalten von erledigten und unerledgten Handlungen. *Psychologische Forschung*, 1927, *9*, 1-85. Portion translated in W. S. Sahakian (Ed.), *History of psychology: A source book in systematic psychology*. Itasca, IL: F. E. Peacock, 1968. Pp. 441-444.

Zilboorg, G. *A history of medical psychology*. New York: Norton, 1967.

Zinchenko, P. I. Problems of involuntary recall. *Nauch. Zap. Karkov. Gos. Pedag. Inst. Inos. Yaz.*, 1939, *1*.

NAME INDEX

SUBJECT INDEX